TIME AND DECISION

TIME AND DECISION

Economic and Psychological Perspectives on Intertemporal Choice

GEORGE LOEWENSTEIN, DANIEL READ, AND ROY BAUMEISTER

Editors

RUSSELL SAGE FOUNDATION　　　NEW YORK

The Russell Sage Foundation

The Russell Sage Foundation, one of the oldest of America's general purpose foundations, was established in 1907 by Mrs. Margaret Olivia Sage for "the improvement of social and living conditions in the United States." The Foundation seeks to fulfill this mandate by fostering the development and dissemination of knowledge about the country's political, social, and economic problems. While the Foundation endeavors to assure the accuracy and objectivity of each book it publishes, the conclusions and interpretations in Russell Sage Foundation publications are those of the authors and not of the Foundation, its Trustees, or its staff. Publication by Russell Sage, therefore, does not imply Foundation endorsement.

Library of Congress Cataloging-in-Publication Data

Time and decision : economic and psychological perspectives on intertemporal choice / George Loewenstein, Daniel Read, Roy Baumeister, editors.

    p.   cm.

"The papers were all first presented during a meeting at the Russell Sage Foundation in New York"—Introd.

    Includes bibliographical references and index.

    ISBN 0-87154-549-7

    1. Decision making—Congresses.   2. Time—Economic aspects—Congresses. 3. Time—Psychological aspects—Congresses.   4. Choice (Psychology)— Congresses.   5. Economics—Psychological aspects—Congresses.   I. Loewenstein, George.   II. Read, Daniel, 1958–   III. Baumeister, Roy F.

BF448 .T55 2003
153.8'3—dc21

2002036743

Text design by Suzanne Nichols

RUSSELL SAGE FOUNDATION
112 East 64th Street, New York, New York 10021
10 9 8 7 6 5 4 3 2 1

Contents

Contributors   ix

Acknowledgments   xiii

Introduction   1
*George Loewenstein, Daniel Read, and
Roy F. Baumeister*

1. Time Discounting and Time Preference:
A Critical Review   13
*Shane Frederick, George Loewenstein, and
Ted O'Donoghue*

**PART I · Philosophical, Evolutionary, and
Neurobiological Underpinnings**

2. Time Preference and Personal Identity   89
Shane Frederick

3. The Evolution of Patience   115
Alex Kacelnik

4. A Neurobiology of Intertemporal Choice   139
*Stephen B. Manuck, Janine D. Flory,
Matthew F. Muldoon, and Robert E. Ferrell*

PART II · Theoretical Perspectives

5. Sustaining Delay of Gratification over Time:
   A Hot-Cool Systems Perspective   175
   Walter Mischel, Ozlem Ayduk, and
   Rodolfo Mendoza-Denton

6. Willpower, Choice, and Self-Control   201
   Roy F. Baumeister and Kathleen D. Vohs

7. Self-Awareness and Self-Control   217
   Ted O'Donoghue and Matthew Rabin

8. Construal Level Theory of Intertemporal
   Judgment and Decision   245
   Nira Liberman and Yaacov Trope

9. Self-Signaling and Self-Control   277
   Drazen Prelec and Ronit Bodner

PART III · Patterns of Preference

10. Subadditive Intertemporal Choice   301
    Daniel Read

11. Summary Assessment of Experiences: The Whole
    Is Different from the Sum of Its Parts   323
    Dan Ariely and Ziv Carmon

12. Predicting and Indulging Changing Preferences   351
    George Loewenstein and Erik Angner

PART IV · Applications

13. Time Discounting of Health Outcomes   395
    Gretchen B. Chapman

14. Delay Discounting: A Fundamental Behavioral
    Process of Drug Dependence   419
    Warren K. Bickel and Matthew W. Johnson

15. Fear as a Policy Instrument   441
    Andrew Caplin

16. Dieting as an Exercise in Behavioral Economics   459
    C. Peter Herman and Janet Polivy

17. Self-Rationing: Self-Control in Consumer Choice   491
       Klaus Wertenbroch

18. The Hyperbolic Consumption Model: Calibration,
       Simulation, and Empirical Evaluation   517
       George-Marios Angeletos, David Laibson,
       Andrea Repetto, Jeremy Tobacman, and
       Stephen Weinberg

Index   545

Contributors

George Loewenstein is professor of economics and psychology in the Department of Social and Decision Sciences at Carnegie Mellon University.

Daniel Read is reader in operational research at the London School of Economics and Political Science.

Roy F. Baumeister is the Eppes Professor of Psychology at Florida State University.

George-Marios Angeletos is assistant professor of economics at the Massachusetts Institute of Technology.

Erik Angner is a graduate student in the Department of History and Philosophy of Science and the Department of Economics at the University of Pittsburgh.

Dan Ariely is the Luis Alvarez Renta Professor at the Sloan School of Management and the Media Laboratory at the Massachusetts Institute of Technology.

Ozlem Ayduk is assistant professor of psychology at the University of California, Berkeley.

Warren K. Bickel is professor of psychiatry and psychology at the University of Vermont.

Ronit Bodner is director of Learning Innovations.

Andrew Caplin is professor of economics at New York University and codirector of the Center for Experimental Social Science.

Ziv Carmon is associate professor of marketing at INSEAD.

Gretchen B. Chapman is associate professor of psychology at Rutgers University.

Robert E. Ferrell is professor and chair of human genetics at the University of Pittsburgh Graduate School of Public Health.

Janine D. Flory is research assistant professor of psychology at the University of Pittsburgh.

Shane Frederick is assistant professor of management science at the Massachusetts Institute of Technology.

C. Peter Herman is professor of psychology at the University of Toronto.

Matthew W. Johnson is a doctoral student in experimental psychology at the University of Vermont.

Alex Kacelnik is professor of behavioral ecology at the University of Oxford and a fellow of the Institute for Advanced Studies in Berlin.

David Laibson is professor of economics at Harvard University.

Nira Liberman is a senior lecturer in psychology at Tel Aviv University, Israel.

Stephen B. Manuck is professor of psychology and psychiatry at the University of Pittsburgh.

Rodolfo Mendoza-Denton is assistant professor of psychology at the University of California, Berkeley.

Walter Mischel is the Robert Johnston Niven Professor of Humane Letters in Psychology at Columbia University.

Matthew F. Muldoon is associate professor of medicine at the University of Pittsburgh School of Medicine.

Ted O'Donoghue is assistant professor of economics at Cornell University.

Janet Polivy is professor of psychology at the University of Toronto.

Drazen Prelec is the Digital Equipment LFM Professor of Management at the Massachusetts Institute of Technology Sloan School of Management.

Matthew Rabin is professor of economics at the University of California, Berkeley.

Andrea Repetto is assistant professor of industrial engineering at the University of Chile, Santiago, Chile.

Jeremy Tobacman is a graduate student in economics at Harvard University.

Yaacov Trope is professor of psychology at New York University.

Kathleen D. Vohs is a research fellow funded by the National Institutes of Mental Health to conduct research at the University of Utah and Case Western Reserve University.

Stephen Weinberg is a graduate student in economics at Harvard University.

Klaus Wertenbroch is associate professor of marketing at INSEAD, Fontainebleau, France, and Singapore.

Acknowledgments

With thanks to Rosa Stipanovic for all the hard work, Suzanne Nichols for keeping us on track, and Eric Wanner for making the whole thing happen.

Introduction

GEORGE LOEWENSTEIN, DANIEL READ,
AND ROY F. BAUMEISTER

PSYCHOLOGY and economics have a classic love-hate relationship. Members of each discipline often express positive sentiments about the other in the abstract, and acknowledge complementarities between disciplines in methods, subject matter, and levels of analysis. Yet actual encounters often produce glassy eyes or, worse, overt hostility. Both disciplines set out to use scientific method to explain and describe human behavior. They differ, however, in the details of their respective paradigms. Psychology is mainly empirically based, embracing a great variety of theories (frequently incompatible, as some economists are not shy about pointing out). Psychologists usually start from phenomena, develop a local theory based on that phenomenon, then test this theory against further observations. Economics, in contrast, is more theory-based, with a single theoretical approach that can be tailored to a wide range of applications. Psychologists and economists converge on at least one point: both wish that members of the other discipline would be more like them. Psychologists wish economists were less theory-driven and more responsive to empirical data. Economists accuse psychologists of being too willing to interpret quirky behavior as evidence of irrationality, and wish that psychologists would subject their theories to the discipline of formal modeling. Each group tends to view the other's theories as invalid or trivial, with very few evaluations falling between these extremes.

A dispassionate mediator might think that both sides have merit, but might also propose that the two disciplines find some way of sorting out their differences and agree on a common ground that combines both their strengths into a greater whole. Now, more than ever before, there are grounds for optimism that such a reconciliation is beginning to occur. This book is a record of what may be the greatest success story in the unfolding interdisciplinary relationship: the development of our knowledge of intertemporal choice and its application to important economic and psychological problems.

1

Intertemporal choice is what we do when we make trade-offs between costs and benefits occurring at different points in time. We are always making intertemporal choices—when we choose between a hamburger now or a fine meal (or thinner body) later; between increasing our pension fund contribution or going to Hawaii; or between a sinful moment on earth or an eternity in heaven. Indeed, so broad is the domain of intertemporal choice that it is difficult to think of a consequential decision that is *not* an intertemporal choice. Given the importance of intertemporal choice, that it is a central theme in both psychology and economics is not surprising.

Basic research on intertemporal choice by contemporary economists has revolved mainly around testing the validity and implications of the discounted utility (DU) model, which posits that people have a single unitary rate of time preference that they use to discount the value of delayed events. This means, for instance, that if something is worth 10 percent less to you if it is delayed by one year, it should be worth a further 10 percent less when delayed by a second year, and so on. DU is a *normative* model because if we don't treat the future in this fashion, we won't be able to make plans that we can be sure we will implement in the future. Whether DU is a valid *descriptive* model of behavior is a matter of debate among economists (and the central focus of the following chapter).

Basic research by psychologists on intertemporal choice (a term psychologists rarely use) has tended to focus on different issues. Some have been concerned with measuring individual differences in the propensity to delay gratification, others with situational determinants of impulsivity, and still others with cognitive and emotional mechanisms underlying intertemporal choice. The chapters in this volume represent a sort of academic "busing" intended to speed up the integration of psychology and economics in the domain of intertemporal choice. These were papers first presented during a meeting at the Russell Sage Foundation in New York, where distinguished researchers with common interests (who in many cases had not heard of one another) shared their work. For many of us the meeting was revelatory. We differed in our terminology, disciplinary assumptions, and research methods, but serious efforts were made to speak a common language. Whenever possible, the economists stripped their talks of equations—and when they did not, were called to task by the psychologists. The psychologists took great pains to express theories in terms that economists could digest. In the end, all left the meeting with a somewhat changed perspective and certainly with an enhanced understanding of diverse aspects of intertemporal choice. We can only hope that these chapters will have a similar effect on the reader.

Completion of this volume occurs almost exactly ten years after the publication of a previous compendium on intertemporal choice (also published by the Russell Sage Foundation) titled *Choice Over Time*. Despite substantial overlap in authorship and subject matter between the two volumes, the differences are striking and underline the pace of progress that occurred in the intervening decade. Much of the original volume (fully six of fifteen chapters) was occupied with discussions of *hyperbolic time discounting*—that is, the observation that people tend to be more impatient toward trade-offs involving earlier rewards than those involving later rewards. These discussions focused mainly on its theoretical development and implications. Hyperbolic time discounting continues to be a central theme in the current volume (see chapters 7, 10, 14, and 18), but most chapters herein are oriented toward examining its implications rather than documenting the phenomenon, as in the earlier volume. Moreover, a variety of other important themes have emerged. For example, there is much more discussion of intra-individual variability in time discounting— why people sometimes behave as if there is no tomorrow and at other times seem obsessively focused on the future (chapters 1, 5, 6, 7, 8, 11, and 12); more discussion of the role played by emotions (chapters 1, 5, 13, 14, and 18); and a plethora of intriguing new theoretical perspectives (chapters 5 through 9). The applications have become far more sophisticated both in terms of underlying theory and quality of empirical research (chapters 13 through 18). Moreover, there is even research questioning the robustness of hyperbolic time discounting (chapters 1 and 10).

On top of the appeal of a round number, the decade gap between the two volumes seems close to ideal from the standpoint of scientific progress. Only a few years earlier, it might have been difficult to fill a volume with new research sufficiently distinct from that published in the original volume. Given the rapid pace of research in the field, doing justice to the breadth of the topic a few years from now may well require two volumes instead of one. As it is, we have inevitably neglected to include much important and high quality research, as well as a number of theoretical perspectives.

The remainder of the introduction provides a map to the thematic concerns in the chapters that follow. Part I looks at some basic issues: the philosophy of intertemporal choice, how it evolved, and what has evolved. Part II describes some theoretical contributions around the question of what is intertemporal choice. Most of these chapters focus on the problem of self-control, an issue that looms large throughout the book. Part III turns to specific patterns of time preference, looking at what we know about how people value future outcomes. Part IV, the final section, deals with applications in the domains of health, drug addiction, dieting, marketing, savings, and public policy. The categorization is necessarily crude. Many of the more theoretical chapters are heavily informed by applied findings, and the applied chapters all derive novel basic theoretical insights from the specific domains they explore. Chapter 1 presents an overview of research on time discounting and time preference. The chapter focuses on the descriptive validity of the DU model, which remains the dominant economic theory of intertemporal choice. Frederick, Loewenstein, and O'Donoghue observe that virtually every assumption and implication of the DU model has been contradicted by empirical research. Moreover, they argue that the model cannot be salvaged by merely assuming a different—hyperbolic, for example—discount function. Rather, they argue, understanding intertemporal choice behavior requires an account of several distinct motives that can vary greatly across decisions—a theme that resounds throughout the book.

While Frederick and colleagues focus on the descriptive question of how people do discount the future, chapter 2, by Frederick, addresses the normative question of whether we *should* discount the future at all. Many argue that there is no good reason to weight utility in the near future more than utility in the more distant future—at least no reason other than the uncertainty of obtaining that future utility. Yet some philosophers, in particular Derek Parfit, have argued that our relation to future selves is fundamentally the same as our relation to other distinct individuals, that our connection to future selves diminishes over time, and that to give lesser weight to selves with whom we are less connected is reasonable—just as we would care less about strangers than about close relations. Along with examining both sides of this issue, Frederick presents a descriptive study that assesses whether diminishing identity might not only justify time preference, but also help explain it. In chapter 3, Kacelnik discusses the evolutionary basis of time discounting, and specifically provides an evolutionary account of anomalous patterns of discounting behavior observed both in humans and animals. Experiments with animals have sometimes been interpreted as showing that, contrary to evolutionary theory, animals do not maximize expected rewards. Kacelnik argues that the findings that support such conclusions are an artifact of research in which animals are placed in artificial environments unlike the natural environments they have evolved to deal with. Kacelnik also devotes considerable attention to drawing linkages between experimental results dealing with humans and other animals, and cautions against the temptation of automatically concluding that they are the product of similar underlying mechanisms and evolutionary forces. Kacelnik's chapter underlines the crucial role that the ability to optimally delay gratification must have played in evolution. Not surprisingly, therefore, as reviewed in chapter 4 by Manuck and colleagues, a great deal of evidence has emerged showing that patience is influenced by specific brain structures and chemical processes. One such brain structure is the prefrontal cortex. People with damage to this area of the brain or to its connections with other brain structures (such as those involved in emotional experiences and motivation) do not take into account the future consequences of their actions, and so choose based on immediate rewards only (Damasio 1994). The ability to withstand impulses is also modulated by activity of the neurotransmitter serotonin. In laboratory animals, for example, administering drugs that reduce serotonin activity in the brain increases the likelihood of impulsive choice, whereas increasing serotonin activity (as by Prozac) makes animals more willing to wait. Variability in serotonergic activity also predicts variability in impulsive choices in humans, including suicide and aggression, as well as scores on a personality test of impulsivity. Manuck and colleagues also discuss genetic variation in a component of the serotonin system that is correlated, in humans, with both impulsivity and brain serotonergic activity.

The ability to wait is not only correlated with brain activity, but also with age and dispositional person variables. Mischel, Ayduk, and Mendoza-Denton describe Mischel's studies of delay ability using the classic *preschool delay of gratification paradigm*, which measures the time children wait for a preferred but delayed reward over a less desirable but immediately available reward. As children mature they become increasingly able to wait for longer periods, due to the development of cognitive-attentional strategies to prevent the immediate desirability of the small rewards from overwhelming their long-term interests. This development is seen as reflecting the maturation of a rational and far-sighted, cognitive, "cool" system (probably located in the frontal lobe and hippocampus) that gradually becomes able to moderate the impulses of the "hot" system (amygdala) and enables self-regulation. Independent of maturational level, stable individual differences also exist in the ability to access cool-system strategies in dealing with the frustration of the delay situation. This ability is predictive of social, emotional, and cognitive competencies throughout adolescence and adulthood. For instance, research showed that five-year-olds who resisted longer in the preschool delay paradigm also did better in college later in life. The authors summarize findings elucidating the attentional mechanisms that underlie this ability. They also highlight recent research exploring how delay ability protects against destructive behavior in interpersonal relationships.

Mischel and colleagues found that four-year-olds who waited longer in the preschool delay paradigm also did better in college later in life. We often speak of the ability to overcome temptation as involving the use of *willpower*. In chapter 6, Baumeister and Vohs report research suggesting that this term can be taken literally. They argue that people have a limited pool of resources that they can use to resist temptation. Successful resistance draws on this resource pool and makes people less able to resist subsequent (immediate) temptations. Indeed, they suggest that self-control is like a muscle that can be temporarily fatigued (and may also be able to be strengthened with judicious use). Baumeister and Vohs describe experiments in which people are required to exert willpower in one domain (resisting tempting food) and then called on to exert it in an unrelated domain (persistence on an unsolvable task). They find that there appears to be less willpower left at the second stage.

The contributions of Mischel, Ayduk, and Mendoza-Denton and Baumeister and Vohs focus on how difficult it can be to overcome the desire for immediate gratification. O'Donoghue and Rabin, in chapter 7, are concerned with the importance of people's awareness of their own self-control problems. They distinguish between two extreme states of awareness: at one extreme is sophistication, or full awareness of future self-control problems; at the other extreme is naivete, or full unawareness. O'Donoghue and Rabin show that to be sophisticated is sometimes better, and at times to be naive is better. A sophisticate will resist procrastinating too much because she knows she will have no more willpower tomorrow than today, while a naïf will (incorrectly) count on his future selves to do the job. Yet a naïf might persist despite inevitable (but unanticipated) future self-control failures, whereas a sophisticate, who predicts these failures, might never even try. Their chapter also describes the more realistic case of partial naivete: you know you will have trouble getting up when the alarm rings, but you underestimate how much. Indeed, one of the results of their analysis will be familiar to many readers—namely, that even a little naivete about the tendency to procrastinate can lead one to delay completing a task until the last minute.

O'Donoghue and Rabin discuss as well how our beliefs affect *when* we want to do things. Although their approach is different, this question is also at the heart of Liberman and Trope's *temporal construal theory* described in chapter 8. They argue that choice objects can be characterized in terms of their high-level and low-level features, and that our *construal*, or mental representations, of those objects will have more high-level features the more the object is delayed. Consequently, choices concerning delayed events will be based on higher-level construals than will choices for immediate events. To illustrate, a high-level construal of writing a book chapter might be "building a career," while a low-level construal would be "sitting in front of the computer." The decision of whether to write a chapter in six months will be based on its effects on one's career, while the decision to work on it *tonight* will depend on whether typing is more fun than watching television. As Trope and Liberman show in numerous experiments, this seems to be precisely how we do decide. Theoretical approaches to self-control have largely focused on the conflict between immediate gratification and long-term objectives. In chapter 9, Prelec and Bodner note that many self-control problems also involve a problem of scale: success in the long run requires persistence and endurance over many smaller decisions, each of which has a negligible impact on the larger goal. To deal with this, they develop a self-signaling model of self-control, in which success "in the small" is a motivating signal of success "in the long run." The model rests on a distinction between two types of reward: reward experienced directly from the consequences of a choice; and diagnostic reward, which is the moral pleasure or pain derived from learning something positive or negative about one's own disposition or future prospects. Anticipation of diagnostic reward or fear of diagnostic pain promotes self-control. In the model, whether a person is aware of the attempt to self-signal matters. Unawareness of self-signaling promotes good behavior and self-esteem. Awareness can trigger an excess of self-control, where good behavior is discounted for diagnostic motives, and being reasonably good is no longer "good enough." The fully aware self-signaler is on a self-control treadmill, engaged in perfect behavior with no commensurate improvement in self-esteem.

As previously mentioned, DU theory has been widely judged deficient. The most widely discussed deficiency—one that has led to the greatest degree of consensus between psychologists and economists—is the idea that the discount rate is not a single number but rather a function. As noted, a strong consensus has developed around the notion of hyperbolic time discounting. The experiments reported in Read's chapter 10 may therefore be met by some dismay by both economists and psychologists who, having finally acknowledged the limitations of exponential time discounting, were on the verge of throwing in their hat with hyperbolic discounting. These experiments show that much of the data adduced as evidence for a hyperbolic discount function are faulty. Read's studies show that the measured discount rate depends critically on the length of the interval being evaluated and may have little to do with when the interval occurs. This is called *subadditive intertemporal choice*, and Read questions the strength of the evidence for hyperbolic time discounting once this subadditivity of time discounting is taken into account.

Although DU theory and its alternatives, such as hyperbolic discounting, are often studied with experiments comparing preferences for single outcomes, in practical terms their most important application is to sequences or streams of consequences, such as the value of a lifetime of paychecks or living with a chronic disease. According to DU theory, the value of such a sequence is the sum of the discounted values of each element in that sequence. These discounted values are assumed to be separable, meaning that the utility experienced at one period does not influence utility at a later period. Ariely and Carmon's review of the evidence (much from their own experimental research) in chapter 11 shows that this assumption is far from true. Rather, the value placed on a sequence of good or bad feelings is apparently based on the combination of a host of gestalt properties of that sequence. For instance, people weigh heavily on how good the end of a sequence is, its peak, and whether it is improving or getting worse (people like improvement). Ariely and Carmon's bottom line is that people encode or evaluate sequences based on abstract mental representations containing summary information (such as the mean, slope, and variance) about the pleasure of experiences, and not on representations of entire sequences. When people decide what *future* sequences they want to experience, they take these gestalt properties into account, thereby violating the assumption of separability. If the assumption of additivity—that the value of a sequence is the sum of the values of its parts—is unrealistic, an even more unrealistic (though all too common) assumption in modeling intertemporal choice is that tastes are fixed over time. Loewenstein and Angner, in chapter 12, underscore the artificiality of this assumption by enumerating some of the most important sources of preference change. They also review the burgeoning literature on predictions of future tastes, showing that, while many reasons exist for why people mispredict changes in their own tastes, these diverse reasons generally produce a common pattern of misestimation that Loewenstein, O'Donoghue, and Rabin (2002) call *projection bias*. Finally, Loewenstein and Angner challenge the universal applicability of a common assumption made in most research that does allow for changing preferences—namely, that people want to satisfy whatever preferences they expect to have in the future. This certainly is often true, but situations occur (which they discuss) in which people attempt to impose their current preferences on their own future selves.

One area in which time discounting plays an especially important role is that of decisions concerning health. For the consumer, virtually all health-related decisions involve trade-offs between short-term and long-term gains. Taking medication, seeing the doctor, undergoing withdrawal—these are all behaviors that are good for us in the long term but can range from annoying to unbearable in the short term. Studies of discounting health outcomes are also theoretically important because health may be the only nonfungible domain of choice that we can study: whereas consumption of money is (in principle) independent of when it is received, health can *only* be consumed when it is received. An important question is whether qualitative findings reported in studies of monetary discounting are also found in studies of health; Chapman, in chapter 13, shows that some are and some aren't. For instance, people discount larger health effects at a lower rate than smaller ones, which is also true for monetary outcomes, but they sometimes would rather their health got worse rather than better (holding total health constant) when they usually want their income to increase (again, holding total income constant). A perhaps more important question is whether health discounting is correlated with discounting for other things; Chapman suggests it is not. This finding appears to challenge the common view that time discounting is a reliable individual difference.

One domain in which the future values of money and health, or at least health-related behavior, do seem to coincide is discussed by Bickel and Johnson in chapter 14. They find that addicts do indeed discount future money much more than do nonaddicts, suggesting that at least in this domain, discounting is related to health-related decisions. One might think that this is because people who discount the future more become addicts, but research suggests that perhaps the addiction creates the heavy discounting. The authors observe that heroin addicts and smokers discount the future heavily, but once they have fought off their addiction, their discount rates fall. Evidence that longtime ex-smokers discount the future the same way as non-smokers also supports this notion.

Both Chapman's and Bickel and Johnson's chapters show how health-related behaviors are often quite shortsighted. Caplin's chapter 15 examines policy implications of this observation. He analyzes the common tendency to avoid learning about, or discovering if one has, a disease. Many people put off seeing the doctor because they fear what they might discover. For them, myopia arises not because they weigh too little on the future but because contemplating bad futures is frightening, and not making an appointment with the doctor is one way to avoid doing so. Many campaigns to increase the public take-up of testing for serious conditions (such as testicular cancer) use fear appeals that emphasize the consequences of the undiagnosed disease.

In line with current psychological theory, Caplin suggests that these fear appeals may have the paradoxical effect of making at-risk individuals less willing to undertake the preventive act. This is especially likely to happen in cases such as self-examination for testicular cancer, in which the preventive act itself triggers fear. In such cases the fear appeal may backfire by making the preventive act even more frightening, prompting greater efforts at avoidance. Caplin's work shows one way in which economic analyses can enhance psychological thinking: his model specifies circumstances under which fear appeals are likely to be effective and those when they are not. He also examines differences between economists and psychologists in how they judge the success of policy interventions, and proposes a hybrid approach that draws on both traditions.

Herman and Polivy, in chapter 16, provide an in-depth examination of a case of dynamic inconsistency that has actually served as the poster child for much writing about intertemporal choice. At the meeting in New York, almost everyone used failure to stick to a diet as the "perfect example" of dynamic inconsistency. The prototypical example is that we plan to eat healthily before dinner, but at dinnertime our good intentions fail and we take some frightfully fattening food. The cycle repeats itself dinner after dinner. Herman and Polivy, who have spent most of their careers studying dieters, pointed out that this is not exactly what happens; dieters do plan to diet when meals are still far away, but they do not necessarily fall prey when the moment for dessert arrives. Rather, dieters break down usually because some particular disruptive event (albeit often minor) disinhibits them enough to make them break their diet momentarily; then the fact that the diet has been broken often leads to a catastrophic binge. Herman and Polivy's skeptical conclusions are in line with many of the other chapters, pointing out that the road to understanding intertemporal choice is not through developing better discount functions but through understanding the variety of psychological processes that enter into future-based decision making. One such psychological process, investigated by Wertenbroch, is in the domain of consumer choice. In chapter 17, he starts with the well-established phenomenon that people seem to consume at a rate that is an increasing function of their immediately available (local) resources. What this means is intuitively compelling: we will eat more cheese if we have ten pounds in the fridge instead of five, and more if we have five pounds instead of one. Wertenbroch suggests that consumption decisions often are driven by lax local constraints (for example, what we have stockpiled in inventory) rather than by more stringent global constraints (such as long-term health concerns). Thus, for example, if we purchase beer by the case (as is virtually mandated by Pennsylvania law), we are likely to consume more beer over the course of the month than if we buy by the six-pack. Wertenbroch presents wide-ranging evidence for the proposition that a large paycheck makes people overspend, a large box of chocolates makes people overeat, and the lack of an explicit deadline makes people squander time. He argues that consumers are partially sophisticated in dealing with this problem, and so respond by self-imposing rationing rules that tighten local constraints on consumption ("never borrow," "only $50 per month for clothes"). Such rationing strategies include, for example, self-imposing costly deadlines to prevent procrastination and *purchase quantity rationing* (buying small amounts at a time) to prevent overconsumption: many smokers, for instance, buy cigarettes one pack at a time rather than economizing by buying cartons. In chapter 18—the final chapter—the focus shifts from the individual to the entire population and asks, What are the consequences of a society of shortsighted decision makers? Angeletos, Laibson, Repetto, Tobacman, and Weinberg investigate the implications of hyperbolic discounting for predictions of national savings data. If consumers conform to the DU model, their rate of spending would be more or less even over their lifetime: early in life they would borrow on future income, then they would save in midlife and retire on their savings. In fact, consumers' spending seems to closely fit their current incomes. Early in life they spend little, in midlife they spend a lot, and they retire in relative poverty. Angeletos and colleagues conducted computer simulations of economies composed of either hyperbolic consumers (who spend too much too soon) or exponential consumers (who spend the right amount at the right time). The hyperbolic economies predicted real consumer behavior extraordinarily well.

As is clear from these synopses, the contributions to this book are remarkably wide ranging and comprehensive. The study of intertemporal choice is now a truly interdisciplinary project. We hope that you'll invest the time in familiarizing yourself with this exciting and active area of research. Please don't procrastinate; there's no time like the present.

References

Damasio, Antonio R. 1994. *Descartes' Error: Emotion, Reason, and the Human Brain.* New York: G.P. Putnam.

Loewenstein, George, Ted O'Donoghue, and Matthew Rabin. 2000. "Projection Bias in the Prediction of Future Utility." Working paper, Department of Social Science and Decision Sciences, Carnegie Mellon University.

· 1 ·

Time Discounting and Time Preference: A Critical Review

SHANE FREDERICK, GEORGE LOEWENSTEIN,
AND TED O'DONOGHUE

INTERTEMPORAL choices—decisions involving trade-offs among costs and benefits occurring at different times—are important and ubiquitous. Such decisions not only affect one's health, wealth, and happiness, but may also, as Adam Smith first recognized, determine the economic prosperity of nations. In this chapter, we review empirical research on intertemporal choice, and present an overview of recent theoretical formulations that incorporate insights gained from this research.

Economists' attention to intertemporal choice began early in the history of the discipline. Not long after Adam Smith called attention to the importance of intertemporal choice for the wealth of nations, the Scottish economist John Rae was examining the sociological and psychological determinants of these choices. We will briefly review the perspectives on intertemporal choice of Rae and nineteenth- and early twentieth-century economists, and describe how these early perspectives interpreted intertemporal choice as the joint product of many conflicting psychological motives.

All of this changed when Paul Samuelson proposed the discounted-utility (DU) model in 1937. Despite Samuelson's manifest reservations about the normative and descriptive validity of the formulation he had proposed, the DU model was accepted almost instantly, not only as a valid normative standard for public policies (for example, in cost-benefit analyses), but as a descriptively accurate representation of actual behavior. A central assumption of the DU model is that all of the disparate motives underlying intertemporal choice can be condensed into a single parameter—the discount rate. We do not present an axiomatic derivation of the DU model, but instead focus on those features that highlight the implicit psychological assumptions underlying the model.

Samuelson's reservations about the descriptive validity of the DU model were justified. Virtually every assumption underlying the DU model has been tested and found to be descriptively invalid in at least some situations. Moreover, these anomalies are not anomalies in the sense that they are regarded as errors by the people who commit them. Unlike many of the better-known expected-utility anomalies, the DU anomalies do not necessarily violate any standard or principle that people believe they should uphold.

The insights about intertemporal choice gleaned from this empirical research have led to the proposal of numerous alternative theoretical models. Some of these modify the discount function, permitting, for example, declining discount rates or "hyperbolic discounting." Others introduce additional arguments into the utility function, such as the utility of anticipation. Still others depart from the DU model more radically, by including, for instance, systematic mispredictions of future utility. Many of these new theories revive psychological considerations discussed by Rae and other early economists that were extinguished with the adoption of the DU model and its expression of intertemporal preferences in terms of a single parameter.

While the DU model assumes that people are characterized by a single discount rate, the literature reveals spectacular variation across (and even within) studies. The failure of this research to converge toward any agreed-upon average discount rate stems partly from differences in elicitation procedures. But it also stems from the faulty assumption that the varied considerations that are relevant in intertemporal choices apply equally to different choices and thus that they can all be sensibly represented by a single discount rate.

Throughout, we stress the importance of distinguishing among the varied considerations that underlie intertemporal choices. We distinguish *time discounting* from *time preference*. We use the term *time discounting* broadly to encompass *any* reason for caring less about a future consequence, including factors that diminish the expected utility generated by a future consequence, such as uncertainty or changing tastes. We use the term *time preference* to refer, more specifically, to the preference for immediate utility over delayed utility. We push this theme further by examining whether time preference itself might consist of distinct psychological traits that can be separately analyzed.

Historical Origins of the Discounted Utility Model

The historical developments that culminated in the formulation of the DU model help to explain the model's limitations. Each of the major figures in its development—John Rae, Eugen von Böhm-Bawerk, Irving Fisher, and Paul Samuelson—built upon the theoretical framework of his predecessors, drawing on little more than introspection and personal observation. When the DU model eventually became entrenched as the dominant theoretical framework for modeling intertemporal choice, it was due largely to its simplicity and its resemblance to the familiar compound interest formula, and not as a result of empirical research demonstrating its validity.

Intertemporal choice became firmly established as a distinct topic in 1834, with John Rae's publication of *The Sociological Theory of Capital*. Like Adam Smith, Rae sought to determine why wealth differed among nations. Smith had argued that national wealth was determined by the amount of labor allocated to the production of capital, but Rae recognized that this account was incomplete because it failed to explain the determinants of this allocation. In Rae's view, the missing element was "the effective desire of accumulation"—a psychological factor that differed across countries and determined a society's level of saving and investment.

Along with inventing the topic of intertemporal choice, Rae also produced the first in-depth discussion of the psychological motives underlying intertemporal choice. Rae believed that intertemporal choices were the joint product of factors that either promoted or limited the effective desire of accumulation. The two main factors that promoted the effective desire of accumulation were the bequest motive—"the prevalence throughout the society of the social and benevolent affections"—and the propensity to exercise self-restraint: "the extent of the intellectual powers, and the consequent prevalence of habits of reflection, and prudence, in the minds of the members of society" (Rae 1905 [1834], 58). One limiting factor was the uncertainty of human life.

> When engaged in safe occupations, and living in healthy countries, men are much more apt to be frugal, than in unhealthy, or hazardous occupations, and in climates pernicious to human life. Sailors and soldiers

are prodigals. In the West Indies, New Orleans, the East Indies, the expenditure of the inhabitants is profuse. The same people, coming to reside in the healthy parts of Europe, and not getting into the vortex of extravagant fashion, live economically. War and pestilence have always waste and luxury, among the other evils that follow in their train. (Rae 1905 [1834], 57)

A second factor that limited the effective desire of accumulation was the excitement produced by the prospect of immediate consumption, and the concomitant discomfort of deferring such available gratifications.

Such pleasures as may now be enjoyed generally awaken a passion strongly prompting to the partaking of them. The actual presence of the immediate object of desire in the mind by exciting the attention, seems to rouse all the faculties, as it were to fix their view on it, and leads them to a very lively conception of the enjoyments which it offers to their instant possession. (Rae 1905 [1834], 120)

Among the four factors that Rae identified as the joint determinants of time preference, one can glimpse two fundamentally different views. One, which was later championed by William S. Jevons (1888) and his son, Herbert S. Jevons (1905), assumes that people care only about their immediate utility, and explains farsighted behavior by postulating utility from the anticipation of future consumption. On this view, deferral of gratification will occur only if it produces an increase in "antical" utility that more than compensates for the decrease in immediate consumption utility. The second perspective assumes equal treatment of present and future (zero discounting) as the natural baseline for behavior, and attributes the overweighting of the present to the miseries produced by the self-denial required to delay gratification. N. W. Senior, the best-known advocate of this "abstinence" perspective, wrote, "To abstain from the enjoyment which is in our power, or to seek distant rather than immediate results, are among the most painful exertions of the human will" (Senior 1836, 60).

The anticipatory-utility and abstinence perspectives share the idea that intertemporal trade-offs depend on immediate feelings—in one case, the immediate pleasure of anticipation, and in the other, the immediate discomfort of self-denial. The two perspectives, however, explain variability in intertemporal-choice behavior in different ways. The anticipatory-utility perspective attributes variations in intertemporal-choice behavior to differences in people's abilities to imagine the future and to differences in situations that promote or inhibit such mental images. The abstinence perspective, on the other hand, explains variations in intertemporal-choice behavior on the basis of individual and situational differences in the psychological discomfort associated with self-denial. In this view, one should observe high rates of time discounting by people who find it painful to delay gratification, and in situations in which deferral is generally painful—for example, when one is, as Rae worded it, in the "actual presence of the immediate object of desire."

Eugen von Böhm-Bawerk, the next major figure in the development of the economic perspective on intertemporal choice, added a new motive to the list proposed by Rae, Jevons, and Senior, arguing that humans suffer from a systematic tendency to underestimate future wants.

> It may be that we possess inadequate power to imagine and to abstract, or that we are not willing to put forth the necessary effort, but in any event we limn a more or less incomplete picture of our future wants and especially of the remotely distant ones. And then there are all those wants that never come to mind at all. (Böhm-Bawerk 1970 [1889], 268–69)[1]

Böhm-Bawerk's analysis of time preference, like those of his predecessors, was heavily psychological, and much of his voluminous treatise, *Capital and Interest*, was devoted to discussions of the psychological constituents of time preference. However, whereas the early views of Rae, Senior, and Jevons explained intertemporal choices in terms of motives uniquely associated with time, Böhm-Bawerk began modeling intertemporal choice in the same terms as other economic tradeoffs—as a "technical" decision about allocating resources (to oneself) over different points in time, much as one would allocate resources between any two competing interests, such as housing and food.

Böhm-Bawerk's treatment of intertemporal choice as an allocation of consumption among time periods was formalized a decade later by the American economist Irving Fisher (1930). Fisher plotted the intertemporal consumption decision on a two-good indifference diagram, with consumption in the current year on the abscissa, and consumption in the following year on the ordinate. This representation made clear that a person's observed (marginal) rate of time preference—the marginal rate of substitution at her chosen consumption bundle—depends on two considerations: time preference and diminishing marginal utility. Many economists have subsequently expressed discomfort with using the term *time preference* to include the effects of differential marginal utility arising from unequal consumption levels between time periods (see in particular Olson and Bailey 1981). In Fisher's formulation, *pure* time preference can be interpreted as the marginal rate of substitution on the diagonal, where consumption is equal in both periods.

Fisher's writings, like those of his predecessors, included extensive discussions of the psychological determinants of time preference. Like Böhm-Bawerk, he differentiated "objective factors," such as projected future wealth and risk, from "personal factors." Fisher's list of personal factors included the four described by Rae, "foresight" (the ability to imagine future wants—the inverse of the deficit that Böhm-Bawerk postulated), and "fashion," which Fisher believed to be "of vast importance . . . in its influence both on the rate of interest and on the distribution of wealth itself" (Fisher 1930, 88).

> The most fitful of the causes at work is probably fashion. This at the present time acts, on the one hand, to stimulate men to save and become millionaires, and, on the other hand, to stimulate millionaires to live in an ostentatious manner. (Fisher 1930, 87)

Hence, in the early part of the twentieth century, "time preference" was viewed as an amalgamation of various intertemporal motives. While the DU model condenses these motives into the discount rate, we will argue that resurrecting these distinct motives is crucial for understanding intertemporal choices.

The Discounted Utility Model

In 1937, Paul Samuelson introduced the DU model in a five-page article titled "A Note on Measurement of Utility." Samuelson's paper was intended to offer a generalized model of intertemporal choice that was applicable to multiple time periods (Fisher's graphical indifference-curve analysis was difficult to extend to more than two time periods) and to make the point that representing intertemporal trade-offs required a cardinal measure of utility. But in Samuelson's simplified model, all the psychological concerns discussed in the previous century were compressed into a single parameter, the discount rate.

The DU model specifies a decision maker's intertemporal preferences over consumption profiles $(c_t, \ldots, c_T)$. Under the usual assumptions (completeness, transitivity, and continuity), such preferences can be represented by an intertemporal utility function $U^t(c_t, \ldots, c_T)$. The DU model goes further, by assuming that a person's intertemporal utility function can be described by the following special functional form:

$$U^t(c_t, \ldots, c_T) = \sum_{k=0}^{T-t} D(k)u(c_{t+k})$$

$$\text{where } D(k) = \left(\frac{1}{1+\rho}\right)^k.$$

In this formulation, $u(c_{t+k})$ is often interpreted as the person's cardinal instantaneous utility function—her well-being in period $t + k$—and $D(k)$ is often interpreted as the person's discount function—the relative weight she attaches, in period t, to her well-being in period $t + k$. ρ represents the individual's pure rate of time preference (her discount rate), which is meant to reflect the collective effects of the "psychological" motives discussed earlier.[2]

Samuelson did not endorse the DU model as a normative model of intertemporal choice, noting that "any connection between utility as discussed here and any welfare concept is disavowed" (1937, 161). He also made no claims on behalf of its descriptive validity, stressing, "It is completely arbitrary to assume that the individual behaves so as to maximize an integral of the form envisaged in [the DU model]" (1937, 159). Yet despite Samuelson's manifest reservations, the simplicity and elegance of this formulation was irresistible, and the DU model was rapidly adopted as the framework of choice for analyzing intertemporal decisions.

The DU model received a scarcely needed further boost to its dominance as the standard model of intertemporal choice when Tjalling C. Koopmans (1960) showed that the model could be derived from a superficially plausible set of axioms. Koopmans, like Samuelson, did not argue that the DU model was psychologically or normatively plausible; his goal was only to show that under some well-specified (though arguably unrealistic) circumstances, individuals were logically compelled to possess positive time preference. Producers of a product, however, cannot dictate how the product will be used, and Koopmans's central technical message was largely lost while his axiomatization of the DU model helped to cement its popularity and bolster its perceived legitimacy.

We next describe some important features of the DU model as it is commonly used by economists, and briefly comment on the normative and positive validity of these assumptions. These features do not represent an axiom system—they are neither necessary nor sufficient conditions for the DU model—but are intended to highlight the implicit psychological assumptions underlying the model.[3]

Integration of New Alternatives with Existing Plans

A central assumption in most models of intertemporal choice—including the DU model—is that a person evaluates new alternatives by integrating them with one's existing plans. To illustrate, consider a person with an existing consumption plan $(c_t, \ldots, c_T)$ who is offered an intertemporal-choice prospect X, which might be something like an option to give up \$5,000 today to receive \$10,000 in five years. Integration means that prospect X is not evaluated in isolation, but in light of how it changes the person's aggregate consumption in all future periods. Thus, to evaluate the prospect X, the person must choose what his or her new consumption path $(c'_t, \ldots, c'_T)$ would be if he or she were to accept prospect X, and should accept the prospect if $U^t(c'_t, \ldots, c'_T) > U^t(c_t, \ldots, c_T)$.

An alternative way to understand integration is to recognize that intertemporal prospects alter a person's budget set. If the person's initial endowment is E_0, then accepting prospect X would change his or her endowment to $E_0 \cup X$. Letting $B(E)$ denote the person's budget set given endowment E—that is, the set of consumption streams that are feasible given endowment E—the DU model says that the person should accept prospect X if:

$$\max_{(c_t, \ldots, c_T) \in B(E_0 \cup X)} \sum_{\tau = t}^{T} \left(\frac{1}{1 + \rho} \right)^{\tau - t} u(c_\tau) > \max_{(c_t, \ldots, c_T) \in B(E_0)} \sum_{\tau = t}^{T} \left(\frac{1}{1 + \rho} \right)^{\tau - t} u(c_\tau)$$

While integration seems normatively compelling, it may be too difficult to actually do. A person may not have well-formed plans about future consumption streams, or be unable (or unwilling) to recompute the new optimal plan every time he or she makes an intertemporal choice. Some of the evidence we will review supports the plausible presumption that people evaluate the results of intertemporal choices independently of any expectations they have regarding consumption in future time periods.

Utility Independence

The DU model explicitly assumes that the overall value—or "global utility"—of a sequence of outcomes is equal to the (discounted) sum of the utilities in each period. Hence, the distribution of *utility* across time makes no difference beyond that dictated by discounting, which (assuming positive time preference) penalizes utility that is experienced later. The assumption of utility independence has rarely been discussed or challenged, but its implications are far from innocuous. It rules out any kind of preference for patterns of utility over time— for example, a preference for a flat utility profile over a roller-coaster utility profile with the same discounted utility.[4]

Consumption Independence

The DU model explicitly assumes that a person's well-being in period $t + k$ is independent of his or her consumption in any other period— that is, that the marginal rate of substitution between consumption in periods τ and τ' is independent of consumption in period τ''.

Consumption independence is analogous to, but fundamentally different from, the independence axiom of expected-utility theory. In expected-utility theory, the independence axiom specifies that preferences over uncertain prospects are not affected by the consequences that the prospects share—that is, that the utility of an experienced outcome is unaffected by other outcomes that one might have experienced (but did not). In intertemporal choice, consumption independence says that preferences over consumption profiles are not affected by the nature of consumption in periods in which consumption is identical in the two profiles—that is, that an outcome's utility is unaffected by outcomes experienced in prior or future periods. For example, consumption independence says that one's preference between an Italian and Thai restaurant tonight should not depend on whether one had Italian last night nor whether one expects to have it tomorrow. As the example suggests, and as Samuelson and Koopmans both recognized, there is no compelling rationale for such an assumption. Samuelson (1952, 674) noted that "the amount of wine I drank yesterday and will drink tomorrow can be expected to have effects upon my today's indifference slope between wine and milk." Similarly, Koopmans (1960, 292) acknowledged, "One cannot claim a high degree of realism for [the independence assumption], because there is no clear reason why complementarity of goods could not extend over more than one time period."

Stationary Instantaneous Utility

When applying the DU model to specific problems, it is often assumed that the cardinal instantaneous utility function $u(c_\tau)$ is constant across time, so that the well-being generated by any activity is the same in different periods. Most economists would acknowledge that stationarity of the instantaneous utility function is not sensible in many situations, because people's preferences in fact do change over time in predictable and unpredictable ways. Though this unrealistic assumption is often retained for analytical convenience, it becomes less defensible as economists gain insight into how tastes change over time (see Loewenstein and Angner, chapter 12 herein, for a discussion of different sources of preference change).[5]

Independence of Discounting from Consumption

The DU model assumes that the discount function is invariant across all forms of consumption. This feature is crucial to the notion of *time preference*. If people discount utility from different sources at different rates, then the notion of a unitary time preference is meaningless. Instead we would need to label time preference according to the object being delayed—"banana time preference," "vacation time preference," and so on.

Constant Discounting and Time Consistency

Any discount function can be written in the form

$$D(k) = \Pi_{n=0}^{k-1}\left(\frac{1}{1 + \rho_n}\right),$$

where ρ_n represents the per-period discount rate for period n—that is, the discount rate applied between periods n and $n + 1$. Hence, by assuming that the discount function takes the form

$$D(k) = \left(\frac{1}{1 + \rho}\right)^k,$$

the DU model assumes a constant per-period discount rate ($\rho_n = \rho$ for all n).[6]

Constant discounting entails an evenhandedness in the way a person evaluates time. It means that delaying or accelerating two dated outcomes by a common amount should not change preferences between the outcomes—if in period t one prefers X at τ to Y at $\tau + d$ for *some* τ, then in period t one must prefer X at τ to Y at $\tau + d$ for *all* τ. The assumption of constant discounting permits a person's time preference to be summarized as a single discount *rate*. If constant discounting does not hold, then characterizing one's time preference requires the specification of an entire discount *function*.

Constant discounting implies that a person's intertemporal preferences are *time-consistent*, which means that later preferences "confirm" earlier preferences. Formally, a person's preferences are time-consistent if, for any two consumption profiles $(c_t, \ldots, c_T)$ and $(c'_t, \ldots, c'_T)$, with $c_t = c'_t$, $U^t(c_t, c_{t+1}, \ldots, c_T) \geq U^t(c'_t, c'_{t+1}, \ldots, c'_T)$ if and only if $U^{t+1}(c_{t+1}, \ldots, c_T) \geq U^{t+1}(c'_{t+1}, \ldots, c'_T)$.[7] For an interesting discussion that questions the normative validity of constant discounting see Albrecht and Weber (1995).

Diminishing Marginal Utility and Positive Time Preference

While not core features of the DU model, virtually all analyses of intertemporal choice assume both diminishing marginal utility (that the instantaneous utility function $u(c_t)$ is concave) and positive time preference (that the discount rate ρ is positive).[8] These two assumptions create opposing forces in intertemporal choice: diminishing marginal utility motivates a person to spread consumption over time, while positive time preference motivates a person to concentrate consumption in the present.

Since people do, in fact, spread consumption over time, the assumption of diminishing marginal utility (or some other property that has the same effect) seems strongly justified. The assumption of positive time preference, however, is more questionable. Several researchers have argued for positive time preference on logical grounds (Hirshleifer 1970; Koopmans 1960; Koopmans, Diamond, and Williamson 1964; Olson and Bailey 1981). The gist of their arguments is that a zero or negative time preference, combined with a positive real rate of return on saving, would command the infinite deferral of all consumption.[9] But this conclusion assumes, unrealistically, that individuals have infinite life spans and linear (or weakly concave) utility functions. Nevertheless, in econometric analyses of savings and intertemporal substitution, positive time preference is sometimes treated as an identifying restriction whose violation is interpreted as evidence of misspecification.

The most compelling argument supporting the logic of positive time preference was made by Derek Parfit (1971, 1976, 1982), who contends that there is no enduring self or "I" over time to which all future utility can be ascribed, and that a diminution in psychological connections gives our descendent future selves the status of other people—making that utility less than fully "ours" and giving us a reason to count it less.[10]

> We care less about our further future . . . because we know that less of what we are now—less, say, of our present hopes or plans, loves or ideals—will survive into the further future . . . [if] what matters holds to a lesser degree, it cannot be irrational to care less. (Parfit 1971, 99)

Parfit's claims are normative, not descriptive. He is not attempting to explain or predict people's intertemporal choices, but is arguing that conclusions about the rationality of time preference must be grounded in a correct view of personal identity. If this is the only compelling normative rationale for time discounting, however, it would be instructive to test for a positive relation between observed time discounting and changing identity. Frederick (chap. 2 herein) conducted the only study of this type, and found no relation between monetary discount rates (as imputed from procedures such as "I would be indifferent between $100 tomorrow and $_____ in five years") and self-perceived stability of identity (as defined by the following similarity ratings: "Compared to now, how similar were you five years ago [will you be five years from now]?"), nor did he find any relation between such monetary discount rates and the presumed correlates of identity stability (for example, the extent to which people agree with the statement "I am still embarrassed by stupid things I did a long time ago").

DU Anomalies

Over the last two decades, empirical research on intertemporal choice has documented various inadequacies of the DU model as a descriptive model of behavior. First, empirically observed discount rates are not constant over time, but appear to decline—a pattern often referred to as hyperbolic discounting. Furthermore, even for a given delay, discount rates vary across different types of intertemporal choices: gains are discounted more than losses, small amounts more than large amounts, and explicit sequences of multiple outcomes are discounted differently than outcomes considered singly.

Hyperbolic Discounting

The best documented DU anomaly is hyperbolic discounting. The term *hyperbolic discounting* is often used to mean that a person has a declining rate of time preference (in our notation, ρ_n is declining in n), and we adopt this meaning here. Several results are usually interpreted as evidence for hyperbolic discounting. First, when subjects are asked to compare a smaller-sooner reward to a larger-later reward (to be discussed), the implicit discount rate over longer time horizons is lower than the implicit discount rate over shorter time horizons. For example, Thaler (1981) asked subjects to specify the amount of money they would require in one month, one year, and ten years to make them indifferent to receiving $15 now. The median responses— $20, $50, $100—imply an average (annual) discount rate of 345 percent over a one-month horizon, 120 percent over a one-year horizon, and 19 percent over a ten-year horizon.[11] Other researchers have found a similar pattern (Benzion, Rapoport, and Yagil 1989; Chapman 1996; Chapman and Elstein 1995; Pender 1996; Redelmeier and Heller 1993).

Second, when mathematical functions are explicitly fit to such data, a hyperbolic functional form, which imposes declining discount rates, fits the data better than the exponential functional form, which imposes constant discount rates (Kirby 1997; Kirby and Marakovic 1995; Myerson and Green 1995; Rachlin, Raineri, and Cross 1991).[12]

Third, researchers have shown that preferences between two delayed rewards can reverse in favor of the more proximate reward as the time to both rewards diminishes—for example, someone may prefer $110 in thirty-one days over $100 in thirty days, but also prefer $100 now over $110 tomorrow. Such "preference reversals" have been observed both in humans (Green, Fristoe, and Myerson 1994; Kirby and Herrnstein 1995; Millar and Navarick 1984; Solnick et al. 1980) and in pigeons (Ainslie and Herrnstein 1981; Green et al. 1981).[13]

Fourth, the pattern of declining discount rates suggested by these studies is also evident *across* studies. Figure 1.1 plots the average estimated discount factor ($= 1/(1 + \text{discount rate})$) from each of these studies against the average time horizon for that study.[14] As the regression line reflects, the estimated discount factor increases with the time horizon, which means that the discount rate declines. We note, however, that after excluding studies with very short time horizons (one year or less) from the analysis (see figure 1.2), there is no evidence that discount rates continue to decline. In fact, after excluding the studies with short time horizons, the correlation between time horizon and discount factor is almost exactly zero (-0.0026).

Although the collective evidence outlined here seems overwhelmingly to support hyperbolic discounting, a recent study by Read (2001) points out that the most common type of evidence—the finding that implicit discount rates decrease with the time horizon—

Figure 1.1   Discount Factor as a Function of Time Horizon (All Studies)

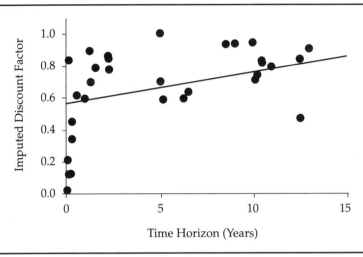

Source: Frederick, Loewenstein, and O'Donoghue (2002).

could also be explained by "subadditive discounting," which means that the total amount of discounting over a temporal interval increases as the interval is more finely partitioned.[15] To demonstrate subadditive discounting and distinguish it from hyperbolic discounting, Read elicited discount rates for a two-year (twenty-four-month) interval and for its three constituent intervals, an eight-month interval beginning at the same time, an eight-month interval beginning eight months later, and an eight-month interval beginning sixteen months later. He found that the average discount rate for the twenty-four-month interval was lower than the compounded average discount rate over the three eight-month subintervals—a result predicted by subadditive discounting but not predicted by hyperbolic discounting (or any type of discount function, for that matter). Moreover, there was no evidence that discount rates declined with time, as the discount rates for the three eight-month intervals were approximately equal. Similar empirical results were found earlier by Holcomb and Nelson (1992), although they did not interpret their results the same way.

If Read is correct about subadditive discounting, its main implication for economic applications may be to provide an alternative psychological underpinning for using a hyperbolic discount function, because most intertemporal decisions are based primarily on discounting from the present.[16]

Figure 1.2   Discount Factor as a Function of Time Horizon (Studies with Average Horizons Greater Than One Year)

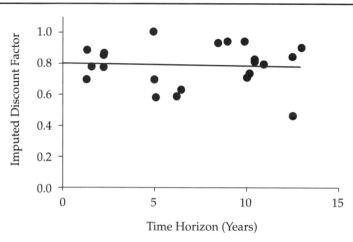

Source: Frederick, Loewenstein, and O'Donoghue (2002).

Other DU Anomalies

The DU model not only dictates that the discount rate should be constant for all time periods, it also assumes that the discount rate should be the same for all types of goods and all categories of intertemporal decisions. There are several empirical regularities that appear to contradict this assumption, namely: gains are discounted more than losses; small amounts are discounted more than large amounts; greater discounting is shown to avoid delay of a good than to expedite its receipt; in choices over sequences of outcomes, improving sequences are often preferred to declining sequences though positive time preference dictates the opposite; and in choices over sequences, violations of independence are pervasive, and people seem to prefer spreading consumption over time in a way that diminishing marginal utility alone cannot explain.

The "Sign Effect" (Gains Are Discounted More than Losses)   Many studies have concluded that gains are discounted at a higher rate than losses. For instance, Thaler (1981) asked subjects to imagine they had received a traffic ticket that could be paid either now or later and to state how much they would be willing to pay if payment could be delayed (by three months, one year, or three years). The discount rates imputed from these answers were much lower than the discount rates imputed from comparable questions about monetary gains. This pattern is prevalent in the literature. Indeed, in many studies, a substantial proportion of subjects prefer to incur a loss immediately rather than delay it (Benzion, Rapoport, and Yagil 1989; Loewenstein 1987; MacKeigan et al. 1993; Mischel, Grusec, and Masters 1969; Redelmeier and Heller 1993; Yates and Watts 1975).

The "Magnitude Effect" (Small Outcomes Are Discounted More than Large Ones)   Most studies that vary outcome size have found that large outcomes are discounted at a lower rate than small ones (Ainslie and Haendel 1983; Benzion, Rapoport, and Yagil 1989; Green, Fristoe, and Myerson 1994; Green, Fry, and Myerson 1994; Holcomb and Nelson 1992; Kirby 1997; Kirby and Marakovic 1995; Kirby, Petry, and Bickel 1999; Loewenstein 1987; Raineri and Rachlin 1993; Shelley 1993; Thaler 1981). In Thaler's (1981) study, for example, respondents were, on average, indifferent between $15 immediately and $60 in a year, $250 immediately and $350 in a year, and $3,000 immediately and $4,000 in a year, implying discount rates of 139 percent, 34 percent, and 29 percent, respectively.

The "Delay-Speedup" Asymmetry   Loewenstein (1988) demonstrated that imputed discount rates can be dramatically affected by whether the change in delivery time of an outcome is framed as an acceleration or a delay from some temporal reference point. For example, respondents who didn't expect to receive a VCR for another year would pay an average of $54 to receive it immediately, but those who thought they would receive it immediately demanded an average of $126 to delay its receipt by a year. Benzion, Rapoport, and Yagil (1989) and Shelley (1993) replicated Loewenstein's findings for losses as well as gains (respondents demanded more to expedite payment than they would pay to delay it).

Preference for Improving Sequences   In studies of discounting that involve choices between two outcomes—for example, X at τ versus Y at τ'—positive discounting is the norm. Research examining preferences over *sequences* of outcomes, however, has generally found that people prefer improving sequences to declining sequences (for an overview see Ariely and Carmon, chapter 11 herein; Frederick and Loewenstein 2002; Loewenstein and Prelec 1993). For example, Loewenstein and Sicherman (1991) found that, for an otherwise identical job, most subjects prefer an increasing wage profile to a declining or flat one (see also Frank 1993). Hsee, Abelson, and Salovey (1991) found that an increasing salary sequence was rated as highly as a decreasing sequence that conferred much more money. Varey and Kahneman (1992) found that subjects strongly preferred streams of decreasing discomfort to streams of increasing discomfort, even when the overall sum of discomfort over the interval was otherwise identical. Loewenstein and Prelec (1993) found that respondents who chose between sequences of two or more events (for example, dinners or vacation trips) on consecutive weekends or consecutive months generally preferred to save the better thing for last. Chapman (2000) presented respondents with hypothetical sequences of headache pain that were matched in terms of total pain that either gradually lessened or gradually increased with time. Sequence durations included one hour, one day, one month, one year, five years, and twenty years. For all sequence durations, the vast majority (from 82 percent to 92 percent) of subjects preferred the sequence of pain that lessened over time. (See also Ross and Simonson 1991.)

Violations of Independence and Preference for Spread   The research on preferences over sequences also reveals strong violations of independence. Consider the following pair of questions from Loewenstein and Prelec (1993):

Imagine that over the next five weekends you must decide how to spend your Saturday nights. From each pair of sequences of dinners below, circle the one you would prefer. "Fancy French" refers to a dinner at a fancy French restaurant. "Fancy Lobster" refers to an exquisite lobster dinner at a four-star restaurant. Ignore scheduling considerations (e.g., your current plans).

First Weekend	Second Weekend	Third Weekend	Fourth Weekend	Fifth Weekend	
		Option A			
Fancy French	Eat at home	Eat at home	Eat at home	Eat at home	[11%]
		Option B			
Eat at home	Eat at home	Fancy French	Eat at home	Eat at home	[89%]
		Option C			
Fancy French	Eat at home	Eat at home	Eat at home	Fancy Lobster	[49%]
		Option D			
Eat at home	Eat at home	Fancy French	Eat at home	Fancy Lobster	[51%]

As discussed earlier, consumption independence implies that preferences between two consumption profiles should not be affected by the nature of the consumption in periods in which consumption is identical in the two profiles. Thus, anyone preferring profile B to profile A (which share the fifth period "Eat at home") should also prefer profile D to profile C (which share the fifth period "Fancy Lobster"). As the data reveal, however, many respondents violated this prediction, preferring the fancy French dinner on the third weekend, if that was the only fancy dinner in the profile, but preferring the fancy French dinner on the first weekend if the profile contained another fancy dinner. This result could be explained by the simple desire to spread consumption over time—which, in this context, violates the dubious assumption of independence that the DU model entails.

Loewenstein and Prelec (1993) provide further evidence of such a preference for spread. Subjects were asked to imagine that they were given two coupons for fancy ($100) restaurant dinners, and were asked to indicate when they would use them, ignoring considerations such as holidays, birthdays, and such. Subjects were told either that "you can use the coupons at any time between today and two years from today" or were told nothing about any constraints. Subjects in the two-year constraint condition actually scheduled both dinners at a *later* time than those who faced no explicit constraint—they delayed the first dinner for eight weeks (rather than three) and the second dinner for thirty-one weeks (rather than thirteen). This counterintuitive result can be explained in terms of a preference for spread if the explicit two-year interval was greater than the implicit time horizon of subjects in the unconstrained group.

Are These "Anomalies" Mistakes?

In other domains of judgment and choice, many of the famous "effects" that have been documented are regarded as errors by the people who commit them. For example, in the "conjunction fallacy" discovered by Tversky and Kahneman (1983), many people will—with some reflection—recognize that a conjunction cannot be more likely than one of its constituents (for example, that it *can't* be more likely for Linda to be a feminist bank teller than for her to be "just" a bank teller). In contrast, the patterns of preferences that are regarded as "anomalies" in the context of the DU model do not necessarily violate any standard or principle that people believe they should uphold. Even when the choice pattern is pointed out to people, they do not regard themselves as having made a mistake (and probably have not made one!). For example, there is no compelling logic that dictates that one who prefers to delay a French dinner should also prefer to do so when that French dinner will be closely followed by a lobster dinner.

Indeed, it is unclear whether *any* of the DU "anomalies" should be regarded as mistakes. Frederick and Read (2002) found evidence that the magnitude effect is *more* pronounced when subjects evaluate both "small" and "large" amounts than when they evaluate either one. Specifically, the difference in the discount rates between a small amount ($10) and a large amount ($1,000) was larger when the two judgments were made in close succession than when made separately. Analogous results were obtained for the sign effect as the differences in discount rates between gains and losses were slightly larger in a within-subjects design, where respondents evaluated delayed gains and delayed losses, than in a between-subjects design, where they evaluate only gains or only losses. Since respondents did not attempt to coordinate their responses to conform to DU's postulates when they evaluated rewards of different sizes, it suggests that they consider the different discount rates to be normatively appropriate. Similarly, even after Loewenstein and Sicherman (1991) informed respondents that a decreasing wage profile ($27,000, $26,000, . . . $23,000) would (via appropriate saving and investing) permit strictly more consumption in every period than the corresponding increasing wage profile with an equivalent nominal total ($23,000, $24,000, . . . $27,000), respondents still preferred the increasing sequence. Perhaps they suspected that they could not exercise the required self-control to maintain their desired *consumption* sequence, or felt a general leeriness about the significance of a declining wage, either of which could justify that choice. As these examples illustrate, many DU "anomalies" exist as "anomalies" only by reference to a model that was constructed without regard to its descriptive validity, and which has no compelling normative basis.

Alternative Models

In response to the anomalies just enumerated, and other intertemporal-choice phenomena that are inconsistent with the DU model, a variety of alternate theoretical models have been developed. Some models attempt to achieve greater descriptive realism by relaxing the assumption of constant discounting. Other models incorporate additional considerations into the instantaneous utility function, such as the utility from anticipation. Still others depart from the DU model more radically, by including, for instance, systematic mispredictions of future utility.

Models of Hyperbolic Discounting

In the economics literature, Strotz was the first to consider alternatives to exponential discounting, seeing "no reason why an individual
should have such a special discount function" (1955–1956, 172).
Moreover, Strotz recognized that for any discount function other than
exponential, a person would have time-inconsistent preferences.[17] He
proposed two strategies that might be employed by a person who
foresees how her preferences will change over time: the "strategy of
precommitment" (wherein she commits to some plan of action) and
the "strategy of consistent planning" (wherein she chooses her behavior ignoring plans that she knows her future selves will not carry
out).[18] While Strotz did not posit any specific alternative functional
forms, he did suggest that "special attention" be given to the case of
declining discount rates.

Motivated by the evidence discussed earlier, there has been a recent surge of interest among economists in the implications of declining discount rates (beginning with Laibson 1994, 1997). This literature
has used a particularly simple functional form that captures the essence of hyperbolic discounting:

$$D(k) = \begin{cases} 1 & \text{if } h = 0 \\ \beta\delta^k & \text{if } k > 0. \end{cases}$$

This functional form was first introduced by Phelps and Pollak (1968)
to study intergenerational altruism, and was first applied to individual decision making by Elster (1979). It assumes that the per-period
discount rate between now and the next period is $(1 - \beta\delta)/\beta\delta$
whereas the per-period discount rate between any two future periods
is

$$\frac{1 - \delta}{\delta} < \frac{1 - \beta\delta}{\beta\delta}.$$

Hence, this (β,δ) formulation assumes a declining discount rate between this period and next, but a constant discount rate thereafter.
The (β,δ) formulation is highly tractable, and captures many of the
qualitative implications of hyperbolic discounting.

Laibson and his collaborators have used the (β,δ) formulation to
explore the implications of hyperbolic discounting for consumption-
saving behavior. Hyperbolic discounting leads one to consume more
than one would like to from a prior perspective (or, equivalently, to
undersave). Laibson (1997) explores the role of illiquid assets, such as

housing, as an imperfect commitment technology, emphasizing how one could limit overconsumption by tying up one's wealth in illiquid assets. Laibson (1998) explores consumption-saving decisions in a world without illiquid assets (or any other commitment technology). These papers describe how hyperbolic discounting might explain some stylized empirical facts, such as the excess comovement of income and consumption, the existence of asset-specific marginal propensities to consume, low levels of precautionary savings, and the correlation of measured levels of patience with age, income, and wealth. Laibson, Repetto, and Tobacman (1998), and Angeletos and colleagues (2001) calibrate models of consumption-saving decisions, using both exponential discounting and (β,δ) hyperbolic discounting. By comparing simulated data to real-world data, they demonstrate how hyperbolic discounting can better explain a variety of empirical observations in the consumption-saving literature. In particular, Angeletos and colleagues (2001) describe how hyperbolic discounting can explain the coexistence of high preretirement wealth, low liquid asset holdings (relative to income levels and illiquid asset holdings), and high credit-card debt.

Fischer (1999) and O'Donoghue and Rabin (1999c, 2001) have applied (β,δ) preferences to procrastination, where hyperbolic discounting leads a person to put off an onerous activity more than she would like to from a prior perspective.[19] O'Donoghue and Rabin (1999c) examine the implications of hyperbolic discounting for contracting when a principal is concerned with combating procrastination by an agent. They show how incentive schemes with "deadlines" may be a useful screening device to distinguish efficient delay from inefficient procrastination. O'Donoghue and Rabin (2001) explore procrastination when a person must not only choose *when* to complete a task, but also *which* task to complete, They show that a person might never carry out a very easy and very good option because they continually *plan* to carry out an even better but more onerous option. For instance, a person might never take half an hour to straighten the shelves in her garage because she persistently plans to take an entire day to do a major cleanup of the entire garage. Extending this logic, they show that providing people with new options might make procrastination more likely. If the person's only option were to straighten the shelves, she might do it in a timely manner; but if the person can either straighten the shelves or do the major cleanup, she now may do nothing. O'Donoghue and Rabin (1999d) apply this logic to retirement planning.

O'Donoghue and Rabin (1999a, 2000), Gruber and Koszegi (2000), and Carrillo (1999) have applied (β,δ) preferences to addiction. These researchers describe how hyperbolic discounting can lead people to overconsume harmful addictive products, and examine the degree of harm caused by such overconsumption. Carrillo and Mariotti (2000) and Benabou and Tirole (2000) have examined how (β, δ) preferences might influence a person's decision to acquire information. If, for example, one is deciding whether to embark on a specific research agenda, one may have the option to get feedback from colleagues about its likely fruitfulness. The standard economic model implies that people should always choose to acquire this information if it is free. Carrillo and Mariotti show, however, that hyperbolic discounting can lead to "strategic ignorance"—a person with hyperbolic discounting who is worried about withdrawing from an advantageous course of action when the costs become imminent might choose not to acquire free information if doing so increases the risk of bailing out.

Self-Awareness

A person with time-inconsistent preferences may or may not be aware that his or her preferences will change over time. Strotz (1955–1956) and Pollak (1968) discussed two extreme alternatives. At one extreme, a person could be completely "naive" and believe that her future preferences will be identical to her current preferences. At the other extreme, a person could be completely "sophisticated" and correctly predict how his or her preferences will change over time. While casual observation and introspection suggest that people lie somewhere between these two extremes, behavioral evidence regarding the degree of awareness is quite limited.

One way to identify sophistication is to look for evidence of commitment. Someone who suspects that his or her preferences will change over time might take steps to eliminate an inferior option that might tempt one later. For example, someone who currently prefers $110 in thirty-one days to $100 in thirty days but who suspects that in a month she will prefer $100 immediately to $110 tomorrow, might attempt to eliminate the $100 reward from the later choice set, and thereby bind herself *now* to receive the $110 reward in thirty-one days. Real-world examples of commitment include "Christmas clubs" or "fat farms."

Perhaps the best empirical demonstration of a preference for commitment was conducted by Ariely and Wertenbroch (2002). In that study, MIT executive-education students had to write three short papers for a class and were assigned to one of two experimental conditions. In one condition, deadlines for the three papers were imposed by the instructor and were evenly spaced across the semester. In the other condition, each student was allowed to set his or her own deadlines for each of the three papers. In both conditions, the penalty for delay was 1 percent per day late, regardless of whether the deadline was externally or self-imposed. Although students in the free-choice condition could have made all three papers due at the end of the semester, many in fact did choose to impose deadlines on themselves, suggesting that they appreciated the value of commitment. Few students chose evenly spaced deadlines, however, and those who did not performed worse in the course than those with evenly spaced deadlines (whether externally imposed or self-imposed).[20]

O'Donoghue and Rabin (1999b) examine how people's behaviors depend on their sophistication about their own time inconsistency. Some behaviors, such as using illiquid assets for commitment, require some degree of sophistication. Other behaviors, such as overconsumption or procrastination, are more robust to the degree of awareness, though the degree of misbehavior may depend on the degree of sophistication. To understand such effects, O'Donoghue and Rabin (2001) introduce a formal model of *partial naivete*, in which a person is aware that he or she will have future self-control problems but underestimates their magnitude. They show that severe procrastination cannot occur under complete sophistication, but can arise if the person is only a little naive. (For more discussion on self-awareness see O'Donoghue and Rabin, chapter 7 herein.)

The degree of sophistication versus naivete has important implications for public policy. If people are sufficiently sophisticated about their own self-control problems, providing commitment devices may be beneficial. If people are naive, however, policies might be better aimed at either educating people about loss of control (making them more sophisticated), or providing incentives for people to use commitment devices, even if they don't recognize the need for them.

Models That Enrich the Instantaneous Utility Function

Many discounting anomalies, especially those discussed earlier, can be understood as a misspecification of the instantaneous utility function. Similarly, many of the confounds discussed in the section on measuring time discounting are caused by researchers attributing to the discount rate aspects of preference that are more appropriately considered as arguments in the instantaneous utility function. As a result, alternative models of intertemporal choice have been advanced that add additional arguments, such as utility from anticipation, to the instantaneous utility function.

Habit-Formation Models James Duesenberry (1952) was the first economist to propose the idea of "habit formation"—that the utility from current consumption ("tastes") can be affected by the level of past consumption. This idea was more formally developed by Pollak (1970) and Ryder and Heal (1973). In habit formation models, the period-τ instantaneous utility function takes the form u $(c_\tau; c_{\tau-1}, c_{\tau-2}, \ldots)$ where $\partial^2 u / \partial c_\tau \partial c_{\tau'} > 0$ for $\tau' < \tau$. For simplicity, most such models assume that all effects of past consumption for current utility enter through a state variable. That is, they assume that period-τ instantaneous utility function takes the form $u(c_\tau; z_\tau)$ where z_τ is a state variable that is increasing in past consumption and $\partial^2 / \partial c_\tau \partial z_\tau > 0$. Both Pollak (1970) and Ryder and Heal (1973) assume that z_τ is the exponentially weighted sum of past consumption, or $z_\tau \Sigma_{i=1}^{\infty} \gamma^i c_{\tau-i}$.

Although habit formation is often said to induce a preference for an increasing consumption profile, it can, under some circumstances, lead a person to prefer a decreasing or even nonmonotonic consumption profile. The direction of the effect depends on things such as how much one has already consumed (as reflected in the initial habit stock), and perhaps most important, whether current consumption increases or decreases future utility.

In recent years, habit-formation models have been used to analyze a variety of phenomena. Becker and Murphy (1988) use a habit-formation model to study addictive activities, and in particular to examine the effects of past and future prices on the current consumption of addictive products.[21] Habit formation can help explain asset-pricing anomalies such as the equity-premium puzzle (Abel 1990; Campbell and Cochrane 1999; Constantinides 1990). Incorporating habit formation into business-cycle models can improve their ability to explain movements in asset prices (Jermann 1998; Boldrin, Christiano, and Fisher 2001). Some recent papers have shown that habit formation may help explain other empirical puzzles in macroeconomics as well. Whereas standard growth models assume that high saving rates cause high growth, recent evidence suggests that the causality can run in the opposite direction. Carroll, Overland, and Weil (2000) show that, under conditions of habit formation, high growth rates can cause people to save more. Fuhrer (2000) shows how habit formation might explain the recent finding that aggregate spending tends to have a gradual "hump-shaped" response to various shocks. The key feature of habit formation that drives many of these results is that, after a shock, consumption adjustment is sluggish in the short term but not in the long term.

Reference-Point Models Closely related to, but conceptually distinct from, habit-formation models are models of reference-dependent utility, which incorporate ideas from prospect theory (Kahneman and Tversky 1979; Tversky and Kahneman 1991). According to prospect theory, outcomes are evaluated using a value function defined over departures from a reference point—in our notation, the period-τ instantaneous utility function takes the form $u(c_\tau, r_\tau) = v(c_\tau - r_\tau)$. The reference point, r_τ, might depend on past consumption, expectations, social comparison, status quo, and such. A second feature of prospect theory is that the value function exhibits *loss aversion*—negative departures from one's reference consumption level decrease utility by a greater amount than positive departures increase it. A third feature of prospect theory is that the value function exhibits *diminishing sensitivity* for both gains and losses, which means that the value function is concave over gains and convex over losses.[22]

Loewenstein and Prelec (1992) applied a specialized version of such a value function to intertemporal choice to explain the magnitude effect, the sign effect, and the delay-speedup asymmetry. They show that if the elasticity of the value function is increasing in the magnitude of outcomes, people will discount smaller magnitudes more than larger magnitudes. Intuitively, the elasticity condition captures the insight that people are responsive to both differences and ratios of reward amounts. It implies that someone who is indifferent between, say, $10 now and $20 in a year should prefer $200 in a year over $100 now because the larger rewards have a greater difference (and the same ratio). Consequently, even if one's time preference is actually constant across outcomes, a person will be more willing to wait for a fixed proportional increment when rewards are larger and, thus, one's imputed discount rate will be smaller for larger outcomes. Similarly, if the value function for losses is more elastic than the value function for gains, then people will discount gains more than losses. Finally, such a model helps explain the delay-speedup asymmetry (Loewenstein 1988). Shifting consumption in any direction is made less desirable by loss aversion, since one loses consumption in one period and gains it in another. When delaying consumption, loss aversion reinforces time discounting, creating a powerful aversion to delay. When expediting consumption, loss aversion opposes time discounting, reducing the desirability of speedup (and occasionally even causing an aversion to it).

Using a reference-dependent model that assumes loss aversion in consumption, Bowman, Minehart, and Rabin (1999) predict that "news" about one's (stochastic) future income affects one's consumption growth differently than the standard Permanent Income Hypothesis predicts. According to (the log-linear version of) the Permanent Income Hypothesis, changes in future income should not affect the rate of consumption growth. For example, if a person finds out that his or her permanent income will be lower than formerly thought, he or she would reduce consumption by, say, 10 percent in every period, leaving consumption growth unchanged. If, however, this person were loss averse in current consumption, he or she would be unwilling to reduce this year's consumption by 10 percent—forcing that person to reduce future consumption by *more* than 10 percent, and thereby reducing the growth rate of consumption. Two studies by Shea (1995a, 1995b) support this prediction. Using both aggregate U.S. data and data from teachers' unions (in which wages are set one year in advance), Shea finds that consumption growth responds more strongly to future wage decreases than to future wage increases.

Models Incorporating Utility from Anticipation Some alternative models build on the notion of "anticipal" utility discussed by the elder and younger Jevons. If people derive pleasure not only from current consumption but also from anticipating future consumption, then current instantaneous utility will depend positively on future consumption—that is, the period-τ instantaneous utility function would take the form $u(c_\tau;c_{\tau+1},c_{\tau+2},\ldots)$ where $\partial u/\partial c_{\tau'} > 0$ for $\tau' > \tau$. Loewenstein (1987) advanced a formal model that assumes that a person's instantaneous utility is equal to the utility from consumption in that period plus some function of the discounted utility of consumption in future periods. Specifically, if we let $v(c)$ denote utility from actual consumption, and assume this is the same for all periods, then:

$$u(c_\tau;c_{\tau+1},c_{\tau+2},\ldots) = v(c_\tau) + \alpha[\gamma v(c_{\tau+1}) + \gamma^2 v(c_{\tau+2}) + \ldots]$$
$$\text{for some } \gamma < 1.$$

Loewenstein describes how utility from anticipation may play a role in many DU anomalies. Because near-term consumption delivers only consumption utility whereas future consumption delivers both consumption utility and anticipatory utility, anticipatory utility provides a reason to prefer improvement and for getting unpleasant outcomes over with quickly instead of delaying them as discounting would predict. It provides a possible explanation for why people discount different goods at different rates, because utility from anticipation creates a downward bias on estimated discount rates, and this downward bias is larger for goods that create more anticipatory utility. If, for instance, dreading future bad outcomes is a stronger emotion than savoring future good outcomes, which seems highly plausible, then utility from anticipation would generate a sign effect.[23]

Finally, anticipatory utility gives rise to a form of time inconsistency that is quite different from that which arises from hyperbolic discounting. Instead of planning to do the farsighted thing (for example, save money) but subsequently doing the shortsighted thing (splurging), anticipatory utility can cause people to repeatedly plan to consume a good after some delay that permits pleasurable anticipation, but then to delay again for the same reason when the planned moment of consumption arrives.

Loewenstein's model of anticipatory utility applies to deterministic outcomes. In a recent paper, Caplin and Leahy (2001) point out that many anticipatory emotions, such as anxiety or suspense, are driven by uncertainty about the future, and they propose a new model that modifies expected-utility theory to incorporate such anticipatory emotions. They then show that incorporating anxiety into asset-pricing models may help explain the equity premium puzzle and the risk-free rate puzzle, because anxiety creates a taste for risk-free assets and an aversion to risky assets. Like Loewenstein, Caplin and Leahy emphasize how anticipatory utility can lead to time inconsistency. Koszegi (2001) also discusses some implications of anticipatory utility.

Visceral Influences   A final alternative model of the utility function incorporates "visceral" influences such as hunger, sexual desire, physical pain, cravings, and such. Loewenstein (1996, 2000b) argues that economics should take more seriously the implications of such transient fluctuations in tastes. Formally, visceral influences mean that the person's instantaneous utility function takes the form $u(c_\tau, d_\tau)$ where d_τ represents the vector of visceral states in period τ. Visceral states are (at least to some extent) endogenous—for example, one's current hunger depends on how much one has consumed in previous periods—and therefore lead to consumption interdependence.

Visceral influences have important implications for intertemporal choice because, by increasing the attractiveness of certain goods or activities, they can give rise to behaviors that look extremely impatient or even impulsive. Indeed, for every visceral influence, it is easy to think of one or more associated problems of self-control—hunger and dieting, sexual desire and various "heat-of-the-moment" behaviors, craving and drug addiction, and so on. Visceral influences provide an alternate account of the preference reversals that are typically attributed to hyperbolic time discounting, because the temporal proximity of a reward is one of the cues that can activate appetitive visceral states (see Laibson 2001; Loewenstein 1996). Other cues—such as spatial proximity, the presence of associated smells or sounds, or similarity in current setting to historical consumption sites—may also have such an effect. Thus, research on various types of cues may help to generate new predictions about the specific circumstances (other than temporal proximity) that can trigger myopic behavior.

The fact that visceral states are endogenous introduces issues of state-management (as discussed by Loewenstein 1999, and Laibson 2001 under the rubric of "cue management"). While the model (at least the rational version of it) predicts that one would want oneself to use drugs if one were to experience a sufficiently strong craving, it also predicts that one might want to prevent ever experiencing such a strong craving. Hence, visceral influences can give rise to a preference for commitment in the sense that the person may want to avoid certain situations.

Visceral influences may do more than merely change the instantaneous utility function. First, evidence shows that people don't fully appreciate the effects of visceral influences, and hence may not react optimally to them (Loewenstein 1996, 1999, 2000b). When in a hot state, people tend to exaggerate how long the hot state will persist, and, when in a cold state, people tend to underestimate how much future visceral influences will affect their future behavior. Second, and perhaps more importantly, people often would "prefer" not to respond to an intense visceral factor such as rage, fear, or lust, even at the moment they are succumbing to its influence. A way to understand such effects is to apply the distinction proposed by Kahneman (1994) between "experienced utility," which reflects one's welfare, and "decision utility," which reflects the attractiveness of options as inferred from one's decisions. By increasing the decision utility of certain types of actions more than the experienced utility of those actions, visceral factors may drive a wedge between what people do and what makes them happy. Bernheim and Rangel (2001) propose a model of addiction framed in these terms.

More "Extreme" Alternative Perspectives

The alternative models discussed thus far modify the DU model by altering the discount function or adding additional arguments to the instantaneous utility function. The alternatives discussed next involve more radical departures from the DU model.

Projection Bias In many of the alternative models of utility discussed thus far, the person's utility from consumption—her tastes—change over time. To properly make intertemporal decisions, one must correctly predict how one's tastes will change. Essentially all economic models of changing tastes assume (as economists typically do) that such predictions are correct—that people have "rational expectations." Loewenstein, O'Donoghue, and Rabin (2000), however, propose that, while people may anticipate the qualitative nature of their changing preferences, they tend to underestimate the magnitude of these changes—a systematic misprediction they label *projection bias*.

Loewenstein, O'Donoghue, and Rabin review a broad array of evidence that demonstrates the prevalence of projection bias, then model it formally. To illustrate their model, consider projection bias in the realm of habit formation. As discussed earlier, suppose the period-τ instantaneous utility function takes the form $u(c_\tau;z_\tau)$, where z_τ is a state variable that captures the effects of past consumption. Projection bias arises when a person whose current state is z_t must predict his or her future utility given future state z_τ. Projection bias implies that the person's prediction $\tilde{u}(c_\tau;z_\tau \mid z_t)$ will lie between his or her true future utility $u(c_\tau;z_\tau)$ and his or her utility given the person's current state $u(c_\tau;z_t)$. A particularly simple functional form is $\tilde{u}(c_\tau;z_\tau \mid z_t) = (1 - \alpha)$ $u(c_\tau;z_\tau) + \alpha u(c_\tau;z_t)$ for some $\alpha \in [0, 1]$.

Projection bias may arise whenever tastes change over time, whether through habit formation, changing reference points, or changes in visceral states. It can have important behavioral and welfare implications. For instance, people may underappreciate the degree to which a present consumption splurge will raise their reference consumption level, and thereby decrease their enjoyment of more modest consumption levels in the future. When intertemporal choices are influenced by projection bias, estimates of time preference may be distorted.

Mental-Accounting Models Some researchers have proposed that people do not treat all money as fungible, but instead assign different types of expenditures to different "mental accounts" (see Thaler 1999 for a recent overview). Such models can give rise to intertemporal behaviors that seem odd when viewed through the lens of the DU model. Thaler (1985), for instance, suggests that small amounts of money are coded as spending money, whereas larger amounts of money are coded as savings, and that a person is more willing to spend out of the former account. This accounting rule would predict that people will behave like spendthrifts for small purchases (for example, a new pair of shoes), but act more frugally when it comes to large purchases (for example, a new dining-room table).[24] Benartzi and Thaler (1995) suggest that people treat their financial portfolios as a mental account, and emphasize the importance of how often people "evaluate" this account. They argue that if people review their portfolios once a year or so, and if people experience joy or pain from any gains or losses, as assumed in Kahneman and Tversky's (1979) prospect theory, then such "myopic loss aversion" represents a plausible explanation for the equity premium puzzle.

Prelec and Loewenstein (1998) propose another way in which mental accounting might influence intertemporal choice. They posit that payments for consumption confer immediate disutility or "pain of paying," and that people keep mental accounts that link the consumption of a particular item with the payments for it. They also assume that people engage in "prospective accounting." According to prospective accounting, when consuming, people think only about current and future payments; past payments don't cause pain of paying. Likewise, when paying, the pain of paying is buffered only by thoughts of future, but not past, consumption. The model suggests that different ways of financing a purchase can lead to different decisions, even holding the net present value of payments constant. Similarly, people might have different financing preferences depending on the consumption item (for example, they should prefer to prepay for a vacation that is consumed all at once versus a new car that is consumed over many years). The model generates a strong preference for prepayment (except for durables), for getting paid after rather than before doing work, and for fixed-fee pricing schemes with zero marginal costs over pay-as-you-go schemes that tightly couple marginal payments to marginal consumption. The model also suggests that interindividual heterogeneity might arise from differences in the degree to which people experience the pain of paying rather than differences in time preference. On this view, the miser who eschews a fancy restaurant dinner is not doing so because he or she explicitly considers the delayed costs of the indulgence, but rather because enjoyment of the dinner would be diminished by the immediate pain of paying for it.

Choice Bracketing   One important aspect of mental accounting is that a person makes at most a few choices at any one time, and generally ignores the relation between these choices and other past and future choices. Which choices are considered at the same time is a matter of what Read, Loewenstein, and Rabin (1999) label *choice bracketing*. Intertemporal choices, like other choices, can be influenced by the manner in which they are bracketed, because different bracketing can highlight different motives. To illustrate, consider the conflict between impatience and a preference for improvement over time. Loewenstein and Prelec (1993) demonstrate that the relative importance of these two motives can be altered by the way that choices are bracketed. They asked one group of subjects to choose between having dinner at a fine French restaurant in one month versus two months. Most subjects chose one month, presumably reflecting impatience. They then asked another group to choose between eating at home in one month followed by eating at the French restaurant in two months versus eating at the French restaurant in one month followed by eating at home in two months. The majority now wanted the French dinner in two months. For both groups, dinner at home was the most likely alternative to the French dinner, but it was only when the two dinners were expressed as a sequence that the preference for improvement became a basis for decision.

Analyzing how people frame or bracket choices may help illuminate the issue of whether a preference for improvement merely reflects the combined effect of other motives, such as reference dependence or anticipatory utility, or whether it is something unique. Viewed from an integrated decision-making perspective, the preference for improvement seems derivative of these other concepts, because it is unclear why one would value improvement for its own sake. But when viewed from a choice-bracketing perspective, it seems plausible that a person would adopt this choice heuristic for evaluating sequences. Specifically, a preference-for-improvement choice heuristic may have originated from considerations of reference dependence or anticipatory utility, but a person using this choice heuristic may come to feel that improvement for its own sake has value.[25]

Loewenstein and Prelec (1993) develop a choice-heuristic model for how people evaluate choices over sequences. They assume that people consider a sequence's discounted utility, its degree of improvement, and its degree of spread. The key ingredients of the model are "gestalt" definitions for improvement and spread. In other words, they develop a formal measure of the degree of improvement and the degree of spread for any sequence. They show that their model can explain a wide range of sequence anomalies, including observed violations of independence, and that it predicts preferences between sequences much better than other models that incorporate similar numbers of free parameters (even a model with an entirely flexible time discount function).

Multiple-Self Models   An influential school of theorists has proposed models that view intertemporal choice as the outcome of a conflict between multiple selves. Most multiple-self models postulate myopic selves who are in conflict with more farsighted ones, and often draw analogies between intertemporal choice and a variety of different models of interpersonal strategic interactions. Some models (for example, Ainslie and Haslam 1992; Schelling 1984; Winston 1980) assume that there are two agents, one myopic and one farsighted, who alternately take control of behavior. The main problem with this approach is that it fails to specify why either type of agent emerges when it does. Furthermore, by characterizing the interaction as a battle between the two agents, these models fail to capture an important asymmetry: farsighted selves often attempt to control the behaviors of myopic selves, but never the reverse. For instance, the farsighted self may pour vodka down the drain to prevent tomorrow's self from drinking it, but the myopic self rarely takes steps to ensure that tomorrow's self will have access to the alcohol he or she will then crave.

Responding in part to this problem, Thaler and Shefrin (1981) proposed a "planner-doer" model that draws upon principal-agent theory. In their model, a series of myopic "doers," who care only about their own immediate gratification (and have no affinity for future or past doers), interact with a unitary "planner" who cares equally about the present and future. The model focuses on the strategies employed by the planner to control the behavior of the doers. The model highlights the observation, later discussed at length by Loewenstein (1996), that the farsighted perspective is often much more constant than the myopic perspective. For example, people are often consistent in recognizing the need to maintain a diet. Yet they periodically violate their own desired course of action—often recognizing even at the moment of doing so that they are not behaving in their own self-interest.

Yet a third type of multiple-self model draws connections between intertemporal choice and models of multiperson strategic interactions (Elster 1985). The essential insight that these models capture is that, much like cooperation in a social dilemma, self-control often requires the cooperation of a series of temporally situated selves. When one self "defects" by opting for immediate gratification, the consequence can be a kind of unraveling or "falling off the wagon" when subsequent selves follow the precedent.

Few of these multiple-self models have been expressed formally, and even fewer have been used to derive testable implications that go much beyond the intuitions that inspired them in the first place. However, perhaps it is unfair to criticize the models for these shortcomings. These models are probably best viewed as metaphors intended to highlight specific aspects of intertemporal choice. Specifically, multiple-self models have been used to make sense of the wide range of self-control strategies that people use to regulate their own future behavior. Moreover, these models provided much of the inspiration for more recent formal models of sophisticated hyperbolic discounting (following Laibson 1994, 1997).

Temptation Utility   Most models of intertemporal choice—indeed, most models of choice in any framework—assume that options not chosen are irrelevant to a person's well-being. In a recent paper, Gul and Pesendorfer (2001) posit that people have "temptation preferences," wherein they experience disutility from not choosing the option that is most enjoyable now. Their theory implies that a person might be better off if some particularly tempting option were not available, even if he or she doesn't choose that option. As a result, the person may be willing to pay in advance to eliminate that option, or in other words, he or she may have a preference for commitment.

Combining Insights from Different Models   Many behavioral models of intertemporal choice focus on a single modification to the DU model and explore the additional realism produced by that single modification. Yet many empirical phenomena reflect the interaction of multiple phenomena. For instance, a preference for improvement may interact with hyperbolic discounting to produce preferences for U-shaped sequences—for example, for jobs that offer a signing bonus and a salary that increases gradually over time. As discussed by Loewenstein and Prelec (1993), in the short term, the preference-for-improvement motive is swamped by the high discount rates, but as the discount rate falls over time, the preference-for-improvement motive may gain ascendance and cause a net preference for an increasing payment sequence.

As another example, introducing visceral influences into models of hyperbolic discounting may more fully account for the phenomenology of impulsive choices. Hyperbolic-discounting models predict that people respond especially strongly to immediate costs and benefits, and visceral influences have powerful transient effects on immediate utilities. In combination, the two assumptions could explain a wide range of impulsive choices and other self-control phenomena.

Measuring Time Discounting

The DU model assumes that a person's time preference can be captured by a single discount rate, ρ. In the past three decades there have been many attempts to measure this rate. Some of these estimates are derived from observations of "real-world" behaviors (for example, the choice between electrical appliances that differ in their initial purchase price and long-run operating costs). Others are derived from experimental elicitation procedures (for example, respondents' answers to the question "Which would you prefer: $100 today or $150 one year from today?"). Table 1.1 summarizes the implicit discount rates from all studies that we could locate in which discount rates were either directly reported or easily computed from the reported data.

Figure 1.3 plots the estimated discount factor for each study against the publication date for that study, where the discount factor is $\delta = 1/(1 + \rho)$.[26] This figure reveals three noteworthy observations. First, there is tremendous variability in the estimates (the corresponding implicit annual discount rates range from -6 percent to infinity). Second, in contrast to estimates of physical phenomena such as the speed of light, there is no evidence of methodological progress; the range of estimates is not shrinking over time. Third, high discounting predominates, as most of the data points are well below 1, which represents equal weighting of present and future.

In this section, we provide an overview and critique of this empirical literature with an eye toward understanding these three observations. We then review the procedures used to estimate discount rates.

Figure 1.3   Discount Factor by Year of Study Publication

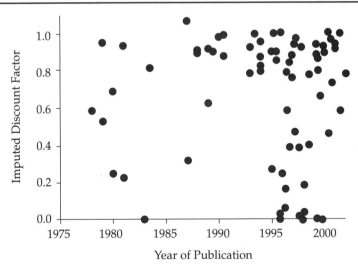

Source: Authors' configuration.

Table 1.1   Empirical Estimates of Discount Rates

Study	Type	Good(s)	Real or Hypo?	Elicitation Method
Maital and Maital 1978	experimental	money and coupons	hypo.	choice
Hausman 1979	field	money	real	choice
Gateley 1980	field	money	real	choice
Thaler 1981	experimental	money	hypo.	matching
Ainslie and Haendel 1983	experimental	money	real	matching
Houston 1983	experimental	money	hypo.	other
Loewenstein 1987	experimental	money and pain	hypo.	pricing
Moore and Viscusi 1988	field	life years	real	choice
Benzion et al. 1989	experimental	money	hypo.	matching
Viscusi and Moore 1989	field	life years	real	choice
Moore and Viscusi 1990a	field	life years	real	choice
Moore and Viscusi 1990b	field	life years	real	choice
Shelley 1993	experimental	money	hypo.	matching
Redelmeier and Heller 1993	experimental	health	hypo.	rating
Cairns 1994	experimental	money	hypo.	choice
Shelley 1994	experimental	money	hypo.	rating
Chapman and Elstein 1995	experimental	money and health	hypo.	matching
Dolan and Gudex 1995	experimental	health	hypo.	other
Dreyfus and Viscusi 1995	field	life years	real	choice
Kirby and Marakovic 1995	experimental	money	real	matching
Chapman 1996	experimental	money and health	hypo.	matching
Kirby and Marakovic 1996	experimental	money	real	choice
Pender 1996	experimental	rice	real	choice
Wahlund and Gunnarson 1996	experimental	money	hypo.	matching
Cairns and van der Pol 1997	experimental	money	hypo.	matching

Table 1.1 *Continued*

Study	Type	Good(s)	Real or Hypo?	Elicitation Method
Green, Myerson, and McFadden 1997	experimental	money	hypo.	choice
Johannesson and Johansson 1997	experimental	life years	hypo.	pricing
Kirby 1997	experimental	money	real	pricing
Madden et al. 1997	experimental	money and heroin	hypo.	choice
Chapman and Winquist 1998	experimental	money	hypo.	matching
Holden, Shiferaw, and Wik 1998	experimental	money and corn	real	matching
Cairns and van der Pol 1999	experimental	health	hypo.	matching
Chapman, Nelson, and Hier 1999	experimental	money and health	hypo.	choice
Coller and Williams 1999	experimental	money	real	choice
Kirby, Petry, and Bickel 1999	experimental	money	real	choice
van der Pol and Cairns 1999	experimental	health	hypo.	choice
Chesson and Viscusi 2000	experimental	money	hypo.	matching
Ganiats et al. 2000	experimental	health	hypo.	choice
Hesketh 2000	experimental	money	hypo.	choice
van der Pol and Cairns 2001	experimental	health	hypo.	choice
Warner and Pleeter 2001	field	money	real	choice
Harrison, Lau, and Williams 2002	experimental	money	real	choice

Table 1.1 *Continued*

Study	Time Range	Annual Discount Rate(s)	Annual Discount Factor(s)
Maital and Maital 1978	1 year	70%	0.59
Hausman 1979	undefined	5% to 89%	0.95 to 0.53
Gateley 1980	undefined	45% to 300%	0.69 to 0.25
Thaler 1981	3 mos. to 10 yrs.	7% to 345%	0.93 to 0.22
Ainslie and Haendel 1983	undefined	96000% to ∞	0.00
Houston 1983	1 yr. to 20 yrs.	23%	0.81
Loewenstein 1987	immediately to 10 yrs.	−6% to 212%	1.06 to 0.32
Moore and Viscusi 1988	undefined	10% to 12%	0.91 to 0.89
Benzion et al. 1989	6 mos. to 4 yrs.	9% to 60%	0.92 to 0.63
Viscusi and Moore 1989	undefined	11%	0.90
Moore and Viscusi 1990a	undefined	2%	0.98
Moore and Viscusi 1990b	undefined	1% to 14%	0.99 to 0.88
Shelley 1993	6 mos. to 4 yrs.	8% to 27%	0.93 to 0.79
Redelmeier and Heller 1993	1 day to 10 yrs.	0%	1.00
Cairns 1994	5 yrs. to 20 yrs.	14% to 25%	0.88 to 0.80
Shelley 1994	6 mos. to 2 yrs.	4% to 22%	0.96 to 0.82
Chapman and Elstein 1995	6 mos. to 12 yrs.	11% to 263%	0.90 to 0.28
Dolan and Gudex 1995	1 month to 10 yrs.	0%	1.00
Dreyfus and Viscusi 1995	undefined	11% to 17%	0.90 to 0.85
Kirby and Marakovic 1995	3 days to 29 days	3678% to ∞	0.03 to 0.00
Chapman 1996	1 yr. to 12 yrs.	negative to 300%	1.01 to 0.25
Kirby and Marakovic 1996	6 hours to 70 days	500% to 1500%	0.17 to 0.06
Pender 1996	7 mos. to 2 yrs.	26% to 69%	0.79 to 0.59
Wahlund and Gunnarson 1996	1 month to 1 yr.	18% to 158%	0.85 to 0.39
Cairns and van der Pol 1997	2 yrs. to 19 yrs.	13% to 31%	0.88 to 0.76

Table 1.1   *Continued*

Study	Time Range	Annual Discount Rate(s)	Annual Discount Factor(s)
Green, Myerson, and McFadden 1997	3 mos. to 20 yrs.	6% to 111%	0.94 to 0.47
Johannesson and Johansson 1997	6 yrs. to 57 yrs.	0% to 3%	0.97
Kirby 1997	1 day to 1 month	159% to 5747%	0.39 to 0.02
Madden et al. 1997	1 week to 25 yrs.	8% to ∞	0.93 to 0.00
Chapman and Winquist 1998	3 months	426% to 2189%	0.19 to 0.4
Holden, Shiferaw, and Wik 1998	1 yr.	28% to 147%	0.78 to 0.40
Cairns and van der Pol 1999	4 yrs. to 16 yrs.	6%	0.94
Chapman, Nelson, and Hier 1999	1 month to 6 mos.	13% to 19000%	0.88 to 0.01
Coller and Williams 1999	1 month to 3 mos.	15% to 25%	0.87 to 0.80
Kirby, Petry, and Bickel 1999	7 days to 186 days	50% to 55700%	0.67 to 0.00
van der Pol and Cairns 1999	5 yrs. to 13 yrs.	7%	0.93
Chesson and Viscusi 2000	1 year to 25 yrs.	11%	0.90
Ganiats et al. 2000	6 mos. to 20 yrs.	negative to 116%	1.01 to 0.46
Hesketh 2000	6 mos. to 4 yrs.	4% to 36%	0.96 to 0.74
van der Pol and Cairns 2001	2 yrs. to 15 yrs.	6% to 9%	0.94 to 0.92
Warner and Pleeter 2001	immediately to 22 yrs.	0% to 71%	0 to 0.58
Harrison, Lau, and Williams 2002	1 month to 37 mos.	28%	0.78

Source: Frederick, Loewenstein, and O'Donoghue (2002).

This section reiterates our general theme: To truly understand intertemporal choices, one must recognize the influence of many considerations besides pure time preference.

Confounding Factors

A wide variety of procedures have been used to estimate discount rates, but most apply the same basic approach. Some actual or reported intertemporal preference is observed, and researchers then compute the discount rate that this preference implies, using a "financial" or net present value (NPV) calculation. For instance, if a person demonstrates indifference between one hundred widgets now and one hundred-twenty widgets in one year, the implicit (annual) discount rate, ρ, would be 20 percent, because that value would satisfy the equation $100 = (1/(1 + \rho))120$. Similarly, if a person is indifferent between an inefficient low-cost appliance and a more efficient one that costs $100 extra but saves $20 a year in electricity over the next ten years, the implicit discount rate, ρ, would equal 15.1 percent, because that value would satisfy the equation $100 = \Sigma_{t=1}^{10} (1/(1 + \rho))^t 20$.

Although this is an extremely widespread approach for measuring discount rates, it relies on a variety of additional (and usually implicit) assumptions, and is subject to several confounding factors.

Consumption Reallocation   The foregoing calculation assumes a sort of "isolation" in decision making. Specifically, it treats the objects of intertemporal choice as discrete, unitary, dated events; it assumes that people entirely "consume" the reward (or penalty) at the moment it is received, as if it were an instantaneous burst of utility. Furthermore, it assumes that people don't shift consumption around over time in anticipation of the receipt of the future reward or penalty. These assumptions are rarely exactly correct, and may sometimes be bad approximations. Choosing between $50 today versus $100 next year, or choosing between fifty pounds of corn today versus one hundred pounds next year, are not the same as choosing between fifty utils today and one hundred utils on the same day next year, as the calculations imply. Rather, they are more complex choices between the various streams of consumption that those two dated rewards make possible.

Intertemporal Arbitrage   In theory, choices between tradable rewards, such as money, should not reveal anything about time preferences. As Fuchs (1982) and others have noted, if capital markets operate effectively (if monetary amounts at different times can be costlessly exchanged at a specified interest rate), choices between dated monetary outcomes can be reduced to merely selecting the reward with the greatest net present value (using the market interest rate).[27] To illustrate, suppose a person prefers $100 now to $200 ten years from now. While this preference *could* be explained by imputing a discount rate on future utility, the person might be choosing the smaller immediate amount because he or she believes that through proper investment the person can turn it into more than $200 in ten years, and thus enjoy more than $200 worth of consumption *at that future time*. The presence of capital markets should cause imputed discount rates to converge on the market interest rate.

Studies that impute discount rates from choices among tradable rewards assume that respondents ignore opportunities for intertemporal arbitrage, either because they are unaware of capital markets or unable to exploit them.[28] The latter assumption may sometimes be correct. For instance, in field studies of electrical-appliance purchases, some subjects may have faced borrowing constraints that prevented them from purchasing the more expensive energy-efficient appliances. More typically, however, imperfect capital markets cannot explain choices; they cannot explain why a person who holds several thousand dollars in a bank account earning 4 percent interest should prefer $100 today over $150 in one year. Because imputed discount rates in fact do not converge on the prevailing market interest rates, but instead are much higher, many respondents apparently are neglecting capital markets and basing their choices on some other consideration, such as time preference or the uncertainty associated with delay.

Concave Utility The standard approach to estimating discount rates assumes that the utility function is linear in the magnitude of the choice objects (for example, amounts of money, pounds of corn, duration of some health state). If, instead, the utility function for the good in question is concave, estimates of time preference will be biased upward. For example, indifference between $100 this year and $200 next year implies a *dollar* discount rate of 100 percent. If the utility of acquiring $200 is less than twice the utility of acquiring $100, however, the *utility* discount rate will be less than 100 percent. This confound is rarely discussed, perhaps because utility is assumed to be approximately linear over the small amounts of money commonly used in time-preference studies. The overwhelming evidence for reference-dependent utility suggests, however, that this assumption may be invalid—that people may not be integrating the stated amounts with their current and future wealth, and therefore that curvature in the utility function may be substantial even for these small amounts (see Bateman et al. 1997; Harless and Camerer 1994; Kahneman and Tversky 1979; Rabin 2000; Rabin and Thaler 2001; Tversky and Kahneman 1991).

Three techniques could be used to avoid this confound. First, one could request direct utility judgments (for example, attractiveness ratings) of the same consequence at two different times. Then, the ratio of the attractiveness rating of the distant outcome to the proximate outcome would directly reveal the implicit discount factor. Second, to the extent that utility is linear in probability, one can use choices or judgment tasks involving different probabilities of the same consequence at different times (Roth and Murnighan 1982). Evidence that probability is weighted nonlinearly (see, for example, Starmer 2000) would, of course, cast doubt on this approach. Third, one can separately elicit the utility function for the good in question, and then use that function to transform outcome amounts into utility amounts, from which utility discount rates could be computed. To our knowledge, Chapman (1996) conducted the only study that attempted to do this. She found that *utility* discount rates were substantially lower than the *dollar* discount rates, because utility was strongly concave over the monetary amounts subjects used in the intertemporal choice tasks.[29]

Uncertainty   In experimental studies, subjects are typically instructed to assume that delayed rewards will be delivered with certainty. Whether subjects do (or can) accept this assumption is unclear, because delay is ordinarily—and perhaps unavoidably—associated with uncertainty. A similar problem arises for field studies, in which it is typically assumed that subjects believe that future rewards, such as energy savings, will materialize. Due to this subjective (or *epistemic*) uncertainty associated with delay, it is difficult to determine to what extent the magnitude of imputed discount rates (or the shape of the discount function) is governed by time preference per se, versus the diminution in subjective probability associated with delay.[30]

Empirical evidence suggests that introducing objective (or *aleatory*) uncertainty to both current and future rewards can dramatically affect estimated discount rates. For instance, Keren and Roelofsma (1995) asked one group of respondents to choose between 100 florins (a Netherlands unit of currency) immediately and 110 florins in one month, and another group to choose between a 50 percent chance of 100 florins immediately and a 50 percent chance of 110 florins in one month. While 82 percent preferred the smaller immediate reward when both rewards were certain, only 39 percent preferred the smaller immediate reward when both rewards were uncertain.[31] Also, Albrecht and Weber (1996) found that the present value of a future lottery (for example, a 50 percent chance of receiving 250 deutsche marks) tended to exceed the present value of its certainty equivalent.

Inflation   The standard approach assumes that, for instance, $100 now and $100 in five years generate the same level of utility at the times they are received. However, inflation provides a reason to devalue future monetary outcomes, because in the presence of inflation, $100 worth of consumption now is more valuable than $100 worth of consumption in five years. This confound creates an upward bias in estimates of the discount rate, and this bias will be more or less pronounced depending on subjects' experiences with and expectations about inflation.

Expectations of Changing Utility   A reward of $100 now might also generate more utility than the same amount five years hence because a person expects to have a larger baseline consumption level in five years (for example, due to increased wealth). As a result, the marginal utility generated by an additional $100 of consumption in five years may be less than the marginal utility generated by an additional $100 of consumption now. Like inflation, this confound creates an upward bias in estimates of the discount rate.

Habit Formation, Anticipatory Utility, and Visceral Influences   To the extent that the discount rate is meant to reflect *only* time preference, and not the confluence of *all* factors influencing intertemporal choice, the modifications to the instantaneous utility function discussed in the previous section represent additional biasing factors, because they are typically not accounted for when the discount rate is imputed. For instance, if anticipatory utility motivates one to delay consumption more than one otherwise would, the imputed discount rate will be lower than the true degree of time preference. If a person prefers an increasing consumption profile due to habit formation, the discount rate will be biased downward. Finally, if the prospect of an immediate reward momentarily stimulates visceral factors that temporarily increase the person's valuation of the proximate reward, the discount rate could be biased upward.[32]

An Illustrative Example   To illustrate the difficulty of separating time preference per se from these potential confounds, consider a proto-typical study by Benzion, Rapoport, and Yagil (1989). In this study, respondents equated immediate sums of money and larger delayed sums (for example, they specified the reward in six months that would be as good as getting $1,000 immediately). In the cover story for the questionnaire, respondents were asked to imagine that they had earned money (amounts ranged from $40 to $5,000), but when they arrived to receive the payment they were told that the "financially solid" public institute is "temporarily short of funds." They were asked to specify a future amount of money (delays ranged from six months to four years) that would make them indifferent to the amount they had been promised to receive immediately. Surely, the description "financially solid" could scarcely be sufficient to allay uncertainties that the future reward would actually be received (particularly given that the institute was "temporarily" short of funds), and it seems likely that responses included a substantial "risk premium." Moreover, the subjects in this study had "extensive experience with . . . a three-digit inflation rate," and respondents might well have considered inflation when generating their responses. Even if respondents assumed no inflation, the real interest rate during this time was positive, and they might have considered intertemporal arbitrage. Finally, respondents may have considered that their future wealth would be greater and that the later reward would therefore yield less marginal utility. Indeed, the instructions cued respondents to consider this, as they were told that the questions did not have correct answers, and that the answers "might vary from one individual to another depending on his or her present or future financial assets."

Given all of these confounding factors, it is unclear exactly how much of the imputed annual discount rates (which ranged from 9 percent to 60 percent) actually reflected time preference. It is possible that the responses in this study (and others) can be entirely explained in terms of these confounds, and that once these confounds are controlled for, no "pure" time preference would remain.

Procedures for Measuring Discount Rates

Having discussed several confounding factors that greatly complicate assigning a discount rate to a particular choice or judgment, we next discuss the methods that have been used to measure discount rates. Broadly, these methods can be divided into two categories: *field studies*, in which discount rates are inferred from economic decisions people make in their lives, and *experimental studies*, in which people are asked to evaluate stylized intertemporal prospects involving real or hypothetical outcomes. The different procedures are each subject to the confounds discussed earlier and, as shall be seen, are also influenced by a variety of other factors that are theoretically irrelevant, but that can greatly affect the imputed discount rate.

Field Studies   Some researchers have estimated discount rates by identifying real-world behaviors that involve trade-offs between the near future and more distant future. Early studies of this type examined consumers' choices among different models of electrical appliances, which presented purchasers with a trade-off between the immediate purchase price and the long-term costs of running the appliance (as determined by its energy efficiency). In these studies, the discount rates implied by consumers' choices vastly exceeded market interest rates and differed substantially across product categories. The implicit discount rate was 17 percent to 20 percent for air conditioners

(Hausman 1979); 102 percent for gas water heaters, 138 percent for freezers, 243 percent for electric water heaters (Ruderman, Levine, and McMahon 1987); and from 45 percent to 300 percent for refrigerators, depending on assumptions made about the cost of electricity (Gately 1980).[33]

Another set of studies imputes discount rates from wage-risk trade-offs, in which individuals decide whether to accept a riskier job with a higher salary. Such decisions involve a trade-off between quality of life and expected length of life. The more that future utility is discounted, the less important is length of life, making risky but high-paying jobs more attractive. From such trade-offs, Viscusi and Moore (1989) concluded that workers' implicit discount rate with respect to future life years was approximately 11 percent. Later, using different econometric approaches with the same data set, Moore and Viscusi (1990a) estimated the discount rates to be around 2 percent, and Moore and Viscusi (1990b) concluded that the discount rate was somewhere between 1 percent and 14 percent. Dreyfus and Viscusi (1995) applied a similar approach to auto-safety decisions and estimated discount rates ranging from 11 percent to 17 percent.

In the macroeconomics literature, researchers have imputed discount rates by estimating structural models of life-cycle–saving behavior. For instance, Lawrence (1991) used Euler equations to estimate household time preferences across different socioeconomic groups. She estimated the discount rate of median-income households to be between 4 percent and 13 percent depending on the specification. Carroll (1997) criticizes Euler equation estimation on the grounds that most households tend to engage mainly in "buffer-stock" saving early in their lives—they save primarily to be prepared for emergencies—and only conduct "retirement" saving later on. Recent papers have estimated rich, calibrated, stochastic models in which households conduct buffer-stock saving early in life and retirement saving later in life. Using this approach, Carroll and Samwick (1997) report point estimates for the discount rate ranging from 5 percent to 14 percent, and Gourinchas and Parker (2001) report point estimates of 4.0 percent to 4.5 percent. Field studies of this type have the advantage of not assuming isolation, because integrated decision making is built into the model. Yet such estimates often depend heavily on the myriad assumptions included in the structural model.[34]

Recently, Warner and Pleeter (2001) analyzed decisions made by U.S. military servicemen. As part of military downsizing, over 60,000 military employees were given the choice between a onetime, lump-sum payment and an annuity payment. The sizes of the payments depended on the employee's current salary and number of years of service—for example, an "E-5" with nine years of service could choose between $22,283 now versus $3,714 every year for eighteen years. In general, the present value of the annuity payment equaled the lump-sum payment for a discount rate of 17.5 percent. Although the interest rate was only 7 percent at the time of these decisions, more than half of all military officers and more than 90 percent of enlisted personnel chose the lump-sum payment.[35] This study is particularly compelling in terms of credibility of reward delivery, magnitude of stakes, and number of subjects.[36]

The benefit of field studies, as compared with experimental studies, is their high *ecological* validity. There is no concern about whether estimated discount rates would apply to real behavior because they are estimated from such behavior. Yet field studies are subject to additional confounds due to the complexity of real-world decisions and the inability to control for some important factors. For example, the high discount rates implied by the widespread use of inefficient electrical appliances might not result from the discounting of future cost savings per se, but from other considerations, including: a lack of information among consumers about the cost savings of the more efficient appliances; a disbelief among consumers that the cost savings will be as great as promised; a lack of expertise in translating available information into economically efficient decisions; or hidden costs of the more efficient appliances, such as reduced convenience or reliability, or, in the case of lightbulbs, because the more efficient bulbs generate less aesthetically pleasing light spectra.[37]

Experimental Studies Given the difficulties of interpreting field data, the most common methodology for eliciting discount rates is to solicit "paper and pencil" responses to the prospect of real and hypothetical rewards and penalties. Four experimental procedures are commonly used: choice tasks, matching tasks, pricing tasks, and ratings tasks.

Choice tasks are the most common experimental method for eliciting discount rates. In a typical choice task, subjects are asked to choose between a smaller, more immediate reward and a larger, more delayed reward. Of course, a single choice between two intertemporal options only reveals an upper or lower bound on the discount rate— for example, if a person prefers one hundred units of something today over one hundred-twenty units a year from today, the choice merely implies a discount rate of *at least* 20 percent per year. To identify the discount rate more precisely, researchers often present subjects with a series of choices that vary the delay or the amount of the rewards. Some studies use real rewards, including money, rice, and corn. Other studies use hypothetical rewards, including monetary gains and losses, and more or less satisfying jobs available at different times. (See table 1.1 for a list of the procedures and rewards used in the different studies.)

Like all experimental elicitation procedures, the results from choice tasks can be affected by procedural nuances. A prevalent problem is an anchoring effect: when respondents are asked to make multiple choices between immediate and delayed rewards, the first choice they face often influences subsequent choices. For instance, people would be more prone to choose $120 next year over $100 immediately if they first chose between $100 immediately and $103 next year than if they first chose between $100 immediately and $140 next year. In general, imputed discount rates tend to be biased in the direction of the discount rate that would equate the first pair of options to which they are exposed (see Green et al. 1998). Anchoring effects can be minimized by using titration procedures that expose respondents to a series of opposing anchors—for example, $100 today or $101 in one year? $100 today or $10,000 in one year? $100 today or $105 in one year? and so on. Since titration procedures typically only offer choices between an immediate reward and a *greater* future reward, however, even these procedures communicate to respondents that they should be discounting, and potentially bias discount rates upward.

Matching tasks are another popular method for eliciting discount rates. In matching tasks, respondents "fill in the blank" to equate two intertemporal options (for example, $100 now = _____ in one year). Matching tasks have been conducted with real and hypothetical monetary outcomes and with hypothetical aversive health conditions (again, see table 1.1 for a list of the procedures and rewards used in different studies). Matching tasks have two advantages over choice tasks. First, because subjects reveal an indifference point, an exact discount rate can be imputed from a single response. Second, because the intertemporal options are not fully specified, there is no anchoring problem and no suggestion of an expected discount rate (or range of discount rates). Thus, unlike choice tasks, matching tasks cannot be accused of simply recovering the expectations of the experimenters that guided the experimental design.

Although matching tasks have some advantages over choice tasks, there are reasons to be suspicious of the responses obtained. First, responses often appear to be governed by the application of some simple rule rather than by time preference. For example, when people are asked to state the amount in n years that equals $100 today, a very common response is $100 \times n$. Second, the responses are often very "coarse"—often multiples of two or ten of the immediate reward, suggesting that respondents do not (or cannot) think very carefully about the task. Third, and most important, there are large differences in imputed discount rates among several theoretically equivalent procedures. Two intertemporal options could be equated or matched in one of four ways: respondents could be asked to specify the amount of a delayed reward that would make it as attractive as a given immediate reward (which is the most common technique); the amount of an immediate reward that makes it as attractive as a given delayed reward (Albrecht and Weber 1996); the maximum length of time they would be willing to wait to receive a larger reward in lieu of an immediately available smaller reward (Ainslie and Haendel 1983; Roelofsma 1994); or the latest date at which they would accept a smaller reward in lieu of receiving a larger reward at a specified date that is later still.

While there is no theoretical basis for preferring one of these methods over any other, the small amount of empirical evidence comparing different methods suggests that they yield very different discount rates. Roelofsma (1994) found that implicit discount rates varied tremendously depending on whether respondents matched on amount or time. One group of subjects was asked to indicate how much compensation they would demand to allow a purchased bicycle to be delivered nine months late. The median response was 250 florins. Another group was asked how long they would be willing to delay delivery of the bicycle in exchange for 250 florins. The mean response was only three weeks, implying a discount rate that is twelve times higher. Frederick and Read (2002) found that implicit discount rates were dramatically higher when respondents generated the future reward that would equal a specified current reward than when they generated a current reward that would equal a specified future reward. Specifically, when respondents were asked to state the amount in thirty years that would be as good as getting $100 today, the median response was $10,000 (implying that a future dollar is $\frac{1}{100}$th as valuable), but when asked to specify the amount today that is as good as getting $100 in thirty years, the median response was $50 (implying that a future dollar is $\frac{1}{2}$ as valuable).

Two other experimental procedures involve rating or pricing temporal prospects. In *rating tasks*, each respondent evaluates an outcome occurring at a particular time by rating its attractiveness or aversiveness. In *pricing tasks*, each respondent specifies a willingness to pay to obtain (or avoid) some real or hypothetical outcome occurring at a particular time, such as a monetary reward, dinner coupons, an electric shock, or an extra year added to the end of one's life. (Once again, see table 1.1 for a list of the procedures and rewards used in the different studies.) Rating and pricing tasks differ from choice and matching tasks in one important respect. Whereas choice and matching tasks call attention to time (because each respondent evaluates two outcomes occurring at two different times), rating and pricing tasks permit time to be manipulated *between* subjects (because a single respondent may evaluate either the immediate or delayed outcome, by itself).

Loewenstein (1988) found that the timing of an outcome is much less important (discount rates are much lower) when respondents evaluate a single outcome at a particular time than when they compare two outcomes occurring at different times, or specify the value of delaying or accelerating an outcome. In one study, for example, two groups of students were asked how much they would pay for a $100 gift certificate at the restaurant of their choice. One group was told that the gift certificate was valid immediately. The other was told it could be used beginning six months from now. There was no significant difference in the valuation of the two certificates *between* the two groups, which implies negligible discounting. Yet when asked how much they would pay (have to be paid) to use it six months earlier (later), the timing became important—the delay group was willing to pay $10 to expedite receipt of the delayed certificate, while the immediate group demanded $23 to delay the receipt of a certificate they expected to be able to use immediately.[38]

Another important design choice in experimental studies is whether to use real or hypothetical rewards. The use of real rewards is generally desirable for obvious reasons, but hypothetical rewards actually have some advantages in this domain. In studies involving hypothetical rewards, respondents can be presented with a wide range of reward amounts, including losses and large gains, both of which are generally infeasible in studies involving real outcomes. The disadvantage of hypothetical choice data is the uncertainty about whether people are motivated to, or capable of, accurately predicting what they would do if outcomes were real.

To our knowledge, only two studies have compared discounting between real and hypothetical rewards. Kirby and Marakovic (1995) asked subjects to state the immediate amount that would make them indifferent to some fixed delayed amount (delayed reward sizes were $14.75, $17.25, $21, $24.50, $28.50; delays were three, seven, thirteen, seventeen, twenty-three, and twenty-nine days). One group of subjects answered all thirty permutations for real rewards, and another group of subjects answered all thirty permutations for hypothetical rewards. Discount rates were *lower* for hypothetical rewards.[39] Coller and Williams (1999) asked subjects to choose between $500 payable in one month and $500 + $x payable in three months, where $x was varied from $1.67 to $90.94 across fifteen different choices. In one condition, all choices were hypothetical; in five other conditions, one person was randomly chosen to receive her preferred outcome for one of her fifteen choices. The raw data suggest again that discount rates were considerably lower in the hypothetical condition, although they suggest that this conclusion is not supported after controlling for censored data, demographic differences, and heteroskedasticity (across demographic differences and across treatments).[40] Thus, as of yet there is no clear evidence that hypothetical rewards are discounted differently than real rewards.[41]

What Is Time Preference?

Figure 1.3 reveals spectacular disagreement among dozens of studies that all purport to be measuring time preference. This lack of agreement likely reflects the fact that the various elicitation procedures used to measure time preference consistently fail to isolate time preference, and instead reflect, to varying degrees, a blend of both pure time preference and other theoretically distinct considerations, including: intertemporal arbitrage, when tradeable rewards are used; concave utility; uncertainty that the future reward or penalty will actually obtain; inflation, when nominal monetary amounts are used; expectations of changing utility; and considerations of habit formation, anticipatory utility, and visceral influences.

Figure 1.3 also reveals a predominance of high implicit discount rates—discount rates well above market interest rates. This consistent finding may also be due to the presence of the aforementioned various extra-time-preference considerations, because nearly all of these work to bias imputed discount rates upward—only habit formation and anticipatory utility bias estimates downward. If these confounding factors were adequately controlled, we suspect that many intertemporal choices or judgments would imply much lower—indeed, possibly even zero—rates of time preference.

Our discussion in this section highlights the conceptual and semantic ambiguity about what the concept of time preference ought to include—about what properly counts as time preference per se and what ought to be called something else (for further discussion see Frederick 1999). We have argued here that many of the reasons for caring when something occurs (for example, uncertainty or utility of anticipation) are not time preference, because they pertain to the expected amount of utility consequences confer, and not to the weight given to the utility of different moments (see figure 1.4, adapted from Frederick 1999). However, it is not obvious where to draw the line

Figure 1.4   Factors Affecting Intertemporal Choices

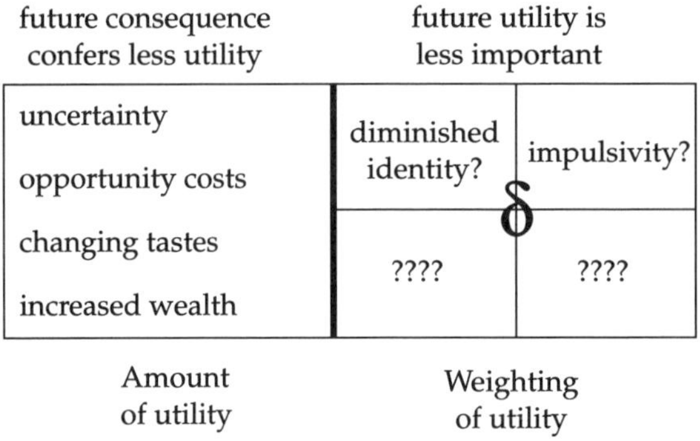

future consequence confers less utility	future utility is less important	
uncertainty opportunity costs	diminished identity?	impulsivity?
changing tastes increased wealth	????	????
Amount of utility	Weighting of utility	

Source: Adapted from Frederick (1999).

between factors that operate through utilities and factors that make up time preference.

Hopefully, economists will eventually achieve a consensus about what is included in, and excluded from, the concept of time preference. Until then, drawing attention to the ambiguity of the concept should improve the quality of discourse by increasing awareness that, in discussions about time preference, different people may be using the same term to refer to significantly different underlying constructs.[42]

Unpacking Time Preference

Early twentieth-century economists' conceptions of intertemporal choice included detailed accounts of disparate underlying psychological motives. With the advent of the DU model in 1937, however, economists eschewed considerations of specific motives, proceeding as if all intertemporal behavior could be explained by the unitary construct of time preference. In this section, we question whether even time preference itself should be regarded as a unitary construct.

Issues of this type are hotly debated in psychology. For example, psychologists debate the usefulness of conceptualizing intelligence in terms of a single unitary "g" factor. Typically, a posited psychological construct (or "trait") is considered useful only if it satisfies three criteria: it remains relatively constant across time within a particular individual; it predicts behavior across a wide range of situations, and different measures of it correlate highly with one another. The concept of intelligence satisfies these criteria fairly well.[43] First, performance in tests of cognitive ability at early ages correlates highly with performance on such tests at all subsequent ages. Second, cognitive ability (as measured by such tests) predicts a wide range of important life outcomes, such as criminal behavior and income. Third, abilities that we regard as expressions of intelligence correlate strongly with each other. Indeed, when discussing the construction of intelligence tests, Herrnstein and Murray (1994, 3) note, "It turned out to be nearly impossible to devise items that plausibly measured some cognitive skill and were *not* positively correlated with other items that plausibly measured some cognitive skill."

The posited construct of time preference does not fare as well by these criteria. First, no longitudinal studies have been conducted to permit any conclusions about the temporal stability of time preference.[44] Second, correlations between various measures of time preference or between measures of time preference and plausible real-world expressions of it are modest, at best. Chapman and Elstein (1995) and Chapman, Nelson, and Hier (1999) found only weak correlations between discount rates for money and for health, and Chapman and Elstein found almost no correlation between discount rates for losses and for gains. Fuchs (1982) found no correlation between a prototypical measure of time preference (for example, "Would you choose $1,500 now or $4,000 in five years?") and other behaviors that would plausibly be affected by time preference (for example, smoking, credit card debt, seat belt use, and the frequency of exercise and dental checkups). Nor did he find much correlation among any of these reported behaviors (see also Nyhus 1995).[45] Chapman and Coups (1999) found that corporate employees who chose to receive an influenza vaccination did have significantly lower discount rates (as inferred from a matching task with monetary losses), but found no relation between vaccination behavior and hypothetical questions involving health outcomes. Munasinghe and Sicherman (2000) found that smokers tend to invest less in human capital (they have flatter wage profiles), and many others have found that for stylized intertemporal choices among monetary rewards, heroin addicts have higher discount rates (for example, Alvos, Gregson, and Ross 1993; Kirby, Petry, and Bickel 1999; Madden et al. 1997; Murphy and De Wolfe 1986; Petry, Bickel, and Arnett 1998).

Although the evidence in favor of a single construct of time preference is hardly compelling, the low cross-behavior correlations do not necessarily disprove the existence of time preference. Suppose, for example, that someone expresses low discount rates on a conventional elicitation task, yet indicates that she rarely exercises. While it is possible that this inconsistency reflects true heterogeneity in the degree to which she discounts different types of utility, perhaps she rarely exercises *because* she is so busy at work earning money for her future or because she simply cares much more about her future finances than her future cardiovascular condition. Or, perhaps she doesn't believe that exercise improves health. As this example suggests, many factors could work to erode cross-behavior correlations, and thus, such low correlations do not mean that there can be no single unitary time preference underlying all intertemporal choices (the intertemporal analog to the hypothesized construct of "g" in analyses of cognitive performance). Notwithstanding this disclaimer, however, in our view the cumulative evidence raises serious doubts about whether in fact there is such a construct—a stable factor that operates identically on, and applies equally to, all sources of utility.[46]

To better understand the pattern of correlations in implied discount rates across different types of intertemporal behaviors, we may need to unpack time preference itself into more fundamental motives, as illustrated by the segmentation of the delta component of figure 1.4. Loewenstein and his colleagues (2001) have proposed three specific constituent motives, which they labeled *impulsivity* (the degree to which an individual acts in a spontaneous, unplanned fashion), *compulsivity* (the tendency to make plans and stick with them), and *inhibition* (the ability to inhibit the automatic or "knee-jerk" response to the appetites and emotions that trigger impulsive behavior).[47] Preliminary evidence suggests that these subdimensions of time preference can be measured reliably. Moreover, the different subdimensions predict different behaviors in a highly sensible way. For example, repetitive behaviors such as flossing one's teeth, exercising, paying one's bills on time, and arriving on time at meetings were all predicted best by the compulsivity subdimension. Viscerally driven behaviors, such as reacting aggressively to someone in a car who honks at you at a red light, were best predicted by impulsivity (positively) and behavioral inhibition (negatively). Money-related behaviors such as saving money, having unpaid credit card balances, or being maxed out on one or more credit cards were best predicted by conventional measures of discount rates (but impulsivity and compulsivity were also highly significant predictors).

Clearly, further research is needed to evaluate whether time preference is best viewed as a unitary construct or a composite of more basic constituent motives. Further efforts hopefully will be informed by recent discoveries of neuroscientists, who have identified regions of the brain whose damage leads to extreme myopia (Damasio 1994) and areas that seem to play an important role in suppressing the behavioral expression of urges (LeDoux 1996). If some behaviors are best predicted by impulsivity, some by compulsivity, some by behavioral inhibition, and so on, it may be worth the effort to measure preferences at this level and to develop models that treat these components separately. Of course, such multidimensional perspectives will inevitably be more difficult to operationalize than formulations like the DU model, which represent time preference as a unidimensional construct.

Conclusions

The DU model, which continues to be widely used by economists, has little empirical support. Even its developers—Samuelson who originally proposed the model, and Koopmans, who provided the first axiomatic derivation—had concerns about its descriptive realism, and it was never empirically validated as the appropriate model for intertemporal choice. Indeed, virtually every core and ancillary assumption of the DU model has been called into question by empirical evidence collected in the past two decades. The insights from this empirical research have spawned new theories of intertemporal choice that revive many of the psychological considerations discussed by early students of intertemporal choice—considerations that were effectively dismissed with the introduction of the DU model. Additionally, some of the most recent theories show that intertemporal behaviors may be dramatically influenced by people's level of understanding of how their preferences change—by their "metaknowledge" about their preferences (see, for example, O'Donoghue and Rabin 1999b; Loewenstein, O'Donoghue, and Rabin 2000).

While the DU model assumes that intertemporal preferences can be characterized by a single discount rate, the large empirical literature devoted to measuring discount rates has failed to establish any stable estimate. There is extraordinary variation across studies, and sometimes even within studies. This failure is partly due to variations in the degree to which the studies take account of factors that confound the computation of discount rates (for example, uncertainty about the delivery of future outcomes or nonlinearity in the utility function). But the spectacular cross-study differences in discount rates also reflect the diversity of considerations that are relevant in intertemporal choices and that legitimately affect different types of intertemporal choices differently. Thus there is no reason to expect that discount rates *should* be consistent across different choices.

The idea that intertemporal choices reflect an interplay of disparate and often competing psychological motives was commonplace in the writings of early twentieth-century economists. We believe that this approach should be resurrected. Reintroducing the multiple-motives approach to intertemporal choice will help us to better understand and better explain the intertemporal choices we observe in the real world. For instance, it permits more scope for understanding individual differences (for example, why one person is a spendthrift while his neighbor is a miser, or why one person does drugs while her brother does not), because people may differ in the degree to which they experience anticipatory utility or are influenced by visceral factors.

The multiple-motive approach may be even more important for understanding *intra*individual differences. When one looks at the behavior of a single individual across different domains, there is often a wide range of apparent attitudes toward the future. Someone may smoke heavily, but carefully study the returns of various retirement packages. Another may squirrel money away while at the same time giving little thought to electrical efficiency when purchasing an air conditioner. Someone else may devote two decades of his life to establishing a career, and then jeopardize this long-term investment for some highly transient pleasure. Since the DU model assumes a unitary discount rate that applies to all acts of consumption, such intraindividual heterogeneities pose a theoretical challenge. The multiple-motive approach, by contrast, allows us to readily interpret such differences in terms of more narrow, more legitimate, and more stable constructs—for example, the degree to which people are skeptical of promises, experience anticipatory utility, are influenced by visceral factors, or are able to correctly predict their future utility.

The multiple-motive approach may sound excessively open-ended. We have described a variety of considerations that researchers could potentially incorporate into their analyses. Including every consideration would be far too complicated, while picking and choosing which considerations to incorporate may leave one open to charges of being ad hoc. How, then, should economists proceed?

We believe that economists should proceed as they typically do. Economics has always been both an art and a science. Economists are forced to intuit, to the best of their abilities, which considerations are likely to be important in a particular domain and which are likely to be largely irrelevant. When economists model labor supply, for instance, they typically do so with a utility function that incorporates consumption and leisure, but when they model investment decisions, they typically assume that preferences are defined over wealth. Similarly, a researcher investigating charitable giving might use a utility function that incorporates altruism but not risk aversion or time preference, whereas someone studying investor behavior is unlikely to use a utility function that incorporates altruism. For each domain, economists choose the utility function that is best able to incorporate the essential considerations for that domain, and then evaluate whether the inclusion of specific considerations improves the predictive or explanatory power of a model. The same approach can be applied to multiple-motive models of intertemporal choice. For drug addiction, for example, habit formation, visceral factors, and hyperbolic discounting seem likely to play a prominent role. For extended experiences, such as health states, careers, and long vacations, the preference for improvement is likely to come into play. For brief, vivid experiences, such as weddings or criminal sanctions, utility from anticipation may be an important determinant of behavior.

In sum, we believe that economists' understanding of intertemporal choices will progress most rapidly by continuing to import insights from psychology, by relinquishing the assumption that the key to understanding intertemporal choices is finding the right discount rate (or even the right discount function), and by readopting the view that intertemporal choices reflect many distinct considerations and often involve the interplay of several competing motives. Since different motives may be evoked to different degrees by different situations (and by different descriptions of the *same* situation), developing descriptively adequate models of intertemporal choice will not be easy; but we hope this discussion will help.

This chapter was reprinted with the permission of the American Economic Association. It was originally published in 2002 as "Time Discounting and Time Preference: A Critical Review." *Journal of Economic Literature* XL(June): 351–401.

Notes

1. In a frequently cited passage from *The Economics of Welfare*, Arthur Pigou (1920, 25) proposed a similar account of time preference, suggesting that it results from a type of cognitive illusion: "our telescopic faculty is defective, and we, therefore, see future pleasures, as it were, on a diminished scale."

2. The continuous-time analogue is $U^t(\{c_\tau\}_{\tau \in [t,T]}) = \int_{\tau=t}^{T} e^{-\rho(\tau-t)} u\,(c_\tau)$. For expositional ease, we shall restrict attention to discrete-time throughout.

3. There are several different axiom systems for the DU model—in addition to Koopmans see Fishburn (1970), Lancaster (1963), Meyer (1976), and Fishburn and Rubinstein (1982).

4. "Utility independence" has meaning only if one literally interprets $u(c_{t+k})$ as well-being experienced in period $t + k$. We believe that this is, in fact, the common interpretation. For a model that relaxes the assumption of utility independence see Hermalin and Isen 2000, who consider a model in which well-being in period t depends on well-being in period $t - 1$— that is, they assume $u_t = u(c_t, u_{t-1})$. See also Kahneman, Wakker, and Sarin (1997), who propose a set of axioms that would justify an assumption of additive separability in instantaneous utility.

5. As will be discussed, endogenous preference changes, due to things such as habit formation or reference dependence, are best understood in terms of consumption interdependence and not nonstationary utility. In some situations, nonstationarities clearly play an important role in behavior—for example, Suranovic, Goldfarb, and Leonard (1999) and O'Donoghue and Rabin (1999a, 2000) discuss the importance of nonstationarities in the realm of addictive behavior.

6. An alternative but equivalent definition of constant discounting is that $D(k)/D(k + 1)$ is independent of k.

7. Constant discounting implies time-consistent preferences only under the ancillary assumption of stationary discounting, for which the discount function $D(k)$ is the same in all periods. As a counterexample, if the period-t discount function is

$$D_t(k) = \left(\frac{1}{1 + \rho}\right)^k$$

while the period-$t + 1$ discount function is

$$D_{t+1}(k) = \left(\frac{1}{1 + \rho'}\right)^k$$

for some $\rho' \neq \rho$, then the person exhibits constant discounting at both dates t and $t + 1$, but nonetheless has time-inconsistent preferences.

8. Discounting is not inherent to the DU model, because the model could be applied with $\rho \leq 0$. The inclusion of ρ in the model, however, strongly implies that it may take a value other than zero, and the name *discount rate* certainly suggests that it is greater than zero.

9. In the context of intergenerational choice, Koopmans (1967) called this result the *paradox of the indefinitely postponed splurge*. See also Arrow (1983); Chakravarty (1962); and Solow (1974).

10. As noted by Frederick (2002), there is much disagreement about the nature of Parfit's claim. In her review of the philosophical literature, Jennifer Whiting (1986, 549) identifies four different interpretations: the *strong absolute claim*: that it is irrational for someone to care about their future welfare; the *weak absolute claim*: that there is no rational requirement to care about one's future welfare; the *strong comparative claim*: that

it is irrational to care more about one's own future welfare than about the welfare of any other person; and the *weak comparative claim*: that one is not rationally required to care more about his or her future welfare than about the welfare of any other person. We believe that all of these interpretations are too strong, and that Parfit endorses only a weaker version of the weak absolute claim. That is, he claims only that one is not rationally required to care about one's future welfare to a degree that exceeds the degree of psychological connectedness that obtains between one's current self and one's future self.

11. That is, $15 = $20 \times (e^{-(3.45)(1/12)}) = $50 \times (e^{-(1.20)(1)}) = $100 \times (e^{-(0.19)(10)})$. While most empirical studies report average discount rates over a given horizon, it is sometimes more useful to discuss average "per-period" discount rates. Framed in these terms, Thaler's results imply an average (annual) discount rate of 345 percent between now and one month from now, 100 percent between one month from now and one year from now, and 7.7 percent between one year from now and ten years from now. That is, $15 = $20 \times (e^{-(3.45)(1/12)}) = $50 \times (e^{-(3.45)(1/12)} e^{-(1.00)(11/12)}) = $100 \times (e^{-(3.45)(1/12)} e^{-(1.00)(11/12)} e^{-(0.077)(9)})$.

12. Several hyperbolic functional forms have been proposed: Ainslie (1975) suggested the function $D(t) = 1/t$, Herrnstein (1981) and Mazur (1987) suggested $D(t) = 1/(1 + \alpha t)$, and Loewenstein and Prelec (1992) suggested $D(t) = 1/(1 + \alpha t)^{\beta/\alpha}$.

13. These studies all demonstrate preference reversals in the synchronic sense—subjects simultaneously prefer $100 now over $110 tomorrow and prefer $110 in thirty-one days over $100 in thirty days, which is consistent with hyperbolic discounting. Yet there seems to be an implicit belief that such preference reversals would also hold in the diachronic sense—that if subjects who currently prefer $110 in thirty-one days over $100 in thirty days were brought back to the lab thirty days later, they would prefer $100 at that time over $110 one day later. Under the assumption of stationary discounting (as discussed earlier), synchronic preference reversals imply diachronic preference reversals. To the extent that subjects anticipate diachronic reversals and want to avoid them, evidence of a preference for commitment could also be interpreted as evidence for hyperbolic discounting (to be discussed).

14. In some cases, the discount rates were computed from the median respondent. In other cases, the mean discount rate was used.

15. Read's proposal that discounting is subadditive is compatible with analogous results in other domains. For example, Tversky and Koehler (1994) found that the total probability assigned to an event increases the more finely the event is partitioned—for example, the probability of "death by accident" is judged to be more likely if one separately elicits the probability of "death by fire," "death by drowning," "death by falling," and so on.

16. A few studies have actually found *increasing* discount rates. Frederick (1999) asked 228 respondents to imagine that they worked at a job that

consisted of both pleasant work ("good days") and unpleasant work ("bad days") and to equate the attractiveness of having additional good days this year or in a future year. On average, respondents were indifferent between twenty extra good days this year, twenty-one the following year, or forty in five years, implying a one-year discount rate of 5 percent and a five-year discount rate of fifteen percent. A possible explanation is that a desire for improvement is evoked more strongly for two successive years (this year and next) than for two separated years (this year and five years hence). Rubinstein (2000) asked students in a political science class to choose between the following two payment sequences:

	March 1	June 1	Sept. 1	Nov. 1
A:	$997	$997	$997	$997

	April 1	July 1	Oct. 1	Dec. 1
B:	$1,000	$1,000	$1,000	$1,000

Then, two weeks later, he asked them to choose between $997 on November 1 and $1,000 on December 1. Fifty-four percent of respondents preferred $997 in November to $1,000 in December, but only 34 percent preferred sequence A to sequence B. These two results suggest increasing discount rates. To explain them Rubinstein speculated that the three more proximate additional elements may have masked the differences in the timing of the sequence of dated amounts, while making the differences in amounts more salient.

17. Strotz implicitly assumes stationary discounting.
18. Building on Strotz's strategy of consistent planning, some researchers have addressed the question of whether a consistent path exists for general nonexponential discount functions. See in particular Pollak (1968); Peleg and Yaari (1973); and Goldman (1980).
19. While not framed in terms of hyperbolic discounting, Akerlof's (1991) model of procrastination is formally equivalent to a hyperbolic model.
20. A similar "natural" experiment was recently conducted by the Economic and Social Research Council of Great Britain. They recently eliminated submission deadlines and now accept grant proposals on a "rolling" basis (though they are still reviewed only periodically). In response to this policy change, submissions have actually declined by 15 to 20 percent (direct correspondence with Chris Caswill at ESRC).
21. For rational-choice models building on Becker and Murphy's framework see Orphanides and Zervos (1995); Wang (1997); and Suranovic, Goldfarb, and Leonard (1999). For addiction models that incorporate hyperbolic discounting see O'Donoghue and Rabin (1999a, 2000); Gruber and Koszegi (2000); and Carrillo (1999).
22. Reference-point models sometimes assume a direct effect of the consumption level or reference level, so that $u(c_\tau, r_\tau) = v(c_\tau - r_\tau) + w(c_\tau)$ or $u(c_\tau, r_\tau) = v(c_\tau - r_\tau) + w(r_\tau)$. Some habit-formation models could be in-

terpreted as reference-point models, where the state variable z_τ is the reference point. Indeed, many habit-formation models, such as Pollak (1970) and Constantinides (1990), assume instantaneous utility functions of the form $u(c_\tau - z_\tau)$, although they typically assume neither loss aversion nor diminishing sensitivity.

23. Waiting for undesirable outcomes is almost always unpleasant, but waiting for desirable outcomes is sometimes pleasurable and sometimes frustrating. Despite the manifest importance for intertemporal choice of these emotions associated with waiting, we are aware of no research that has sought to understand when waiting for desirable outcomes is pleasurable or aversive.

24. While it seems possible that this conceptualization could explain the magnitude effect as well, the magnitude effect is found for very "small" amounts (for example, between $2 and $20 in Ainslie and Haendel [1983]), and for very "large amounts" (for example, between $10,000 and $1,000,000 in Raineri and Rachlin [1993]). It seems highly unlikely that respondents would consistently code the lower amounts as spending and the higher amounts as savings across all of these studies.

25. Thus, to the extent that the preference for improvement reflects a choice heuristic, it should be susceptible to framing or bracketing effects, because what constitutes a sequence is highly subjective, as noted by Loewenstein and Prelec (1993) and by Beebe-Center (1929, 67) several decades earlier:

> *What enables one to decide whether a given set of affective experiences does, or does not, constitute a unitary temporal group?* . . . what of series involving experiences of different modalities— . . . visual and auditory experiences, for instance? . . . And what of such complex events as "arising in the morning" or "eating a good meal" or "enjoying a good book?" (Emphasis added)

26. In some cases, the estimates are computed from the median respondent. In other cases, the authors reported the mean discount rate.

27. Meyer (1976, 426) expresses this point: "if we can lend and borrow at the same rate . . . , then we can simply show that, regardless of the fundamental orderings on the c's [consumption streams], the induced ordering on the x's [sequences of monetary flows] is given by simple discounting at this given rate. . . . We could say that the market assumes command and the market rate prevails for monetary flows."

28. Arguments about violations of the discounted utility model assume, as Pender (1996, 282–83) notes,

> that the results of discount rate experiments reveal something about intertemporal preferences directly. However, if agents are optimizing an intertemporal utility function, their opportunities for intertemporal arbitrage are also important in determining how they respond to such experiments . . . when tradable rewards are

offered, one must either abandon the assumption that respondents in experimental studies are optimizing, or make some assumptions (either implicit or explicit) about the nature of credit markets. The implicit assumption in some of the previous studies of discount rates appears to be that there are no possibilities for intertemporal arbitrage.

29. Chapman also found that magnitude effects were much smaller after correcting for utility function curvature. This result supports Loewenstein and Prelec's (1992) explanation of magnitude effects as resulting from utility function curvature (see section on reference-point models herein).

30. There may be complicated interactions between risk and delay, because uncertainty about future receipt complicates and impedes the planning of one's future consumption stream (Spence and Zeckhauser 1972). For example, a 90 percent chance to win $10,000,000 in fifteen years is worth much less than a guarantee to receive $9,000,000 at that time, because, to the extent that one cannot insure against the residual uncertainty, there is a limit to how much one can adjust one's consumption level during those fifteen years.

31. This result cannot be explained by a magnitude effect on the expected amounts, because 50 percent of a reward has a *smaller* expected value, and, according to the magnitude effect, should be discounted more, not less.

32. Whether visceral factors should be considered a determinant of time preference or a confounding factor in its estimation is unclear. If visceral factors increase the attractiveness of an immediate reward without affecting its experienced enjoyment (if they increase wanting but not liking), they are probably best viewed as a legitimate determinant of time perference. If, however, visceral factors alter the amount of utility that a contemplated proximate reward actually delivers, they might best be regarded as a confounding factor.

33. These findings illustrate how people seem to ignore intertemporal arbitrage. As Hausman (1979) noted, it does not make sense for anyone with positive savings to discount future energy savings at rates higher than the market interest rate. One possible explanation for these results is that people are liquidity constrained. Consistent with such an account, Hausman found that the discount rate varied markedly with income—it was 39 percent for households with under $10,000 of income, but just 8.9 percent for households earning between $25,000 and $35,000. Conflicting with this finding, however, a study by Houston (1983, 245) that presented individuals with a decision of whether to purchase a hypothetical "energy-saving" device, found that income "played no statistically significant role in explaining the level of discount rate."

34. These macroeconomics studies are not included in the tables and figures, which focus primarily on individual-level choice data.

35. It should be noted, however, that the guaranteed payments in the annu-

ity program were not indexed for inflation, which averaged 4.2 percent during the four years preceding this choice.

36. Warner and Pleeter (2001) noted that if everyone had chosen the annuity payment, the present value of all payments would have been $4.2 billion. Given the choices, however, the present value of the government payout was just $2.5 billion. Thus offering the lump-sum alternative saved the federal government $1.7 billion.

37. For a criticism of the hidden-costs explanation, however, see Koomey and Sanstad (1994); and Howarth and Sanstad (1995).

38. Rating tasks (and probably pricing tasks as well) are subject to anchoring effects. Shelley and Omer (1996), Stevenson (1992), and others have found that a given delay (for example, six months) produces greater time discounting when it is considered alongside shorter delays (for example, one month) than when it is considered alongside longer delays (for example, three years).

39. The two results were not strictly comparable, however, because they used a different procedure for the real rewards than for the hypothetical rewards. An auction procedure was used for the real-rewards group only. Subjects were told that whoever, of three subjects, stated the lowest immediate amount would receive the immediate amount, and the other two subjects would receive the delayed amount. Optimal behavior in such a situation involves overbidding. Since this creates a downward bias in discount rates for the real-rewards group, however, it does not explain away the finding that real discount rates were higher than hypothetical discount rates.

40. It is hard to understand which control eliminates the differences that are apparent in the raw data. It would seem not to be the demographic differences per se, because the hypothetical condition had a "substantially higher proportion of non-white participants" and "non-whites on average reveal discount rates that are nearly 21 percentage points higher than those revealed by whites" (Coller and Williams 1999, 121, 122).

41. There has been considerable recent debate outside of the context of intertemporal choice about whether hypothetical choices are representative of decisions with real consequences. The general conclusion from this debate is that the two methods typically yield qualitatively similar results (see Camerer and Hogarth 1999 for a recent review), though systematic differences have been observed in some studies (Cummings, Harrison, and Rutstrom 1995; Kroll, Levy, and Rapoport 1988).

42. Not only do people use the same term to refer to different concepts (or sets of concepts), they also use different terms to represent the same concept. The welter of terms used in discussions of intertemporal choice include: discount factor, discount rate, marginal private rate of discount, social discount rate, utility discount rate, marginal social rate of discount, pure discounting, time preference, subjective rate of time preference, pure time preference, marginal rate of time preference, social rate of time preference, overall time preference, impatience, time bias, temporal orientation, consumption rate of interest, time positivity inclination,

and "the pure futurity effect." Broome (1995, 128–29) notes that some of the controversy about discounting results from differences in how the term is used:

> On the face of it . . . typical economists and typical philosophers seem to disagree. But actually I think there is more misunderstanding here than disagreement . . . When economists and philosophers think of discounting, they typically think of discounting different things. Economists typically discount the sorts of goods that are bought and sold in markets [whereas] philosophers are typically thinking of a more fundamental good, people's *well-being* . . . It is perfectly consistent to discount commodities and not well-being.

43.   Debates remain, however, about whether traditional measures exclude important dimensions, and whether a multidimensional account of intelligence would have even greater explanatory power. Sternberg (1985), for example, argues that intelligence is usefully decomposed into three dimensions: analytical intelligence, which includes the ability to identify problems, compute strategies, and monitor solutions, and is measured well by existing IQ tests; creative intelligence, which reflects the ability to generate problem-solving options, and practical intelligence, which involves the ability to implement problem-solving options.

44.   Although there have been no longitudinal studies of time preference per se, Mischel and his colleagues did find that a child's capacity to delay gratification was significantly correlated with *other* variables assessed decades later, including academic achievement and self-esteem (Ayduk et al. 2000; Mischel, Shoda, and Peake 1988; Shoda, Mischel, and Peake 1990). Of course, this provides evidence for construct validity only to the extent that one views these other variables as expressions of time preference. We also note that while there is little evidence that intertemporal behaviors are stable over long periods, there is some evidence that time preference is not strictly constant over time for all people. Heroin addicts discount both drugs and money more steeply when they are craving heroin than when they are not (Giordano et al. 2001).

45.   A similar lack of *intraindividual* consistency has been observed in risk taking (MacCrimmon and Wehrung 1990).

46.   Note that one can also *over*estimate the strength of the relationship between measured time preference and time-related behaviors or between different time-related behaviors if these variables are related to characteristics such as intelligence, social class, or social conformity, that are not adequately measured and controlled for.

47.   Recent research by Baumeister, Heatherton, and Tice (1994) suggests that such "behavioral inhibition" requires an expenditure of mental effort that, like other forms of effort, draws on limited resources—a "pool" of willpower (Loewenstein 2000a). Their research shows that behavioral inhibition in one domain (for example, refraining from eating desirable food) reduces the ability to exert willpower in another domain (for example, completing a taxing mental or physical task).

References

Abel, Andrew. 1990. "Asset Prices Under Habit Formation and Catching Up with the Joneses." *American Economic Review* 80: 38–42.

Ainslie, George. 1975. "Specious Reward: A Behavioral Theory of Impulsiveness and Impulse Control." *Psychological Bulletin* 82(4): 463–96.

Ainslie, George, and Varda Haendel. 1983. "The Motives of the Will." In *Etiologic Aspects of Alcohol and Drug Abuse*, edited by E. Gottheil, K. Durley, T. Skodola, and H. Waxman. Springfield, Ill.: Charles C. Thomas.

Ainslie, George, and Nick Haslam. 1992. "Hyperbolic Discounting." In *Choice Over Time*, edited by George Loewenstein and Jon Elster. New York: Russell Sage Foundation.

Ainslie, George, and Richard J. Herrnstein. 1981. "Preference Reversal and Delayed Reinforcement." *Animal Learning Behavior* 9(4): 476–82.

Akerlof, George A. 1991. "Procrastination and Obedience." *American Economic Review* 81(2): 1–19.

Albrecht, Martin, and Martin Weber. 1995. "Hyperbolic Discounting Models in Prescriptive Theory of Intertemporal Choice." *Zeitschrift Fur Wirtschafts-U Sozialwissenschaften* 115(S): 535–68.

———. 1996. "The Resolution of Uncertainty: An Experimental Study." *Journal of Theoretical Economics* 152(4): 593–607.

Alvos, Leanne, R. A. Gregson, and Michael W. Ross. 1993. "Future Time Perspective in Current and Previous Injecting Drug Users." *Drug and Alcohol Dependency* 31: 193–97.

Angeletos, George-Marios, David Laibson, Andrea Repetto, Jeremy Tobacman, and Stephen Weinberg. 2001. "The Hyperbolic Consumption Model: Calibration, Simulation, and Empirical Evaluation." *Journal of Economic Perspectives* 15(3): 47–68.

Ariely, Daniel, and Klaus Wertenbroch. 2002. "Procrastination, Deadlines, and Performance: Using Precommitment to Regulate One's Behavior." *Psychological Science* 13(3): 219–24.

Arrow, Kenneth J. 1983. "The Trade-Off Between Growth and Equity." In *Social Choice and Justice: Collected Papers of Kenneth J. Arrow*, edited by Kenneth J. Arrow. Cambridge, Mass.: Belknap Press.

Ayduk, Ozlem, Rodolfo Mendoza-Denton, Walter Mischel, G. Downey, Philip K. Peake, and Monica Rodriguez. 2000. "Regulating the Interpersonal Self: Strategic Self-Regulation for Coping with Rejection Sensitivity." *Journal of Personality and Social Psychology* 79(5): 776–92.

Bateman, Ian, Alistair Munro, Bruce Rhodes, Chris Starmer, and Robert Sugden. 1997. "A Test of the Theory of Reference-Dependent Preferences." *Quarterly Journal of Economics* 112(2): 479–505.

Baumeister, Roy F., Todd F. Heatherton, and Diane M. Tice. 1994. *Losing Control: How and Why People Fail at Self-Regulation*. San Diego: Academic Press.

Becker, Gary, and Kevin M. Murphy. 1988. "A Theory of Rational Addiction." *Journal of Political Economy* 96(4): 675–701.

Beebe-Center, John G. 1929. "The Law of Affective Equilibrium." *American Journal of Psychology* 41: 54–69.

Benabou, Roland, and Jean Tirole. 2000. "Self-Confidence: Intrapersonal Strategies." Discussion paper 209, Princeton University.

Benartzi, Shlomo, and Richard H. Thaler. 1995. "Myopic Loss Aversion and the Equity Premium Puzzle." *Quarterly Journal of Economics* 110(1): 73–92.

Benzion, Uri, Amnon Rapoport, and Joseph Yagil. 1989. "Discount Rates Inferred from Decisions: An Experimental Study. *Management Science* 35: 270–84.

Bernheim, Douglas, and Antonio Rangel. 2001. "Addiction, Conditioning, and the Visceral Brain." Unpublished paper, Stanford University, Palo Alto, Calif.

Böhm-Bawerk, Eugen von. 1970 [1889]. *Capital and Interest*. South Holland: Libertarian Press.

Boldrin, Michele, Lawrence Christiano, and Jonas Fisher. 2001. "Habit Persistence, Asset Returns, and the Business Cycle." *American Economic Reveiw* 91: 149–66.

Bowman, David, Deborah Minehart, and Matthew Rabin. 1999. "Loss Aversion in a Consumption-Savings Model." *Journal of Economic Behavior and Organization* 38(2): 155–78.

Broome, John. 1995. "Discounting the Future." *Philosophy & Public Affairs* 20: 128–56.

Cairns, John A. 1992. "Discounting and Health Benefits." *Health Economics* 1: 76–79.

———. 1994. "Valuing Future Benefits." *Health Economics* 3: 221–29.

Cairns, John A., and Marjon M. van der Pol. 1997. "Constant and Decreasing Timing Aversion for Saving Lives." *Social Science and Medicine* 45(11): 1653–59.

———. 1999. "Do People Value Their Own Future Health Differently than Others' Future Health?" *Medical Decision Making* 19(4): 466–72.

Camerer, Colin F., and Robin M. Hogarth. 1999. "The Effects of Financial Incentives in Experiments: A Review and Capital-Labor Production Framework." *Journal of Risk Uncertainty* 19: 7–42.

Campbell, John, and John Cochrane. 1999. "By Force of Habit: A Consumption-Based Explanation of Aggregate Stock Market Behavior." *Journal of Political Economy* 107: 205–51.

Caplin, Andrew, and John Leahy. 2001. "Psychological Expected Utility Theory and Anticipatory Feelings." *Quarterly Journal of Economics* 166: 55–79.

Carrillo, Juan D. 1999. "Self-Control, Moderate Consumption, and Craving." CEPR discussion paper 2017.

Carrillo, Juan D., and Thomas Mariotti. 2000. "Strategic Ignorance·as a Self-Disciplining Device." *Review of Economic Studies* 67(3): 529–44.

Carroll, Christopher. 1997. "Buffer-Stock Saving and the Life Cycle/Permanent Income Hypothesis." *Quarterly Journal of Economics* 112: 1–55.

Carroll, Christopher, Jody Overland, and David Weil. 2000. "Saving and Growth with Habit Formation." *American Economic Reveiw* 90: 341–55.

Carroll, Christopher, and Andrew Samwick. 1997. "The Nature of Precautionary Wealth." *Journal of Monetary Economics* 40: 41–71.

Chakravarty, S. 1962. "The Existence of an Optimum Savings Program." *Econometrica* 30(1): 178–87.

Chapman, Gretchen B. 1996. "Temporal Discounting and Utility for Health and Money." *Journal of Experimental Psychology: Learning, Memory, Cognition* 22(3): 771–91.

———. 2000. "Preferences for Improving and Declining Sequences of Health Outcomes." *Journal of Behavioral Decision Making* 13: 203–18.

Chapman, Gretchen B., and Elliot J. Coups. 1999. "Time Preferences and Preventive Health Behavior: Acceptance of the Influenza Vaccine." *Medical Decision Making* 19(3): 307–14.

Chapman, Gretchen B., and Arthur S. Elstein. 1995. "Valuing the Future: Temporal Discounting of Health and Money." *Medical Decision Making* 15(4): 373–86.

Chapman, Gretchen, Richard Nelson, and Daniel B. Hier. 1999. "Familarity and Time Preferences: Decision Making About Treatments for Migraine Headaches and Crohn's Disease." *Journal of Experimental Psychology: Applied* 5(1): 17–34.

Chapman, Gretchen B., and Jennifer R. Winquist. 1998. "The Magnitude Effect: Temporal Discount Rates and Restaurant Tips." *Psychonomic Bulletin and Review* 5(1): 119–23.

Chesson, Harrell, and W. Kip Viscusi. 2000. "The Heterogeneity of Time-Risk Trade-offs." *Journal of Behavioral Decision Making* 13: 251–58.

Coller, Maribeth, and Melonie B. Williams. 1999. "Eliciting Individual Discount Rates." *Experimental Economy* 2: 107–27.

Constantinides, George M. 1990. "Habit Formation: A Resolution of the Equity Premium Puzzle." *Journal of Political Economy* 98(3): 519–43.

Cummings, Ronald G., Glenn W. Harrison, and E. Elisabet Rutstrom. 1995. "Homegrown Values and Hypothetical Surveys: Is the Dichotomous Choice Approach Incentive-Compatible?" *American Economic Review* 85: 260–66.

Damasio, Antonio R. 1994. *Descartes' Error: Emotion, Reason, and the Human Brain.* New York: G. P. Putnam.

Dolan, Paul, and Claire Gudex. 1995. "Time Preference, Duration and Health State Valuations." *Health Economics* 4: 289–99.

Dreyfus, Mark K., and W. Kip Viscusi. 1995. "Rates of Time Preference and Consumer Valuations of Automobile Safety and Fuel Efficiency." *Journal of Law and Economics* 38(1): 79–105.

Duesenberry, James. 1952. *Income, Saving, and the Theory of Consumer Behavior.* Cambridge, Mass.: Harvard University Press.

Elster, Jon, 1979. *Ulysses and the Sirens: Studies in Rationality and Irrationality.* Cambridge: Cambridge University Press.

———. 1985. "Weakness of Will and the Free-Rider Problem." *Economics and Philosophy* 1: 231–65.

Fischer, Carolyn. 1999. "Read This Paper Even Later: Procrastination with Time-Inconsistent Preferences." Discussion paper 99–20, Resources for the Future.

Fishburn, Peter C. 1970. *Utility Theory and Decision Making*. New York: Wiley.

Fishburn, Peter C., and Ariel Rubinstein. 1982. "Time Preference." *International Economic Review* 23(2): 677–94.

Fisher, Irving. 1930. *The Theory of Interest*. New York: Macmillan.

Frank, Robert. 1993. "Wages, Seniority, and the Demand for Rising Consumption Profiles." *Journal of Economic Behavior and Organization* 21: 251–76.

Frederick, Shane. 1999. "Discounting, Time Preference, and Identity." Ph.D. diss., Carnegie Mellon University.

Frederick, Shane, and George Loewenstein. 2002. "The Psychology of Sequence Preferences." Working paper. Cambridge, Mass.: Sloan School, MIT.

Frederick, Shane, George Loewenstein, and Ted O'Donoghue. 2002. "Time Discounting and Time Preference: A Critical Review." *Journal of Economic Literature* XL(June): 351–401.

Frederick, Shane, and Daniel Read. 2002. "The Empirical and Normative Status of Hyperbolic Discounting and Other DU Anomalies." Working paper. Cambridge and London: MIT and London School of Economics.

Fuchs, Victor. 1982. "Time Preferences and Health: An Exploratory Study." In *Economic Aspects of Health*, edited by Victor Fuchs. Chicago: University of Chicago Press.

Fuhrer, Jeffrey. 2000. "Habit Formation in Consumption and Its Implications for Monetary-Policy Models." *American Economic Review* 90: 367–90.

Ganiats, Theodore G., Richard T. Carson, Robert M. Hamm, Scott B. Cantor, Walton Sumner, Stephen J. Spann, Michael Hagen, and Christopher Miller. 2000. "Health Status and Preferences: Population-Based Time Preferences for Future Health Outcome." *Medical Decision Making* 20(3): 263–70.

Gately, Dermot. 1980. "Individual Discount Rates and the Purchase and Utilization of Energy-Using Durables: Comment." *Bell Journal of Economics* 11: 373–74.

Giordano, Louis A., Warren Bickel, George Loewenstein, Eric Jacobs, Lisa Marsch, and Gary J. Badger. 2001. "Opioid Deprivation Affects How Opioid-Dependent Outpatients Discount the Value of Delayed Heroin and Money." Working paper. University of Vermont, Burlington, Psychiatry Department Substance Abuse Treatment Center.

Goldman, Steven M. 1980. "Consistent Plans." Review Economic Studies 47(3): 533–37.

Gourinchas, Pierre-Olivier, and Jonathan Parker. 2001. "The Empirical Importance of Precautionary Saving." *American Economic Review* 91(2): 406–12.

Green, Donald, Karen Jacowitz, Daniel Kahneman, and Daniel Mcfadden. 1998. "Referendum Contingent Valuation, Anchoring, and Willingness to Pay for Public Goods." *Resource Energy Economics* 20: 85–116.

Green, Leonard, E. B. Fischer, Jr., Steven Perlow, and Lisa Sherman. 1981. "Preference Reversal and Self Control: Choice as a Function of Reward Amount and Delay." *Behavioral Analysis Letters* 1(1): 43–51.

Green, Leonard, Nathanael Fristoe, and Joel Myerson. 1994. "Temporal Discounting and Preference Reversals in Choice Between Delayed Outcomes." *Psychonomic Bulletin and Review* 1(3): 383–89.

Green, Leonard, Astrid Fry, and Joel Myerson. 1994. "Discounting of Delayed Rewards: A Life-Span Comparison." *Psychological Science* 5(1): 33–36.

Green, Leonard, Joel Myerson, and Edward McFadden. 1997. "Rate of Temporal Discounting Decreases with Amount of Reward." *Memory & Cognition* 25(5): 715–23.

Gruber, Jonathan, and Botond Koszegi. 2000. "Is Addiction 'Rational'? Theory and Evidence." NBER working paper 7507.

Gul, Faruk, and Wolfgang Pesendorfer. 2001. "Temptation and Self-Control." *Econometrica* 69: 1403–35.

Harless, David W., and Colin F. Camerer. 1994. "The Predictive Utility of Generalized Expected Utility Theories." *Econometrica* 62(6): 1251–89.

Harrison, Glenn W., Morten I. Lau, and Melonie B. Williams. 2002. "Estimating Individual Discount Rates in Denmark." *Quarterly Journal of Economics* 116(4): 1261–1303.

Hausman, Jerry. 1979. "Individual Discount Rates and the Purchase and Utilization of Energy-Using Durables." *Bell Journal of Economics* 10(1): 33–54.

Hermalin, Benjamin, and Alice Isen. 2000. "The Effect of Affect on Economic and Strategic Decision Making." Mimeo, University of California, Berkeley, and Cornell University.

Herrnstein, Richard. 1981. "Self-Control as Response Strength." In *Quantification of Steady-State Operant Behavior*, edited by Christopher M. Bradshaw, Elmer Szabadi, and C. F. Lowe. North Holland: Elsevier.

Herrnstein, Richard J., George F. Loewenstein, Drazen Prelec, and William Vaughan. 1993. "Utility Maximization and Melioration: Internalities in Individual Choice." *Journal of Behavioral Decision Making* 6(3): 149–85.

Herrnstein, Richard J., and Charles Murray. 1994. *The Bell Curve: Intelligence and Class Structure in American Life.* New York: Free Press.

Hesketh, Beryl. 2000. "Time Perspective in Career-Related Choices: Applications of Time-Discounting Principles." *Journal of Vocational Behavior* 57: 62–84.

Hirshleifer, Jack. 1970. *Investment, Interest, and Capital.* Englewood Cliffs, N.J.: Prentice-Hall.

Holcomb, J. H., and P. S. Nelson. 1992. "Another Experimental Look at Individual Time Preference." *Rationality Society* 4(2): 199–220.

Holden, Stein T., Bekele Shiferaw, and Mette Wik. 1998. "Poverty, Market Imperfections and Time Preferences of Relevance for Environmental Policy?" *Environmental Development Economics* 3: 105–30.

Huouston, Douglas A. 1983. "Implicit Discount Rates and the Purchase of Untried, Energy-Saving Durable Goods." *Journal of Consumer Resources* 10: 236–46.

Howarth, Richard B., and Alan H. Sanstad. 1995. "Discount Rates and Energy Efficiency." *Contemporary Economic Policy* 13(3): 101–9.

Hsee, Christopher K., Robert P. Abelson, and Peter Salovey. 1991. "The Relative Weighting of Position and Velocity in Satisfaction." *Psychological Science* 2(4): 263–66.

Jermann, Urban. 1998. "Asset Pricing in Production Economies." *Journal of Monetary Economics* 41: 257–75.

Jevons, Herbert S. 1905. *Essays on Economics*. London: Macmillan.

Jevons, William S. 1888. *The Theory of Political Economy*. London: Macmillan.

Johannesson, Magnus, and Per-Olov Johansson. 1997. "Quality of Life and the WTP for an Increased Life Expectancy at an Advanced Age." *Journal of Public Economics* 65: 219–28.

Kahneman, Daniel. 1994. "New Challenges to the Rationality Assumption." *Journal of Institutional and Theoretical Economics* 150: 18–36.

Kahneman, Daniel, and Amos Tversky. 1979. "Prospect Theory: An Analysis of Decision Under Risk." *Econometrica* 47: 263–92.

Kahneman, Daniel, Peter Wakker, and Rakesh Sarin. 1997. "Back to Bentham? Explorations of Experienced Utility." *Quarterly Journal of Economics* 112: 375–405.

Keren, Gideon, and Peter Roelofsma. 1995. "Immediacy and Certainty in Intertemporal Choice." *Organizational Behavior and Human Decision Processes* 63(3): 287–97.

Kirby, Kris N. 1997. "Bidding on the Future: Evidence Against Normative Discounting of Delayed Rewards." *Journal of Experimental Psychology: General* 126: 54–70.

Kirby, Kris N., and Richard J. Herrnstein. 1995. "Preference Reversals Due to Myopic Discounting of Delayed Reward." *Psychological Science* 6(2): 83–89.

Kirby, Kris N., and Nino N. Marakovic. 1995. "Modeling Myopic Decisions: Evidence for Hyperbolic Delay-Discounting with Subjects and Amounts." *Organizational Behavior and Human Decision Processes* 64: 22–30.

———. 1996. "Delay-Discounting Probabilistic Rewards: Rates Decrease as Amounts Increase." *Psychonomic Bulletin and Review* 3(1): 100–4.

Kirby, Kris N., Nancy M. Petry, and Warren Bickel. 1999. "Heroin Addicts Have Higher Discount Rates for Delayed Rewards than Non-Drug-Using Controls." *Journal of Experimental Psychology: General* 128(1): 78–87.

Koomey, Jonathan G., and Alan H. Sanstad. 1994. "Technical Evidence for Assessing the Performance of Markets Affecting Energy Efficiency." *Energy Policy* 22(10): 826–32.

Koopmans, Tjalling C. 1960. "Stationary Ordinal Utility and Impatience." *Econometrica* 28: 287–309.

———. 1967. "Objectives, Constraints, and Outcomes in Optimal Growth Models." *Econometrica* 35(1): 1–15.

Koopmans, Tjalling C., Peter A. Diamond, and Richard E. Williamson. 1964. "Stationary Utility and Time Perspective." *Econometrica* 32: 82–100.

Koszegi, Botond. 2001. "Who Has Anticipatory Feelings." Working paper. Berkeley: University of California.

Kroll, Yoram, Haim Levy, and Amnon Rapoport. 1988. "Experimental Tests of the Separation Theorem and the Capital Asset Pricing Model." *American Economic Review* 78: 500–19.

Laibson, David. 1994. "Essays in Hyperbolic Discounting." Ph.D. diss., MIT.

———. 1997. "Golden Eggs and Hyperbolic Discounting." *Quarterly Journal of Economics* 112: 443–77.

———. 1998. "Life-Cycle Consumption and Hyperbolic Discount Functions." *European Economic Review* 42: 861–71.

————. 2001. "A Cue-Theory of Consumption." *Quarterly Journal of Economics* 116: 81–119.

Laibson, David, Andrea Repetto, and Jeremy Tobacman. 1998. "Self-Control and Saving for Retirement." *Brookings Papers on Economic Activity* 1: 91–196.

Lancaster, K. J. 1963. "An Axiomatic Theory of Consumer Time Preference." *International Economic Review* 4: 221–31.

Lawrence, Emily. 1991. "Poverty and the Rate of Time Preference: Evidence from Panel Data." *Journal of Political Economy* 119: 54–77.

LeDoux, Joseph E. 1996. *The Emotional Brain: The Mysterious Underpinnings of Emotional Life.* New York: Simon & Schuster.

Loewenstein, George. 1987. "Anticipation and the Valuation of Delayed Consumption." *Economy Journal* 97: 666–84.

————. 1988. "Frames of Mind in Intertemporal Choice." *Management Science* 34: 200–14.

————. 1996. "Out of Control: Visceral Influences on Behavior." *Organizational Behavior and Human Decision Processes* 65: 272–92.

————. 1999. "A Visceral Account of Addiction." In *Getting Hooked: Rationality and Addiction*, edited by Jon Elster and Ole-Jorgen Skog. Cambridge: Cambridge University Press.

————. 2000a. "Willpower: A Decision-Theorist's Perspective." *Law Philosophy* 19: 51–76.

————. 2000b. "Emotions in Economic Theory and Economic Behavior." *American Economic Review Papers Proceedings* 90: 426–32.

Loewenstein, George, Ted O'Donoghue, and Matthew Rabin. 2000. "Projection Bias in the Prediction of Future Utility." Center for Analytic Economics Working paper #02-11, Cornell University.

Loewenstein, George, and Drazen Prelec. 1991. "Negative Time Preference." *American Economic Review* 81: 347–52.

————. 1992. "Anomalies in Intertemporal Choice: Evidence and an Interpretation." *Quarterly Journal of Economics* 107(2): 573–97.

————. 1993. "Preferences for Sequences of Outcomes." *Psychological Review* 100(1): 91–108.

Loewenstein, George, and Nachum Sicherman. 1991. "Do Workers Prefer Increasing Wage Profiles?" *Journal of Labor Economics* 9(1): 67–84.

Loewenstein, George, Roberto Weber, Janine Flory, Stephen Manuck, and Matthew Muldoon. 2001. "Dimensions of Time Discounting." Paper presented at Conference on Survey Research on Household Expectations and Preferences. Ann Arbor, Mich. (November 2–3, 2001).

MacCriminon, Kenneth R., and Donald A. Wehrung. 1990. "Characteristics of Risk-Taking Executives." *Management Science* 36(4): 422–35.

MacKeigan, L. D., L. N. Larson, J. R. Draugalis, J. L. Bootman, and L. R. Burns. 1993. "Time Preference for Health Gains vs. Health Losses." *Pharmacoeconomics* 3(5): 374–86.

Madden, Gregory J., Nancy M. Petry, Gary J. Badger, and Warren Bickel. 1997. "Impulsive and Self-Control Choices in Opioid-Dependent Patients and Non-Drug-Using Control Participants: Drug and Monetary Rewards." *Experimental and Clinical Psychopharmacology* 5(3): 256–62.

Maital, S., and S. Maital. 1978. "Time Preference, Delay of Gratification, and Intergenerational Transmission of Economic Inequality: A Behavioral Theory of Income Distribution." In *Essays in Labor Market Analysis*, edited by Orley Ashenfelter and Wallace Oates. New York: Wiley.

Martin, John L. 2001. "The Authoritarian Personality, 50 Years Later: What Lessons Are There for Political Psychology?" *Political Psychology* 22(1): 1–26.

Mazur, James E. 1987. "An Adjustment Procedure for Studying Delayed Reinforcement." In *The Effect of Delay and Intervening Events on Reinforcement Value*, edited by Michael L. Commons, James E. Mazur, John A. Nevin, and Howard Rachlin. Hillsdale, N.J.: Erlbaum.

Meyer, Richard F. 1976. "Preferences Over Time." In *Decisions with MultipleObjectives*, edited by Ralph Keeney and Howard Raiffa. New York: Wiley.

Millar, Andrew, and Douglas Navarick. 1984. "Self-Control and Choice in Humans: Effects of Video Game Playing as a Positive Reinforcer." *Learning and Motivation* 15: 203–18.

Mischel, Walter, Joan Grusec, and John C. Masters. 1969. "Effects of Expected Delay Time on Subjective Value of Rewards and Punishments." *Journal of Personality and Social Psychology* 11(4): 363–73.

Mischel, Walter, Yuichi Shoda, and Philip K. Peake. 1988. "The Nature of Adolescent Competencies Predicted by Preschool Delay of Gratification." *Journal of Personality and Social Psychology* 54(4): 687–96.

Moore, Michael J., and W. Kip Viscusi. 1988. "The Quantity-Adjusted Value of Life." *Economic Inquiry* 26(3): 369–88.

———. 1990a. "Discounting Environmental Health Risks: New Evidence and Policy Implications." *Journal of Environmental Economics and Management* 18: S51–S62.

———. 1990b. "Models for Estimating Discount Rates for Long-Term Health Risks Using Labor Market Data." *Journal of Risk Uncertainty* 3: 381–401.

Munasinghe, Lalith, and Nachum Sicherman. 2000. "Why Do Dancers Smoke? Time Preference, Occupational Choice, and Wage Growth." Working paper. New York: Columbia University and Barnard College.

Murphy, Thomas J., and Alan S. De Wolfe. 1986. "Future Time Perspective in Alcoholics, Process and Reactive Schizophrenics, and Normals." *International Journal of Addictions* 20: 1815–22.

Myerson, Joel, and Leonard Green. 1995. "Discounting of Delayed Rewards: Models of Individual Choice." *Journal of Experimental Analysis and Behavior* 64: 263–76.

Nisan, Mordecai, and Abram Minkowich. 1973. "The Effect of Expected Temporal Distance on Risk Taking." *Journal of Personality and Social Psychology* 25(3): 375–80.

Nyhus, E. K. 1995. "Item and Non Item-Specific Sources of Variance in Subjective Discount Rates. A Cross Sectional Study." Paper presented 15th Conference on Subjective Probability, Utility and Decision Making, Jerusalem.

O'Donoghue, Ted, and Matthew Rabin. 1999a. "Addiction and Self-Control." In *Addiction: Entries and Exits*, edited by Jon Elster. New York: Russell Sage Foundation.

———. 1999b. "Doing It Now or Later." *American Economic Review* 89(1): 103–24.

———. 1999c. "Incentives for Procrastinators." *Quarterly Journal of Economics* 114(3): 769–816.

———. 1999d. "Procrastination in Preparing for Retirement." In *Behavioral Dimensions of Retirement Economics*, edited by Henry Aaron. New York: Brookings Institution and Russell Sage Foundation.

———. 2000. "Addiction and Present-Biased Preferences." Cornell University, Ithaca, and University of California, Berkeley. Center for Analytic Economics Working paper #02-10, Cornell University.

———. 2001. "Choice and Procrastination." *Quarterly Journal of Economics* 116(1): 121–60.

Olson, Mancur, and Martin J. Bailey. 1981. "Positive Time Preference." *Journal of Political Economy* 89(1): 1–25.

Orphanides, Athanasios, and David Zervos. 1995. "Rational Addiction with Learning and Regret." *Journal of Political Economy* 103(4): 739–58.

Parfit, Derek. 1971. "Personal Identity." *Philosophical Review* 80(1): 3–27.

———. 1976. "Lewis, Perry, and What Matters." In *The Identities of Persons*, edited by Amelie O. Rorty. Berkeley: University of California Press.

———. 1982. "Personal Identity and Rationality." *Synthese* 53: 227–41.

Peleg, Bezalel, and Menahem E. Yaari. 1973. "On the Existence of a Consistent Course of Action When Tastes Are Changing." *Review of Economic Studies* 40(3): 391–401.

Pender, John L. 1996. "Discount Rates and Credit Markets: Theory and Evidence from Rural India." *Journal of Developmental Economy* 50(2): 257–96.

Petry, Nancy M., Warren Bickel, and Martha M. Arnett. 1998. "Shortened Time Horizons and Insensitivity to Future Consequences in Heroin Addicts." *Addiction* 93: 729–38.

Phelps, E. S., and Robert Pollak. 1968. "On Second-Best National Saving and Game-Equilibrium Growth." *Review of Economic Studies* 35: 185–99.

Pigou, Arthur C. 1920. *The Economics of Welfare*. London: Macmillan.

Pollak, Robert A. 1968. "Consistent Planning." *Review of Economic Studies* 35: 201–8.

———. 1970. "Habit Formation and Dynamic Demand Functions." *Journal of Political Economy* 78(4): 745–63.

Prelec, Drazen, and George Loewenstein. 1998. "The Red and the Black: Mental Accounting of Savings and Debt." *Marketing Science* 17(1): 4–28.

Rabin, Matthew. 2000. "Risk Aversion and Expected-Utility Theory: A Calibration Theorem." *Econometrica* 68(5): 1281–92.

Rabin, Matthew, and Richard H. Thaler. 2001. "Anomalies: Risk Aversion." *Journal of Economic Perspectives* 15(1): 219–32.

Rachlin, Howard, Andres Raineri, and David Cross. 1991. "Subjective Probability and Delay." *Journal of Experimental Analysis and Behavior* 55(2): 233–44.

Rae, John. 1905 [1834]. *The Sociological Theory of Capital*. London: Macmillan.

Raineri, Andres, and Howard Rachlin. 1993. "The Effect of Temporal Constraints on the Value of Money and Other Commodities." *Journal of Behavioral Decision Making* 6: 77–94.

Read, Daniel. 2001. "Is Time-Discounting Hyperbolic or Subadditive?" *Journal of Risk Uncertainty* 23: 5–32.

Read, Daniel, George F. Loewenstein, and Matthew Rabin. 1999. "Choice Bracketing." *Journal of Risk Uncertainty* 19: 171–97.

Redelmeier, Daniel A., and Daniel N. Heller. 1993. "Time Preference in Medical Decision Making and Cost-Effectiveness Analysis." *Medical Decision Making* 13(3): 212–17.

Roelofsma, Peter. 1994. "Intertemporal Choice." Free University Amsterdam.

Ross, Jr., W. T., and I. Simonson. 1991. "Evaluations of Pairs of Experiences: A Preference for Happy Endings." *Journal of Behavioral Decision Making* 4: 155–61.

Roth, Alvin E., and J. Keith Murnighan. 1982. "The Role of Information in Bargaining: An Experimental Study." *Econometrica* 50(5): 1123–42.

Rubinstein, Ariel. 2000. "Is It 'Economics and Psychology'? The Case of Hyperbolic Discounting." Tel Aviv University, Israel, and Princeton University, New Jersey.

Ruderman, H., M. D. Levine, and J. E. McMahon. 1987. "The Behavior of the Market for Energy Efficiency in Residential Appliances Including Heating and Cooling Equipment." *Energy Journal* 8(1): 101–24.

Ryder, Harl E., and Geoffrey M. Heal. 1973. "Optimal Growth with Intertemporally Dependent Preferences." *Review of Economic Studies* 40: 1–33.

Samuelson, Paul. 1937. "A Note on Measurement of Utility." *Review of Economic Studies* 4: 155–61.

———. 1952. "Probability, Utility, and the Independence Axiom." *Econometrica* 20(4): 670–78.

Schelling, Thomas C. 1984. "Self-Command in Practice, in Policy, and in a Theory of Rational Choice." *American Economic Review* 74(2): 1–11.

Senior, N. W. 1836. *An Outline of the Science of Political Economy*. London: Clowes and Sons.

Shea, John. 1995a. "Myopia, Liquidity Constraints, and Aggregate Consumption." *Journal of Money, Credit, Banking* 27(3): 798–805.

———. 1995b. "Union Contracts and the Life-Cycle/Permanent-Income Hypothesis." *American Economic Review* 85(1): 186–200.

Shelley, Marjorie K. 1993. "Outcome Signs, Question Frames and Discount Rates." *Management Science* 39: 806–15.

———. 1994. "Gain/Loss Asymmetry in Risky Intertemporal Choice." *Organizational Behavior and Human Decision Processes* 59: 124–59.

Shelley, Marjorie K., and Thomas C. Omer. 1996. "Intertemporal Framing Issues in Management Compensation." *Organizational Behavior and Human Decision Processes* 66(1): 42–58.

Shoda, Yuichi, Walter Mischel, and Philip K. Peake. 1990. "Predicting Adolescent Cognitive and Self-Regulatory Competencies from Preschool Delay of Gratification." *Developmental Psychology* 26(6): 978–86.

Solnick, Jay, Catherine Kannenberg, David Eckerman, and Marcus Waller. 1980. "An Experimental Analysis of Impulsivity and Impulse Control in Humans." *Learning and Motivation* 11: 61–77.

Solow, Robert M. 1974. "Intergenerational Equity and Exhaustible Resources."

Review of Economic Studies 41: Symposium on the Economics of Exhaustible Resources, 29–45.

Spence, Michael, and Richard Zeckhauser. 1972. "The Effect of Timing of Consumption Decisions and Resolution of Lotteries on Choice of Lotteries." *Econometrica* 40(2): 401–3.

Starmer, Chris. 2000. "Developments in Non-Expected Utility Theory: The Hunt for a Descriptive Theory of Choice Under Risk." *Journal of Economic Literature* 38(2): 332–82.

Sternberg, Robert J. 1985. *Beyond IQ: A Triarchic Theory of Human Intelligence.* New York: Cambridge University Press.

Stevenson, Mary Kay. 1992. "The Impact of Temporal Context and Risk on the Judged Value of Future Outcomes." *Organizational Behavior and Human Decision Processes* 52(3): 455–91.

Strotz, R. H. 1955–1956. "Myopia and Inconsistency in Dynamic Utility Maximization." *Review of Economic Studies* 23(3): 165–80.

Suranovic, Steven, Robert Goldfarb, and Thomas C. Leonard. 1999. "An Economic Theory of Cigarette Addiction." *Journal of Health Economics* 18(1): 1–29.

Thaler, Richard H. 1981. "Some Empirical Evidence on Dynamic Inconsistency." *Economic Letters* 8: 201–7.

———. 1985. "Mental Accounting and Consumer Choice." *Management Science* 4: 199–214.

———. 1999. "Mental Accounting Matters." *Journal of Behavioral Decision Making* 12: 183–206.

Thaler, Richard H., and Hersh M. Shefrin. 1981. "An Economic Theory of Self-Control." *Journal of Political Economy* 89(2): 392–410.

Tversky, Amos, and Daniel Kahneman. 1983. "Extensional vs. Intuitive Reasoning: The Conjunction Fallacy in Probability Judgment." *Psychological Review* 90: 293–315.

———. 1991. "Loss Aversion in Riskless Choice: A Reference Dependent Model." *Quarterly Journal of Economics* 106: 1039–61.

Tversky, Amos, and Derek J. Koehler. 1994. "Support Theory: Nonextensional Representation of Subjective Probability." *Psychological Review* 101(4): 547–67.

van der Pol, Marjon M., and John A. Cairns. 1999. "Individual Time Preferences for Own Health: Application of a Dichotomous Choice Question with Follow Up." *Applied Economic Letters* 6(10): 649–54.

———. 2001. "Estimating Time Preferences for Health Using Discrete Choice Experiments." *Social Science and Medicine* 52: 1459–70.

Varey, C. A., and Daniel Kahneman. 1992. "Experiences Extended Across Time: Evaluation of Moments and Episodes." *Journal of Behavioral Decision Making* 5(3): 169–85.

Viscusi, W. Kip, and Michael J. Moore. 1989. "Rates of Time Preference and Valuation of the Duration of Life." *Journal of Public Economics* 38(3): 297–317.

Wahlund, Richard, and Jonas Gunnarsson. 1996. "Mental Discounting and Financial Strategies." *Journal of Economic Psychology* 17(6): 709–30.

Wang, Ruqu. 1997. "The Optimal Consumption and Quitting of Harmful Addictive Goods." Working paper. Queens University, New York.

Warner, John T., and Saul Pleeter. 2001. "The Personal Discount Rate: Evidence from Military Downsizing Programs." *American Economic Review* 91(1): 33–53.

Whiting, Jennifer. 1986. "Friends and Future Selves." *Philosophical Review* 95(4): 547–80.

Winston, Gordon C. 1980. "Addiction and Backsliding: A Theory of Compulsive Consumption." *Journal of Economic Behavioral Organization* 1: 295–324.

Yates, J. Frank, and Royce A. Watts. 1975. "Preferences for Deferred Losses." *Organizational Behavior and Human Performance* 13(2): 294–306.

PART I

Philosophical,
Evolutionary, and
Neurobiological
Underpinnings

· 2 ·

Time Preference and Personal Identity

SHANE FREDERICK

ECONOMISTS usually regard time preference as any other type of preference. A preference for current utility over future utility is treated the same as the preference for an apple over an orange—as a personal taste, whose rationality cannot be disputed. There is one important difference, however. Choosing an apple over an orange is compatible with utility maximization: while one cannot be certain that the apple conferred more utility than the orange, it seems reasonable to assume so. Such an assumption is not tenable in the case of time preference: someone who chooses a smaller amount of utility now over a greater amount in some future period is clearly *not* maximizing utility over that interval.[1]

Since time preference runs counter to utility maximization, it requires more justification than other types of preferences. Many have argued that no such justification can be found; that there is no good reason to care less about future utility than current utility (see, for example, Jevons 1871; Sidgwick 1930 [1874]; Pigou 1920; Ramsey 1928; Lewis 1946; Rawls 1971; Elster 1986; Broome 1991). Those who advocate temporal neutrality argue that one should want their life *as a whole* to go as well as possible, and that counting some parts of life more than others interferes with this goal. On this view, preferring a smaller immediate pleasure over a greater future pleasure (or a greater future pain over a smaller immediate pain) is irrational, because now and later are equally parts of one life, and choosing the smaller good or the greater bad reduces the quality of one's life as a whole.

The belief that a person should weight all utility the same, regardless of its temporal position, implicitly assumes that all parts of one's future are *equally* parts of oneself; that there is a single, enduring, irreducible entity to whom all future utility can be ascribed. However, some philosophers—most notably Derek Parfit (1971, 1984)—deny this assumption. They argue that a person is nothing more than a succession of overlapping selves related to varying degrees by physical continuities, memories, and similarities of character and interests. On this view, the separation between selves may be just as significant as the separation between persons, and discounting one's "own" future utility may be no more irrational than discounting the utility of someone else.[2]

To illustrate this argument with an extreme example, consider the plight of Seth Brundle, the main character in the movie *The Fly*. In a scientific experiment gone awry, Seth becomes genetically fused with a housefly and gradually metamorphoses into "Brundlefly" (a human-fly hybrid). Under these exceptional circumstances, it seems rational for Seth to discount "his" future utility—to give less weight (perhaps no weight at all) to the future utility of Brundlefly.

The foregoing example lends credibility to the idea that it *could*, at least under *some* circumstances, be rational to discount future utility. This of course leaves open the questions of exactly which *types* of changes justify diminished concern for future selves and what *degree* of discounting might ordinarily be appropriate.

Personal Identity

Philosophical debates about the nature of personal identity are dominated by two competing views: the simple and the complex. According to the simple view, we are the same person through time, despite the physical and psychological changes we undergo; our existence across time is unified by some indivisible and irreducible entity or essence or soul to which all of our future experiences can be assigned.[3] The complex view of identity, by contrast, denies the existence of some irreducible entity or "I" that remains unchanged over time. This view argues instead that our identity across time is based only on continuity of memories, interests, and other characteristics that can diminish.[4]

The complex view is not new. Plato articulated it in his *Symposium*:

A man is said to be the same person from childhood until he is advanced in years: yet though he is called the same he does not at any time possess the same properties; he is continually becoming a new person . . . not only in his body but in his soul besides we find none of his manners or habits, his opinions, desires, pleasures, pains or fears, ever abiding the same in his particular self; some things grow in him, while others perish. (207D–208B, cited in Borowski 1976)

David Hume later echoed the implicit question in Plato's statement. In *An Enquiry Concerning the Principles of Morals* (1927 [1751], 253) he asks, "What . . . gives us so great a propension to ascribe an identity to these successive perceptions, and to suppose ourselves possest of an invariable and uninterrupted existence thro' the whole course of our lives?" Among modern philosophers, the complex view is endorsed by Parfit (1971, 1973, 1976, 1984), Wachsberg (1983), Zemach (1978, 1987), Lewis (1976), and others. The complex view also appears to be endorsed by the economist Robert H. Strotz (1956, 179), who writes, "The individual over time is an infinity of individuals, and the familiar problems of interpersonal utility comparisons are there to plague us."

Once one accepts the complex view of personal identity, which denies the existence of a single entity persisting across time, it is a small step to further conclude that discounting "our" own future utility is as rational as discounting the utility experienced by someone else— because the utility experienced by the later selves is not fully one's "own."[5] Although philosophers have appreciated this implication for some time (see, for example, Butler 1975 [1736], 99, 105; Sidgwick 1930 [1874], 419), this view is now most strongly associated with Parfit, who was among the first to explicitly endorse it:

> My concern for my future may correspond to the degree of connectedness between me now and myself in the future . . . since connectedness is nearly always weaker over long periods, I can rationally care less about my further future. (1984, 313)

Parfit's provocative views—and their implications for analyses of intertemporal choice—have largely been ignored outside of philosophy journals (though see Broome 1985, 286–89; Baron 1988, 442, 446; Harvey 1994, 40, 48). Among philosophers, however, they have spawned a lively debate. The following briefly summarizes the three primary bases for philosophical opposition to Parfit's claims.

Three Critiques of the Parfitian View

Critics of Parfit attack him by denying his proposition that the degree of connectedness with a future self is closely related to the degree of concern for that self that is rationally mandated. Some offer examples (typically, thought experiments) in which a diminution in connectedness does not seem to permit diminished concern. Others construct examples in which concern does not seem to be required despite full connectedness. Still others argue that we construct our identity; that changes in our character, values, goals, and beliefs are something we *initiate* and do not merely *experience*, and that this continuity of agency integrates our existence through time. A brief sketch of each of these three criticisms follows.

Concern for Future Welfare May Be Required in the Absence of Connectedness

Many have attacked the Parfitian view by asking the reader to imagine a profound change in our psychology, followed by a horrific pain (see, for example, Madell 1981; Williams 1970). These critics maintain that, in a deep and undeniable sense, the one who feels the future pain will still be "you," however different "you" might be. For example, Williams (1970, 170, 180) writes,

> Physical pain . . . is minimally dependent on character or belief. No amount of change in my character or my beliefs would seem to affect substantially the nastiness of tortures applied to me; correspondingly, no degree of predicted change in my character and beliefs can unseat the fear of torture which . . . is predicted for me . . . the principle that one's fears can extend to future pain whatever psychological changes precede it seems positively straightforward.

Concern May Not Be Required Despite Full Connectedness

Others have criticized Parfit's view by arguing that connectedness per se cannot be the appropriate basis for our future concern (Robinson 1988, 323; Korsgaard 1989, 107). These critics argue that if connectedness is what matters, we ought to be indifferent about whether "we" survive or whether someone who is sufficiently psychologically connected to us does, including a replica of ourselves whom we have never met. The unacceptability of this conclusion is assumed to be self-evident.

> Suppose that scientists on Mars are mass-producing bio-programmed people to populate other planets. They are able to imprint various information on the brains of these creatures, including personalities, apparent memories, interests, and so on. Suppose that by purely random coincidence they program a man to have a personality, memories, skill,

interests, and so on just like mine, so that they unwittingly create a coincidental replica, who would be just as he is if I had never been born. I am about to die. If identity isn't what matters, the fact that this coincidental replica will continue ought to be just as good as survival. . . . This is plainly mistaken. (Stone 1988, 526)

While replacement with a replica does not seem as good as ordinary survival, it surely seems better than ordinary death. Suppose, for example, that in the airports of the future you enter a special type of scanner that records all of your physical and psychological characteristics (including dispositions, memories, and so on). Prior to boarding, you are given your disk containing this information. You may either throw the disk away or give it to the ticket agent for safekeeping. If you throw the disk away, then the result of a plane crash is as it is now. However, if you give the disk to the ticket agent, in the event of a plane crash the information would be sent to the airport of your destination and an exact replica of you would be reconstituted from the information on the disk. It seems unlikely that the fate of the disk would be a matter of indifference for people. This suggests that *something* important *is* preserved on the disk. Indeed, I suspect that some people would be willing to pay a substantial premium to be "backed up" in this way.

Agency Unifies Successive Selves Despite Diminishing Connectedness

A third criticism of Parfit is less easily captured by an intuitively compelling thought experiment. However, like the other objections, it denies Parfit's assertion that selves are linked principally by connectedness. This third critique denies that selves are merely spatio-temporally continuous passive loci of experiences. Instead, these critics suggest that selves are active agents whose choices forge the identity of descendent selves, and that this continuity of agency connects selves more tightly than an assessment of connectedness alone would imply. For example, Elster (1986) argues,

I have no argument against Parfit's view that a person who expected his future states to be weakly connected would not be irrational in discounting the future. I believe, however, that a person who takes his future states as given, rather than something to be created, is fundamentally irrational. (See also Daniels 1979, 273; McClennen 1990, 218; Whiting 1986; Korsgaard 1989)

Elster's objection is not entirely convincing, though. While it may be rational to strive for psychological connectedness, this does not make it irrational to discount for any loss of connectedness that might occur despite such efforts. As an analogy, though one should strive to stay vigorous, this does not make it irrational to account for the likelihood of becoming less vigorous with age.

Discussion

Parfit's claims about time preference are normative, not descriptive. He is not attempting to explain or predict people's intertemporal choices. Rather, he is arguing that theories of rational choice must be grounded on a correct view of personal identity, and the correct view permits people to discount future utility. It is important to be clear about this claim. Parfit is not claiming that people *should* not care about their future welfare, but that one is not rationally compelled to care about his or her future welfare to a degree that exceeds their level of connectedness with those future selves.[6]

However, even if one correctly interprets and accepts Parfit's claims, they provide precious little guidance about the degree of time preference that would be rationally permissible. First, he offers no precise definition of *connectedness*, suggesting only that it is related to "ambitions, achievements, commitments, emotions, memories, and several other psychological features" (1984, 284).[7] Second, Parfit never quite spells out the relation between connectedness and concern, claiming only that the two concepts "correspond" (1984, 313). Third, he never specifies how much connectedness diminishes over time, saying only that it "is nearly always weaker over longer periods" (1984, 313).

The following section describes a study that attempts to measure connectedness (and its diminution across time) by asking people to report their self-perceived similarity with their past and future selves. These assessments in turn are compared with imputed discount rates to determine whether Parfit's views about identity have descriptive as well as normative content—whether they might *explain* as well as *justify* intertemporal choices.

A Measure of Psychological Connectedness

Sample

Two hundred twenty-eight respondents participated in this study. Their ages ranged from thirteen to eighty-three (M = 38, σ = 16). Respondents were drawn from five convenience samples: travelers at the Pittsburgh International Airport, employees of the U.S. Forest Service, competitors at a Pittsburgh Scrabble tournament, Carnegie Mellon undergraduates, and elderly residents of a Jewish Community center. Of the 228 respondents, 207 produced usable responses.[8] Each respondent received a $1 lottery ticket for completing the questionnaire.

Procedure

In this study, connectedness was operationalized in terms of "similarity." Respondents were first asked to indicate, on a 100-point scale, how similar they expected to be to their future selves and how similar they are now to their former selves. In these judgments, respondents were told to think of characteristics such as "personality, temperament, likes and dislikes, beliefs, values, ambitions, goals, ideals, etc." (See appendix 2.1 for a full description of the procedure.) Although similarity to future selves would be the relevant consideration for choices, I assumed that reported similarity of past selves might be a more meaningful measure than future projections, and that these retrospective reports might serve as proxies for the degree of future connectedness that could be expected (under the strong assumption that those who changed substantially in the past would continue to do so in the future).

Concern for future selves was operationalized through two measures of discount rates. Monetary discount rates were elicited by asking respondents to report the amount of money they would require in one, five, ten, twenty, thirty, and forty years to make them indifferent to receiving $100 tomorrow. Nonmonetary discount rates were then elicited by asking respondents to imagine that they worked at a job that had equal proportions of pleasant and unpleasant work ("good days" and "bad days") and to report the number of additional good days in one, five, ten, twenty, and thirty years that would make them indifferent to receiving twenty additional good days (and thus twenty fewer bad days) this year.[9] It was assumed that respondents who cared less about their future selves would require more future money (or more future good days) to make them indifferent to the immediate reward. (See appendices 2.3 and 2.4 for a full description of the elicitation procedure.)

Results

Similarity with Past and Future Selves   Table 2.1 reports the mean similarity judgments, both overall and disaggregated by age group

Table 2.1 Mean Self-Assessed Similarity of Current Self to Past Selves and Future Selves

	(Reported Similarity)						(Predicted Similarity)				
Age group	Forty Years Ago	Thirty Years Ago	Twenty Years Ago	Ten Years Ago	Five Years Ago	Now	Five Years Ahead	Ten Years Ahead	Twenty Years Ahead	Thirty Years Ahead	Forty Years Ahead
Teens					55	100	65	55	49	46	42
Twenties				43	64	100	75	66	59	53	49
Thirties			35	56	73	100	81	72	67	60	55
Forties		35	60	75	87	100	78	72	64	55	46
Fifties	29	38	47	61	74	100	80	69	53	38	
Sixty +	40	46	56	73	84	100	72	57	49		
Overall	33	39	48	59	72	100	76	66	58	51	49
Kruskall-Wallis sig lev	0.13	0.31	0.00	0.00	0.00	—	0.05	0.01	0.03	0.01	0.25

Source: Author's compilation.

Figure 2.1   Self-Assessed Similarity of Past and Future Selves as Judged by Different Age Groups

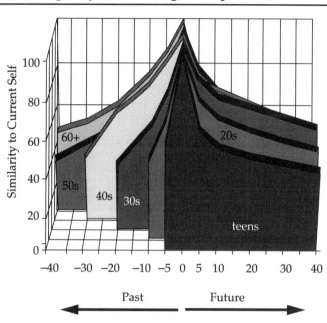

Source: Author's configuration.

(teenagers, people in their twenties, thirties, forties, fifties, and those sixty and over). For example, teenagers looking five, ten, twenty, thirty, forty years into the future predicted a degree of similarity of 65, 55, 49, 46, 42, respectively (read the Teens row left to right, starting from Now). For people over sixty looking five, ten, twenty, thirty, forty years into the past, the reported mean degree of similarity was 84, 73, 56, 46, 40, respectively (read the Sixty+ row right to left, starting from Now). Figure 2.1 depicts these data graphically, with the six age groups plotted along the z axis ascending from Teens to Sixty+.

The shape of these similarity discount functions defy any simple interpretation, because it is unclear exactly how respondents used the response scale. Similarity has no natural zero point, and the judged degree of similarity between two selves depends on the breadth of the judgmental context that one adopts. For example, if the judgmental context is one's twin brother or one's close friends, a former self may be judged as "very different" than one's current self, but if the judgmental context is a randomly selected person (for example, an Australian aborigine), one's former self may seem "very similar."[10]

Thus, it isn't clear exactly what a similarity of 60 means. Nor is it clear whether a drop from 90 to 80 represents the same reduction in similarity as a drop from 50 and 40.[11]

However, notwithstanding the problems posed by forcing similarity judgments onto a ratio-scale response format, the results do permit some interesting comparisons. First, the projected similarity of future selves suggests a curvilinear relation with age. In general, the "very young" (teens and twenties) and "very old" (fifties and sixty +) believe that they will change more than people who are "middle aged" (thirties and forties). This can be seen by looking down the columns in table 2.1 (or into the z axis of figure 2.1). (The bottom row of table 2.1 shows the significance level of a Kruskall-Wallis test against the null hypothesis of equal responses among all six age categories.) Perhaps the younger respondents predict greater change because their adult personalities have not yet crystallized, whereas older respondents predict greater change because they anticipate senile dementia or physical debilitation that is profound enough to change their conception of self.[12]

Reported similarity showed a simpler pattern. Looking back any given number of years into the past, older respondents report having changed less. For example, respondents sixty and older reported that the similarity between their current self and "−5" self was 84, whereas teenagers reported the similarity to their "−5" self to be only 55. (Again, the bottom row of table 2.1 shows the significance level of a Kruskall-Wallis test against the null hypothesis of equal responses among all six age categories.)

Since this was not a longitudinal study, respondents' predicted similarity of a future self could not be compared with their *own* reported similarity after that interval had elapsed. However, respondents' prospective judgments could be compared with the corresponding retrospective judgments of *other* older respondents. For example, the "+5" judgments of all thirteen-year-olds could be compared to the "−5" judgments of all eighteen-year-olds, and so on. Table 2.2 reports the average differences between predicted and reported similarity for matched age groups, both overall and for a given age range (see appendix 2.2 for a description of this calculation). Most of the entries are positive, which indicates that respondents generally predicted more similarity looking forward than they reported looking backward over the same age interval. Since there is no objective measure of similarity with which to compare these judgments, it is unclear whether people underpredict how much they will change, overreport how much they have changed, or some of each. (It is also possible that respondents use the response scale differently as they age.)

**Table 2.2   Difference Between Predicted Future Similarity and
Reported Past Similarity of Older Matched Age Groups**

Predicting Group	Length of Interval				
	Five Years	Ten Years	Twenty Years	Thirty Years	Forty Years
Teens	3.4	8.2	8.3	−1.1	14.6
Twenties	5.0	10.5	−0.2	15.9	12.7
Thirties	−0.8	−1.7	22.2	16.7	18.4
Forties	−6.2	6.5	3.0	28.4	17.0
Fifties	2.5	−7.0	13.8	13.7	
Sixty +	−2.1	−13.8			
Overall	0.4	2.4	8.9	14.7	14.9

Source: Author's compilation.

Does Predicted Reduction in Similarity Influence Discount Rates?   Tables 2.3 and 2.4 show median responses and corresponding imputed discount rates, both overall and disaggregated by age category.[13] If the predicted similarity of future selves affects the weighting of future welfare, discount rates should be inversely correlated with these similarity judgments (because if the utility from future rewards were discounted, people would need greater rewards to make them indifferent to an immediate reward). This was not found. In general, neither predicted nor reported similarity correlated significantly with either monetary discount rates or nonmonetary discount rates (see tables 2.5 and 2.6).[14]

The failure to find any correlation between future similarity and discount rates may have several explanations. First, it might indicate that people (implicitly) endorse the simple view of personal identity— they believe they *are* the same person through time, and that change in personality (or connectedness) is not one of the things that should affect their valuation of future rewards.

Second, even if people believe that diminishing connectedness justifies discounting, they may fail to incorporate this consideration when assigning numbers to the matching tasks.[15] The matching tasks may be so abstract that the responses reflect idiosyncratic algorithms for "solving the task" as much as they reflect anything about time preference per se.[16] Of course, to the extent that the matching tasks are not measuring time preference, one would not expect the responses to correlate with similarity judgments, even if similarity was a proxy for connectedness and projected connectedness was, in fact, an important determinant of concern for future welfare.

Table 2.3   Median Number of Future Dollars Judged to Be Equally Attractive to $100 Tomorrow

	One Year	Five Years	Ten Years	Twenty Years	Thirty Years	Forty Years
Teens	$150 (50)	$500 (38)	$800 (23)	$1,000 (12)	$1,800 (10)	$1,800 (7)
Twenties	$180 (50)	$500 (38)	$900 (25)	$2,000 (16)	$3,000 (12)	$4,500 (10)
Thirties	$160 (60)	$500 (38)	$1,000 (26)	$1,500 (15)	$2,000 (11)	$3,500 (9)
Forties	$150 (50)	$500 (38)	$1,000 (26)	$2,000 (16)	$2,500 (11)	$3,500 (9)
Fifties	$150 (50)	$400 (32)	$1,000 (26)	$2,000 (16)	$7,500 (15)	
Sixty +	$163 (63)	$450 (35)	$900 (25)	$2,000 (16)		
Overall	$150 (50)	$500 (38)	$1,000 (26)	$2,000 (16)	$3,000 (12)	$3,750 (9)

Source: Author's compilation.
Note: Implicit discount rates (percentage) in parentheses.

**Table 2.4   Median Number of Future Extra "Good Days"
Judged Equally Attractive to Twenty Extra Good
Days This Year**

	One Year	Five Years	Ten Years	Twenty Years	Thirty Years
Teens	25 (25)	35 (12)	40 (7)	60 (6)	85 (5)
Twenties	21 (5)	38 (14)	50 (10)	84 (7)	100 (5)
Thirties	20 (0)	33 (11)	50 (10)	50 (5)	55 (3)
Forties	21 (5)	50 (20)	100 (17)	183 (12)	
Fifties	21 (5)	80 (32)	120 (20)		
Sixty +	25 (25)				
Overall	21 (5)	40 (15)	56 (11)	70 (6)	80 (5)

Source: Author's compilation.
Note: Implicit discount rates (percentage) in parentheses.

Third, although respondents were instructed to base their similarity judgments on features that Parfit views as central components of connectedness ("personality, temperament, likes and dislikes, beliefs, values, ambitions, goals, ideals, etc."), at least some things that fall under these broad terms may have little to do with how much one ought to care about his or her future self. For example, suppose someone predicts that her passion for Scrabble will wither with age. She will, accordingly, be somewhat dissimilar with respect to "likes and dislikes" (one component of connectedness). Nevertheless, she may not believe that this particular change has *any* significance for how much she should care about future monetary rewards or future pleasurable work experiences. Furthermore, her similarity judgments might well have been heavily influenced by factors (such as anticipated changes in physical characteristics) that are relatively unimportant determinants of how "connected" she feels to a future self.

Final Remarks

Economic analyses of intertemporal choice typically assume positive time preference and focus on the implications of that assumption. The normative question about how much one *ought* to care about one's future welfare is usually avoided.[17]

Philosophical analyses of intertemporal choice, by contrast, have sought to establish a normative basis for time preference—to articulate reasons why future utility should or should not be counted the same. Conclusions often rest on the view of personal identity that is

Table 2.5 Rank Correlations Between Similarity Judgments and One-, Five-, Ten-, Twenty-, Thirty-, and Forty-Year Monetary Discount Rates

Years Until Receipt of Money	Reported Similarity						Predicted Similarity				
	Forty Years Ago	Thirty Years Ago	Twenty Years Ago	Ten Years Ago	Five Years Age	Now	Five Years Ahead	Ten Years Ahead	Twenty Years Ahead	Thirty Years Ahead	Forty Years Ahead
One	0.13	0.03	−0.01	−0.05	−0.04	—	0.00	−0.02	−0.07	−0.05	−0.01
Five	0.37*	0.23	0.00	0.01	0.07	—	0.09	0.07	0.04	0.01	0.07
Ten	0.41*	0.26	0.03	0.04	0.09	—	0.09	0.08	0.04	0.00	−0.00
Twenty	0.49*	0.26	0.11	0.10	0.13	—	0.08	0.07	0.05	0.02	−0.00
Thirty	0.55*	0.24	0.08	0.08	0.12	—	0.07	0.03	−0.00	−0.02	−0.04
Forty		−0.01	−0.08	−0.03	0.04	—	0.05	0.00	−0.04	−0.02	−0.04

Source: Author's compilation.
Note: * Indicates statistically significant positive correlation.

Table 2.6 Rank Correlations Between Similarity Judgments and One-, Five-, Ten-, Twenty-, and Thirty-Year "Good Days" Discount Rates

Years Until Receipt of Good Days	Reported Similarity						Predicted Similarity				
	Forty Years Ago	Thirty Years Ago	Twenty Years Ago	Ten Years Ago	Five Years Age	Now	Five Years Ahead	Ten Years Ahead	Twenty Years Ahead	Thirty Years Ahead	Forty Years Ahead
One	0.12	−0.01	0.10	−0.08	0.02	—	−0.11	−0.13	−0.10	−0.08	−0.02
Five	0.24	0.01	0.02	0.03	0.05	—	0.08	0.04	−0.05	−0.08	−0.07
Ten	0.44	0.02	0.12	0.16	0.15	—	0.10	0.07	−0.01	−0.04	−0.07
Twenty		−0.31	0.00	0.12	0.14	—	0.03	0.01	−0.02	−0.03	−0.06
Thirty			−0.13	0.04	0.08	—	0.04	0.04	0.03	0.03	−0.02

Source: Author's compilation.
Note: * Indicates statistically significant positive correlation.

adopted. Those who regard a person as a single irreducible entity that persists across time generally believe that any degree of time preference is irrational. Others, such as Parfit, who deny the existence of an enduring irreducible entity may view future selves as partially distinct individuals and, correspondingly, may believe that some degree of time preference is rational (though very little is said about how much discounting is allowed).

However, while diminishing connectedness of future selves may *permit* one to weight future utility less, it does not *require* one to do so. One might reasonably regard descendent future selves as children or close friends—others whose welfare is important enough to justify the sacrifice of one's "own" utility (see Whiting 1986). Moreover, while diminishing connectedness may make it rationally permissible to discount future utility, it may render it *morally* impermissible to do so. As future selves gain the status of other people, rational mandates give way to ethical obligations. Regarding his decision to smoke, Parfit (1973, 240–41) comments:

> If I am not acting irrationally there is surely an objection to what I am doing. For the sake of smaller benefits now, I am bringing upon myself in old age greater burdens. This may not be irrational. But it is surely open to criticism. . . . By acting against my interest in my old age I am doing what, impartially considered, has worse effects, or reduces the sum of benefits minus burdens. We should perhaps begin to claim that this is morally wrong, even when it will be me who will bear the increased burdens.

Appendix 2.1

Below, I would like you to rate how similar you expect to be in the future compared to how you are now, and how similar you were in the past compared to how you are now. By similar, I mean characteristics such as personality, temperament, likes and dislikes, beliefs, values, ambitions, goals, ideals, etc.

For each of the questions below, rate similarity by using a number from 0 to 100, where 0 means you (were / will be) *completely different* and 100 means you (were / will be) *exactly the same*. You may use decimals if you wish.

0   100
├──┼──┼──┼──┼──┼──┼──┼──┼──┤
completely   exactly
different   the same

Similarity   Rating

Compared to now, how similar will you be *5 years* from now?   _____

Compared to now, how similar will you be *10 years* from now?   _____

Compared to now, how similar will you be *20 years* from now?   _____

Compared to now, how similar will you be *30 years* from now?   _____

Compared to now, how similar will you be *40 years* from now?   _____

Compared to now, how similar were you *5 years* ago?   _____

Compared to now, how similar were you *10 years* ago?   _____

Compared to now, how similar were you *20 years* ago?   _____

Compared to now, how similar were you *30 years* ago?   _____

Compared to now, how similar were you *40 years* ago?   _____

Appendix 2.2

(1) "k" year perspective effect =

$$\sum_{x=13}^{x=83}\left[\frac{\sum_i sim_x(x + k,x)}{i} - \frac{\sum_j sim_{x+k}(x,x + k)}{j}\right],$$

where:

x = age

k = length of interval being considered

i = number of respondents of age x who made predictions

j = number of respondents of age $x + k$ who made reports

$sim_x(x + k,x)$ = similarity of age $x + k$ to age x, as judged from the perspective of age x

$sim_{x+k}(x, x + k)$ = similarity of age x to age $x + k$ as judged from the perspective of age $x + k$

Appendix 2.3

On each of the seven lines below, circle the option that you would prefer

1) $100 tomorrow   or $500 in 1 year

2) $100 tomorrow   or $25 in 1 year

3) $100 tomorrow   or $250 in 1 year

4) $100 tomorrow   or $50 in 1 year

5) $100 tomorrow   or $125 in 1 year

6) $100 tomorrow   or $75 in 1 year

7) $100 tomorrow   or $100 in 1 year

Now, for each of the lines below, fill in the blank so that you would be indifferent between the immediate and the delayed payment—i.e., so that you would have a very hard time deciding between them.

I would be indifferent between $100 tomorrow and $_____ in 1 year.

I would be indifferent between $100 tomorrow and $_____ in 5 years.

I would be indifferent between $100 tomorrow and $_____ in 10 years.

I would be indifferent between $100 tomorrow and $_____ in 20 years.

I would be indifferent between $100 tomorrow and $_____ in 30 years.

I would be indifferent between $100 tomorrow and $_____ in 40 years.

Appendix 2.4

Imagine that you will have the same job for the rest of your life. At this job, you get to spend about half of the days doing something that you love (good days). The other half of the days, you must spend doing something that you hate (bad days).

Suppose that you were given a chance to choose between having some extra good days (and, thus, fewer bad days) this year, or in a future year. For each of the six lines below, circle the option that you would prefer.

1) 20 extra good days this year   or   100 extra good days next year

2) 20 extra good days this year   or   5 extra good days next year

3) 20 extra good days this year   or   50 extra good days next year

4) 20 extra good days this year   or   10 extra good days next year

5) 20 extra good days this year   or   25 extra good days next year

6) 20 extra good days this year   or   15 extra good days next year

7) 20 extra good days this year   or   20 extra good days next year

Now, complete the blanks below so that you would be indifferent.

I would be indifferent between 20 extra good days this year and _____ extra good days *next year*.

I would be indifferent between 20 extra good days this year and _____ extra good days in *5 years*.

I would be indifferent between 20 extra good days this year and _____ extra good days in *10 years*.

I would be indifferent between 20 extra good days this year and _____ extra good days in *20 years*.

I would be indifferent between 20 extra good days this year and _____ extra good days in *30 years*.

Notes

1. Note that if future utility is discounted, there is some $\epsilon > 0$ such that the utility sequence $(1 - \epsilon, 0)$ would be preferred to the sequence $(0, 1)$. However, choosing $(1 - \epsilon, 0)$ over $(0, 1)$ fails to maximize utility over the two-period interval, because $1 - \epsilon < 1$. As an analogy, suppose that you are asked to choose between \$99 on the left side of the table and \$100 on the right side. If you choose the \$99, you can hardly claim that you are maximizing because that amount is on the *left* side of the table. Correspondingly, preferring $1 - \epsilon$ units of utility now over 1 unit in the future requires some account for why the *temporal* position of utility is any more relevant than the *spatial* position of the two monetary quantities in the foregoing example.

2. Although the analogy between selves and persons is strong, there are some distinctions. First, selves have identical genetic structure, whereas individuals do not (except for identical twins). Second, selves are spatiotemporally continuous, whereas individuals are not (except for Siamese twins). Finally, by some philosophical and religious views, selves possess the same soul, whereas distinct individuals do not. Of course, this final alleged disanalogy is precisely what many philosophers deny and is the basis for debate among those championing differing views on the nature of personal identity.

3. Thus, the simple view holds that persons are fundamentally unlike other objects, such as ships, whose identity over time can hold to intermediate degrees, depending on objective empirical relations between the object at two points in time (for example, the proportion of original planks that remain, whether the sail has been replaced by an engine, and so on).

4. In one widely cited argument in support of the complex view of identity, we are invited to imagine a machine that, by the gradual replacement of cells, can transform Derek Parfit into Greta Garbo. Those who ascribe to the simple view of personal identity are forced to adopt the untenable position that somewhere along this spectrum is a sharp borderline on one side of which we have Derek Parfit and on the other side, Greta Garbo. The complex view handles this puzzle more easily, because it permits intermediate degrees of identity. We are allowed to speak of the resulting person as being more Parfitlike or more Garbolike, without having to specify exactly where Parfit ends and Garbo begins (see Parfit 1984, 277).

5. Indeed, philosophers often turn the discounting issue on its head. Rather than seeking to articulate a basis for giving less than full weight to future outcomes, they seek to establish reasons why we should have any special concern about "our" future selves (any concern beyond that which we would feel for any stranger). For example, Perry (1976, 74) asks,

> If I am told that by pushing a button I will prevent someone from being in great pain tomorrow, I will have a reason to push it. But

intuitively, if the person is *me*, I will have more reason, or perhaps special reasons, for pushing it. What basis can the theory of personal identity sketched provide for this feeling?

Whiting (1986, 551–52) suggests that most cannot. "Of any candidate for what constitutes such identity—for example, bodily continuity or sameness of immaterial soul—we can always ask how that candidate justifies concern. And it's not clear that any account has a very satisfactory answer." (See also Korsgaard 1989, 112.)

6. Some readings of Parfit could perhaps interpret a stronger claim: that it is irrational to care more about one's "own" future self than about the welfare of any other person whose connectedness is equally high. Of course, if the degree of connectedness with other persons is generally lower than the degree of connectedness with future selves (as seems likely), this distinction is irrelevant.

7. Shoemaker (1996, 320) defines connectedness of a later self in terms of the degree to which the later self remembers actions, carries out the intentions, or has the same character, desires, and goals as the earlier self. Nozick (1981, 69) comments on the difficulty of defining an objective measure of connectedness:

> Which particular properties, features, and dimensions constitute the measure of closeness, and with what relative weights? . . . what are the relevant subcomponents of psychological continuity or similarity (for example, plans, ambitions, hobbies, preferences in flavors of ice cream, moral principles) and what relative weights are these to be given in measuring closeness?

8. Respondents were excluded if their similarity judgments were not monotonically declining. For example, a person whose predicted degrees of similarity for five, ten, twenty, thirty, and forty years into the future were 95, 41, 90, 35, and 10 would be excluded, because 90 is greater than 41. Although nothing is inherently illogical about a teenager predicting that he or she is more similar to his or her fifty-year-old self than his or her forty-year-old self, it seems unlikely, and suggests a misunderstanding of the task.

9. I assumed that people would retire by age seventy, and excluded responses that required the assumption of working past seventy. Many respondents older than forty did not answer all of the questions, writing "will be retired" or "doesn't apply" in at least one of the blanks.

10. In many other studies that have elicited similarity judgments, the judgmental context can be inferred from the set of experimental stimuli explicitly presented, which often are a small set of abstract, impoverished figures that vary along only two or three dimensions, such as sixteen squares that vary in size and brightness (Tversky and Gati 1982), sixteen drawings of plants that vary in form of pot and elongation of leaves (Gati and Tversky 1982), four schematic faces varying in the shape of the mouth, eyebrows, and nose (Tversky 1977), or on the presence or absence of beard, glasses, and mustache (Sattath and Tversky 1987).

11. If literally interpreted as a ratio-scale measure of similarity, the judgments suggest an inconsistency: forward-looking predictions indicate higher rates of change at younger ages, whereas backward-looking reports indicate higher rates of change at older ages. For example, collectively, respondents predicted similarity to diminish by 34 points over the first ten years (from 100 to 66), but only 8 additional points over the next ten years (from 66 to 58). Looking in the opposite direction, however, perceived similarity diminished more quickly in the near past than the more distant past. For example, collectively, respondents reported a decline of 41 similarity points going ten years back (from 100 to 59), but an additional decline of only 11 more points going twenty years back (from 59 to 48).

12. Although physical characteristics were not included among the adjectives used to cue similarity judgments, respondents may have thought that they were part of the "etc."—that is, they might also have chosen to account for physical characteristics even if they did not consider them part of the explicit or implicit instructions.

13. For the monetary question, implicit discount rates were computed from responses using the formula $r = [(\# \text{ of future dollars}/\$100)^{1/t}] - 1$. For the nonmonetary question, implicit discount rates were computed from indifference values using the formula $r = [(\# \text{ of future days}/20)^{1/t}] - 1$.

14. In fact, the only statistically significant correlations are *positive*. Among respondents fifty and older, there was a significant positive correlation between the reported similarity of past selves and the monetary discount rate (see Forty Years Ago column of table 2.5). There was also a significant correlation between the perceived similarity of distant past selves and the nonmonetary discount rate for a ten-year time horizon (see Forty Years Ago column of table 2.6). In other words, older respondents who viewed themselves as being very similar to their more youthful selves had higher implicit discount rates. I have no explanation for these results. Perhaps they require none, as only 5 of 109 correlations are significant, and this is almost exactly what would be expected by chance.

15. This explanation predicts that if people were reminded of the concept of personal identity immediately before making intertemporal choices or rendering intertemporal judgments, those who projected a greater reduction in similarity would indeed display higher discount rates. Although this remains to be tested, the similarity judgments *did* precede the matching tasks, so one might conclude that such a reminder was in fact provided in this study.

16. For example, for the more distant time horizons in the monetary matching task, the median and modal response for $100 tomorrow = $_____ in X years is, simply, $100X. Moreover, the matching task is so difficult or unengaging that fewer than half of the respondents in the sample generated answers that could be considered "reasonable." Specifically, fewer than half generated a set of numbers that were strictly monotonically ascending in X. (Restricting the sample to these respondents did not alter the qualitative conclusions.)

17. Sometimes, however, the issue does make its way to the surface. In their economic analysis of addiction, Becker and Murphy (1988, 684) comment, "Although fully myopic behavior is formally consistent with our definition of rational behavior, should someone who entirely or largely neglects future consequences of his actions be called rational?"

References

Baron, Jon. 1988. *Thinking and Deciding*. Cambridge: Cambridge University Press.

Becker, Gary, and Kevin M. Murphy. 1988. "A Theory of Rational Addiction." *Journal of Political Economy* 96: 675–700.

Borowski, E. J. 1976. "Identity and Personal Identity." *Mind* 85(340): 481–502.

Broome, John. 1985. "The Economic Value of Life." *Economica* 52: 281–94.

————. 1991. *Weighing Goods: Equality, Uncertainty, and Time*. Oxford: Basil Blackwell.

Butler, Joseph. 1975 [1736]. "The Analogy of Religion." In *Personal Identity*, edited by John Perry. University of California Press.

Daniels, Norman. 1979. "Moral Theory and the Plasticity of Persons." *Monist* 6: 265–87.

Elster, Jon. 1986. "Introduction." In *Rational Choice*, edited by Jon Elster. New York: New York University Press.

Gati, Itamar, and Amos Tversky. 1982. "Representations of Qualitative and Quantitative Dimensions." *Journal of Experimental Psychology: Human Perception and Performance* 8(2): 325–40.

Harvey, Charles M. 1994. "The Reasonableness of Non-Constant Discounting." *Journal of Public Economics* 53: 31–51.

Hume, David. 1927 [1751]. *An Enquiry Concerning the Principles of Morals*. In *Hume Selections*, edited by C. W. Hendel. New York: Scribners.

Jevons, W. Stanley. 1871. *The Theory of Political Economy*. London: MacMillan.

Korsgaard, Christine M. 1989. "Personal Identity and the Unity of Agency: A Kantian Response to Parfit." *Philosophy and Public Affairs* 18(2): 101–32.

Lewis, Clarence I. 1946. *An Analysis of Knowledge and Valuation*. La Salle, Ill.: Open Court.

Lewis, David. 1976. "Survival and Identity." In *The Identities of Persons*, edited by Amelie O. Rorty. Berkeley: University of California Press.

Madell, Geoffrey. 1981. *The Identity of the Self*. Edinburgh: Edinburgh University Press.

McClennen, Edward F. 1990. *Rationality and Dynamic Choice: Foundational Explorations*. Cambridge: Cambridge University Press.

Nozick, Robert. 1981. *Philosophical Explanations*. Cambridge, Mass.: Harvard University Press.

Parfit, Derek. 1971. "Personal Identity." *Philosophical Review* 80(1): 3–27.

————. 1973. "Later Selves and Moral Principles." In *Philosophy and Personal*

Relations: An Anglo-French Study, edited by Alan Montefiore. Montreal: McGill-Queen's University Press.

———. 1976. "Lewis, Perry and What Matters." In *The Identities of Persons*, edited by Amelie O. Rorty. Berkeley: University of California Press.

———. 1982. "Personal Identity and Rationality." *Synthese* 53: 227–41.

———. 1984. *Reasons and Persons*. Oxford: Clarendon Press.

Perry, John. 1976. "The Importance of Being Identical." In *The Identities of Persons*, edited by Amelie O. Rorty. Berkeley: University of California Press.

Pigou, Arthur C. 1920. *The Economics of Welfare*. London: Macmillan.

Ramsey, Frank P. 1928. "A Mathematical Theory of Saving." *Economic Journal* 38(December): 543–49.

Rawls, John. 1971. *A Theory of Justice*. Cambridge, Mass.: Harvard University Press.

Robinson, John. 1988. "Personal Identity and Survival." *Journal of Philosophy* 85(6): 319–28.

Sattath, Shmuel, and Amos Tversky. 1987. "On the Relation Between Common and Distinctive Feature Models." *Psychological Review* 94(1): 16–22.

Shoemaker, David. 1996. "Theoretical Persons and Practical Agents." *Philosophy and Public Affairs* 25(4): 318–32.

Sidgwick, Henry. 1930 [1874]. *The Methods of Ethics*. 7th ed. London: Macmillan.

Stone, Jim. 1988. "Parfit and the Buddha: Why There Are No People." *Philosophy and Phenomenological Research* 48(3): 519–32.

Strotz, Robert H. 1956. "Myopia and Inconsistency in Dynamic Utility Maximization." *Review of Economic Studies* 23(3): 165–80.

Tversky, Amos. 1977. "Features of Similarity." *Psychological Review* 84(4): 327–52.

Tversky, Amos, and Itamar Gati. 1982. "Similarity, Separability, and the Triangle Inequality." *Psychological Review* 89(2): 123–54.

Wachsberg, Milton. 1983. "Personal Identity, the Nature of Persons, and Ethical Theory." Ph.D. diss., Princeton University.

Whiting, Jennifer. 1986. "Friends and Future Selves." *Philosophical Review* 95(4): 547–80.

Williams, Bernard. 1970. "The Self and Future." *Philosophical Review* 79: 161–80.

Zemach, Eddy. 1978. "Love the Neighbor as Thyself or Egoism and Altruism." *Midwest Studies in Philosophy* 3: 148–58.

———. 1987. "Looking Out for Number One." *Philosophy and Phenomenological Research* 48(2): 209–33.

· 3 ·

The Evolution of Patience

Alex Kacelnik

THE YOUNG couple beholds the forbidden fruit with both longing and misapprehension. They suspect that biting the apple will yield immediate pleasure, but are concerned that given that it is forbidden, it may cause unpleasantness in the future. How can they decide if the delayed woes are worth paying in exchange for the immediate joy? They face an intertemporal problem that is also plagued by uncertainty, because they do not know the magnitude of either positive or negative consequences nor over how long will they persist. They may or may not care whether the forthcoming misery will affect their descendents. If they do care, they will not find it easy to judge the number of generations over which they should bother.

Meanwhile, the tree that yielded the fruit also faces intertemporal problems, but it is on safer grounds. Every spring the tree determines the amount of root, branch, leaf, and flower growth, taking into account that each of them distracts resources that, if stored, may be used in growing more apples later on. Its decisions are accurately tuned to the expected time and relative probability of factors such as the density of pollinating insects, the weather, and the presence of seed-distributing birds. Its problems are intertemporal because flowering early cuts into the growing season and many seeds one year may compromise the number of seeds the following year. The tree's timing takes good account of this.

Similarly, birds nesting in the tree's branches lay their eggs at a carefully chosen date so that the moment at which the chicks reach their greater need coincides with the time when the abundance of caterpillars (their main food) is greatest. They too handle stochastic intertemporal trade-offs, because they gain by laying their eggs early so as to give their chicks an edge against the others and good chances of growth before the fall sets in. Impatient parents would, however, pay a heavy cost if their chicks hatch too early in the season, because the chicks would then be growing at maximum rate before the caterpillars hatch.

The actions of trees, birds, and other animals including humans are subject to intertemporal compromises in many respects. The extreme uncertainty of Adam and Eve arises from not having evolved or even developed, having instead been created from mud. Fortunately for the rest of us, we have been shaped by evolution with the same criteria used for other organisms and develop individually over many years of facing similar problems repeatedly, so that our decision making should be expected to be well designed to cope with intertemporal problems. The design of behavior to handle intertemporal trade-offs is a universal peculiarity of living systems; they may be expected to solve these trade-offs as if they took into account the costs, benefits, and temporal relations of all their actions. As efficient decision makers, living things take into account that cost can be paid earlier if it leads to sufficiently large gains later on. They also know that immediate satisfaction such as that expected from biting a forbidden fruit should be avoided, because it may have nasty and long-lasting consequences to be paid by an infinite number of generations of genetic descendents. In this context, cost and gains are measured in the universal currency of evolution by natural selection, that biologists call *fitness* and is roughly defined as relative success in passing inherited characteristics to the next generations. In the case of the behavioral issues discussed in this volume, the characteristics that concern us are mechanisms of choice.

Contrast the previous examples with the behavior of a nonliving system such as a river. The course of a river can be described and predicted with metaphorical goal-seeking language similar to that used by biologists when they say that trees, humans, and birds do things "in order to achieve the goal of fitness maximization," and that they are in some sense capable of optimal decisions. The river behaves as if its goal is to descend as fast as possible, and following the same metaphor, takes optimal decisions at every fork in its path; but water cannot handle intertemporal trade-offs. A river never pays the immediate cost of running uphill, even when this would allow it to descend through a steeper valley later on.

Living things can choose efficiently between actions whose consequences are separated in time, because through natural selection, consequences of choices shape mechanisms of choice. Hence at the scale of an individual organism, these mechanisms of choice behave as if they were anticipating consequences, even when no such anticipation may be transparent to the individual decision maker. This view of things is so compelling that when an organism is seen taking decisions that violate the maximization of fitness, biologists and evolutionarily minded psychologists are startled and normally make a big fuss; and so they must. It is nobody's worry if an individual makes a mistake. If an organism takes the wrong decision in an unusual ecological setting, this is also of scant concern: starlings crash against lighthouses as a consequence of using usually effective night navigation mechanisms; trout get hooked on fishermen's decoys while snapping at the stimuli normally associated with floating insects; people in rich countries overeat sweets and fats because they have taste mechanisms evolved to cope with scarce resources. These accidents are evolutionarily unproblematic. If research shows, however, that members of one species—or worse, of many species—typically take decisions in a way that is incompatible with fitness maximization in ecologically relevant situations, an evolutionarily minded biologist or psychologist should not just sit back and enjoy the flight: something is shouting for an explanation.

This is precisely the reason why there is a great deal of interest in intertemporal choice by humans and other animals. As many chapters of this book make clear, ample evidence shows that decision makers care "too much" for things that happen immediately, and seem incapable to attribute proper value to delayed events.

Bickel and Johnson (chap. 14, herein) for instance, discuss the similarities between the discounting functions of pigeons, rats, and humans (see their figure 14.1) and find that while all humans seem to discount imminent events sharply and distant events less so, in drug-dependent subjects this tendency is exaggerated. Hence, they postulate, drug dependence as a proclivity may be the expression of a disorder of discounting. Further, they show that manipulating access to drugs of dependence seems to affect discounting functions for different commodities, showing a bidirectional determination.

In another important analysis, Angeletos and collaborators (chap. 18 herein) start from the empirical observations of discounting being greater than expected in the short run and implement a simulation of the consequences of this behavior for households living in a realistic economic environment. They show that their simulation fits consumption patterns of real households better than predictions of classical, optimal strategy models, and that this leads to a higher drop in consumption at retirement time, thereby leading to substantial economic consequences and reduction in quality of life.

With regard to temporal discounting, in the same vein as Bickel and Johnson, Frederick and colleagues (chap. 1 herein) refer to the similarity between human and nonhuman results, raising the possibility that a fundamental mechanism used by species as different as humans, pigeons, and rats leads to suboptimal intertemporal choice (that is, different from that predicted by the Discounted Utility model). If the DU model really describes some form of optimum, how such a universal deviation from optimal choice mechanisms may evolve and be maintained against adverse selection is, and should be, a major puzzle.

Examples such as these are ubiquitous across the literature dealing with intertemporal choice, including the behavioral ecology literature. In a recent paper using blue jays as subjects, Stephens and Anderson (2001) show that in a self-control paradigm, the animals sacrifice long-term gains for the sake of more immediate and less valuable food rewards. They propose that this is the result of using the same decision rule that is used in the so-called patch problem, in which a subject decides when to abandon a resource of declining value. The prevalence among economists of the notion that temporal discounting is a result of uncertainty is exemplified by a recently published account (Fehr 2002) of the Nobel Symposium on Experimental and Behavioral Economics, tellingly entitled "The Economics of Impatience." This summary puts the problem thus: "In experiments, animals often prefer smaller, immediate rewards over larger rewards that are deferred—thus failing to maximise their total gain. Many people exhibit similar behaviour." Ernst Fehr, the author of this summary, offers as an explanation the fact that

> throughout evolutionary history, future rewards have been uncertain. An animal foraging for food may be interrupted, or, in the case of reproductive opportunities, die before it is successful. For humans, the promise of future rewards may be broken. And if the risk faced by a person varies over time, he or she applies various discounts to future events and so behaves inconsistently. (1)

Notice that preference of a smaller, sooner reward over a larger, later reward is taken to imply a failure of maximization. Under this vision, any temporal discounting is suboptimal under the experimental conditions. The putative reason for this suboptimal behavior would be the history of the decision mechanisms, evolved in environments where delayed rewards were uncertain. The next step in most analyses of animal experiments is to accept this history of uncertainty, then deduce the properties that the discounting function ought to have given this assumption. In other words, although animals in the laboratory ought not to discount at all, if they do so it is because they respond to the ghost of uncertainty in their environment of evolutionary adaptation. As a consequence, the exhibited discounting function should have some properties, notably, a constant rate of discounting that reflects the constant probability of losing the delayed reward per unit of waiting time. Animals are found not to show a constant discount rate, hence they appear not to maximize gains even according to their evolutionary history. The claims that animals fall into this trap and thus fail to function effectively are often substantiated with the description of classical experiments on pigeons (Green et al. 1981), to which we shall return in a later section.

The important point here is that were we to accept uncritically this literature, we would have to live with the conclusion that people and other animals live their lives consistently yielding to the temptation of attributing too much value to immediate pleasure, even though they would achieve a higher expected gain by exhibiting greater self-control. Indeed, they appear to behave more like water than like living organisms. To the extent that any temporal discounting is seen as adaptive, it is in the context of handling probabilistic loss of reward during waiting time (Houston and McNamara 1999; Kagel, Green, and Caraco 1986; Kagel, Battalio, and Green 1995). Uneasy with this conclusion, my goal here is to provide an alternative explanation for temporal discounting and for the shape of the relevant function, based on the notion that animals do maximize gains under ecologically relevant conditions. When they do not, an adaptive interpretation is at hand that is not based on the influence of the ghost of interruptions past. Scattered ideas related to this material can be found elsewhere (Bateson and Kacelnik 1996; Kacelnik 1997; Stephens and Anderson 2001). Frederick and colleagues (chap. 1 herein) discuss the superficiality of the assumptions that allow for the DU model to be derived axiomatically. Here a similar path is followed, with an emphasis on the nonhuman evidence.

Case 1: One-Shot Choice, Fixed Outcome

Assume an imaginary decision maker choosing between two options (the term *option* is used to identify possible actions in a simultaneous choice), each leading to an amount of money earned after a given delay. The assumptions are: (1) this is a one-shot choice; (2) each of the two options has a fixed outcome; (3) the chooser is fully knowledgeable of all aspects of the situation; (4) neither the subject nor the environment change during the intervening delays; and (5) satisfaction is proportional to the expected magnitude of the reward (probability times size).

Within this scenario we consider two ways in which the choice that maximizes expected utility may depend on delay, namely, *growth* and *loss*. As we will see, the two are mathematically equivalent, but imply different physical processes and hence are worth a distinction.

Problem 1: Growth

Let's assume that the outcome of option A (if chosen) is received as soon as it is chosen (in real situations we should always talk of at least some small delay, but for the present purpose this is not necessary), while that of B is delivered τ time units later. If we assume that A starts yielding some benefit immediately, then by the time that B would have been received, A will have produced some accumulated benefit. For instance, a tree in early spring invests in growing leaves by metabolizing stored sugar, as opposed to storing the sugar to grow fruit later in the season. The new leaves generate extra sugar by photosynthesis during the time gap, and the tree may accrue greater longer-term benefit (seed production) than it would have had by keeping those resources under the mattress, so to speak. If A were money that is received immediately and can be put at compound interest, its value after τ time units can be compared with that of a delayed reward B taking the interest into account. The value of A after delay τ is given by $S_A(1 + \alpha)^\tau$ where S_i is the size of reward i and α is the interest rate. A and B will have equal value when

$$S_B = S_A(1 + \alpha)^\tau. \tag{3.1}$$

Since the interest rate is positive, S_B needs to be larger than S_A for the two options to be equally attractive. This is expressed by saying that B is "discounted" exponentially as a function of its delay.

Two features of equation 3.1 are important here. First, if a constant delay is added to both alternatives, the ratio of their values remains constant. If we call this added delay k, so that A is delivered after k time units and B after $\tau + k$ time units, then from equation 3.1 we get $S_B(1 + \alpha)^k = S_A(1 + \alpha)^{\tau+k}$, so that the ratio between the two sizes remains the same ($\frac{S_B}{S_A} = (1 + \alpha)^\tau$) for any value of k. Second, the size of the rewards does not affect the discount rate, so that if the immediate reward is modified, the size of the delayed reward at indifference will be modified by the same factor, so their ratio remains the same.

Problem 2: Loss

If instead of postulating that more immediate rewards generate value during the time gap we assume that delayed payoffs may be lost during the wait, the results are almost identical. To see it, let us assume that there is a chance β per unit of time that the delayed option B may be lost during the time gap. For example, a monkey that discovers an unripe fig may wonder whether to take it now or wait another day. Its immediate option is the fig as it is, and the delayed option is the more valuable ripe fig that could be eaten tomorrow. The problem is that if it decides to wait, another monkey may take the fig. In a monetary example, the subject considers money to be safe if and only if it is in the pocket (or has been spent and produced satisfaction). Money promised for some time in the future is considered vulnerable to loss. To formalize this, even if we assume that the delayed reward is either lost totally or received in its integrity, its value can be represented as a smaller expected value as time lapses, according to the accumulated probability of being lost. In the monkey example, we assume that the benefits from eating the fig drop continuously as a function of waiting time, because implicitly we are averaging over many instances of the same kind. Since the probability that the item is not lost in one time unit is $1 - \beta$, the probability that it will still be there after a delay of τ time units is $(1 - \beta)^\tau$. Consequently, the value of a delayed reward B after a delay τ is $S_B(1 - \beta)^\tau$. Here the equal value of the two options occurs when

$$S_A = S_B(1 - \beta)^\tau. \tag{3.2}$$

Since $\beta > 0$, S_B has to be larger than S_A for equal attractiveness. Once again, we can say that B is discounted exponentially as a function to its delay. The discounting function has the same two properties emphasized for problem 1: the relative value is unaffected by adding a constant delay to both options and by the size of the rewards.

The putative greater uncertainty for more delayed rewards due to probability of losses or interruptions has been the main argument in evolutionary accounts for discounting in intertemporal choice (Kagel, Green, and Caraco 1986; Kagel, Battalio, and Green 1995; Houston and McNamara 1999; Sozou 1998), probably because considering gains in value of the immediate reward during the delay is unrealistic for very short delays.

Theoretical Shortcomings of Case 1

Case 1 in its two variants of growth and loss illustrates the discounted utility perspective, and is based on starting from some simplifying assumptions. Simplification is a universal need for theoretical modeling, and hence to argue that the assumptions do not reflect reality in its richness would be trivial, but the process of simplification may have fundamental consequences on the conclusions reached, and one must think about it carefully. Let us then consider these assumptions again.

One-Shot Choice   In the animal literature, discounting is studied by making subjects choose between stimuli (such as right or left levers for rats or differentially colored pecking keys for birds) that lead to rewards of different sizes and delays. To get animals to respond to these stimuli, they are trained with repeated exposure to each stimulus followed by the assigned reward and assigned delay. Animals never choose between the rewards themselves, always between stimuli that have been associated with those rewards in repeated presentations. In spite of this, most authors examine data on animal choice in the one-shot frame. This theoretical weakness is crucial to understand animal data on intertemporal choice, as will be discussed. In the human literature, intertemporal choice has been studied much more by psychologists, who tend to study choices by presenting the problem linguistically to their subjects, than by experimental economists, who prefer to examine choices for real monetary payoffs and hence use techniques more akin to those used in the animal experiments (Hertwig and Ortmann 2001). This is a major obstacle in comparing human and animal results.

Fixed Outcomes   In real life most actions have a range of possible outcomes, and in attributing value to an option the subject must integrate across these various outcomes. We focus here on cases where each action (the choice of an option) leads to one outcome. This is an important issue, because results of multiple outcome experiments challenge most present theoretical accounts. We will return to this problem when examining the failures of rate maximization accounts, but the problem is examined in more detail elsewhere (Bateson and Kacelnik 1996, 1997).

Full Knowledge   The prediction of exponential discounting assumes that delayed rewards are assessed with perfect knowledge of the rate of growth or probability of loss. This is highly unlikely in the real world and completely unjustified in animal experiments. Some authors (Kagel, Battalio, and Green 1995) do refer to the fact that in most animal experiments rewards are never lost, and therefore according to the single-choice DU model, experimental animals should not discount at all. Yet even these authors argue that since they do discount, they must still respond to an evolutionarily fixed tuning to the probability of interruptions in nature. This assumption sits uncomfortably with attributing to the same subjects the ability to learn perfectly the parameters of the experiments related to delay and size of rewards.

Stability of the Subject's State and Its Environment During the Delay
This assumption is not warranted for long delays, but since the focus here is mainly on short intervals, for simplicity it will not be further discussed.

Satisfaction Is Proportional to Expected Reward Amount   Again, strictly speaking, this is indefensible, because utility and fitness gains are usually concave functions of reward amount, but for amounts that are sufficiently small the assumption can be temporarily kept without much damage. In reality, to assess value not only expected size but variance in reward size is also important, precisely because this proportionality does not hold. Issues related to the importance of variance in related contexts have been reviewed from theoretical and empirical perspectives elsewhere (Shafir 2000; McNamara and Houston 1992; Kacelnik and Bateson 1996, 1997; Houston and McNamara 1999). A further problem, to be addressed, is that under this assumption satisfaction is judged on a trial-by-trial basis and not over a continuous time base. Although experimenters may think in trial units, from a functional perspective to assume that value is tallied by the subjects on a continuous time base makes more sense; the concept of a trial may be meaningless to a foraging animal. To this problem we turn in the next case.

Descriptive Shortcomings of Case 1

Experimental work in both humans and animals shows that the predictions derived from both versions of case 1 (exponential discounting) are incompatible with observed behavior. In particular, the two features of equation 3.1 discussed at the end of problem 1 are violated by existing data. First, while exponential discounting states that the ratio of the value of two rewards is unaffected when a constant time is added to both options, subjects show increasing preference for the more delayed reward as the delay to both options increases by a constant amount, leading to preference reversals (Green et al. 1981). Second, while exponential discounting and its underlying logic states that discount rate should be independent of reward size, observed discount rate is sensitive to it: smaller rewards are discounted more steeply than larger ones (Green and Myerson 1996; Green, Myerson, and McFadden 1997; Myerson and Green 1995).

Exponential discounting in its basic form is thus derived from unrealistic assumptions and is not supported by the majority of data in either humans or animals. Given this performance, both scenarios implied by case 1 seem unhelpful to promote understanding of short-term intertemporal decision making, other than as a reference landmark that serves to clarify ideas. This conclusion does not imply that the reasoning behind exponential discounting is wrong, only that it is not appropriate to describe natural behavior of organisms. The rationale is perfectly adequate to take monetary decisions when the assumptions apply, but if our target is to understand human and animal intertemporal choice mechanisms, we must modify the assumptions and model intertemporal choice in entirely different fashion.

Case 2: Repeated Choice, Fixed Outcome

Case 1 started with an agent making an isolated choice between two rewards with different delays. Here we can use the image of an animal that chooses between committing itself to hunting using either of two incompatible foraging strategies. This is realistic because animals often have to choose between foraging "modes" (Vance and Soluk 2001). While pursuing prey of one kind they miss the opportunity of capturing other prey that require plainly being elsewhere or different hunting techniques. Leopards, for instance, sometimes lie at the edge of a pond where they capture small fish (tilapia) at brief intervals, while at other times (or other leopards) stalk larger prey, such as antelopes, from the branches of trees, sometimes waiting days between opportunities. In the context of intertemporal choice, the leopard chooses between the actions leading to delayed large antelopes and more immediate small fish, but the choice is not arranged in separate trials. In an optimality analysis the payoff must be judged for a given period of foraging, not as a single choice between a single tilapia and a single antelope. In a laboratory analogue, a rat may be offered repeated choices between a lever associated with a single food pellet after a short delay and another whose operation causes the delivery of a larger number of pellets after a longer wait. As in the case of the leopard, from a foraging point of view the value of each option must be considered in continuous time. To examine this situation, we modify the assumptions used for case 1 as follows.

(Assumption 1) From one shot to repeated choice. Choices are considered in a repetitive cycle: after choosing one option the subject cannot pursue other goals during the waiting time, and after each outcome it faces a new choice.

Assumptions 2, 3, and 4 remain unaltered.

(Assumption 5) Satisfaction is proportional to the sum of the rewards obtained after a given time interval. Assuming a long time horizon (that is, many cycles), this sum is proportional to the rate of gain per unit of time. An appropriate natural model to formalize this scenario is that of a foraging starling (starlings tend to be more manageable for laboratory experiments than leopards). These birds forage sometimes by walking on the ground while poking the soil with their beaks to dig for hidden grubs, and sometimes by taking short flights to hawk small aerial insects. Hawking yields more immediate, smaller captures and is more expensive, because flying uses more energy per unit of time than walking. Let us say that S_{aw} and τ_w are respectively the size (in energy units) and delay (in time units) per prey from walking, while S_f and τ_f are the size and delay from flying. Delay here means all the times taken to find, capture, and consume a prey item, and for simplicity assume a constant metabolic rate throughout the whole delay. Foraging theorists usually refer to the return rate of energy over time for an option i as γ_i, and compute it as the energy content of the payoff minus the energy spent in procuring it, divided over the involvement time. In this case, the two foraging modes yield equal net return rates when $\gamma_w = \gamma_f$ as expressed by

$$\frac{S_w - m_w \tau_w}{\tau_w} = \frac{S_f - m_f \tau_f}{\tau_f} \tag{3.3a}$$

or

$$\frac{S_w}{\tau_w} - m_w = \frac{S_f}{\tau_f} - m_f \tag{3.3b}$$

where m_w and m_f are the metabolic rates of walking and flying, respectively.

The trade-off between amount and delay is then given by

$$S_w = \frac{\tau_w}{\tau_f} S_f - \tau_w (m_f - m_w) \qquad (3.4)$$

This relation misbehaves if one of the foraging modes involves no delay at all, because it means dividing by 0, but this is an unlikely problem because each capture includes minimum times, such as those required to consume the reward. The equality is also meaningless if the parameters are such that to achieve equal rate one or both of the reward sizes or delays need to be negative. According to equation 3.4, a rate maximizer discounts rewards as a function of delay using time in the denominator of the value equation and not in the exponent as in case 1, where one-shot choices were considered. In the language used throughout this volume and more widely in economics and psychology, these expressions imply *hyperbolic discounting*.

We now can return to the two features of exponential discounting that were most problematic for case 1. The first is that equation 3.1 does not allow for preference reversals if a constant time is added to both delays, while experimental subjects do show these reversals. Figure 3.1 shows how the value expressions in equation 3.3a behave when constant times are added to both delays. Figure 3.1 uses realistic physiological parameters for the starling, and plots the net rate (value) for each option as a function of a common added time interval of length k. We see that when k is small, the flying option yields higher rate and should then be preferred, while for greater values of k the opposite is true. At some intermediate value the preference should reverse. The second important issue is the relation between size of reward and discount rate. According to the assumptions in case 1, and its embodiment in equation 3.1, discount rate is independent of reward size. Equation 3.4 instead is not a strict proportionality, and this means that we should not expect apparent discount rate to be unaffected by size.

Although its application to choice between foraging modes is more recent, the idea that animals might use net rate of gain as a currency for decision making has been at the core of optimal foraging theory (OFT) since its beginnings in the mid 1970s (see Stephens and Krebs 1986 for a review of earlier literature, and Krebs and Kacelnik 1984 for an application to foraging modes with differential metabolic costs). The approach is attractive because it not only leads to reasonable qualitative predictions but can be used with known physiological parameters to predict choice in precise quantitative terms. While the account of temporal discounting based on assumed adaptation to uncertainty needs to postulate a rate of loss that is never measured or controlled and is not actually experienced by animals in experiments, all the ingredients of equations 3.3a and 3.4 are independently accessi-

Figure 3.1 Rational Preference Reversals and Rate Maximization

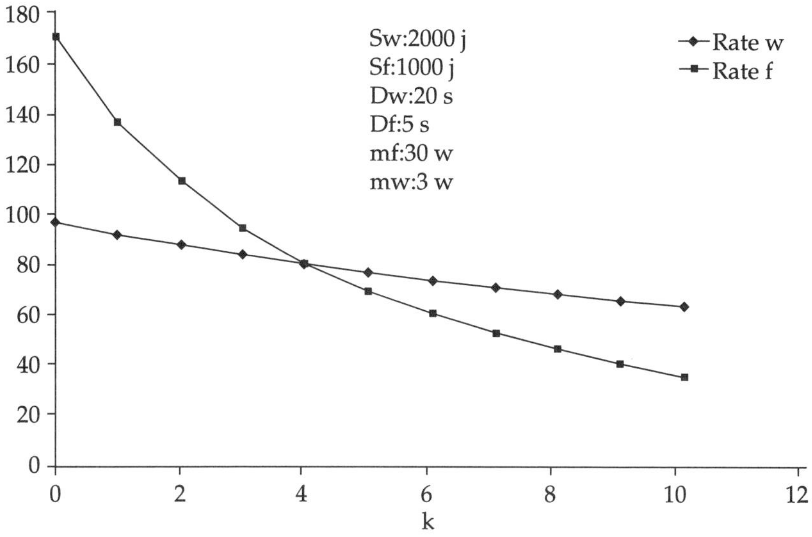
180
160
140
120
100
80
60
40
20
0
0
2
4
6
8
10
12
k
Sw:2000 j
Sf:1000 j
Dw:20 s
Df:5 s
mf:30 w
mw:3 w
Rate w
Rate f

Source: Author's configuration.

Note: Rational preference reversals and rate maximization. Net rate of gain $\left(\frac{S_i - m_i\tau_i}{\tau_i}\right)$ for starlings using two foraging modes (walking and flying) as a consequence of adding a time constant (k) to both options. The foraging modes are denoted by the suffixes f and w. For k small, flying should be preferred while the opposite is true if k > 4s. S_i: Reward size in joules, D_i: time per prey in seconds, m_i: metabolic rate in joules s^{-1}. Numerical parameters are given in the figure legend.

ble to experimentation. Metabolic costs, for instance, can be put into the equations using appropriate values for each individual animal (cost of flight is very sensitive to body mass).

The quantitative predictive value of equation 3.4 was tested directly by Bautista, Tinbergen, and Kacelnik (2001). These authors gave captive starlings a choice between working for food by walking or flying. They fixed the flying time per reward (by varying the number of flights) at various levels, then found for each number of flights the walking time (number of walks) that made the two options equally attractive, using a titration technique that increased or decreased the required walking depending on the animal's previous choice. In their experiment, reward sizes were equal between the two foraging modes, in order to focus on the intertemporal trade-off alone. Following equation 3.4, when reward sizes are equal, the intertemporal trade-off is given by

$$\tau_w = \cfrac{1}{\cfrac{1}{\tau_f} + \cfrac{m_w - m_f}{S}},$$ (3.5)

where S is the common size of both rewards. The results of Bautista and colleague's experiment are shown in figure 3.2, where, for comparison, the predictions of two alternative models are also included.

The two alternative models included in figure 3.2 are Gross Rate and Efficiency. According to the Gross Rate model, the subject disregards the difference in metabolic costs so that if reward sizes are equal, the bird is indifferent between foraging modes when the delays are equal. According to the Efficiency model, the subject does take into account metabolic costs but not time costs. It chooses the option that yields greater ratio of gain to expenditure, disregarding the opportunity cost of longer delays. In this case the subject is not discounting according to time, except for the fact that reward delays affect the energy costs and hence the net value of rewards resulting from each foraging mode. As figure 3.2 shows, net rate maximization is extremely successful in predicting the way delay is traded against metabolic expenditure, but neither of the alternative models is close to the data.

This result demonstrates that starlings can and do handle intertemporal choice so as to maximize net rate of gain. In this situation they are neither excessively impatient nor do they fail to maximize reward gains. Hyperbolic discounting is derived from realistic theoretical assumptions and not used to fit data a posteriori. Net rate of gain is good at coping with qualitative features of discounting data in general and in precisely describing what the subjects do. In summary, hyperbolic discounting occurs and it is the rational solution.

In the behavioral analysis literature, an equation very similar to the rate expression used in foraging studies and adapted here in equation 3.3a has emerged independently, driven by empirical results rather than by normative modeling. For instance, Mazur (1984, 1987) found that the following relation describes well the trade-off between amount and delay in pigeons working in Skinner boxes:

$$\frac{S_1}{1 + k\tau_1} = \frac{S_2}{1 + k\tau_2}$$ (3.6)

where S_i is the value that reward i would have if delivered immediately, and k is a dimensional constant that can be approximated to 1 when τ is expressed in seconds. Notice that equation 3.3a, when the two metabolic costs are equal, reduces to equation 3.6 with the only

Figure 3.2   How Birds Choose Among Foraging Modes

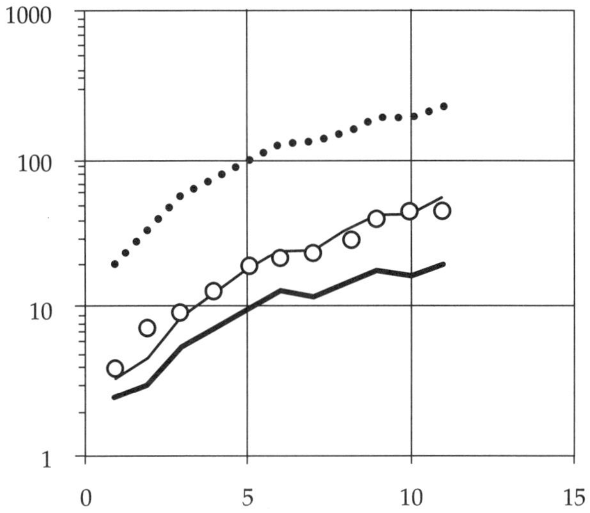

Source: Author's configuration.

Note: Number of walks (ordinate) preferred as often as the corresponding number of flights (abscissa) by four starlings in the experiment run by Bautista et al. (2001). The lines (from top to bottom) show the predictions of three putative currencies of choice: energy gained per unit of energy spent (efficiency), net energy gain per unit of time, and gross energy gain per unit of time. The mean results (circles) coincide with the predictions of the net gain model.

difference of adding 1 to the denominator. Adding unity has the main function of avoiding the discontinuity for rewards delivered with no delay at all, but becomes insignificant if delays are above a few seconds and k is close to $1\ s^{-1}$, as is the case in most experiments. Hence the standard hyperbolic equation derived empirically in behavioral analysis is consistent with a particular case of the rate expression used in optimal foraging theory. One caveat is that equation 3.6 has units of subjective value (or behavioral preference) and not of physically identifiable dimensions such as energy per unit of time, as is the case with the energy rate equations derived from foraging theory.

The apparent success of the rate maximizing approach should be tempered by two systematic deviations from its predictions observed in animal data. One relates to the problems posed by variable outcomes, and the other to cases where the experimental cycles include times other than those used to procure rewards. I believe that these

two deviations have a common theoretical explanation and will turn
to them in the next two sections.

Case 3: Repeated Choices, Multiple Outcomes

Case 2 makes considerable progress toward marrying rational decision-making theory to data in animal results, but it is only applicable
when assumption 2—that each choice has a fixed outcome—applies.
In most real-life instances, actions such as making a choice have a
range of possible outcomes, at best with well-defined probabilities. In
such cases, the choice mechanism makes at least two distinct operations (not necessarily separated in time). First, it assigns value to each
possible outcome, taking into account size and delay. Second, it combines the different outcomes and their probabilities to assign value to
each option. The way these two operations are combined can be critical to determine relative preference between options. Two rather intuitive possibilities are: to compute the average reward size, then discount this expectation by the average delay; and to compute the
discounted value of each possible outcome considering its amount
and delay, then compute the average value of the set of discounted
rewards. A numerical example may help at this point. Say that a subject faces two options, one with fixed and one with variable outcomes
(to simplify the example, let's assume that metabolic costs are equal
in both options). The fixed option's outcome (O_f) has size 2 units and
delay 50 s, namely, a rate of 0.04 units s^{-1}. The variable option has
two equally frequent outcomes (O_x and O_y). Outcome O_x has size 1
and delay 10 s (a rate of 0.1 units s^{-1}); outcome O_y has size 3 and
delay 120 s (a rate of 0.025 units s^{-1}). Which option should a rate
maximizer that follows equation 3.3a prefer? Since choice of the variable option will yield the two outcomes equally often, you may be
forgiven to believe that its overall rate of payoff would be the average
of the rates for each outcome $(0.1 + 0.025)/2 = 0.0625$ units s^{-1}.
Computed this way, the variable option yields 56 percent extra gains
and should be preferred. Under repeated choice, however, this option
gives an average amount of 2 units $((1 + 3)/2)$ and an average delay
of 65 s $((10 + 120)/2)$. Its resulting rate of returns is $2/65 = 0.03$
units s^{-1}, 25 percent less than the fixed alternative. Thus the two
computing processes lead to opposite predictions: if the subject discounts the amounts and then averages the discounted values, it prefers the variable option, while if it averages the amounts and delays
and then discounts using these averages, it prefers the fixed option.
Theories dealing with preference among options yielding multiple

outcomes cannot avoid dealing with the processes of averaging and discounting. At this point, however, normative predictions may run into difficulties that are worth examining in detail.

According to the rate maximizing logic, subjects should compute averages first and then discount, because this yields the true rates of gain. Thus in the numerical example they should prefer the fixed to the variable option. Observed preferences, however, are much closer to the opposite (averaging the discounted outcomes), even when this leads to choosing options with lower overall payoff. This issue has been discussed in the foraging literature (Bateson and Kacelnik 1996; Stephens and Anderson 2001). Yet it has been mostly ignored in the behavioral analysis literature, where the latter algorithm is the only one considered owing to its descriptive superiority, without acknowledgment that, given its apparent maladaptiveness, it is in need of explanation.

Thus the first paradox we face is that experimental animals indeed behave as if maximizing rate of energy over time when dealing with fixed options, but fail to do so when facing options with variable outcomes.

The second paradox is another failure of rate maximization: animals assign greater value to intervals between choice and outcome than to intervals between outcome and later choices, even when all times imply lost opportunity and thus have the same impact on rate of gain. This second issue is highlighted in experiments such as that reported by Green and colleagues (1981), and will be discussed to introduce a functional explanation for both paradoxes. Both problems can be solved by examining the process by which animals learn the value of each option.

Failures of Rate Maximization and the Role of Learning Processes

The argument presented here is based on recognizing that animal subjects choose between options by responding to levers or pecking keys to which they have been trained. We can see this by examining each of these two deviations from rate maximizing in turn. Let us first examine the problem exposed by using multiple outcomes.

Using a variety of protocols, experimenters make subjects experience the consequences of acting on each option. For instance, pressing the left lever (fixed option) may be followed by a rat receiving two pellets after fifty seconds, while pressing the right lever (variable option) may result in the rat receiving either one pellet after ten seconds or three pellets after one hundred-twenty seconds, equally often. As discussed earlier, the variable lever yields lower average rate than the fixed option and should not be chosen.

Consider, however, the way the subject may come to learn the outcomes of pressing either lever. At the beginning of training, lever pressings occur at random as the naive rat moves around the cage, followed by delivery of the programmed rewards. With time, the animal incorporates the fact that two-pellet rewards are preceded systematically by its own contacts with the left lever, while rewards of one or three pellets are preceded by contacts with the right lever. This is the problem of *credit attribution*. The rat behaves as if it attributes to these contacts the responsibility for the outcome just experienced, and the attribution process is sensitive to how fresh the lever pressing is in its memory at the time of the outcome. The salience of the outcome depends positively on its size, and the strength of the attribution depends negatively on the interval between lever presses and outcomes. The key here is that the rat learns whenever the significant event, or outcome, occurs. The credit attribution process implements the discounting, and the rat is naturally rather insensitive to times other than the gap between the lever pressing and its consequence. It is easy to see why such a learning mechanism is a very efficient way to credit events causing that in which the animal is interested: the outcomes. Empiricist philosophers have long been aware of the role of experience in the inference of causal links and have called attention to the fact that causes tend to precede effects, be proximate to them in time, be correlated with them probabilistically, and belong in some relevant domain. These are exactly the properties of mechanisms for associative learning that command credit attribution in animals (Dickinson 1980). While it makes sense to assume that evolution has resulted in brains that are good at establishing causal links, learning in this way leads to averaging individually discounted outcomes rather than averaging different dimensions of the outcomes (such as amount and delay), then implementing the discounting relation. In this case, this implies using the alternative value-assignment algorithm and, consequently, to a preference for the variable option. I believe that applying the principles of associative learning to experiments designed for other purposes can account for a number of other apparent irrationalities in the animal literature.

To discuss the second deviation from rate maximizing we turn our attention to the influential experiment reported by Green and colleagues (1981). The main features of the experimental design are shown in figure 3.3. In this experiment, pigeons appeared to be excessively impatient and also inconsistent, because their preference re-

Figure 3.3   A Self-Control Experiment in Pigeons: Green et al. 1981

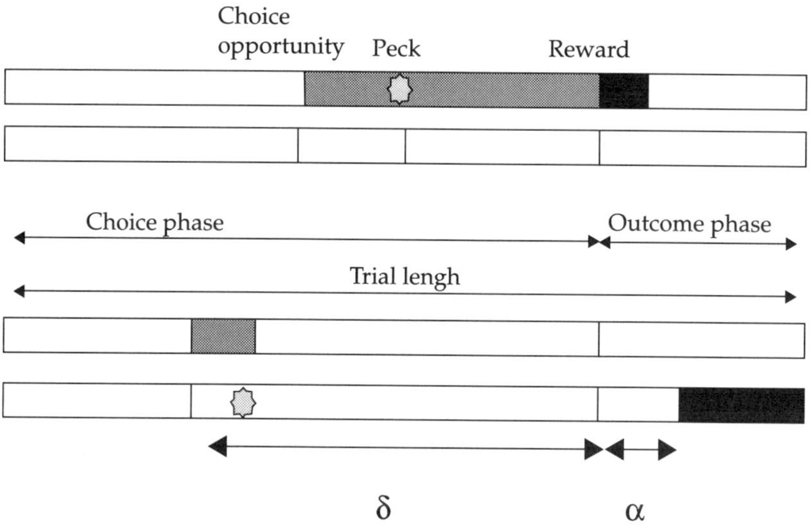

Source: Author's configuration.

Note: Design of the experiment by Green et al. (1981) using pigeons. Each trial was divided in two phases, "choice phase" and "outcome phase." The former lasted always 30 s and the latter 10 s. White bars indicate that no key was enabled and the pigeon was forced to wait. At some point during the choice phase, the pigeons had the opportunity to choose between two options, identified by different colored keys. A single peck determined the choice and had the effect of extinguishing the alternative colored key. Two exemplar trials are shown, one (two top bars) in which the pigeon chooses the Small-Soon reward and the other (two bottom bars) where the pigeon chooses the Large-Late reward. Rewards were times of access to a food hopper, shown in solid black during the outcome phase. δ: time from onset of the relevant stimulus to the onset of the outcome phase; α: time waiting for the Large-Late reward during the outcome phase. Notice that trial length, choice phase, and outcome phase did not vary.

versed between treatments when the choice was made at different temporal distances in advance of the outcomes.

Green and colleagues offered pigeons a choice between two pecking keys. One option led to a Small-Soon (SS) reward (2 s of access to a food hopper immediately after pecking the relevant key), and the alternative yielded a Large-Late (LL) reward (6 s of hopper access 4 s after pecking the other key). Choosing SS led to a neutral period of 8 s after the outcome and before the start of the next trial, but choosing LL led to the next trial without further delays, so that the total time of the "outcome" section of each trial was independent of the option

(2 s + 8 s for SS and 4 s + 6 s for LL). In different treatments, the pigeons were allowed to choose between these two options with varying anticipation (between 28 s and 2 s) respect to the outcomes. Similarly to the design of the outcome phase, in the choice phase, varying choice times were controlled by compensatory intervals before the choice, so that the total time in the "choice" portion of the trial was always 30 s across all treatments. Since the total times (choice plus outcome phases) per trial were fixed at 40 s, the choice that maximizes the number of food hopper seconds per total time is to take always LL regardless of the choice delay. Green and colleagues found that this was not what happened. Pigeons did take LD when the choice opportunity was a relatively long time before the outcome (> 10 s), but they preferred the small reward when choice and outcome were separated by a shorter gap. In one of the most explicit attempts to apply economic theory to animal research, Kagel and colleagues (1995) discuss this experiment, and propose an adaptive account of its results based on the effects of stochastic probability of interruption. In this account, pigeons would discount temporally only as a relict of the interruptions present in their natural environment. Additional speculations are used to deal with the nonexponential shape of discounting, so as to generate an excessive bias for immediacy and explain the associated inconsistency of preference, even though the experimental pigeons were never interrupted. This account is substantially different from the approach proposed here.

According to the foregoing analysis of learning, the intervals after SS in the outcome phase or before the opportunity to choose in the choice phase had no reason to be associated to specific outcomes, and were probably ignored by the animals. This alone is sufficient to explain discounting using only the temporal gap between choice and outcome.

The observed preference reversal results from the nonexponential effect of the relevant interval, which itself derives from including time in a rate equation. In fact, the point of reversal can be predicted subject to some speculation. In this experiment, pigeons did not receive a controlled amount of food. Instead they were allowed controlled times of access to feeders. The amount of food collected from a hopper will not normally be strictly proportional to hopper time, due to the discrete nature of pigeons' scoops (Epstein 1981). Although the relation between amount of food scooped and time of access to the hopper is measurable, I do not have this information and will thus use a free parameter, assuming that food collected obeys a power function of time of exposure. We can use equation 3.3a with equal metabolic rates to find when the two options would be equivalent in rate of gain for a subject that ignores all times other than intervals between choice and the onset of the outcome. The rate equivalence is given by

$$\frac{S^x}{\delta} = \frac{L^x}{\delta + \alpha} \tag{3.7}$$

where S and L are the durations of hopper access, x is a constant relating length of hopper access to intake, δ is the time between the opportunity to choose and the start of the outcome phase, and α is the waiting time for LL at the beginning of the outcome phase (see figure 3.3). Strictly speaking, as rate has dimensions of energy over time, S and L are multiplied by a constant equal to a unit of energy per unit of time, but this constant cancels out and we do not need to include it.

From equation 3.7, the value of δ at which the pigeons should be indifferent is

$$\delta = \frac{\alpha}{\left(\dfrac{L}{S}\right)^x - 1} \tag{3.8}$$

or, for the specific values used by Green and colleagues,

$$\delta = \frac{4}{3^x - 1} \tag{3.9}$$

Equation 3.9 shows that we should expect a reversal of preference as δ changes. To predict a priori when this should occur, we would need to measure the constant x for the given apparatus and foodstuff. We can proceed inversely to explore if equation 3.9 is at least reasonable. The pigeons tended to prefer SS for anticipations of less than 10 s and LL for longer values. For $\delta = 10$ s, equation 3.9 would require that $x \approx 0.3$. This value is a bit smaller than one might expect, but certainly within a reasonable range.

Again, note that this treatment of the problem does not assume any role for interruptions or other form of stochastic loss: hyperbolic time discounting is a product of rate maximizing, and the deviations from objective rate maximization are due to adaptive laws of learning. From an adaptationist viewpoint, the circle is closed by assuming that having good rules for learning (that is, rules that are good at establishing causal links between events distributed in time) must have had greater overall significance in evolution than the occasional loss

of reward in ecologically unusual situations. The fact that these results show in many species suggests the not implausible hypothesis
that indeed learning about the world according to the laws of causa-
tion may be a regular and strong selective pressure.

How Do These Ideas Apply to
Discounting in Humans?

Animal experiments examining the role of amount and delay on preference produce "discounting" functions that appear hyperbolic (apparent rate of discounting drops with time), and hence are isomorphic
with results obtained using human subjects. An equation for net rate
of gain, normally used by optimal foraging theorists, is good at predicting the shape of these functions and the points of indifference
between rewards with different net values and delays. When metabolic rate (or similar cost of waiting) while pursuing different options
differs, the rate function also produces an effect of amount of reward
on discount rate.

The rate equation fails to accommodate two experimental results:
when options have multiple outcomes, animals average individually
discounted outcomes rather than discounting average gains by average delays; and animals tend to disregard time components outside
the gap between action and outcome. I propose that these two departures can be explained by direct reference to adaptive laws of associative learning.

Direct comparisons of animal and human results on discounting
(Kagel, Battalio, and Green 1995; Fehr 2002; Dasgupta and Maskin
2002; Sozou 1998, 2002) are undermined owing to substantial procedural differences between the two sets of results: while animal subjects are repeatedly exposed to the conditions of the tests before they
are allowed to choose, human subjects in most experiments are presented each choice as a one-shot problem. Animals have opportunity
to learn the lack of stochasticity and the lost opportunity during waiting, while humans can only be informed by their previous life outside
the experiment. We may, however, ask whether there may still be a
common interpretation for the observation of hyperbolic discounting
in both cases. I am skeptical of replies that imply that laboratory animals show temporal discounting because they bring to their situation
a baggage of uncertainty experienced in the wild. Yet I am more
hopeful for the idea that humans treat the one-shot problems with
which they are presented as if they were repeated choices involving
lost opportunity. If they do, humans would subjectively be in condi-

tions under which hyperbolic discounting is the right answer. In other words, maybe it is us, not them, that really get it wrong.

References

Bateson, Melissa, and Alex Kacelnik. 1996. "Rate Currencies and the Foraging Starling: The Fallacy of the Averages Revisited." *Behavioural Ecology* 7: 341–52.

———. 1997. "Starlings' Preferences for Predictable and Unpredictable Delays to Food." *Animal Behavior* 53: 1129–42.

Bautista, Luis M., Joost Tinbergen, and Alex Kacelnik. 2001. "To Walk or to Fly: How Birds Choose Among Foraging Modes." *Proceedings of the National Academy of Sciences* 98: 1089–94.

Dasgupta, Partha, and Eric Maskin. 2002. "Uncertainty, Waiting Costs, and Hyperbolic Discounting." Unpublished paper, faculty of Economics, University of Cambridge and Institute for Advanced Study, Princeton University.

Dickinson, Anthony. 1980. *Contemporary Animal Learning Theory*. Cambridge: Cambridge University Press.

Epstein, Robert. 1981. "Amount Consumed as a Function of Magazine-Cycle Duration." *Behavioral Analysis Letters* 1: 63–66.

Fehr, Ernst. 2002. "The Economics of Impatience." *Nature* 415: 269–72.

Green, Leonard, Ewin B. Fisher, Steven Perlow, and Lisa Sherman. 1981. "Preference Reversal and Self-Control: Choice as a Function of Reward Amount and Delay." *Behavioral Analyses Letters* 1: 43–51.

Green, Leonard, and Joel Myerson. 1996. "Exponential Versus Hyperbolic Discounting of Delayed Outcomes: Risk and Waiting Time." *American Zoology* 36: 496–505.

Green, Leonard, Joel Myerson, and Edward McFadden. 1997. "Rate of Temporal Discounting Decreases with Amount of Reward." *Memory and Cognition* 25: 715–23.

Hertwig, Ralph, and Andreas Ortmann. 2001. "Experimental Practices in Economics: A Methodological Challenge for Psychologists?" *Behavioral and Brain Sciences* 24: 383–403.

Houston, Alasdair I., and John M. McNamara. 1999. *Models of Adaptive Behaviour: An Approach Based on State*. Cambridge: Cambridge University Press.

Kacelnik, Alex. 1997. "Normative and Descriptive Models of Decision Making: Time Discounting and Risk Sensitivity." In *Characterizing Human Psychological Adaptations*, edited by G. R. Bock and G. Cardew. Chichester: Wiley.

Kacelnik, Alex, and Melissa Bateson. 1996. "Risky Theories—The Effects of Variance on Foraging Decisions." *American Zoology* 36: 402–34.

Kagel, John H., Ray C. Battalio, and Leonard Green. 1995. *Economic Choice Theory: An Experimental Analysis of Animal Behavior*. Cambridge: Cambridge University Press.

Kagel, John H., Leonard Green, and Tom Caraco. 1986. "When Foragers Discount the Future: Constraint or Adaptation?" *Animal Behavior* 34: 271–83.

Krebs, John R., and Alex Kacelnik. 1984. "Time Horizons of Foraging Animals." *Annals of the New York Academy of Science* 423: 278–91. Special volume on *Timing and Time Perception*, edited by J. Gibbon and L. Allan.

Mazur, James E. 1984. "Tests of an Equivalence Rule for Fixed and Variable Reinforcer Delays." *Journal of Experimental Psychology: Animal Behavioral Processes* 10: 426–36.

———. 1987. "An Adjusting Procedure for Studying Delayed Reinforcement." In *Quantitative Analyses of Behaviour: The Effect of Delay and of Intervening Events on Reinforcement Value*, edited by Michael L. Commons, James E. Mazur, John A. Nevin, and Howard Rachlin. Hillsdale, N.J.: Erlbaum.

McNamara, John M., and Alasdair I. Houston. 1992. "Risk-Sensitive Foraging: A Review of the Theory." *Bulletin of Mathematical Biology* 54: 355–78.

Myerson, Joel, and Leonard Green. 1995. "Discounting of Delayed Rewards: Models of Individual Choice." *Journal of Experimental Analyses of Behavior* 64: 263–76.

Shafir, Sharoni. 2000. "Risk-Sensitive Foraging: The Effect of Relative Variability." *Oikos* 88: 663–69.

Sozou, Peter D. 1998. "On Hyperbolic Discounting and Uncertain Hazard Rates." *Proceedings of the Royal Society of London* 265: 2015–20.

———. 2002. "Discounting Delayed Rewards: A Trade-Off Between Risk of Loss and Cost of Protection or Information Storage." Unpublished paper, London School of Economics and Political Science.

Stephens, David W., and Dack Anderson. 2001. "The Adaptive Value of Preference for Immediacy: When Shortsighted Rules Have Farsighted Consequences." *Behavioral Ecology* 12: 330–39.

Stephens, David W., and John R. Krebs. 1986. *Foraging Theory*. Princeton, N.J.: Princeton University Press.

Vance, Heather D., and Daniel A. Soluk. 2001. "Technique for Assessing the Foraging Modes of Four Stream Predator Species: Ambush or Active?" North American Banthological Society annual meeting, La Crosse, Wisconsin (June 2).

· 4 ·

A Neurobiology of Intertemporal Choice

STEPHEN B. MANUCK, JANINE D. FLORY,
MATTHEW F. MULDOON, AND ROBERT E. FERRELL

LIFE'S PROBLEMS have a certain sameness for most people. As the evolutionary psychologists tell it, these problems have to do largely with survival and reproduction, with getting resources and begetting offspring in an uncertain world inhabited by others struggling to do the same. True perhaps, ultimately, but ultimate goals are reached by a succession of present acts, and the here and now generally finds us engaged in more mundane problem solving, occasioned by the myriad dilemmas of daily life. As illustrated throughout this volume, one such dilemma is called *intertemporal choice* and concerns decision making in situations where we must choose between two differently valued outcomes that cannot both be obtained at the same time (Loewenstein and Elster 1992; Mischel, Shoda, and Rodriguez 1989). Selecting immediate (or sooner) rewards of lesser preference is often referred to as impulsive choice, whereas waiting for a more desired outcome requires the restraint of impulse and is said therefore to reflect self-control. Neither we nor other creatures always prefer the prospect of larger, later rewards over lesser but more immediate gratifications; as a result, many organisms, ourselves included, tend to devalue (or discount) outcomes for which we must wait. Since enabling choice and effecting the behaviors that choice entails subsumes much of what brains do, one may ask whether a neurobiology of intertemporal choice also exists. Although intertemporal choice as the economist understands it is not a topic much discussed at the high table of neuroscience, it is nonetheless a subject addressed both directly and indirectly in a growing body of neurobiological research. In this chapter we consider two aspects of this question: where in the brain time-dependent choice might be regulated, and how features of brain chemistry may inform an understanding of delayed gratification, time discounting, impulsivity, and self-control.

Blueprint for a Planning Brain

No one really knows why we evolved such a large brain. Unless Darwin got it wrong, this surely had to do with solving life's abiding challenges: securing food, aid and shelter, avoiding threats to life and livelihood, acquiring mates, and rearing offspring that themselves survived to reproduce. Still, why a big brain, and why us? Many have suggested that toolmaking, at which humans are notably adept, required a great expansion of mental capacity and was achieved by an ever-growing brain. Yet others note that for more than two million years the basic hominid toolkit acquired few new items, even as our brains more than doubled in size (Miller 2000; Boyd and Silk 2000). Where was the adaptive advantage of brain enlargement if tools that purportedly gave that advantage changed so little? Other evolutionary arguments have been advanced as well, invoking such novelties as an expanded diet, the acquisition of language, a capacity to deceive others, and even sexual selection, but the initial impetus for an expanding hominid brain remains elusive.

Whatever its origins, our now enormous brain clearly possesses prodigious capacities for complex cognition, a feature of human biology unmet elsewhere in vertebrate evolution. In fact, natural selection's codiscoverer, Alfred Russel Wallace, found these capacities so prodigious that he exempted human intellect from the catalogue of evolutionary adaptations, thinking it instead the product of purposeful design by an omniscient, creative power (Wallace 1889). Perhaps understandably, Wallace had difficulty conceiving adaptive advantages conferred in ancestral environments by such abilities as abstraction, mathematical reasoning, or aesthetic appreciation. Yet unlike Darwin, neither could Wallace envision the possibility that traits evolved for one purpose might serve other ends in other contexts (for example, that the same capacities for fine motor control needed to fabricate archaic tools might also permit a performance of Rachmaninov's second piano concerto). Neuroanatomists of the nineteenth century also weighed in on the uniqueness of the human brain. The most eminent of these, Sir Richard Owen, claimed to have identified a neural structure in humans that was absent in apes and other primates, the so-called hippocampus minor (Gould 1980). This assertion was quickly refuted, though, by the comparative studies of Thomas Henry Huxley, Darwin's ardent defender and Owen's archnemesis (Huxley 1863). Following the Owen–Huxley encounter, which was widely publicized (and parodied) at the time, little further controversy ensued regarding the phylogenetic continuity of vertebrate neuroanatomy.

Lurking behind hopes of a fundamental difference in the brains of man and ape was the thornier conundrum of mind and body. Prior to the debate on evolution, the Cartesian duality of mind and brain had already been challenged. The Austrian physician Franz Joseph Gall held that the functions of mind inhere in the brain itself and that these functions are distributed topographically over the surface of the brain (Finger 2000). In these assertions Gall was preceded by the still largely unknown Emanuel Swedenborg, whose review of mid-eighteenth-century comparative anatomy and brain pathology (such as it was) suggested to him that "higher" mental functions (for example, imagination, memory, thought, intention, voluntary motor action) could be traced to discrete areas of the cerebral cortex. Gall went further: he believed that attributes of character and cognition comprise fundamental organs of the brain (mind), that individual differences in each of these attributes reflect corresponding variability in the size of their associated cortical areas, and that these differences can be "read" from variations in the surface of the overlying crania. Amended later and termed *phrenology* by Johann Spurzheim and George Combe, Gall's mental topography attracted a good deal of public interest in the early nineteenth century and probably contributed to popular belief in biological bases of personality and intellect (Finger 2000; Secord 2000).

One of the mind's larger "organs" was identified by Gall as the seat of "circumspection and forethought" and retained as "cautiousness" in the Spurzheim–Combe system. Cautiousness is really too narrow a term for what might best be construed as prudent character and self-control. Located beneath the skull's large parietal bone, cautiousness was said to be the faculty by which we apprehend danger and trace the consequences of our actions. When well developed, caution inhibits impulsive behavior and gives scope for "mature deliberation," thereby promoting the satisfaction of our desires in circumstances most appropriate to their expression. In this way, a "most beautiful provision [is] made for supporting the activity of, and affording legitimate gratification to, the lower propensities. These powers are conferred on us clearly to support our animal nature, and to place us in harmony with the external objects of creation" (Combe 1827, 26). If nothing else, this seems a remarkable anticipation of Freud's executive ego, the mental agency charged with achieving gratification of impulses under the aegis of the reality principle. Insofar as an inhibition of impulsive behavior postpones the satisfaction of desire to a more propitious moment, such delay may be thought to afford a better and therefore more highly valued outcome. Viewed in these terms, the phrenologists' organ of "cautiousness" might be seen as a first neurobiological theory of intertemporal choice. The theory was also wrong.

Despite its early popularity, phrenology pretty much expired in the 1840s, a victim of its inadequate methodology (Finger 2000). Gall was an accomplished neuroanatomist, but he eschewed both experimentation and the clinical study of neurological patients. Instead, he and his followers simply measured the crania of diverse individuals and sought to correlate observed differences with purported variability in the various faculties of mind (Combe 1835). Normal variations in cranial features, however, do not mirror contours of the cerebral cortex (the skull is not shrink-wrap for the brain), and therefore skulls could not, as the phrenologists believed, act as signposts to neural structures underlying traits of personality and cognition. Yet Gall was quite correct in asserting the localization of brain function; it was the localities he got wrong, led astray by preconception and insupportable method. More informative were later studies based in clinical neuroanatomy, the experimental lesioning of discrete cortical regions in animals, and subsequently, electrical stimulation of areas of the human brain.

For instance, it was discovered that persons unable to express themselves in speech or writing but still capable of reading and following a conversation suffered damage to a posterior region of the left frontal lobe, called Broca's area. Others might vocalize, yet prove incoherent and unable to comprehend speech; these patients also had significant brain damage, but at another site located toward the back of the temporal lobe (Wernicke's area). In experimental animals, destruction of other cortical regions produced various forms of paralysis, while electrically stimulating these areas in intact animals induced precise movements of paw and limbs. Similarly, localized stimulation of the brain in patients undergoing neurosurgery—conscious patients—elicits a range of experiences, including discrete movements of the body, physical sensations, even memories and feelings.

Over time the cortical topography and its correlated functions became known in ever-greater detail. Briefly, the cerebral cortex contains areas devoted both to processing information derived from the senses and to producing movement. Adjacent to the primary sensory and motor cortices are larger expanses of cortex that underlie such "higher" processes as perception, learning and memory, decision making, and the formation of plans and goals. In the association cortices sensory input acquires meaning (objects are recognized, words comprehended), and this information is integrated with prior experience, consolidated across modalities, and interpreted. Elsewhere, analogous operations effect the coordination of complex motor sequences, presumably by accessing previously learned representations of such actions.

All this and, in humans, there is still remaining cortex to explain. Most of this "residuum" lies in the forward (anterior) regions of the frontal lobe, a rather enigmatic area at the front of the brain known as the prefrontal cortex. The enigma lies in giving precise definition to functions served by the prefrontal cortices. When most areas of the brain suffer damage due to stroke or injury, their roles are revealed by the incapacities they leave behind. Yet patients with damage to the prefrontal cortex—even those with extensive lesions—may have no notable abnormalities of sensation, perception, motor control, speech, or intelligence.

At least among students, the story of the prefrontal cortex is also the story of Phineas Gage. No tale of neurology is told in lectures more often than that of this unfortunate railway worker who accidentally dynamited a thirteen-pound tamping rod through his cheek, brain, and skull while supervising roadwork in Vermont, in 1848. Gage survived the accident, sat up and conversed with coworkers while transported to a local physician, was treated in the manner of the day, and recovered with his intellect intact. The recovered Gage, however, was not his old self. The previously temperate, conscientious, industrious Gage was now an intemperate, impulsive, and capricious man. Unable to plan ahead or to adhere to a plan, Gage drifted in the moment, from South America to California, from one lost or abandoned job to another until expiring early, dead at age thirty-eight (Damasio 1994; Macmillan 2000).

Gage's injury was difficult to accommodate within the neurophysiology of his time. To many, the discovery of discrete sensory and motor areas of the cortex suggested that the brain acts on the same principles as sensorimotor reflexes in the spinal cord. Since Gage suffered no obvious sensory or motor deficits (after all, he could walk, read, write, and converse), they simply denied he had suffered any functional impairment. Others, however, most notably the British physiologist David Ferrier, acknowledged Gage's difficulties in impulse control and his newly irascible temperament. Ferrier reasoned that *because* Gage's sensory and motor functions were spared, despite extensive injury to the most anterior regions of the frontal lobes, these cortical areas must ordinarily serve a different purpose. Given Gage's manifest impulsivity, perhaps that purpose is to modulate, or inhibit, motor function (Ferrier 1876, 1878). By severing a mechanism of inhibitory control in the prefrontal region, then, Gage's injuries could have led to the very behavioral anomalies noted by his physician and acquaintances following this horrific accident. Although Ferrier later retreated from his theory of inhibitory motor control, possibly for lack of more direct evidence, concepts of behavioral inhibition remain a prominent metaphor of prefrontal function (Macmillan 1992, 2000).

It is common now to think of the prefrontal cortices as engaged in a variety of executive activities needed to orchestrate planned behavior (Gazzaniga, Ivry, and Mangun 1998; Roberts, Robbins, and Weiskrantz 1998). These functions entail the recruitment and integration of diverse inputs from elsewhere in the brain (for example, sensory information, remembered events, affective experiences—both current and past) to effect advantageous decision making—decisions enacted in real time, informed by anticipated consequences, and subservient to both near and long-term goals (Shallice and Burgess 1998). As with Phineas Gage, disruption of these executive processes by trauma or clinical event (such as stroke) can derail the coherent progress of an ordered life. The perplexing combination of altered personality and motivation, loss of insight, and disinhibition of previously well-regulated behavior that may occur with prefrontal damage often is accorded the vague diagnosis *frontal lobe syndrome*. Frontal lobe symptoms are not uniform, though, and vary somewhat by location of lesion. When one region of the prefrontal cortex is affected, for instance, prominent symptoms might include problems of impulse control, irritability, and a coarsening of social intercourse; in a second area, inattentiveness, disinterest, and apathy; and in yet a third, an inability to conceive and execute planful behavior (Fuster 2001). Nonetheless, there is typically much overlap in these symptoms, as brain damage rarely respects fine neuroanatomic boundaries. Recent work in cognitive neuroscience, however, has given clearer definition to the working of the prefrontal cortex.

Consider that to decide a course of action we must weigh options in relation to our current situation and knowledge of our alternatives, as derived from prior experience. One function of the prefrontal cortex, located mainly in its lateral regions, is to maintain a temporary store of mental representations relevant to the decision or task at hand. This store, referred to as *working memory*, sustains relevant information retrieved from other areas of the brain during periods of active processing (Goldman-Rakic 1998). This is facilitated by extensive connections between the prefrontal cortex and most other brain regions. The prefrontal cortex is also highly compartmentalized, with various areas of representational memory "specialized" for different stimulus and task features, such as object recognition, spatial orientation, temporality, and context. Another function (and region) of the prefrontal cortex regulates attentional processes, aiding decision making by heightening the salience of immediately relevant information and screening from processing the currently irrelevant (Shimamura 1995). Interestingly, the motor inhibition postulated by Ferrier as a primary activity of the frontal lobes was conceived as a means of promoting *attentive ideation*, time bought for intelligent deliberation by the suppression of motoric responses otherwise dictated by stimuli of the moment (Ferrier 1876; Macmillan 1992).

One other region, the ventromedial prefrontal cortex (located above the orbits of the eyes, and therefore also known as the oribitofrontal or orbital prefrontal cortex), is especially interesting for its extensive connections with subcortical (under the cortex) structures involved in motivation and emotion. These structures, such as the amygdala, hippocampus, fornix, septum, and cingulate cortex (the latter actually located on the medial, or midline, surface of the neocortex), form what is known loosely as the limbic system. Damasio (1994) argues that effective decision making stems not from working memory, selective attention, and other purely cognitive functions alone, but also from emotion and, in particular, emotional tags (or visceral feelings) attached to stimuli by prior experience. Activation of these affective (limbic) representations—*somatic markers*—in the ventromedial prefrontal cortex biases choice against actions previously associated with negative emotional experiences and toward options of more positive valence.

Disrupting connections between the limbic system and ventromedial prefrontal cortex (as by injury to the latter) compromises our ability to optimize choice. Indeed, such damage does so even when patients may otherwise seem to have reasoned social judgment, such as understanding how one "ought" to act under the same circumstances in which their own behavior is impaired. This is nicely demonstrated in studies of Bechara and colleagues (Bechara et al. 1994, 1996, 1997, 1998, 1999; Bechara, Tranel, and Damasio 2000), who presented patients having ventromedial prefrontal lesions, as well as control subjects, with several decks of cards in a simulated gambling experiment. In all decks, successively selected cards generated either gains or losses. In some decks, both the gains and losses were moderate, and playing these decks generated positive earnings. In other decks, winning cards produced larger rewards, but these were offset by even higher penalties for losing cards, yielding significant losses overall. Through trials, control subjects learned to select from the low-risk decks, whereas prefrontal patients showed a consistent preference for the decks that gave high immediate rewards and, over time, a losing outcome. Consistent with Damasio's hypothesis, a measure of skin conductance—which indexes autonomic nervous system response and, thereby, subjects' emotional arousal—revealed anticipatory emotional reactions among the control subjects when they happened to select high-risk cards; some control subjects even exhibited these responses before they could articulate the difference between decks. Prefrontal patients did not show such responses and, in many cases, failed to do so even after they knew that playing the high-risk decks was a bad idea. These findings obtained despite the fact that both patients and controls experienced emotional arousal *after* receiving losing cards. Patients with prefrontal lesions therefore could react emotionally to a negative event (as could controls), but could not do so in predictable anticipation of such an event—and in consequence gambled to their ultimate disadvantage, seduced by the false promise of an attractive gain on each turn of the card. Alternative explanations suggesting that prefrontal patients may be overly attracted to large, immediate rewards or simply insensitive to punishment also failed to account for these observations (Bechara, Tranel, and Damasio 2000). Thus investigators conclude that patients with ventromedial prefrontal lesions are myopic with respect to the future, "oblivious to the . . . consequences of their actions, and seem to be guided by immediate prospects only" (Bechara et al. 1994, 7).

The primary defect here appears to involve patients' inability to reconstitute the affective (somatic) states that attended reward and punishment previously when selecting cards from the high- and low-risk decks, thereby preventing the emotion evoked by prior experience from informing (biasing) current decisions. Interestingly, similarly impaired decision making may arise among patients with an intact prefrontal cortex if they have sustained damage to the amygdala, one of the principal subcortical structures comprising the limbic system (Bechara et al. 1999). In the amygdala affective states become attached to events and experiences and, without the amygdala, such emotional learning, or conditioning, will not occur. In this case, there is no affect to reexperience in anticipation of an imprudent act, because no previously established connection exists between the act and its accompanying emotion. These patients, for example, fail to show autonomic arousal (skin conductance responses) not only when deciding from which deck to select, but even when punished for a losing draw. In this instance, impaired decision making is a by-product of impaired emotional learning, whereas prefrontal patients attach affect to experience normally (as registered in the amygdala), but cannot access or take advantage of this information when it comes to making a decision. (See Mischel et al., chap. 5 herein, for further discussion of cognitive and emotional aspects of decision making, as seen from a developmental and systems perspective.)

Analogous deficits are documented in animal studies involving experimentally induced brain lesions. In one study, laboratory rats were given the choice of receiving either one pellet of food immediately or two pellets after varying intervals of delay. Not surprisingly, preference for the larger, later reward declined as a function of the length of delay imposed by the experimenter. Moreover, selective destruction of the orbitofrontal cortex caused animals to spurn the two-pellet, delayed reward (and therefore opt for a smaller, immediate outcome) at briefer intervals of delay than did intact control animals (Mobini et al. 2002). In earlier experiments, also using laboratory rats, animals' preferences for delayed reinforcement were likewise altered by damage to the septum, which lies behind the anterior cingulate in a circuit linking other limbic structures with the orbitofrontal cortex (Newman, Gorenstein, and Kelsey 1983). Thirsty rats were given a choice between assured access to water after a ten-second delay and a less than certain probability of receiving water immediately. By a far margin, lesioned rats selected the immediate, uncertain reinforcement more frequently than sham-lesioned controls, and as a result they also received less total reward. When animals were given the same choice between certain and uncertain access to water, but were required to wait for both, each group showed a clear preference for the schedule of continuous (certain) reinforcement. Thus lesioned rats' diminished propensity to wait for assured rewards when offered an immediate but uncertain alternative did not stem from simple failure to discriminate between the two reward contingencies. More recent findings indicate that selectively lesioning portions of another subcortical structure, the core of the nucleus accumbens, similarly impairs preferences for larger, delayed rewards among food-deprived rats. Like the septum, the nucleus accumbens has long been implicated in processes of motivation and reinforcement, and may possibly affect choice over time through neural pathways involving both limbic system nuclei (for example, the basolateral amygdala) and certain prefrontal regions, such as the orbitofrontal cortex (Cardinal et al. 2001).

It is intriguing that the foregoing studies demonstrate similarly altered choice behavior in both brain-damaged humans and brain-lesioned rats. This suggests that the neural machinery of decision making may have certain common elements, some of which are continuous in phylogeny and preserved through much of vertebrate evolution (see Kacelnik, chap. 3 herein, for a discussion of evolutionary considerations). Of course, the scope of human decision making is hardly to be compared with that of other animals, and rates of time-dependent discounting differ by orders of magnitude between the rat and human. That there are homologous features to the neurobiology of rodents and humans, however, and that these extend to the level of neural circuitry is well established and underlies much of contemporary neuroscience. Perhaps it is in the complexity of human sociality that we differ most from other animals, our lives being lived in enlarged circles of acquaintance, with multiple and often conflicting spheres of cooperative and competitive endeavor, replete with ambiguity and choices good and bad. If the anterior regions of the frontal lobes (those areas of exceptional expansion in human evolution) oversee goal-directed behavior, they surely have much work to do in the human brain, advancing goals nested within goals, in hierarchies of aspiration reaching to distant futurities. In negotiating our daily lives, we have much to bring "forward" into our prefrontal cortices, the mental scratchpad for processing sensory experience, memory and affect needed to conceive, sequence, and monitor planned behavior. We therefore also differ from other species in the objects over which we exercise choice, these projecting for us far further into the future and extending over wider expanses of space and resources. Accordingly, our expanding frontal lobe may have retained (in the orbitofrontal area) much of a previously evolved apparatus for choice itself, while adding the capacities that permit such choices to be elaborated in thought and language and to range over ever larger physical, social, and temporal landscapes. When the shared mechanisms of decision making are disrupted by injury or experiment, though, similar impairments may be seen across diverse species, even from rat to human.

Aspects of a Neurochemistry of Impulse Control

Neurobiological explanations of behavior might be thought to address at least two kinds of questions: Where and how? *Where* questions would refer to regions, structures, or patterns of connectivity—that is, circuitry of the brain—that underlie some aspect of behavior and that, save for the damaged brain, we all have in common. This is the scaffolding of evolved mentality, tangibly present in brains both alive and dead. Yet only the living brain registers, represents, and processes information, and by such processing instructs the body it inhabits. Though channeled by the wiring within, the actual work of the brain is evanescent, an activity in time. Because it falls to the brain's primary functional component, the neuron, to do this work, *how* questions often have to do with attributes of neurons and the forms of communication that occur between neurons. Also, we find much of our individuality in neuronal functioning, from the contents of memory to individual differences in temperament and personality—what the neuroscientist Joseph LeDoux calls our *synaptic self* (LeDoux 2002). In the following we discuss some of the properties of neurons and address their potential role in intertemporal choice.

Neurons, Neurotransmitters, and Neuromodulators

As noted, the neuron is the fundamental information-conveying unit of the nervous system. All neurons have a cell body (the soma), which contains the nucleus and various cellular organelles, with two classes of structure extending outward from the soma, the dendrites and the axon. Dendrites resemble branches on a tree, reaching out profusely to provide surfaces on which information may be received from other neurons. The axon projects away from the cell body and carries neuronal information *to* other cells.

Within neurons, messages are conducted down the axon as "action potentials" propagated by electrochemical events occurring at the cell membrane. When conduction of an action potential is complete, information is delivered to neighboring neurons by *chemical* means. The extremities of the axon are defined by a proliferation of small budlike structures called *terminal buttons*, which house tiny vesicles containing the chemical substances known as neurotransmitters. To effect neurotransmission, these vesicles fuse with nearby areas of the cell membrane and disgorge their stored transmitter molecules into the surrounding extracellular space. Specialized receptors on the dendrites and cell bodies of neighboring neurons provide recognition sites to which newly released neurotransmitter may bind. This form of chemical communication between neurons is termed *synaptic neurotransmission* and the gap between the terminal button of a transmitting (or presynaptic) nerve cell and the membrane of a receiving (or postsynaptic) neuron is referred to as the synapse, or synaptic cleft.

Neurons typically have a large number of dendrites, as well as a profusion of terminal buttons. A single neuron can receive inputs from many cells (termed *convergence*) and through its numerous terminals convey messages to many other neurons (called *divergence*), thus accounting for much of the brain's potential and realized complexity. Activating receptors on the dendrites or soma of a neuron can affect functioning of the postsynaptic cell in a variety of ways, depending on the neurotransmitter released and the nature and class of receptor to which the neurotransmitter binds. For instance, synaptic transmission might be either excitatory or inhibitory with respect to the initiation of an action potential. When the aggregate of postsynaptic influences converging on a neuron depolarizes the cell's membrane beyond what is called its "threshold of excitation," an action potential is then propagated in the postsynaptic neuron. These effects occur almost immediately, as within a span of milliseconds. Other receptors act more slowly, on the order of seconds to minutes, but can also influence the expression of certain proteins in the neuron and exert an impact on the cell that may last for days. These effects can extend even to the cell's nucleus and modulate many important features of nerve cell functioning, including (among other things) the regulation of transmitter synthesis and release, as well as the rate of production of membrane-bound receptors. Finally, neurotransmitters are themselves synthesized within the neuron and transported down the axon and stored for release in the synaptic vesicles. After release, neurotransmitter molecules do not remain in the synapse long, but in most instances are quickly taken back up into the presynaptic neuron. This process, called *reuptake*, is accomplished by special transporter "pumps" located in the cell membrane. The returning neurotransmitter molecules are then either repackaged in synaptic vesicles for re-release or broken down (inactivated) by degradative enzymes.

Of the several dozen neurotransmitters identified to date, just two—glutamate and GABA (gamma-aminobutyric acid)—account for most synaptic transmission in the brain. The integrated actions of these two neurotransmitters, one excitatory (glutamate) and the other inhibitory (GABA), conduct most ordinary cell-to-cell communication, generally in neural circuits localized to particular brain areas or structures (Carlson 2001). In contrast, most other neurotransmitters facilitate or inhibit activity within larger functional systems that coordinate communication between different neural structures and usually encompass multiple regions of the brain; these neurotransmitters are also referred to as *neuromodulators*. The so-called monoamine neurotransmitters, which comprise one prominent category of neuromodulators, include norepinephrine, dopamine, and serotonin. All three of these transmitters influence neural activity across large expanses of the brain and therefore also modulate many aspects of cognition, affect, and behavior. These include several features of individual temperament, such as responsiveness to novelty and threat, sensitivity to reward or reinforcement, and our ability to restrain impulses of the moment (see, for example, Cloninger 1987; Depue and Collins 1999; Depue and Spoont 1986; Zuckerman 1995). Notably, much research indicates that serotonin in particular is deeply involved in the regulation of impulsive behavior (Coccaro and Kavoussi 1997; Coscina 1997; Fairbanks et al. 2001; Manuck et al. 1998; Soubrie 1986), and from this it follows that serotonin might also play a role in time-dependent decision making. Of course, no neurotransmitter is actually designated for a particular behavior or class of behaviors, and by the same token, many complex psychological processes are influenced by multiple neuromodulators, including possibly all of the monoamine neurotransmitters. As discussed further, however, evidence regarding the serotonergic modulation of impulsive behavior is now extensive and provides at least one stepping-stone to a neurochemistry of intertemporal choice.

Serotonin and Impulse Control

Neurons of the serotonergic system originate in a region of the brain stem called the *raphe nuclei*, and from there project to diverse areas of the forebrain, including subcortical structures such as the thalamus, basal ganglia, hypothalamus, hippocampus, and septum, as well as much of the cerebral cortex (encompassing, not least, the prefrontal cortex). Serotonin is also known as 5-hydroxytryptamine (5-HT) and is synthesized from the amino acid tryptophan. When serotonin is released from an axon terminal, its effects on a postsynaptic neuron are mediated by one of several serotonin receptors. As with other neurotransmitters, shortly after serotonin is released it is removed from the synapse and taken back up into the presynaptic (releasing) neuron. This reuptake is accomplished by another molecule, called the *serotonin transporter*, and ultimately serotonin is metabolized by an enzyme, monoamine oxidase. Noteworthy too is that the axons of serotonergic neurons branch extensively as they ascend through the forebrain, thereby permitting the near-simultaneous stimulation of serotonin receptors at multiple sites in the brain. Functionally, serotonin modulates responses evoked by other neurotransmitters at its many sites of action and, to a first approximation, exerts inhibitory (or stabilizing) effects on behavior. The domains of behavior affected by serotonin include, among others, locomotor activity, consummatory and sexual behavior, sleep, appetite, and aggression. Enhanced serotonergic activity typically restrains, rather than facilitates, behavioral responding and does so in a variety of contexts, including conditions of uncertainty, conflict, and punishment (Depue and Spoont 1986; Spoont 1992; Soubrie 1986). Conversely, decreased serotonergic neuro-transmission "disinhibits" goal-directed activity and impairs regulation of behavioral and affective responses activated by other transmitter systems.

Writing on the psychology of self-control, Logue (1995) suggests that impulsive choice may underlie such wide-ranging human problems as fiscal imprudence, alcohol and other substance abuse, pathological gambling, health-impairing habits of behavior and lifestyle, impulsive aggression, and even suicide. Many of these domains of behavioral variability and psychopathology also figure prominently in recent research on brain serotonin. We start with the last in Logue's list—suicide—which embodies, at least metaphorically, the furthest extremity of intertemporal choice, a place in mind where the future collapses onto the present in shared hopelessness. To the suicidal patient, writes the psychologist Kay Redfield Jamison (1999, 93), "the future cannot be separated from the present, and the present is painful beyond solace." Suicide is thus a tragic reckoning, in which the relief of current anguish extinguishes time itself, and with it, the value (utility) of all future outcomes.

It is now well established that persons with histories of attempted suicide, repeated suicide attempts, or completed suicide have low levels of serotonin's principal metabolite, 5-hydroxyindoleacetic acid (5-HIAA), in their cerebral spinal fluid (CSF) (Asberg 1998; Lester 1995). This observation is noteworthy because the CSF concentration of 5-HIAA is an indirect measure of serotonin release in the brain. Postmortem studies similarly show abnormalities of serotonergic function, such as altered serotonin receptor binding, in the brains of suicide victims, including the ventral area of the prefrontal cortex (Arrango et al. 1995; Mann 1998).

A third indicator of decreased brain serotonergic activity is likewise associated with attempted suicide. Activation of serotonin receptors in the brain (particularly in the hypothalamus) causes the pituitary gland to release various hormones, such as prolactin, into the bloodstream. An in vivo measure of central nervous system serotonergic response can be obtained by administering drugs that enhance serotonin neurotransmission acutely, then measuring the stimulated rise of a pituitary-derived hormone in peripherally sampled blood. One such drug is fenfluramine, which causes serotonin to be released from nerve terminals and inhibits its reuptake. In a fenfluramine "challenge," the rise in plasma prolactin concentration occurring after the drug is administered is believed to be proportional to serotonergic responsivity in the brain, as influenced by both pre- and postsynaptic processes. Among depressed and personality disordered psychiatric patients, persons with histories of attempted suicide show a blunted prolactin release when given fenfluramine, thereby reflecting reduced central serotonergic responsivity, compared with patients of similar diagnosis without history of suicide attempt (Coccaro et al. 1989; Mann et al. 1995). Hence, studies of CSF 5-HIAA concentrations, postmortem evaluations of suicide victims, and tests by neuroendocrine challenge all suggest a consistent relation between diminished serotonergic function and suicidal behavior. So consistent is this literature that in fact it is frequently cited as the most highly replicated observation in biological psychiatry.

Acts of suicide are often impulsive, as are many instances of human aggression; nor are these two forms of injurious behavior unrelated. In a recent study of several hundred psychiatric hospital admissions, for instance, correlated measures of aggressive disposition and impulsivity predicted patients' histories of attempted suicide, irrespective of their clinical diagnosis, severity of suicidal ideation, or recency of attempt (Mann et al. 1999). Not surprisingly, many investigations also show an inverse relation between measures of brain serotonergic activity and both behavioral and psychometric indices of aggression. These studies involve numerous clinical and forensic populations, including patients with personality and substance abuse disorders, men incarcerated for impulse-related crimes (for example, impulsive fire setting, unpremeditated homicide), criminal recidivists, and children with disruptive behavior disorders (for example, Brown et al. 1979, 1982; Coccaro et al. 1989, 1996; Coccaro, Kavoussi, and Hauger 1995; Kruessi et al. 1990; Linnoila et al. 1983; Virkkunen et al. 1994). Importantly, even normative variation in aggressiveness, as seen in healthy, nonpatient populations, correlates negatively with brain seronotergic function (Manuck et al. 1998). This generality of association in turn suggests the influence of an underlying neurobehavioral dimension of individual differences, described previously by temperament theorists as a continuum of behavioral constraint, inhibition, or harm avoidance (Soubrie 1986; Depue and Spoont 1986; Cloninger 1987; Gray 1987; Zuckerman 1995). In these dimensional models, persons who exhibit low serotonergic activity are thought to have a diminished capacity to restrain impulses, a disinhibition of otherwise constrained behavior reflecting impaired learning, a disregard for future consequences, or insensitivity to cues for punishment. When conjoined with an antagonistic motivation, reduced impulse control is experienced as impulsive aggression and expressed as irritability, acts of verbal aggression or physical assault, property destruction, or other antisocial behavior. When self-injurious, however, impulsive aggression may predispose to suicide or attempted suicide.

That serotonin helps regulate impulsive behavior is supported by several recent studies of nonhuman primates. Among rhesus monkeys housed in a natural social environment, for instance, males having the lowest CSF 5-HIAA concentrations engage in high rates of unrestrained aggression. These animals are apparently unable to "appropriately" modulate their aggressive responses to other monkeys, thereby escalating otherwise ordinary altercations to fights of heightened severity and increasing risk of both injury and premature mortality (Higley et al. 1992, 1997). Consistent with previous speculation, "low" 5-HIAA animals act imprudently even in contexts unrelated to the expression of antagonistic behavior. Such animals readily reenter baited cages in which they have been captured previously, risk long-distance leaps in the forest canopy, and among juvenile males, emigrate early from their natal groups, at an age when they are more susceptible to attack and predation (Higley, Suomi, and Linnoila 1996; Kaplan et al. 1995; Mehlman et al. 1994, 1995). Other research demonstrates that vervet monkeys with low CSF 5-HIAA concentrations also exhibit heightened *social* impulsivity, as indicated by their uninhibited approach to social strangers in laboratory testing (Fairbanks et al. 2001). Conversely, these animals engage strangers more hesitantly when administered the serotonin reuptake inhibitor fluoxetine, which increases serotonergic neurotransmission by blocking the presynaptic reuptake mechanism in serotonin-releasing neurons (and over time possibly inducing other serotonin-regulating adaptations in affected neural circuits). Thus brain serotonergic activity varies appreciably in monkeys, and this variability correlates inversely with individual differences in impulsive behavior (including impulsivity-associated aggression). Furthermore, impulsivity declines when serotonergic function is augmented by pharmacologic intervention.

Is there also an impulsive dimension to variation of serotonergic activity in humans? We have already noted that psychometric indices of impulsivity and aggressiveness predict histories of attempted suicide in hospitalized patients, and that suicide itself is associated with diminished serotonergic function. In addition, the aggressive and antisocial behaviors of persons exhibiting low serotonergic activity often contain an impulsive element, lacking in premeditation or provocation proportional to the act (Linnoila et al. 1983). Nonetheless, assessing impulsivity as an independent construct has proven difficult in human research, not least because so many different operational definitions have been proposed. Standardized questionnaires measuring

Figure 4.1   Mean Values on the Barratt Impulsiveness Scale

Quartiles of Prolactin
Response to Fenfluramine

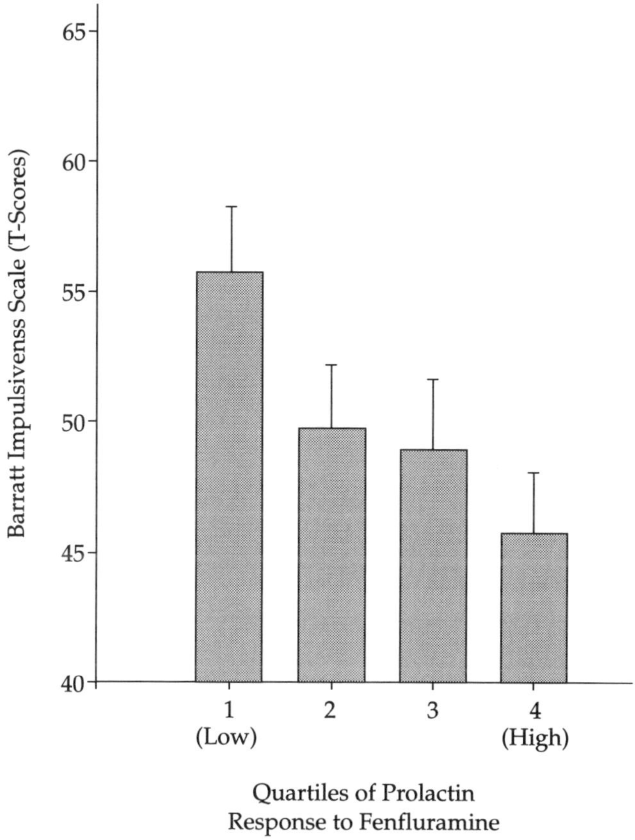

Source: Authors' compilation.
Note: Mean values on the Barratt Impulsiveness Scale (expressed as T-scores [± SEM]) of men ranked by quartile of central nervous system serotonergic responsivity, as indexed by the peak prolactin response to fenfluramine hydrochloride (adjusted for several relevant covariates, including age, body weight, weight-relative fenfluramine dose, and drug and metabolite concentrations in plasma over the 3.5-hour challenge). 1 = lowest quartile of prolactin response; 4 = highest quartile. N = 59.

impulsivity as a personality trait, for instance, number at least a dozen and often index poorly correlated dimensions of putatively impulsive behavior—processes described variously as functional or dysfunctional, attentional, decisional, inhibitory, or ideomotor impulsivity, to name a few (Evenden 1999). One instrument, the Barratt Impulsiveness Scale, measures variability in planfulness, deliberation before action, and motor inhibition (Barratt 1994). Unlike most other measures of impulsivity, this instrument has been administered in several studies that include a neuropharmacologic assessment of central serotonergic function. Moreover, in both clinical and nonpatient populations, subjects' neuroendocrine responses to the fenfluramine challenge (described earlier) correlated inversely with their scores on the Barratt Impulsiveness Scale (Coccaro et al. 1989, 1996; Manuck et al. 1998). For instance, figure 4.1 presents data derived from an analysis we conducted on the fenfluramine-induced prolactin responses of healthy men having no history of major psychiatric disorder.

The columns depict mean values for impulsiveness, as indexed by the Barratt scale, among subjects ranked by quartile of peak prolactin concentration following administration of fenfluramine. Reported impulsivity is clearly greatest among men who showed the lowest prolactin response to fenfluramine (quartile 1), least in the most responsive quartile (4), and intermediate in the quartiles of similarly intermediate prolactin response.

In addition to an overall measure of impulsivity, the Barratt scale yields scores on three subscales, labeled *motor, cognitive,* and *non-planning* impulsiveness. In these data, subjects' prolactin responses to fenfluramine correlated significantly, albeit modestly, with the Barratt total score ($r = -.36$, $p < .005$), but varied in strength among the subscales. Our results reflect primarily a relation between brain serotonergic function and "nonplanning impulsiveness" ($r = -.37$, $p < .004$), as "motor impulsivity" (acting "on the spur of the moment") correlated only weakly with serotonergic responsivity ($r = -.24$, $p < .05$) and "cognitive impulsivity" (roughly, disciplined thought) not at all. Items comprising the *non-planning* subscale are nearly all referenced to time, foresight, and prudent action. Persons who score high on this subscale (that is, impulsively) tend to report that they value the present more than the future, often spend more than they earn, avoid current inconveniences at the expense of future gain (for example, neglect routine medical or dental checkups), fail to save regularly, and only occasionally plan for the future. These items seem to capture much of the essence of intertemporal choice—decisions made between alternatives in time, where choosing the rewarded present yields satisfactions of lesser magnitude than anticipated gains reasonably achieved by postponed or delayed gratification.

Interestingly, individual differences in both brain serotonergic activity and impulsive behavior (when addressed as a personality trait) stem from genetic as well as environmental influences (Higley et al. 1993; Matthews et al. 2000; Serocynski, Bergeman, and Coccaro 1999). On the genetic side, heritable variation may be expressed through

Figure 4.2   Non-Planning Impulsiveness

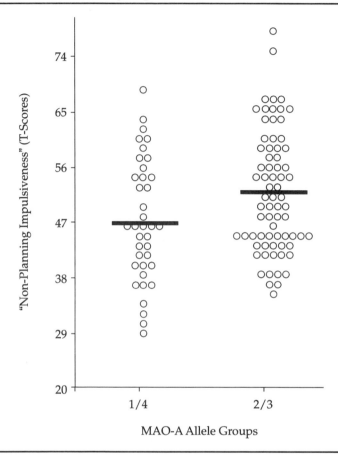

MAO-A Allele Groups

Source: Authors' compilation.
Note: Non-planning impulsiveness (expressed as T-scores) among men grouped by alleles of a promoter region polymorphism in the gene encoding monoamine oxidase A ("Low" transcription alleles: group 1/4; "high" transcription alleles: group 2/3). N = 110.

differences in serotonin-regulating genes, such as those involved in transmitter synthesis, release and reuptake, metabolism, or receptor activation. One example is the enzyme monoamine oxidase A (MAO-A), which inactivates the monoamine neurotransmitters, including serotonin. If anything should retard the enzymatic degradation of serotonin we would expect the synaptic availability of this neurotransmitter to increase, and indeed, inhibitors of monoamine oxidase do just that. Furthermore, if reducing MAO-A activity increases synaptic serotonin, it follows that any naturally occurring genetic variation that alters the rate at which this enzyme is synthesized might similarly modulate serotonergic neurotransmission. This appears to be the case for four recently identified variants (called *alleles*) of the MAO-A gene. Two of these alleles (here designated alleles 1 and 4) are associated with less transcription of the MAO-A gene and with greater serotonergic activity than the alternate alleles, numbered 2 and 3 (Manuck et al. 2000; Sabol, Hu, and Hamer 1998). Since the MAO-A gene is located on the X chromosome, men carry only one copy of the gene and women carry two.

When we assessed allelic variation in this gene among 110 men, we found "total" scores on the Barratt Impulsiveness Scale to be highest in subjects having either allele 2 or 3—that is, the "high" transcription alleles associated with reduced serotonergic activity. In addition, of the three Barratt subscales, *non-planning impulsiveness* showed the strongest genetic association. This is illustrated in figure 4.2, which depicts the scores of individual subjects in each of the two allele groups (alleles 1–4 versus 2–3). Again, *non-planning impulsiveness* comprises the subscale most reminiscent of time-dependent decision making, containing items that explicitly contrast preferences for near-term (or present-oriented) satisfactions against delayed gain of higher value or postponed gratification (for example, spending within earned resources, valuing the future more than the present, planning for future outcomes, saving regularly, or accepting inconveniences now against implied benefits later). Also apparent from figure 4.2 is that the strength of this association is only moderate, as substantial overlap exists in the distribution of scores among the two allele groups. MAO-A is but one of many elements of the serotonin system, however, and numerous environmental variables undoubtedly influence serotonergic activity as well, the latter also interacting with genetic factors to influence trajectories of both neurobiological and behavioral development (Bennett et al. 2002). Other sources of genetic variation likely will soon be found similarly associated with aspects of impulsivity and gene-environment interactions elucidated. For the present, though, we find it noteworthy that individual differences in a behavioral trait descriptively related to intertemporal choice may be shown to correlate with both an *in vivo* index of brain serotonergic function and genetic variability in at least one regulatory component of the serotonin system.[1]

Serotonin and Intertemporal Choice

Endorsing questionnaire items indicative of "non-planning impulsiveness" indeed *may* denote a dispositional analogue of intertemporal choice. Yet asserting that one has a preference for immediate reward, a tendency to spend beyond earnings, and a disinclination to plan for the future, is still distanced from the decisions of moment and circumstance that define intertemporal choice in daily experience. Choices that appear in hindsight to reflect a disregard for later consequences (a discounting of future benefits), for instance, may have seemed different at the time these choices were made. Unfortunately, we rarely have the opportunity to observe people choosing among known outcomes (rewards) of varying magnitude and delay under identical conditions and on repeated occasions. To the experimentalist, this is the laboratory animal's raison d'être. Indeed we already know that rats are capable of intertemporal choice, that such behavior may rest in part on the integrity of neural pathways in the brain linking areas of the prefrontal cortex with certain subcortical structures of the limbic system, and that the axons of serotonin-releasing neurons project to these same forebrain regions. Would experimental manipulations of brain serotonergic function also modulate qualities of intertemporal choice?

In a common experimental paradigm, hungry laboratory rats may be offered a choice of two rewards, perhaps a pellet or two of rat chow available immediately, against a larger reward (say eight pellets) delayed by ten, twenty-five, or thirty seconds. The rat can express its preference by pressing either of two levers in a testing chamber or by scurrying to one or another goal box across the arms of a simple T-maze; the experimenter records how often an animal selects the later, larger reward and thus obtains a measure of the rat's relative tolerance for delay. Alternatively, awaited outcomes may be delayed incrementally over successive trials until rats show an equal preference for immediate (smaller–sooner) and delayed (larger–later) rewards. This "indifference" point is indicative of increasingly impulsive behavior when reached at ever-shorter intervals of delayed reinforcement (Mazur 1987).

If serotonin enhances preference for delayed reward, administering drugs known to augment brain serotonergic function would be expected to increase an animal's capacity to await deferred but larger outcomes. We have previously described several pharmacologic interventions that facilitate serotonergic neurotransmission, such as blocking the reuptake of synaptic serotonin, inhibiting enzymatic degradation of serotonin by monoamine oxidase, or directly stimulating serotonin release by the drug fenfluramine. The reuptake inhibitors exert a modest effect on the availability of serotonin in the synapse when administered acutely and have been shown to increase tolerance for delay among rats given any of several such agents (Thiebot et al. 1985; Bizot et al. 1988, 1999). Although comparable effects of reuptake inhibitors are not seen in all studies (for example, Cherrier and Thiebot 1996; Evenden and Ryan 1996), heightened preferences for delayed–larger reinforcers have also been reported for two other drugs, the monoamine oxidase inhibitor nialamide and the serotonin-releasing agent fenfluramine (Bizot et al. 1988; Poulos, Parker, and Le 1996). In one of the few studies of similar design involving human subjects, conduct-disordered men asked to perform an analogous experimental task also showed greater tolerance for delayed responding (diminished impulsivity) when pretreated with fenfluramine, compared with their performance of the same task under placebo-controlled conditions (Cherek and Lane 1999).

Conversely, impulsive behavior may be *increased* by manipulations that reduce central serotonergic function. The drug *para*-Chlorophenylalanine (*p*CPA), for instance, inhibits tryptophan hydroxylase, the rate-limiting enzyme in serotonin biosynthesis, thereby diminishing serotonin production in serotonergic neurons. Rats administered *p*CPA show an enhanced preference for smaller, immediate rewards when tested in the T-maze paradigm, relative to control animals (Bizot et al. 1999).

Similar effects may be achieved with other pharmacologic agents. A drug that stimulates the receptors for a neurotransmitter is called a *direct-acting agonist*, and such agonists may vary in strength; hence, some drugs are known as "partial" agonists and others as "full" agonists. An interesting fact is that one kind of receptor, an autoreceptor, binds to transmitter molecules of the type released by the cell on which the autoreceptor is itself located. Activation of these autoreceptors generally causes a *decrease* in neurotransmitter synthesis or release as a means of regulating synaptic transmission in the affected neuron. In the serotonergic system, the so-called 5-HT_{1a} receptors act both as autoreceptors on presynaptic neurons and as postsynaptic receptors. Partial 5-HT_{1a} agonists appear to reduce cell firing (decrease serotonergic neurotransmission) by activation of the 5-HT_{1a} autoreceptors, while minimally stimulating postsynaptic receptors of the same class. Consistent with these pharmacologic actions, rats administered a variety of 5-HT_{1a} partial agonists show an increased preference for immediate reinforcement, thus shifting toward more impulsive behavior (Bizot et al. 1999). In contrast, the 5-HT_{1a} full agonist, 8-OH-DPAT (the tongue-twisting 8-hydroxy-[2-di-n-propylamino]tetralin), stimulates not only the autoreceptor, but *postsynaptic* 5-HT_{1a} receptors too, thereby also effecting serotonergic transmission at postsynaptic neurons. As a result, animals treated with 8-OH-DPAT might be expected to show intermediate effects in a delay of reward procedure, or possibly even increased tolerance for delay. In fact, Bizot and colleagues (1999) reported heightened preference for delayed responding in 8-OH-DPAT–treated animals, while other investigators have shown biphasic effects of this same drug—greater impulsivity at small doses (when stimulatory effects on autoreceptors may predominate) and reduced impulsivity at a higher dose that presumably activates postsynaptic 5-HT$_{1a}$ receptors as well (Poulos, Parker, and Le 1996).

Together, these studies suggest a certain complexity of serotonergic effects on choice behavior, in which preferences for immediate or delayed outcomes may depend on subtle shifts in receptor populations, rates of transmitter synthesis, release, reuptake and metabolism, and patterns of receptor-specific activation. Perhaps for this reason some inconsistencies also exist in this literature, with the same effect not always seen in all drugs of a given class, at all doses of a given drug, or under all intervals of delayed reward. A more compelling test of serotonergic effects on intertemporal choice might be made if we could inactivate the serotonergic system more globally. Several investigators have done this by injecting the serotonin-specific neurotoxin 5,7-DHT (5,7-dihydroxytryptamine) into the brainstem raphe nuclei of experimental animals. This agent effectively destroys ascending serotonergic pathways, including those terminating in the various forebrain structures implicated in decision making, affect, and impulse control. To our knowledge, all studies employing this methodology show that chemically lesioned animals exhibit a diminished tolerance for delay when compared with sham-lesioned controls (Al-Ruwaitea et al. 1999; Bizot et al. 1999; Mobini et al. 2000a, 2000b; Wogar, Bradshaw, and Szabadi 1993). This heightened impulsiveness obtains under widely varying choice procedures, including T-maze testing and variations on Mazur's adjusting-delay paradigm. One recent study also suggests differential effects of serotonin on two ordinarily confounded attributes of intertemporal choice procedures, length of delay and magnitude of reward. Mobini and colleagues (2000b) applied a multiplicative model of delay discounting (Ho et al. 1999), in which both time and reward magnitude are modeled, and experimentally varied delay intervals to both smaller and larger rewards. As in other studies, they demonstrated that depleting central serotonin diminishes animals' ability to delay gratification; in addition, their results indicate that the more impulsive behavior of chemically lesioned rats stems specifically from an accelerated rate of temporal discounting. In a parallel experiment, depleting serotonin did not alter animals' preferences for probabilistic outcomes (namely, "small, certain" versus "large, less certain" rewards). Curiously, in a previously cited study by the same investigators (Mobini et al. 2002), lesioning the orbitofrontal cortex altered both delay *and* probability discounting. This suggests that effects on decision making due to gross prefrontal damage may differ somewhat from those associated with functional alterations in brain serotonin, at least in this animal model and under these experimental conditions.

The foregoing literature notwithstanding, serotonin is surely not the only neurotransmitter affecting choice over time. For example, the near-total destruction of serotonergic projections causes a quantitative change in tolerance for delayed reward among chemically lesioned rats, but does not altogether eliminate delayed choice (Wogar, Bradshaw, and Szabadi 1993). This is what we would expect of a neuromodulator, which does just that—it modulates, but does not cause the behavior of interest to occur or not occur. Some evidence shows that delay discounting can be influenced by other neurotransmitters as well, including the two other monoamine neuromodulators, norepinephrine (Bizot et al. 1999) and dopamine (for example, Evenden and Ryan 1996; Wade, de Wit, and Richards 2000). Of these, dopamine is especially interesting for its extensive involvement in hedonic motivation and reward mechanisms of the brain (Carlson 2001; Wise 1996). In general, rats administered amphetamine or its analogue methamphetamine (dopamine agonists) show an increased preference for delayed rewards of larger magnitude (Cardinal, Robbins, and Everitt 2000; Richards et al. 1997; Richards, Sabol, and de Wit 1999; Wade, de Wit, and Richards 2000), whereas blocking certain dopamine receptors shifts preferences in the opposite direction, toward more immediate (impulsive) responding (Cardinal, Robbins, and Everitt 2000; Wade, de Wit, and Richards 2000). Nonetheless, this literature is not entirely consistent: an increased preference for smaller, sooner rewards has also been shown occasionally in amphetamine-treated animals (Cherrier and Thiebot 1996; Evenden and Ryan 1996); and across studies, findings show a somewhat fragile sensitivity to methodological factors, such as the presence of cued reinforcement during testing procedures, acute or chronic drug administration, whether rats are rewarded by food or water, and the extent of animals' prior exposure to choice contingencies (Cardinal, Robbins, and Everitt 2000; Richards, Sabol, and de Wit 1999). Additionally, extensive interaction exists between serotonin and dopamine-releasing neurons in brain areas likely to be involved in intertemporal choice, such as the nucleus accumbens, where dopamine levels have been shown to vary with alterations in serotonergic stimulation (Benloucif, Keegan, and Galloway 1993; Parsons and Justice 1993).

Concluding Comments

In his 1861 volume, *On the Study of Character*, the Scottish philosopher Alexander Bain excoriated phrenologists' claims to a neurobiological understanding of temperament and intellect. One might think that by this date attacking phrenology amounted to beating a dead horse, and indeed Bain's critique often relies on extended quotation from earlier criticisms by Samuel Bailey. One target of his attack is the previously discussed organ of "cautiousness," the seat of apprehension, circumspection and foresight residing beneath the parietal bone in phrenological thinking. How, asks Bailey, can such incommensurable qualities coexist in a single "organ," qualities that experience tells us "'are heterogeneous and disparate, and bear no sort of regular proportion to each other'" (Bain 1861; 100)? True enough, and since roughly the time of Bain we have known that complex mental processes entail integrated actions of many specialized brain structures, enabled by patterns of neural connectivity. In a sense, this has long been implicit in the ways we construe relations of intellect and affect. Whether conceived as a battle for the control of imperious impulse by an "executive" frontal lobe (the heroic, if beleaguered, ego of an earlier day) or as a cooperative endeavor by which emotion informs intellect of the probable outcomes ensuing from alternative courses of action (affect as a partner in wisdom, as argued by Damasio and Bechara), our central metaphors for such relations share a presumption of coordinated circuitry between cortical processes of a controlling, decisional nature and subcortical structures mediating aspects of motivation and emotion. This circuitry is instantiated in neuroanatomy and brought together by evolution to effect adaptive, goal-directed behavior. Clinical and experimental evidence also gives credence to these views. As we have seen, damage to certain areas of the prefrontal cortex, certain limbic structures, and by implication their circuits of connectivity, impairs judgments underlying prudent action, including matters of choice over time.

Influencing all of the foregoing structures are the long arms (axons) of neurons arising from many of the brain's neuromodulatory systems, including those conveying messages of vigilance, value, restraint, and activation, as mediated by the monoamine neurotransmitters. Among the monoamines, we have focused in this chapter on serotonin, as there is now ample reason to believe that brain serotonergic function is implicated in intertemporal choice. By a preponderance of evidence, manipulating serotonergic activity alters delay preferences of laboratory animals and does so under a variety of pharmacologic agents. Drugs that decrease serotonergic neurotransmission by blocking transmitter synthesis, activating inhibitory autoreceptors, or selectively destroying ascending serotonin neurons all heighten impulsive behavior in intertemporal choice paradigms, whereas increasing serotonergic activity by blocking synaptic reuptake, potentiating the neuronal release of serotonin stores, or inhibiting enzymatic degradation of serotonin enhances animals' preferences for delayed, larger rewards. Additionally, in vivo indices of brain serotonergic activity covary inversely with more broadly defined expressions of impulsive behavior, such as trait measures of impulsivity, impulsive aggression, and suicide, and among nonhuman primates, escalated aggression, risk-taking, and laboratory tests of social impulsivity.

Recent clinical research also helps bring together the *where* and *how* issues addressed in this chapter. Recall that patients with damage to the ventromedial prefrontal cortex tend to choose disadvantageously in a contrived gambling task that pits immediate rewards against the specter of long-term loss. Similarly impaired choice is also seen in at least some patients with psychopathologies of impulse control, including substance abuse, gambling, and obsessive-compulsive disorder (OCD) (Bechara et al. 2001, Bechara and Damasio 2002; Bechara, Dolan, and Hindes 2002; Cavedini, Riboldi, Keller, et al. 2002; Grant, Contoreggi, and London 2000; Petry, Bickel, and Arnett 1998; see also Bickel and Johnson, chap. 14 herein). Dysregulation of the serotonergic system is suspected in each of these conditions, and serotonin reuptake inhibitors have been used to treat both OCD and pathological gambling (Hollander et al. 2000; LeMarquand, Pihl, and Benkelfat 1994; Micallef and Blin 2001). Indeed, when tested on the gambling task, OCD patients who responded therapeutically to such drugs performed in the range of healthy controls (Cavedini, Riboldi, D'Annucci, et al. 2002). Conversely, normal volunteers given a tryptophan-depleting "cocktail" in order to *lower* central serotonergic activity show deficits in decision making like those of patients with damage to the orbitofrontal cortex (Rogers et al. 1999). This further supports the notion that serotonin modulates neural functioning in forebrain structures underlying prudent choice, including decisions informed by time and future consequence.

In sum, these observations suggest that variability in central nervous system serotonergic activity reflects a basic neurobiologic dimension of individual differences affecting diverse manifestations of impulsive action. As we have cautioned previously, though, brain serotonergic function alone can neither cause, nor by its absence abolish, an animal's preference for delayed, larger rewards in experimental paradigms, and in both humans and nonhuman primates serotonergic activity can account for some, but not all, naturally occurring variability in impulsive behavior. For these reasons, as well as the probable involvement of other neurotransmitter systems, we believe it reasonable to conclude that serotonin plays an important and large, but not exclusive, role in the processes of time discounting and intertemporal choice.

Clearly, then, much also remains to be discovered. Moreover, the continued, ineluctable gap between neuron and conscious experience offers a potent reminder that neurotransmitters and neural pathways speak a language still distanced from the phenomena they are invoked to explain. Closing this gap is perhaps the ultimate aspiration of neuroscience, yet short of that goal lie large expanses of contemporary neurobiological research, each offering many insights into the mechanisms of mentality, reaching even to the intersection of choice and time.

Preparation of this chapter was supported by National Institutes of Health grants P01 HL40962, R01 HL46328, and R01 HL65137.

Note

1. Consistent with the foregoing observations, "high" transcription alleles of the MAO-A regulatory polymorphism may also be more common in children with Attention Deficit Hyperactivity Disorder (ADHD) compared with healthy controls (Manor et al. 2002). Impulsivity is a prominent clinical feature of ADHD, and intolerance for delay when choosing between smaller–immediate and larger–later rewards has been demonstrated previously among ADHD patients (Schweitzer and Sulzer-Azaroff 1995).

References

Al-Ruwaitea, A. S. A., T.-J. Chiang, S. S. A. Al-Zahrani, M.-Y. Ho, C. M. Bradshaw, and E. Szabadi. 1999. "Effect of Central 5-Hydroxytryptamine Depletion on Tolerance of Delay of Reinforcement: Evidence from Performance in a Discrete-Trials 'Time-Left' Procedure." *Psychopharmacology* 141: 22–29.

Arrango, V., M. D. Underwood, A. V. Gubbi, and J. J. Mann. 1995. "Localized Alterations in Pre- and Postsynaptic Serotonin Binding Sites in the Ventrolateral Prefrontal Cortex of Suicide Victims." *Brain Research* 688: 121–33.

Asberg, M. 1998. "Neurotransmitters and Suicidal Behavior: The Evidence from Cerebrospinal Fluid Studies." *Annals of the New York Academy of Sciences* 836: 158–81.

Bain, Alexander. 1861. *On the Study of Character*. London: Parker, Son, and Bourn.

Barratt, Ernest S. 1994. "Impulsiveness and Aggression." In *Violence and Mental Disorder: Developments in Risk Assessment*, edited by John Monahan and Henry J. Steadman. Chicago: University of Chicago Press.

Bechara, Antoine, Antonio R. Damasio, Hanna Damasio, and Steven W. Anderson. 1994. "Insensitivity to Future Consequences Following Damage to Human Prefrontal Cortex." *Cognition* 50: 7–15.

Bechara, Antoine, Antonio R. Damasio, Daniel Tranel, and Steven W. Anderson. 1998. "Dissociation of Working Memory from Decision Making Within the Human Prefrontal Cortex." *Journal of Neuroscience* 18(1): 428–37.

Bechara, Antoine, Antonio R. Damasio, Daniel Tranel, and Hanna Damasio. 1997. "Deciding Advantageously Before Knowing the Advantageous Strategy." *Science* 275: 1293–95.

Bechara, Antione, and Hanna Damasio. 2002. "Decision Making and Addiction (Part I): Impaired Activation of Somatic States in Substance-Dependent Individuals When Pondering Decisions with Negative Future Consequences." *Neuropsychologia* 40: 1675–89.

Bechara, Antoine, Hanna Damasio, Antonio R. Damasio, and Gregory P. Lee. 1999. "Different Contributions of the Human Amygdala and Ventromedial Prefrontal Cortex to Decision Making." *Journal of Neuroscience* 19: 5473–81.

Bechara, Antoine, S. Dolan, N. Denburg, A. Hindes, Steven W. Anderson, and Peter E. Nathan. 2001. "Decision-Making Deficits, Linked to a Dysfunctional Ventromedial Prefrontal Cortex, Revealed in Alcohol and Stimulant Abusers." *Neuropsychologia* 39: 376–89.

Bechara, Antoine, S. Dolan, and A. Hindes. 2002. "Decision Making and Addiction (Part II): Myopia for the Future or Hypersensitivity to Reward?" *Neuropsychologia* 40: 1690–1705.

Bechara, Antoine, Daniel Tranel, and Hanna Damasio. 2000. "Characterization of the Decision-Making Deficit of Patients with Ventromedial Prefrontal Cortex Lesions." *Brain* 123: 2189–202.

Bechara, Antoine, Daniel Tranel, Hanna Damasio, and Antonio R. Damasio. 1996. "Failure to Respond Autonomically to Anticipated Future Outcomes Following Damage to Prefrontal Cortex." *Cerebral Cortex* 6(2): 215–25.

Benloucif, Susan, M. J. Keegan, and M. P. Galloway. 1993. "Serotonin-Facilitated Dopamine Release In Vivo: Pharmacological Characterization." *Journal of Pharmacology and Experimental Therapeutics* 265: 373–77.

Bennett, A. J., K. P. Lesch, A. Heils, J. C. Long, J. G. Lorenz, S. E. Shoaf, M. Champoux, S. J. Suomi, M. V. Linnoila, and J. D. Higley. 2002. "Early Experience and Serotonin Transporter Gene Variation Interact to Influence Primate CNS Function." *Molecular Psychiatry* 7: 118–22.

Bizot, J. C., C. Le Bihan, A. J. Puech, M. Hamon, and M. Thiebot. 1999. "Serotonin and Tolerance to Delay of Reward in Rats." *Psychopharmacology* 146(4): 400–12.

Bizot, J. C., M. H. Thiebot, C. Le Bihan, P. Soubrie, and P. Simon. 1988. "Effects of Imipramine-Like Drugs and Serotonin Uptake Blockers on Delay of Reward in Rats. Possible Implication in the Behavioral Mechanism of Action of Antidepressants." *Journal of Pharmacology and Experimental Therapeutics* 246(3): 1144–51.

Boyd, Robert, and Joan B. Silk. 2000. *How Humans Evolved*. New York: Norton.

Brown, G. L., M. H. Ebert, P. F. Goyer, D. C. Jimerson, W. J. Klein, W. E. Bunney, and F. K. Goodwin. 1982. "Aggression, Suicide, and Serotonin: Relationships to CSF Amine Metabolites." *American Journal of Psychiatry* 139: 741–46.

Brown, G. L., F. K. Goodwin, J. C. Ballenger, P. F. Goyer, and L. F. Major. 1979. "Aggression in Humans Correlates with Cerebrospinal Fluid Amine Metabolites." *Psychiatry Research* 1: 131–39.

Cardinal, R. N., D. R. Pennicott, C. L. Sugathapala, T. W. Robbins, and B. J. Everitt. 2001. "Impulsive Choice Induced by Lesions of the Nucleus Accumbens Core." *Science* 292: 2499–2501.

Cardinal, R. N., T. W. Robbins, and B. J. Everitt. 2000. "The Effects of D-Amphetamine, Chlordiazepoxide, Alpha-Flupenthixol and Behavioural Manipulations on Choice of Signalled and Unsignalled Delayed Reinforcement in Rats." *Psychopharmacology* 152(4): 362–75.

Carlson, Neil R. 2001. *Physiology of Behavior*. Needham Heights, Mass.: Allyn and Bacon.

Cartwright, John. 2000. *Evolution and Human Behavior*. Cambridge, Mass.: MIT Press.

Cavedini, Paolo, Giovanna Riboldi, Arcangela D'Annucci, P. Belotti, M. Cisima, and Laura Bellodi. 2002. "Decision-Making Heterogeneity in Obsessive-Compulsive Disorder: Ventromedial Prefrontal Cortex Function Predicts Different Treatment Outcomes." *Neuropsychologia* 40: 205–11.

Cavedini, Paolo, Giovanna Riboldi, Roberto Keller, Arcangela D'Annucci, and Laura Bellodi. 2002. "Frontal Lobe Dysfunction in Pathological Gambling Patients." *Biological Psychiatry* 51: 335–41.

Cherek, D. R., and S. D. Lane. 1999. "Effects of D,1-Fenfluramine on Aggressive and Impulsive Responding in Adult Males with a History of Conduct Disorder." *Psychopharmacology* 146(4): 473–81.

Cherrier, D., and M. H. Thiebot. 1996. "Effects of Psychotropic Drugs on Rat Responding in an Operant Paradigm Involving Choice Between Delayed Reinforcers." *Pharmacology, Biochemistry and Behavior* 54: 149–57.

Cloninger, C. R. 1987. "A Systematic Method for Clinical Description and Classification of Personality Variants." *Archives of General Psychiatry* 44: 573–88.

Coccaro, E. F., M. E. Berman, R. J. Kavoussi, and R. L. Hauger. 1996. "Relationship of Prolactin Response to D-Fenfluramine to Behavioral and Questionnaire Assessments of Aggression in Personality-Disordered Men." *Biological Psychiatry* 40: 157–64.

Coccaro, E. F., and R. J. Kavoussi. 1997. "Fluoxetine and Impulsive Aggressive Behavior in Personality-Disordered Subjects." *Archives of General Psychiatry* 54(12): 1081–88.

Coccaro, E. F., R. J. Kavoussi, and R. L. Hauger. 1995. "Physiological Responses to D-Fenfluramine and Ipsapirone Challenge Correlate with Indices of Aggression in Males with Personality Disorders." *International Clinical Psychopharmacology* 10: 177–79.

Coccaro, E. F., L. J. Siever, H. M. Klar, G. Maurer, K. Cochrane, T. B. Cooper, R. C. Mohs, and K. L. Davis. 1989. "Serotonergic Studies in Patients with Affective and Personality Disorders." *Archives of General Psychiatry* 46: 587–99.

Combe, George. 1827. *Essay on the Constitution of Man and Its Relations to External Objects*. Edinburgh: P. Neill.

————. 1835. *The Constitution of Man Considered in Relation to External Objects.* Boston: Sanborn, Carter, Bazin.

Coscina, Donald V. 1997. "The Biopsychology of Impulsivity: Focus on Brain Serotonin." In *Impulsivity*, edited by Christopher D. Webster and Margaret A. Jackson. New York: Guilford.

Damasio, Antonio R. 1994. *Descartes' Error*. New York: G. P. Putnam's Sons.

Depue, R. A., and P. F. Collins. 1999. "Neurobiology of the Structure of Personality: Dopamine, Facilitation of Incentive Motivation, and Extraversion." *Behavioral and Brain Sciences* 22: 491–569.

Depue, R. A., and M. R. Spoont. 1986. "Conceptualizing a Serotonin Trait: A Behavioral Dimension of Constraint." *Annals of the New York Academy of Sciences* 487: 47–62.

Evenden, J. L. 1999. "Varieties of Impulsivity." *Psychopharmacology* 146(4): 348–61.

Evenden, J. L., and C. N. Ryan. 1996. "The Pharmacology of Impulsive Behaviour in Rats: The Effects of Drugs on Response Choice with Varying Delays of Reinforcment." *Psychopharmacology* 128: 161–70.

Fairbanks, L. A., W. P. Melega, M. J. Jorgensen, J. R. Kaplan, and M. T. McGuire. 2001. "Social Impulsivity Inversely Associated with CSF 5-HIAA and Fluoxetine Exposure in Vervet Monkeys." *Neuropsychopharmacology* 24(4): 370–78.

Ferrier, David. 1876. *The Functions of the Brain*. London: Smith, Elder.

————. 1878. *Localization of Cerebral Disease*. London: Smith, Elder.

Finger, Stanley. 2000. *Minds Behind the Brain*. New York: Oxford University Press.

Fuster, J. M. 2001. "The Prefrontal Cortex B, an Update: Time Is of the Essence." *Neuron* 30: 319–33.

Gazzaniga, Michael S., Richard B. Ivry, and George R. Mangun. 1998. *Cognitive Neuroscience*. New York: Norton.

Goldman-Rakic, P. S. 1998. "The Prefrontal Landscape: Implications of Functional Architecture for Understanding Human Mentation and the Central Executive." In *The Prefrontal Cortex*, edited by A. C. Roberts, T. W. Robbins, and L. Weiskrantz. New York: Oxford University Press.

Gould, Stephen J. 1980. *The Panda's Thumb*. New York: Norton.

Grant, S., C. Contoreggi, and E. D. London. 2000. "Drug Abusers Show Impaired Performance in a Laboratory Test of Decision Making." *Neuropsychologia* 38: 1180–87.

Gray, J. A. 1987. "The Neuropsychology of Emotion and Personality." In *Cognitive Neurochemistry*, edited by S. M. Stahl, S. D. Iverson, and E. C. Goodman. Oxford: Oxford University Press.

Higley, J. D., and A. J. Bennett. 1999. "Central Nervous System Serotonin and Personality as Variables Contributing to Excessive Alcohol Consumption in Non-Human Primates." *Alcohol and Alcoholism* 34: 402–18.

Higley, J. D., P. T. Mehlman, S. B. Higley, B. Fernald, J. Vickers, S. G. Lindell, D. M. Taub, S. J. Suomi, and M. Linnoila. 1996. "Excessive Mortality in Young Free-Ranging Male Nonhuman Primates with Low Cerebrospinal Fluid 5-Hydroxyindoleacetic Acid Concentrations." *Archives of General Psychiatry* 53: 537–42.

Higley, J. D., P. T. Mehlman, R. E. Poland, D. M. Taub, J. Vickers, S. J. Suomi, and M. Linnoila. 1997. "CSF Testosterone and 5-HIAA Correlate with Different Types of Aggressive Behaviors." *Biological Psychiatry* 40(11): 1067–82.
Higley, J. D., P. T. Mehlman, D. M. Taub, S. B. Higley, S. J. Suomi, M. Linnoila, and J. H. Vickers. 1992. "Cerebrospinal Fluid Monoamine and Adrenal Correlates of Aggression in Free-Ranging Rhesus Monkeys." *Archives of General Psychiatry* 49: 436–41.
Higley, J. D., S. J. Suomi, and M. Linnoila. 1996. "A Nonhuman Primate Model of Type II Excessive Alcohol Consumption? Part 1. Low Cerebrospinal Fluid 5-Hydroxyindoleacetic Acid Concentrations and Diminished Social Competence Correlate with Excessive Alcohol Consumption." *Alcohol: Clinical and Experimental Research* 20: 629–42.
Higley, J. D., W. W. Thompson, M. Champous, D. Goldman, M. F. Hasert, G.-W. Draemer, J. M. Scanlan, S. J. Suomi, and M. Linnoila. 1993. "Paternal and Maternal Genetic and Environmental Contributes to Cerebrospinal Fluid Monoamine Metabolites in Rhesus Monkeys (*Macaca Mullata*)." *Archives of General Psychiatry* 50: 615–23.
Ho, M.-Y., S. Mobini, T.-J. Chiang, C. M. Bradshaw, and E. Szabadi. 1999. "Theory and Method in the Quantitative Analysis of 'Impulsive Choice' Behaviour: Implications for Psychopharmacology." *Psychopharmacology* 146(4): 362–72.
Hollander, Eric, Concetta M. DeCaria, Jared N. Finkell, Tomer Begaz, Cheryl M. Wong, and Charles Cartwright. 2000. "A Randomized Double-Blind Fluvoxamine/Placebo Crossover Trial in Pathologic Gambling." *Biological Psychiatry* 47(9): 813–17.
Huxley, Thomas H. 1863. *Evidence as to Man's Place in Nature.* New York: Appleton.
Jamison, Kay Redfield. 1999. *Night Falls Fast: Understanding Suicide.* New York: Knopf.
Kaplan, J. R., M. B. Fontenot, J. Berard, S. B. Manuck, and J. J. Mann. 1995. "Delayed Dispersal and Elevated Monoaminergic Activity in Free-Ranging Rhesus Monkeys." *American Journal of Primatology* 35: 229–34.
Kruessi, M. J. P., J. L. Rapoport, S. Hamburger, E. Hibbs, W. Z. Potter, M. Lenane, and G. L. Brown. 1990. "Cerebrospinal Fluid Monoamine Metabolites, Aggression, and Impulsivity in Disruptive Behavior Disorders of Children and Adolescents." *Archives of General Psychiatry* 47: 419–26.
LeDoux, Joseph. 2002. *Synaptic Self.* New York: Viking.
LeMarquand, D., R. O. Pihl, and C. Benkelfat. 1994. "Serotonin and Alcohol Intake, Abuse, and Dependence." *Biological Psychiatry* 36: 326–37.
Lester, D. 1995. "The Concentration of Neurotransmitter Metabolites in the Cerebrospinal Fluid of Suicidal Individuals: A Meta-Analysis." *Pharmacopsychiatry* 28: 45–50.
Linnoila, M., M. Virkkunen, M. Scheinin, A. Nuutila, R. Pimon, and F. K. Goodwin. 1983. "Low Cerebrospinal Fluid 5-Hydroxyindoleacetic Acid Concentration Differentiates Impulsive from Nonimpulsive Violent Behavior." *Life Sciences* 33: 2609–14.
Loewenstein, George, and Jon Elster, eds. 1992. *Choice Over Time.* New York: Russell Sage Foundation.

Logue, A. W. 1988. "Research on Self-Control: An Integrating Framework." *Behavioral and Brain Sciences* 11: 665–79.

——. 1995. *Self-Control*. Upper Saddle River, N.J.: Prentice Hall.

Macmillan, Malcolm. 1992. "Inhibition and the Control of Behavior: From Gall to Freud via Phineas Gage and the Frontal Lobes." *Brain and Cognition* 19: 72–104.

——. 2000. *An Odd Kind of Fame*. Cambridge, Mass.: MIT Press.

Mann, J. J. 1998. "The Neurobiology of Suicide." *Nature Medicine* 4: 25–30.

Mann, J. J., P. A. McBride, K. M. Malone, M. D. DeMeo, and J. Keilp. 1995. "Blunted Serotonergic Responsivity in Depressed Patients." *Neuropsychopharmacology* 13: 53–64.

Mann, J. J., C. Waternaux, G. L. Haas, and K. M. Malone. 1999. "Toward a Clinical Model of Suicidal Behavior in Psychiatric Patients." *American Journal of Psychiatry* 156: 181–89.

Manor, I., S. Tyano, E. Mel, J. Eisenberg, R. Bachner-Melman, M. Kotler, and R. P. Ebstein. 2002. "Family-Based and Association Studies of Monoamine Oxidase A and Attention Deficit Hyperactivity Disorder (ADHD): Preferential Transmission of the Long Promoter-Region Repeat and Its Association with Impaired Performance on a Continuous Performance Test (TOVA)." *Molecular Psychiatry* 7: 626–32.

Manuck, S. B., J. D. Flory, R. E. Ferrell, J. J. Mann, and M. F. Muldoon. 2000. "A Regulatory Polymorphism of the Monoamine Oxidase-A Gene May Be Associated with Variability in Aggression, Impulsivity, and Central Nervous System Serotonergic Responsivity. *Psychiatry Research* 95: 9–23.

Manuck, S. B., J. D. Flory, J. M. McCaffery, K. A. Matthews, J. J. Mann, and M. F. Muldoon. 1998. "Aggression, Impulsivity, and Central Nervous System Serotonergic Responsivity in a Nonpatient Sample." *Neuropsychopharmacology* 19(4): 287–99.

Matthews, K. A., J. D. Flory, M. F. Muldoon, and S. B. Manuck. 2000. "Does Socioeconomic Status Relate to Central Serotonergic Responsivity in Healthy Adults?" *Psychosomatic Medicine* 62: 231–37.

Mazur, J. E. 1987. "An Adjusting Procedure for Studying Delayed Reinforcement." In *Quantitative Analyses of Behavior*. Vol. 5. *The Effects of Delay and of Intervening Events on Reinforcement Value*, edited by M. L. Commons, J. E. Mazur, J. A. Nevin, and H. Rachlin (55–73). Mahwah, N.J.: Erlbaum.

Mehlman, P. T., J. D. Higley, I. Faucher, A. A. Lilly, D. M. Taub, J. Vickers, S. J. Suomi, and M. Linnoila. 1994. "Low CSF 5-HIAA Concentrations and Severe Aggression and Impaired Impulse Control in Nonhuman Primates." *American Journal of Psychiatry* 151: 1485–91.

——. 1995. "Correlation of CSF 5-HIAA Concentration with Sociality and the Timing of Emigration in Free-Ranging Primates." *American Journal of Psychiatry* 152: 907–13.

Micallef, Joelle, and Olivier Blin. 2001. "Neurobiology and Clinical Pharmacology of Obsessive-Compulsive Disorder." *Clinical Neuropharmacology* 24(4): 191–207.

Miller, Geoffrey F. 2000. *The Mating Mind*. New York: Doubleday.

Mischel, Walter, Yuichi Shoda, and M. L. Rodriguez. 1989. "Delay of Gratification in Children." *Science* 244: 933–38.

Mobini, Sirous, S. Body, M.-Y. Ho, C. M. Bradshaw, E. Szabadi, J. F. W. Deakin, and I. M. Anderson. 2002. "Effects of Lesions in the Orbitofrontal Cortex on Sensitivity to Delayed and Probabilistic Reinforcement." *Psychopharmacology* 160: 290–98.

Mobini, Sirous, T.-J. Chiang, A. S. A. Al-Ruwaitea, M.-Y. Ho, C. M. Bradshaw, and E. Szabadi. 2000a. "Effect of Central 5-Hydroxytryptamine Depletion on Inter-Temporal Choice: A Quantitative Analysis." *Psychopharmacology* 149: 313–18.

Mobini, Sirous, T.-J. Chiang, M.-Y. Ho, C. M. Bradshaw, and E. Szabadi. 2000b. "Effects of Central 5-Hydroxytryptamine Depletion on Sensitivity to Delayed and Probabilistic Reinforcement." *Psychopharmacology* 152(4): 390–97.

Newman, J. P., E. E. Gorenstein, and J. E. Kelsey. 1983. "Failure to Delay Gratification Following Septal Lesions in Rats: Implications for an Animal Model of Disinhibitory Psychopathology." *Personality and Individual Differences* 4: 147–56.

Parsons, L. H., and J. B. Justice. 1993. "Perfusate Serotonin Increases Extracellular Dopamine in the Nucleus Accumbans of the Rat as Measured by In Vivo Microdialysis." *Brain Research* 606: 195–99.

Pedersen, N. L., R. Plomin, G. E. McClearn, and L. Friberg. 1988. "Neuroticism, Extraversion, and Related Traits in Adult Twins Reared Apart and Reared Together." *Journal of Personality and Social Psychology* 55: 950–57.

Petry, Nancy, Warren K. Bickel, and Martha Arnett. 1998. "Shortened Time Horizons and Insensitivity to Future Consequences in Heroin Addicts." *Addiction* 93(5): 729–38.

Poulos, C. X., J. L. Parker, and A. D. Le. 1996. "Dexfenfluramine and 8-OH-DPAT Modulate Impulsivity in a Delay-of-Reward Paradigm: Implications for a Correspondence with Alcohol Consumption." *Behavioural Pharmacology* 7: 395–99.

Pribram, K. H. 1998. "A Century of Progress?" *Annals of the New York Academy of Sciences* 843: 11–19.

Richards, J. D., S. H. Mitchell, H. de Wit, and L. S. Seiden. 1997. "Determination of Discount Functions with an Adjusting Amount Procedure in Rats." *Journal of the Experimental Analysis of Behavior* 67: 353–66.

Richards, J. D., K. E. Sabol, and H. de Wit. 1999. "Effects of Methamphetamine on the Adjusting Amount Procedure: A Model of Impulsive Behavior in Rats." *Psychopharmacology* 146(4): 432–39.

Roberts, A. C., T. W. Robbins, and L. Weiskrantz. 1998. *The Prefrontal Cortex.* New York: Oxford University Press.

Rogers, R. D., B. J. Everitt, A. Baldacchino, A. J. Blackshaw, R. Swainson, K. Wynne, N. B. Baker, J. Hunter, T. Carthy, E. Booker, M. London, J. F. W. Deakin, B. J. Ahakian, and T. W. Robbins. 1999. "Dissociable Deficits in the Decision-Making Cognition of Chronic Amphetamine Abusers, Opiate Abusers, Patients with Focal Damage to Prefrontal Cortex, and Tryptophan-Depleted Normal Volunteers: Evidence for Monoaminergic Mechanisms." *Neuropsychopharmacology* 20(4): 323–39.

Sabol, S. Z., S. Hu, and D. Hamer. 1998. "A Functional Polymorphism in the Monoamine Oxidase A Gene Promoter." *Human Genetics* 103: 273–79.

Schweitzer, J. B., and Beth Sulzer-Azaroff. 1995. "Self-Control in Boys with Attention Deficit Hyperactivity Disorder: Effects of Added Stimulation and Time." *Journal of Child Psychology and Psychiatry* 36: 671–86.

Secord, James A. 2000. *Victorian Sensation*. Chicago: University of Chicago Press.

Serocynski, A. L., C. S. Bergeman, and E. F. Coccaro. 1999. "Etiology of the Impulsivity/Aggression Relationship: Genes or Environment?" *Psychiatry Research* 86: 41–57.

Shallice, Tim, and Paul Burgess. 1998. "The Domain of Supervisory Processes and the Temporal Organization of Behavior." In *The Prefrontal Cortex*, edited by A. C. Roberts, T. W. Robbins, and L. Weiskrantz. New York: Oxford University Press.

Shimamura, A. P. 1995. "Memory and Frontal Lobe Function." In *The Cognitive Neurosciences*, edited by M. S. Gazzaniga. Cambridge, Mass.: MIT Press.

Soubrie, P. 1986. "Reconciling the Role of Central Serotonin Neurons in Human and Animal Behavior." *Behavioral and Brain Sciences* 9: 319–64.

Spoont, M. R. 1992. "Modulatory Role of Serotonin in Neural Information Processing: Implications for Human Psychopathology." *Psychological Bulletin* 112: 330–50.

Thiebot, M.-H., C. Le Bihan, P. Soubrie, and P. Simon. 1985. "Benzodiazepines Reduce the Tolerance to Research Delay in Rats." *Psychopharmacology* 86: 147–52.

Virkkunen, M. R. Rawlings, R. Rokola, R. E. Poland, A. Guidotti, C. Nemeroff, G. Bissette, K. Kalogeras, S.-L. Laronen, and M. Linnoila. 1994. "CSF Biochemistries, Glucose Metabolism, and Diurnal Activity Rhythms in Alcoholic, Violence Offenders, Fire Setters, and Health Volunteers." *Archives of General Psychiatry* 51: 20–27.

Wade, T. R., H. de Wit, and J. B. Richards. 2000. "Effects of Dopaminergic Drugs on Delayed Reward as a Measure of Impulsive Behavior in Rats." *Psychopharmacology* 150: 90–101.

Wallace, Alfred Russel. 1889. *Darwinism*. London: Macmillan.

Wise, R. A. 1996. "Addictive Drugs and Brain Stimulation Reward." *Annual Review of Neuroscience* 19: 319–40.

Wogar, M. A., C. M. Bradshaw, and E. Szabadi. 1993. "Effect of Lesions of the Ascending 5-Hydroxytryptaminergic Pathways on Choice Between Delayed Reinforcers." *Psychopharmacology* 111: 239–43.

Zuckerman, M. 1995. "Good and Bad Humors: Biochemical Bases of Personality and Its Disorders." *Psychological Science* 6: 325–32.

PART II

Theoretical Perspectives

· 5 ·

Sustaining Delay of Gratification over Time: A Hot-Cool Systems Perspective

WALTER MISCHEL, OZLEM AYDUK, AND
RODOLFO MENDOZA-DENTON

T HE DIETER'S decision to forgo the pizza, the smoker's vow never to light another cigarette, and the compulsive shopper's resolution to steer clear of the latest sale all too often turn out to be choices and commitments that soon turn into failed good intentions. Successful implementation of initial choices to delay immediate gratification for the sake of delayed but larger benefits requires not only making the initial choice, but also maintaining that choice in the face of the temptations and obstacles encountered along the route. In this sense, turning good intentions into willpower requires a continuous choice to defer immediate gratification until the long-term goal is actually attained.

Our goal in this chapter is to demystify and elucidate the psychological mechanisms that operate in long-term goal commitment and pursuit of temporally delayed but valued outcomes or goals (see also Mischel et al. 1996). Many of the insights into these mechanisms—the dynamics of "willpower"—come from research on children's ability to delay gratification (Mischel 1974; Mischel, Shoda, and Rodriguez

1989). The early phases of this research focused on differences among children in their willingness to choose more valuable but delayed rewards over less valuable but immediately available ones. The emphasis thus was on the *motivational* factors influencing people's initial choice to delay gratification. In a nutshell, this work revealed that the initial choice to wait for a larger but delayed reward is determined predominantly by an expectancy-value mechanism. First, the incentive value of the delayed rewards must be sufficiently high for the individual to be motivated to prefer it to an immediately available reward. Second, there must be a reasonable level of expectation that the delayed reward can be attained upon waiting. This expectation in turn depends on the level of trust the individual has in the agents or in the system who will deliver the delayed rewards as well as in his or her own efficacy in being able to meet the requirements for success. We begin this chapter with a brief summary of these factors.

Our primary concern for most of the chapter, however, will be on those later studies addressing the issue of successful goal pursuit after the initial choice to delay gratification has been made. Thus the focus will be on whether children have the actual *competency* to utilize strategies that will help sustain their initial choice until the long-term goal is successfully attained. Using findings from the classic preschool delay of gratification paradigm (Mischel, Shoda, and Rodriguez 1989), we discuss the cognitive and attentional mechanisms that underlie the ability to sustain delay behavior to attain a more valued but delayed outcome—without reversing the initial choice. Discussion here is guided by a framework that casts these mechanisms in terms of the interaction between two systems: a hot, impulsive, "go" system and a cool, cognitive, "know" system (Metcalfe and Mischel 1999).

Finally, we show with relevant research findings that similar mechanisms also operate to enable delay of gratification in social, interpersonal contexts. Specifically, we focus on examples in which desired but temporally distant goals (for example, long-term interpersonal relationship maintenance and enhancement) require inhibition of impulsive reactions (such as anger-aggression or withdrawal in defensive responses under momentary pressure or threat).

Understanding Initial Choice: The Role of Motivation in Goal Commitment

Early studies examined differences among people in their preferences for valuable but delayed rewards over less valuable but immediately available ones—for example, their decision to take one dollar today rather than to get a dollar and fifty cents tomorrow. In studies conducted with children on the island of Trinidad, for example, sizable differences in choice behavior were initially found between blacks and East Indians, with East Indian participants often preferring the delayed reward and black participants preferring the immediate reward (Mischel 1961). The differences between these groups, however, disappeared when statistically controlling for the effect of father absence. That is, those children coming from homes with absent fathers were likely to have fewer experiences where male social agents kept their promises to provide future rewards; subsequently, these same children showed less trust or lower expectancy to receive rewards promised by a male experimenter following time delay. These findings illustrate how *outcome expectations*—that future delayed rewards for which one would have to work or wait would actually materialize—can be of particular importance for initial choice (Mischel 1974). Such expectations, of course, are closely related to whether one believes that one can control the allocation of rewards. The effect of *control beliefs* in goal commitment at the societal level was clearly observed on the island of Trinidad (for example, Mischel 1958). Whereas the islanders did not save money in conventional ways (for example, savings in banks with colonial heritages) because they did not believe there would be fair resource allocation by the colonialists, they did save carefully, however, for yearly festivals over which they could exert more control.

When the attainment of delayed gratification requires one to reach particular achievement levels, then the willingness to work and wait for these outcomes also hinges on expectations that one *will be able* to adequately fulfill the necessary contingencies. Thus, another factor related to choice preferences is individuals' *self-efficacy beliefs* (Bandura 1986; Mischel, Cantor, and Feldman 1996). To illustrate, Mischel and Staub (1965) gave adolescent participants bogus success or failure feedback for their performance on a series of verbal reasoning problems. Then the participants had to make many choices, including one between a highly valued reward contingent on their successful performance on a similar reasoning task and a less preferred but noncontingent reward. As expected, individuals for whom success expectations had been situationally primed (through false positive feedback for their performance on a set of verbal tasks) chose much more often to work for the contingent-preferred reward than did those who were primed with failure. In a control group where participants were given no performance feedback, chronic, preexperimental success expectancies were a significant determinant of people's choice to work for contingent rewards.

The motivation to forgo immediate gratification depends not only on outcome expectations and self-efficacy expectations, but also on the *subjective value* of a delayed reward. The subjective value of rewards depends on both its magnitude and the amount of time before it becomes available. For example, Mischel and Metzner (1962) showed experimentally the effects of *delay interval* on the initial choice, indicating that the longer the future rewards were delayed, the less willing children were to wait for them. Through temporal discounting, rewards that are delayed have less value than equivalent rewards available immediately (Ainslie 1992). The choice to delay increases with the relative magnitude of the delayed reward and decreases with the required time for its attainment (Mischel 1966, 1974).

In summary, then, the initial choice for delayed but more valued rewards reflects individuals' motivation to pursue this long-term goal (Mischel and Ayduk 2002). Such goal commitment is determined at least in part by an individual's beliefs about the trustworthiness of the sources who hold access to future rewards, expectations about one's own capacity to successfully attain those future outcomes, and the subjective value of the delayed reward in comparison to immediately available rewards.

Processes Involved in Goal Pursuit: Fulfilling the Preliminaries

Beyond initial choice, a second aspect of successful self-regulation involves the ability to *sustain* the delay over time so that the individual actually attains the selected but deferred outcome, without reversing the initial choice. James (1981 [1890], 486) foreshadowed the relationship between goal commitment and goal pursuit over a century ago.

> Desire, wish, will are states of mind which everyone knows and which no definition can make plainer. . . . If with the desire there goes a sense that attainment is not possible we simply *wish*; but if we believe the end is in our power, we *will* that the desired feeling, having, or doing shall be real . . . and real it presently becomes, either immediately upon the willing or after certain preliminaries have been fulfilled.

Differentiating *wish* from *will*, James not only recognized the significance of self-efficacy and control expectations reviewed earlier, but also stressed that often we can realize our intentions in the pursuit of difficult goals and outcomes only after having fulfilled certain "preliminaries." The next section focuses on demystifying these preliminaries, stressing the link between cognitive-affective mechanisms and voluntary delay behavior during the actual waiting period.

Insights into these preliminaries have come from research on the preschool delay paradigm, in which young children wait for two cookies (or other little treats) that the children want and have chosen to get. They are faced with this dilemma: they can continue to wait for the treats until the experimenter comes back on his or her own, or they are free to ring a little bell to summon the adult at any time. The contingency, however, is such that if they ring the bell they can have one cookie right away but they will not get their two cookies later. The situation thus is constructed to create a strong conflict between the temptation to stop the delay and take the immediately available smaller reward or to continue waiting for the children's original, larger, more preferred choice albeit not knowing how long the wait will be. After children understand the situation, they are left alone in the room until they signal. To reiterate, the child has a continuous free choice, and can resolve the conflict about whether or not to stop at any time by ringing the bell, which instantly brings back the adult. If they continue to wait, the adult returns spontaneously (after a maximum of twenty minutes).

Although this situation may seem trivial from an adult perspective, it has been shown to be compelling for the young child and indeed highly diagnostic of conceptually relevant long-term outcomes, such as self-control and self-regulation in goal pursuit decades later in adulthood. For example, the number of seconds children can wait in certain diagnostic situations (that is, when no regulatory strategies are provided by the experimenter and children have to access their own competencies) predict higher SAT scores as well as better personal and interpersonal competencies years later (for example, Mischel, Shoda, and Peake 1988; Shoda, Mischel, and Peake 1990). Remarkably, these positive correlations between seconds of preschool delay time and positive life outcomes in diverse social and cognitive domains persist into adulthood (Ayduk et al. 2000). Given the existence and psychological importance of these individual differences as tapped in this situation, the question becomes: What is happening psychologically that makes some children ring soon and others wait for what seems an eternity?

Hot-Cool Model: The Interface Between Affect and Cognition

Recently, Metcalfe and Mischel (1999) have proposed two interacting systems—a cognitive "cool" system and an emotional "hot" system—to understand and help account for the dynamics of self-regulation in general and of delay of gratification in particular. This hot-cool model, the essentials of which are summarized here, guides much of the following discussion. The novelty of the model is that it tries to integrate research on self-regulation that emerged from different research traditions at different levels of analysis. Specifically, the model bridges social psychological perspectives with its focus on social-cognitive processes and individual differences in self-regulation with cognitive approaches examining attentional processes, memory, and information-processing mechanisms. This model also links with recent developments in cognitive-neuroscience focusing on the brain mechanisms that affect self-regulation.

Metcalfe and Mischel (1999) cast this model, at least as a metaphor, at the level of a parallel-processing neural network, and use the basic principles of connectionist systems in their conceptualization (for example, Anderson 1983; Rumelhart and McClelland 1986; Read and Miller 1998). Briefly, in connectionist systems concepts are represented as *nodes* that are related to each other through *links*. Links designate the relation between any two nodes, which differ in strength as a function of the frequency of previous activation and which can be either excitatory or inhibitory. Information processing works through spreading activation—that is, activation at each initial concept spreads through the links to the other related concepts, and from them to those concepts related to them, and so on.

Within this general framework, Metcalfe and Mischel (1999) propose primarily two kinds of representations—one cognitive and the other affective, controlled by two different subsystems. The cool system is an emotionally neutral, *know* system: cognitive, complex, slow, and contemplative. Attuned to the informational, cognitive, and spatial aspects of stimuli, the cool system consists of a network of informational, *cool nodes* elaborately interconnected to each other and that generates rational, reflective, strategic, and planful behavior. Its activation increases with age but is attenuated under high stress levels, whether acute or chronic. The cool system is thought to be associated with hippocampal and frontal lobe processing (Metcalfe and Mischel 1999; also see Manuck et al., chap. 4 herein), two structures of the brain that begin to develop around the age of four—which is also roughly when young children begin to be able to delay gratification.

The hot system, in contrast, is a *go* system, specialized for quick, emotional processing. It is simple and fast, consisting of relatively few representations or *hot spots* (that is, feeling fragments) that when activated trigger virtually reflexive approach (for example, consummatory) or avoidance (for example, fight or flight) reactions. The hot system develops early in life and is most dominant in the young infant. Contemporary neural models of information processing suggest that the amygdala—a small, almond-shaped region in the forebrain thought to enable fight or flight responses—may be the bed of hot system processing (Gray 1982, 1987; LeDoux 1996; Metcalfe and Jacobs 1996, 1998).

Individual differences in starting levels of activation in both systems in part reflect biological predispositions, which influence chronic accessibility of specific constructs. Yet the hot system is also heavily influenced by learning, whereby environmental contingencies lead to "changes in the chronic activation levels of nodes, in the transition probabilities among nodes, and in the probability and speed of responses" (Metcalfe and Mischel 1999, 7). New hot spots also develop through learning when initially neutral stimuli become associated with biologically significant triggers. Similarly, increasing interconnections in the cool system may result in the development of new informational nodes. Thus biological predispositions, maturation, and learning all interact to affect the development of both the impulsive hot and the regulatory cool systems.

Interactions Between the Hot and Cool Systems

The study of the affect-cognition interface in human behavior has a long history in psychology (James 1981 [1890]; Lange 1967 [1885]). At the turn of the century, James and Lange suggested that phenomenological experience of emotion was preceded by cognitive perceptions of one's reactions. Later appraisal theories of emotion, however, argued that for emotion to be felt, there needed to be first a generalized affective arousal state but that the emotional impact of this generalized arousal state depended on the cognitive interpretation of the context (Schachter and Singer 1962; also see Lazarus 1993). Two controversial points dominate much current debate surrounding the conceptualization of cognition-emotion interactions. One comes from recent findings in cognitive-neuroscience research suggesting that different emotions may have distinct neurological activation patterns that are at least partly independent of cognitive appraisal (see Ekman and Davidson 1994). The second controversy questions the idea of a single serial process (irrespective of whether affect precedes cognition or vice versa) and raises the possibility that cognition and affect operate in a continuously interactive sequence (see Ellsworth 1991, 1994).

From the perspective of the hot-cool model, the common denominator of these different approaches is the notion of a complicated interplay between cognition and affect, even though our knowledge of the exact nature of this interaction is still rudimentary. Building on this basic idea and consistent with a parallel-processing neural network metaphor, the hot-cool model assumes that cognition and affect operate in a continuous interaction with one another in producing phenomenological experiences as well as behavioral responses. Specifically, the model argues that hot spots and cool nodes that have the same external referent are directly connected to one another, and thus link the two systems (Metcalfe and Mischel 1999; see also Metcalfe and Jacobs, 1996, 1998). Hot spots can be evoked by activation of corresponding cool nodes; alternately, hot representations can be cooled through intersystem connections to the corresponding cool nodes. Consequential for self-control are the conditions under which hot spots do not have, or cannot access, corresponding cool representations, because under these conditions cool system regulation of hot impulses is expected to be radically impaired or nonexistent. One basic factor that affects the balance between hot and cool systems is the developmental phase of the organism due to the developmental lag between the two systems: the hot system is well developed at birth, whereas the cool system develops with age. Thus the young child is responsive primarily to the urgencies of internally activated hot spots and the pushes and pulls of hot stimuli in the external world, as many of the hot spots do not have corresponding cool nodes that can regulate and inhibit hot system processing.

A second important factor is stress, because it affects the two systems differently. Whereas the activation of the hot system increases as stress levels increase, the relationship between stress and the level of cool system activation is curvilinear: it increases at moderate levels but shuts off under high levels of stress. Under relatively low levels of stress, then, the cool system can modulate and restrict the reactivity of the hot system through interconnections between hot spots and cool nodes. Metcalfe and Mischel (1999, 13) propose that "the cross-system interconnections, along with selective activation of the relevant cool nodes, enable the individual to divert activation away from the hot system and its attendant immediate action by engaging instead, automatically as well as strategically and purposefully, in cool thinking." Under high arousal, however, hot system processing is likely to dominate cool system mediational processes. Since stress and hot system activation are likely to feed into each other (that is, stress potentiates the hot system and hot system activation in turn increases negative arousal), effective self-regulation in stressful situations may hinge on preventing escalation of emotional arousal in the first place and attenuating hot system activation.

This conceptualization is also consistent with Loewenstein's (1996) account of self-regulatory failure in behavioral economics. He argues that visceral influences—drive states associated with biologically significant functions such as hunger, sex, and fear and that conceptually correspond to the hot system in the hot-cool systems model—lead to impulsive behavior, especially at high levels of intensity. That is, when the individual is in a high-arousal affective state, that person acts in accordance with a short-term goal to fulfill or avoid these states, which more often than not is in conflict with and undermines one's long-term goals.

Hot-Cool Analyses of Delay of Gratification

The hot-cool model provides a heuristic framework for understanding intertemporal choice, as the hot system works on a here-and-now principle relying mostly on biologically significant affective triggers, and the cool system's hallmark is deliberation and planning that involve a long-term perspective. The hot-cool framework allows an analysis of the processes that work for or against successful exertion of willpower in the context of the delay studies, and predicts those findings on theoretical grounds.

Effects of Attention to Rewards   Almost a century ago Freud (1959 [1911]) theorized that the ability to endure delay of gratification begins to develop when the young child comes to construct a "hallucinatory wish-fulfilling image" of the delayed object. According to Freud, this mental image or representation of the object of desire (for example, the maternal breast) enables the child to "bind time" and ultimately sustain delay of gratification volitionally. In this view, delay behavior should be facilitated by cues that make the delayed rewards more salient and psychologically vivid or immediate. Learning psychologists made similar predictions, albeit for different reasons (see Mischel 1974). Studies with animals suggested that in learning, behavior toward a goal may be maintained by "fractional anticipatory goal responses" that essentially cognitively represent the desired rewards and sustain goal pursuit—for example, as the animal in a learning task tries to find its way back to the food at the end of a maze. In this sense, anticipation and self-instructions through which the delayed rewards are made salient should sustain delay behavior in pursuit of those rewards. Thus, together, these views suggest that focusing attention on the delayed rewards should make it easier to sustain delay of gratification.

To explore this hypothesis, a series of experimental studies varied whether or not the reward objects in the choice were available for attention while the children were waiting (Mischel and Ebbesen 1970). In one condition, children waited with the rewards, both immediate and delayed, in full view. In a second condition, both options also were present but obscured from sight (placed under an opaque cover rather than on top of it). In two other conditions, either the delayed rewards only or the immediately available one only was exposed during the delay period. On average, the children waited more than eleven minutes when none of the rewards was exposed, but they waited only a few minutes when any of them were exposed during delay.

These results were the opposite of those initially anticipated by the psychodynamic and animal learning traditions, but are compatible with the hot-cool model. Namely, when the rewards are in full view, the salience of the rewards makes the consummatory representations of the rewards more accessible, activating the hot system and triggering the reflexive response to ring the bell and get the immediately available treats. When the rewards are obscured from sight, however, the eliciting power of the hot stimulus is diminished and the delay task becomes less difficult and frustrating, enabling children to wait for longer periods of time. Thus, preventing the activation of the hot spots and the hot system is one of the routes toward willpower in the delay of gratification situation.

The Role of Distraction   The pull of the hot stimulus in the delay situation also can be reduced by shifting attention away from the tempting rewards. This can be done through either external (for example, a toy to play with for the child in the delay situation) or self-generated distraction. In one experiment, for example (Mischel, Ebbesen, and Zeiss 1972), children were provided with a distracting toy (Slinky) while the rewards were exposed. More than half of the children in this condition were able to wait up to the criterion period (fifteen minutes), whereas none of the children who were left waiting for the exposed rewards without the distracting toy were able to do so. Self-generated cognitive distractions, however, can serve to enhance control by attenuating the power of the hot stimulus as effectively as externally provided distraction. In a study that tested for this (Mischel, Ebbesen, and Zeiss 1972), children were primed to think about fun thoughts while they waited as follows: "while you're waiting, if you want to, you can think of mommy pushing you on a swing at a birthday party." As in the Slinky condition, more than half of the children cued to distract themselves with fun thoughts waited for the whole fifteen minutes. In contrast, children who were cued to distract by thinking about negative thoughts (for example, minor accidents in which they were hurt) were unable to delay past a few minutes.

As these experiments demonstrate, the effectiveness of distraction depends on how involving it is for shifting attention away from the hot, tempting stimulus. In other words, Slinky toys and fun thoughts are effective because they successfully draw attention away from the rewards without undue effort. When the distracting object is itself intriguing, it has an even greater effect on diverting activation away from the relevant hot spot (Metcalfe and Mischel 1999; also see Peake, Hebl, and Mischel 2002). Slinky toys and fun thoughts in many ways are themselves hot, and their effectiveness may lie in that they divert attention from the relevant hot spot by activating *irrelevant* hot nodes. Ideation about such hot stimuli may provide particularly powerful distractions—vivid fantasies—capturing children's attention and in-advertently facilitating goal-directed delay. In one test of this idea, when children waiting for marshmallows were cued to think about the crunchy and salty taste of pretzels, they were able to wait for the delayed rewards (in this case, marshmallows) for almost seventeen minutes on average (Mischel and Baker 1975).

From Distraction to Abstraction: Alternative Representations of the Rewards   The idea that two types of representation exist—one fundamentally emotional and reactive and the other essentially cognitive and deliberative—also has a long history both of research and explanatory metaphors. Such a history is seen, for example, in the distinction made between the motivational (consummatory, arousal, action-oriented) and informational (cognitive cue) functions of a stimulus (Berlyne 1960; Estes 1972). In an arousing representation, the focus is on the motivating, hot qualities of the stimulus (for example, the chewy quality of the marshmallows, the crunchiness of the pretzels) that activate the relevant hot spots and elicit completion of the action sequence associated with them. In a cool representation, however, the focus is on the more abstract, cognitive, informational aspects of the stimulus, which are contained in the cool nodes. The hot-cool analysis predicts that the meaning of a hot stimulus can be transformed from hot to cool by activating the cool nodes associated with an object, leading to the inhibition of the impulsive behavior tendencies that otherwise would be activated by the hot spots. This reconstrued meaning can be accomplished externally, by presenting the cool rather than the hot features of the stimulus, as when a picture of the object rather than the actual object is shown. To illustrate, in one study (Mischel and Moore 1973), most children who saw images of rewards for which they were waiting (shown life-size and realistically on slides) waited for fifteen minutes until they obtained the delayed reward. Yet those exposed to actual rewards were able to wait less than a few minutes.

The hot-cool framework suggests that a pictorial representation of the desired object enhances control efforts by activating the cool nodes associated with the object rather than hot spots. More specifically, the pictorial representation of a marshmallow makes salient cool information such as figure-ground relations, the knowledge that the representation is a depiction of a marshmallow, and the two-dimensional quality of the picture itself. The actual object, however, connects directly to the object's hot spots, including the sensations of it's taste and smell. Owing to these direct connections, the treats themselves are more likely to trigger the *go* response associated with the hot system than the object's pictorial representation. In the words of one child participant, "you can't eat the picture" (Metcalfe and Mischel 1999).

As with distraction, though, individuals need not rely exclusively on changing the external world to help them in a self-regulatory task. In a study by Moore, Mischel, and Zeiss (1976), children looking at the real objects were instructed, "If you want to, when you want to, you can pretend they [the pretzels] are not real, but just pictures, just put a frame around them in your head, like in a picture." Other children saw the picture of the rewards but were cued to think about the objects as if they were real: "In your head, you can make believe they're really there in front of you, just make believe they're there." As expected, thinking about the rewards as real made delay much more difficult, while thinking about them as pictures made it easy, regardless of what was actually in front of the child. Children facing pictures delayed almost eighteen minutes, but when they pretended that the real rewards—rather than the pictures—were in front of them, they waited less than six minutes. Even when they faced real rewards, the children could wait almost eighteen minutes by imagining that they were pictures. In sum, these studies suggest that cognitive control also should be increased by *self-generated* cool ideation about the hot stimulus—that is, by mentally turning a real treat into "just a picture."

Further direct support for effect of hot versus cool representations comes from a study (Mischel and Baker 1975) in which children were cued to think of the exposed rewards either in terms of their hot, consummatory features (for example, the sweet, chewy taste of marshmallows the crunchy, salty taste of pretzels) or their cool, cognitive features (for example, marshmallows as round and puffy clouds; pretzels as long, brown logs). When encouraged to focus on the cool qualities of the rewards in the choice situation, children waited an average of more than thirteen minutes. Yet when thinking hot about the rewards, children were able to wait for only five minutes on average.

Delay of Gratification Across Species   The mechanisms that underlie delay of gratification behavior across species have been studied most extensively in pigeons, but also in rats, and point to interesting cross-species parallels (for example, Grosch and Neuringer 1981; Siegel and Rachlin 1995). For example, it has been established that the absence versus presence of rewards and availability of distractions for attention during the delay task affect pigeons' delay of gratification behavior in the same manner that they do the human child's. This cross-species generalizability suggests that the hot and cool strategies studied under the Mischel paradigm may constitute basic, fundamental mechanisms that govern self-control. Likewise, research with animals underlies, and is consistent with, the idea that similar specific brain areas are the locus for hot and cool system activation in humans (for example, LeDoux 1996).

Effects of Age on Delay Ability   Age and stress are two of the most important factors likely to determine whether the hot or cool system will be dominating processes of self-regulation. At birth, the hot system is thought to be already well developed, with the cool system having only limited cool nodes and with very sparse within-system (that is, cool ←→ cool) as well as cross-system (that is, cool ←→ hot) connections, thus allowing hot system processing to dominate the still minimal cool system in early childhood. With age and maturity, however, the cool system becomes elaborated: many more cool nodes get developed and connected to one another, increasing the network of cool system associations and thus the number of cool nodes corresponding to the hot spots.

Empirical evidence supports these expectations. Whereas delay of gratification in the paradigm described seems almost impossible for children younger than four years old (Mischel 1974), by age twelve almost 60 percent of children are able to wait to criterion (twenty minutes maximum). Furthermore, the spontaneous use of cooling strategies such as distraction is positively related to both age and verbal intelligence (Rodriguez, Mischel, and Shoda 1989). In children between the ages of six and twelve, the exposure to the desired object within the immediate stimulus environment ceases to influence delay time, as the cool system continues to develop and internal control strategies become increasingly available (Rodriguez, Mischel, and Shoda 1989). Instead, delay time depends on the individual's attention deployment strategies—that is, longer delay times depend on whether children can spontaneously use "cooling" strategies such as looking away from the rewards and self-distraction while at the same time facing the tempting rewards.

Effects of Stress   As described earlier, the research on traumatic memory indicates that the hot system is increasingly potentiated by stress (Metcalfe and Mischel 1999). In contrast, although low to moderate levels of stress increase cool system activation, at high levels of stress the cool system shuts off. The implication of these premises for the ability to delay gratification is that waiting should be more difficult when children are put under additional psychological stress. We have seen that instructing children to "think fun," thereby decreasing stress, facilitated control (Mischel, Ebbesen, and Zeiss 1972). In the same experiment, some children were given cues to think sad thoughts, such as "think about the last time you fell off the swing and got a bloody nose, which hurt a lot." As expected, such negative thoughts had an adverse effect on delay time, presumably because they increased stress and frustration. In summary, distraction that is stress inducing is likely to be ineffective, or under stressful conditions, inhibition of the hot system becomes increasingly difficult.

Regulatory Strength and Automatization   These effects of stress on self-regulation failure are also consistent with the strength model of self-regulation (see Baumeister and Vohs, chap. 6 herein). According to this model, people have a limited resource for self-regulation that is depleted with exertion of willpower. With each successive or additional self-regulatory task, therefore, self-regulatory failure is more likely. From the perspective of this model, stress is thus likely to deplete the limited resources or strength that one has momentarily, leading children to give up and lose control in the delay of gratification task.

The idea that self-regulation failure is more likely under stress or cognitive load because effective self-regulation requires mental resources raises the question of what happens if access to effective self-control strategies under certain circumstances becomes automatic so that their application requires minimal energy. This issue has been most extensively addressed by Gollwitzer and colleagues in their research on *implementation plans* (see Gollwitzer 1999 for review; also see Patterson and Mischel 1975). These plans specify where, when, and how to pursue a goal intention by linking a specific situation to a specific response (for example, I will read the textbook for my course from 5 to 8 P.M. every day). When planned and rehearsed, implementation intentions help self-control because goal-directed action is initiated relatively automatically when the relevant trigger cues become situationally salient (for example, when the clock hits 5 P.M., I will go to the gym). Implementation intentions help self-regulation across a wide range of regulatory tasks, such as action initiation (for example,

I will start writing the paper the day after Thanksgiving), inhibition of unwanted habitual responses (for example, when the dessert menu is served, I will not order the chocolate cake), and resistance to temptation (for example, whenever the distraction arises, I will ignore it).

These findings have further implications for the question of whether strategic and effective self-control necessarily requires controlled, effortful processes. As becomes clear in Gollwitzer's work, some effortful, deliberative process of linking action plans to specific situational triggers is necessary in the initial phases of automatization. Yet once this link has been established and rehearsed, effective self-regulatory behavior can be activated, and ability may not lie so much in whether or not people can deliberately access effective control strategies but rather in whether they can turn on the cool system activation automatically, even under stressful or cognitively busy situations.

Flexible Attention Deployment   An important point that arises out of recent research in delay of gratification is the notion of *flexible* attention deployment: that of strategic cooling and warming, as required by the demands of the situation. To illustrate, in one study, attentional mechanisms in self-regulation were assessed in the attachment context in mother-child interactions during toddlerhood, then linked prospectively to attention deployment during the delay task at age four (Sethi et al. 2000). It was found that toddlers' use of distraction strategies in interacting with the mother was differentially linked to delay ability, depending on the mother's parenting style. For example, toddlers who moved away from a highly controlling mother to explore the toys at a distance when she tried to engage the child used more effective delay strategies at age four, compared to toddlers who did not distance themselves from an aversive mother. The pattern was reversed for toddlers whose mothers were not controlling: this time, distancing oneself from a noncontrolling mother was related to lower delay times and the use of ineffective attentional strategies in preschool. These findings thus suggest that effective self-regulation in the preschool delay paradigm taps into children's ability to flexibly deploy attention to or away from the mother, depending on the aversiveness of the maternal interactional style.

Even more direct evidence for the notion of flexible attention deployment was found in a study by Peake, Hebl, and Mischel (2002), which examined the role of attention in delaying gratification when children were required to complete a task (rather than passively wait) in order to get the larger, delayed reward. They found that when the task was interesting and engaging (that is, feeding a toy bird with marbles), deploying attention to the rewards present was detrimental. Yet when the task was not engaging (that is, sorting marbles into cups according to color), attention to rewards motivated instrumental work by reminding children of their long-term goals and facilitated delay as long as attention deployment stayed flexible and did not become fixed on rewards.

In summary, when the instrumental work toward attaining long-term goals is boring, strategic cooling and warming may be most effective, rather than an unconditional utilization of cooling strategies. The findings regarding flexible attention deployment are consistent with the view that being sensitive to the demands of different situations and adjusting one's behavior flexibly in accordance with the situational constraints is basic for adaptive social and emotional behavior (Cantor and Kihlstrom 1987; Chiu et al. 1995; Mendoza-Denton et al. 2001; Shoda, Mischel, and Wright 1993). They also draw attention to the complex relationship between affect, motivation, and cognition, suggesting that hot system and affect can be strategically used in the service of motivation if the cool system can be effectively used to keep arousal under control.

Individual Differences in Delay of Gratification Ability: Differences in Hyperbolic Discounting Functions?

Although most of the original delay of gratification studies involved experimental manipulations of ideation in reward representation, chronic individual differences also emerged in certain diagnostic conditions. Specifically, when rewards were exposed in front of the children, and the experimenter did not offer them any one way of thinking about the exposed rewards, children were left to their own devices to deal with this "hot" situation. Thus individual differences in the number of seconds children were able to wait in this diagnostic situation reflected their own spontaneous strategies and ability to delay. These differences proved to be predictive of important long-term outcomes. Children who were able to delay gratification longer in preschool had higher SAT scores at age seventeen (Shoda, Mischel, and Peake 1990), and also were described by their parents in late adolescence as having high social-cognitive competence (Mischel, Shoda, and Peake 1988). As adults, these former children indicated that they took their long-term goals seriously, and that they carefully planned for them. Even in this very homogeneous sample of upper-middle-class participants, by approximately age twenty-eight, those who delayed longer at age four had attained significantly higher education levels (Ayduk et al. 2000).

This network of empirical evidence brings up the question of whether the differences in children's ability to delay can be explained by differences in hyperbolic discount functions (for example, Loewenstein and Prelec 1992). Some researchers (for example, Rachlin 2000) have indeed argued that waiting time in the delay experiments depends on hyperbolic delay discount functions—specifically, on the rate at which children discount future rewards. Those who have higher discount rates—and thus have steeper hyperbolic functions—reach the point of preference reversal much sooner than those who have flatter discount functions with lower discount rates. What presumably is happening psychologically is that for the former group, as waiting time progresses, the value of the delayed reward is discounted at such a higher rate that its current value sinks below that of the immediately available reward much sooner, and therefore reversal of choice is observed. Our research program has not investigated the relationship between discount functions and delay times directly; nevertheless, the idea that low delayers should have steeper discount functions is consistent with our thinking and data. What our program of research does speak to directly are the psychological mechanisms that *underlie* rate of discounting in delay of gratification behavior.

Summary

Adaptive and intelligent functioning in the social world requires one to voluntarily postpone immediate gratification in the pursuit of preferred but delayed goals and outcomes. The frustration and conflict involved in such delay is particularly challenging when the immediate situation includes hot cues that activate a biologically hardwired automatic response system. According to the hot-cool model, the challenge in delaying gratification is to inhibit this hot, reflexive system in favor of the activation of the cool system, with its problem-solving cognitive skills and strategies. The classic studies on delay of gratification behavior in children illustrate that the predictions generated by this model closely fit the empirical results. Findings indicate that children can delay gratification to the extent that their attention is diverted away from arousing, hot features. This can be accomplished by distraction, via either the physical presence of pleasant and engaging distracting objects or by self-generated positive thoughts. Second, a hot stimulus can be mentally represented in cool terms, for example, by thinking of it as a picture that can't be eaten, or by focusing on its cognitive, cool properties such as its shape and color. Notably, these principles generalize beyond consumable rewards—whether edible treats such as pretzels or symbolic ones such as shiny poker chips, attention to the motivating, desired aspects of delayed outcomes activates impulsive approach tendencies leading at least young children to terminate delay (see Peake, Hebl, and Mischel 2002 for a discussion). Overall, the hot-cool analyses of delay of gratification studies implicate effective attention deployment strategies as underlying exertion of willpower in attaining valued long-term goals.

Implications of a Hot-Cool Analysis for Regulation of Defensive Systems

The dilemmas in most of the delay of gratification studies have involved conflicts between immediately available smaller rewards and delayed larger outcomes in essentially simple "less now" versus "more later" dilemmas, but similar psychological processes underlie the subtler interpersonal economics of many human relationships and the conflicts experienced within them. Resolutions to maintain harmony and to work toward common goals in business or in romantic partnerships all too often give way to the explosion of anger, hostility, and jealousy under the emotional arousal of the immediate situation within the tensions of everyday life. In the heat of the moment the need to delay hot, automatic—potentially destructive—reactions becomes most difficult in social relationships, particularly when those relationships are of high importance and emotional significance to the individual.

Interdependence theory (Kelley 1979; Kelley and Thibaut 1978; Arriaga and Rusbult 1998) distinguishes between *given* preferences and *effective* preferences that guide people's behavior in interactions with significant others. Given preferences reflect immediate, self-centered responses to an event, whereas effective preferences are based on long-term consequences and implications for the partner. In hot-cool system analysis terms, given preferences are the response tendencies generated by the hot system and effective preferences are based on cool system processing. Interdependence theory argues that when a partner behaves in destructive ways, people experience an *accommodation dilemma* between their given and effective preferences. For instance, on the one hand, they may want to lash out and hurt the partner back, which would serve an immediate self-interest toward taking revenge and also may be the most readily accessible automatic response. On the other hand, they may also be motivated to protect and maintain their relationship and think about what would be the best way to handle the situation for the long-term stability of the relationship.

Accommodation in this context refers to the inhibition of given preferences and instead acting on one's effective preferences. "The shift from given preferences to effective preferences is guided by transformation of motivation, a process by which immediate, self-interested preferences are replaced by preferences that take into account broader concerns, including considerations to some degree that transcend the immediate situation" (Arriaga and Rusbult 1998, 928). In a deep sense, then, attainment of accommodation involves delay of gratification: making and sustaining a choice between immediate but smaller self-interest and a delayed but larger interest (larger in the sense that it is good both for the self and for the relationship). In line with this analysis, evidence suggests that cooling attentional processes that underlie delay ability also help in the regulation of defensive reactions in interpersonal contexts.

Recently, the role of delay ability was examined in the context of rejection sensitivity (RS) (Downey and Feldman 1996)—a chronic processing disposition characterized by anxious expectations of rejection. These expectations stem from prior rejection experiences and get activated when people encounter interpersonal situations in which rejection is a possibility. Thus, in such situations, people who are high in RS experience a sense of threat and foreboding. In such a state, the person's defensive, fight or flight systems are activated. Attention narrows on detection of threat-related cues, which in turn makes the high RS person ready to see the actualization of the threatening outcome.

Anticipation of threat also creates action readiness and potentiation of the fight or flight response system so that people high in RS are likely to react automatically, defensively, and intensely (that is, in a self-protective way) when the threat is experienced as having occurred. In hot-cool system terms, this personality disposition reflects individual differences in how readily the defensive, fear-driven aspects of the hot system get activated in interpersonal situations. Unsurprisingly, when high RS people perceive rejection, they respond to it with hostility and aggression as well as depression and withdrawal symptoms (Ayduk et al. 1999; Ayduk, Downey, and Kim 2001; Downey et al. 1998). These negative behaviors in turn elicit actual rejection from partners, leading to a self-fulfilling prophecy, and romantic relationships of high RS people are likely to end sooner than those of low RS people (Downey et al. 1998). Repeated rejection and disillusionment of relationships are likely to erode self-worth, and low self-esteem is a common characteristic of people high in RS.

Similar to the dilemma of waiting in the delay of gratification paradigm, effective coping in threatening interpersonal contexts among high RS individuals should involve cooling the hot, emotional features associated with the situation, allowing problem-solving strategies to be accessed (Arriaga and Rusbult 1998; Mischel, Shoda, and Rodriguez 1989). One study exploring these links was an adult follow-up of the children who had participated in the original Bing delay of gratification studies (Ayduk et al. 2000). This study showed that among vulnerable (high RS) individuals, the number of seconds participants were able to wait as preschoolers in the delay situation predicted their adult resiliency against the potentially destructive effects of RS. That is, high RS adults who had high delay ability in preschool had more positive functioning (high self-esteem, self-worth, and coping ability) compared with similarly high RS adults who were not able to delay in preschool. High RS participants showed higher levels of cocaine–crack use and lower levels of education than those low in RS, unless they were good delayers in preschool. In contrast, high RS people who had high delay ability in preschool had relatively lower levels of drug use and higher education levels, and in these respects were similar to low RS participants.

A similar pattern of results was found in a second study with middle school children. Namely, whereas high RS children with low delay ability were more aggressive toward their peers and thus had less positive peer relationships than children low in RS, high RS children who were able to delay longer were even less aggressive and more liked by their peers than low RS children. Likewise, a cross-sectional study of preadolescent boys with behavioral problems characterized by heightened hostile reactivity to potential interpersonal threats also showed that the spontaneous use of cooling strategies in the delay task (that is, looking away from the rewards and self-distraction) predicted reduced verbal and physical aggression (Rodriguez, Mischel, et al. 1989).

An even more direct test of the effect of hot and cool systems on hostile reactivity to rejection comes from a study in which college students imagined an autobiographical rejection experience focusing either on their physiological and emotional reactions during the experience (hot ideation) or contextual features of the physical setting where this experience happened (cool ideation). In a subsequent lexical decision task, hostility and anger words were less accessible to those individuals primed with cool ideation than those primed with hot ideation. More important, this was true for both high RS and low RS participants. The same pattern of anger reduction in the cool condition was found in people's self-report measures of angry mood and in the level of angry affect expressed in their descriptions of the rejection experience (Ayduk, Mischel, and Downey 2002).

Collectively, these studies suggest that in threatening interpersonal situations that activate the hot system, attention deployment on emotional information perpetuates hot system processing by maintaining stress and inhibiting access to complex cognitive mediation. In contrast, "cooling" attention deployment strategies such as self-distraction from the arousing aspects of the situation attenuate hot system processing, enable cool, cognitive, thoughtful processing that takes account of long-term temporal considerations, and thus help regulate the self in interpersonal situations.

In addition to such cognitive and attentional strategies in dealing with negative interpersonal experiences, individuals' motivation to attain long-term relationship goals (for example, maintenance of a relationship) should also impact their affective and behavioral responses. Research shows that greater availability and chronic accessibility of long-term goals (Bargh 1990) may in fact play a pivotal role in whether people are able to inhibit their impulses to behave negatively and transcend the often engulfing salience of their short-term goals when they are emotionally aroused under threat. For example, in close relationships, commitment plays an important role in mediating willingness to accommodate (Rusbult et al. 1991). Thus it is possible and even likely that both motivational and cognitive-attentional processes operate simultaneously and in interaction with one another in self-regulation. On the one hand, the attention control mechanisms of the cool system inhibit hot system processing, at least in part by making people's long-term goals take precedence over the immediate situation; on the other hand, the strength and commitment to one's long-term goals affect how readily one can utilize cooling strategies.

Conclusion

As the research reviewed here illustrates, successful self-regulation extends over time and thus often depends not on a single choice but rather on a *continuous* series of choices that often need to be made in the face of considerable frustrations, temptations, and barriers. Such sustained choices are influenced by multiple factors, including the construals, expectations, beliefs, and values relevant to the choices and temptations that the individual confronts and creates (Mischel and Shoda 1995). This chapter has focused on only a small but crucial component of these diverse determinants: the role of attention control and the interaction of cognitive cool and emotional hot processes in ways that enable delay of gratification, albeit not as isolated factors. The complexity and fundamental difficulties of effective self-regulation often under harsh life conditions and emotional arousal seem self-evident and need not be belabored here. Thus the present analysis is not intended to imply a simplistic, preemptive explanation nor a fast cure waiting to solve complex lifelong problems of self-regulation that characterize so much of the human condition. Understanding some of the core processes involved in successful self-regulation over time, however, hopefully brings us one step closer to making volition and willpower a possibility in the pursuit of desired yet distal rewards.

The preparation of this chapter was supported by a grant from the National Institute of Mental Health (MH39349). Correspondence concerning this article should be sent to Walter Mischel, Department of Psychology, 406 Schermerhorn Hall, New York, N.Y. 10027. Electronic mail can be sent to wm@psych.columbia.edu.

References

Ainslie, George. 1992. *Picoeconomics: The Strategic Interaction of Successive Motivational States Within the Person*. New York: Cambridge University Press.

Anderson, John R. 1983. *The Architecture of Cognition*. Cambridge, Mass.: Harvard University Press.

Arriaga, Ximena B., and Caryl E. Rusbult. 1998. "Standing in My Partner's Shoes: Partner Perspective Taking and Reactions to Accommodative Dilemmas." *Personality and Social Psychology Bulletin* 24(9): 927–48.

Ayduk, Ozlem, Rodolfo Mendoza-Denton, Walter Mischel, Geraldine Downey, Philip Peake, and Monica Rodriguez. 2000. "Regulating the Interpersonal Self: Strategic Self–Regulation for Coping with Rejection Sensitivity." *Journal of Personality and Social Psychology* 79(5): 776–92.

Ayduk, Ozlem, Geraldine Downey, Alessandra Testa, Ying Yen, and Yuichi Shoda. 1999. "Does Rejection Elicit Hostility in High Rejection Sensitive Women?" *Social Cognition* 17(2): 245–71.

Ayduk, Ozlem, Geraldine Downey, and Minji Kim. 2001. "Rejection Sensitivity and Depression in Women." *Personality and Social Psychology Bulletin* 27(7): 868–77.

Ayduk, Ozlem, Walter Mischel, and Geraldine Downey. 2002. "Attentional Mechanisms Linking Rejection to Hostile Reactivity: The Role of 'Hot' Versus 'Cool' Focus." *Psychological Science* 13(5): 443–48.

Bandura, Albert. 1986. *Social Foundations of Thought and Action: A Social Cognitive Theory*. Englewood Cliffs, N.J.: Prentice-Hall.

Bargh, John A. 1990. "Auto-motives: Preconscious Determinants of Social Interaction." In *Handbook of Motivation and Cognitions: Foundations of Social Behavior*, edited by Edward T. Higgins and Richard M. Sorrentino. New York: Guilford Press.

Berlyne, Daniel. 1960. *Conflict, Arousal, and Curiosity*. New York: McGraw-Hill.

Cantor, Nancy, and John F. Kihlstrom. 1987. *Personality and Social Intelligence*. Englewood Cliffs, N.J.: Prentice-Hall.

Chiu, Chi-yue, Ying-yi Hong, Walter Mischel, and Yuichi Shoda. 1995. "Discriminative Facility in Social Competence: Conditional Versus Dispositional Encoding and Monitoring-Blunting of Information." *Social Cognition* 13(1): 49–70.

Downey, Geraldine, and Scott Feldman. 1996. "Implications of Rejection Sensitivity for Intimate Relationships." *Journal of Personality and Social Psychology* 70(6): 1327–43.

Downey, Geraldine, Antonio Freitas, Benjamin Michealis, and Hala Khouri. 1998. "The Self-Fulfilling Prophecy in Close Relationships: Do Rejection Sensitive Women Get Rejected by Romantic Partners?" *Journal of Personality and Social Psychology* 75(2): 545–60.

Ekman, Paul, and Richard J. Davidson, eds. 1994. *The Nature of Emotion*. New York: Oxford University Press.

Ellsworth, Phoebe. 1991. "Some Implications of Cognitive Appraisal Theories of Emotion." In *International Review of Studies of Emotion*, edited by Ken T. Strongman. Vol. 2. New York: Wiley.

———. 1994. "William James and Emotion: Is a Century of Fame Worth a Century of Misunderstanding?" *Psychological Review* 101(2): 222–29.

Estes, William K. 1972. "Reinforcement in Human Behavior." *American Scientist* 60(6): 723–29.

Freud, Sigmund. 1959 [1911]. "Formulations Regarding the Two Principles of Mental Functioning." *Collected Papers*. Vol. 4. New York: Basic Books.

Gollwitzer, Peter M. 1999. "Implementation Intentions: Strong Effects of Simple Plans." *American Psychologist* 54(7): 493–503.

Gray, Jeffrey A. 1982. *The Neuropsychology of Anxiety*. London: Oxford.

———. 1987. *The Psychology of Fear and Stress*. 2d ed. New York: McGraw-Hill.

Grosch, James, and Allen Neuringer. 1981. "Self-Control in Pigeons Under the Mischel Paradigm." *Journal of the Experimental Analysis of Behavior* 35(1): 3–21.

James, William. 1981 [1890]. *The Principles of Psychology*. Vol. 2. Cambridge, Mass.: Harvard University Press.

Kelley, Harold H. 1979. *Personal Relationships: Their Structures and Processes*. Hillsdale, N.J.: Erlbaum.

Kelley, Harold H., and John W. Thibaut. 1978. *Interpersonal Relations: A Theory of Interdependence*. New York: Wiley.

Lange, James C. 1967 [1885]. "The Emotions. Translation of Lange's 1885 Monograph." In *The Emotions*, edited by James C. Lange and William James. New York: Hafner. Facsimile of 1922 ed.

Lazarus, Richard A. 1993. "From Psychological Stress to the Emotions: A History of Changing Outlooks." *Annual Review of Psychology* 44: 1–21.

LeDoux, Joseph. 1996. *The Emotional Brain*. New York: Touchstone.

Loewenstein, George. 1996. "Out of Control: Visceral Influences on Behavior." *Organizational Behavior and Human Decision Processes* 65(3): 272–92.

Loewenstein, George, and Drazen Prelec. 1992. "Anomalies in Intertemporal Choice: Evidence and Interpretation." In *Choice Over Time*, edited by George Loewenstein and Drazen Prelec. New York: Russell Sage Foundation.

Mendoza-Denton, Rodolfo, Ozlem Ayduk, Walter Mischel, Shoda Yuichi, and Alessandra Testa. 2001. "Person X Situation Interactionism in Self-Encoding (*I Am . . . When . . .*): Implications for Affect Regulation and Social Information Processing." *Journal of Personality and Social Psychology* 80(4): 533–44.

Metcalfe, Janet, and Jake W. Jacobs. 1996. "A 'Hot-System/Cool-System' View of Memory Under Stress." *PTSD Research Quarterly* 7: 1–6.

———. 1998. "Emotional Memory: The Effects of Stress on 'Cool' and 'Hot' Memory Systems." In *The Psychology of Learning and Motivations*. Vol. 38. *Advances in Research and Theory*, edited by Douglas L. Medin. San Diego: Academic.

Metcalfe, Janet, and Walter Mischel. 1999. "A Hot/Cool System Analysis of Delay of Gratification: Dynamics of Willpower." *Psychological Review* 106(1): 3–19.

Mischel, Walter. 1958. "Preference for Delayed and Immediate Reinforcement: An Experimental Study of a Cultural Observation." *Journal of Abnormal and Social Psychology* 56: 57–61.

———. 1961. "Preference for Delayed Reinforcement and Social Responsibility." *Journal of Abnormal and Social Psychology* 62: 1–7.

———. 1966. "Theory and Research on the Antecedents of Self-Imposed Delay of Reward." In *Progress in Experimental Personality Research*. Vol. 3, edited by Brendan A. Maher. New York: Academic Press.

———. 1974. "Cognitive Appraisals and Transformations in Self-Control." In *Cognitive Views of Human Motivation*, edited by Bernard Weiner. New York: Academic Press.

Mischel, Walter, and Ozlem Ayduk. 2002. "Self-Regulation in a Cognitive-Affective Personality System: Attentional Control in the Service of the Self." *Self and Identity* 1: 113–20.

Mischel, Walter, and Nancy Baker. 1975. "Cognitive Appraisals and Transformations in Delay Behavior." *Journal of Personality and Social Psychology* 31(2): 254–61.

Mischel, Walter, Nancy Cantor, and Scott Feldman. 1996. "Principles of Self-Regulation: The Nature of Willpower and Self-Control." In *Social Psychology: Handbook of Basic Principles*, edited by Edward T. Higgins and Arie W. Kruglanski. New York: Guilford Press.

Mischel, Walter, and Ebbe B. Ebbesen. 1970. "Attention in Delay of Gratification." *Journal of Personality and Social Psychology* 16(2): 329–37.

Mischel, Walter, Ebbe B. Ebbesen, and Antonette R. Zeiss. 1972. "Cognitive and Attentional Mechanisms in Delay of Gratification." *Journal of Personality and Social Psychology* 21(2): 204–18.

Mischel, Walter, and Ralph Metzner. 1962. "Preference for Delayed Reward as a Function of Age, Intelligence, and Length of Delay Interval." *Journal of Abnormal and Social Psychology* 64(6): 425–31.

Mischel, Walter, and Bert Moore. 1973. "Effects of Attention to Symbolically-Presented Rewards on Self-Control." *Journal of Personality and Social Psychology* 28(2): 172–79.

Mischel, Walter, and Yuichi Shoda. 1995. "A Cognitive-Affective System Theory of Personality: Reconceptualizing Situations, Dispositions, Dynamics and Invariance in Personality Structure." *Psychological Review* 102(2): 246–68.

Mischel, Walter, Yuichi Shoda, and Philip Peake. 1988. "The Nature of Adolescent Competencies Predicted by Preschool Delay of Gratification." *Journal of Personality and Social Psychology* 54(4): 687–96.

Mischel, Walter, Yuichi Shoda, and Monica L. Rodriguez. 1989. "Delay of Gratification in Children." *Science* 244(4907): 933–38.

Mischel, Walter, and Ervin Staub. 1965. "Effects of Expectancy on Working and Waiting for Larger Rewards." *Journal of Personality and Social Psychology* 2(5): 625–33.

Moore, Bert, Walter Mischel, and Antonette R. Zeiss. 1976. "Comparative Effects of the Reward Stimulus and Its Cognitive Representation in Voluntary Delay." *Journal of Personality and Social Psychology* 34(3): 419–24.

Patterson, Charlotte J., and Walter Mischel. 1975. "Plans to Resist Distraction." *Developmental Psychology* 11(3): 369–78.

Peake, Philip, Michelle Hebl, and Walter Mischel. 2002. "Strategic Attention Deployment for Delay of Gratification in Waiting and Working Situations." *Developmental Psychology* 38(2): 313–26.

Rachlin, Howard. 2000. *The Science of Self-Control*. Cambridge, Mass.: Harvard University Press.

Read, Stephen J., and Lynn C. Miller, eds. 1998. *Connectionist Models of Social Reasoning and Social Behavior*. New Jersey: Erlbaum.

Rodriguez, Monica L., Walter Mischel, and Yuichi Shoda. 1989. "Cognitive Person Variables in the Delay of Gratification of Older Children at Risk." *Journal of Personality and Social Psychology* 57(2): 358–67.

Rodriguez, Monica L., Walter Mischel, Yuichi Shoda, and Jack Wright. 1989. "Delay of Gratification and Children's Social Behavior in Natural Settings." Paper presented at the Eastern Psychological Association, Boston.

Rumelhart, David E., and James L. McClelland. 1986. *Parallel Distributed Processing: Explorations in the Microstructure of Cognition*. Vol. 1. *Foundations*. Cambridge, Mass.: MIT Press/Bradford Books.

Rusbult, Caryl E., Julie Verette, Gregory A. Whitney, Linda F. Slovik, and Isaac Lipkus. 1991. "Accommodation Processes in Close Relationships: Theory and Preliminary Empirical Evidence." *Journal of Personality and Social Psychology* 60(1): 53–78.

Schachter, Stanley, and Jerome E. Singer. 1962. "Cognitive, Social, and Physiological Determinants of Emotional State." *Psychological Review* 69(5): 379–99.

Sethi, Anita, Walter Mischel, Lawrence J. Aber, Yuichi Shoda, and Monica L. Rodriguez. 2000. "The Role of Strategic Attention Deployment in Development of Self-Regulation: Predicting Preschoolers' Delay of Gratification from Mother-Toddler Interactions." *Developmental Psychology* 36(6): 767–77.

Shoda, Yuichi, Walter Mischel, and Philip Peake. 1990. "Predicting Adolescent Cognitive and Self-Regulatory Competencies from Preschool Delay of Gratification: Identifying Diagnostic Conditions." *Developmental Psychology* 26(6): 978–86.

Shoda, Yuichi, Walter Mischel, and Jack C. Wright. 1993. "The Role of Situational Demands and Cognitive Competencies in Behavior Organization and Personality Coherence." *Journal of Personality and Social Psychology* 65(5): 1023–35.

Siegel, Eric, and Howard Rachlin. 1995. "Soft Commitment: Self-Control Achieved by Response Persistence." *Journal of the Experimental Analysis of Behavior* 64(2): 117–28.

· 6 ·

Willpower, Choice, and Self-Control

ROY F. BAUMEISTER AND KATHLEEN D. VOHS

T HE SELF cannot be described as reactive, disinterested, or apathetic. Quite the contrary: most activities in which a person engages are willfully initiated, chosen, or controlled in one form or another. Self-regulation is involved in a multitude of tasks such as getting out of bed, suppressing a worrisome thought, forcing oneself to smile through disappointment, overriding the temptation of an extramarital affair, running for exercise, and staying alert through a dull lecture.

The capacity of the human self to override its initial responses is one of the most important, powerful, and adaptive aspects of human nature. The immense flexibility and variety of human behavior can be directly attributed to people's ability to alter their responses—the essence of self-regulation. In many species, response follows directly from the stimulus and flows along well-programmed, highly regular and predictable patterns. Humans too are animals and have many of these innately prepared or well-learned responses. Yet humans can often prevent themselves from responding in these ways if they make the effort to override their initial response. We use the terms *self-regulation* and *self-control* interchangeably.

The ability to change, alter, or override responses is crucial to understanding the wealth and complexity of human behavior. By overriding initial responses and acting in different ways, people have managed to break free from the way nature designed these standard responses and produce an immense assortment of diverse, sophisti-

201

cated behavior, even culminating in the rise of culture and civilization. Indeed, acts of choice and self-control have become greatly important in modern Western cultures. Instead of merely following a prescribed script of rituals and behaviors, people are now given a vast array of options for how they live their lives (see Schwartz 2000 on the "tyranny of choice").

The adaptive, beneficial effects of self-regulation seem intuitively obvious and have also received support from research findings. Most of the major personal and social problems that afflict human beings in our society center on some failure to control or regulate ourselves. Thus, drug and alcohol abuse (including addiction), debt and bankruptcy, violence and criminality, gambling, unwanted pregnancy, school failure and underachievement, emotional problems such as anger and anxiety, and sexually transmitted diseases all arise when people fail to control their behavior. Research by Mischel and his colleagues (for example, Mischel et al. 1988; Shoda et al. 1990) has shown that children who are better able to delay gratification at age four go on to become more successful academically and more adept socially as adults. Adult college students who score high on self-control get better grades, have better interpersonal relationships, suffer fewer psychopathological symptoms, are better adjusted psychologically, and are less prone to problems of eating and drinking disorders than students who score lower on self-control (Engels et al. 2002; Finkel and Campbell 2001; Tangney and Baumeister 2000; Vohs et al. 2002).

The thrust of this chapter is to examine this remarkable human ability of self-regulation. From years of laboratory studies, we have developed a picture of this ability that is far from what we initially suspected. More specifically, we have come to think that self-regulation—along with other crucial functions of the self, including effortful choice and responsible decision making in general—draws on a limited resource, akin to strength or energy. The human self contains a small pool of this precious energy and tries to manage it judiciously. The aim of such prudence is to use the resources where most effective and appropriate, conserve them where possible, and meanwhile cope with the myriad challenges and problems that each day presents.

The Nature of Self-Control

A review of past writings about self-control concluded that three different kinds of theoretical models predominated. Hence we tried to think of experimental tests that would pit these three theories against one another and allow us to determine which was correct.

The first theory uses traditional folk concepts of willpower. This view depicts self-regulation as based on a kind of strength or energy, and probably gained appeal from the common experience of battling temptation. When people are tempted, they have a strong or weak desire to do something of which they do not approve. To resist that temptation, the self has to have at least as much strength as the impulse or desire it is battling.

The second theory depicts self-control as a set of cognitive schemas and processes. In this view, the self employs schematic knowledge about itself and about the world. It attends to certain possibilities and opportunities, calculates the costs and benefits, plans strategies, and these cognitive calculations determine the course of action.

The third theory understands self-control as a kind of skill. This kind of thinking has perhaps been popular among child psychologists, who like to understand the processes of human development as a matter of a child slowly acquiring skills.

How could we distinguish which of these three theories was correct? One arena in which competing predictions could be tested involves what would happen when people have to perform two seemingly unrelated acts of self-control in a row. The three theories have different predictions about how the second act of self-control would be affected by having performed the first.

The willpower theory would predict that the first act of self-control would deplete some of the self's energy, and so less would be left over for the second act. Hence the second act of self-control would be somewhat less effective than it would normally be (that is, if it had not been preceded by the first act of self-control). In contrast, the schema theory would predict that self-control would actually be better on the second act because of the first. Cognitive processes show "priming" effects, in which continuing to use some module or process is easier when it has already been active in one's mind. To use a computer analogy, the self would already have loaded its self-control program into active memory by the first act of self-control, and since it is already up and running it will perform the second act more easily and readily. The skill theory would predict little or no effect of the first act of self-control on the second. Skill improves gradually through many trials but remains essentially constant from one trial to the next. Unless the first act of self-control managed to instill some major new skill, the second act of self-control would be about as successful as it would have been had the first act never happened.

When we began testing this theory, our findings very consistently supported the first (willpower) theory—that is, performing a first act of self-regulation weakened people's ability to regulate themselves subsequently. This pattern was found repeatedly, with many different manipulations and measures of self-regulation.

Thus in a first study, some people were (by random assignment) instructed to regulate their emotions and moods while watching an upsetting video clip. Other people watched the same clip without any such instructions. Afterward we measured people's stamina by timing how long they could squeeze a handgrip muscle exerciser. The people who had regulated their moods—either amplifying and intensifying their emotional reactions, or stifling and suppressing them— gave up significantly faster on the handgrip task compared with people who had not tried to regulate their moods. This finding suggests that the attempt to control one's emotional reactions used up some resource that was therefore not available to help them overcome muscle fatigue so that they could keep squeezing the handgrip (Muraven et al. 1998).

In another study, people were instructed to list their thoughts. They were told that they could think about anything they wanted, except that in the crucial condition, they were instructed to avoid thinking about a white bear. This is a procedure for studying thought suppression developed by Wegner, Schneider, Carter, and White (1987). Afterward, all participants were given anagram problems to solve. In reality, the anagrams were unsolvable, and the procedure was used to measure how long they kept trying until they gave up. The people who had sought to suppress the white bear thoughts gave up significantly faster on the anagrams compared with people who had listed their thoughts without trying to regulate them (Muraven et al. 1998).

Impulse control was the focus of yet another study (Baumeister et al. 1998). Participants had been requested to avoid eating anything for several hours prior to this experiment, and this entailed that many were deprived of food and presumably hungry when they arrived. Appetite was further stimulated by baking fresh chocolate-chip cookies in the laboratory room in a microwave oven. The laboratory room was filled with the tempting aroma of cookies, and the participant was seated at a table in front of a plate of these cookies, along with chocolate candies. A bowl of radishes was also on the table. In the crucial condition, participants were instructed to eat only the radishes and were left alone for five minutes (ostensibly to permit them to eat their radishes, but actually in order to maximize their temptation to filch a couple of cookies—and hence require a bigger exertion of self-control to resist that temptation). Others were permitted to eat the cookies instead of the radishes, and yet another control group involved no food at all. Afterward, all food was cleared away, and participants were given some geometric puzzles to solve. As in the previous study, these were in fact unsolvable, and the procedure was designed to measure how long they persisted before giving up. Once again, the results suggested that self-control depletes some energy or strength, because participants who had resisted the chocolate temptation gave up significantly faster than those in the control conditions.

The idea that self-initiated inhibition acts as a vulnerability with regard to self-regulatory depletion was tested by Vohs and Heatherton (2000). Chronic dieters are the ideal example of self-control, because they must repeatedly suppress the desire to eat and emphasize long-term weight goals (see also Herman and Polivy, chap. 16 herein). Studies of dieters found that situations that called for an overriding of the desire to eat (for example, the presence of tempting candies) weakened subsequent attempts to engage in self-control. In several studies, dieters were found to eat more ice cream and persist less on a cognitive task after depletion. In contrast, nondieters were not affected by situational manipulations involving food, which supports the notion that self-standards and chronic inhibitions are important parameters in understanding ego depletion.

Additional work has begun to connect the self-regulatory resource model to areas directly related to problematic personal behavior. One such investigation involves the area of personal spending, and two studies reveal that self-regulatory resources may play an important role in understanding when people engage in impulsive spending (see also Angeletos et al., chap. 18 herein; Wertenbroch, chap. 17 herein). In these studies (Vohs and Faber 2002), self-regulatory resource depletion was manipulated using an attention-control task. In this task, participants are asked to watch a video (with no audio) of a woman being interviewed off-camera, while inhibiting their desire to look at irrelevant words appearing at the bottom of the screen. Other participants are not asked to inhibit their gaze and are left to watch the video in whatever manner they wish. In both studies, participants who were depleted of regulatory resources after the attention-control task made more impulsive purchasing responses. Specifically, depleted participants said they would pay more money for a variety of items and also reported that statements from an impulsive buying measure were more descriptive of them, relative to nondepleted participants.

Additional studies were done to rule out alternative explanations. For example, it seemed plausible that quitting early on unsolvable tasks was a sign of good self-regulation rather than ego depletion and poor self-regulation. Hence we repeated the studies using solvable problems. The results confirmed that self-regulation is impaired; after an act of self-control, people's performance on solvable problems was relatively poor. Another potential alternate explanation for these results is that drawing on the limited resource changes mood states in a way that has implications for subsequent self-control. Across more than a dozen empirical studies, however, we have found almost no suggestion that ego depletion alters mood (see Baumeister et al. 1998; Muraven et al. 1998; Vohs and Heatherton 2000).

We had shown that the capacity for self-regulation gets weaker after use, just as a muscle grows tired; but we also wanted to show that exercise could gradually improve the capacity for self-regulation, just as a muscle gets stronger. In one longitudinal study, participants were given assignments to perform self-regulation exercises for two weeks (Muraven et al. 1999). For example, one group of participants was assigned to work on their posture whenever they could remember to do it, such as by sitting up straight or standing erect. The participants who performed these exercises did in fact show improvements in self-control relative to a control group (who had no such assigned exercises).

In another study, participants were given one of two self-control practice regimens of using their nondominant hand or curbing their verbal dysfluencies, or were given no self-control exercises (Oaten et al. 2002). After two weeks of practice, all three groups were compared on a Stroop task, which measures one's ability to override habitual impulses to achieve an opposing goal. The results showed that participants who engaged in self-control exercises for the two weeks prior to the test performed much better than participants in the no-exercise control group.

Both study's results had some statistical noise, and the findings need to be replicated more strongly before one can express high confidence in the conclusions, but the findings do suggest that regular exertion of self-regulation can strengthen the individual's capacity. The muscle analogy is thus a promising model for understanding self-control.

This series of studies points to several conclusions about the nature of self-control. Apparently, efforts to regulate one's own behavior depend on a limited resource, akin to strength or energy. This resource appears to be common to a broad spectrum of seemingly very different kinds of self-control, insofar as the same resource is used for: regulating emotions, suppressing thoughts, physical stamina, persisting in the face of failure in a difficult task, overriding the desire to procrastinate on an undesirable chore (see O'Donoghue and Rabin, chap. 7 herein), curbing impulsive spending, and resisting temptation. Moreover, the resource appears to be quite limited, because even a seemingly brief exertion can produce a noticeable drop in performance.

Exhaustion or Conservation?

Is the self's capacity to control itself indeed seriously depleted after just a couple of minutes of resisting temptation? Our studies suggested that participants did indeed experience some kind of significant depletion that impaired their performance. Yet were they less able to control themselves—or merely less willing?

Both views are plausible. We had found repeatedly that self-control was impaired in the aftermath of using it, and this might suggest that the capacity was in fact so low that the person really could not control him- or herself any further. Then again, it might well be that once the stock of self-regulatory energy began to be depleted, people would seek to conserve what remained.

The potentially immense advantages of being able to regulate one's behavior would make it imperative not to reach the state of full exhaustion. Moreover, the muscle analogy was again relevant: athletes do not normally use their muscles at full capacity until they are fully exhausted. Rather, once they begin to suffer from fatigue, they regulate their efforts carefully so as to conserve their energy, such as by not running after every ball.

Findings by Muraven (1998) supported the conservation view. He found, first, that even when people are experiencing ego depletion, they can regulate themselves effectively if the incentive is large enough. In one study, he varied how much money participants were offered to drink a bad-tasting beverage. When the incentive was low, he found the usual ego depletion effect, which was that people who had already exerted self-control performed worse than other people. Yet this deficit vanished when participants were offered a relatively large amount of money.

In another study, Muraven (1998) tested the conservation hypothesis by telling people that they would have a third self-control task to perform. In other words, participants performed a first act of self-regulation (or not, in the control group), then they performed a second self-control task after being told that a third task was pending (or not, in another control condition). Sure enough, people who had been depleted by the first task and anticipated the third task showed the biggest drop in self-control on the second task. Moreover, how much they had exerted themselves on the second task was inversely related to how well they did on the third task, which is precisely what an energy conservation model would predict.

These results shed further light on the nature of self-regulation: it consumes a limited resource, but the resource is not as limited as might appear at first blush. The impairments in self-regulation that follow an initial exertion may be motivated by the desire to conserve the remaining resource, rather than being a sign that the resource is dangerously near exhaustion. People can "suck it up" and exert further self-control if necessary, although the cost in subsequent performance is high.

Decision Fatigue

In summarizing what social psychology has learned about the self, Baumeister (1998) proposed that self-regulation is part of what may be broadly termed the executive function. Self-regulation is thus akin to other executive processes, including decision making, exerting control, active (instead of passive) responding, initiative, responsibility, and other acts of volition. This view of self-regulation raises the possibility that the energy used in self-regulation may also be involved in other processes of the self's executive function.

Anecdotal impressions underscored the plausibility of the view that the energy resource used in self-regulation would also be used in decision making. One colleague described how utterly depleted she had felt after making all the decisions involved in bridal registry. Meanwhile, a spate of political scandals suggested that dangerous failures of impulse control can often be found in the private lives of men whose occupational and public lives include the burden of substantial decision making.

We conducted several laboratory tests to investigate the possible links between self-regulation and decision making. In one study, participants agreed to make a speech contrary to their established attitudes, under conditions of either high or low choice. This is a standard method used in cognitive dissonance research (Linder et al. 1967). Sure enough, people who had made an active choice agreeing to make the speech subsequently showed ego depletion, as indicated by reduced persistence on unsolvable laboratory tasks (Baumeister et al. 1998). Participants in the low-choice condition showed no such reduction in persistence. In another series of studies, participants were asked to make a long series of choices between products—or, in the control condition, simply to report on their usage of those same products. Afterward, with a new experimenter, their ability to make themselves consume a bad-tasting beverage was assessed. The people who had made many choices exhibited a significant decrement in how much they could make themselves drink compared with people in the control condition. These results suggest that the same resource is used in decision making as in self-regulation. They also suggest that in fact to make decisions and choices is psychologically draining.

Self-Regulation and Intertemporal Choice

Self-regulation is often crucial to intertemporal choice, and indeed the early studies on the capacity to delay gratification (for example, Mischel and Ebbesen 1970; Mischel et al., chap. 5 herein)—itself an important form of intertemporal choice—constitute the most important foundation of modern research on self-regulation. The link involves resisting the strong impulse to seize the immediate reward rather than pursue the greater but delayed reward.

We assume that behavioral tendencies arise when latent motivations encounter some activating stimulus. When a hungry person sees food, he or she will experience an impulse to eat it. Immediately available stimuli will therefore elicit the strongest impulses, by and large. Accordingly, in nature, a short-term focus predominates: animals respond to the immediate environment. Animals have no concept of planning for the future, which is one of the premises underlying self-regulation (for a discussion of animal self-control see Kacelnik, chap. 3 herein). Saving money in case of crisis, dieting to lose weight and therefore live longer, and putting forth extra effort to soothe a loved one are deliberate behaviors that center on an individual's desire to lay the foundation for his or her future. In contrast, animals' future-minded behaviors, such as the squirrel that gathers acorns for the winter, are preprogrammed and do not require intent or advanced thought.

To override the impulse stimulated by the immediate outcome, it is therefore necessary to pursue a delayed one. Such overriding is the essence of self-regulatory operations. The normal or natural sequence would be for the stimulus to elicit the impulse, which in turn would produce the behavior. Pursuing the distal goal, however, requires resisting that impulse.

Pursuing long-term benefits instead of immediately available ones therefore is difficult. Doing so may also be highly adaptive. By storing food instead of consuming it all, our ancestors may have been able to survive periods of scarcity (see Kacelnik, chap. 3 herein). Even today, the financial sacrifices necessary to obtain a college education produce substantial (though delayed) benefits in terms of lifetime earnings (Vohs and Faber 2002; see also Angeletos et al., chap. 18 herein; Wertenbroch, chap. 17 herein).

In fact, we suspect that the adaptive benefits of delaying gratification were one of the crucial reasons that human beings evolved the capacity for self-regulation. Developing the ability to resist impulses induced by immediate stimuli probably conferred a huge competitive advantage on some of the earliest human beings and thereby enabled them to survive and reproduce better than others.

Futuremindedness and Transcendence

The psychological requirements of futuremindedness can be understood by considering the problem of delayed gratification. For people to pursue a distal goal instead of a less appealing but more immediate one, what is necessary?

First, clearly, the individual must be able to hold a cognitive representation of the distal goal. The proximal goal has the advantage of salience, and the distal goal can only compete if the person can imagine or visualize it. This factor encompasses more than the simple cognitive capacity to form mental representations. Variations in how well the distal goal can be imagined may well have a substantial impact on how powerfully it competes with proximal temptations. For example, that medieval Christians sought to depict Heaven and Hell with vivid, concrete descriptions rather than allowing them to remain mere abstractions may be no accident. The clear images may well have had more power for inducing believers to regulate their current behavior on the basis of contingencies that extended to after their death. Baumeister, Heatherton, and Tice (1994) used the term *transcendence* to refer to the ability to see beyond the immediate circumstances, especially in terms of mentally representing distal goals and abstract standards instead of allowing one's behavior to be driven entirely by proximal stimuli.

A second requirement is to believe that the distal goal can possibly be reached. One may well imagine a distal goal, even vividly, but if one does not believe that one can ever reach it, it will lose much of its motivational power. Snyder's (forthcoming) writing on hope captures this aspect effectively, for Snyder insists that hope depends on both visualizing a goal and being able to conceptualize pathways to reach it from one's current situation. At the level of pursuing body weight self-standards, Vohs and colleagues (Vohs et al. 1999; Vohs et al. 2001) have found that when perfectionistic, low self-esteem women believe they are overweight, they enter into a negative spiral of binge eating and subsequent purging. Indeed, these perfectionistic, low self-esteem women can all too vividly imagine the distal goal—but they do not believe that they have the ability to reach their desired level of thinness.

The capacity to organize behavior toward the pursuit of distal goals is also essential. That is, the person must be able to plan and carry out behaviors designed to bring about the realization of the distal goal. Gollwitzer, for example (1999), has researched the benefits of implementation intentions, which involve making conditional statements about behaviors that will be performed if one encounters an obstacle to goal pursuit. (For example, "If I feel discouraged, I will think of the high-paying job I'll get with a college degree.") Making these statements helps the individual know which behaviors to perform and also renders the behaviors less effortful when enacted. The pursuit of some future benefit is typically more than a matter of making a single choice at the present time. Rather, the person may have to make a series of choices conducive to making further choices, spanning a long period. Each may require some faith that one will have the consistency to make all the others.

Last, to resist the recurrent temptations to pursue immediate satisfactions is necessary, when these compete with distal goals. Long-term success often depends on some degree of short-term self-denial, and this in turn requires overriding the proximal impulses so that one's behavior can be effectively directed toward the distal goal.

Losing the Future

Thus far we have argued that self-regulation is important for enabling people to pursue distal goals instead of succumbing to the temptation of proximal stimuli. That intertemporal choices will be altered by events or factors that weaken self-control follows. Impairment of self-regulation will often be accompanied by a shift of focus toward a heightened orientation to the present, which will undermine pursuit of distal goals.

One factor that emerged from our own laboratory is ego depletion (as mentioned). The ability to override responses and alter one's behavior depends on a limited resource that operates like an energy or strength. After it has been used, the resource is depleted, and the self is less able to carry out its functions. This resource corresponds to the traditional concept of willpower, and indeed the concept of power does entail several relevant aspects of the resources (such as being limited and being subject to depletion). In laboratory studies, people who initially exert self-regulation (such as by trying to suppress certain thoughts, increase or diminish their emotional responses, or resist the temptation to eat chocolates and cookies) subsequently are less able to regulate themselves effectively on other, seemingly unrelated tasks (Baumeister et al. 1998; Muraven et al. 1998; Vohs and Heatherton 2000).

The weakening of self-regulation during ego depletion often is accompanied by signs of a shift toward a present focus. Although somewhat speculative, the measures used in ego depletion studies suggest a shift away from futuremindedness and toward emphasizing immediate, present concerns. Such concerns include giving up more rapidly on painful, unpleasant, or discouraging tasks, and yielding more readily to emotionally evocative stimuli (Baumeister et al. 1998; Muraven et al. 1998). In support of the idea that ego threat elevates the importance of immediate interests are data showing that depletion (in the form of emotion regulation) leads to greater eating among chronic dieters (Vohs and Heatherton 2000). Under neutral conditions, they are able to maintain their caloric restrictions, but after ego depletion people whose explicit goal is to lose weight are overcome by the temptation of available (but fattening) desserts (see also Herman and Polivy, chap. 16 herein).

Self-regulation also alters the perception of time, as new data indicate. Vohs and Schmeichel (2002) randomly assigned people to suppress their emotions during a video clip or were given no instructions, and afterward they were instructed to estimate the duration of the video clip (retrospective time perception). Participants who suppressed their feelings estimated the clip as having been significantly longer than the other participants, suggesting that the exertion of self-regulation made the time drag by more slowly. In another study, participants were asked to either suppress their emotions, psychologically distance themselves from the emotion-provoking event (a strategy called *reappraisal* that has been shown to effectively control emotions; see Richards and Gross 2000), or were given no instructions. Emotion suppression—but not reappraisal or no regulation—led to longer retrospective estimates of the duration of the video clip. In a third study, participants were first asked to write a pro- or counterattitudinal essay (corresponding to no depletion and depletion, respectively), then asked to prospectively estimate the duration of a specific time interval. In this study, no differences in prospective time estimates were found as a function of depletion condition. In a fourth study, time perception was manipulated such that participants believed either more, less, or a veridical amount of time had passed during a regulatory task. Participants who believed that time was moving slowly (more slowly than actual time) were more likely to quit the self-regulation task early. A further study showed that time perceptions of duration of a regulatory episode can statistically account for differences in self-regulatory efforts after previous self-regulatory resource expenditure. Thus self-regulatory resource depletion may lengthen people's perceptions of the duration of a regulatory task, which leads people to exert less regulatory energy subsequently (for a related discussion see Liberman and Trope, chap. 8 herein).

Emotional distress is an important cause of self-regulation failure, and indeed a review of widely assorted findings about different patterns of self-regulation failure repeatedly found evidence of emotional distress contributing to such failure (Baumeister et al. 1994). Recent work suggests that one important reason that emotional distress undermines self-regulation is that it brings about a priority shift. Specifically, emotional distress causes people to want to feel better immediately, by whatever means.

Unfortunately, the means that promise immediate good feelings often are precisely the ones that people may seek to regulate and restrain in order to pursue their long-term goals and standards. Eating fattening foods, drinking, taking drugs, spending money, and wasting time in frivolous pleasures all hold the promise of short-term pleasures. Many people seek to restrain their indulgence in those pleasures, but when they become emotionally distraught they may abandon their long-term concern with restraint and indulge themselves—hoping to feel better as a result. Tice, Bratslavsky, and Baumeister (2001) found that emotionally distraught people indulged in such pleasures specifically because they hoped to feel better. When people were told that their moods were fixed and would not be susceptible to change for a short period of time, people lost interest in indulging in those pleasures. Bushman, Baumeister, and Phillips (2001) found the same for aggression. That is, people who believed that venting their anger was a good way to feel better tended to respond to a provocation with high aggression—unless they had been told that the pill they had just taken would render their moods unable to change for the next hour, in which case they were no more aggressive than others.

One way to interpret these findings is that emotional distress raises the priority of the immediate present, at the expense of the future. Emotional distress tends to be present-oriented, because emotions are temporary states that exist in the here and now. A person may be dieting successfully in the hope of looking good in a swimsuit next summer—but intense emotional distress makes next summer seem impossibly far away and hence irrelevant, whereas consuming that entire cheesecake holds the (possibly illusory) promise of feeling better in the next few minutes.

Another common cause of self-regulation failure is alcohol intoxication. As with emotional distress, alcohol intoxication has been implicated in most spheres and varieties of self-regulation failure (Baumeister et al. 1994). Why does this happen? One explanation is that alcohol intoxication narrows the focus of attention to the here and now, thereby giving greater power to proximal stimuli and weakening any motivation to pursue the distal ones. Steele and Josephs (1990) coined the term *alcohol myopia* to refer to the narrowing of attention that occurs under the influence of alcohol. Under this myopia, a few salient stimuli seem to gain power and influence, whereas others recede. Since effective self-regulation depends on maintaining the focus on the distal goals and outcomes, self-regulation will be undermined when attention recedes from them and focuses instead on the temptations and provocations in the here and now.

Conclusion

The resource appears to be common to a broad spectrum of important activities of the self. We found that the same resource is used in many seemingly different and unrelated spheres of self-regulation, including mood and emotion control, thought suppression, impulse control, and task performance. Moreover, we found that the same resource is used in other kinds of volition, notably decision making. Hence this limited resource deserves to be recognized as one of the self's most important aspects. Self-regulation is quite relevant to intertemporal choice. Many such choices require the person to forgo the temptation to respond to immediate stimuli in order to pursue what is more desirable or beneficial in the long run. When the capacity for self-control is impaired, such as during ego depletion, the person is less able to transcend the immediate situation and pursue distal goals.

References

Baumeister, Roy F. 1998. "The Self." In *Handbook of Social Psychology*, 4th ed., edited by Dan T. Gilbert, Susan T. Fiske, and Gardner Lindzey. New York: McGraw-Hill.

Baumeister, Roy F., Ellen Bratslavsky, Mark Muraven, and Dianne M. Tice. 1998. "Ego Depletion: Is the Active Self a Limited Resource?" *Journal of Personality and Social Psychology* 74: 1252–65.

Baumeister, Roy F., Todd F. Heatherton, and Dianne M. Tice. 1994. *Losing Control: How and Why People Fail at Self-Regulation*. San Diego: Academic Press.

Bushman, Brad J., Roy F. Baumeister, and Coleen M. Phillips. 2001. "Do People Aggress to Improve Their Mood? Catharsis Beliefs, Affect Regulation Opportunity, and Aggressive Responding." *Journal of Personality and Social Psychology* 81: 17–32.

Engels, Rutger, Catrin Finkenauer, Endy den Exter Blokland, and Roy F. Baumeister. 2002. "Parental Influences on Self-Control and Juvenile Delinquency." Unpublished paper. Utrecht University, Netherlands.

Finkel, Eli J., and W. Keith Campbell. 2001. "Self-Control and Accommodation in Close Relationships: An Interdependence Analysis." *Journal of Personality and Social Psychology* 81: 263–77.

Gollwitzer, P. M. 1999. "Implementation Intentions: Strong Effects of Simple Plans." *American Psychologist* 54: 493–503.

Linder, Darwyn E., Joel Cooper, and Edward E. Jones. 1967. "Decision Freedom as a Determinant of the Role of Incentive Magnitude in Attitude Change." *Journal of Personality and Social Psychology* 6: 245–54.

Mischel, Walter, and Ebbe B. Ebbesen. 1970. "Attention in Delay of Gratification." *Journal of Personality and Social Psychology* 16: 329–37.

Mischel, Walter, Yuichi Shoda, and Philip K. Peake. 1988. "The Nature of Adolescent Competencies Predicted by Preschool Delay of Gratification." *Journal of Personality and Social Psychology* 54: 687–96.

Muraven, Mark. 1998. *Mechanisms of Self-Control Failure: Motivation and Limited Resource.* Ph.D. diss., Case Western Reserve University, Cleveland, Ohio.

Muraven, Mark, Roy F. Baumeister, and Dianne M. Tice. 1999. "Longitudinal Improvement of Self-Regulation Through Practice: Building Self-Control Strength Through Repeated Exercise." *Journal of Social Psychology* 139: 446–57.

Muraven, Mark, Dianne M. Tice, and Roy F. Baumeister. 1998. "Self-Control as Limited Resource: Regulatory Depletion Patterns." *Journal of Personality and Social Psychology* 74: 774–89.

Oaten, Megan, Kathleen D. Vohs, Ken Cheng, and Roy F. Baumeister. 2002. "Strengthening the Regulatory Muscle: The Longitudinal Benefit of Exercising Self-Control." Unpublished paper. Case Western Reserve University, Cleveland, Ohio.

Richards, Jane M., and James J. Gross. 2000. "Emotional Regulation and Memory: The Cognitive Costs of Keeping One's Cool." *Journal of Personality and Social Psychology* 79: 410–24.

Schwartz, Barry. 2000. "Self-Determination: The Tyranny of Freedom." *American Psychologist* 55: 79–88.

Shoda, Yuichi, Walter Mischel, and Philip K. Peake. 1990. "Predicting Adolescent Cognitive and Self-Regulatory Competencies from Preschool Delay of Gratification: Identifying Diagnostic Conditions." *Developmental Psychology* 26: 978–86.

Snyder, C. Richard. Forthcoming. "Hope Theory: Rainbows in the Mind." *Psychological Inquiry.*

Steele, Claude M., and Robert A. Josephs. 1990. "Alcohol Myopia: Its Prized and Dangerous Effects." *American Psychologist* 45: 921–33.

Tangney, June P., and Roy F. Baumeister. 2000. "High Self-Control Predicts Good Adjustment, Less Pathology, Better Grades, and Interpersonal Success." Unpublished paper. George Mason University, Fairfax, Va.

Tice, Dianne M., Ellen Bratslavsky, and Roy F. Baumeister. 2001. "Emotional Distress Regulation Takes Precedence over Impulse Control: If You Feel Bad, Do It!" *Journal of Personality and Social Psychology* 80: 53–67.

Vohs, K. D., Anna M. Bardone, Thomas E. Joiner Jr., Lyn Y. Abramson, and Todd F. Heatherton. 1999. "Perfectionism, Perceived Weight Status, and Self-Esteem Interact to Predict Bulimic Symptoms: A Model of Bulimic Symptom Development." *Journal of Abnormal Psychology* 108: 695–700.

Vohs, Kathleen D., Natalie Ciarocco, and Roy F. Baumeister. 2002. "Interpersonal Functioning Requires Self-Regulatory Resources." Unpublished paper. Case Western Reserve University, Cleveland, Ohio.

Vohs, Kathleen D., and Ron Faber. October 2002. "Self-Regulation and Impulsive Spending Patterns." Association for Consumer Research, Atlanta, Ga.

Vohs, Kathleen D., and Todd F. Heatherton. 2000. "Self-Regulatory Failure: A Resource-Depletion Approach." *Psychological Science* 11: 249–54.

Vohs, Kathleen D., and Brandon J. Schmeichel. 2002. "Subjective Time Perception and Self-Regulation." Unpublished paper. University of Utah, Salt Lake City.

Vohs, Kathleen D., Zachary R. Voelz, Jeremy W. Pettit, Anna M. Bardone, Jennifer Katz, Lyn Y. Abramson, Todd F. Heatherton, and Thomas E. Joiner Jr. 2001. "Perfectionism, Body Dissatisfaction, and Self-Esteem: An Interactive Model of Bulimic Symptom Development." *Journal of Social and Clinical Psychology* 20: 476–97.

Wegner, Daniel M., David J. Schneider, Samuel R. Carter, and Teri L. White. 1987. "Paradoxical Effects of Thought Suppression." *Journal of Personality and Social Psychology* 53: 5–13.

· 7 ·

Self-Awareness and Self-Control

TED O'DONOGHUE AND MATTHEW RABIN

P EOPLE have self-control problems: from a prior perspective, they want to behave relatively patiently, but as the moment of action approaches, they want to behave relatively impatiently.[1] While the existence of self-control problems is well established and much discussed in psychological research, a standard assumption used in economic models of intertemporal choice is that a person's preferences cannot change over time. Recently, however, a small set of economists have studied the implications of self-control problems for a variety of economic behaviors, including consumption-saving decisions, procrastination, addiction, information acquisition, and job search.

When a person has self-control problems and his preferences change over time, the question arises to what extent is that person aware of his own future self-control problems. While there is very little behavioral evidence, much of the economic research on self-control problems has assumed full awareness. This chapter will discuss alternative assumptions to full awareness, ranging from full unawareness to partial awareness. We argue with some simple illustrations that the degree to which a person is aware of self-control problems is a crucial determinant of the implications of those self-control problems, and hence analyses that assume complete awareness can sometimes be misleading.

Self-Control Problems and Self-Awareness

A standard assumption used in economic models of intertemporal choice is that people have *time-consistent preferences*: a person's relative preference for well-being at an earlier date over a later date is the same no matter when she is asked. If, for example, from a prior perspective a person prefers a larger, later reward to a smaller, sooner reward, the passage of time cannot change this preference. More concretely, if on Monday a person chooses to work on Saturday rather than Sunday, the person cannot change her mind when Saturday arrives; and if someone decides to save next year, that person cannot change her mind when next year arrives.

Self-Control Problems

Psychology has a long tradition that seeks to identify the discount function used for intertemporal choice. Perhaps the most robust conclusion from this literature is that people have declining discount rates: a person's relative preference for date τ over date $\tau + \Delta$ is larger the closer is τ to the present moment (now). In other words, from a prior perspective, people want to behave relatively patiently, but as the moment of action approaches, they want to behave relatively impatiently. While the evidence is sometimes explicitly framed in terms of declining discount rates, it is sometimes framed in other ways. For instance, a large strand of research discusses how hyperbolic discount functions—which impose declining discount rates—better fit the data than do exponential discount functions—which impose constant discount rates. Another strand of research discusses how people exhibit *preference reversals*, wherein a larger, later reward is preferred to a smaller, sooner reward when both dates are far in the future, but the smaller, sooner reward becomes preferred if both dates are moved close enough to now.[2]

In recent years, a number of economists have incorporated such self-control problems into their analyses. The goal of this research has been to understand the implications of self-control problems in specific economic environments; we discuss specific applications in a later section.[3] These researchers have modeled self-control problems in a particularly simple way, using a model originally developed by Phelps and Pollak (1968) in the context of intergenerational altruism, and later used by Laibson (1994, 1997) to model self-control problems within an individual. Let u_t be the instantaneous utility a person gets in period t, by which we mean well-being in period t. The person's intertemporal preferences at time t, U^t, can be represented by the following intertemporal utility function:

$$U^t (u_t, u_{t+1}, \ldots, u_T) \equiv u_t + \beta \sum_{\tau=t+1}^{T} \delta^{\tau-1} u_\tau.$$

This model is a simple modification of the standard discounted-utility model. The parameter δ is the standard discount rate, and represents "time-consistent" impatience. The parameter β introduces a time-inconsistent preference for immediate gratification, and represents the person's self-control problem. In particular, for any $\beta < 1$, at any given moment the person has an extra bias for the present over the future.

To better understand how these preferences incorporate self-control problems, consider the following example.

Example 1   Suppose a person can choose to see either *Sleepy Hollow* in period 2 or *Ed Wood* in period 3, and these options yield the following instantaneous utilities:

Sleepy Hollow in period 2: $u_1 = 0$, $u_2 = 4$, $u_3 = 0$.

Ed Wood in period 3: $u_1 = 0$, $u_2 = 0$, $u_3 = 6$.

Consider the person's preferences when $\delta = 1$ and $\beta = 1/2$. From a period-1 perspective, the person's preferences are $U^1 (u_1, u_2, u_3) \equiv u_1 + (1/2)u_2 + (1/2)u_3$. Hence the person prefers to see *Ed Wood*, because doing so yields intertemporal utility of $(1/2)6 = 3$, whereas seeing *Sleepy Hollow* would only yield intertemporal utility of $(1/2)4 = 2$. When period 2 arrives, the person's preferences change to $U^2(u_2, u_3) \equiv u_2 + (1/2)u_3$. As a result, he now prefers to see *Sleepy Hollow*, because doing so yields intertemporal utility of $(1)4 = 4$, whereas seeing *Ed Wood* would only yield intertemporal utility of $(1/2)6 = 3$. This example illustrates how these (β, δ) preferences give rise to a self-control problem: whereas from a prior perspective the person wants to behave relatively patiently and attend the better movie, at the moment of action he wants to behave relatively impatiently and see the inferior movie now.

Self-Awareness

When a person has self-control problems and her preferences change over time, a question arises: to what extent is she aware of her own future self-control problems? Two extreme assumptions about self-awareness have appeared in the economics literature on self-control problems. Most researchers assume that people are *sophisticated*, fully aware of their future self-control problems, and therefore prone to correctly predict how they will behave in the future. Fewer researchers have assumed people are *naive*, fully unaware of their future self-control problems, and therefore prone to (wrongly) predict that they will behave themselves in the future.[4]

While casual observation and introspection suggest that people lie somewhere between these two extremes—that people are aware that they will have self-control problems but underestimate their magnitude—the behavioral evidence is quite limited. One study worth mentioning (Ariely and Wertenbroch 2002) is discussed in Wertenbroch (chap. 17 herein). They offer one group of subjects the ability to impose costly deadlines on themselves (for example, binding deadlines for course papers), while for a second group evenly spaced deadlines are exogenously imposed. Subjects in the first group chose to impose deadlines on themselves, suggesting that they are not completely naive. But the deadlines they chose allowed more delay than evenly spaced deadlines, and by some performance measures—for example, their grade for the course—they fared worse than people with exogenously imposed, evenly spaced deadlines. These results are consistent with people being to some degree aware, but not completely aware, of future self-control problems.

O'Donoghue and Rabin (2001) formulate an approach to the more realistic assumption *partial naivete*. We suppose that a person has true self-control problem β, but perceives that in the future he will have self-control problem $\hat{\beta}$. Formally, we assume the person believes that in the future he will behave like a sophisticated person with self-control problem $\hat{\beta}$. Given these beliefs, the person chooses current behavior to maximize current preferences, which are of course determined by his true self-control problem β. With this formulation, people with standard time-consistent preferences—to whom we refer as TCs—have $\hat{\beta} = \beta = 1$, sophisticates have $\hat{\beta} = \beta < 1$, naifs have $\beta < \hat{\beta} = 1$, and partial naifs have $\beta < \hat{\beta} < 1$.

To illustrate this approach, consider what it implies in example 1. As argued earlier, in period 1 the person prefers to see *Ed Wood*, while in period 2 he prefers to see *Sleepy Hollow*. What does the person believe in period 1 about his period-2 preferences? Given beliefs $\hat{\beta}$, the person perceives his period-2 preferences to be $\hat{U}^2(u_2,u_3) \equiv u_2 + \hat{\beta}u_3$. If $\hat{\beta} < 2/3$, the person believes that in period 2 he will prefer to see *Sleepy Hollow*—that is, the person correctly predicts that his preferences will change. If, in contrast, $\hat{\beta} > 2/3$, the person believes that in period 2 he will prefer to see *Ed Wood*—that is, the person incorrectly predicts that his preferences will not change.

The next section will explore how the different beliefs about future preferences influence choice behavior.

Basic Principles

In this section, we explore the role of awareness in some simple environments. Our goal is to outline some basic principles, which will then be used to frame our discussion of specific applications. Throughout this section, we apply the (β, δ) preferences described earlier, where we assume for simplicity that $\delta = 1$.

"One-Shot" Decisions

In some situations, a person's awareness of future self-control problems does not affect her behavior. The most obvious such case is a simple one-shot decision. Consider, for instance, a person who is choosing whether to have dessert. Suppose the dessert would yield an immediate benefit of 5, but would create future costs of 10. If these were truly the only payoff consequences of having dessert, then the person's decision is simple: eat the dessert if $5 - \beta(10) > 0$, or $\beta < 1/2$. In other words, the person simply implements what she currently feels to be the best decision, and her awareness of future self-control problems is irrelevant.

Several comments about this conclusion help illustrate the ways in which awareness will matter. First, one-shot decisions need not involve only short-term behavior. If, for instance, someone must commit in January to a sequence of desserts for the next three months, the person will merely choose what he currently feels to be the best sequence, and again his awareness of future self-control problems would be irrelevant. More generally, for any decisions involving long-term commitments, awareness will not play an important role.[5]

Second, if someone faces a series of completely disconnected one-shot decisions, her awareness of future self-control problems still does not matter. Suppose, for instance, that on seven consecutive nights the person must choose whether to have dessert that night. These decisions are disconnected if eating dessert on any given night does not affect the payoffs from eating dessert on any other night. If the aforementioned payoffs apply for all nights, then the person will eat dessert on all seven nights if $\beta < 1/2$, and no desserts if $\beta > 1/2$. Notice that, because the benefit is smaller than the cost, on each night the person would like to skip dessert on every future night. Also notice that her beliefs about whether she will eat desserts on future nights depends on her awareness—if $\hat{\beta} < 1/2$, the person predicts that she will eat dessert on all future nights, whereas if $\hat{\beta} > 1/2$, the person predicts that she will not eat dessert on any future night. When the payoffs for the different decisions are disconnected, however, neither of these concerns influences the person's decision whether to have dessert tonight.

What makes two decisions disconnected? Formally, two decisions are disconnected if the choice for each decision does not affect the payoffs for the other decision. Whether this condition is satisfied of course depends on what the two decisions are. Should a person's beliefs about whether he will rent *Ed Wood* versus *Sleepy Hollow* next weekend affect his decision whether to have dessert tonight? Probably not. Should his beliefs about whether to have a hamburger versus a salad for lunch tomorrow matter? Perhaps. Should his beliefs about whether to have a banana versus cake late tonight matter? Probably yes.

This discussion suggests that true one-shot decisions are rare. In the dessert example, if eating dessert tonight affects the payoffs from eating dessert tomorrow night—for example, because the cost of desserts is not linear in the number of desserts, or because the person will develop a taste for desserts, or because the person has a limited budget for desserts—then it is no longer a one-shot decision, and awareness of future self-control problems matters.[6]

When to Do an Activity

When decisions are connected, awareness can sometimes mitigate and sometimes exacerbate misbehavior due to self-control problems, depending on the environment. To demonstrate these possibilities, we present a modified version of the one-activity environment introduced by O'Donoghue and Rabin (1999a, 2000). Suppose a person must do some activity exactly once in some finite number of periods. In each period, the person chooses only whether to do the activity then, with no external commitment devices available to commit future behavior. In such an environment, the implications of self-control problems—and the role of awareness—depend on whether the activity is onerous or pleasurable. First consider the case of an onerous activity, such as writing a paper.

Example 2 Suppose a person must carry out an onerous task in one of the next T periods, where T might be large. The task is onerous in the sense that carrying out the task requires that the person incur an immediate cost of 10. Completing the task generates a future reward, but delay in completing the task reduces this future reward. Specifically, if the person completes the task in period 1 then she gets reward V, but each period of delay reduces the reward by $1/2$. Hence, if the person completes the task in period $k + 1$ (that is, she delays for k periods), then the reward is $V - (1/2)k$.

We examine behavior in this environment when $\delta = 1$ and $\beta = .9$. Given $\delta = 1$, standard time-consistent agents merely complete the task in the period that maximizes the reward minus the cost, which is period 1. The behavior of time-consistent agents is a useful benchmark, because it represents how people with self-control problems would like to behave if asked from some prior perspective. In each period, people with self-control problems trade off their desire to put off incurring the onerous task cost against the lost reward from a short delay.

Naifs, who are fully unaware of future self-control problems, procrastinate completing the task until the last possible moment–that is, until period T. Since naifs always believe they will behave themselves and choose optimally in the future, they always believe that if they delay this period then they will complete the task next period (because any further delay would be suboptimal). Hence, in each period they compare the benefit of incurring the onerous task cost in the future rather than now, which is $(1 - \beta)10 = 1$, to the (discounted) lost reward from a one-period delay, which is $\beta(1/2) = .45$. Since the benefit of delay is larger than the lost reward, naifs always prefer to complete the task next period rather than this period, and so they wait in all periods and end up completing the task in period T.

Sophisticates, in contrast, who are fully aware of future self-control problems, complete the task early on—specifically, in one of the first three periods. Like naifs, sophisticates would like to delay incurring the onerous task cost. Unlike naifs, sophisticates correctly predict when they would complete the task in the future were they to delay now. Hence, if in period 1 sophisticates choose to delay, then they must be at peace with the actual realized delay. In other words, if sophisticates delay until period τ, then in period 1 they must have preferred completion in period τ to completion in period 1. In this example, sophisticates are willing to tolerate a two-period delay (until period 3) but not a three-period delay (until period 4). Thus sophisticates must complete the task in one of the first three periods.[7]

Partial naifs with beliefs $\hat{\beta} < .909$ behave exactly like sophisticates and complete the task early on, and partial naifs with $\hat{\beta} > .909$ behave exactly like naifs and complete the task at the last possible moment. Partial naifs would like to delay, but are willing to tolerate at most a two-period delay. If their beliefs are sufficiently well cali-brated—$\hat{\beta}$ close enough to β—then partial naifs predict the same future behavior as sophisticates, and hence behave exactly as sophis-ticates do. Suppose instead that their beliefs are sufficiently over-opti-mistic that they view their future tolerance for delay to be at least one day shorter than their current tolerance for delay—that is, their per-ceived future tolerance for delay is less than two periods. Then in all periods partial naifs believe that, if they wait now, they will complete the task within two periods. As a result, they wait in all periods and end up completing the task in period T. In this example, the per-ceived future tolerance for delay is less than two if $(1 - \hat{\beta})10 < \hat{\beta}(2 \times 1/2)$ or $\hat{\beta} > .909$.[8]

Example 2 illustrates how, for an onerous activity, a preference for im-mediate gratification implies a tendency to procrastinate—delay com-pletion relative to TCs. More important for our discussion of the role of awareness, this example illustrates how naivete exacerbates mis-behavior in this environment. An overoptimistic belief that you won't procrastinate in the future makes it more likely that you procrastinate now. Example 2 also illustrates how it only takes a small amount of naivete to generate severe procrastination of the form we see for com-plete naifs. In particular, the person severely procrastinates whenever he perceives his future self-control problem to be $\hat{\beta} > .909$, and the critical level is not much larger than his true future self-control prob-lem of $\beta = .9$.

Our conclusion that only a little naivete is required to generate severe procrastination of an onerous task is quite robust. The basic intuition is exactly as in example 2: whenever a person is willing to tolerate, say, a k-period delay, that person only needs to be sufficiently overoptimistic to make her perceived future tolerance for delay less than or equal to $k - 1$ to generate severe procrastination. This conclu-sion illustrates how the assumption of complete sophistication can sometimes be nonrobust to a little naivete. Indeed, one can show that, while sophisticates are immune to severe procrastination, a person with any degree of naivete is subject to the possibility of severe pro-crastination.

We next turn our attention to the case of a pleasurable activity, such as seeing a movie.

Example 3 Suppose a person gets to carry out a pleasurable activity exactly once in the next T periods, where T may be large. The activity is pleasurable in the sense that carrying out the activity yields some immediate reward, and this reward is growing over time. Specifically, if the person completes the activity in period T, then he gets reward

V, but if the person completes the activity prior to period T, then the reward is reduced by factor $.99$ per period. Hence, if the person completes the activity in period t, then the reward is $(.99)^{T-t}V$. Finally, no costs are associated with the activity.

We again examine behavior when $\delta = 1$ and $\beta = .9$. Time-consistent agents complete the activity in the period with the largest reward, which is period T. Hence, if asked from a prior perspective, people with self-control problems would most like to wait until period T. Each period, however, they trade off their desire to grab the reward now against the larger reward that comes from waiting.

Naifs are able to delay until period $T - 10$.[9] As before, naifs always believe they will behave themselves and choose optimally in the future, which here means that they always believe that if they wait, they will end up completing the activity in period T. In period t, therefore, they compare grabbing the reward now, which has value $(.99)^{T-t}V$, to waiting until period T, which has value $\beta(V)$. The larger is t, the larger is the value of grabbing the reward now. Thus naifs do the activity the first time they prefer receiving the reward now as opposed to waiting until period T, which is period $T - 10$.

Sophisticates, sadly, are unable to delay at all, and grab the reward in period 1. In each period, sophisticates are willing to delay only if they believe they will wait more than 10 periods, because $(.99)^{T-t}V < \beta(.99)^{T-t-d}V$ only if $d > 10$. But an unraveling similar to that of the finitely repeated prisoner's dilemma leads them to always believe that if they delay now they'll just grab the reward next period. Since sophisticates correctly predict that they would complete the activity on date $T - 1$, on date $T - 2$ they realize that waiting merely means waiting one additional period, which is not worth it. Hence sophisticates would complete the activity in period $T - 2$. This means that in period $T - 3$ they correctly realize that waiting merely means waiting one additional period, and so they would complete the activity in period $T - 3$. This logic iterates until sophisticates decide in period 1 that they might as well complete the activity now.

Partial naifs with beliefs $\hat{\beta} > .99$ behave exactly like naifs and delay until period $T - 10$, and partial naifs with $\hat{\beta} < .99$ behave exactly like sophisticates and don't delay at all. Intuitively, when $\hat{\beta} > .99$, partial naifs, like naifs, believe that if they wait, they will end up completing the activity in period T. When $\hat{\beta} < .99$, however, partial naifs experience the same unraveling logic as sophisticates, and hence, like sophisticates, always believe that if they delay now they'll just grab the reward next period.

Example 3 illustrates how, for a pleasurable activity, a preference for immediate gratification implies a tendency to *preoperate*—accelerate completion relative to TCs. In this environment, it is *sophistication* that exacerbates misbehavior. An accurate belief that you'll just preproperate in the future reduces the value of waiting, and therefore makes you more prone to preproperate now. Moreover, even a little awareness can induce severe preproperation. This example illustrates that sophistication effects can arise even for small degrees of awareness. Hence merely observing that people make commitments, or seem to be worried about their own future behavior, does not mean that people are completely sophisticated.

A Richer Environment

In the simple, discrete, one-activity model, the effects of awareness are straightforward: for onerous activities, awareness mitigates misbehavior, while for pleasurable activities, awareness exacerbates misbehavior. In richer environments, the effects of awareness are more complicated. To illustrate, consider a simple three-period consumption-saving example. Suppose a person has an income of $100,000 to allocate over three years of consumption, and assume for simplicity that the interest rate is 0 percent. In year 1, the person chooses how to divide this income between year-1 consumption (c_1) and saving for years 2 and 3 ($s_1 = \$100,000 - c_1$). Then in year 2, the person chooses how to divide these savings between year-2 consumption (c_2) and year-3 consumption (c_3). We assume the person's instantaneous utility (well-being) in year t is given by $u(c_t)$.

As a benchmark, we note that if u has diminishing marginal utility—if u is concave—then TCs would merely divide their income evenly across the three years, and so they would choose $c_1 = c_2 = c_3 = \$33,333$. People with self-control problems are prone to consume more than $33,333 in year 1 (and less than $33,333 in years 2 and 3). How much more, however, depends (among other things) on their awareness of future self-control problems. Naifs believe that whatever they save they will divide equally between years 2 and 3, and so they believe they will choose $c_2 = c_3 = s_1/2$. People who are aware of their future self-control problems recognize that in year 2 they'll consume more than half of their savings. Whether this awareness leads them to save more or less depends on their utility function.

Table 7.1 describes year-1 consumption as a function of awareness. For simplicity, we assume no time-consistent impatience ($\delta = 1$). We use $\beta = .7$, and we consider three different utility functions. Table 7.1 presents year-1 consumption for four levels of awareness: complete unawareness ($\hat{\beta} = 1$), two levels of partial awareness ($\hat{\beta} = .9$ and $\hat{\beta} = .8$), and complete awareness ($\hat{\beta} = \beta = .7$).

Table 7.1   Year-1 Consumption (c_1) Given \$100,000 to Allocate over Three Years[a]

Utility Function	Naifs $\hat{\beta} = 1$	Partial Naifs		Sophisticates $\hat{\beta} = .7$
		$\hat{\beta} = .9$	$\hat{\beta} = .8$	
$u(c) = c^{1/2}$	$c_1 = \$50,505$	$c_1 = \$50,574$	$c_1 = \$50,812$	$c_1 = \$51,271$
$u(c) = \ln c$	$c_1 = \$41,667$	$c_1 = \$41,667$	$c_1 = \$41,667$	$c_1 = \$41,667$
$u(c) = -c^{-1/2}$	$c_1 = \$38,809$	$c_1 = \$38,801$	$c_1 = \$38,776$	$c_1 = \$38,725$

Source: Authors' compilation.
[a]Assuming $r = 0$ percent, $\delta = 1$, and $\beta = .7$.

For all three utility functions, all types overconsume in year 1 relative to the benchmark of \$33,333. The role of awareness differs across the three utility functions. For the first utility function, increased awareness exacerbates overconsumption; for the second utility function, awareness has no effect on consumption; and for the third utility function, awareness mitigates overconsumption. This ambiguity reflects the more complicated role of awareness in more general environments.[10]

The implications of awareness in this example are not nearly as dramatic as in examples 2 and 3, particularly relative to the main effect of overconsumption due to self-control problems. For utility function $u(c) = c^{1/2}$, people with self-control problems overconsume by more than \$17,000, while the difference between sophisticates and naifs is only \$766. Similarly, for utility function $u(c) = -c^{-1/2}$, people with self-control problems overconsume by more than \$5,000, while the difference between sophisticates and naifs is only \$84. These results reflect that in some circumstances, while the degree of awareness qualitatively affects behavior, the magnitudes of these effects are small relative to the main effect of having self-control problems. We return to this theme in the next section.

Welfare Implications

Many researchers are interested in studying self-control problems because of their welfare implications. People with self-control problems may not behave in their own best interests—that is, self-control problems may cause people to harm themselves. By better understanding the ways in which self-control problems cause harm, we can (eventually) analyze policy interventions that might help. We now discuss some simple welfare lessons in the context of the environments discussed earlier.

For our welfare criterion, we ask what would the person prefer if asked at some prior (long-run) perspective. To formalize this approach, we define a person's long-run utility to be

$$U^0(u_1, u_2, \ldots, u_T) \equiv \sum_{\tau=1}^{T} \delta^{\tau-1}\, u_\tau,$$

then conduct welfare analysis in terms of these preferences.[11] Specifically, we measure the harm generated from self-control problems by comparing long-run utility from the person's actual behavior to long-run utility from the best thing she could have done (from a long-run perspective). Our main welfare concern is to understand when self-control problems generate severe harm versus minor suboptimalities.

In one-shot decisions, self-control problems can generate harm, but this harm cannot be significant unless the person's self-control problem is large. To illustrate, consider an extended version of our dessert example, wherein the dessert yields an immediate benefit of V but creates future costs of C. Self-control problems generate harm whenever $V - \beta(C) \geq 0 > V - C$, because the person chooses to have dessert when from a long-run perspective she would prefer not to. One can show, however, that the harm generated can be at most $V(1 - \beta)/\beta$. Hence, unless the person's self-control problem is large—β significantly less than 1—the harm generated by this one-shot decision is small. The more general point is that, for modest self-control problems, the harm generated by any single decision to indulge must be small.

At the same time, the harm generated by many decisions to indulge can be quite large. If life consists of 100,000 unrelated opportunities to indulge, even small self-control problems can generate severe net harm. This suggests one way in which a person's awareness of future self-control problems can play an important role in determining the magnitude of harm generated by those problems. If a person is aware of her future self-control problems, and in particular recognizes the situations in which she is likely to indulge, then she may make "commitments" that help prevent this indulgence. One might, for instance, alter a situation in a way that will reduce the likelihood of indulging—for example, by making sure to have only healthy desserts in the house—or she might avoid the situation altogether—for example, by choosing to have no desserts in the house. Naivete about future self-control problems can generate harm, because the person fails to engage in such "self-management."[12]

When decisions are connected, as in the one-activity model, a person's awareness of future self-control problems has a more direct effect on the harm generated by those problems. In example 2, self-control problems generate harm when they cause the person to delay, and the harm suffered is the total delay cost incurred. Since sophisticates delay at most two periods, they suffer harm of at most $2 \times (1/2) = 1$. Naifs, however, delay until period T, and therefore suffer harm $(T - 1) \times (1/2)$, which can be much larger.

The welfare conclusions in example 2 reflect more general intuitions. For onerous activities, one can show that sophisticates suffer at most small harm. Intuitively, when sophisticates choose to delay, they know exactly when in the future they will complete the task, and (at the moment of action) they approve of the delay. Hence this decision to delay is essentially a single decision to indulge, and therefore the harm generated is small. Naifs, on the other hand, can suffer severe harm, because they might *repeatedly* decide to complete the task in the near future. While each decision to delay generates only small harm, the net effects of many decisions to delay can be large. Since partial naifs can also severely procrastinate, they too can suffer severe harm. Indeed, one can show that for any degree of naivete, no matter how small, environments exist in which the person suffers severe harm. Hence, for completion of an onerous activity, a person can suffer at most minor harm if he is completely sophisticated but may sometimes suffer severe harm if he has any degree of naivete.

For the case of a pleasurable activity, just as our behavioral results are reversed—awareness exacerbates misbehavior—so are our welfare conclusions. In example 3, the harm suffered by naifs is $V - (.99)^{10} V = .096V$, while the harm suffered by sophisticates can be much larger—for $T = 200$, for instance, the harm for sophisticates is $V - (.99)^{199}V = .865V$. More generally, one can show for pleasurable activities that naifs suffer at most small harm. When naifs grab the reward, they directly compare grabbing it now to grabbing it in period T, and so they approve of their preproperation. Hence naifs are essentially making a single decision to indulge, and the harm generated is small. Sophisticates can suffer large harm because the unraveling logic leads them to always compare grabbing the reward now versus grabbing the reward next period. Although the harm caused by each step in this unraveling is small, the net harm can be large. Hence, for completion of a pleasurable activity, a person can suffer at most minor harm if she is completely naive but may sometimes suffer severe harm if she has any degree of sophistication.

While we believe long-run preferences are the appropriate welfare criterion, other researchers have been troubled by the question of how to conduct welfare analysis for people with time-inconsistent preferences, since people themselves evaluate their well-being differently at different times. Some researchers (for example, Goldman 1979; Laibson 1994, 1996, 1997) have avoided this problem by using a Pareto criterion, which says one outcome is better than another outcome when the person prefers the first outcome from all perspectives. In example 2, for instance (and assuming T is large), the Pareto criterion says completion in period 3 is better than completion in period T, because from all perspectives the person prefers completion in period 3 to completion in period T. At the same time, the Pareto criterion does not rank completion in period 3 versus completion in period 1, because completion in period 3 is preferred from a period-1 perspective, while completion in period 1 is preferred from the period-2 and period-3 perspectives.

We prefer using long-run preferences for welfare analysis for several reasons. First is our personal belief that a preference for immediate gratification (the β) is an "error" that does not reflect true well-being. On every other day of a person's life, he disagrees with his March 1, 2005, preference for immediate gratification, and so to give this preference for immediate gratification any weight in the person's welfare function seems wrong. Second, the Pareto criterion is too weak, because it refuses to rank outcomes when one perspective barely prefers one outcome and all other perspectives vastly prefer a second outcome. For example, suppose one outcome yields utilities $u_1 = 0$ and $u_2 = 1$, while another outcome yields utilities $u_1' = 1,000,000$ and $u_2' = 0.99$. The second outcome is clearly better, and yet the Pareto criterion refuses to rank these two outcomes.[13] This usual critique of the Pareto criterion is particularly problematic when applied to intertemporal choice, because we're talking about the same person. Finally, even when the Pareto criterion does make a prediction, it does not permit an analysis of the *magnitude* of harm. Indeed, one can even show that Pareto-inefficient outcomes need not generate significant harm. This limitation is problematic if we are interested in analyzing which situations we should be particularly concerned about, or which types of policy interventions are most useful (and most worth the costs of implementing the policy).

Specific Applications

This section will discuss the role of awareness in specific applications. In some situations, awareness is relatively unimportant; but in other situations, awareness plays an important role in the implications of self-control problems, and analyses that restrict attention to complete sophistication can be misleading.

Procrastination

Prelec (1989), Akerlof (1991), O'Donoghue and Rabin (1999b, 1999c, 2001), and Fischer (1999) consider the role of self-control problems for procrastination.[14] Procrastination seems a natural application for self-control problems, because most people delay doing unpleasant tasks that they wish they would do sooner. Moreover, procrastination may be a realm in which the extreme assumption of complete sophistication is likely to be highly misleading. Our onerous activity example illustrates this point in a very simple way, by showing that severe procrastination and severe harm can arise if and only if a person has some naivete. This section will further discuss this point by describing how sophistication rules out realistic-sounding behaviors that can arise if a person is naive.

In O'Donoghue and Rabin (2001), we examine the implications of choice for procrastination. In many complete-a-task situations, people have some choice over what exactly they will do. In particular, people often can put in a small amount of effort to receive small benefits, or a larger amount of effort to receive larger benefits. If, for instance, the task represents choosing how to invest some money, you might thoughtlessly follow the advice of a friend, or thoroughly investigate investment strategies.

In such environments, the two aspects of the person's decision—which task to do and when to do it—are determined by two different criteria. A person plans to do the task that yields the highest net benefits; when she completes this task depends on her desire to put off incurring the immediate task cost. This basic insight has important implications. For instance, a naive person who would not otherwise procrastinate can be induced to severely procrastinate if offered a new option. This outcome occurs when the new option is better than existing options but more onerous. If the new option is better than existing options, the person plans to carry it out; but if at the same time the new option is sufficiently onerous, the person procrastinates.

A second implication is that a naive person may be more prone to procrastinate in pursuit of important goals than unimportant ones. The more important the person's goals, the more ambitious the person is—that is, he plans to carry out a more onerous task. The more ambitious the person is, however, the more likely he is to severely procrastinate. While increasing importance indeed can make procrastination more likely, this phenomenon is clearly not universal. Increasing importance makes a person less likely to procrastinate with regard to any fixed amount of effort. Yet, as emphasized in the aforementioned intuition, increasing importance can exacerbate procrastination through inducing the person to plan to exert more effort.

Naivete about future self-control problems is crucial for these results. For a completely sophisticated person, additional options or increasing importance always makes performance more likely. In O'Donoghue and Rabin (2001), however, we show that additional options or increasing importance can lead to procrastination if the person has *any degree of naivete*. Moreover, we show that environments exist in which for sufficiently important goals, a person surely procrastinates *unless she is completely sophisticated*.

We believe these ideas may be quite relevant for important economic contexts. In O'Donoghue and Rabin (1999c), for instance, we apply these ideas to the question of whether and how a person invests savings for retirement. We argue that people may be significantly delaying transferring their savings from low-interest bank accounts into more profitable investments. We show with some simple calibrations that for complete sophistication, such delays can only be short and not very costly (in terms of lost retirement savings), while even a little naivete can generate significant and costly delays. We also demonstrate how people may be more prone to procrastinate when they have the option to exert extra effort to find a better investment, and how people may be more prone to procrastinate the larger is their principal.

Consumption-Saving Decisions

Laibson (1994, 1996, 1997, 1998), Laibson and colleagues (1998), and Angeletos and colleagues (2001) consider the role of self-control problems for consumption-saving decisions. Since consumption-saving decisions are all about trading off current well-being for future well-being, they are a natural realm in which to consider self-control problems.

As our simple consumption-saving example discussed earlier suggests, this application is a realm where awareness sometimes does not play an important role. The main effect of having self-control problems is overconsumption or, equivalently, undersaving. Being aware of future self-control problems might mitigate or exacerbate this overconsumption, but such effects are often small relative to the main effect.

Angeletos and colleagues (2001) demonstrate how self-control problems may help explain a variety of empirical observations in the consumption-saving literature that seem anomalous when viewed through the lens of the standard economic model. They calibrate models of consumption-saving decisions using both the standard assumption that households are time-consistent and the assumption that households have sophisticated self-control problems. By comparing their simulated data for the two cases to real-world data, the researchers demonstrate that sophisticated self-control problems are better able to explain things such as people's liquid asset holdings (relative to monthly income and relative to illiquid asset holdings), consumption-income comovement, drops in consumption at retirement, and high credit card debt. Moreover, Angeletos and colleagues claim that their conclusions would be the same if they were to consider naive self-control problems instead of sophisticated self-control problems, again reflecting that in some ways, awareness may not matter in this realm.

Even so, for some consumption-savings decisions, awareness is clearly more important. Laibson, for instance, focuses on the use of illiquid assets such as housing in creating commitment opportunities, and the detrimental effects of credit cards in creating liquidity (Laibson 1997). The intentional use of illiquid assets to influence future behavior clearly relies on people being aware of their self-control problems. That people do in fact engage in such behavior—for example, Christmas clubs—suggests that people are to some degree aware. Even so, whether people in the real world are using as many commitment devices as one might expect from completely sophisticated people is unclear.

A closely related point is that if people are naive, then they won't fully recognize the commitment value of certain savings instruments, and creating *incentives* for people to use these savings instruments might have value. Consider the use of 401k retirement plans. Since such plans typically impose significant penalties for early withdrawals, they represent a commitment device to help keep oneself from consuming one's savings. If people are sophisticated, this commitment feature makes these instruments quite valuable independent of their tax-exempt features (see Laibson et al. 1998 for a more complete discussion of the sophisticated case). If people are not completely aware, however, the tax-exempt features may be crucial, because people may not see the commitment value of 401k plans. In other words, naive people may use 401k plans because of the tax benefits and end up reaping unexpected commitment benefits as well.

Addiction

O'Donoghue and Rabin (1999d, 2002), Gruber and Koszegi (2001), and Carrillo (1999) consider the role of self-control problems for ad-

diction. One key feature of harmful addictive products such as cigarettes is that current consumption creates future costs, and hence the
decision whether to consume boils down to whether the current desire to consume outweighs the future cost of this consumption. Since
self-control problems make a person more prone to conclude that current consumption is worthwhile, the main effect of self-control problems is a tendency to overconsume addictive products.

A second key feature of harmful addictive products is that current
consumption increases the future desire to consume, and thus awareness of future self-control problems may be particularly important in
this realm. O'Donoghue and Rabin (1999d, 2002) and Gruber and
Koszegi (2001) both show that for stationary environments in which
the desire to consume depends on past consumption but is otherwise
constant over one's lifetime, sophistication exacerbates overconsumption for relatively unaddicted people but mitigates overconsumption
for relatively addicted people. The intuition behind this dichotomy is
that the implications of sophistication depend on two effects. First is a
pessimism effect. Sophisticates expect more future consumption than
do naifs, and this pessimism tends to exacerbate overconsumption: if
you're going to consume in the future, you might as well start now.
Second is an incentive effect. Sophisticates may restrict current consumption so as to reduce the desire to smoke in the future: by consuming less now, you're less likely to consume in the future. The latter effect becomes more powerful as a person gets more addicted.

O'Donoghue and Rabin (2002) go further, attempting to identify
the situations in which self-control problems can generate *severe* harm
in the realm of addiction. Under the assumption of complete sophistication, addiction is problematic only to the extent that the person
feels that future consumption is inevitable. Sophisticates suffer severe
harm when they feel that they will consume in the future no matter
what they do now, and because future consumption is inevitable, they
decide they might as well start consuming now. This inevitability
might take the extreme form of expecting to consume throughout
one's life or the less extreme form of expecting to consume throughout one's years at college. Since in real-world environments extreme
inevitability seems unlikely, though, sophisticated self-control problems may not represent a realistic source of harmful addictions.

Naifs, in contrast, suffer severe harm when they repeatedly plan to
consume only in the short run but end up consuming in the long run.
As a result, naive self-control problems can give rise to more realistic-
sounding and plausibly harmful behaviors. For instance, an addicted
person might suffer severe harm because he procrastinates quitting—
he wants to quit, and always plans to quit in the near future, but

never gets around to it. Moreover, naifs might develop severely harmful addictions in the first place because they naively give in to temporarily high temptations believing they'll just quit after the temptation subsides, when in fact they end up with long-term addictions.

Acquiring Information

Carrillo and Mariotti (2000), Benabou and Tirole (2001, 2002), and Brocas and Carrillo (1999, 2000) apply self-control problems to information-acquisition decisions. In many situations, people have the option to acquire information about the costs and benefits of their actions. If, for instance, a person is deciding whether to embark on a specific research agenda, she has the option to get feedback from colleagues about the likely fruitfulness of that research agenda. The standard economic model implies that, if such information is free, people should always choose to acquire it. The intuition is simple: having more information allows people to make better decisions.

Carrillo and Mariotti (2000) point out, however, that sophisticated self-control problems might change this intuition, because better decisions as viewed from the future—that is, after receiving the information—may not correspond to better decisions as viewed from the present moment. Carrillo and Mariotti emphasize the possibility of "strategic ignorance"—not acquiring free information, because doing so increases the likelihood of future misbehavior. Benabou and Tirole (2001, 2002) explore strategic ignorance in more detail, and explore the role of memory manipulation in this regard.

These results about self-control problems leading to the active manipulation of information (relative to optimal information acquisition) obviously require some degree of sophistication, because they are driven by a desire to reduce future misbehavior. While the literature has focused on strategic ignorance, a variety of other embodiments of sophisticated information manipulation may in fact exist. For instance, whereas strategic ignorance involves people not gathering information they should because the information *increases* the likelihood of future misbehavior, people might also gather (costly) information they shouldn't when the information *decreases* the likelihood of future misbehavior (Carrillo and Mariotti briefly mention this possibility in their conclusion). More generally, sophisticated information manipulation might involve selective information gathering: when multiple sources of information are available, people will be biased against information that increases the likelihood of future misbehavior, and biased in favor of information that decreases the likelihood of future misbehavior.

Given its focus on complete sophistication, however, this literature ignores what we suspect may be an important source of distortions in information acquisition: procrastination in information gathering. Since information gathering itself is likely to be onerous—and create immediate costs—people with self-control problems may be prone to put off incurring these costs. As a result, our procrastination results have implications for information acquisition. For instance, people might fail to acquire information not because they are worried about future behavior but because they never get around to it. Or if people are choosing from among multiple sources of information, they may be biased toward information that is less onerous to acquire. Moreover, while mild versions of such distortions may arise even for people who are sophisticated, these distortions are likely to be particularly pronounced for people who are not completely aware of their self-control problems.

Boundedly Rational Incomplete Awareness

This section briefly speculates on an alternative, boundedly rational approach to incomplete awareness. To motivate this approach, consider the problem faced by naifs. To choose their current behavior, naifs merely need to know their current preferences, then simply follow their most preferred behavior path.

Sophisticates of course also need to know their current preferences; but to carry out the backward-induction logic required to derive the sophisticated path, they must know much more. They must know what their preferences will be in the last period, so that they can derive the behavioral rule that they will follow in that period. They also must know what their preferences will be in the second-to-last period, which they must then combine with their behavioral rule for the last period to determine the behavioral rule that they will follow in the second-to-last period. They also must know what their preferences will be in the third-to-last period, which they must then combine with their behavioral rules for the last and second-to-last periods to determine the behavioral rule that they will follow in the third-to-last period, and so forth.

Clearly, for sophisticated people, deciding what to do can involve a rather complicated reasoning process. Hence, even though sophisticated people are fully aware of their future self-control problems, they might follow some simplified procedure in deciding how to behave. We consider one particular simplification: they don't do all the rounds of backward induction. In other words, instead of starting the

Table 7.2 Year-1 Consumption (c_1) Given \$100,000 to Allocate over Four Years[a]

Utility Function	Naifs	Sophisticates	Boundedly Rational Sophisticates
$u(c) = c^{1/2}$	$c_1 = \$40,486$	$c_1 = \$41,781$	$c_1 = \$41,229$
$u(c) = \ln c$	$c_1 = \$32,258$	$c_1 = \$32,258$	$c_1 = \$32,258$
$u(c) = -c^{-1/2}$	$c_1 = \$29,717$	$c_1 = \$29,601$	$c_1 = \$29,650$

Source: Authors' compilation.
[a]Assuming $r = 0$ percent, $\delta = 1$, and $\beta = .7$.

backward-induction logic in the last period, they might start the process, say, three periods hence. What would this mean? Merely that in deciding what to do, sophisticates first ask what their preferences will be three periods hence, and use those preferences to derive the behavioral rule that they will follow from that period onward. They then continue the backward induction from there. Sophisticates might think in this way as a useful heuristic to simplify their decision-making process. Such boundedly rational sophisticates would have incorrect predictions about future behavior, and might be aware of this fact, but they would view it as too costly to think through their decisions more carefully.

To illustrate this approach, reconsider the simple consumption-saving example, except that now assume the person must allocate his \$100,000 income over four years of consumption. As before, we assume no interest ($r = 0$ *percent*) and no time-consistent impatience ($\delta = 1$), and we use $\beta = .7$. Table 7.2 describes year-1 consumption for three types: naifs, complete sophisticates who do the entire backward induction starting from the end (year 3), and boundedly rational sophisticates who do the backward induction starting from year 2.[15] We note as a benchmark that time-consistent people would consume \$25,000 in each year.

The simplified solution procedure fares quite well in this environment. For all three utility functions, boundedly rational sophisticates consume roughly the same amount as both sophisticates and naifs. This conclusion is largely driven by our earlier conclusion that in this environment the degree of awareness is relatively unimportant. Our point, however, is that even if people are fully aware of their future self-control problems, to assume that they carry out the complete, complicated, backward-induction logic when making their decisions might not make sense.

What does this approach rule out? In this example, boundedly rational sophisticates exhibit what might be called first-order sophistication effects: they recognize that they will overconsume in year 2, and their year-1 consumption partially reflects a reaction to this future overconsumption. Boundedly rational sophisticates do not exhibit what might be called second-order sophistication effects. That is, complete sophisticates also recognize that they will overconsume in year 3, and that their year-2 behavior will partially be driven by reactions to year-3 overconsumption. Hence their year-1 consumption also reflects reactions to future first-order sophistication effects.

We find it appealing that this approach rules out higher-order sophistication effects, because we feel that results driven by higher-order sophistication effects rely a little too heavily on the game-theoretic approach. The standard game-theoretic approach to sophistication that is used in the literature represents a nice formal way to understand the behavior of a person who is aware of future self-control problems. To assume, however, that the person literally carries out the complicated backward-induction procedure seems to push the framework a little too far. While results that rely on first-, second-, and perhaps even third-order sophistication effects seem quite reasonable, results that rely on higher-order sophistication effects seem less reasonable.

An important issue for this approach is how often people revise their plans. In our consumption-saving example, when year 2 arrives, does the person stick to the year-1 plan, or does the person reevaluate the plan, doing the backward induction starting from year 3? In some situations—for example, the one-activity model discussed earlier—the answer to this question is critical. If the person sticks to the plan and only occasionally reevaluates, then his or her behavior will be closer to sophisticated behavior. If the person constantly reevaluates, then his or her behavior will be closer to naive behavior. This approach suggests that another interpretation of naivete is as an approximation of what a boundedly rational sophisticate might do.

Discussion

We have attempted to illustrate throughout this chapter how the degree to which a person is aware of her own future self-control problems can be a crucial determinant of the implications of those self-control problems. Perhaps our main point is directed at economists prone to assume complete awareness: since awareness can play such a crucial role, and people appear to be at least to some degree naive, economists must seriously address the possibility of naivete to fully understand the implications of self-control problems. Indeed, we have shown how even a small degree of unawareness can give rise to realistic behaviors that could not arise under complete awareness, and how even a small degree of unawareness can give rise to different welfare conclusions.

We conclude with a few thoughts about how researchers might proceed in exploring the implications of self-control problems. First, one reason to study naivete is tractability. We have illustrated how in some circumstances the implications of sophistication versus naivete are small relative to the direct effect of people having self-control problems. Our analysis also makes clear that the sophisticated path can be complicated to derive, whereas the naive path—or something similar—is relatively easy to derive. Hence from a modeling perspective, and perhaps also from the agent's own perspective, the simpler case of naivete may make more sense. Indeed, tractability was exactly the motivation behind Pollak (1968) first introducing a formalization of the naive path. Pollak was interested in the sophisticated path, but since it was difficult to solve for, he identified a situation for which he could prove that the sophisticated path coincides with the easy-to-solve-for naive path.

Second, we believe the literature on self-control problems should focus more explicitly on when small self-control problems can cause severe harm. Much of the recent literature has focused on the ways in which models with self-control problems can better explain observed real-world behavior. We think this agenda is very important. At the same time, at least implicit in these analyses is the policy concern of what types of policies might help people make better decisions. To seriously address this policy concern, and evaluate the costs and benefits of proposed policies, studies must formally analyze the magnitude of harm caused by self-control problems. As we have emphasized here, in some situations, self-control problems may lead people to misbehave, and yet this misbehavior may not be very important.

A related comment is that welfare concerns may be the main reason for being concerned with people's awareness of self-control problems. We have argued in the past that welfare concerns are perhaps the main reason for considering models of self-control problems (as well as other behavioral errors). Even if we can explain some behavior with a rational-choice model, an interest in welfare analysis implies that we should still be concerned whether this explanation is correct. This same argument applies to the question of sophistication versus naivete. In some situations, we may be able to explain some behavior with a model of self-control problems and complete sophistication; but an interest in welfare analysis implies that we should still ask whether the behavior is driven by sophistication versus naivete, because there might be dramatically different welfare implications.

Indeed, we believe that in real-world situations sophisticated self-control problems may be even less problematic than suggested by simple economic models. Situations likely exist in the real world in which sophisticates would suffer severe harm, but real-world sophisticates would constantly be on the lookout to avoid such situations. This type of meta-behavior would not be carried out by naifs.

It has not yet been established whether we are right or wrong about people being naive. By demonstrating the specialness of the extreme assumption of complete awareness, we hope we have convinced economists and other researchers that we ought to be interested in finding out.

Notes

1. This basic phenomenon goes by a variety of names in addition to *self-control problems*—for example, *hyperbolic discounting, present-biased preferences,* and *preference for immediate gratification.*
2. For an overview of this evidence see Frederick, Loewenstein, and O'Donoghue (chap. 1 herein); also Ainslie (1975, 1991, 1992); Ainslie and Haslam (1992a, 1992b); Loewenstein and Prelec (1992); Thaler (1991); and Thaler and Loewenstein (1992). See, however, Read (chap. 10 herein) for a critique of much of the evidence for hyperbolic discounting, which is confounded with a subadditivity in discounting.
3. An older literature in economics pioneered by Strotz (1956) and Pollak (1968) analyzes general abstract models of time-inconsistent preferences. This literature does not make any assumptions about the form of time inconsistency—allowing for self-control problems but also other forms of time inconsistency—nor does it discuss much the implications of time inconsistency.
4. Strotz (1956) and Pollak (1968) carefully lay out these two assumptions (and develop the labels), but do not much consider the implications of assuming one versus the other.
5. As another example, the decision whether to buy a durable good—for example, an automobile—can be interpreted as a long-term commitment, and hence awareness should not be important.
6. Recent research in psychology suggests that seemingly unrelated decisions may in fact be connected through limited "willpower." For instance, while the decision about which movie to watch tonight may seem unrelated to the decision about whether to eat dessert tonight, having to make the former decision first may affect the willpower available for the latter decision. For an overview see Baumeister and Vohs (chap. 6 herein).
7. Exactly when sophisticates complete the task depends on T. Doing the backward induction, we can derive that sophisticates' plan must involve

planning to complete the task in periods T, $T - 3$, $T - 6$, and so on, and planning to wait in all other periods. Hence, if, for instance, $T = 63$, then sophisticates complete the task in period 3; if $T = 64$, then sophisticates complete the task in period 1; and if $T = 65$, then sophisticates complete the task in period 2.

8.   This logic is more carefully formalized in O'Donoghue and Rabin (2001).

9.   If $T < 10$, then naifs do the activity in period 1.

10.   The three utility functions are from the family of constant-relative-risk-aversion (CRRA) utility functions, and have coefficients of relative risk aversion equal to $1/2$, 1, and $3/2$, respectively. Pollak (1968) showed that awareness is irrelevant for logarithmic utility; more generally, within the family of CRRA utility functions, awareness exacerbates overconsumption for relative risk aversion less than unity, and awareness mitigates overconsumption for relative risk aversion greater than unity. Also note that the degree of overconsumption is decreasing in the degree of risk aversion (amount of curvature in the utility function).

11.   These preferences are the same as the preferences represented by

$$U^0(u_1, u_2, \ldots, u_T) \equiv \beta \sum_{\tau=1}^{T} \delta^{\tau-1} u_\tau.$$

Also, for "small" self-control problems (β close to 1), long-run preferences are quite similar to period-1 preferences

$$U^1(u_1, u_2, \ldots, u_T) \equiv u_1 + \beta \sum_{\tau=2}^{T} \delta^{\tau-1} u_\tau,$$

and yield similar welfare conclusions.

12.   While such commitments are often discussed in the literature, most formal models incorporate rather limited commitment technologies. As a result, such models may overstate the harm caused by sophisticated self-control problems.

13.   The Pareto criterion's unwillingness to designate the first outcome as inefficient *holds even for time-consistent agents*, illustrating that the Pareto criterion is not what is used for welfare analysis in standard models of intertemporal choice. Indeed, the long-run-utility criterion (or perhaps the closely related period-1-utility criterion) is equivalent to what is used in standard analyses.

14.   While Akerlof (1991) does not frame his analysis in terms of self-control problems, his model implicitly corresponds to (β, δ) preferences.

15.   Since in year 4 the person merely consumes whatever is left over, the last substantive decision occurs in year 3.

References

Ainslie, George. 1975. "Specious Reward: A Behavioral Theory of Impulsiveness and Impulse Control." *Psychological Bulletin* 82(4): 463–96.

————. 1991. "Derivation of 'Rational' Economic Behavior from Hyperbolic Discount Curves." *American Economic Review* 81(2): 334–40.

————. 1992. *Picoeconomics: The Strategic Interaction of Successive Motivational States Within the Person.* New York: Cambridge University Press.

Ainslie, George, and Nick Haslam. 1992a. "Self-Control." In *Choice Over Time,* edited by George Loewenstein and Jon Elster. New York: Russell Sage Foundation.

————. 1992b. "Hyperbolic Discounting." In *Choice Over Time,* edited by George Loewenstein and Jon Elster. New York: Russell Sage Foundation.

Akerlof, George. 1991. "Procrastination and Obedience." *American Economic Review* 81(2): 1–19.

Angeletos, George-Marios, David Laibson, Andrea Repetto, Jeremy Tobacman, and Stephen Weinberg. 2001. "The Hyperbolic Buffer Stock Model: Calibration, Simulation, and Empirical Evaluation." *Journal of Economic Perspectives* 15(3): 47–68.

Ariely, Daniel, and Klaus Wertenbroch. 2002. "Procrastination, Deadlines, and Performance: Self-Control by Precommitment." *Psychological Science* 13(3): 219–24.

Benabou, Roland, and Jean Tirole. 2001. "Willpower and Personal Rules." Unpublished paper. Princeton University and Massachusetts Institute of Technology.

————. 2002. "Self-Confidence and Personal Motivation." *Quarterly Journal of Economics* 117(3): 871–915.

Brocas, Isabelle, and Juan Carrillo. 1999. "A Theory of Haste with Applications to Impulse Buying and Destruction of the Environment." Centre for Economic Policy Research discussion paper no. 2027.

————. 2000. "The Value of Information When Preferences Are Dynamically Inconsistent." *European Economic Review* 44: 1104–15.

Carrillo, Juan. 1999. "Self-Control, Moderate Consumption, and Craving." Centre for Economic Policy Research discussion paper no. 2017.

Carrillo, Juan, and Thomas Mariotti. 2000. "Strategic Ignorance as a Self-Disciplining Device." *Review of Economic Studies* 67: 529–44.

Fischer, Carolyn. 1999. "Read This Paper Even Later: Procrastination with Time-Inconsistent Preferences." Resources for the Future discussion paper no. 99–20.

Frederick, Shane, George Loewenstein, and Ted O'Donoghue. 2002. "Time Discounting and Time Preference: A Critical Review." *Journal of Economic Literature* 40(2): 351–401.

Goldman, Steven. 1979. "Intertemporally Inconsistent Preferences and the Rate of Consumption." *Econometrica* 47(3): 621–26.

Gruber, Jonathan, and Botond Koszegi. 2001. "Is Addiction 'Rational'? Theory and Evidence." *Quarterly Journal of Economics* 116(4): 1261–1303.

Laibson, David. 1994. "Essays in Hyperbolic Discounting." Ph.D. diss., Massachusetts Institute of Technology.

————. 1996. "Hyperbolic Discount Functions, Undersaving, and Savings Policy." National Bureau of Economic Research working paper no. 5635.

————. 1997. "Hyperbolic Discounting and Golden Eggs." *Quarterly Journal of Economics* 112(2): 443–77.

————. 1998. "Life-Cycle Consumption and Hyperbolic Discount Functions." *European Economic Review* 42: 861–71.

Laibson, David, Andrea Repetto, and Jeremy Tobacman. 1998. "Self-Control and Saving for Retirement." *Brookings Papers on Economic Activity* 1: 91–196.

Loewenstein, George, and Drazen Prelec. 1992. "Anomalies in Intertemporal Choice: Evidence and an Interpretation." *Quarterly Journal of Economics* 107(2): 573–97.

O'Donoghue, Ted, and Matthew Rabin. 1999a. "Doing It Now or Later." *American Economic Review* 89(1): 103–24.

————. 1999b. "Incentives for Procrastinators." *Quarterly Journal of Economics* 114(3): 769–816.

————. 1999c. "Procrastination in Preparing for Retirement." In *Behavioral Dimensions of Retirement Economics*, edited by Henry Aaron. Washington, D.C., and New York: Brookings Institution Press and Russell Sage Foundation.

————. 1999d. "Addiction and Self-Control." In *Addiction: Entries and Exits*, edited by Jon Elster. New York: Russell Sage Foundation.

————. 2000. "The Economics of Immediate Gratification." *Journal of Behavioral Decision Making* 13(2): 233–50.

————. 2001. "Choice and Procrastination." *Quarterly Journal of Economics* 116(1): 121–60.

————. 2002. "Addiction and Present-Biased Preferences." Center for Analytic Economics working paper 02-10, Cornell University.

Phelps, Edmund S., and Robert A. Pollak. 1968. "On Second-Best National Saving and Game-Equilibrium Growth." *Review of Economic Studies* 35: 185–99.

Pollak, Robert A. 1968. "Consistent Planning." *Review of Economic Studies* 35: 201–8.

Prelec, Drazen. 1989. "Decreasing Impatience: Definition and Consequences." Unpublished paper. Harvard Business School, Cambridge.

Strotz, Robert. 1956. "Myopia and Inconsistency in Dynamic Utility Maximization." *Review of Economic Studies* 23(3): 165–80.

Thaler, Richard. 1991. "Some Empirical Evidence on Dynamic Inconsistency." In *Quasi Rational Economics*. New York: Russell Sage Foundation.

Thaler, Richard, and George Loewenstein. 1992. "Intertemporal Choice." In *The Winner's Curse: Paradoxes and Anomalies of Economic Life*, edited by Richard Thaler. New York: Free Press.

· 8 ·

Construal Level Theory of Intertemporal Judgment and Decision

NIRA LIBERMAN AND YAACOV TROPE

CONSTRUAL level theory (CLT) posits that temporal distance influences the evaluation and choice of future events by systematically changing the way they are construed. We propose that individuals form higher-level construals of distant future events than near future events. High-level construals are schematic, abstract, and include central features of events, whereas low-level construals are less schematic, more concrete, and may also include incidental, peripheral features of events. We argue, then, that judgment and choice regarding the more temporally distant events are based on higher-level construals of the events. Thus temporal distance affects level of construal, which in turn affects evaluation of future events. We first introduce in more depth the concept of construal level, discuss our research on the influences of temporal perspective on construal level, then turn to examine the implications of these findings for time-dependent changes in evaluation and choice. Finally, we discuss how CLT relates to theories of motivational gradients, dreading and savoring, intertemporal preference reversals, self-control, and magnitude effects.

Level of Construal

To elaborate on the cognitive properties of schemas and schematic representations is beyond the scope of this chapter. Instead, we would like to emphasize here the unifying principle behind the various manifestations of level of construal. Let us start with the basic notion that objects and events are classified into categories despite the fact that no two objects or events are identical. Categorizing an object means disregarding its unique features, and thus involves an implicit decision about which features are more central and important and which features are incidental and less important (and thus can be disregarded). For example, categorizing an object as a table emphasizes its similarity to other tables and involves a decision that the function of the object is central, whereas its specific size and color are secondary. An alternative categorization of the same target, for instance, as a "wooden object" would involve a different decision about which feature is central and which is peripheral. As another example, categorizing an event as a lecture implies a decision that the presence of speaker and audience is important, whereas refreshment is not. Of course, there might be idiosyncratic variations in schemas. For example, refreshment for some people could be a central and indispensable part of talks. Such variations notwithstanding, there is wide agreement between members of a culture on the content of schemas (Abelson 1981). Consistent with the common use in social psychology, we use the term *schema* to encompass categories of objects, actions, or events as well as scripts, scenarios, and implicit theories (Fiske and Taylor 1991; Smith 1998). Schematic representations and categorization are not all-or-none phenomena. Representations get more abstract or schematic the more unique, incidental features are omitted. Thus many schemas may be thought of as organized hierarchically, with representations that are higher in the hierarchy having less concrete features (Hampson, John, and Goldberg 1986; Rosch 1978; Semin and Fiedler 1988).

Many categories (for example, foods to eat when on a diet) are organized around goals. In such categories, features that are related to the goal (for example, the calories of the food) are more central than goal-irrelevant features (for example, crunchiness). Like other categories, categories of goal-directed actions form hierarchies, as goals could be translated into more concrete subgoals (Miller, Galanter, and Pribram 1960; Carver and Scheier 1990, 1999; Vallacher and Wegner 1987). In such hierarchies, each action (for example, studying for an exam) has a superordinate level, which answers the question of why the action is performed (for example, doing well) and a subordinate level, which answers the question how the action is to be performed (for example, reading a textbook).

As noted before, we use the term *high-level construal* to refer to a schematic, abstract representation that gives more weight to central features, and *low-level construal* to refer to less schematic, concrete representations that may also include less central, incidental features. Operationally, one could distinguish between higher- and lower-level features by asking how much difference would it make if this feature is altered or removed. Altering high-level features should produce more substantial change in the concept in question than altering a low-level feature. For example, suppose that a change in the topic of a conference is announced, as opposed to a change in its time. The result of the first change is more likely to be classified as an altogether different conference than the result of the second change, and thus the topic comprises a higher-level feature of "a conference" than its timing.

Intertemporal Changes in Construal

CLT proposes that the same information will be construed at a higher level when it pertains to distant future activities and objects than when it pertains to near future activities and objects. To test this prediction, we asked participants to imagine engaging in different activities (for example, reading a science-fiction book, watching TV, moving into a new apartment) either "tomorrow" or "next year" (Liberman and Trope 1998, study 1). The descriptions were content analyzed as conveying a high-level construal (reflecting a superordinate goal or answering a why question) or a low-level construal (reflecting a subordinate goal or answering a how question). For example, a description of the activity "reading a science-fiction book" as "broadening my horizons" was classified as a high-level construal of the activity, whereas the description "flipping pages" was classified as a low-level construal of the activity. As predicted by CLT, high-level descriptions were more common in the distant future condition compared to the near future condition, and the reverse was true for low-level descriptions. "Watching TV," for example, was often described as "being entertained" in the distant future, but as "sitting on the sofa, flipping channels" in the near future. Similarly, "moving into a new apartment" was often described as "starting a new life" in the distant future, but as "packing and carrying boxes" in the near future.

The second part of the same study used an adapted version of Vallacher and Wegner's (1989) "Levels of Personal Agency" questionnaire. The questionnaire presented nineteen activities, each followed by two restatements, one corresponding to the "why" (high-level) aspects of the activity and the other corresponding to the "how" (low-level) aspects of the activity. For example, "locking a door" was followed by the alternative restatements (a) putting a key in the lock; (b) securing the house. Participants chose the restatement they felt better described the action. To manipulate temporal perspective, we added a time indicator to each activity, which was either "tomorrow" or "sometime next year." As predicted by CLT, the proportion of high-level, "why" restatements was higher in the distant future condition than in the near future condition.

In another study Liberman, Sagristano, and Trope (forthcoming) examined time-dependent changes in the breadth of categories. Participants in this study imagined four different events (for example, going to a camping trip, showing NYC to a stranger) occurring in either the near future (the upcoming weekend) or the distant future (the weekend a few months later). For each event, they received a list of relevant objects (for example, tent, brush, camera for a camping trip, West Village, Madison Square Garden, tickets to *Stomp* for a NYC visit), which they had to classify into as many mutually exclusive and exhaustive groups as they deemed appropriate. We found that people used fewer categories in distant future scenarios than in near future scenarios. Thus, consistent with CLT, the same set of objects was classified into broader categories when the objects were part of a distant future situation than a near future situation.

Interestingly, the association between level of construal and time perspective seems to be bidirectional—not only does more distant time perspective foster construal in higher level terms, but also construing activities in high-level terms fosters perception of the more distant future as appropriate for their enactment. In support of this idea, Liberman, Trope, Mccrae, and Sherman (2002) found that describing their own and other people's activities in superordinate "why" (as opposed to subordinate "how") terms and in abstract (as opposed to concrete) terms made participants plan to do or expect others to do these activities in the more distant future.

What are the origins of the association between time-perspective and level of construal? It seems intuitive that more details are seen from a close perspective, whereas a distant perspective allows a more general view, in which the details are lost but the overall picture emerges—seeing the forest instead of the trees. One must remember, however, that this visual analogy is only a metaphor that does little in terms of explanation. After all, one does not really "see" either the near future or the distant future. What then drives CLT and makes the visual analogy intuitively compelling? One possibility is that temporal construal—the tendency to construe the more distant future in higher-level terms—evolved as a result of repeated association between temporal distance and people's knowledge about future situations. Ordinarily, low-level information regarding distant future situations is unreliable or even unavailable. Details about concrete, secondary aspects of future events often become available only as one gets closer in time to the events. It could be, then, that people overgeneralize this tendency and continue to construe the distant future on a higher level even when details about the distant future are available or may be obtained.

In addition, people are often free to delay or change their decisions regarding distant future events. This in turn may allow them to postpone consideration of low-level information about the means they are going to use or other specific, secondary details until they get close in time to the event. One can therefore start thinking about a future situation in high-level terms—in terms of one's superordinate goals, general knowledge, and central aspects of the situation—and only later start thinking in low-level terms—in terms of means, specific knowledge, and secondary aspects of the situation. An association thus may be established between temporal distance and level of construal. High-level construals become prominent and guide responses to distant future situations, and low-level construals become prominent and guide responses to near future situations.

Notably, CLT proposes that individuals continue to use high-level construals for distant future events and low-level construals for near future events even when the above mentioned reasons do not exist—that is, when the information about near future and distant future events is the same and an irreversible decision has to be made at both points in time. Our research suggests that temporal construal is an overgeneralized tendency that is applied in situations in which it is neither appropriate nor necessary. We turn now to review the research on the implications of CLT for evaluation and choice.

CLT Explanation of Intertemporal Changes in Value

CLT proposes that the value people assign to events reflects the way they construe those events (see Herman and Polivy, chap. 16 herein; Mischel, Ayduk, and Mendoza-Denton, chap. 5 herein for other examples of a construal-based approach to evaluation and choice). We also assume that different construals of the same activity or event could influence how positively they are viewed. For example, the construal "running subjects in the lab" may be less positive than "conducting a psychology study." CLT proposes that people use higher-level construals for distant future events than for near future events. It therefore predicts that the value associated with low-level construals should be more prominent in a subjective evaluation of near future events, whereas the value associated with high-level construals should be more prominent in evaluating distant future events. In other words, we predict that the value that is associated with high-level construals would be enhanced with increasing temporal distance, while the value associated with low-level construals would be diminished with temporal distance.

Thus CLT predicts that when the value associated with high-level construals is more positive than that associated with low-level construals, the attractiveness of an option should increase with temporal distance. Yet when the value associated with low-level construals is more positive than that associated with high-level construals, the attractiveness of an option should decrease with temporal distance. For example, suppose that the abstract construal "helping another person" is more positive than the concrete construal "giving a dollar to a homeless person in a NYC subway late at night." We predict that the former construal is more likely to be used for a situation in the distant future than in the near future, whereas the reverse would hold for the latter construal. Hence the action in this case would seem more positive in the distant future than in the near future. To use another example, assuming that the abstract construal "cheating" is more negative than the more concrete construal "peeking at my neighbor's exam to compare answers," CLT would predict that the action described by these construals would seem more negative in the distant future than in the near future. We propose then that as temporal distance increases, preferences are more likely to reflect the value associated with high-level construals of events than the value associated with low-level construals of the same events.

Primary Versus Secondary Sources of Value

A number of studies, involving both hypothetical and real choice, tested these predictions of CLT. In one study (Trope and Liberman 2000, study 4), participants in a two-session experiment evaluated two alternative activities. Some of the participants were told that they would perform one of the activities in the same session (the near future condition), whereas other participants were told that they would perform one of the activities in a later session, to be held two months later (the distant future condition). Participants in both time-perspective conditions were told that activities would be allocated according to their preferences, and had to indicate how much they wanted to do each of two activities on scales ranging from one (not interested at all) to nine (very interested). The first activity consisted of an interesting main task and a boring filler task, whereas the second activity consisted of a boring main task and an interesting filler task. Each of the two alternative activities was described as consisting of three sessions of performing the main task, with the filler task performed between these sessions to provide rest and distraction from the main task. Counterbalancing across participants, we used the same contents for both the main and the filler tasks. For example, an activity entitled "Judging humor" was described as follows: "The main task is judging humor, and will ask you to evaluate the funniness of cartoons. The filler task in between the three sessions is checking data, and will ask you to compare two lists of numbers to check for discrepancies." In the other version of this activity, the roles of the same tasks as main and filler were reversed. Thus the activity was entitled "Checking data," and was described as follows: "The main task is checking data, and will ask you to compare two lists of numbers to check for discrepancies. The filler task in between the three sessions is judging humor, and will ask you to evaluate the funniness of cartoons."

We reasoned that the filler task constitutes a less central feature of the experimental procedure than the main task, and therefore would be less likely to be retained in a high-level, abstract construal of the experimental procedure. We predicted, therefore, that the valence of the filler task would affect desirability ratings for the distant future less than the desirability ratings for the near future. We predicted the reverse (that is, greater effect on distant future ratings than on near future ratings) for the valence of the main task, which would be more dominant. The findings (see figure 8.1) confirmed these predictions, showing that the ratings given to the activity with the interesting main task and the boring filler task were higher in the distant future than in the near future, whereas the ratings given to the activity with the boring main task and the interesting filler task showed the reverse pattern.

Another study (Trope and Liberman 2000, study 3) examined the effect of temporal distance on evaluating products with multiple features. We reasoned that construing a product in terms of features related to its primary function, compared to features unrelated to this function, constitutes a higher level of construal. In the study, participants indicated how satisfied they would be in either the near future or the distant future with purchasing one of two radio sets: one had good sound but a poor built-in clock, and the other had poor sound but a good clock. The radio was rated on a scale ranging from one (not at all satisfied) to nine (very satisfied). Given that one's goal in buying the radio set is listening to programs, sound quality should be more central than the quality of the clock in the construal of the radio

Figure 8.1   Attractiveness Ratings of Near Future and Distant Future Experimental Tasks

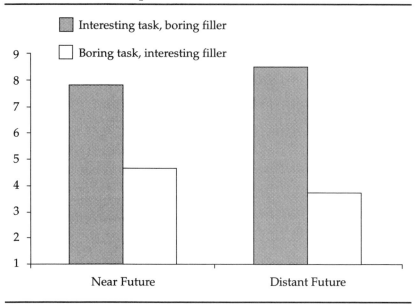

Source: Based on data from Trope and Liberman (2000).
Note: Ratings were made on a 1 (not attractive at all) to 9 (very attractive) scale.

set. CLT predicts, therefore, that the advantage in ratings of the radio that has good sound over the radio that has poor sound should be stronger in the distant than near future, with the ratings given to the former increasing and the ratings given to the latter decreasing with temporal distance. The results confirmed the predictions of CLT.

These findings have implications for decision situations in which the available options entail a trade-off between one's primary and secondary considerations. For example, imagine a situation that involves a conflict between interpersonal motives and achievement motives (for example, one can get ahead by pushing down another person). While all people typically hold both motives, their relative importance may vary across individuals, with interpersonal goals being more important for some people and achievement goals being more important for other people (Schwartz 1992). CLT predicts that from a distance, the conflict would be resolved unequivocally in favor of the primary motive, but as one gets closer in time to the situation, the secondary motive would become increasingly influential, causing hesitation and conflict and "contaminating" one's decision. Interestingly, it seems that in these situations, as in our studies, temporal construal actually produces clearer preferences regarding the distant future than the near future, despite the greater uncertainty inherent to the more distant future.

It is interesting to examine our results from the perspective of valence-dependent time-discounting theories. Conflict theories (Lewin 1951; Miller 1944) maintain that negative aspects of options are discounted over temporal distance more steeply than positive aspects (see also Shelley 1994). For example, parachute jumping is both fun and scary, but fear has a steeper gradient over time perspective, giving rise to an approach-avoidance conflict: from a distance, fun is predominant and the response is approach, but from a close perspective fear is predominant and the response is avoidance (Epstein and Fenz 1965). Conflict theory would predict that ambivalent options (that is, options with both positive and negative aspects) would be more attractive in the more distant future. The literature on intertemporal choice, however, has widely documented the sign effect, showing that losses are discounted less steeply than gains (for a review see Frederick, Loewenstein, and O'Donoghue, chap. 1 herein). If extended to ambivalent options, the sign effect would predict that such options would be less attractive in the more distant future, an effect opposite to that of conflict theories.

The results of our studies depart from both predictions. Specifically, we show that options that had a positive high-level construal and a negative low-level construal were seen as more attractive over greater delay, whereas options that had a negative high-level construal and a positive low-level construal were seen as less attractive over delay.

Perhaps in many situations, level of construal and valence are correlated and the predictions of CLT and conflict theory coincide. For example, positive outcomes are often part of individuals' goals, whereas negative outcomes are often incidental and imposed by circumstances. In such situations, positive outcomes constitute a higher level of construal than negative outcomes and, as a result, would be discounted over temporal distance less steeply than negative outcomes.

Affective and Cognitive Sources of Value

The literature on delay of gratification (Mischel et al. 1989; Mischel, Ayduk, and Mendoza-Denton, chap. 5 herein) and self-control (Baumeister and Vohs, chap. 6 herein; Baumeister and Heatherton 1996; Loewenstein 1996; Metcalfe and Mischel 1999) commonly distinguishes between affective, appetitive or "hot" stimuli and cognitive or "cold" stimuli. To explain why self-control problems occur with affective stimuli more than with cognitive stimuli, it is sometimes assumed that cognition-based value is discounted less steeply (and even augmented) with temporal distance than affect-based value. For example, the positive value of watching a funny movie is affective or "hot," whereas the positive value of studying for an exam is cognitive or "cold." If the value of watching the movie is discounted more steeply than the value of studying, a temporally inconsistent pattern of preferences emerges whereby studying is preferred a long time in advance but watching the film seems more attractive from a closer perspective. According to this approach, then, temporal distance should always increase the relative weight of cognitive (versus affective) value in preference.

An interesting prediction of CLT is that both affective and cognitive types of value could be either high level or low level, and therefore could be both augmented and discounted over time perspective. This prediction was tested in a study that independently manipulated the affective-cognitive dimension and level of construal (Trope and Liberman 2000, study 5). In this study, we assessed desirability ratings (indicated on a one to ten scale) of four films varying in affective value (funniness) and cognitive value (informativeness). The films thus were funny and informative, funny but uninformative, not funny but informative, or neither funny nor informative. Some of our participants expected to watch the films in the same experimental session, whereas other participants expected to watch them in the second session of the study, two months later. The goal of watching the films was also manipulated: it was either affective (getting oneself into a good mood) or cognitive (learning about a topic). We assumed that the features of the film that are related to the goal would be more central than the goal-irrelevant features, and thus would constitute a high-level construal of the film. Thus, depending on the goal, either affective features or cognitive features of the films were more central (constituted the high-level construal of the films), whereas the other type of features was rendered goal-irrelevant (and thus part of the low-level construal of the films).

We examined how time perspective, goal, affective value, and cognitive value influenced the desirability ratings of the films. Consistent with the predictions of CLT, we found that temporal distance increased the influence of informativeness versus funniness of the films when the goal was cognitive, but decreased the influence of informativeness versus funniness of the films when the goal was affective. Thus the effect of high-level, goal-relevant value increased over delay relative to the effect of low-level, goal-irrelevant value.

The results of our study are not predicted by the affect-dependent time-discounting approach, according to which near future decisions, compared with distant future decisions, should be more influenced by affective value and less influenced by cognitive value. Of course, funniness, although more "affective" than informativeness, is not quite as "hot" as drives related to food, sex, or pain. To examine real life or experimental situations in which more intense emotional aspects comprise a high level of construral would be interesting. For example, one could think that for some people, romantic love and sexual attraction are primary characteristic in a spouse, whereas financial prospects are secondary. Would it be the case, as CLT would predict, that for those people, considerations related to money would be absent from distant future contemplations about romantic candidates, but nevertheless would creep into near future decisions?

Are the predictions of CLT at odds with the observation that impulsive behavior and difficulties in self-control occur predominantly with affective, hot outcomes rather than cognitive, cold outcomes (Baumeister and Vohs, chap. 6 herein; Baumeister and Heatherton 1996; Metcalfe and Mischel 1999)? We believe that this is not the case, because CLT only explains intertemporal changes in value, whereas impulsive behavior often results from processes other than intertemporal changes in value. Thus, as noted by Loewenstein (1996), the value of some hot stimuli (for example, food) is enhanced under the influence of visceral factors (that is, in a corresponding state of need, such as hunger). Some intertemporal changes in preferences and evaluation thus may reflect a (mis)prediction of a change in one's state rather than discounting of future value. For example, when hungry, people may prefer an immediate bad meal to a better meal in a week as a result of assuming (either correctly or erroneously) that they are unlikely to be as hungry in a week. In a similar way, a satiated person may prefer to eat later rather than immediately. Notably, in these examples the differential evaluation of delayed versus immediate rewards does not occur as a result of time delay per se, but rather because people associate time with a change in their level of hunger. More generally, some intertemporal variations in value occur as a result of an anticipated change in one's state, rather than because of time delay per se (see Frederick, Loewenstein, and O'Donoghue, chap. 1 herein for a related discussion). Depending on whether people predict their own future states accurately, underestimate the intensity of those states (Loewenstein 1996), or overestimate it (Gilbert and Wilson 2000; Wilson et al. 2000), their choice pattern would exhibit stability over time, impulsiveness (preference for sooner rewards), or procrastination (preference for delayed rewards), respectively. Thus, if, as suggested by Loewenstein (1996), people systematically under-estimate future visceral needs, they would be impulsive about stimuli that are related to those needs.

CLT is also consistent with those theories of affective discounting that associate affective stimuli with a low level of construal. For example, Metcalfe and Mischel (1999) proposed that affective (hot) value is typically represented at a concrete level, whereas cognitive (cold) value may be represented more abstractly. Moreover, one may contend that affective value (for example, funniness) can be consumed for its own sake without considering higher-level goals, whereas cognitive value (for example, informativeness) derives its positivity from higher-level goals (for example, doing well on an exam) and therefore must be represented in terms of these goals to be appreciated. Such differences in construal level thus possibly contribute to the steeper discounting of affective value than cognitive value.

Feasibility and Desirability

Liberman and Trope (1998) examined the implications of CLT for time-dependent changes in the role of two particularly important types of high-level and low-level aspects of activities, namely, desirability and feasibility. According to theories of action control (Miller, Galanter, and Pribram 1960; Carver and Scheier 1990, 1999; Vallacher and Wegner 1987), goal-directed actions are organized in means-ends hierarchical structures, in which each action is superordinate to the means of achieving it and subordinated to its goal. For example, studying may be subordinate to doing well (people study in order to do well) and superordinate to reading (people study by reading). Superordinate goals are more abstract and are typically more important than subordinate goals (Carver and Scheier 1990, 1999; Vallacher and Wegner 1987). Our analysis of feasibility and desirability derives from this hierarchical analysis of goals. Specifically, desirability considerations pertain to why an activity is performed (a superordinate goal) and thus refer to a higher-level of construal, whereas feasibility aspects pertain to how an activity is performed (subordinate goal) and thus refer to a lower level of action identification. CLT predicts therefore that temporal distance would increase the weight of desirability concerns and decrease the weight of feasibility concerns in preferences regarding future activities.

Our studies supported this prediction using a variety of realistic as well as hypothetical choice situations. In our studies, people made irreversible decisions regarding an action to be performed in either the near or distant future. Information about the feasibility and desir-

Figure 8.2   Attractiveness Ratings of Near Future and Distant Future Academic Assignments

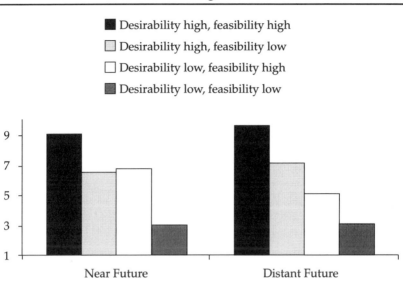

■ Desirability high, feasibility high
▨ Desirability high, feasibility low
☐ Desirability low, feasibility high
▨ Desirability low, feasibility low

Near Future   Distant Future

Source: Based on data from Liberman and Trope (1998).
Note: Ratings were made on a 1 (not attractive at all) to 10 (very attractive) scale.

ability of the action was provided, and was of course similar in the two time-perspective conditions. In one study, for example, four different groups of participants indicated on a one-to-ten scale how likely they are to attend a guest lecture that was either interesting or boring (that is, either high or low in desirability) and given in either a convenient or an inconvenient time (that is, either high or low in feasibility). Our results showed that the rated likelihood of attending the interesting but inconvenient lecture increased over delay, the likelihood of attending the boring but convenient lecture decreased over delay, while the likelihood of attending the interesting and convenient and boring and inconvenient lectures remained unchanged. This pattern of change in likelihood ratings over time indicated that a distant future lecture was chosen according to the interest of its topic (desirability), whereas a near future lecture was chosen according to the convenience of its timing (feasibility). A similar pattern of results was obtained in the same study with other decisions. Specifically, a word processor for distant future use was chosen according to its quality, whereas a word processor for the near future was chosen according to how easy it was to master. Decision to buy tickets for a distant future show was influenced by the quality of the show, whereas buying tickets for a show in the near future was relatively more influenced by the ticket price.

In a realistic field study, students chose course assignments to be performed in either the near future or the distant future. In both time-perspective conditions participants had one week to do the assignments, but this week was either the next week or a week two months later. Participants stated how much they would like to do each of four assignments, varying in interest (desirability) and difficulty (feasibility). They were told that assignments would be distributed according to their preferences. Consistent with the predictions of CLT, we found that the ratings of the interesting but difficult assignment increased over delay, the ratings of the boring but easy assignment decreased over delay, while the ratings of the interesting and easy and the boring and difficult assignments remained unchanged (see figure 8.2). Thus distant future academic assignments were chosen according to interest level, whereas near future assignments were chosen according to difficulty.

These findings cannot be explained by temporal differences in availability of feasibility versus desirability information or ability to postpone the use of one of these types of information when it pertained to distant future options. This is because in all of these cases, an irreversible decision was made at the same point regarding near or distant future options, and similar feasibility and desirability information was available for both near and distant future options at the time of the decision.

We must distinguish both empirically and theoretically between our approach and the notion of future optimism, which states that people tend to hold more positive expectancies for distant future than for immediate future outcomes (see, for example, Gilovich et al. 1993; Mitchell et al. 1997; Taylor and Brown 1988; Weinstein 1980). Future optimism suggests that temporal distance increases the perceived feasibility of outcomes. Empirically, future optimism may explain the increase over time in preference for the difficult but highly desirable options, as individuals presumably become increasingly confident over time in attaining the future outcome (that is, people think that they can be more efficient in the distant future than in the near future). Yet future optimism cannot account for the decreased preference for easy but less desirable options. Nor can future optimism explain the null effect of time on preference for difficult and undesirable options. That is, if temporal distance makes learning a new word processor seem easy, then it should enhance the value of both low- and high-quality difficult-to-master word processors. Our findings, however, show that this is not the case. Future optimism cannot explain these findings, because unlike CLT, it does not predict that temporal distance would affect people's view of desirability.

There is also a subtle but potentially important theoretical distinction between future optimism and CLT. Future optimism suggests that individuals undertake harder activities for the more distant future because time perspective changes the subjective estimates of feasibility by making distant future activities seem more feasible. Temporal construal, however, suggests that individuals undertake harder activities for the more distant future because feasibility receives less weight in distant future activities. CLT proposes, then, that overoptimistic decisions regarding future activities may reflect underweighting rather than overestimating feasibility.

Probabilities and Payoffs in Gambling

In positive gambles—characterized by a probability to win a desirable prize—one could conceptualize the prize as the desirability "why" dimension (that is, people play lotteries to get prizes) and the probability of winning as an uncontrollable feasibility consideration having to do with the random mechanism that determines the likelihood of winning (that is, the process of how wins are generated). In this view, the prize value, like other desirability aspects, pertains to a high-level construal of a gamble, whereas probability, like other feasibility dimensions, pertains to a low-level construal of a gamble. If this analysis is correct, then CLT must predict that in deciding on gambles, the weight given to probability would decrease over time perspective, whereas the weight given to amounts would increase over time perspective.

A series of studies conducted by Sagristano, Trope, and Liberman (2002) supports this prediction. Specifically, Sagristano and colleagues invited participants to bid on and rate the attractiveness of gambles they expected to play either in the same session or in the next session a few weeks later. The gambles systematically varied probabilities and expected utility. In different studies, bets were to be played by drawing balls from an urn, drawing cards, or drawing raffle tickets. Consistent with CLT, relatively safe bets—those with a high probability of winning a small prize—were more attractive in the near future than in the distant future, whereas risky bets—those with a low probability of winning a large prize—were more attractive in the distant future than in the near future (see figure 8.3). Most important, in two of the studies conducted by Sagristano and colleagues, participants evaluated a large number of gambles (between twelve and twenty), and it was possible to assess, within subjects, the independent effects of probability and value on people's bids and ratings of

Figure 8.3   Bids (In Dollars) for Near Future and Distant Future Bets of Equal Expected Utility by Probability of Winning

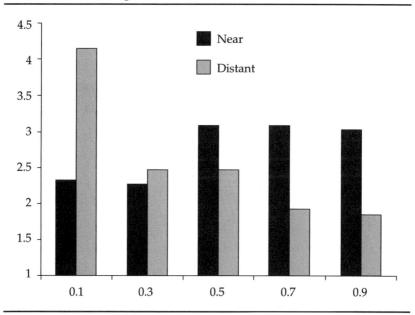

Source: Based on data from Sagristano, Trope, and Liberman (2002).

bets. Thus for each participant, bids in dollars and desirability ratings were regressed on the probability and value of the bets, and the regression slopes were averaged within each time-perspective condition. Consistent with the predictions of CLT, temporal distance significantly increases the weight of the payoff (independent of its effect on probability) and significantly decreases the weight of probability of winning (independent of its effect on payoffs) in evaluating future gambles. For example, in one study, payoffs predicted the bids participants placed on distant future bets (average slope .34) more than they predicted the bids placed on near future bets (average slope −.02). Probabilities showed the reverse intertemporal pattern—they predicted the bids placed on near future bets (average slope .48) more than the bids placed on distant future bets (average slope .10).

In addition, one of the studies assessed people's stated reasons for their preferences. These reasons were coded as referring to probabilities, amounts, neither, or both. People stated more probability-related reasons and less amounts-related reasons in explaining their preferences for near future gambles compared to distant future gambles. Thus, consistent with CLT, two independent effects emerged: the weight given to probabilities decreased over time delay, while the weight given to amounts increased over time delay.

We should note that the probability dimension in bets is distinct from other types of feasibility, such as difficulty or convenience. A person may think that he or she will overcome difficulty or inconvenience by putting in extra effort, but that person cannot think in the same way about probability. Our findings on time-dependent preferences of bets thus extend CLT to preferences among options with uncontrollable outcomes.

Controlling Intertemporal Variations in Evaluation and Choice

CLT suggests that intertemporal patterns of evaluation and preference could be altered if construals are controlled. For example, to prevent potentially harmful consequences of neglecting low-level aspects of distant future situations, one could try harder to construe such situations in low-level, concrete terms. Furthermore, CLT suggests that one way to control construal is to mentally place the events in question in different points in time. Thus one could try to think of a distant future situation as if it were close, and think of a near future situation as if it were distant. In fact, a variety of socially enforced procedures, such as practice talks, practice exams, and practice interviews simulate a close perspective on distant situations, and often force individuals to rehearse, practice, or plan in full detail distant future academic, social, or physical tasks.

People may also use construal processes to try to overcome harmful consequences of insensitivity to high-level aspects of near future situations. Mischel's (1974) work, for example, demonstrates that an effective way to overcome immediate temptations and successfully delay gratification is to turn attention away from the concrete qualities of the immediate temptation (for example, a tasty cookie) and focus on its abstract qualities (Mischel et al. 1989; see also Mischel, Ayduk, and Mendoza-Denton, chap. 5 herein). Thinking how a near future choice might affect distant future outcomes may also promote high-level construal of current options. Merely imagining a distant future retrospective evaluation of a near future decision also may facilitate high-level construal of the available options.

These mental control strategies may act to offset undesirable consequences of the default linkage between temporal distance and level of construal. This, however, may be easier to say than do. For example, construal processes were suggested to mediate overconfidence in social prediction (Griffin, Dunning, and Ross 1990) and the planning fallacy effect (Buehler, Griffin, and Ross 1994; Newby-Clark et al. 2000). In both lines of research, however, prompting participants to change their default construals proved to be fairly difficult.

Other Perspective-Dependent Construals

Future temporal distance is an important but not sole determinant of level of construal. Other dimensions of distance may affect level of construal in a similar way, such as past time perspective, social distance (self versus other, similar other versus dissimilar other, ingroup versus outgroup member), distance as measured in "stages" (that is, the number of nodes along a decision tree), hypotheticality, probability, and geographical distance. This idea seems to be in line with some of the literature in these domains. The literature on memory, for example, suggests that concrete details fade from memory more rapidly than general abstractions (Bartlett 1932; Hastie 1981; Wyer and Srull 1986), so that memories of the distant past tend to be more abstract than recent memories. The memory literature explains these effects of past temporal distance in terms of differential retention of abstract versus concrete information in memory rather than differential construal (Bartlett 1932; Hastie 1981; Wyer and Srull 1986). Nevertheless, that construal processes, on top of memory retention processes, also contributed to the greater abstractness of more distant memories is possible. Demonstrating the effects of past time perspective on construal, as distinct from retention, would be an interesting direction for future research. For example, one could examine whether higher-level construals are formed of imaginary events in the more distant past: suppose, for instance, that you learn now that a friend of yours interviewed for a job either a year ago or yesterday. When picturing the interview in your mind, would the more distant interview be construed on a higher level than the recent interview?

Level of construal may also be related to social distance dimensions, such as self versus other and ingroup versus outgroup (see Rachlin and Raineri 1992 for a related idea drawing a parallel between the effect of temporal and social distances on evaluation). Social cognitive research is consistent with the idea that more abstract construals are applied to other people and outgroup members compared with self and ingroup members. Thus many studies have documented the tendency to explain others' behaviors in dispositional (high-level, abstract) terms and one's own behavior in situational (that is, low-level, concrete) terms (Fiedler et al. 1995; Jones 1976; Jones and Nisbett 1972; for a review see Robins et al. 1996). Similarly, research on group perception suggests that outgroups are construed more schematically than ingroups, being perceived as more homogeneous (Jones, Wood, and Quattrone 1981; Park, Ryan, and Judd 1990), less differentiated into subgroups (Brewer and Lui 1984; Linville 1982; Park et al. 1992), possessing more structured, predictable sets of properties (Linville, Fischer, and Yoon 1996), and described in more abstract terms (Fiedler et al. 1995; Werkman, Wigboldus, and Semin 1999).

Uncertainty also may enhance psychological distance, with relatively uncertain events (that is, "remote possibilities") being represented in higher-level, more abstract terms. Consistent with this idea is Loewenstein and Prelec's (1991, 1992) notion that the effects of probability parallel those of temporal distance. Although Prelec and Loewenstein did not explain the similarity of time and uncertainty effects in terms of psychological distance and construal processes, these processes may have contributed to the effect.

Possibly, then, past temporal distance, uncertainty, social and geographical distance as well as other dimensions of distance would produce effects similar to future time distance on evaluations and choice. This prediction, however, must be made with caution, because many of these dimensions incorporate factors other than distance (for example, people tend to hold more negative attitudes toward outgroup members than toward ingroup members), which may have independent effects on evaluation and choice.

CLT and Other Theories of Intertemporal Evaluation and Choice

In this section, we outline the similarities and the differences between CLT and other theoretical approaches and findings in the field of intertemporal decision and choice, examine how these approaches could account for some of our results, and comment on how CLT may account for some of the results generated by these theories. In doing so, we attempt to delineate the scope of application of CLT versus other theories and suggest potentially interesting questions for future research.

Motivational Intensity Gradients over Temporal Distance

CLT predicts and our studies actually show that temporal distance may both diminish and intensify the value of outcomes. Is this prediction at odds with the notion of overall intertemporal discounting, which seems to be so central in the field of intertemporal choice (see Frederick, Loewenstein, and O'Donoghue, chap. 1 herein for a review)? We believe that this is not the case, because temporal distance may discount not only the value of outcomes but also, independently, the motivation to exert effort toward achieving those outcomes. Since CLT is a theory of intertemporal changes in value and is silent with respect to intertemporal changes in motivation, it does not contradict the existence of intertemporal gradients of motivation.

What is temporal discounting of motivation? Let us assume that the motivation to pursue a goal is proportional to the product of the value of the goal and the expectancy of achieving it (Atkinson 1957). Consider Brown's (1948) classic finding, that rats will pull a harness stronger the closer they are to an unconditioned stimulus (food or shock). One explanation for this effect (see, for example, Foerster, Higgins, and Idson 1998) is that in close proximity to an appetitive stimulus (two steps away from it), each unit of effort (one step by the rat) produces a relatively large change in the distance from the stimulus (a 50 percent reduction in distance), whereas further away from the stimulus (ten steps away from it) the same amount of effort produces a relatively smaller change (a 10 percent reduction in distance). In this case, the increased motivation (harder pulling) closer to the outcome may be due to changes in the perceived instrumentality of one's efforts rather than changes in the subjective value of the stimulus in question. Kacelnik (chap. 3 herein) provides another example of motivational gradients due to opportunity loss: going for a distant prey is more costly than going for a proximal prey, because it involves losing more alternative opportunities in the time between the decision to get the prey and actually achieving it. The cost of opportunity loss may be conceptualized as another variant of expectancy. More generally, some distance-related gradients in motivation may be produced not by changes in the subjective value of an outcome, but rather by changes in the perceived instrumentality of one's efforts, or changes in the strength of the perceived contingency between one's efforts and the outcome. This distinction is of little consequence for the behaviorist tradition, which identifies the value of stimuli with the organism's motivation to approach or avoid it. Economic and psychological models of behavior, however, conceptualize expectancy and value as distinct components of motivation, and thus cannot equate motivation with value.

Let us consider an example closer to human reality: People are more likely to diet shortly before a vacation than long in advance, because they want to look good in their beachwear (Herman and Polivy, chap. 16 herein). One may conceptualize failing to lose weight as omitting a one in x opportunity to do so. As one gets closer to the vacation, fewer opportunities remain to lose weight and failing to do so becomes more irreversible and consequential. In other words, dieting becomes objectively more instrumental closer to the vacation. Note that given the foregoing analysis, an enhanced motivation to diet does not have to reflect an increase in the subjective value (importance) of losing weight closer to the vacation. Rather, it could reflect an objectively justified perception that one's efforts toward achieving this goal are more crucial and efficient the closer one is to the relevant situation.

To sum up, in all the foregoing examples, distance causes an objective (real, normatively justified) change in expectancy, and thus enhanced motivation closer to the goal (or the deadline) could reflect change in expectancy rather than change in value. Note that no new theory is invoked to explain motivational gradients. Rather, they are explained within the traditional expectancy value model of motivation.

What are the implications of this analysis for the measurement of intertemporal changes in value? Theoretically, if one could measure value independently of motivation, time-dependent changes in motivation would not cause any problem for the assessment of temporal discounting of value. In reality, however, both researchers and laypersons may use motivation as a proxy for value. For example, researchers may ask how much effort a person is willing to exert in dieting as a proxy for the value of losing weight. Measures of arousal and emotional intensity also are likely to reflect motivational strength, so that the question, "How important is it for you to lose weight?" may prompt participants to consult their own level of anxiety about dieting as a basis for evaluation. In both cases, motivation would contaminate the measure of value, thereby creating an appearance of discounting in value over time.

Expectancy does not always increase closer to the outcome. For example, in many of our studies, outcomes were assigned to people according to their ratings, but the contingency between the expressed ratings and the assignment of outcomes was not stronger in the near future than the distant future. The measurement of such ratings therefore was not contaminated with time-dependent changes in motivational factors unrelated to value. As another example, uncontrollable events (for example, gambles) by definition do not depend on one's actions. Therefore, time-dependent changes in the motivation to experience such events cannot reflect objective changes in the instrumentality of one's actions, and thus is more easily attributable to changes in the subjective value of the event.

Two points emerge from this discussion. First, some findings and intuitions that are commonly interpreted in terms of discounting in value over time (for example, Brown's results) may actually stem from changes in motivation attributable to objective changes in expectancy. Such expectancy-related changes in motivation are outside of the scope of CLT or any other theory about the effect of temporal distance on value. Therefore, as noted earlier, CLT's notion that temporal distance could cause an augmentation in value and not only discounting in value is entirely consistent with motivational discounting. Second, the discussion obviates the need to distinguish more clearly between motivation and value in theories and measures of the effect of intertemporal choice (see Higgins 2000 for a related discussion of the importance of this distinction).

Dread and Savoring

Loewenstein (1987; see also Elster and Loewenstein 1992; Lovallo and Kahneman 2000) proposed that expecting an event has value and thus can be consumed in its own right. This can lead to a preference to delay positive events and speed up the occurrence of negative events. For example, waiting to see a good movie may be pleasurable, and the positive valence of waiting could be added to the positive valence of a movie and thus enhance its attractiveness over delay. Contrary to this, waiting for an electric shock is aversive, and adding the aversiveness of waiting to that of the shock may result in a delayed shock being more aversive than an immediate shock. Savoring and dreading thus could account for value enhancement over delay.

Obviously, dreading and savoring and the construal processes proposed by CLT could coexist and both contribute to intertemporal variations in evaluation of events. It is interesting, however, to examine more closely some of the predictions that these two approaches make. According to Loewenstein (1987, 672), augmenting of value over time delay is more likely when consumption is fleeting rather than prolonged, and with outcomes that "can be readily imagined and that are pleasurable [or painful] to contemplate." CLT could predict more augmentation of fleeting experiences than prolonged experiences if duration is conceptualized as a low-level construal of an event. For example, an electric shock causes an aversive reaction, but the fact that it is brief may undermine its negative value. If duration is a low-level, concrete feature of the event, then such undermining of negativity would be more pronounced with a shock in the near future than with a distant future shock, resulting in a perception of a distant future shock as more negative. Similarly, the value of a positive experience may be undermined by acknowledging its shortness, and if duration comprises a low level of construal, then such undermining will be more pronounced closer to the event.

CLT and the dreading-savoring hypothesis make different predictions when duration is central to an event and thus comprises a high-level of construal. For example, suppose that duration is a central feature of an aversive experience of waiting. CLT would predict, in this case, that briefness would be given more weight in the distant future than in the near future, and thus a distant future brief waiting would seem less aversive than a near future brief waiting. Dreading and savoring, however, would continue to predict that a brief waiting would seem more negative in the distant future than in the near future.

Intertemporal Preference Reversals

An important observation in the literature on intertemporal choice has been that in choosing between a smaller, sooner (SS) reward and a larger, later (LL) reward, people may reverse preferences toward the larger, later reward if a constant amount of time is added to both delays. For example, a person may prefer one apple today over two apples tomorrow, and at the same time prefer two apples in fifty-one days over one apple in fifty days (Thaler 1981). A widely accepted explanation of this effect is that discounting rate changes over temporal distance, such that discounting is steeper closer in time than at more distant intervals (for example, discounting is steeper from day one to day two than from day fifty to day fifty-one). Hyperbolic discounting functions capture this property and were proposed to explain preference reversals (Ainslie 1975; Ainslie and Haslam 1992; Green, Fristoe, and Myerson 1994; Loewenstein and Prelec 1992; Prelec and Loewenstein 1991; Rachlin 1995; Read et al. 1999—but see Frederick, Loewenstein, and O'Donoghue, chap. 1 herein, and Read, chap. 10 herein, for critical discussions of hyperbolic discounting).

According to hyperbolic discounting, when a future activity has earlier and later outcomes, more weight should be given to the earlier outcome than to the later outcome in near compared to distant future decisions. As a result, temporal distance should increase preference for activities with relatively more valuable later outcomes and decrease preference for activities with relatively more valuable earlier outcomes. One could argue that the activities in some of our studies had immediate and delayed outcomes. For example, in a word processor, learning comes before enjoying the quality of the product. Therefore, by hyperbolic time discounting, ease of learning should receive smaller weight in distant future than near future decisions. One should point out, however, that in other studies low-level outcomes and high-level outcomes were concurrent. For example, participants in the task preference study expected to experience the boring or interesting main and filler task in the same occasion. The same holds true for the quality of the sound and quality of the clock radio in the product preference study, and the goal-relevant versus goal-irrelevant features of the films in the film preference study. Hyperbolic time discounting thus can account for some but not all of our findings.

An alternative account of intertemporal preference reversals is found in attribute-based models of intertemporal choice (Roelofsma and Read 2000), which view the SS and LL options as trading off quality and delay (that is, LL is better but later, whereas SS is sooner but worse). It has been proposed that in this type of trade-off, the delay dimension receives less weight when the decision is removed in time (Rubinstein 2001). This explanation assumes, in line with general principles of psychophysics, a diminishing sensitivity to delay without making assumptions about the shape of the function of discounting of value over time. (A diminishing sensitivity to delay is perceiving the difference between one day and two days, for instance, as subjectively bigger than the difference between fifty days and fifty-one days; see, for example, Gibbon 1977.)

Can CLT account for the tendency to choose SS now and LL when delayed? We think that a CLT explanation would be closer to the attribute-based account of intertemporal preference reversals (Roelofsma and Read 2000; Rubinstein 2001) than to hyperbolic discounting. Specifically, CLT would suggest that if amount is central and thus high-level—whereas delay is peripheral and thus low-level—then people would choose according to amount in the distant future more than in the near future, which is the typical finding of intertemporal preference reversals.

Note, however, that in CLT, delay is less important in the distant future than in the near future not because of general psychophysical processes, but because it is a low-level feature. Therefore, CLT makes the unique prediction that a reverse pattern of choice (that is, more LL choice in the near future) would emerge in situations in which delay comprises a high-level rather than a low-level aspect. For example, imagine an instructor who struggles to extinguish procrastination in her students (that is, the issue of delay is of some centrality to her). Suppose that a student asks for a one-day extension of the deadline, saying that this would enable him to write a better paper (that is, presents the instructor with a version of an SS versus LL dilemma). CLT would predict that the instructor will be less likely to grant the student the requested extra day if the request is made long in advance compared to right before the deadline, because delay—being a high-level feature—would be weighted more in the more distant future. Of course, in practice both psychophysical processes and construal processes may coexist and independently contribute to changes in the perceived magnitude and importance of delay.

Self-Control

Some problems of self-control (failure to quit smoking) are not easily conceptualized as a preference for an immediately available smaller reward (smoking a cigarette) over a larger reward that is available later (good health). This is because, as Rachlin (1995) noted, in those instances a single failure of self-control does not mean forgoing the larger, later reward—that is, there is no trade-off between SS and LL, because one can both smoke the cigarette and be healthy. In fact, smoking one cigarette is enjoyable but has very little effect on one's health, an effect that can be fully counteracted later. Thus it is very likely that smoking one cigarette should not be avoided from the perspective of a cost-benefit analysis. We should also note that the larger reward (good health) is not restricted to any specific point in the future, but rather comprises an extended desirable state. These considerations make it difficult to apply hyperbolic discounting to explain an important class of self-control failures.

To address this difficulty, Rachlin (1995) proposed to distinguish between a single act and a pattern of behavior. When viewed as a single act, smoking one cigarette is enjoyable and has no serious negative consequences. When viewed as part of a behavioral pattern, however, smoking one cigarette undermines the desirable pattern of healthy behavior and as such is negative. Thus, according to Rachlin (1995), maintaining a desirable pattern has a positive valence, and the negativity of a failure of self-control stems from interrupting that pattern, rather than from thwarting an important long-term goal.

It is interesting to relate this conceptualization to CLT. Specifically, viewing a behavior as part of a pattern rather than a single act may be analogous to construing the behavior in abstract rather than concrete terms. Thus Rachlin's conceptualization, restated in terms of CLT, would be that a self-control failure stems from failing to attend to the high-level aspects of an immediate behavior. Both Rachlin's act-pattern theory and CLT offer a similar explanation of the fact that self-control failures (deciding to smoke a cigarette) are more likely in a close temporal perspective than long in advance. Both theories would explain it as a consequence of construing a distant future behavior in high-level, "pattern" terms and a near future behavior in low-level, "act" terms.

A related conceptualization was offered by Kahneman and Lovallo (2000), who distinguished between an inside and an outside perspective on a decision. An inside perspective views a situation as a unique, one-time event, whereas an outside perspective views it as a case within a category of similar events. According to Kahneman and Lovallo (2000), adopting an outside view is associated with less risk aversion than an inside view, for the same reason that people are less risk averse with an aggregate of gambles than with an isolated gamble (for example, Lopes 1996). Specifically, when each choice is seen as one in a series of similar choices, then a prospective failure could be compensated by a successful outcome later and does not seem so crucial. Possibly, an outside view is analogous to a more abstract, high-level construal of an action, whereas an inside view is akin to a low-level construal. CLT would predict, then, a more outside view for distant future events than for near future events. Kahneman and Lovallo's (2000) theorizing on less risk aversion due to adopting an outside view is thus consistent with our findings of more risky choice for the distant future than for the near future.

Applying Kahneman and Lovallo's (2000) conceptualization to self-control situations would suggest that one could adopt either an inside or outside view of self-control behavior. For example, one could think of smoking a cigarette as a one-time, isolated event that is unrelated to other incidents of smoking, or, alternatively, as one event in a category of similar behaviors (for example, smoking this cigarette is similar to smoking other cigarettes on other occasions). Clearly, in the latter case, one is more likely to realize that what someone decides now would apply equally well to decisions in other incidents, and hence health damage would be imminent if one decides to smoke the cigarette. In this case, just as with risk taking, an outside view would make people decide on an aggregate of behaviors rather than on an isolated case, to make a strategic rather than a local decision. Again, CLT would predict that because a high-level construal or an outside view are more likely for the more distant future, self-controlling (that is, strategic, aggregate) decisions would become more likely for more temporally removed situations.

Conclusion

CLT proposes that temporal distance changes preferences regarding responses for future events by changing the way people mentally represent those events. The greater the temporal distance, the more likely are events to be represented in terms of a few central and abstract features (high-level construals), rather than in terms of more concrete and incidental details of the events (low-level construals). The evaluative implications of high-level construals compared with those of low-level construals should therefore have more impact on responses to distant future events than near future events. Our research on interpretation and categorization of future events supports our assumptions regarding temporal construal, and our research on future preference supports the implications of temporal construal for temporal changes in value. Based on this research, we propose that temporal construal is a general mechanism that can integrate a wide range of previous findings and generate novel predictions regarding intertemporal choice.

Our research so far has been primarily concerned with the consequences of temporal construal for temporal changes in preference and choice, but CLT also applies to temporal changes in predictions. According to CLT, predictions for the more distant future should be primarily based on the informational implications of high-level construals rather than low-level construals of future situations. The distinction between high-level and low-level construals may also apply to other types of proximal versus distal perspectives, such as near versus distant past, distance in decision trees, self versus other, and ingroup versus outgroup. Research along these lines can significantly extend past research on intertemporal choice and help uncover the general psychological principles underlying perspective-driven responses to events.

References

Abelson, Robert P. 1981. "Psychological Status of the Script Concept." *American Psychologist* 36(7): 715–29.

Ainslie, George. 1975. "Specious Reward: A Behavioral Theory of Impulsiveness and Impulse Control." *Psychological Bulletin* 82(4): 463–96.

Ainslie, George, and Nick Haslam. 1992. "Hyperbolic Discounting." In *Choice Over Time*, edited by George Loewenstein and Jon Elster. New York: Russell Sage Foundation.

Atkinson, John W. 1957. "Motivational Determinants of Risk-taking Behavior." *Psychological Review* 64: 359–72.

Bartlett, C. Frederic. 1932. *Remembering: A Study in Experimental and Social Psychology*. New York: Cambridge University Press.

Baumeister, Roy F., and Todd F. Heatherton. 1996. "Self Regulation Failure: An Overview." *Psychological Inquiry* 7(1): 1–15.

Benzion, Uri, Amnon Rappoport, and J. Yagil. 1989. "Discount Rates Inferred from Decisions: An Experimental Study." *Management Science* 35, 270–84.

Brewer, Marilynn B., and Layton Lui. 1984. "Categorization of the Elderly by the Elderly: Effects of Perceiver's Category Membership." *Personality and Social Psychology Bulletin* 10(4): 585–95.

Brown, Judson S. 1948. "Gradients of Approach and Avoidance Responses and Their Relation to Motivation." *Journal of Comparative and Physiological Psychology* 41: 450–65.

Buehler, Roger, Dale Griffin, and Michael Ross. 1994. "Exploring the 'Planning Fallacy': Why People Underestimate Their Task Completion Times." *Journal of Personality and Social Psychology* 67(3): 366–81.

Burhans, K. Karen. 1995. "Trading off Time-Structured Goals: An Alternative to Discounted Value Theories." Ph.D. diss., Columbia University, New York.

Carver, Charles S., and Michael F. Scheier. 1990. "Principles of Self-Regulation." In *Handbook of Motivation and Cognition: Foundations of Social Behavior*, edited by Tory E. Higgins and Richard M. Sorrentino. New York: Guilford Press.

———. 1999. "Themes and Issues in the Self-Regulation of Behavior." In *Perspectives on Behavioral Self-Regulation: Advances in Social Cognition*, edited by Robert S. Wyer Jr. Mahwah, N.J.: Erlbaum.

Chapman, Gretchen B. 1996. "Temporal Discounting and Utility of Health and Money." *Journal of Experimental Psychology: Learning, Memory and Cognition* 22(3): 771–91.

Elster, Jon, and George Loewenstein. 1992. "Utility from Memory and Anticipation." In *Choice Over Time*, edited by George Loewenstein and Jon Elster. New York: Russell Sage Foundation.

Epstein, Seymour, and Walter D. Fenz. 1965. "Steepness of Approach and Avoidance Gradient in Humans as a Function of Experience: Theory and Experiment." *Journal of Experimental Psychology* 70(1): 1–12.

Fiedler, Klaus, Guen R. Semin, Catrin Finkenauer, and Ingrid Berkel. 1995. "Actor-Observer Bias in Close Relationships: The Role of Self-Knowledge and Self-Related Language." *Personality and Social Psychology Bulletin* 21(5): 525–38.

Fiske, Susan T., and Shelley E. Taylor. 1991. *Social Cognition*. 2d ed. New York: McGraw-Hill.

Foerster, Jens, Tory E. Higgins, and Lorraine C. Idson. 1998. "Approach and Avoidance Strength During Goal Attainment: Regulatory Focus and the 'Goal Looms Larger' Effect." *Journal of Personality and Social Psychology* 75(5): 1115–31.

Gibbon, John. 1977. "Scalar Expectancy Theory and Weber's Law in Animal Timing." *Psychological Review* 84(3): 279–325.

Gilbert, Daniel T., and Timothy D. Wilson. 2000. "Miswanting: Some Problems in Affective Forecasting of Future Affective States." In *Feeling and Thinking: The Role of Affect in Social Cognition*, edited by Joseph Forgas. New York: Cambridge University Press.

Gilovich, Thomas, Margaret Kerr, and Victoria H. Medvec. 1993. "Effect of Temporal Perspective on Subjective Confidence." *Journal of Personality and Social Psychology* 64(4): 552–60.

Green, Leonard, Nathanael Fristoe, and Joel Myerson. 1994. "Temporal Discounting and Preference Reversals in Choice Between Delayed Outcomes." *Psychonomic Bulletin and Review* 1(3): 383–89.

Green, Leonard, Joel Myerson, and Edward McFadden. 1997. "Rate of Temporal Discounting Decreases with Amount of Reward." *Memory and Cognition* 25(5): 715–23.

Griffin, Dale W., David Dunning, and Lee Ross. 1990. "The Role of Construal Processes in Overconfident Predictions About Self and Others." *Journal of Personality and Social Psychology* 59(6): 1128–39.

Hampson, Sarah E., Oliver P. John, and Lewis R. Goldberg. 1986. "Category Breadth and Hierarchical Structure in Personality: Studies of Asymmetries in Judgments of Trait Implications." *Journal of Personality and Social Psychology* 51(1): 37–54.

Hastie, Reid. 1981. "Schematic Principles in Human Memory." In *Social Cognition: The Ontario Symposium*, edited by E. Tory Higgins, P. Herman, and Mark P. Zanna. Hillsdale, N.J.: Erlbaum.

Higgins, Tory E. 2000. "Making a Good Decision: Value from Fit." *American Psychologist* 55(11): 1217–30.

Jones, Edward E. 1976. "How Do People Perceive the Causes of Behavior?" *American Scientist* 64(3): 300–5.

Jones, Edward E., and Richard E. Nisbett. 1972. "The Actor and the Observer: Divergent Perceptions of the Causes of Behavior." In *Attribution: Perceiving the Causes of Behavior*, edited by Edward E. Jones, David E. Kanouse, Harold H. Kelley, Richard E. Nisbett, Stuart Valins, and Bernard Weiner. Hillsdale, N.J.: Erlbaum.

Jones, Edward E., George C. Wood, and George A. Quattrone. 1981. "Perceived Variability of Personal Characteristics in In-groups and Out-groups: The Role of Knowledge and Evaluation." *Personality and Social Psychology Bulletin* 7(3): 523–28.

Kahneman, Daniel, and Dan Lovallo. 2000. "Timid Choices and Bold Forecasts: A Cognitive Perspective on Risk Taking." In *Choices, Values, and Frames*, edited by Daniel Kahneman and Amos Tversky. New York: Cambridge University Press.

Kirby, Kris N. 1997. "Bidding on the Future: Evidence Against Normative Discounting of Delayed Rewards." *Journal of Experimental Psychology: General* 126(1): 54–70.

Lewin, Kurt. 1951. *Field Theory in Social Science: Selected Theoretical Papers*. New York: Harper.

Liberman, Nira, Michael Sagristano, and Yaacov Trope. Forthcoming. "The Effect of Temporal Distance on Level of Construal." *Journal of Experimental Social Psychology*.

Liberman, Nira, and Yaacov Trope. 1998. "The Role of Feasibility and Desirability Considerations in Near and Distant Future Decisions: A Test of Temporal Construal Theory." *Journal of Personality and Social Psychology* 75(1): 5–18.

Liberman, Nira, Yaacov Trope, Sean Mccrae, and Steven J. Sherman. 2002. "The Effect of Construal Level on Perceived Temporal Distance." Unpublished paper. Indiana University.

Linville, Patricia W. 1982. "The Complexity-Extremity Effect and Age-Based Stereotyping." *Journal of Personality and Social Psychology* 42(2): 193–211.

Linville, Patricia W., George W. Fischer, and Carolyn Yoon. 1996. "Perceived

Covariation among the Features of Ingroup and Outgroup Members: The Outgroup Covariation Effect." *Journal of Personality and Social Psychology* 70(3): 421–36.

Loewenstein, George F. 1987. "Anticipation and the Valuation of Delayed Consumption." *Economic Journal* 97: 666–84.

———. 1996. "Out of Control: Visceral Influences on Behavior." *Organizational Behavior and Human Decision Processes* 65(3): 272–92.

Loewenstein, George F., and Drazen Prelec. 1992. "Anomalies in Intertemporal Choice: Evidence and an Interpretation." In *Choice Over Time*, edited by George F. Loewenstein and Jon Elster. New York: Russell Sage Foundation.

Lopes, Lola L. 1996. "When Time Is of the Essence: Averaging, Aspiration and the Short Run." *Organizational Behavior and Human Decision Processes* 65(3): 179–89.

Lovallo, Dan, and Daniel Kahneman. 2000. "Living with Uncertainty: Attractiveness and Resolution Timing." *Journal of Behavioral Decision Making* 13(2): 179–90.

Metcalfe, Janet, and Walter Mischel. 1999. "A Hot/Cool System Analysis of Delay of Gratification: Dynamics of Willpower." *Psychological Review* 106(1): 3–19.

Miller, George A., Eugene Galanter, and Karl H. Pribram. 1960. *Plans and the Structure of Behavior*. New York: Holt, Rinehart and Winston.

Miller, Neil E. 1944. "Experimental Studies of Conflict." In *Personality and the Behavior Disorders*, edited by Joseph McVicker Hunt. New York: Ronald Press.

Mischel, Walter. 1974. "Processes in Delay of Gratification." In *Advances in Experimental Social Psychology*, edited by L. Berkowitz. New York: Academic Press.

Mischel, Walter, Yuichi Shoda, and Monica L. Rodriguez. 1989. "Delay of Gratification in Children." *Science* 244(4907): 933–38.

Mitchell, Terence R., Leigh Thompson, Erika Peterson, and Randy Cronk. 1997. "Temporal Adjustments in the Evaluation of Events: The 'Rosy View.'" *Journal of Experimental Social Psychology* 33(4): 421–48.

Newby-Clark, Lan R., Michael Ross, Roger Buehler, Derek Koehler, and Dale Griffin. 2000. "People Focus on Optimistic Scenarios and Disregard Pessimistic Scenarios While Predicting Task Completion Times." *Journal of Experimental Psychology: Applied* 6(3): 171–82.

Park, Bernadette, Carey S. Ryan, and Charles M. Judd. 1992. "Role of Meaningful Subgroups in Explaining Differences in Perceived Variability for Ingroups and Outgroups." *Journal of Personality and Social Psychology* 63(4): 553–67.

Prelec, Drazen, and George Loewenstein. 1991. "Decision Making over Time and Under Uncertainty: A Common Approach." *Management Science* 37: 770–86.

Rachlin, Howard. 1995. "Self-Control: Beyond Commitment." *Behavioral and Brain Sciences* 18(1): 109–59.

Rachlin, Howard, and Andres Raineri. 1992. "Irrationality, Impulsiveness, and Selfishness as Discount Reversal Effects." In *Choice Over Time*, edited by George F. Loewenstein and Jon Elster. New York: Russell Sage Foundation.

Raineri, Andres, and Howard Rachlin. 1993. "The Effect of Temporal Constraints on the Value of Money and Other Commodities." *Journal of Behavioral Decision Making* 6(2): 77–94.

Read, Daniel, George Loewenstein, and Shobana Kalyanaraman. 1999. "Mixing Virtue with Vice: Combining the Immediacy Effect and the Diversification Heuristic." *Journal of Behavioral Decision Making* 12(4): 257–73.

Robins, Richard W., Mark D. Spranca, and Gerald A. Mendelsohn. 1996. "The Actor-Observer Effect Revisited: Effects of Individual Differences and Repeated Social Interactions on Actor and Observer Attributions." *Journal of Personality and Social Psychology* 71(2): 375–89.

Roelofsma, Peter H. M. P., and Daniel Read. 2000. "Intransitive Intertemporal Choice." *Journal of Behavioral Decision Making* 13(2): 161–77.

Rosch, Eleanor. 1978. "Principles of Categorization." In *Cognition and Categorization*, edited by Eleanor Rosch and Barbara B. Lloyd. Hillsdale, N.J.: Erlbaum.

Rubinstein, Ariel. 2001. "A Theorist's View of Experiments." *European Economic Review* 45(4–6): 615–28.

Sagristano, Michael, Yaacov Trope, and Nira Liberman. 2002. "Odds Now, Money Later: Temporal Distance Effects on Weighting Risk and Outcomes in Positive Bets: A Temporal Construal Perspective." *Journal of Experimental Psychology: General.*

Schwartz, Shalom H. 1992. "Universals in the Content and Structure of Values: Theoretical Advances and Empirical Tests in 20 Countries." In *Advances in Experimental Social Psychology,* edited by Mark P. Zanna. Vol. 25. New York: Academic Press.

Semin, Guen R., and Klaus Fiedler. 1988. "The Cognitive Functions of Linguistic Categories in Describing Persons: Social Cognitive and Language." *Journal of Personality and Social Psychology* 54(4): 558–68.

Shelley, Marjorie K. 1994. "Gain/Loss Asymmetry in Risky Intertemporal Choice." *Organizational Behavior and Human Decision Processes* 59(1): 124–59.

Smith, Eliot R. 1998. "Mental Representation and Memory." In *The Handbook of Social Psychology,* edited by Daniel T. Gilbert, Susan T. Fiske, and Gardner Lindzey. New York: McGraw-Hill.

Taylor, Shelley E., and Jonathon D. Brown. 1988. "Illusion and Well-Being: A Social Psychological Perspective on Mental Health." *Psychological Bulletin* 103(2): 193–210.

Thaler, Richard. 1981. "Some Empirical Evidence on Dynamic Inconsistency." *Economics Letters* 8: 201–7.

Trope, Yaacov, and Nira Liberman. 2000. "Temporal Construal and Time-Dependent Changes in Preference." *Journal of Personality and Social Psychology* 79(6): 876–89.

Vallacher, Robin R., and Daniel M. Wegner. 1987. "What Do People Think They're Doing? Action Identification and Human Behavior." *Psychological Review* 94(1): 3–15.

———. 1989. "Levels of Personal Agency: Individual Variation in Action Identification." *Journal of Personality and Social Psychology* 57(4): 660–71.

Weinstein, Neil D. 1980. "Unrealistic Optimism About Future Life Events." *Journal of Personality and Social Psychology* 39(5): 806–20.

Werkman, Wolanda M., Daniel H. J. Wigboldus, and Guen R. Semin. 1999. "Children's Communication of the Linguistic Intergroup Bias and Its Impact upon Cognitive Inferences." *European Journal of Social Psychology* 29(1): 95–104.

Wilson, Timothy D., Thalia Wheatley, Jonathan M. Meyers, Daniel T. Gilbert, and Danny Axsom. 2000. "Focalism: A Source of Durability Bias in Affective Forecasting." *Journal of Personality and Social Psychology* 78(5): 821–36.

Wyer, Robert S., and Thomas K. Srull. 1986. "Human Cognition in its Social Context." *Psychological Review* 93(3): 322–59.

· 9 ·

Self-Signaling and Self-Control

Drazen Prelec and Ronit Bodner

Sᴇʟꜰ-ᴄᴏɴᴛʀᴏʟ is a hallmark virtue of human character. To lack self-control is to be governed by momentary pleasures even when these pleasures place larger values at risk. Willing the tired body to exercise or the tired mind to another hour of work are but two examples of active self-control—the tolerance of pain in return for a larger but more remote and uncertain gain. Turning down a chocolate dessert or an attractive sexual encounter are examples of passive self-control—avoiding immediate gratification to preserve broader personal objectives or self-esteem. The importance of self-control for individual happiness and social welfare is not controversial (Baumeister et al. 1994).

Motivation Without Causality

Theoretical approaches to self-control have largely focused on the temporal aspect of the problem, the conflict between the near and far. This conflict, however, does not capture one key issue present in many if not most self-control dilemmas. Let us take a workhorse example—dieting. The dieter faces a series of temptations, each of which involves a choice between yielding and eating the tempting morsel, or resisting temptation and gaining . . . what precisely? At the level of a single action, the benefits of self-control are obscure. The caloric impact of one act of indulgence is negligible and will not affect the waistline, let alone any larger objectives. As described by Herman and Polivy (chap. 16 herein),

> She [the dieter] can resist that tempting plate of cookies, but there's no certainty that she will become slim as a result. The stubborn fact of the matter is that weight loss is only vaguely connected to food intake. . . . Finally, it may be that the reward that the dieter is after is something more than slimness. For some dieters, slimness may be an end in itself; but for many other dieters, slimness is simply a means to an end. Being slim is how one becomes attractive; being slim is how one becomes healthy; being slim is how one displays one's virtue.

The gap between a single act of dietary self-sacrifice and its benefits—slimness, leading to beauty, health, and virtue—is not only temporal but also *causal*. A single low-calorie salad does not cause slimness, beauty, health, or virtue. Rather, the benefits or costs are properties of a long-run policy or lifestyle, and an integral policy or lifestyle cannot be obtained with a single decision, except in extreme cases, such as joining the Foreign Legion. In earlier work (Prelec 1991; Prelec and Herrnstein 1991), one of us referred to this as a mismatch of "scale," where the effects of an action only become visible if the action is repeated many times, across different contexts, and in conjunction with other supporting activities (for example, exercise in the case of dieting).

Our ability to persevere in spite of the tenuous connection between individual actions and broad lifestyle objectives is both essential to normal functioning and a major challenge for psychology and economics. As several authors have pointed out (for example, Elster 1989), the theoretical problem resembles the paradox of voting in political science. Voters go through some trouble to cast their vote, though their individual effort cannot affect the outcome (no major election has been, or is likely to be decided by, exactly one vote). Here too we have an instance of motivation without clear causality. Whatever motivates the voter, it cannot be only the ceremonial or participatory pleasures of the exercise. Few would stand for hours to vote at a broken polling booth. People want their vote to count, and they will vote only if they think there is some chance their vote *will count*—that is, affect the final outcome.

The feeling that larger objectives are put at risk even by small-stakes choices seems essential to self-control, to persistence and endurance over the long haul. Intuitively, success in a small matter is a *signal* of success in larger matters; it allows one to enjoy for a moment the expectations of attaining the larger good.[1] As such, the signal—

whatever its intrinsic nature—is an independent source of immediate pleasure, as nicely described by Herman and Polivy (chap. 16 herein):

> Indeed the very hunger pangs that signal abstention, and that are allegedly so difficult to bear, provide a clear signal of success. Going to bed hungry is usually regarded as an aversive experience; for the dieter, however, it may provide a sense of accomplishment. This hedonic dialectic—in which pain confers pleasure, and dieting is an exercise in masochism—makes the application of standard behavioral economic calculations questionable.

In a recent paper (Bodner and Prelec 1997, 2002) we proposed a "self-signaling" model of diagnostic motivation, which we now apply to self-control. The model rests on a distinction between two types of reward (or utility): *causal* reward that flows directly from the consequences of choice (whether these consequences are immediate or delayed), and *diagnostic* reward, which is the pleasure or pain derived from learning something positive or negative about one's internal state, disposition, ability, or future prospects. People are presumed to be chronically uncertain about where they stand with respect to these broad attributes, which in turn makes their choices diagnostic. For example, taking a drink before noon is diagnostic of alcoholism; hard exercise is diagnostic of health, willpower, perhaps even financial success, and so on. Anticipation of such diagnostic reward or fear of diagnostic pain promotes self-control and inhibits self-indulgence.

The model is an exercise in behavioral economics in that the person's choices are governed by maximization of utility, albeit with the diagnostic component added to the equation. More important, economic analysis provides determinate predictions about the amount of good or bad news that any given action might yield—it provides, in other words, a precise theory of what actions *mean*. The core idea is that if you believe that your choices are governed by maximization of total utility, then any choice you make triggers a recognition (possibly gratifying or damaging) that you are the kind of person for whom that choice maximizes total utility. The choice brings your tastes out into the open, as it were.

Self-Signaling in the Lab and in Everyday Life

A self-signaling action is an action taken precisely in order to obtain good news about these tastes or dispositions, even when this action has no causal impact on tastes or dispositions. The definition immediately raises philosophical problems—if I take an action to get good news, doesn't that invalidate the "good news" (Campbell and Sowden 1985; Elster 1985)?

Whatever its logical status, self-signaling is a real phenomenon, as several studies have shown (Dunning, Leuenberger, and Sherman 1995; Quattrone and Tversky 1984; Sanitioso, Kunda, and Fong 1990; Shafir and Tversky 1992). The cold water test by Quattrone and Tversky (1984) is especially elegant, both as a definition of self-signaling and demonstration of existence. Quattrone and Tversky began by asking subjects to keep their hand submerged in a container of cold water until they could no longer tolerate the pain. Subjects were then told (via a "scientific" lecture) that a certain inborn heart condition, leading to a shorter-than-average life expectancy, could be diagnosed by the effect of exercise on cold tolerance. One half of the subjects were told that having a bad heart would increase cold tolerance, the other half that it would decrease cold tolerance following exercise. Having absorbed this interesting piece of information, subjects then rode a treadmill vigorously for about a minute and repeated the cold water test. The vast majority showed changes in tolerance on the second cold trial in the direction correlated with "good news," thereby demonstrating the influence of diagnostic motivation on behavior. Most subjects were not aware of any attempt to bias their test results.

Although the setup in this experiment is somewhat unusual, the results fit well with a great deal of other psychological research. We know that people manipulate personality self-reports (Sanitioso, Kunda, and Fong 1990; Kunda 1990; Dunning, Leuenberger, and Sherman 1995), problem-solving strategies (Ginossar and Trope 1987), and charitable pledges (Bodner 1995) in a diagnostically favorable direction. From the literature on "self-handicapping," we know that a person might get too little sleep or underprepare for an examination to create a situation where successful performance could be attributed to ability, while unsuccessful performance could be externalized as due to lack of proper preparation (for example, Berglas and Jones 1978). The general notion that people adopt the perspective of an outside observer when interpreting their own actions is the core hypothesis in Bem's influential (1972) self-perception theory. This idea can also be traced back at least to the James-Lange theory of emotions (Burkhardt and Bowers 1981), which claimed that people infer their own emotions from behavior (for example, they feel afraid if they see themselves running). This broader context of psychological research suggests that the phenomenon reported by Quattrone and Tversky is not an isolated laboratory curiosity. If anything, the experimental results should underestimate the impact of diagnosticity in realistic decisions, where the absence of causal links between actions and dispositions is less transparent.

A key difference between the laboratory and the real world is that in the real world, it is hard to identify decisions with no causal consequences whatsoever. Here, for example, are five situations where part of the motive for engaging or not engaging in an activity is diagnostic. Each example identifies an action that might provide evidence of an underlying state.

1.   Donating time or money to a charitable cause as evidence of true concern for the cause.
2.   Taking a drink before noon as evidence of a drinking problem.
3.   Jogging during a heat wave as evidence of willpower.
4.   Purchasing an expensive item on credit as evidence of financial irresponsibility.
5.   Voting as evidence that one is dedicated to the candidate, and hence that other people like me will also take the trouble to vote.

In many of the examples—certainly in the first, second, third, and fourth—the action in question also has causal implications. Going out on the jog in the third example does lead to an incremental improvement in fitness, but this improvement seems insufficient to explain the compulsive quality of the behavior. With diagnostic motivation the significance of an action need not bear any relation to the actual stakes: a small-scale action—a breaking of a routine or a norm—can be just as diagnostic as a large one. If you take a dollar from the collection plate when no one is looking, that reveals that you are a thief just as much as if you had taken all the money on the plate.[2]

Looking over these examples, we can discern at least three distinct motives for self-signaling that may be labeled *intrinsic, instrumental,* and *magical.* Self-signaling is intrinsic when a person cares about an underlying trait or disposition independent of behaviors that might flow from this. For example, one might wish to believe that one has a good heart or soul, loves one's spouse and family, cares about those in need, appreciates good wine, has a particular sexual orientation, and so on. With instrumental self-signaling, however, a person is concerned only with the specific consequences that a particular disposition promotes. For instance, a person may not care about endurance and perseverance per se, but only the career benefits that he or she expects to derive from this trait.[3] Finally, magical self-signaling applies to cases such as example five, where one cares about an underlying disposition because it correlates across the population, and hence predicts how others will behave. The feeling is that by taking an action one is "magically" causing other people to behave in the same way. We shall not discuss the magical case further here (for experimental evidence see Quattrone and Tversky 1984; Shafir and Tversky 1992).

The Self-Signaling Model

In economic theory, a person is defined by their desires (as formalized with utilities) and beliefs (as formalized with probability distributions). Individual differences in traits, dispositions, and character resolve into differences in desires or beliefs. To say that a person is not sure of some underlying trait or disposition is to say that a person is not sure of his or her true utility function (the person might not be sure of his or her beliefs as well, but we will avoid this complication here).

To capture this notion formally, we let θ be the index of the unknown underlying disposition, x a possible choice outcome, and $u(x, \theta)$ the *outcome-utility* generated by x if there were no choice in the matter. For example, a compulsory charitable contribution (via a tax, say) will make a generous person (high θ on the generosity dimension) feel better than a selfish person, other things being equal. A person's current beliefs about θ—or current "self-image"—are defined by a probability distribution, $f(\theta)$ over possible θ. The value of this self-image in turn is determined by a second utility function, $V(\theta)$, which indicates how much pleasure or pain a person would feel if he or she found out his or her θ for sure—for example, by taking some kind of infallible psychological test. A person's initial endowment of self-esteem, before making a choice, equals the expectation of $V(\theta)$, or $\Sigma\theta V(\theta)f(\theta)$.

The range of internal characteristics that fall under the notion of a disposition is broad. Stable traits such as endurance, perseverance, or intelligence, which establish expectations of future success, would be one category. A second category would be inclinations to deviant behavior, addictions, sexual proclivities, and such. A third category would be moral dispositions, altruism, virtue, and so on. All of these dispositions contribute to the self-image and hence to self-esteem. The necessary property of a disposition is that it can influence behavior. This leads to an apparent paradox: How can an unknown disposition have any effect on choice? The question brings to the surface the distinction between conscious and implicit knowledge of θ. A dispositional parameter is implicitly "known" by the decision-making mechanism, even though it cannot be introspected before the choice.[4] The "gut" knows θ but the conscious mind does not. Willpower, inclination to alcoholism, altruism, or cold-water tolerance exert influence at the moment of choice but cannot be deduced by merely imagining what one might do in a given situation.

By choosing one outcome over others, therefore, a person reveals something about his or her dispositions. Hence the choice leads to an updating of the self-image, from $f(\theta)$ to $f(\theta \mid x)$. The change in self-image marked by the choice generates a separate form of utility—*diagnostic utility*—equal to the gain or loss in self-esteem when the prior beliefs $f(\theta)$ are revised in light of the choice to $f(\theta \mid x)$: $\Sigma\theta$ $V(\theta)f(\theta \mid x) - \Sigma\theta V(\theta)f(\theta)$. Diagnostic utility registers the extent one is "morally" impressed or disappointed by one's choices.

Our first assumption is that diagnostic utility is fully taken into account before a choice is made. The "hand" that chooses maximizes total utility, which is the sum of outcome *and* diagnostic utility:

$$\text{Total utility} = \text{Outcome utility} + \text{Diagnostic utility},$$

$$= u(x,\theta) + \Sigma\theta\, V(\theta)\, (f(\theta \mid x) - f(\theta)).$$

This looks straightforward, until one considers the revised self-image as given by the revised distribution $f(\theta \mid x)$. Where does this distribution come from? The simplest assumption, though perhaps not the most accurate one psychologically, is that inferences are *true*, which means that the revised distribution $f(\theta \mid x)$ is consistent with maximization of both components of total utility. What does this mean psychologically? It means that the decision maker is fully aware that he or she is partly motivated by the desire to get good news. Whatever action he or she chooses will thereby be revealed as the best action, all things considered, including in "all things" the desire to find out something good about themselves. More precisely, by choosing x over other options y, z, and so forth, the person reveals him- or herself to be exactly the kind of person for whom x produces more total utility than either y, z, and others. This assumption precludes unrealistic, self-serving inferences. For example, suppose that the disposition in question is altruism, and a person interprets a 25¢ donation as evidence of altruism. This would not be a true interpretation of the action, because the generous portion of diagnostic utility would make it worth giving the quarter even when there was no real concern for the poor. In other words, the diagnostic value of an action is properly discounted for the presence of diagnostic motivation.

The assumption of true inferences carries to a logical conclusion the basic idea in self-perception theory (Bem 1972), namely, that the

process of inferring underlying beliefs and desires from external behavior is the same, irrespective of whether the inferences pertain to
someone else's or to our own states. Just as we might discount someone else's good behavior as being due only to a desire to impress, so
too we discount our own behavior for ulterior motives, according to
the true inferences assumption.

Self-Control with Intrinsic and Instrumental Self-Signaling

We now look at how self-signaling promotes self-control in a simple
example. Imagine a person facing a decision whether to *indulge* or
abstain in some problematic activity—let's say an opportunistic sexual
encounter. In the situation we have in mind, the person faces a desire,
but does not know—before deciding—how strong the desire truly is,
nor whether the desire arises because he or she is "loose" (which is a
permanent disposition or trait) or because exceptional attraction or
"chemistry" exists with this partner on this unique occasion. Whatever happens, the decision will be diagnostic and provide some clues
about all of these things. We imagine also that this is the first time
such a situation has arisen.

The effective desire to *indulge* is an example of an unknown disposition, θ, as discussed in the previous section. The desire combines
two parameters, also unknown: a stable inclination toward this kind
of thing, θ^*, and a "pull of the moment" or chemistry variable, τ.

$$\text{Desire} = \text{inclination} + \text{chemistry on this occasion,}$$

$$\theta = \theta^* + \tau.$$

We can think of θ^* and τ as percentages, ranging from 0 to 100 percent with all values equally likely (so that θ^* measures inclination
relative to some underlying population and τ measures chemistry relative to other opportunities). Desire, being the simple sum of these
two factors, ranges from 0 to $+2.00$ (and conforms to a triangular
distribution). A level of desire close to $+2$ means that both inclination
and chemistry are unusually high. A level close to zero means that
both are low. Intermediate levels of desire could be due to a combination of high inclination and low chemistry, to low inclination and high
chemistry, or to moderate levels of both inclination and chemistry.

In this situation, the gain in outcome utility of *indulging* rather than
abstaining is proportional to desire, or more precisely,

$$u(\text{indulge}, \theta) - u(\text{abstain}, \theta) = \theta - T.$$

T is the cost of having such an encounter, capturing the risks and other costs associated with a single episode. A person with no diagnostic motivation would indulge only on those occasions when desire exceeded the cost—that is, when $\theta > T$. We assume that T is small ($T < 1$) so that most people, most of the time, would succumb to desire if self-signaling was not a factor in the decision.

Diagnostic motivation now enters into the picture in one of two ways, exemplified by two individuals, Tom and Harry. Tom is concerned about intrinsic inclination, which he regards as an important and undesirable character trait. He just doesn't want to be the kind of person who enjoys this activity, perhaps because it would reveal a coarse hedonistic nature, or a weakness of character inconsistent with his moral and religious ideals. Harry, on the other hand, is more pragmatic. He is not interested in intrinsic inclination per se, but does care about it insofar as it conveys information about the likelihood of indulging in such escapades in the future. For him too the action is a signal, but it is a signal of his *behavioral propensity* to indulge. For prudential reasons, Harry prefers to believe that such consummated encounters will be few and far between.

Basically, Tom wants to have his true desires—his identity— aligned with his ideals, while Harry wants to believe that he does not engage in sex with strangers, or at least not often. Their V functions are essentially the same, but with respect to different arguments:

For Tom: $V(\theta^*) = 1 - \theta^*$,

For Harry: $V(\theta^*) = 1 - $ (behavioral propensity to indulge, given θ^*).

By "behavioral propensity to indulge" we simply mean Harry's estimate of how likely he is to indulge in *situations of this kind*. This is exactly the estimate that an outside observer would make, using the information about Harry's behavior on this specific occasion.

Our motivating question therefore is whether diagnostic concerns will affect the likelihood of abstaining, for either Tom or Harry. Precisely, we would like to know whether the *threshold level* of desire— the level at which desire is just sufficient to tip the decision in favor of indulging—is higher than the natural level, T, which obtains when diagnostic concerns do not arise. Note that both Tom and Harry believe that their inclination is fixed and unaffected by what they do— that is, self-control is not a "muscle" that gains with exercise, in the sense discussed by Baumeister and Vohs (chap. 6 herein).

Figure 9.1   Tom's Inferences About His Intrinsic Inclination to Indulge

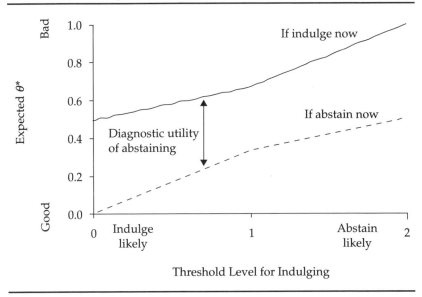

Source: Author's configuration.

Tom's Inferential Problem

Let us consider Tom first. Suppose that Tom passes the test on this occasion and abstains. What can Tom infer about his inclination from this happy outcome? To assess the implications of that single decision, Tom needs to know his threshold level of desire for situations of this kind. He needs to know whether abstaining is a surprising decision, as it would be if the threshold were low, or the expected one, as it would be if the threshold were high.

Figure 9.1 shows how Tom's inferences about his inclination depend on the action chosen and the presumed threshold, given on the x axis. When the threshold is low and abstaining a surprising choice, then abstaining is indeed a strong signal of low θ^*—that is, little inclination for the activity. Indulging, however, which is the expected action, would provide little new information and the estimate of θ^* would remain close to the initial estimate of 0.5 (recall that θ^* ranges from zero to one, with all values equally likely).

The opposite inferences obtain at the right-hand side of the graph, when the threshold is high and abstention nearly certain. Now the single decision to abstain provides little new information, leaving the

Figure 9.2   Harry's Inferences About His Behavioral Propensity of Indulging

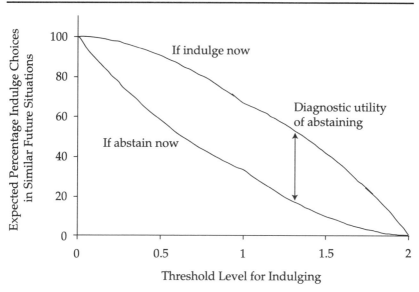

Source: Author's configuration.

best guess of θ^* close to 0.5. Indulging is a big surprise, leading to a sharp negative revision in Tom's self-image. We have here the ingredients for a "compulsive" adherence to a norm, where the virtuous action is taken not because it leads to increased self-esteem but because failure to adhere to the norm would trigger a harsh negative inference. Indeed, as we can see from the upward sloping lines in figure 9.1, as the threshold goes up and abstention becomes more certain, the interpretation of either action—abstaining or indulging—becomes more pessimistic. Positive expectations about behavior depress subsequent inferences about dispositions is the paradoxical conclusion here.

Harry's Inferential Problem

The situation is quite different for Harry, who cares only for the long-run behavioral predictions that flow from the current action. First, the inferential problem involves one extra step. Not only must he infer something about his inclination but also must assess what this particular level of appetite implies about his behavioral tendencies. Harry begins, therefore, with the analysis displayed in figure 9.1. Assuming a particular threshold, indulging or abstaining leads to revised self-

image distributions, from the uniform distribution $f(\theta^*)$ to $f(\theta^* \mid$ indulge) or $f(\theta^* \mid$ abstain). With these distributions in hand, he is able to
assess how likely it is that desire will exceed threshold and lead to
indulging on occasions of this type. These computed probabilities of
indulging and abstaining are displayed in figure 9.2.[5] We see that as
the threshold goes up and abstention becomes more certain, the interpretation of either action—abstaining or indulging—now becomes
more *optimistic*. In Harry's case, positive expectations about behavior
enhance rather than depress subsequent inferences about dispositions.

Figures 9.1 and 9.2 summarize what either action means, as a source
of information about inclination (figure 9.1) or behavioral propensity
(figure 9.2). Since meta-utility is linear in either inclination (for Tom)
or behavioral propensity (for Harry), the diagnostic utility of doing
"the right thing" and abstaining is proportional to the difference between the two graphs in either figure. For Tom, diagnostic utility does
not vary much with threshold—the gap between the two lines in figure 9.1 remains roughly constant. For Harry, diagnostic utility diminishes as the threshold moves toward zero or two, and one or the other
action becomes almost certain. If the threshold is near two, for example, then Harry will indulge only if both his inclination and the pull
of the moment are very high. Under these conditions, an otherwise
surprising "lapse" might reveal high inclination, without shaking
Harry's belief that such lapses will remain relatively rare.

Balancing Diagnostic and Outcome Utilities

Whether Tom or Harry actually indulges on any given occasion depends on the balance between outcome utility (which is desire net of
cost) and diagnostic disutility. Figures 9.3 and 9.4 compare these two
components of total utility, first for Tom (figure 9.3) and then for
Harry (figure 9.4). Both figures are set up to graphically compute the
threshold level of desire, which is the level where the outcome utility
of indulging exactly matches the diagnostic utility of abstaining. The
x axis in both figures represents levels of desire as candidates for such
a threshold. The y axis then displays two graphs: a graph of outcome
utility as function of desire, which is an increasing straight line, and a
graph of diagnostic utility as function of candidate threshold desire
level, which is copied directly from either figure 9.1 (for Tom) or from
figure 9.2 (for Harry).

The benchmark to use here is T, the level of desire that would be
sufficient to motivate indulgence in the absence of diagnostic motivation. This is just the level where the outcome utility graph intersects
the horizontal axis. When diagnostic utility is introduced into the picture, then this level of desire is no longer sufficient.

Figure 9.3   Tom's Threshold Level of Desire

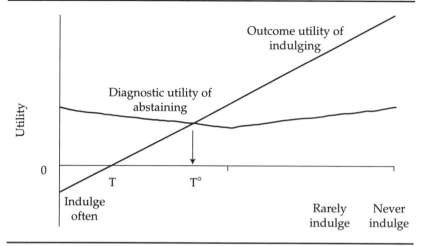

Source: Author's configuration.
T = "Natural" threshold, ignoring diagnostic utility.
T° = Threshold with true interpretations.

Looking at Tom's problem in figure 9.3 first, the point where outcome utility of indulging matches diagnostic utility of abstaining is given by T°. If desire is greater than T°, then outcome utility exceeds diagnostic utility by a positive amount and Tom will indulge. Conversely, if desire falls below T°, then diagnostic utility of abstaining is greater and Tom will abstain. A similar situation obtains for Harry, whose dilemma is captured by the pair of graphs in figure 9.4. Again, the threshold level of desire is given by T°, which is greater than the diagnosticity-free level of T.

A key difference between Tom and Harry becomes evident when the diagnostic component of utility assumes great weight—that is, when there is tremendous concern about the diagnostic significance of indulging. In that case, Tom will exhibit perfect behavior, and never indulge. The outcome utility straight line in figure 9.3 will fall entirely below the diagnostic utility line, indicating that T° = +2. Tom is trapped by the asymmetric diagnosticity of the two actions: abstaining is discounted for diagnostic motivation, and hence provides no reassurance, while indulging signals the worst. With Harry, however, there is always going to be some chance that he will indulge: the two lines in figure 9.4 always intersect. When concern about diagnosticity is high, then the lines intersect near +2. If desire is also high Harry will indulge, but will also attribute this—correctly!—to "special circumstances." His estimate of his behavioral

Figure 9.4   Harry's Threshold Level of Desire

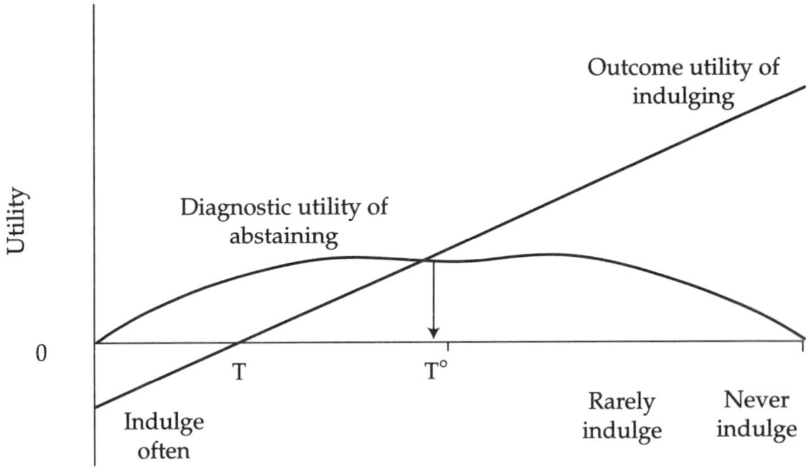

Source: Author's configuration.
T = Natural threshold, ignoring diagnostic utility.
T° = Threshold with true interpretations.

tendency to indulge will remain low—truly an example of "having one's cake and eating it too."

Three important points emerge here. First, *self-signaling promotes self-control*, irrespective of whether a person is intrinsically (Tom) or instrumentally (Harry) concerned about underlying dispositions. Second, this conclusion follows even though there is full awareness of diagnostic motivation. The model therefore instantiates Ainslie's (1992, 203) view that "doing good for its diagnostic value may not invalidate that diagnostic value." Although people may engage in self-deception in many settings, self-deception is not necessary for self-signaling. Third, compulsive behavior—not allowing for any exceptions—is more likely to emerge with intrinsic rather than instrumental self-signaling.

Although the model may look complicated, it is intended to describe something quite simple. A person is looking at his own behavior just as he would look at the behavior of someone else. He observes a particular action (for example, to indulge) and draws from it inferences about what this person is like, and how often he will do this kind of thing in the future. Since the inferences are about his own character and prospects, they are also a source of *immediate* pleasure and pain, which then contribute to his ability to exercise self-control.

Salience and Self-Control

That self-control is not just a matter of time discounting and time preference was evident ever since the classical delay of gratification experiments by Mischel and his associates (Mischel 1974; Mischel et al., chap. 5 herein). In Mischel's paradigm, children were placed in a room by themselves and taught that they could summon the experimenter by ringing a bell. The children would then be shown a superior and inferior prize and told that they would receive the superior prize if they could wait for the experimenter to return. Children found it harder to wait for the delayed reward if made to wait in the physical presence of either one of the reward objects, which presumably induced craving. Time discounting alone cannot explain this, nor can it explain why self-control breaks down especially under the influence of strong physical drives or emotions (Loewenstein 1996) or when a person is fatigued (Muraven and Baumeister 2000).

The negative effect of salience on self-control emerges naturally with the self-signaling framework, for the simple reason that operations that change salience affect the two parts of the total utility equation asymmetrically. If salience is reduced, for example, by making the tempting reward delayed in time or uncertain or physically less available, this changes the outcome utility part of the equation while leaving the diagnostic utility part unchanged. Hence the balance of power will shift in favor of diagnostic considerations.

A conceptually simple demonstration of this arises in context of *contingent resolutions*, which are binding decisions that only take effect if a certain contingency is realized. To continue with the earlier example, suppose that Tom or Harry must decide what to do before knowing for sure whether the opportunity truly exists. Intuition suggests that it will be easier to abstain in that case; the rewards, after all, are somewhat hypothetical.[6]

The model expresses this by proportionally scaling down the outcome utility of indulging, from $u(\text{indulge}, \theta)$ to: $pu(\text{indulge}, \theta)$, where p is the probability that the tempting opportunity will present itself. The discounted line with smaller slope in figure 9.5 gives the reduced levels of outcome utility. Since the outcome utility of indulging is now everywhere lower than the diagnostic utility of abstaining, the person would resolve to abstain irrespective of disposition. Yet if the resolution wasn't binding, then the person might also be inconsistent, resolving to abstain but then reversing his decision and indulging if the opportunity to do so actually came up.

The same argument applies to situations where the consequences are removed in time. Outcome utility is now *temporally* discounted,

Figure 9.5   Contingent Resolutions to Never Indulge

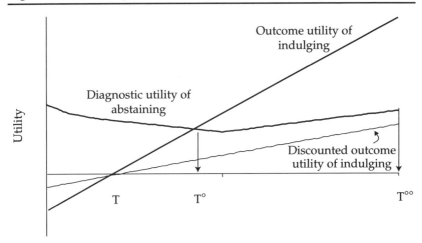

Source: Author's configuration.
T = Outcome utility threshold for indulging.
T° = Threshold.
T°° = Threshold if outcomes are discounted.

again making abstaining more likely. The chronic discrepancy between future plans and actual behavior may therefore be explained by the fact that the diagnostic utility of a resolution is immediate, while the cost of the resolution in outcome utility is delayed; and people fail to anticipate reversals in preference—that is, they are naive in the sense of O'Donoghue and Rabin (1999, chap. 7 herein).

This account provides a common explanation of what are otherwise different categories of dynamic inconsistency. Anything that selectively lowers the weight of outcome utility (low physical salience, uncertainty, time distance, and so forth) will result in choices being more driven by meta-utility. When the weight of outcome utility is restored, by making outcomes salient, certain, imminent, and so forth, the person may regret the earlier choice.

Self-Signaling Without Awareness

The reader may wonder at this point whether the account presented here rests on an odd combination of self-ignorance (that is, of one's own dispositions) and self-insight (that is, of one's propensity to self-signal). While we are certainly able to discount the behavioral signals of other people when we suspect ulterior motives on their part, that we will apply to our own actions the same standards we apply to the actions of others is not at all self-evident. Experimental evidence shows that even inferences about other people's beliefs and tastes are insufficiently discounted for external constraints (Gilbert 2002).

While we do know that people engage in self-signaling, there is little experimental evidence on the level of subjective awareness of the process. In the cold water experiment by Quattrone and Tversky (1984), most of the subjects denied (in a follow-up interview) that they were trying to bias the results of the bogus medical test. Yet a significant minority did confess to the attempt, and these "aware" subjects in fact were quite pessimistic about their heart condition.

As a theoretical matter, one can combine the self-signaling hypothesis with variable levels of awareness, ranging from full awareness (the true inferences model) to complete unawareness. In the latter case, the person is presumed ignorant of the self-signaling motive, and accepts the evidence of his or her actions at *face value*. The updated inferences, $f(\theta \mid x)$, are then based on the assumption that an action reveals the disposition that maximizes only the outcome utility component of total utility, ignoring the diagnostic component. Here, there would be no discounting for diagnostic motivation. Diagnostic utility would be experienced as an unintentional by-product of choice, not something that consciously affected choice.

How does this affect the impact of diagnostic motivation on self-control? The basic result—that diagnostic motivation promotes self-control—holds irrespective of the level of awareness. Yet the interplay of diagnostic motivation with awareness of diagnostic motivation leads to some suggestive distinctions and predictions, summarized in table 9.1. The table shows how the two ways of interpreting actions generate four self-signaling "psychologies." The columns in the table indicate whether diagnostic motivation is present (right column) or absent (left column). The rows indicate whether inferences from actions are discounted for diagnostic motivation (bottom row) or not discounted (top row). The diagonal entries are "rational" in the sense that interpretations and motivations are consistent with each other.

We will not dwell on left side of the table, where preferences are free from diagnostic utility. Case 1 is the rational standard economic model, where you do as you please, and your choices hence directly reveal what you like. Case 4 describes a logical possibility of dubious realism, except perhaps as a model of certain forms of psychosis. Here you are not diagnostically motivated, but interpret your actions as if you were so motivated. The result is a kind of paranoid self-scrutiny, a search for ulterior motives that are not really there.

The interesting contrast is between cases 2 and 3. In case 2, diag-

Table 9.1   Diagnostic Motivation and Awareness: Two Ways of Interpreting Actions

	Preferences Free from Diagnostic Utility	Preferences Subject to Diagnostic Utility
Face-value interpretations of actions	I. Standard economic model • You do as you please • Actions reveal who you are	II. Normal self-deception • You bias behavior toward actions diagnostic of good dispositions • Improve future prospects • Create overly positive intrinsic self-image
Interpretations discounted for diagnostic motivation	IV. Paranoid self-scrutiny • You do as you please • Second-guess actions for nonexistent motives • Overly negative intrinsic self-image and excessive pessimism about future prospects	III. Rational self-signaling • You seek behavioral perfection • Tend toward "always" "never" rules • Improve future prospects • Fail to improve intrinsic self-image (on average)

Source: Authors' compilation.

nostic motivation makes "good" actions more likely, yet this biasing effect is ignored in making inferences. You generously give yourself full credit for doing the good thing, even when part of the motive was precisely to get the credit. The result is an excessively positive self-image.[7] As an empirical hypothesis, case 2 may be quite close to the truth. There is much evidence that self-assessments are excessively positive (for example, Taylor and Brown 1988). What is distinctive about this particular explanation of excessive self-esteem is that it doesn't postulate any direct self-deception; the incorrect self-image is a by-product of a cognitive blind spot, a lack of awareness that good actions were motivated by diagnostic concerns.

The salient feature of the fully rational self-signaling model, shown as case 3 in table 9.1, is that it leads to an escalation of virtuous conduct. Since good behavior is discounted for diagnostic motives, being reasonably good is no longer "good enough." As inferior dispositions mimic behavior diagnostic of superior ones, the superior dispositions need to do even better to differentiate themselves. As we have seen in our analysis of Tom, the process tends toward perfection, where no further improvements on the relevant dimension are possible. At the verbal level, a person may characterize his or her behavior in terms of rules that either proscribe an activity altogether (in the case of vices) or insist that an activity be performed without exception (in the case of virtues).

Perfection, however, doesn't succeed in securing a positive self-image; to the extent that it accomplishes anything, it is to hold an utterly negative self-image at bay. Perfection demands compulsion, with motivation sustained not by positive benefits but fear of negative inferences that would be triggered by a single lapse on the dimension of concern. To a compulsive, washing hands does not guarantee that they are clean, but a failure to wash would confirm that they are dirty. Like Baron von Munchausen's horse, the rational self-signaler drinks but the thirst cannot be quenched.

Summary

We have described here a model that accounts for some of the diagnostic implications of choice. Is this a theory of self-control, however? In an important sense, it is not. One can certainly imagine situations where self-control is needed to *overcome* diagnostic motivation. Consider a case of a person debating whether to enroll in a dating service. Signing up for the service has long-term causal benefits—more partners to choose from, and so on. Yet this also has diagnostic costs: the person must confront a certain kind of personal failure, namely, that unlike so many others he or she was not able to find a partner in the usual "romantic" way. This diagnostic pain is realized the moment the person signs up, before any benefits are realized. In this case, willpower must be applied to overcome the diagnostic hurt associated with an otherwise sensible action. Diagnosticity is a general source of motivation, which often supports long-term objectives but which can sometimes work against them, as in this example.

In our model, diagnostic utility enters the equation as just another source of pleasure, to be balanced against other pleasures. Nothing in the model refers to the problem of effort and willpower, which is intimately involved with self-control (Muraven and Baumeister 2000). A person with strong diagnostic motivation will not feel any conflict—he or she will do "the right thing" smoothly, without strain. The model therefore explains why we get out of bed, brush our teeth, and go about our daily business without much fuss. At least in present form, it does not shed light on intrapersonal conflict per se.

Notes

1. In Ainslie's terms, you "stake the expectation" of long-run success on successful performance in the here and now (Ainslie 1992, 2001). As with voting, the logic follows the Kantian categorical imperative: if I fail now, then I will fail on all subsequent occasions of this type (Gilboa and Gilboa-Schechtman 2002).
2. A second issue that arises in real-world examples is to what extent the signaling is to the self and what extent it is signaling to others. Certainly, the motivational force of many of the examples on the list would be enhanced if others were there to observe the choice. That said, we claim that even if no one is watching, there is still some diagnostic pleasure or pain in these examples.
3. Similarly, Koszegi (1999) distinguishes between "pure self-image" and "anxiety or worry about the future."
4. The assumption that people only remember choices but not the motivational and informational states that led up to those choices is invoked (in very different settings) by Ariely, Loewenstein, and Prelec (forthcoming); Benabou and Tirole (2000); Hirshleifer and Welch (1999); and Koszegi (1999).
5. We are also assuming that Harry does not consider the possibility of learning over successive choices. If we allow for learning, then actions at some point would lose most of their diagnosticity—a lifetime of behavioral evidence would surely overwhelm the information content of the next action. This is psychologically implausible (and we are not aware of any evidence that diagnostic concerns diminish over the life cycle). As anyone who has given a poor lecture knows, we often do ignore the long-run record and give excess weight to current performance.
6. Bodner's (1995) experiments on contingent charitable pledges revealed a version of this phenomenon. Contingent pledges are promises to give in the event that one is called on to do so. Bodner found that the pledges of subjects who regarded themselves as insufficiently altruistic were relatively more sensitive to the stated probability of being called on to give: they were relatively more generous when that probability was small. In effect, such subjects were purchasing self-esteem "on the cheap," by pledging more when the likelihood of actual sacrifice was low.
7. Carrillo and Mariotti (2000), Brocas and Carillo (1999, 2000), Benabou and Tirole (1999), and Koszegi (1999) present other models that give rise to an excessively positive self-image.

References

Ainslie, George. 1992. *Picoeconomics: The Strategic Interaction of Successive Motivational States Within the Person.* New York: Cambridge University Press.
———. 2001. *Breakdown of Will.* Cambridge: Cambridge University Press.
Ariely, Dan, George Loewenstein, and Drazen Prelec. Forthcoming. "Coherent Arbitrariness: Stable Demand Curves Without Stable Preferences." *Quarterly Journal of Economics* (February 2003).
Baumeister, Roy F., Todd F. Heatherton, and Dianne M. Tice. 1994. *Losing Control: How and Why People Fail at Self-Regulation.* San Diego: Academic Press.
Bem, D. J. 1972. "Self-Perception Theory." In *Advances in Experimental Social Psychology.* Vol. 6, edited by L. Berkowitz. New York: Academic Press.
Benabou, R., and J. Tirole. 1999. "Self-Confidence: Intrapersonal Strategies." L'Institut d'Economie Industrielle, mimeograph, June.
———. 2000. "Willpower and Personal Rules." Princeton University, mimeograph, June.
Berglas, S., and E. E. Jones. 1978. "Drug Choice as a Self-Handicapping Strategy in Response to Noncontingent Success." *Journal of Personality and Social Psychology* 36(4): 405–17.
Bodner, Ronit. 1995. "Self-Knowledge and the Diagnostic Value of Actions: The Case of Donating to a Charitable Cause." Ph.D. diss., Massachusetts Institute of Technology, Sloan School of Management.
Bodner, Ronit, and Drazen Prelec. 1997. "The Diagnostic Value of Actions in a Self-Signaling Model." Massachusetts Institute of Technology, mimeograph, January.
———. 2002. "Self-Signaling in a Neo-Calvinist Model of Everyday Decision Making." In *Psychology and Economics,* edited by Juan D. Carrillo and Isabelle Brocas. Oxford: Oxford University Press.
Brocas, Isabelle, and Juan D. Carrillo. 1999. "Entry Mistakes, Entrepreneurial Boldness and Optimism." Université Libre de Bruxelles, European Center for Advanced Research in Economics and Statistics, mimeograph, June.
———. 2002. "Information and Self-Control." In *Psychology and Economics,* edited by Juan D. Carrillo and Isabelle Brocas. Oxford: Oxford University Press.
Burkhardt, Frederick, and Fredson Bowers, eds. 1981. *The Work of William James: The Principles of Psychology.* Vol. 1. Cambridge, Mass.: Harvard University Press.
Campbell, Richmond, and Lanning Sowden, eds. 1985. *Paradoxes of Rationality and Cooperation.* Vancouver: University of British Columbia Press.
Carrillo, Juan, and Thomas Mariotti. 2000. "Strategic Ignorance as a Self-Disciplining Device." *Review of Economic Studies* 76(3): 529–44.
Dunning, D., A. Leuenberger, and D. A. Sherman. 1995. "A New Look at Motivated Inference: Are Self-Serving Theories of Success a Product of Motivational Forces?" *Journal of Personality and Social Psychology* 69: 58–68.
Elster, Jon. 1985. "Weakness of Will and the Free-Rider Problem." *Economics and Philosophy* 1: 231–65.

————. 1989. *The Cement of Society: A Study of Social Order.* Cambridge: Cambridge University Press.

Gilbert, D. 2002. "Inferential Correction." In *Heuristics and Biases: The Psychology of Intuitive Judgment,* edited by T. Gilovitch, D. Griffin, and Daniel Kahneman. Cambridge: Cambridge University Press.

Gilboa, Itzhak, and Eva Gilboa-Schechtman. 2002. "Mental Accounting and the Absentminded Driver." In *Essays in Psychology and Economics,* edited by Juan D. Carrillo and Isabelle Brocas. Oxford: Oxford University Press.

Ginossar, Z., and Y. Trope. 1987. "Problem Solving in Judgment under Uncertainty." *Journal of Personality and Social Psychology* 52: 464–74.

Hirshleifer, David, and Ivo Welch. 1999. "An Economic Approach to the Psychology of Change: Amnesia, Inertia, and Impulsiveness." Yale School of Management, mimeograph, May.

Koszegi, B. 1999. "Self-Image and Economic Behavior." Massachusetts Institute of Technology, mimeograph, October.

Kunda, Ziva. 1990. "The Case for Motivated Reasoning." *Psychological Bulletin* 108: 480–98.

Loewenstein, George F. 1996. "Out of Control: Visceral Influences on Behavior." *Organizational Behavior and Human Decision Processes* 65: 272–92.

Mischel, Walter. 1974. "Processes in Delay of Gratification." In *Advances in Experimental Social Psychology,* edited by L. Berkowitz. New York: Academic Press.

Muraven, Mark, and Roy F. Baumeister. 2000. "Self-Regulation and Depletion of Limited Resources: Does Self-Control Resemble a Muscle?" *Psychological Bulletin* 126: 247–59.

O'Donoghue, Ted, and Matthew Rabin. 1999. "Doing It Now or Later." *American Economic Review* 89(1): 103–24.

Prelec, Drazen. 1991. "Values and Principles: Some Limitations on Traditional Economic Analysis." In *Socioeconomics: Toward a New Synthesis,* edited by Amitai Etzioni and Paul Lawrence. New York: M. E. Sharpe.

Prelec, Drazen, and R. J. Herrnstein. 1991. "Preferences and Principles, Alternative Guidelines for Choice." In *Strategic Reflections on Human Behavior,* edited by Richard Zeckhauser. Cambridge, Mass.: MIT Press.

Quattrone, G. A., and Amos Tversky. 1984. "Causal Versus Diagnostic Contingencies: On Self-Deception and on the Voter's Illusion." *Journal of Personality and Social Psychology* 46(2): 237–48.

Sanitioso, R., Ziva Kunda, and G. T. Fong. 1990. "Motivated Recruitment of Autobiographical Memory." *Journal of Personality and Social Psychology* 59: 229–41.

Shafir, Eldar, and Amos Tversky. 1992. "Thinking Through Uncertainty: Nonconsequential Reasoning and Choice." *Cognitive Psychology* 24: 449–74.

Taylor, S. E., and J. D. Brown. 1988. "Illusion and Well-Being: A Social Psychological Perspective on Mental Health." *Psychological Bulletin* 103: 193–210.

PART III

Patterns of Preference

· 10 ·

Subadditive Intertemporal Choice

Daniel Read

I N THE study of decision making, researchers typically compare the observed pattern of choice with a normative one, meaning the one that people would adopt if they were "rational." The normative model for decision making under risk is expected utility theory, and for intertemporal choice it is *discounted utility* (DU) theory. In a simplified form, DU theory holds that a rational decision maker will discount the costs or benefits from all delayed events by a constant rate per unit of time (Samuelson 1937; Strotz 1955). This constant rate is analogous to a psychological interest rate, and the same equations are used to calculate the present value of an investment given an anticipated future interest rate, and the present value of a delayed outcome for an individual with a given rate of time preference:

$$v_1 = \delta^{t_2 - t_1} v_2.$$

This is *exponential* discounting. The value at an earlier time t_1 of an outcome (v_2) that will be received at a later time t_2, is obtained by discounting the later outcome at a constant rate for the interval separating t_1 and t_2. The parameter δ is a *discount factor*, usually assumed to be between 0 and 1. To illustrate, suppose that the per-period $\delta = 0.8$ and we delay something worth 100 for two periods. Its value is reduced to $v_1 = \delta^2 v_2 = 0.8^2(100) = 64$ by this two-period reduction. Higher values of δ imply more *patience*, because they mean that decision makers demand a smaller premium per unit of time to wait for a reward.[1]

Discounted utility has fared badly when put to empirical test (see Frederick, Loewenstein, and O'Donoghue, chap. 1 herein). The finding that has received the most attention, which I will call *increasing patience*, is that δ apparently increases with delay.[2] This means, for instance, that if δ is 0.8 for the first period, it might be 0.9 for the second. The major *intuitive* evidence for increasing patience is *dynamic inconsistency*, exemplified by a much cited example due to Thaler (1981): someone might well take 1 apple today over 2 apples tomorrow, but he would be unlikely to take 1 apple in 364 days over 2 in 365 days. For both choices only 1 day separates both options (that is, $t_2 - t_1 = 1$ day), so this preference pattern implies that we are less patient over 1 day if it begins now than if it begins in 364 days. Or, put another way, δ appears to be less for day one than for day 364. The conventional view is that this is due to *hyperbolic discounting*, meaning that, as Kirby (1997, 54) puts it, the value of a reward increases "by an increasingly larger proportion per unit time as the reward approaches." Figure 10.1 depicts the relationship between delay and δ proposed by the most widely cited hyperbolic discount function (Mazur 1984).

Increasing patience and hyperbolic discounting are not usually studied with tests of dynamic inconsistency.[3] The usual procedure is to make direct measurements of δ over delays of differing length. In a typical experiment, participants equate pairs of outcomes that differ in their delay. We can label the two outcomes the smaller, sooner (SS) and larger, later one (LL). For instance, $100 now might be judged as equal to $150 in one year. When such an indifference point is reached, δ can be derived as a function of the ratio SS/LL and the interval separating them.

These SS/LL ratios are measured using either *matching* procedures, in which participants state the value of delayed outcomes (for example, Benzion, Rapoport, and Yagil 1989; Bickel and Johnson, chap. 14 herein; Chapman and Elstein 1995; Kirby 1997; Kirby and Marakovic 1995; Raineri and Rachlin 1993; Thaler 1981), or *choice* procedures, in which they choose between pairs of delayed outcomes (for example, Chapman 2001; Green, Fry, and Myerson 1994; Green, Myerson, and McFadden 1997; Holcomb and Nelson 1992; Richards et al. 1999). Matching is illustrated by Kirby's (1997) study, in which participants offered bids (the SS amount, which the winners would have to pay immediately) for $10 or $20 that would be received from two to thirty days from the bidding date (LL). Choice is illustrated by Green and colleagues' (1994) study, in which participants chose between a fixed

Figure 10.1 Patience (δ) Increasing as a Function of Delay: A Hyperbolic Discount Function

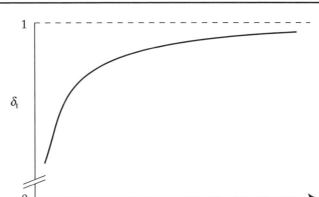

Source: Author's configuration.

delayed amount (LL) and an immediate amount (SS) that was varied until they reached an indifference point. Regardless of whether they use the choice or matching method, all the foregoing studies share a common characteristic: SS occurs immediately or in the very near future, while LL is delayed by differing amounts. The universal finding is that the longer the delay to LL, the higher the value of δ, and the usual inference is δ (patience) increases with delay according to the manner depicted in figure 10.1.

These conventional methods are flawed because they confound two factors, the *delay* and the *interval*. The delay is the time that intervenes between now and when the later outcome is to occur ($t_2 - 0$); the interval is the time separating the outcomes ($t_2 - t_1$). Delay and interval are confounded when, as in the prototypical time-discounting studies just cited, t_1 is set to be equal to 0. This is made more concrete with figure 10.2. A typical study (and all the foregoing studies are typical in this way) might compare discounting over 6- and 12-month delays. Not only does 6 months come before 12 months (these are the delays), but the $0 \to 6$ month interval is shorter than the $0 \to 12$ month one. The standard finding therefore is that the longer the delay *and* interval the higher the value of δ. While this is typically interpreted as support for hyperbolic discounting—a theory about *delay*—equally plausible is that this is due to *interval* length.

To put this more analytically, imagine a study in which discounting is measured over a six-month and a twelve-month delay (as in A and

Figure 10.2   Discount Periods Illustrating the Distinction Between Delay and Interval

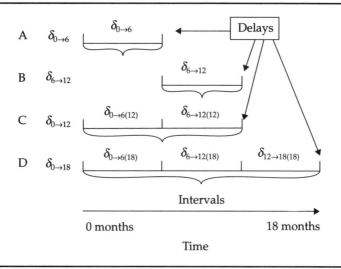

Source: Author's configuration.

C of figure 10.2). The usual finding is that the average level of patience is greater for the twelve-month delay. From this observation, increasing patience is inferred by assuming that the average level of patience over a twelve-month delay can be decomposed into a period during which average patience is equal to the standard rate for a six-month delay (A: $\delta_{0\to6}$), and another period where the average level is higher (B: $\delta_{6\to12}$). If we denote the *implicit* discount factors operating over two six-month intervals when they are embedded in a twelve-month delay as $\delta_{0\to6(12)}$ and $\delta_{6\to12(12)}$, then the full argument is:

Assumption 1: $\delta_{0\to6(12)} = \delta_{0\to6}$. That is, discounting for the first six months is independent of whether that period is embedded in a longer interval (as in C), or is isolated (as in A).

Assumption 2: $\delta_{6\to12(12)} = \delta_{6\to12}$. As with assumption 1, this means that discounting for the second six months is independent of whether it is embedded (C) or isolated (B).

Observation: $\delta_{0\to6} < \delta_{0\to12}$. That is, average discounting for six unbroken months (A) is greater than that for twelve unbroken months (C).

Conclusion: If assumptions 1 and 2 are true, and the observation is made, then increasing patience follows, meaning the discount factor is greater for the second six months than for the first:

$$\delta_{6\rightarrow12} = \frac{\delta^2_{0\rightarrow11}}{\delta_{0\rightarrow6}} > \delta_{0\rightarrow6}.$$

(Since all discount factors are defined over a one-year period and, from assumptions 1 and 2, $\delta_{0\rightarrow12} = \sqrt{(\delta_{0\rightarrow6})(\delta_{6\rightarrow12})}$.) The logic is sound, in that the conclusions follow from the premises. Yet both these premises are untested assumptions. If they are false, then the inference of increasing patience could also be false. In particular, if δ increases with interval length—what I will call *subadditivity*—then, in a typical experiment, δ would also increase with delay, but only because delay and interval are confounded.

This chapter describes several experiments testing assumptions 1 and 2. In the experiments, δ is measured over a long delay (obtaining, for instance, $\delta_{0\rightarrow12}$) and over shorter intervals that span the delay ($\delta_{0\rightarrow6}$ and $\delta_{6\rightarrow12}$). If the two assumptions are true, we will observe two things. First, *additivity*, which means that the average discount factor over two intervals is equal to the discount factor over the unbroken interval, and second, increasing patience:

Additivity: $\delta_{0\rightarrow12} = \sqrt{(\delta_{0\rightarrow6})(\delta_{6\rightarrow12})}$.

Increasing impatience: $\delta_{6\rightarrow12} > \delta_{0\rightarrow6}$

As we will see, the results of all experiments are inconsistent with the two assumptions. First, discounting is in fact *subadditive*, meaning that δ is greater for shorter intervals, regardless of when they occur (that is, their delay).[4] Moreover, although there is a modest amount (substantially less than reported in previous studies) of increasing patience when δ is measured using a matching procedure, there is *no* evidence of it when δ is measured with choice.

Hypotheses

Before describing the hypotheses, the foregoing notation is modified to make it easier to discuss the experimental results. All the studies investigate discounting over a delay, T, which is either undivided or divided into n intervals of equal length. The discount factor operating over the ith subinterval of the delay is $\delta_{T\cdot n \ \cdot i}$. To illustrate, consider a study comparing A and B from figure 10.2. The total delay being investigated is twelve months, the two intervals are $0 \rightarrow 6$ and $6 \rightarrow 12$, so the corresponding values of δ would be $\delta_{12\cdot2 \ \cdot 1}$ and $\delta_{12\cdot2 \ \cdot 2}$. The average value of δ over the entire delay (C, from figure 10.2) is denoted as $\delta_{T\cdot n}$, with $n = 1$ when the delay is undivided. So $\delta_{0\rightarrow12}$ would be denoted $\delta_{T\cdot1}$, and $\sqrt{(\delta_{0\rightarrow6})(\delta_{6\rightarrow12})}$ would be denoted $\delta_{T\cdot2}$. In the experi-

Figure 10.3   Notation and Terminology Used in Experiments

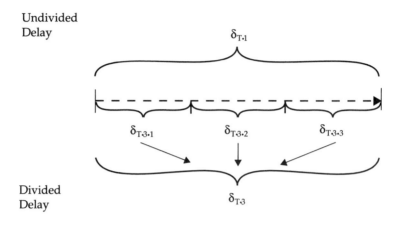

Undivided
Delay

$\delta_{T\cdot1}$

Divided
Delay

$\delta_{T\cdot3}$

$\delta_{T\cdot3\cdot1}$

$\delta_{T\cdot3\cdot2}$

$\delta_{T\cdot3\cdot3}$

Compared to eighteen month interval of figure 10.2:

$$\delta_{T\cdot1} \; = \delta_{0\rightarrow18}$$
$$\delta_{T\cdot3\cdot1} = \delta_{0\rightarrow6}$$
$$\delta_{T\cdot3\cdot2} = \delta_{6\rightarrow12}$$
$$\delta_{T\cdot3\cdot3} = \delta_{12\rightarrow18}$$
$$\delta_{T\cdot3} \; = [(\delta_{0\rightarrow6})(\delta_{6\rightarrow12})(\delta_{12\rightarrow18})]^{1/3}$$

Source: Author's configuration.

ments, delays were decomposed into one or three intervals, so we need only those symbols given in figure 10.3: $\delta_{T\cdot1}$ for the undivided delay T, $\delta_{T\cdot3\cdot1}$, $\delta_{T\cdot3\cdot2}$, and $\delta_{T\cdot3\cdot3}$ for each of the intervals from which it is composed, and $\delta_{T\cdot3}$ for a delay that has been divided into three equal intervals. The discount factor for the divided delay is the geometric mean of the separate discount factors:

$$\delta_{T\cdot3} = [(\delta_{T\cdot3\cdot1})(\delta_{T\cdot3\cdot2})(\delta_{T\cdot3\cdot3})]^{\frac{1}{3}}.$$

(In this chapter, all discount factors are given in a standard form corresponding to average discounting over one year.)

The experiments test three hypotheses. For hypothesis 1, the null hypothesis is *additive discounting*, which means that δ is independent of the number of intervals into which a delay is divided ($\delta_{T\cdot1} = \delta_{T\cdot3}$), and the alternate hypothesis is *subadditive* discounting, which means that δ decreases the more subintervals into which a delay is divided ($\delta_{T\cdot1} > \delta_{T\cdot3}$). Hypothesis 2, the *delay/interval effect*, is a statement of the traditional evidence for increasing patience: the shorter the delay the lower the value of δ:

$$\text{Hypothesis 2: } \delta_{T \cdot 1} > \delta_{T \cdot 3 \cdot 1}.$$

This is because the first interval of a delay is itself a delay of length $T/3$. In contrast, exponential discounting would predict that $\delta_{T \cdot 1} = \delta_{T \cdot 3 \cdot 1}$.

Hypothesis 3 describes the extra evidence needed to infer increasing patience if discounting is subadditive. *True increasing patience* means that δ will increase with delay, holding interval length constant:

$$\text{Hypothesis 3a: } \delta_{T \cdot 3 \cdot 1} < \delta_{T \cdot 3 \cdot 2} < \delta_{T \cdot 3 \cdot 3}.$$

The specific theoretical account of time discounting called *hyperbolic discounting* (seen in figure 10.1) makes the further prediction that patience will increase at a decreasing rate (for example, Mazur 1984; Loewenstein and Prelec 1992):

$$\text{Hypothesis 3b: } \delta_{T \cdot 3 \cdot 2} - \delta_{T \cdot 3 \cdot 1} > \delta_{T \cdot 3 \cdot 3} - \delta_{T \cdot 3 \cdot 2}.$$

Experiments

In four experiments, discount factors were measured for an undivided delay and for a division of the delay into three intervals. In experiments 1 to 3, δ was measured using choice, while experiment 4 compared choice and matching.[5] Although studies of time preference make frequent use of both choice and matching, in these studies the emphasis is on choice because it is the more basic or primitive index of preference. In an everyday context, choice means deciding whether to buy a loaf of bread at a given price, while matching means deciding the price at which one would be indifferent between the bread and the money. Choice is more straightforward than matching—requiring only ranking rather than numerical estimates—and also constitutes the empirical basis for the principle of revealed preference, which holds that what people choose reflects what they really want (for example, Varian 1992). Nonetheless, matching is a frequently used experimental technique, and there is a real need to investigate both methods.[6] Indeed one previous comparison between choice and matching has yielded the interesting conjecture that increasing patience will be found for matching but not for choice (Ahlbrecht and Weber 1997).[7]

The experimental procedure generated pairs of delayed outcomes, one smaller, sooner (SS) and one larger, later (LL), between which the participant was indifferent. From these, a value of δ was derived based on the ratio SS/LL and the time separating them. With the start and end of the interval denoted t_1 and t_2 respectively, and with time measured in one-year units, δ is:

$$\left(\frac{SS}{LL}\right)^{\frac{1}{t_2 - t_1}}.$$

To illustrate, suppose £100 in 12 months (1 year) was judged to be equivalent to £150 in 18 months. The interval would be 6 months (0.5 years), and δ would be:

$$\left(\frac{100}{150}\right)^{\frac{1}{0.5}} = 0.5.$$

This means that if the interval had been one year, and the same level of discounting had been operating over that year, the value of something would be cut in half by being delayed over that interval.

Choice indifference points were obtained using a "splitting the difference" titration procedure. Participants chose between LL and SS amounts presented on a computer screen in the following way:

Amount: £500   £1,000
When received: Sept. 28, 2001 Sept. 27, 2002

After each choice, one amount was adjusted up or down, depending on whether SS or LL was chosen, and in this way the difference between the two amounts was gradually reduced until an indifference point was reached. This set of choices leading to an indifference point is termed a *choice sequence*. The choice sequences were constructed according to a four (*interval*) by two (variable amount *timing*) design. The four *intervals* were one unbroken delay of T months, and three intervals of T/3 months that spanned the period T. Variable amount *timing* referred to whether the SS or LL amount was adjusted following each choice. For each interval, choice and matching questions were repeated once with the SS amount being adjusted (*SS-variable* condition), and once with the LL amount being adjusted (*LL-variable*).

In the matching task participants first saw pairs of delayed options, with one value missing, such as:

Amount: £????   £1,000
When received: Sept. 28, 2001 Sept. 27, 2002

They then typed in an amount that would make the two options equivalent in value.

The four experiments differed in a variety of details, of which the most important are summarized here. In experiment 1, the delay (T) was twenty-four months broken into three eight-month intervals. The endpoints of the intervals were designated using months and years, as in "February 2002." Since the description of the dates in experiment 1 was potentially problematic (participants may have thought that intervals starting in the month they were being tested in were shorter than other intervals), experiment 2 replicated experiment 1 with the delays described in more abstract terms, as in "eight months." In experiment 3, the choices were for "real money," in that the experimental session was immediately followed by a draw in which one participant received his or her preferred outcome for one of his or her choices. For financial reasons, the amounts under consideration were much smaller in this real choice experiment, with a maximum possible value of £250 as opposed to £2,500. Finally, in experiment 4, all participants answered the same questions with both choice and matching.

Results

The results of all experiments are given in tables 10.1 and 10.2. Table 10.1 shows mean values of δ, while table 10.2 shows the results of selected hypothesis tests. Subadditive discounting was observed in every condition of every experiment: δ was greater for undivided than divided delays ($\delta_{T\cdot1} > \delta_{T\cdot3}$), with the ratio $\delta_{T\cdot1}/\delta_{T\cdot3}$ ranging from 1.05 to 1.32, and all statistical tests were highly significant.

Hypothesis 2, the delay/interval effect—usually the only evidence adduced to support the hypothesis of increasing patience—similarly received strong support. In every condition, the value of δ for the entire delay was greater than that for the first third of the delay: $\delta_{T\cdot1} > \delta_{T\cdot3\cdot1}$. The mean difference $\delta_{T\cdot1} - \delta_{T\cdot3\cdot1}$ ranged from 0.01 to 0.17 (average = 0.10), with the smallest differences occurring in experiment 1. The analyses in table 10.2 support this observation, with all relevant comparisons being significant.

The delay/interval effect could be due entirely to subadditivity, or there could be some true increasing patience that subadditivity cannot explain. When this issue was examined with tests of hypothesis 3a and hypothesis 3b, none of the choice conditions showed evidence of true increasing patience. Experiments 1 and 3 do show main effects of interval, but neither of these is due to increasing patience. In experiment 1, δ was *highest* for the first interval ($\delta_{T\cdot3\cdot1}$), when increasing

Table 10.1   Mean Discount Factors Per Year for All Conditions of Experiments 1 to 4

Study	Variable Amount	Cond.	$\delta_{T\cdot1}$	$\delta_{T\cdot3}$	$\delta_{T\cdot3\cdot1}$	$\delta_{T\cdot3\cdot2}$	$\delta_{T\cdot3\cdot3}$
Exp 1: Times given	LL	Choice	76	63	71	61	61
as month and year;	SS	Choice	70	60	67	60	59
T = 24 months;							
N = 32.							
Exp 2: Times given	LL	Choice	73	57	60	54	59
as number of	SS	Choice	66	54	54	58	55
months delay;							
T = 24 months;							
N = 31.							
Exp 3: Times given	LL	Choice	74	55	59	53	57
as exact dates;	SS	Choice	75	58	61	54	62
T = 18 months;							
N = 16; "real"							
choice.							
Exp 4: Times given	LL	Choice	81	72	72	71	72
as exact dates;	SS	Choice	81	77	75	77	80
T = 36 months;	LL	Match	85	78	76	78	79
N = 38; two ses-	SS	Match	85	81	79	83	83
sions at least one							
day apart.							

Source: Author's compilation.
Note: Values of δ are given without leading decimal points.

patience would predict it would be lowest, and in experiment 3, δ was lowest for the middle interval ($\delta_{T\cdot3\cdot2}$). The means of the SS-adjusted choice condition of experiment 4 also suggest increasing patience, but this pattern is not reflected in the median values of δ, is not replicated in the LL-adjusted condition, and was not statistically significant. For choice, therefore, there was no evidence of increasing patience. For matching, however, there was evidence of true increasing patience and hyperbolic discounting. The magnitude of the increase in δ from the first to second period was small (.02 and .04, depending on condition) but statistically reliable.

As seen in table 10.2, the test for hyperbolic discounting was not statistically significant, but the fact that all the means (and medians) are ordered as predicted is important, especially given the absence of any effect for choice. These results therefore support Ahlbrecht and Weber's (1995) conjecture that increasing patience occurs in matching but not in choice.

Table 10.2   ANOVA Results for Crucial Main Effects, All Hypotheses of Experiment 1 to 4

Experiment	Condition	F	MSe	Df	p<
Hypothesis 1: Additivity					
1	Choice	36.8	.03	(1,30)	.0001
2	Choice	68.5	.02	(1,30)	.0001
3	Choice	57.3	.02	(1,15)	.0001
4	Choice	36.8	.004	(1,36)	.0001
4	Matching	26.7	.004	(1,36)	.0001
Hypothesis 2: Delay/interval effect					
1	Choice	5.01	.12	(1,31)	.05
2	Choice	36.8	.03	(1,30)	.0001
3	Choice	47.0	.01	(1,15)	.0001
4	Choice	32.0	.006	(1,36)	.0001
4	Matching	35.5	.005	(1,36)	.0001
Hypothesis 3a: True increasing patience					
1	Choice	16.2*	.02	(2,30)	.0001
2	Choice	0.11	.05	(2,29)	.895
3	Choice	5.0*	.02	(2,14)	.05
4	Choice	2.4	0.012	(2,35)	.13
4	Matching	5.5	0.025	(2,35)	.001
Hypothesis 3b: Hyperbolic discounting					
1	Matching	3.2	0.007	(1,36)	.1

Source: Author's compilation.
*Pattern of means inconsistent with the hypothesis of increasing patience/hyperbolic discounting. See text.

Do Matching Results Fit the Predictions of Hyperbolic Discounting?

The presence of increasing patience in matching warrants further consideration of the extent to which it is as predicted by models of hyperbolic discounting. To determine this, I tested two simple one-parameter models of hyperbolic discounting by estimating discount parameters from the first period δ ($\delta_{T\cdot3\cdot1}$), and then estimating how well the model predicted discounting over the second and third periods.

The first model tested is the most widely cited version of hyperbolic discounting, usually given in the following form:

$$v_1 = \frac{v_2}{1 + kt_2}, \text{ when } t_1 = 0.$$

This equation, due to Mazur (1984), is to be found throughout the literature on time discounting. For an interval of arbitrary length and temporal position, δ corresponding to this equation is given as follows:

$$\delta_{t_1 \to t_2} = \left(\frac{1 + kt_1}{1 + kt_2}\right)^{\frac{1}{t_2 - t_1}},$$

where t_1 and t_2 are the beginning and end of an interval (measured in units of one year) and the parameter k reflects the decision maker's personal rate of time preference. I will refer to this as k-discounting. Given an indifference point, the k parameter can then be obtained as follows:

$$k = \frac{1 - \left(\frac{SS}{LL}\right)}{\left(\frac{SS}{LL}\right)t_2 - t_1}.$$

When the interval is a 1-year delay, as in experiment 4, $SS/LL = \delta$, $t_2 = 1$ and $t_1 = 0$ and therefore $k = (1 - \delta_{T.3.1})/\delta_{T.3.1}$. This k parameter can *only* be derived from first period discounting ($\delta_{T.3.1}$), because many values of SS/LL for later intervals are incompatible with *any* value of k.[8]

A second model comes from Harvey (1992, 1994), who proposed a hyperbolic alternative to a constant value of δ, which he called *proportional discounting*. Ahlbrecht and Weber (1995) give this model in a convenient form that, redescribed for the present purposes, is:

$$\delta_{t_1 \to t_2} = \left(\frac{1 + t_1}{1 + t_2}\right)^h,$$

I will call this *h-discounting*, which is a special one-parameter case of Loewenstein and Prelec's (1992) model. The h parameter can be estimated as:

$$h = \frac{\log\left(\frac{SS}{LL}\right)}{\log\left(\frac{1 + t_1}{1 + t_2}\right)}.$$

For the one year delay of experiment 4, this reduces to $h = \log(\delta_{T \cdot 3 \cdot 1})/\log(0.5)$.

The results of this analysis appear in table 10.3. For each participant a value of k and h was calculated from $\delta_{T \cdot 3 \cdot 1}$, and this was used to predict values for the later subintervals. As can be seen, the observed values of δ were consistently and significantly lower than predicted. In general, conventional hyperbolic discounting models predict a much bigger change from the first to the second period than actually occurs. Moreover, the increase in δ from the second to the third interval was also substantially less than predicted—indeed, δ was essentially identical over the second and third year. The extent of this "badness of fit" is underlined by comparing the obtained results with those predicted by exponential discounting, which holds that δ is constant over time. It turns out that the mean $\delta_{T \cdot 3 \cdot 1}$ is closer to its successors, $\delta_{T \cdot 3 \cdot 2}$ and $\delta_{T \cdot 3 \cdot 3}$, than are the values predicted from the hyperbolic discounting models.

The theoretical benefit of hyperbolic discounting is that it can account for behavior suggesting a very low δ in early periods, followed by a rapid convergence to a very high δ. Even the increasing patience found in the matching data from experiment 4 do not show this effect. What seems clear is that when the confound between date and delay is eliminated, little remains of what previously appeared to be strong evidence for hyperbolic discounting.

Discussion

The results of the present study are clear. First, time discounting is clearly subadditive, with subadditivity occurring in every condition in four experiments. Second, the conventional evidence for increasing patience—lower values of δ for shorter delays—was also observed in every condition. The crucial question therefore is whether this delay/interval effect is due to subadditive or hyperbolic discounting. When discount factors are estimated using a choice procedure, there was no evidence of increasing patience. There was, however, a modest level of increasing patience when time preference was measured using matching rather than choice.

Here I consider two issues raised by these studies. First, I speculate

Table 10.3   Discounting Parameters Estimated from $\delta_{T,3\cdot1}$ and Observed and Predicted Values of $\delta_{T\cdot3\cdot2}$ and $\delta_{T\cdot3\cdot3}$

Interval	Timing	Parameter	δ Observed	δ Predicted	Diff.	t(36)	p
k-discounting							
12 to 24	SS	0.33	83	84	−1	−1.27	0.21
24 to 36	SS		83	87	−4	−3.00	0.00
12 to 24	LL	0.39	78	82	−4	−2.14	0.04
24 to 36	LL		79	85	−6	−3.39	0.00
h-discounting							
12 to 24	SS	0.37	83	87	−4	−3.86	0.00
24 to 36	SS		83	90	−7	−5.64	0.00
12 to 24	LL	0.44	78	85	−7	−4.36	0.00
24 to 36	LL		79	89	−10	−6.24	0.00

Source: Author's compilation.

about why matching might lead to hyperbolic-like discounting while choice does not. The purpose is to suggest some ways that psychological processes of time discounting might depend on the task used. Second, the question of dynamic inconsistency, or time-based preference reversal, is examined. If there is no hyperbolic discounting, then how can dynamic inconsistency occur?

How Do Choice and Matching Differ?

The finding that increasing patience occurs in matching but not choice raises the question of what different psychological processes are used in the two methods. Although the present data cannot answer such process questions, some speculations here are offered that can form the basis for future research. Consider two ways of choosing between the delayed amounts SS and LL. The first, here called the *delay* method, is to compute the present value of each outcome and take the one with the higher present value. The second is the *interval* method, which involves focusing on the interpayoff interval, and deciding if the difference in amount (LL-SS) can compensate for the difference in delay. Analogous processes can be used in matching. The delay method means calculating the present value of the known outcome, then determining what missing amount will make both outcomes equivalent. The interval method means deciding what adjustment to the known amount is needed to correspond to the stated change in delay.

Consider two choices (or matchings) between pairs of options delayed by different amounts. The first choice is between SS_0 and LL_1, and the second is between SS_1 and LL_2, where the subscripts indicate the time of their realization in years. For both choices the *interval* is one year; but the delay is one year for the first choice and two years for the second. If the delay method is used, the decision maker will first calculate the present value of the two alternatives and then decide between them. That is, the task is to set

$$w_0 SS_0 = w_1 LL_1, \text{ and}$$

$$w_1 SS_1 = w_2 LL_2,$$

where w_i is the weight associated with each delay and corresponds to a nonnormalized discount factor. Using the notation introduced here, $w_0 = 1$ (no discounting), $w_1 = \delta_{1\cdot1}$, and $w_2 = \delta_{2\cdot1}^2$ (discounting at rate $\delta_{2\cdot1}$ over two years). Both subadditivity and hyperbolic discounting predict that $1 - \delta_{1\cdot1} > \delta_{1\cdot1} - \delta_{2\cdot1}^2$, so choice or matching based on the delay method does not distinguish between the hypotheses. Yet the predictions of subadditive and hyperbolic discounting do differ when the *interval* method is used. The crucial discount factors for the interval method are those operating over a one-year interval when it is the first year ($\delta_{1\cdot1}$), or the second year ($\delta_{2\cdot2\cdot2}$), so the task is to set:

$$SS_0 = \delta_{1\cdot1} LL_1, \text{ and}$$

$$SS_1 = \delta_{2\cdot2\cdot2} LL_2.$$

If discounting is *exclusively* subadditive, then $\delta_{1\cdot1} = \delta_{2\cdot2\cdot2}$, while hyperbolic discounting predicts that $\delta_{1\cdot1} < \delta_{2\cdot2\cdot2}$ (increasing patience). In experiment 2, the first of these predictions was true for choice, while the second was true for matching.

This analysis does not indicate when (or if) the two methods are used, but it does provide two hypothetical processes that can give rise to the results of both choice and matching studies, can account for the presence and absence of increasing patience, and are also compatible with subadditivity. The difference between tasks may be that the interval method is used almost exclusively during choice, while during matching some mixture of the methods are used. To determine if this is true, or if some other factor distinguishes between matching and choice, future research must be directed toward unearthing the processes underlying intertemporal decision making, as well as observing the decisions themselves.

How Does Dynamic Inconsistency Happen?

The hyperbolic discounting hypothesis was developed to account for a phenomenon that undeniably exists: dynamic inconsistency such as Thaler's 1 apple/2 apple effect.[9] So reliable is this effect that I use a version of the apple problem as a classroom demonstration. While a majority of students choose 1 apple today over 2 tomorrow, no one ever chooses 1 apple in 364 days over 2 in 365. I suggest, however, that to explain these choices with a hyperbolic discount function of the sort widely discussed in the psychological literature leads to absurdities; and moreover, there is no need to call on such a function— one can account for dynamic inconsistency in many other ways. We can address the question of whether hyperbolic discounting can account for everyday dynamic inconsistency by closely examining the apple problem. Someone who chooses 1 apple today but 2 in a year is indicating that:

$$w_0 u(A) > w_1 u(2A), \text{ but } w_{364} u(A) < w_{365} u(2A),$$

where w_i is the weight put on utility received at time i (corresponding to δ defined over intervals of differing length), and $u(A)$ and $u(2A)$ are, respectively, the utility of 1 and 2 apples. It is clear that if

$$\frac{w_0}{w_1} > \frac{u(A)}{u(2A)} > \frac{w_{364}}{w_{365}},$$

then the typical preference reversal will occur. To estimate the various values of w_i we need to know something about $u(A)$ and $u(2A)$. A conservative guess is that 2 apples are only 10 percent better than 1, or that $u(2A) = 1.1u(A)$. To explain the 1 apple/2 apple preference pattern with a hyperbolic discount function, the value of k or h must be compatible with discounting 10 percent over the first day. We will use k discounting because it turns out to be less outrageous. The *minimum* acceptable k parameter is 36.5 (h is 34.8), which means that the one year discount factors are:

$$\delta_{0 \to 1} = .027; \ \delta_{0 \to 1} = .51; \ \delta_{0 \to 1} = .67, \text{ and so on.}[10]$$

These are absurdly low values that are also plainly incompatible with human behavior. Someone who discounts the future in this way would choose £27,000 today over £1 million in one year, £14,000 over the £1 million in two years, £8,000 over the £1 million in three years, and so on. It turns out, therefore, that conventional forms of hyperbolic discounting probably cannot explain the only thing we want them to without committing us to absurd conclusions.

Given that hyperbolic discounting is probably a poor way to account for dynamic inconsistency, how else can it be explained? One way that has been discussed by Kirby (1997) and Green and Myerson (1993) is that it is a manifestation of the magnitude effect. This is the very robust finding that smaller amounts are discounted faster than larger ones (reviewed in Frederick, Loewenstein, and O'Donoghue, chap. 1 herein). Consider two outcomes A and B, where $u(A) < u(B)$, but A is preferred because it is available sooner. The classic result is that if we hold the interoutcome delay constant, but further delay both outcomes, we will eventually reach a point where B is chosen over A. If we describe this in terms of discount factors, we say that a higher discount factor is applied to A than to B. Hyperbolic discounting explains it through absolute increasing patience: since A is available sooner it is discounted more, per unit of time, than is B. Since A is in fact worth less than B, though, the magnitude effect *alone* predicts that A will be discounted faster than B, and therefore also predicts dynamic inconsistency. The reason you might prefer one apple today to two tomorrow is that the δ applied to small numbers of apples *is* extremely low because they are worth very little. The δ applied to two apples, however, is still higher than that applied to one, so when you are choosing for one year away you prefer the two apples. The magnitude effect therefore accounts for both the low discount factors for apples *and* preference reversals. Moreover, this effect does not call on us to generalize from apples to millions of dollars.[11]

A second explanation turns on the nature of the goods between which preference reversals are observed. Hyperbolic discounting is often used to explain impulsivity and myopic choice (for example, Ainslie 1975; Frank 1988; Heyman 1996; Rachlin and Raineri 1992). A conventional example is choosing a high-fat dessert over long-term health. When the dessert is some time away it is easy to resist, but when it gets near its value is magnified (because of the steep slope of the hyperbolic discount function) and so becomes highly attractive. The hyperbolic discounting story is appealing if told about such things as desserts, cigarettes, and alcohol, but then it must be applicable to all goods. Yet clearly we are not impulsive about most things. As Hoch and Loewenstein (1991) point out, we are not overtaken with the desire for gasoline or writing paper. Loewenstein (1996) has argued that impulsive preference reversal is associated with the conjunction of specific kinds of goods and experiences combined with their corresponding "visceral" drive states. When hungry we are impulsive about food, when nicotine deprived we are impulsive about tobacco, and so on, but no single internal discount function is driving our impulses. Moreover, other evidence on impulsivity suggests that temporal proximity alone doesn't lead to preference reversals; usually, temporal proximity is accompanied by the physical proximity of the tempting alternative (see Herman and Polivy, chap. 16 herein). Impulsivity therefore does not require a discount function at all, simply an ability to be overwhelmed by physiological drives under specific circumstances that are unrelated to time discounting.

A further account for dynamic inconsistency comes from Liberman and Trope's (chap. 8 herein) theory of temporal construal. They argue that options can be described in terms of central and peripheral features. The relative weight of central over peripheral features increases over time, so that as delays are increased, goods that are strong on central features become relatively more attractive than those that are strong on more peripheral features. To illustrate, consider a choice between a sports car and a family-size sedan. Many people will take the sports car if they can get it right away, but will take the sedan if it will be delayed for some time. Hyperbolic discounting accounts for this by saying that the sports car has more immediate utility than the sedan, and this immediate utility is discounted at a greater rate than the more distributed utility of the sedan. Liberman and Trope's research, however, suggests that we don't need any discount function at all. For most people the central property of a car is that it is a form of transport, with the fun of driving being a secondary albeit not trivial property. If the car will be available immediately, this secondary property weighs much more heavily in our decision than if we are thinking ahead, when central properties are more important.

Each of these explanations shows how dynamic inconsistency can occur under different circumstances: the magnitude effect when choosing between experiences that differ in quantity and when the larger item is more delayed (Kirby and Herrnstein 1995); variations in visceral drive states and physical proximity when appealing goods are available right now versus delayed by some perhaps very small amount (Read and van Leeuwen 1998); and temporal construal theory when the later good has more (or better) central features than the earlier one (Liberman and Trope, chap. 8 herein). Note that these are not merely alternatives to hyperbolic discounting, because they not only explain what hyperbolic discounting can explain but also what it cannot. Undoubtedly, a host of other accounts are possible, but the main point is that not only is hyperbolic discounting an awkward way of explaining dynamic inconsistency, it is not even a useful one.[12]

Notes

1. Some details: first, when $t_1 = 0$, meaning the first item is available immediately, we call v_1 the *present value*; second, when $\delta = 1$, decision makers are indifferent about the timing of outcomes (that is, they are perfectly patient), while if $\delta > 1$ they will prefer to delay all positive outcomes indefinitely, because the more they are delayed the greater their present value.

2. This is sometimes called *decreasing impatience* (Prelec 1990), *decreasing timing aversion* (Bleichrodt and Johannesson 2001) and, as will be discussed, *hyperbolic discounting* (Kirby 1997).

3. An exception is Kirby and Herrnstein (1995). Their results are discussed herein.

4. A subadditive function is one with the form $f(a) + f(b) > f(a + b)$. Subadditive discounting means that the total amount of discounting over an undivided interval $(a + b)$ is less than that over its component intervals when they are treated separately (a, b).

5. Experiments 1 to 3 are reported elsewhere (Read 2001) although the analyses here differ in some details.

6. To collect matching data is much easier, since it can be done using a paper-and-pencil questionnaire. Choice, however, requires an interactive question-and-answer session, usually (but not necessarily) using a computer.

7. Ahlbrecht and Weber compared two separate studies, one based on choice and another on matching. They observed increasing patience for matching but not choice. Unfortunately, their matching study confounded delay and interval in the usual manner, while their choice study did not. Their result therefore may be due to subadditive discounting.

8. A k parameter can only be derived from an interval as long as $SS/LL > t_1/t_2$.

9. An additional basis for considering hyperbolic discounting comes from studies of animals in studies of operant conditioning. Not at all clear, however, is whether these studies have any relationship to the studies of human choice with which the present chapter is concerned (for example, Kacelnik, chap. 3 herein).

10. Compare this value of h with the values of 0.33 and 0.39 obtained in the matching condition of experiment 4.

11. When Kirby (1997) and Green and colleagues (1997) undertook to rule out the magnitude effect explanation for preference reversals, they did so by using methods that incorporated the delay/interval confound that this chapter explores.

12. One other version of hyperbolic discounting not discussed here remains compatible with the lack of increasing patience observed in the present study. This is a model that incorporates an immediacy effect only, so that

$$v_0 = \beta \delta^n \, v_n, \, \beta < 1,$$

whenever $n > 0$ (see, for example, Angeletos et al., chap. 18 herein; O'Donoghue and Rabin, chap. 7 herein). The β parameter corresponds to a fixed tax that is charged once for delay, and is in addition to a constant discount factor imposed on additional delays. This is not a version of strong hyperbolic discounting as discussed earlier, since the discount factor drops only once—in the delay from "now" to "later." In the experiments described herein no "now" condition existed and so it remains feasible that disproportionate discounting may have occurred in the very short delays from zero to a few days. See Read (2001) and Read and Roelofsma (2002) for more on this.

References

Ahlbrecht, Martin, and Martin Weber. 1995. "Hyperbolic Discounting Models in Prescriptive Theory of Intertemporal Choice." *Zeitschrift fur Wirtschaft- und Sozialwissenschaften* 115: 511–34.

———. 1997. "An Empirical Study on Intertemporal Decision Making Under Risk." *Management Science* 43: 813–26.

Ainslie, George. 1975. "Specious Reward: A Behavioral Theory of Impulsiveness and Impulse Control." *Psychological Bulletin* 82: 463–69.

Benzion, Uri, Amnon Rapoport, and Joseph Yagil. 1989. "Discount Rates Inferred from Decisions: An Experimental Study." *Management Science* 35: 270–84.

Bleichrodt, Han, and Magnus Johannesson. 2001. "Time Preference for Health: A Test of Stationarity Versus Decreasing Timing Aversion." *Journal of Mathematical Psychology* 45: 265–82.

Chapman, Gretchen B. 2001. "Time Preferences for the Very Long Term." *Acta Psychologica* 109: 95–116.

Chapman, Gretchen B., and Arthur S. Elstein. 1995. "Valuing the Future: Temporal Discounting of Health and Money." *Medical Decision Making* 15: 373–86.

Frank, Robert H. 1988. *Passions Within Reason: The Strategic Role of the Emotions.* New York: Norton.

Green, Leonard, Astrid Fry, and Joel Myerson. 1994. "Discounting of Delayed Rewards: A Life-Span Comparison." *Psychological Science* 5: 33–36.

Green, Leonard, and Joel Myerson. 1993. "Alternative Frameworks for the Analysis of Self-Control." *Behavior and Philosophy* 21: 37–47.

Green, Leonard, Joel Myerson, and Edward McFadden. 1997. "Rate of Temporal Discounting Decreases with Amount of Reward." *Memory and Cognition* 25: 715–23.

Harvey, Charles M. 1992. "A Slow-Discounting Model for Social Costs and Benefits." *Interfaces* 22: 47–60.

———. 1994. "The Reasonableness of Non-Constant Discounting." *Journal of Public Economics* 53: 31–51.

Heyman, Gene M. 1996. "Resolving the Contradictions of Addiction." *Behavioral and Brain Sciences* 19: 561–610.

Hoch, Stephen, and George Loewenstein. 1991. "Time-Inconsistent Preferences and Consumer Self-Control." *Journal of Consumer Research* 17: 492–507.

Holcomb, James H., and P. S. Nelson. 1992. "Another Experimental Look at Individual Time Preference." *Rationality and Society* 4: 199–220.

Kirby, Kris N. 1997. "Bidding on the Future: Evidence Against Normative Discounting of Delayed Rewards." *Journal of Experimental Psychology: General* 126: 54–70.

Kirby, Kris N., and Richard J. Herrnstein. 1995. "Preference Reversals Due to Myopic Discounting of Delayed Reward." *Psychological Science* 6: 83–89.

Kirby, Kris N., and Nina Marakovic. 1995. "Modeling Myopic Decisions: Evidence for Hyperbolic Delay-Discounting Within Subjects and Amounts." *Organizational Behavior and Human Decision Processes* 64: 22–30.

Loewenstein, George. 1996. "Out of Control: Visceral Influences on Behavior." *Organizational Behavior and Human Decision Processes* 65: 272–93.

Loewenstein, George, and Drazen Prelec. 1992. "Anomalies in Intertemporal Choice: Evidence and an Interpretation." *Quarterly Journal of Economics* 107: 573–97.

Mazur, James E. 1984. "Tests of an Equivalence Rule for Fixed and Variable Reinforcer Delays." *Journal of Experimental Psychology: Animal Behavior Processes* 10: 426–36.

Prelec, Drazen. 1990. "Decreasing Impatience: Definition and Consequences." Working paper no. 90–015. Harvard Business School.

Prelec, Drazen, and George Loewenstein. 1991. "Decision Making over Time and Under Uncertainty: A Common Approach." *Management Science* 37: 770–76.

Rachlin, Howard, and Andres Raineri. 1992. "Irrationality, Impulsiveness, and Selfishness as Discount Reversal Effects." In *Choice Over Time*, edited by G. F. Loewenstein and J. Elster. New York: Russell Sage Foundation.

Raineri, Andres, and Howard Rachlin. 1993. "The Effect of Temporal Constraints on the Value of Money and Other Commodities." *Journal of Behavioral Decision Making* 6: 77–94.

Read, Daniel. 2001. "Is Time-Discounting Hyperbolic or Subadditive?" *Journal of Risk and Uncertainty* 23: 5–32.

Read, Daniel, and Barbara van Leeuwen. 1998. "Predicting Hunger: The Effects of Appetite and Delay on Choice." *Organizational Behavior and Human Decision Processes* 76: 189–205.

Read, Daniel, and Peter H. M. P. Roelofsma. 2002. "Exploring Subadditive Intertemporal Choice: Tests of Hyperbolic Discounting Using Choice and Matching." London School of Economics working paper.

Richards, Jerry B., Lan Zhang, Suzanne H. Mitchell, and Harriet de Wit. 1999. "Delay or Probability Discounting in a Model of Impulsive Behavior: Effect of Alcohol." *Journal of the Experimental Analysis of Behavior* 71: 121–43.

Samuelson, Paul. 1937. "A Note of Measurement of Utility." *Review of Economic Studies* 4: 155–61.

Strotz, Robert H. 1955. "Myopia and Inconsistency in Dynamic Utility Maximization." *Review of Economic Studies* 23: 165–80.

Thaler, Richard H. 1981. "Some Empirical Evidence on Dynamic Inconsistency." *Economic Letters* 8: 201–7.

Varian, Hal R. 1992. *Microeconomic Analysis*. 3rd ed. New York: Norton.

· 11 ·

Summary Assessment of Experiences: The Whole Is Different from the Sum of Its Parts

DAN ARIELY AND ZIV CARMON

Cᴏᴍᴍᴏɴ experiences such as watching a film, waiting to be served at a restaurant, or undergoing a medical procedure unfold over time through a stream of transient states that may vary from moment to moment in their intensity (for example, become more or less pleasant) and even in sign (for example, change from being pleasant to being unpleasant). A visit to the dentist for example, may begin with a boring wait in the reception room. Treatment can then begin with an unpleasant but not painful checkup, proceed with a painful drilling, and end with a lingering mildly painful sensation. Similarly, dinner at a restaurant can start with a fabulous appetizer, continue with an ordinary entree, during which you become temporarily annoyed when you notice a piece of eggshell that clearly was not supposed to be there, and conclude with a wonderful dessert.

Such evolution of subjective experiences can be depicted by an *experience profile*, whereby time is presented on the *x* axis, and the *y* axis represents the perceived momentary intensity of the experience. As an example, consider figure 11.1, which presents the experience profile of a patient studied by Ariely and Carmon (2000). In that study, patients in the bone marrow transplant unit of a local hospital re-

323

Figure 11.1   Experience Profile

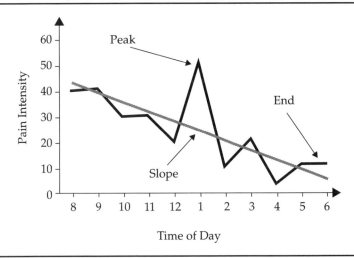

Source: Authors' configuration.
Note: An example (based on Ariely and Carmon [2000]) of an experience profile and three of its gestalt characteristics, based on the data of Subject 17 in the hospital study (assessment of a painful day at a hospital). *Peak* is the maximum intensity, *end* is the intensity at the final moment of the experience, and in this case *slope* is a single measure of the profile's overall linear trend (in gray).

ported the pain they experienced on a 0 to 100 scale (0 represented no pain, and 100 the worst pain they could imagine) every hour from 8 A.M. to 6 P.M. The figure indicates that the pain intensity for this patient was relatively high early in the day, then decreased, picked up around 1 P.M., and generally improved thereafter.

Over the past decade, a substantial body of research has examined summary evaluations of experiences such those previously described. In particular, this research investigated the correspondence between experience profiles and their overall assessments, the topic of this chapter. To illustrate, Ariely and Carmon examined how hourly pain reports such as those depicted in figure 11.1 corresponded to end-of-the-day evaluations in which patients were asked to assess the overall pain they experienced throughout the entire day. A primary motivation for this line of research has been the finding that when people form summary assessments of experiences, they *do not* combine the individual components of the experience profiles. Instead, a large number of studies has repeatedly demonstrated that neither the sum (integral) nor the average of experience profiles corresponds closely to overall evaluations of their components (for reviews of this research see Ariely and Carmon 2000, Huber et al. 1997, Kahneman 2000). Therefore studying experience profiles must focus not only on their components (intensities of the transient states) but also on the rules people use to combine these components into overall evaluations.

Researchers have wanted to understand summary evaluations of experiences for several reasons: overall evaluations of the pain and pleasure associated with different experiences are obviously important as input for future decision making. How positively or negatively people remember an experience is a key determinant of whether they will want to repeat it and whether they will recommend it to others. Retrospective summary assessments of events can also determine how people "consume" memories of these experiences in the future. For instance, a brief exotic vacation can produce fond memories one could savor long after the experience is over. Like retrospective summary evaluations, prospective summary evaluations can also be important. They can evoke sensations, such as anticipation and dread, before the experience ever takes place (Loewenstein 1987) and may thus determine whether or not one pursues an experience. Lottery tickets, for example, may often be purchased not so much because people truly expect to win the prize, but because they offer an opportunity to fantasize for a few days how it would feel to win the money, how to spend it, and so on.

In the rest of this chapter, we first sum up what is known about how prolonged experiences are evaluated. In particular, we describe central features of experiences that appear to dominate their summary evaluation. We briefly describe empirical evidence for the effects of these features and identify variables that can moderate those effects. Next, we discuss the weighting of the duration of experiences in summary evaluations, and list variables that may influence this weighting. In the following section, we present ideas about why the features we described in the first section influence summary evaluations. Specifically, we propose ideas about the role of efficient encoding, and about tendencies to predict future states. Finally, we describe ideas about retrospective reevaluations and reinterpretations of experiences, then suggest directions for future research in this domain.

Gestalt Characteristics of Experiences

An intuitively appealing way to summarize an experience would be to integrate (or perhaps average) across intensities of the subjective states of which the experience is composed (see Kahneman, Wakker, and Sarin 1997 for detailed explanations of this argument). Yet a clear conclusion of research in this domain is that when people summarize experiences, they do not integrate or average the transient states they experienced as the events unfolded. Rather, two types of defining features of the profiles of experiences appear to dominate overall retrospective evaluations. In Ariely and Carmon (2000) we name such defining features *gestalt characteristics*, of which there are two types, static and dynamic.

Static (state) *characteristics* reflect the intensity of the momentary experiences (that is, transient states) at particular key points in time. To illustrate, a variety of studies have found that a weighted average of the momentary experience at the most intense and final moments—often referred to as the *peak* and *end*, respectively—can generally account for the global retrospective evaluations (compare with Fredrickson and Kahneman 1993; Kahneman et al. 1993; Redelmeier and Kahneman 1996; Varey and Kahneman 1992).

Dynamic (configural) *characteristics* reflect the change in the intensity of the transient states as the experience progresses. Prominent examples of such characteristics include the trend of the profile (Ariely 1998; Loewenstein and Prelec 1993) and its rate of change (Hsee and Abelson 1991; Hsee, Salovey, and Abelson 1994).

Note that to distinguish between the two types of gestalt characteristics can often be difficult. For example, an experience with a very positive ending is likely to also have an improving trend, making it difficult to determine whether the ending or the trend made the overall experience as positive as it was.

Evidence for Effects of Static (State) Gestalt Characteristics

The logic underlying static gestalt characteristics is that people retain a few key statistics of their experiences, and these statistics—rather than the complete experience—are stored in memory for later use. An example of this notion of feature (statistic) retention in the context of assessment of experience profiles can be found in the work of Fredrickson and Kahneman (1993), who suggested that memory stores discrete snapshots of experiences. They offered a succinct metaphor inspired by Kundera (1991), according to which "memory does not take film, it takes photographs." In a series of studies exploring different types of experiences, Kahneman and his colleagues repeatedly found that the differences between summary evaluations of different experiences is accounted for by two static characteristics—a weighted average of the most extreme state (peak) and the final (end) state. In one study, for example, Fredrickson and Kahneman (1993) showed respondents either long or short movie clips that were either pleasant (for example, a puppy playing) or unpleasant (for example, an amputation). Their respondents provided both continuous real-time ratings of their affective state and a global retrospective rating of the pleasantness or unpleasantness of the experience when it was over.[1] They examined the correspondence between mean overall evaluations given at the end of each experience and the experience profile composed of the continuous on-line ratings respondents provided. Their results (and those of others) indicate that people appear to rely only on key moments in their experiences when forming overall retrospective evaluations. In another interesting study, Redelmeier and Kahneman (1996) asked patients who underwent colonoscopy or lithotripsy to report the momentary pain they experienced during the procedure as well as to summarize the total pain they experienced after the procedure was over. Those results also suggested that a weighted average of the most intense moment and the final three minutes closely corresponded to the retrospective summary evaluations of the experiences ($r = 0.67$).

Evidence for Effects of Dynamic (Configural) Gestalt Characteristics

The logic underlying dynamic gestalt characteristics is similar to that used for static ones. Individuals extract basic statistics of their experiences, and these statistics—rather than the complete experience—are stored for later use. In the dynamic case, however, the extracted statistics represent *relationships* between different states of the experience rather than states in and of themselves. In particular, indicators of progress over time appear to be important to people (see Loewenstein 1987).

Indeed one of the most robust findings in research about assessment of experiences is the clear preference for improvement over time (see Loewenstein and Prelec 1993). Preference for improvement has been demonstrated in many domains, including monetary payments (Loewenstein and Sicherman 1991; Langer, Sarin, and Weber 2000), experiences such as vacations (Loewenstein and Prelec 1991, 1993; Varey and Kahneman 1992), queuing events (Carmon and Kahneman 2000), pain (Ariely 1998, Ariely and Carmon 2000), discomfort (Kahneman et al. 1993; Ariely and Zauberman 2000; Ariely and Loewenstein 2000), medical outcomes and treatments (Chapman 2000; Redelmeier and Kahneman 1996), gambling (Ross and Simonson 1991), and academic performance (Hsee and Abelson 1991; Hsee, Salovey, and Abelson 1994).

Consider, for example, two different sequences of four dental treatments spaced over a week, for which the intensity of pain is represented by numerical ratings, and greater pain by larger numbers. In these two sequences the pain intensity either increases (2, 3, 4, 5) or decreases (5, 4, 3, 2) from one instance to the next. Although both sequences deliver the same cumulative discomfort, most people prefer the sequence of decreasing pain. To further illustrate, consider the example of the patients described earlier (for example, in figure 11.1). In that study, we found that ratings of overall daily pain were best predicted by the intensity of the final state and the slope of changes in pain ratings throughout the day (R^2 of 0.89). Moreover, in that case neither the average nor the sum of the pain experienced was effective at predicting the ratings of the overall pain.

In two other studies of dynamic gestalt characteristics, Ariely (1998) inflicted moderate levels of pain on participants either by using a heat probe or by pressing their finger in a vise. The experiences differed in their duration as well as in how they progressed over time (pain intensity over time either increased or decreased or increased then decreased, and so on). After each experience, participants rated the overall pain they experienced, and those ratings were then regressed on features of the stimuli. The results suggest that participants were most sensitive to *changes* in intensity. Increasing pain intensity was perceived as very painful, and decreasing intensity was perceived as not painful, even when the sum of momentary intensities was the same. Also, some stimuli used in these experiments were not monotonic (that is, increasing then decreasing or decreasing then increasing), and results showed that sequences that first deteriorated and later improved were perceived as less painful than patterns that first improved and later deteriorated (see also Ariely and Loewenstein 2000). Thus not only did people prefer improving sequences, they also preferred that the improvement take place later rather than earlier in the experience.

Moderators of the Effects of Gestalt Characteristics

The role of gestalt characteristics appears to be influenced by a variety of different factors. Examples include the type of experience, expectations, and the cohesiveness of the experience. These moderators are important because of their direct effect on overall evaluations, but also since they can provide insight into mechanisms that underlie people's summaries of their experiences.

One moderator of gestalt characteristics is the *type of the experience*. Carmon and Kahneman (2000) found that global retrospective evaluations of queuing experiences (experiences consisting of waiting) are dominated by the final affective state (end). In that setting, summary assessments effectively ignored the transient-state components that preceded the ending of the experience. For example, some queuing events that were dissatisfying up until seconds before they ended but concluded on a positive note were summarized positively. To conceptualize the differences between the waiting experiences described by Carmon and Kahneman and the more commonly studied experiences (Kahneman et al. 1993; Ariely 1998), we suggest that experiences fall on a continuum. On one end of the continuum are pure goal-directed experiences, such as fixing a flat tire and waiting for a service. These experiences derive their meaning mostly from their outcome, after the experience is over. In such cases the momentary experience as the event takes place reflects perceived progress toward the goal, whereas the summary assessment reflects the extent to which the goal is reached by the end of the experience (this idea will be further discussed). On the other end of the continuum are experiences that derive their meaning from the event itself rather than its outcome. Examples include receiving a massage, fine dining, and watching a movie. Note that many real-life experiences fall somewhere in between these two ends of the continuum. For example, activities such as driving to work and playing a game of squash are directed at goals of getting to work and winning, respectively. At the same time, however, the ongoing experiences in and of themselves are meaningful and they also influence the overall evaluations (how pleasant or unpleasant the drive was, how good the game was).

Chapman (2000) proposes another moderator. She suggests that people's *expectations* moderate their desire for improvement over time for those events. On one hand, she found that subjects preferred that their skin initially appear young and become increasingly wrinkled with age rather than preferring improvement over time, as they do in most situations. On the other hand, she found that subjects preferred that another aspect of their facial appearance—the state of facial acne—improve over time. In another paper (Chapman 1996), she showed that people preferred declining sequences of health over time, due to people's expectations regarding those experiences. For instance, she argues that since one's skin normally appears more rather than less wrinkled as one ages, people prefer the anticipated sequence of events. In her studies Chapman finds a significant correlation between the patterns of events that people expect to encounter and the patterns they prefer. Read and Powell (forthcoming), however, suggest that the impact of expectations is often indirect, in that people view what they expect as appropriate and want that which is appropriate. When expected outcomes are not viewed as appropriate, people prefer the appropriate.

Another moderator of gestalt characteristics is the *cohesiveness of the experience*. Ariely and Zauberman (2000) showed that the way people summarize an experience depends on whether they perceive it as composed of single or multiple segments (that is, if they see it as continuous or discrete). The authors show that the preference for improving trends over deteriorating ones is substantially reduced if the same experience is composed of discrete segments. Thus they demonstrate that the cohesiveness of an experience influences the relationship between its pattern and overall evaluation. This seems reasonable in light of the idea that summary assessments partly reflect inferences about future states. Specifically, if people naturally extrapolate current states in terms of their meaning for the future, the trend of an experience may appear more diagnostic of future states of continuous experiences than of future states of multiple discrete or segmented experiences (which will be elaborated on further).

Another moderating factor is the *spread*—the duration between the different segments of the overall experience. Loewenstein and Prelec (1993) showed that people preferred an escalating sequence when a later segment was to take place long after an earlier one, even though they displayed the more typical preference for improvement when events were to take place within a relatively short period of time. For example, people would prefer to dine at an excellent restaurant before dining at a mediocre one were the second dinner to take place many months after the first. Yet they would prefer the opposite (first the mediocre dinner, then the excellent one) were the second meal to take place a short time after the first. In other words, they show that the relationship between the pattern of the experience profile and its summary evaluation is moderated by the spread.

In conclusion, the main finding reviewed in this section—that a weighted average of the static and dynamic gestalt characteristics of experiences predicts summary assessments—is robust across the many types of experiences. Variables listed here (extent to which the experience is goal directed, expectations regarding the experience, its cohesiveness and spread) moderate the relative weighting of these characteristics. These variables also moderate the desirability of improvement over time.

The Weighting of Duration in Summary Evaluations of Experiences

An intriguing implication of the role different gestalt characteristics play in overall evaluations of experiences is the possibility that duration of experiences does not significantly impact their summary evaluations (Kahneman, Wakker, and Sarin 1997). After all, if overall evaluations take into account only the gestalt characteristics (slope, peak, and end) of the experience profile, what role remains for the duration of the experience? One empirical generalization that emerged from this research stream is that while other gestalt characteristics indeed influence overall evaluations, duration does not. Varey and Kahneman (1992) were first to draw attention to this phenomenon. In their studies, subjects provided summary evaluations of each of several hypothetical experience profiles that differed in duration and in their intensity pattern over time. Both Varey and Kahneman (1992) and Fredrickson and Kahneman (1993) found that summary evaluations of experiences corresponded closely to a weighted average of the maximum and final intensities of the experiences, while duration had almost no impact on the magnitude of the overall evaluations. Fredrickson and Kahneman (1993) termed this *duration neglect,* since after accounting for the gestalt characteristics of peak and end, duration had no significant effect.

In addition to documenting small marginal effect of duration beyond that of the maximum and final intensities, these authors also observed violations of dominance. Subjects rated the overall pain in the hypothetical sequence 2, 5, 8 as worse than the overall pain in the sequence 2, 5, 8, 4, where larger numbers represented more intense pain; yet any positive number represented some pain. In other words, adding a segment with less severe pain, which represented a *relative* improvement at the end (4), improved rather than hurt the overall evaluations of discomfort. Other examples of dominance violations were documented in a cold water study (Kahneman et al. 1993), and for patients undergoing medical procedures (Redelmeier and Kahneman 1996).

Although such results could be taken to indicate a complete neglect of duration, Ariely and Loewenstein (2000, see also Ariely, Kahneman, and Loewenstein 2000) pointed out that all one can conclude from dominance violations is that subjects neither base their summary evaluations on the integral (sum) of pleasure or pain nor on a simple average (in which each is weighted equally). In fact, deviations from integration or simple averaging—such as giving special weight to peak, end, final slope—can produce violations of dominance, regardless of whether subjects do or do not attend to duration.

The original notion of duration neglect was recently modified to reflect the idea that rather than ignoring or underweighting duration, people do not evaluate sequences in the multiplicative fashion predicted by discounted utility theory—a notion labeled *additive duration effect* (Schreiber and Kahneman 2000). *Additive duration neglect* implies that people do care about duration, but this does not depend on the intensity of the stimuli whose duration is varied. Discounted utility theory, however, predicts that the impact of the duration of an experience depends on its intensity: people presumably would care more about how long a 110-volt shock lasts than about how long a 10-volt shock lasts. Additive duration effect implies that people's aversion to extending a shock would not depend on its intensity, which if true, could lead to undesirable decisions.

Effects of Response Mode on Duration Neglect

The phenomenon of duration neglect is intriguing. An important question both from a theoretical and practical viewpoint is under what circumstances we may expect to observe it. In addressing this issue, Ariely and Loewenstein (2000; see also Ariely, Kahneman, and Loewenstein 2000) point out two mechanisms that may influence the weighting of duration. The first is whether the goal of the judgment is to encode the overall goodness or badness of an event or to facilitate future choices among future events. The second is whether the judgment is comparative or not (compare with Hsee et al. 1999). These two notions are described in what follows.

Ariely and Loewenstein (2000) proposed that while the goal of choice is to maximize one's utility, the goals of encoding are more complex and typically include future use or communicating preferences to others. Under these goals, explicit neglect of duration can be sensible. For example, imagine that a friend asks you, "Overall, how would you rate your recent trip to San Francisco?" In that situation, the suitable answer would not incorporate the trip's duration, since you would mislead your friend were you to rate a trip more positively simply because it lasted longer (except insofar as duration affected your average momentary pleasure from the visit). The typical reason to ask a question of this type is that the questioner is evaluating the desirability of visiting San Francisco for him- or herself. The most useful answer, which would be in line with the questioner's expectations, would offer some average rating of your visit that does not take duration into account. If you responded "wonderful" because you had spent two full weeks of slightly better-than-average days in San Francisco, the questioner would be severely misled. The same would be true if you responded "awful" because you had spent only one though fabulous day in San Francisco. The questioner may not know how long you spent there, and you are unlikely to know in advance how long he or she might spend there were they to go. The questioner indeed may use your answer in part to decide how long to spend in San Francisco.

The argument regarding situations in which you rate extended episodes as input into your own future decisions is similar. For a future decision of whether to repeat a past experience, it seems more useful to encode a summary measure of desirability that does not account for duration. This would allow the decision maker to decide about the duration of the future episode according to the conditions at the time of making that decision. If duration were encoded into the stored representation of desirability, and a decision maker were deciding whether to experience a new episode of different duration from the one he or she had experienced, the new judgment would require the decision maker to partial out the effect of duration from the evaluation recalled, then combine the new duration into it. Such an adjustment requires storing additional information (for example, the duration of the original episode) and in practice is difficult to perform.

The second factor mentioned by Ariely and Loewenstein (2000) is whether the nature of the judgment is comparative or not (for extensive discussion of difficulties in judging attributes in isolation see Hsee et al. 1999; Nowlis and Simonson 1997). Duration may be an attribute difficult to judge in isolation without direct comparison to other events. In such situations, norm theory (Kahneman and Miller 1986) suggests that each evaluation will automatically evoke a norm of comparison—even if the judgment is not explicitly comparative. In rating a visit to the Grand Canyon, for example, people are likely to compare it to some other long trips they took. People are less likely to compare their San Francisco trip to a dinner or sports event. The same notions apply to duration. When evaluating a particular morning's commute, people are unlikely to evaluate it relative to a recent cross-country drive. Duration is one of many variables that people use to classify stimuli for purposes of scale-norming. If people indeed norm on the duration of an experience (comparing short experiences to other short experiences and long experiences to other long experiences), then observing a neglect of duration will follow by design.

To examine these issues Ariely and Loewenstein (2000) conducted a study using four different elicitation methods that varied on whether they involved ratings or choices, and whether evaluations were comparative or separate (see table 11.1). As figure 11.2 shows, results suggest that both factors are important to the weight respondents placed on duration. The role of duration appears to increase when responses are comparative rather than separate, and also when responses involve choices rather than ratings. Additional evidence for the effect of separate versus comparative judgments comes from re-

Table 11.1   Summary of Four Elicitation Methods

	Rating	Decision
Separate evaluation	Experiment 1 (Separate ratings)	Experiment 2 (WTA)
Comparative evaluation	Experiment 3 (Rating relative to standard)	Experiment 4 (Choice)

Source: Ariely and Loewenstein (2000).

cent work by Sonnenschein and Shizgal (2001). In their experiments, rats working for brain stimulation placed much greater weight on the duration of stimulation when the length of the reward could be compared to other rewards. When rewards were presented separately, the role of their duration was vastly diminished. Note that the role of other gestalt characteristics such as the slope, final intensity, and peak intensity did not differ across the four different elicitation modes, suggesting that the role of duration is unique both in its sensitivity to different response modes and with regard to how it is used.

Is Underweighing Duration an Error?

The relatively low impact of duration on overall evaluations (see figure 11.2) may suggest that people underweigh duration. This assumes, however, a normative model of how duration should be integrated, and what that normative model would be is not clear. One complication is that people derive utility not only from the experience in and of itself but also from anticipation and memories of the experience (Loewenstein and Elster 1992). Since these sources of utility can be significant, to prefer a longer sequence of pain (with a larger integral of utility) could be perfectly reasonable, which leads to less disutility from memory or anticipation. To the extent that pleasure or pain from memory and anticipation are not themselves influenced by duration, to weigh duration less heavily in choice can be normatively defensible. Thus to prefer a longer colonoscopy that ends on a good note to a shorter one that ends in excruciating pain can make good sense if the longer procedure is remembered more favorably, or if the next one is dreaded less, even if the sum of discomfort during the longer procedure is greater.

Even if one could measure utility from memory and anticipation, however, which would be exceedingly difficult, whether utility integration is a compelling normative principle would still be question-

Figure 11.2   Responses of Four Elicitation Methods

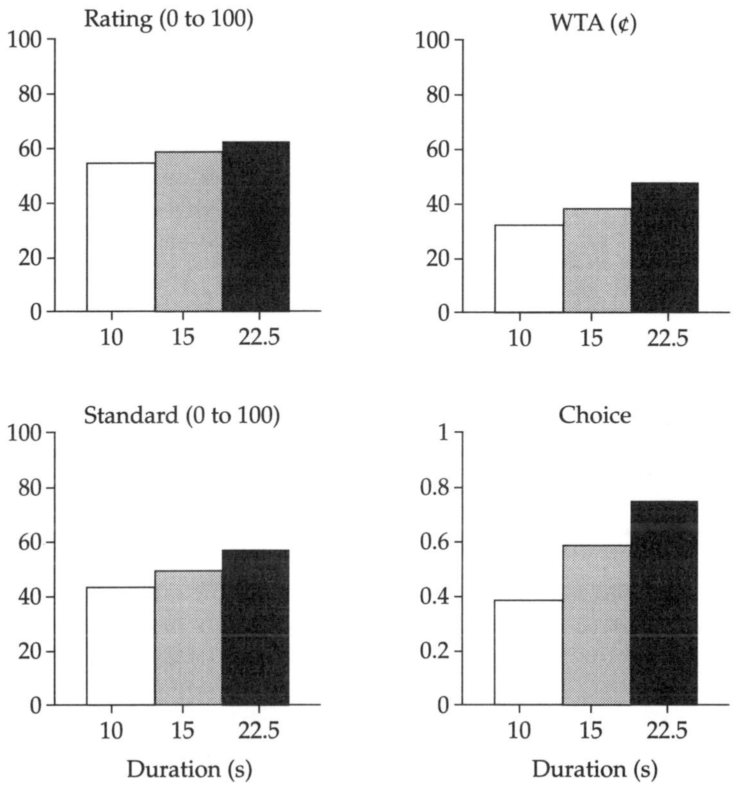

Source: Authors' configuration.
Note: Responses for the four experiments of Ariely and Loewenstein (2000), plotted separately for each experiment, and each duration. The four experiments were: 1) Ratings: ratings overall annoyance on a 0 to 100 scale. 2) Standard: ratings overall annoyance on a 0 to 100 scale, relative to a constant known standard that was 50. 3) WTA: minimum willingness to accept payments (¢) in exchange for the sounds. 4) Choice: choice of each sound relative to a constant known standard. The measures are plotted in the original response scale. Mean annoyance on a 0 to 100 scale for the Ratings and Standard experiments. A monetary scale (¢) for the WTA experiment and the proportion of choice of the standard over the focal stimuli in the choice experiment.

able. For many normative rules of choice, such as dominance (if *A* is better than *B* on all dimensions, then choose *A*) or transitivity (if *A* is preferred to *B* and *B* is preferred to *C*, then *A* should be preferred to *C*), many people are persuaded that the rule should be followed after it is explained to them, and they generally want to change their behavior if they are made aware that they violated the rule. This is not the case for utility integration. People often deviate dramatically from utility integration in prospective studies of preferences for sequences (for example, Loewenstein and Prelec 1993) and they do not tend to change their minds, even when the logic of doing so is explained (Loewenstein and Sicherman 1991). People do care about properties of sequences other than the integral of utility that they provide, and that they do so knowingly and unapologetically should make us wary of labeling their preference a bias. We propose that future work explore in depth how and when duration is (and should be) integrated into overall judgments, both from descriptive and prescriptive perspectives.

Conditions Influencing the Weighting of Duration

We offer the following two distinctions to help understand effects of duration on summary evaluation of experiences. First, when attention is drawn to the duration of an experience, its role clearly increases. This can occur when duration of the experience is an important characteristic (for example, in experiences such as childbirth, prison sentences, or a wait in a restaurant; compare with Carmon et al. 1995), or when a comparison across experiences is explicit, such as comparing a twenty-minute to a forty-minute massage. A second factor is the extent to which duration is inherent to (that is, an integral aspect of) the experience. To illustrate, the duration of an afternoon walk is fairly extrinsic to the experience, and a person thus can decide at any point during the walk about its desired duration. This is not as true of an experience such as a movie or cruise, as the duration of such experiences is more inherent.

The extent to which people will weigh duration depends on a combination of these two factors. We suggest that people will weigh duration least when attention is not drawn to this attribute and when duration of experience is extrinsic to the experiences. In other cases, duration will be weighed more heavily. The role of duration in real decisions therefore depends on what form these factors take in day-to-day decisions (ecological validity).

Toward an Understanding of Why Gestalt Characteristics Matter

The significance of the defining features (gestalt characteristics) of experiences in predicting summary assessments is by now widely accepted. A remaining research challenge is to understand why, how, and when these gestalt characteristics are important. We propose that reliance on gestalt characteristics has two main functions: efficiency in memory and ability to predict future states. Here we describe each of these in turn.

Memory Efficiency

One role of summary evaluations may be to cope with people's cognitive limitations, requiring highly efficient representation of the many detailed characteristics of stimuli such as experienced events. We believe that the notion that people retain key features may be true not only for the assessment of experiences. To illustrate, in a recent study Ariely (2001) showed respondents sets of circles of dissimilar sizes for a brief duration of 500 milliseconds (ms), followed by a single circle also displayed for a period of 500 ms. In some trials, participants were asked to indicate whether they had seen a circle of particular size within the set of circles they were previously shown (that is, if a circle of that size was "a member of the set"). In other trials, participants were asked to indicate whether the single circle was larger or smaller than the mean of the "set" of circles shown in the previous exposure. The results showed that as the number of circles in a set increased, recognition of individual circles (that is, correctly answering questions as to whether the particular circle had been a member of the set of circles shown) dropped rapidly to chance level, but recognition of the mean of the set remained precise. Moreover, respondents appeared to have a good sense of the distribution (variance) of the sizes.

We find it interesting that even with simple visual stimuli, people seem to extract and retain a few key statistics rather than the original complete set of information. Note that in order to represent information efficiently, the visual system "could have" either represented all the information at low resolution (in less detail) or represented highly accurate statistical properties of the stimuli. That the visual system developed to represent statistical properties accurately suggests to us that there is an advantage to statistical representation, perhaps also in domains other than visual perception.

The application of these ideas to gestalt characteristics of prolonged experiences is straightforward. For many situations, parsimonious representation of experiences with a few key characteristics seems reasonable and highly adaptive. The alternative—representing and retaining each of the individual transient states of an experience—may demand too many cognitive resources and offer only marginal benefits. Thus representation by statistical properties seems efficient and effective. The focus on specific statistics of the peak and the end seems adaptive because the peak is the aspect of experience that may often signal the extent to which the experience may be risky, and the ending can often seem important for learning about the effectiveness of the course of action.

Predicting Future States

Another important goal of assessing and summarizing experiences is to facilitate effective decisions by helping to predict future states. To illustrate, imagine a patient undergoing a painful and long medical treatment that becomes less painful over time. Based on aspects such as a trend of decreasing pain, the patient may extrapolate that the future is likely to be less painful, or even infer that he or she is closer to recovery. This extrapolation-based explanation can help us understand why dynamic (configural) aspects of the experience (that is, the manner in which its intensity evolved, such as trend) and the final state (end) are emphasized in summary assessments. The key is that these gestalt characteristics may help—or seem to help—predict future states.

We propose *naive extrapolation* as an underlying concept that can explain the strong preference for improving sequences (see Loewenstein 1987 for related ideas). The notion is that decision makers naturally incorporate into their evaluations their expectations for the future, which they draw from how experiences progress over time. Hence decision makers extrapolate the progression of experiences over time to predict their future state (even if the experience terminates). The notion of naive extrapolation is based on the ideas that decision makers assess implications of the present state for the future, and that the anticipation of future states is incorporated into current evaluations. In the area of pain, for instance, decision makers who experience an increasing pattern of pain are likely to predict that the pain will continue to escalate (or remain high); and this prediction, because of its anticipated negativity, is likely to make the present experience feel worse. Note that this incorporation of future states would be reasonable if the task indeed called for such predictions. We believe, however, that decision makers do so even when there is no apparent reason to do so, and even when they clearly are asked for retrospective evaluations—explicitly instructed to ignore the future and evaluate only the past. We refer to this as the *naive extrapolation hypothesis*.

Currently, the evidence for the naive extrapolation view is very limited. Two experiments by Ariely and Zauberman (2002) are consistent with this idea. In one experiment, the authors showed that breaking an experience into segments reduces the effect of the trend (improvement versus deterioration). The argument is that if people extrapolate from a trend, partitioning will decrease this tendency and thus reduce the impact of trend on summary evaluation. In a second, more direct experimental test, the authors asked respondents not to provide overall evaluations but instead to predict the future state of the hedonic profile. The results showed that manipulations that decreased participants' tendency to extrapolate (partitioning and increased unpredictability) also decreased the effects of the trend of the experiences on overall evaluations. The tentative conclusion is that at least to some degree, people automatically extrapolate the meaning of their current experiences to future ones, and that these extrapolations influence how they experience the present.

Why the Past May Seem Different Than When It Was Present

An interesting aspect of summary assessments of experiences not well understood is the drastic change in how people view some experiences retrospectively compared to how they felt as the events took place. Rosy retrospective sentiments about one's military service, a stormy former romantic relationship, or what the aging refer to as "the good old days," to name a few examples, may well be vastly distorted. Those "misguided" feelings are often supported by specific memories that are consistent with the sentiment but distort what was actually experienced. The memories may be a result of selective recollection and suppression of true events, significant misrepresentation of other events, and possibly even mental construction of events that never actually happened but eventually seem real nevertheless.

Loewenstein (1999) offers several examples of how differently people sometimes think of and remember a past experience compared with how they felt about it as it was taking place. In an illuminating essay about the utility people derive from mountaineering experiences, Loewenstein cites descriptions of conditions people undergo in this activity as "harshly uncomfortable, miserable and exhausting." To explain why people nevertheless engage in such an activity, he further cites descriptions of the change in perspective between the way the activity is experienced as it occurs and how it is remembered after it is over. For example, Simpson, a renowned climber, reports that his perspective changed almost instantly after he reached the top of a mountain. "On the summit my memory edited out the anxiety and tension and fed me happy recollections of superb climbing." Stroud, a famous arctic explorer, offers similar observations. "Even though I can clearly remember saying to myself every day of the journey: 'I must never do this again' I don't feel now as I did then. The memory deficit is playing its tricks already."

Loewenstein's essay suggests that such experiences may be undesirable as they take place but have desirable value (perhaps symbolic) after they end. He further lists a variety of reasons for "consuming" an experience other than for its own sake or for the sake of its direct outcomes. The notion is that in some instances the ending of an experience gives it special meaning. How people feel as the experiences take place therefore may have little to do with how they assess and perhaps even remember the same experiences in retrospect. One such symbolic goal could be self-signaling (see Bodner and Prelec 2001; Dhar and Wertenbroch 2002), whereby a difficult activity can "reveal character." Loewenstein suggests that "This desire for a harsh test . . . along with poor memory for misery, may help explain why the most miserable trips often produce the best memories; pain and discomfort are, to some degree, the *point* of the trip." Completion is another goal that could be related to self-signaling, because the completion of a task defines the task as a whole and thus the value of self-signaling rises mostly from completing a task and not from simply engaging in it. Mastery is yet another goal, about which Loewenstein says, "It is generally pleasant to engage in an activity that you are good at, no matter how useless it might be . . . it is typically aversive to do something you are incompetent at, no matter how instrumental the activity" (319). Finally, Loewenstein also lists the search for meaning of life as a goal whose pursuit could undermine momentary utility and memory.

In a different approach to the same general topic, Tykocinski (2001) suggests that there are instances in which people may alter how they assess an experience after it is over to maintain how they feel about themselves (rather than to enhance it, as in Loewenstein's examples). Specifically, she observes that "pointing out that a tragic event was inescapable, or somehow 'bound to happen,' appears to be a popular tool in our solace repertoire." She proposes that to make disappointing events more palatable, people sometimes alter perceived probabilities of relevant events after the fact. The underlying goal is to help deal with the unpleasant event by making it appear almost inevitable as well as making more positive outcomes seem highly unlikely. This idea offers another possible reason for substantial discrepancies between perceptions of experiences before, during, and after they take place—self-deception.

Such motivated biases in memory can be different for different types of experience profiles and different levels of gestalt characteristics. To the extent that some of the gestalt characteristics are more memorable than others, memory distortions are likely to occur more frequently and rapidly (and with less mental effort) for those aspects of the experience profile that are not remembered well. Such less-remembered aspects could be the parts of experience not captured by gestalt characteristics—or by gestalt characteristics that are not very salient (a low peak, low level of improvement, and so on).

Directions for Future Research

In this section, we highlight a few directions for future research that we view as important for better understanding assessments of experiences, and end with a few concluding thoughts.

Ending Effects

As described earlier, people sometimes view experiences very differently after the fact compared with how they felt as those experiences took place. We propose that future research explore when, why, and how such retrospective "reinterpretation" of experiences tends to happen. One specific approach would be to empirically explore ideas described in Loewenstein (1999) about effects of goals people might pursue as they undertake an activity. One could test, for instance, whether the extent to which an experience has a symbolic value and the degree to which the final goal was achieved influences the ways in which decision makers combine the experience profile into overall evaluations.

The effects of endings may be important not only when goal attainment is defined by the final part of an experience, but also because endings define the boundary of the experience. Moreover, ending points are likely to be natural points in which decision makers summarize their experiences (Ariely and Zauberman 2000). A change in motivation toward the end has been noted in rats and pigeons who increase their effort as a function of temporal distance from the end of the experience—a pattern known as scalloping—even when the increased behavior does not improve their payoffs (Ferster and Skinner 1957). In humans, the effects of endings have been reported to influence many different behaviors, including impatience (Ceci and Bronfenbrenner 1985), the propensity to get agreement in negotiation (Roth, Murnighan, and Schoumaker 1988), as well as bidding behaviors in online auctions (Roth and Ockenfels forthcoming).

To test such effects of endings, consider the following possible experiment (compare with Fredrickson 1991): subjects evaluating an experience occasionally would be prompted to indicate intermediate summary evaluations (a summary of their experience up until that point in time). At some point a subset of the subjects would be told that they had reached the end of the experience and asked to provide the final summary assessment, whereas others would be led to believe that they were merely providing another intermediate summary evaluation. Comparing evaluations across such a manipulation may offer insights into how assessments change when the end is reached.

The effects of endings can be important not only in retrospect but also prospectively. We find it interesting, for example, that patients are often very keen to know when their pain will end or how long treatment will last, even though such knowledge would not alter the actual events they will experience. What value such information may offer and how advance knowledge about the end can reduce the pain are interesting and important questions. Possible underlying factors include perceived control, allocation of coping resources, and decreased tendency to naively extrapolate (see earlier discussion for related ideas). Support for such notions is apparent even from casual observations of people who exercise. Such people routinely want to know how they are doing in relation to their goals to assess how much effort is required to accomplish them. This knowledge presumably can help sustain motivation and increase the probability of achieving the goal.

In a small test of this notion, sixty people exercising in a gym were asked to stretch their dominant arm to the side of their body (parallel to the ground) holding a five-pound weight for as long as they could. The duration for each participant I was recorded and termed X_i. Once participants could no longer hold the weight, they were immediately asked to repeat the process using the other (nondominant) arm. This time, however, the task was to hold the weight for a duration of $X_i + 30$ (thirty seconds longer than they had been able to hold with their stronger arm). Participants were randomly assigned to one of three conditions. In the up-counting condition, the experimenter counted each passing second aloud (from 1 until the time goal, $X + 30$, or until the participant stopped of his or her own accord). In the down-counting condition, the experimenter counted the seconds aloud (from $X_i + 30$ down to 0, or until the participant stopped of his or her own accord). In the no-counting condition, the experimenter provided a free association every second, effectively preventing participants from knowing how they were doing in relation to their goal.

Results show that the different counting conditions greatly influenced how long participants were able to hold the weight with their nondominant arm [$F(2,57) = 43.48$, p < 0.001; all the pairwise differences p $< .001$]. Participants in the down-counting condition managed to hold the weight for the longest time (24.7 seconds longer than with their dominant arm, which was 5.3 seconds less than the requested goal). Participants in the up-counting condition managed to hold the weight for a shorter time (5 seconds more than with their dominant arm, which was 25 seconds less than the requested goal). Participants in the no-counting condition managed to hold the weight for less than participants in the other two conditions. In fact, whereas those in the other conditions were able to hold the weight longer with their nondominant arm, this was not true of participants in the no-counting condition (22.6 seconds less than with their dominant arm, which was 52.6 seconds less than the requested goal). Note that across the conditions only two participants reached the goal, and the results hold if these two respondents are eliminated from the analysis—indicating that it is not simply having a known end point that causes people to reach their goal. In sum, these results show that knowing the end (comparing the up-counting and down-counting conditions versus the no-counting condition) increases tolerance. They also show that having a clearer view of an end point (the 0 in the down-counting condition compared with the $X_i + 30$ in the up-counting condition) further increases tolerance.

Several questions arise from these findings. Why does knowledge of the end point improve coping ability and motivation? What tools can we provide patients to better cope with pain and thereby diminish it? Does the improved coping ability (caused by knowing when the end will arrive) hold for all time frames—is this knowledge as beneficial for a duration of months, weeks, hours, and minutes? Moreover, once the end point has been identified, do the benefits of knowing it increase as time goes by and the end draws nearer? Clearly, more research on the psychological effects of "end-knowledge" regarding endurance and coping ability is needed.

Memory Effects

A research topic related to the effects of endings is how summary assessments and memories associated with them change as a function of the temporal distance from the event: soon after the experience is over, some time afterward, and long after that. For example, would the memory decay be the same for the different gestalt characteristics, or would some gestalt characteristics decay and be forgotten faster than others?

The effects of time may not be limited to memory decay. As suggested by the work of Loewenstein (1999) and Tykocinski (2001), memories of experiences may be constructed in a manner that ignores significant aspects of the original experience, thereby associating different meanings with the experience. Thus to go beyond merely examining the accuracy of overall evaluations of such experiences is important, as well as to assess whether the discrepancies are a result of distortions of specific aspects of the experiences.

Finally, memory can also change the grouping of different experiences into experience profiles. A simple example is that shortly after a vacation, each day in memory may be perceived as an independent experience, while a few years later the boundaries of the individual days may well be blurry and the vacation is likely to be perceived as a single experience. Such grouping effects are not limited to blurry boundaries and can also occur as the meaning of experiences changes. For example, the integration of a single date with the rest of one's relationship with a romantic partner might depend on the length, success, and variability of the relationship.

The Evaluated Dimensions

Another potentially interesting direction for future research is to examine different dimensions of people's evaluations of experiences. Research to date has mostly focused on a single measure of affect: the extent to which one feels positively or negatively about the experience. Yet as discussed earlier, people's motives for pursuing an experience sometimes have little to do with how well it makes them feel as it takes place. In such cases, it may be more productive to examine real-time momentary assessments that relate more directly to the goal the person is pursuing in that instance. The correspondence between the summary assessment of the experience and real-time experience profiles on those dimensions (rather than the affective experience profile) may be more related to each other. If you consider Loewenstein's mountaineering examples, for instance, measuring the experience profile on dimensions such as mastery or goal completion may be more informative than how positively or negatively the person feels as the experience progresses.

Another potential avenue for future investigations is based on research that has identified common coexistence of several distinct types of emotions (it has been suggested, for example, that pain and pleasure are distinct emotions that do not define ends of one continuum). There is no reason to believe that those independent types of emotions would necessarily evolve in the same way throughout an event or even be summarized in the same fashion. In some situations, summary assessments of an experience may therefore be better predicted based on some weighted average of experience profiles along different emotions. In conclusion, while an overall measure of emotions (such as that used in most research on hegemonic integration to date) may often capture much of the needed information effectively, exceptional cases are likely, such as experiences that evoke mixed (conflicting) emotions.

Types of Experiences

Much of the research that explicitly measured experience profiles and examined how they correspond to their summary assessments has focused on unpleasant events. Examples of types of experiences that have been investigated include discomfort (Kahneman et al. 1993; Ariely and Zauberman 2000; Schreiber and Kahneman 2000; Ariely and Loewenstein 2000), medical procedures (Ariely and Carmon 2000; Redelmeier and Kahneman 1996; Katz, Redelmeier, and Kahneman 1997), queuing experiences (Carmon and Kahneman 2000), and pain (Ariely 1998). Yet pleasant experiences have received little attention. One reason pleasant experiences have hardly been investigated is that to cause pleasure to people in a controlled manner is difficult. Food and sex, for example—two major causes of pleasure—are not monotonic with stimulation intensity; that is, more of these two experiences is not always better, and it is hard to control in the lab.

Little attention as well has been devoted to mixed experiences that are at times pleasant and at other times unpleasant (compare with Kahneman 1992). Experiences also can be mixed in other ways. Largely unrelated events may co-occur, for example. One may experience pain in one part of the body and pleasure in another; or one can watch a good movie in the cinema while feeling the urge to urinate. How people would summarize such mixtures of events is not at all obvious. More generally, investigating how people summarize different types and combinations of experiences may help identify additional moderating variables and border conditions. Such research is likely to provide further insights about summary assessments of experiences.

Conclusion

Roughly a decade of extensive research activity on the relationship between how events are experienced as they occur and how they are retrospectively summarized has resulted in a considerable body of knowledge. In this chapter we offered a critical overview of selected aspects of this literature and summarized a handful of findings that are widely accepted. In particular, we described central features of experiences (gestalt characteristics) that seem to govern summary evaluations of those events, and identified variables that can moderate those effects. We next discussed the weighting of the duration of experiences in summary evaluations, and listed variables that could affect this weighting. We continued with a discussion of why the gestalt characteristics we described earlier influence summary evaluations, and proposed ideas about why some experiences are remembered very differently from how they were experienced as they occurred. We concluded by presenting directions for potential future research.

A more complete theory of summary assessments of experiences could offer a better understanding of people's preferences in a very broad variety of domains. Beyond obvious theoretical value, this could have important practical implications, since many types of experiences can be delivered in different ways and can perhaps be structured in a manner that is more effective. Examples of experiences that may benefit from insights about summary evaluations include entertainment events, service encounters (compare with Carmon et al. 1995), medical procedures (compare with Ariely 1998, Redelmeier and Kahneman 1996), and possibly even how people prefer their lives to end (compare with Diener, Wirtz, and Oishi 2001). There may even be ways to write chapters that leave their readers with very favorable overall assessments.

The ideas described in this paper draw on work we have conducted in this domain over the past few years. We draw heavily on ideas developed in Ariely and Carmon (2000) and Ariely and Loewenstein (2000).

Note

1.   Ariely (1998) notes that it is an open question whether people have both momentary and global evaluations and how independent they are.

References

Ariely, Dan. 1998. "Combining Experiences over Time: The Effects of Duration, Intensity Changes and On-Line Measurements on Retrospective Pain Evaluations." *Journal of Behavioral Decision Making* 11: 19–45.

———. 2001. "Seeing Sets: Representation by Statistical Properties." *Psychological Science* 12(2): 157–62.

Ariely, Dan, and Ziv Carmon. 2000. "Gestalt Characteristics of Experiences: The Defining Features of Summarized Events." *Journal of Behavioral Decision Making* 13(2): 191–201.

Ariely, Dan, Daniel Kahneman, and George Loewenstein. 2000. "Joint Commentary on the Importance of Duration in Ratings of, and Choices Between, Sequences of Outcomes." *Journal of Experimental Psychology: General* 129(4): 524–29.

Ariely, Dan, and George Loewenstein. 2000. "When Does Duration Matter in Judgment and Decision Making?" *Journal of Experimental Psychology: General* 129(4): 508–23.

Ariely, Dan, and Gal Zauberman. 2000. "On the Making of an Experience: The Effects of Breaking and Combining Experiences on Their Overall Evaluation." *Journal of Behavioral Decision Making* 13(2): 219–32.

———. 2002. "Differential Partitioning of Extended Experiences." Massachusetts Institute of Technology working paper, Cambridge, Mass.

Bodner, Ronit, and Drazen Prelec. 2001. "Self-Signaling and Diagnostic Utility in Everyday Decision Making." In *Collected Essays in Psychology and Economics*, edited by Isabelle Brocas and Juan Carillo. Oxford: Oxford University Press.

Carmon, Ziv, and Daniel Kahneman. 2000. "The Experienced Utility of Queuing: Real Time Affect and Retrospective Evaluations of Simulated Queues." Working paper. INSEAD, France.

Carmon, Ziv, J. George Shanthikumar, and Tali F. Carmon. 1995. "A Psychological Perspective on Service Segmentation: The Significance of Accounting for Consumers' Perceptions of Waiting and Service." *Management Science* 41(11): 1806–15.

Ceci, Stephen J., and Urie Bronfenbrenner. 1985. "Don't Forget to Take the Cupcakes Out of the Oven: Prospective Memory, Strategic Time-Monitoring, and Context." *Child Development* 56(1): 152–64.

Chapman, Gretchen B. 1996. "Expectations and Preferences for Sequences of Health and Money." *Organizational Behavior and Human Decision Processes* 67: 59–75.

———. 2000. "Preferences for Improving and Declining Sequences of Health Outcomes." *Journal of Behavioral Decision Making* 13(2): 203–18.

Dhar, Ravi, and Klaus Wertenbroch. 2002. "The Costs and Benefits of Temptation: Choice Set Effects on Consumption Utility." Working paper. INSEAD, France.

Diener, Ed, Derrick Wirtz, and Shigehiro Oishi. 2001. "End Effects of Rated Life Quality: The James Dean Effect." *Psychological Science* 12(2): 124–28.

Ferster, Charles B., and B. F. Skinner, 1957. *Schedules of Reinforcement.* New York: Appleton-Century-Croft.

Fredrickson, Barbara L. 1991. "Anticipated Endings: An Explanation for Selective Social Interaction." Ph.D. diss., Stanford University.

Fredrickson, Barbara L., and Daniel Kahneman. 1993. "Duration Neglect in Retrospective Evaluations of Affective Episodes." *Journal of Personality and Social Psychology* 65: 45–55.

———. 2000. "Extracting Meaning from Past Affective Experiences: The Importance of Peaks, Ends, and Specific Emotions." *Cognition and Emotion* 14(4): 577–606.

Hsee, Christopher K., and Robert P. Abelson. 1991. "Velocity Relation: Satisfaction as a Function of the First Derivative of Outcome over Time." *Journal of Personality and Social Psychology* 60: 341–47.

Hsee, Christopher K., George Loewenstein, Sally Blount, and Max Bazerman. 1999. "Preference Reversals Between Joint and Separate Evaluations of Options: A Theoretical Analysis." *Psychological Bulletin* 125 (5): 576–90.

Hsee, Christopher K., Peter Salovey, and Robert P. Abelson. 1994. "The Quasi-Acceleration Relation: Satisfaction as a Function of the Change of Velocity of Outcome over Time." *Journal of Experimental Social Psychology* 30: 96–111.

Huber, Joel, John G. Lynch, Jr., Kim Corfman, Jack Feldman, Morris Holbrook, Don Lehmann, Bertrand Munier, David Schkade, and Itamar Simonson. 1997. "Thinking About Values in Prospect and in Retrospect: Maximizing Experienced Utility." *Marketing Letters* 8(2): 323–34.

Kahneman, Daniel. 1992. "Reference Points, Anchors, Norms, and Mixed Feelings." *Organizational Behavior and Human Decision Processes* 51: 296–312.

———. 2000. "Evaluation by Moments: Past and Future." In *Choices Values and Frames*, edited by Daniel Kahneman and Amos Tversky. New York: Cambridge University Press.

Kahneman, Daniel, Barbara L. Fredrickson, Charles A. Schreiber, and Donald A. Redelmeier. 1993. "When More Pain Is Preferred to Less: Adding a Better End." *Psychological Science* 4: 401–5.

Kahneman, Daniel, and Dale T. Miller. 1986. "Norm Theory: Comparing Reality to Its Alternatives." *Psychological Review* 93: 136–53.

Kahneman, Daniel, Peter P. Wakker, and Rakesh Sarin. 1997. "Back to Bentham? Explorations of Experienced Utility." *Quarterly Journal of Economics* 112: 375–405.

Katz, Joel, Donald A. Redelmeier, and Daniel Kahneman. 1997. "Memories of Painful Medical Procedures." Paper presented to the meeting of the American Pain Society. Washington, D.C. (November 26).

Kundera, Milan. 1991. *Immortality*. New York: Grove Press.

Langer, Thomas, Rakesh Sarin, and Martin Weber. 2000. "The Retrospective Evaluation of Payment Sequences: Duration Neglect, Peak and End Effects." Working paper. Manheim University.

Loewenstein, George. 1987. "Anticipation and the Valuation of Delayed Consumption." *Economic Journal* 97: 666–84.

Loewenstein, George. 1999. "Because It's There: The Challenge of Mountaineering . . . for Utility Theory." *Kyklos* 52: 315–44.

Loewenstein, George, and Jon Elster. 1992. *Choice Over Time*. New York: Russell Sage Foundation.

Loewenstein, George, and Drazen Prelec. 1991. "Negative Time Preference." *American Economic Review: Papers and Proceedings* 82(2): 347–52.

———. 1993. "Preferences for Sequences of Outcomes." *Psychological Review* 100: 91–108.

Loewenstein, George, and Nachum Sicherman. 1991. "Do Workers Prefer Increasing Wage Profiles?" *Journal of Labor Economics* 9: 67–84.

Nowlis, Stephen M., and Itamar Simonson. 1997. "Attribute-Task Compatibility as a Determinant of Consumer Preference Reversals." *Journal of Marketing Research* 34: 205–18.

Read, Daniel, and Melanie Powell. Forthcoming. "Reasons for Sequence Preferences." *Journal of Behavioral Decision Making*.

Redelmeier, Donald A., and Daniel Kahneman. 1996. "Patients' Memories of Painful Medical Treatments: Real-Time and Retrospective Evaluations of Two Minimally Invasive Procedures." *Pain* 66: 3–8.

Ross, William T., Jr., and Itamar Simonson. 1991. "Evaluations of Pairs of Experiences: A Preference for Happy Endings." *Journal of Behavioral Decision Making* 4: 273–82.

Roth, Alvin E., J. K. Murnighan, and Francoise Schoumaker. 1988. "The Deadline Effect in Bargaining: Some Experimental Evidence." *American Economic Review* 78 (4): 806–23.

Roth, Alvin E., and Axel Ockenfels. Forthcoming. "Last-Minute Bidding and the Rules for Ending Second-Price Auctions: Evidence from eBay and Amazon Auctions on the Internet." *American Economic Review*.

Schreiber, Charles A., and Daniel Kahneman. 2000. "Determinants of the Remembered Utility of Aversive Sounds." *Journal of Experimental Psychology: General* 129: 27–42.

Sonnenschein, Bonnie.H., and Peter Shizgal. 2001. "Preference Reversals Displayed by Laboratory Rats Working for Rewarding Brain Stimulation." Society for Judgment and Decision-Making Conference, Orlando, Fla (November 14).

Trope, Yaacov, and Nira Liberman. 2000. "Temporal Construal Theory of Time-Dependent Preferences." In *Economics and Psychology*, edited by Isabelle Brocas and Juan D. Carrillo. New York: Oxford University Press.

Tykocinski, Orit E. 2001. "I Never Had a Chance: Using Hindsight Tactics to Mitigate Disappointment." *Personality and Social Psychology Bulletin* 27: 376–82.

Varey, Carol A., and Daniel Kahneman. 1992. "Experiences Extended Across Time: Evaluation of Moments and Episodes." *Journal of Behavioral Decision Making* 5: 169–85.

· 12

Predicting and Indulging Changing Preferences

GEORGE LOEWENSTEIN AND ERIK ANGNER

The one thing I could be sure of was that I had to leave this apartment, where I had never known a moment's peace of mind, as soon as possible. . . . The trouble, the rub, was that I had to give three months' notice and therefore had to predict how I would be feeling three months hence, which was very difficult. It was all very well deciding today that I wanted to leave but what counted was how I was going to be feeling three months from now. You could be perfectly happy today, I would say to myself, and three months from now you could be suicidal, precisely because you will see the enormity of the mistake you made months earlier.

—Geoff Dyer, *Out of Sheer Rage*

DECISIONS, from the most mundane to the most momentous, often involve a *prediction of future preferences*. Whether one is shopping for groceries, contemplating whether to "tie" the knot, or (as in the epigraph) deciding whether to sign the lease on an apartment, the feelings and tastes that matter may not be those one currently has but rather those that one anticipates having when the consequences of the decision are experienced. Mispredicting future preferences can result in diverse negative consequences, from uneaten groceries to painful divorces to the suicidal feeling of being trapped for another year in an apartment one detests.

The trouble—as Dyer puts it, the *rub*—is that predicting preferences is difficult. The difficulties stem in part from the fact that determinants of tastes are complex and poorly understood. Though social scientists have devoted whole careers to studying the formation of

351

preferences, progress has been painfully slow. To date there is little agreement about the sources of even the most fundamental preferences—for example, for food, drink, and sex. Given the lack of progress by social scientists, the fact—documented by research reviewed here—that people have trouble predicting how their preferences will change should come as no surprise.

The difficulties people have in predicting their future preferences are exacerbated by the fact that to imagine having tastes that are substantially different from those we have at the moment is challenging. We have a tendency to believe that our current tastes and preferences reflect objective features of the external world to a larger extent than they actually do. As Adam Smith (2000 [1759], 283) observed almost two hundred and fifty years ago,

> Few men . . . are willing to allow, that custom or fashion have much influence upon their judgments concerning what is beautiful, or otherwise. [Rather, they] imagine that all the rules which they think ought to be observed . . . are founded upon reason and nature, not upon habit or prejudice.

Ross and Ward (1996) use the term *naive realism* to denote this tendency to believe that our perceptions and tastes are more objective, and hence more universal, than they really are.[1] As a result of our susceptibility to naive realism, current preferences for cars, clothes, music—even body types and intimate relations—simply seem "right," and it is difficult to imagine that were we in a different culture or historical period our preferences might be quite different.

Predicting changes in future preferences is also difficult because tastes and desires are an integral aspect of our personal *identity* (Akerlof and Kranton 2000; Belk 1988; Frederick, chap. 2 herein; Parfit 1971, 1982). People define who they are in part by their tastes and values; imagining oneself with different preferences is therefore similar to imagining oneself as a different person, which is a difficult mental exercise.

Owing to difficulties involved in predicting preferences, mistakes are common (or so we later argue, reviewing available research on the topic). The difficulties just noted here suggest that one kind of mistake will be particularly common: predictions will be too "regressive,"—that is, biased in the direction of current tastes. For example, if people are unaware of certain sources of preference change, they are likely to underestimate the magnitude of changes caused by that source. Similarly, if people have difficulty imagining having preferences different from their current ones—either because they mistakenly view their current tastes as objective or perceive their current tastes as an integral part of their core identity—then they will tend to underestimate the magnitude of those changes. Indeed research suggests that people are prone to exactly such a regressive bias, referred to by Loewenstein, O'Donoghue, and Rabin (2001) as *projection bias*.

Analyses of shifting preferences by economists and decision researchers typically assume that people want to satisfy whatever preferences they expect to hold at the time when the consequences of their decision are enjoyed or suffered (whether or not such analyses acknowledge that people sometimes mispredict their future preferences). This assumption is implicit, for example, in economic models of "habit formation" (Duesenberry 1952; Pollak 1970), including models of addiction (for example, Becker and Murphy 1988). However, the assumption that people attempt to honor future preferences is not always valid. In some cases, people indeed attempt to *deny* their anticipated future preferences. For example, in "cool" moments, people recognize that they may get "hot" in the future and develop transient preferences for things they currently would prefer to avoid (for example, harmful drugs, dangerous sexual practices, or unhealthy foods). To prevent themselves from behaving in this fashion, people sometimes seek to deter themselves from acting on their anticipated future preferences (for example, by taking antabuse, which makes alcohol intake nauseating) or simply remove the undesired behavior from their future choice set (for example, keeping alcohol or tempting snack food out of the house; see Elster 1979; Schelling 1984).

Instead of simply trying to honor the preferences they have or expect to have, people also sometimes attempt to *shape* their own tastes. Rather than attempting to prevent themselves from succumbing to hot future preferences, for example, people sometimes avoid exposing themselves to situations and stimuli that could cause them to become hot, thereby saving themselves from experiencing a transient preference that they do not wish to have. People also sometimes attempt to *refine* their future tastes—for example, they drink fine wines or listen to highbrow music that they don't currently enjoy in the hope of developing a taste for it. To date, very little research has sought to understand the factors that cause people to indulge, deny, or seek to change their own future preferences. Instead most of the attention to this issue has come from philosophers. A later section summarizes this work and attempts to draw out some general conclusions about when people in fact choose to indulge or deny anticipated changes in their tastes. In passing, we also discuss some related normative is sues, namely, under what conditions people *should* indulge or deny anticipated preferences.

Beyond discussing the twin problems of predicting and honoring tastes, this chapter has a third goal, which is to enumerate some of the diverse determinants of preferences and the sources of changes in tastes. This goal is in certain ways more basic, since whether people manage to accurately predict, and whether they choose to honor (or should choose to honor), future preferences may depend on the source of those preferences. Thus an understanding of the determinants of preferences is critical to understanding when people mispredict changes in their own preferences and when they choose to honor or deny such changed preferences.

Sources of Preference Change

Do Preferences Change at All?

In their famous article "De Gustibus Non Est Disputandum," Stigler and Becker (1977, 76) argue that tastes and preferences are stable over time and are identical across people; they write, "tastes neither change capriciously nor differ importantly between people . . . one does not argue over tastes for the same reason that one does not argue over the Rocky Mountains—both are there, will be there next year, too, and are the same to all men." This seemingly obviously false assertion depends crucially on the distinction between two kinds of entities: final preferences (or demand) and underlying preferences (or tastes). Although final preferences may vary, say, when a new fashion appears or when one gets sick of spam after eating too much of it, one can usually identify some set of stable underlying preferences—for example, looking good and experiencing the pleasures of the palate.

Herbert Simon (1981, 58) explicitly challenged the perspective advanced by Stigler and Becker, arguing that the distinction between final and underlying preferences obscures more than it illuminates.

> It is unrealistic to suppose that utility functions are given and remain fixed. New experiences produce new tastes. Some attempts have been made to save the classical theory along this dimension by replacing tangible goods and services as the arguments of the utility function with more basic "wants"—for example, pleasure from music listened to, rather than number of hours of listening. Thus, Becker and Stigler

speak of investing in musical experience to increase the pleasure, per unit of time, in listening to music.

It may be doubted whether anything is gained by trying to rescue the traditional view of utility with such heroic measures. If, to continue the example, we do not wish to speak of a change in utility function as the result of listening to music, then we must postulate within the human head a production function (itself changeable by experience) that manufactures musical pleasure from musical listening. We have merely relocated "taste" from the utility function to that hypothetical new production function. It would seem more parsimonious simply to regard the utility function as an evolving structure.

Clearly, the argument between Stigler and Becker and Simon raises important questions about the proper definition of tastes and taste change. Should momentary changes in behavior—such as those that result from elevated appetites or emotions—be considered to reflect a change in tastes? What about behavior that reflects new information about engaging in some particular activity? Does a friend's suggestion to avoid a certain movie produce a change in tastes, or simply provide us with information that allows us to predict our tastes more accurately? As Stigler and Becker imply, a meaningful distinction exists between fundamental changes in tastes and changes in demand. Our own intellectual proclivities, however, lie more with Simon than with Stigler and Becker. Defining away individual differences and intraindividual changes in preferences only obfuscates the study of taste formation. The problem of predicting and honoring changing preferences remains whether or not we assume that every change in preferences rests on a foundation of stable underlying tastes. On Stigler and Becker's account, predicting such preferences (assuming fundamental tastes are known) boils down to predicting the characteristics of the evolving "production function" mentioned by Simon. We adhere to the more customary terminology, while acknowledging the nontrivial question raised by Stigler and Becker of what forms of changes in demand should rightly be classified as changes in "preferences."

Here we enumerate a number of different determinants of preference, and therefore sources of preference change (see McCauley, Rozin, and Schwartz 2002 for a much more complete treatment). We draw connections between those determinants, by grouping them into broad categories and showing how some of these categories can be modeled using similar mathematical formulations.

Endogenous Change in Tastes: Habit Formation, Satiation, and Refinement

"Endogenous change in tastes" (Hammond 1976) refers to a situation in which what one consumes in the present alters the preferences one has in the future. Within this broad category are several significantly different variants that can be distinguished largely in terms of whether past consumption increases or decreases one's preference for future consumption.

Habit Formation   Habit formation refers to a situation in which consuming a particular substance increases one's preference for it. If s_t is the "habit stock" that summarizes the extent of past consumption of c (with higher values of s corresponding to greater past consumption) and the individual's utility function takes the form $u(c, s)$, then habit formation corresponds to the case in which the marginal utility of c is increasing in s—that is,

$$\frac{\partial^2 u(c_t, s_t)}{\partial c_t \partial s_t} > 0.$$

A common assumption in modeling habit formation (for example, Ryder and Heal 1973, or see Frederick et al., chap. 1 herein) is that the habit stock shifts according to $s_t = \propto s_{t-1} + (1 - \propto) c_t$. At one extreme, when $\propto$ equals 1, then there is no adaptation; the habit stock always remains at whatever level it began. At the opposite extreme, when $\propto$ equals zero, then the habit stock adjusts instantly to the level of consumption in the current period. For intermediate values of $\propto$, this formula implies that s_t is an exponentially weighted sum of past consumption, with more recent consumption given greater weight.

Within the category of habit formation, a distinction is often made between *negative* and *positive* habits. Negative habits—such as harmful addictions—arise when the "habit stock" s has a negative impact on overall utility—that is,

$$\frac{\partial u(c, s)}{\partial s} < 0.$$

Positive habit formation refers to situations in which enhanced liking of certain goods and activities such as good music, fine wine, and so on is thought to enhance overall utility—that is,

$$\frac{\partial u(c, s)}{\partial s} > 0.$$

Satiation   Satiation can be thought of as the opposite of habit formation: it is a situation in which consuming more of a substance decreases its marginal utility. Satiation can be a short-term phenomenon.
For example, after consuming a steak for dinner, one's desire for a
second steak might be minimal or even negative. Yet satiation can
also be a longer-term phenomenon, as might occur after consuming
steak several evenings in a row, or after spending too many summer
vacations in the same spot. Satiation is commonly represented with a
simple utility function that incorporates diminishing marginal utility—that is, $u(c)$, with $u''(c) < 0$. Yet such a formulation is only capable of dealing with the most short-term variant of the phenomenon—
that is, the effect of steak just consumed on the marginal utility of
further consumption of steak; it cannot deal with, for example, the
effect of steak eaten on the previous day on the marginal utility of
steak today.

More complex patterns of satiation can be modeled parsimoniously
using the same state-dependent utility function that is commonly applied to habit formation. Satiation simply corresponds to the case in
which marginal utility is a declining function of the habit stock:

$$\frac{\partial^2 u(c,s)}{\partial c \partial s} < 0,$$

the opposite of the pattern that characterizes habit formation.[2] With
such a formulation, to model the complexities of satiation—for example, by again assuming that s_t is a weighted average of past consumption—is easy. Since satiation diminishes some sources of pleasure
without increasing others, it is probably safe to assume that satiation
decreases (or at least does not increase) an individual's overall utility—that is, that

$$\frac{\partial u(c,s)}{\partial s} \leq 0.$$

Refinement   In addition to habit formation and satiation, it is useful to
distinguish a third pattern of endogenous preference change that
could be termed *refinement*. People often expose themselves to goods
and experiences for the purpose of refining their tastes. There are
various possible interpretations of what refinement involves, but perhaps the most common is that it involves an increase in one's relative
appreciation for higher-quality goods or experiences. If x represents
the quality level of a particular type of good, then refinement would
resemble habit formation in the sense that (though note that this ex-

pression substitutes x—the level of quality—for s, the habit stock). The big difference between positive and negative habit formation on the one hand, and refinement on the other, is in the impact of the habit on overall utility. Presumably, refining one's tastes not only increases one's enjoyment of high-quality goods but also, as illustrated in figure 12.1, decreases one's enjoyment of low-quality goods.

$$\frac{\partial^2 u(c,x)}{\partial c \, \partial x} \geq 0$$

If this is the case, then whether refining one's tastes actually increases overall pleasure will depend on any direct effect of refinement on utility, and on one's budget constraint—that is, on whether one can actually afford the goods for which one's appreciation has been enhanced. If the higher-quality goods one has developed a taste for are unattainably expensive, forcing one to consume goods whose inferiority is now recognized, then refining preferences may not increase utility. Having refined tastes in and of itself may be a source of utility, but certainly it cannot be assumed that having such tastes increases one's overall pleasure from consumption.[3]

Appetites, Emotions, and Other "Visceral Factors"

Tastes are also determined at least in part by biological systems that fluctuate, sometimes dramatically, even over short periods of time. Like other animals, humans are sustained by the operation of numerous homeostatic processes. These processes regulate body temperature, blood pressure, food intake, heart rate, and a whole range of chemical and electrical processes in the body and brain. Homeostatic processes operate by comparing the level of a system that is being regulated (for example, blood oxygenation) to a *set-point*—a desired level. When the actual level of the system departs from the set-point, this triggers processes that shift the system in the direction of the set-point.[4]

A wide range of regulatory processes are devoted to maintaining homeostasis in these diverse systems. Some of these processes are automatic and occur without conscious intention or even knowledge. For example, body temperature is maintained in part by autonomous mechanisms such as sweating; but other processes involve overt, deliberate behaviors. Thus body temperature is also maintained by actions such as turning on the air conditioner or heater or drinking a cold or hot beverage.

People typically are motivated to take these types of homeostasis-

Figure 12.1   Refining Tastes

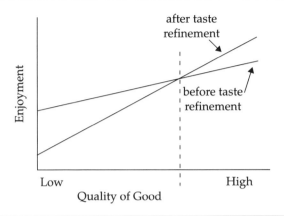

Source: Authors' configuration.

restoring actions through the combined application of a carrot and stick. The stick takes the form of specific discomforts, such as hunger, thirst, and pain that motivate us to take action. The carrot is the increase in pleasure that accompanies such actions. Both effects motivate us to take actions to bring the system back into line. Thus a decrease in our core body temperature produces intense discomfort, and any actions that can increase one's body temperature, such as placing one's hand in a bowl of warm water or drinking a hot beverage, become pleasurable. Our brains in effect produce transient changes in preferences that induce us to take actions to reinstate homeostasis. These combined effects can be modeled with the same state-dependent preferences used to model endogenous change in tastes. If s_t represents the level of a particular homeostatic mechanism such as hunger, then the carrot corresponds to

$$\frac{\partial^2 u(c,s)}{\partial c \partial s} > 0,$$

and the stick to

$$\frac{\partial u(c,s)}{\partial s} \leq 0.$$

Note that these are the same partial derivatives that define a negative habit. Moreover, as some goods and activities become more attractive, others become less attractive, presumably so that the organism does not waste effort pursuing goals with a lower priority for survival (Brendl, Markman, and Irwin 2001).

The cues that signal departures from homeostatic set-points in some cases can be extraordinarily sophisticated. Thus, for example, signals to the brain that trigger hunger come from the stomach, intestines, blood-sugar level, and so on. Moreover, we are sensitive not only to internal signals but also to external signals that indicate the possible *future* scarcity of food, which may help to explain why dieting is so ineffective (see Herman and Polivy, chap. 16 herein). Perhaps when a person begins to diet, the brain receives signals indicating that the body is about to be deprived of food and responds by increasing the person's motivation to eat. The brain is also attuned to opportunities: if it senses an opportunity for low-cost access to food, it again responds by increasing the motivation to eat (again, causing problems for the dieter).

Conditioning

Classical conditioning is one of the most coherent and well-researched sources of preference change. The idea of classical conditioning begins with the basic building blocks of "unconditioned stimuli" (US), which are rewards and punishments, such as food, water, and electrical shock, that we are biologically programmed to find attractive or repellent. During development, organisms, including humans, come to associate certain types of cues with unconditioned stimuli, and these cues become "conditioned stimuli" (CS) that produce reactions similar to those of the US with which they are associated. For example, a baby might enjoy the taste of mother's milk, and when the mother rapidly becomes a cue signaling the availability of milk, it transfers the same positive feelings toward the mother (of course maternal attention may itself also be an unconditioned stimuli). The process need not end here. The individual who has become conditioned to like milk might subsequently develop positive feelings toward locations (for example, rooms) where he or she often consumes milk—a process known as *conditioned place preference*. Thus classical or "evaluative" conditioning (another common label for the process of acquiring preferences via associative connections) can explain how initial fundamental likes and dislikes—unconditional stimuli—can transfer their valence to a wide range of objects, persons, and activities in an ever-widening web.

Evaluative conditioning has been observed in diverse domains and with diverse stimuli (see De Houwer, Thomas, and Baeyens 2001 for a recent review). For example, evaluations of political slogans and human faces have been enhanced or undermined by pairing these CS with pleasant or aversive odors; drink flavors have been enhanced by their pairing with sweetness (that persists when the sweetness is later eliminated); and neutral pictures have been made to appear attractive or unattractive by presenting them simultaneously with pictures that were selected to be attractive or unattractive.

Different conditioned reactions seem to differ in terms of how quickly they are acquired, how rapidly they are lost when not reinforced, and a variety of other properties. Thus fear conditioning and learned taste aversion (in which a person or other type of animal avoids food that has become associated with nausea) occur very rapidly—often in a single trial—whereas positive conditioning effects usually require repeated pairings. Some forms of conditioning seem to be very specific to the environmental settings in which they are learned, while others are not. Different forms of conditioning differ in how rapidly they become "extinguished" when the conditioned stimulus is presented in the absence of the unconditioned stimulus (for further nuances concerning extinction see Bouton 1994; Bouton and Swartzentruber 1991; LeDoux 1996). Moreover, different species, including humans, seem to be biologically "prepared" to learn some types of CS, US associations (for example, between a snake or angry face and a shock) but not others (for example, between a flower or rabbit and a shock) (see, for example, Öhman 1986).

Conditioning effects do not require conscious awareness of US–CS associations. In one study, subjects were shown a series of pictures of a target person engaged in various activities, such as getting into a car and grocery shopping. There were two experimental conditions. In both, prior to the presentation of each photograph, another photograph was flashed subliminally (so rapidly that it was not consciously perceived). In one condition, those photographs were intended to arouse positive affect (for example, kittens or smiling friends), and in the other they were intended to arouse negative affect (for example, a skull, face on fire, bucket of snakes). At the end of the session, subjects were asked a series of questions about how much they liked or disliked the person in the photo. Those who had been exposed to the negative subliminal photos expressed substantially less liking than those exposed to the positive subliminal photos. A second component of the same study showed further that subjects made sense of their own tastes by evaluating various personality attributes of the target person differently. That is, people seemed to seek out rational explanations for why they either liked or disliked the individual shown in the photos, and were of course completely unaware that their like or dislike was in fact powerfully shaped by subliminal conditioning. In general, because people tend to rationalize their tastes and because conditioning is usually an unconscious process, the natural tendency is to underestimate the impact of conditioning—to believe that tastes are, as Adam Smith expressed it, "founded upon reason and nature."

In sum, numerous studies have established the occurrence and robustness of evaluative conditioning effects, and many researchers have asserted the importance of conditioning for processes such as the formation of food tastes, the acquisition of phobias and of sexual fetishes (for example, Bouton, Mineka, and Barlow forthcoming). Yet few if any studies have produced a "smoking gun"—that is, have convincingly demonstrated the ecological importance of conditioning as a determinant of tastes. Indeed there have been some failures to observe evaluative conditioning in situations in which one might have strong expectations that it would occur. Heroin addicts, for example, in treatment whose methadone is diluted in a solution of TANG do not subsequently develop a taste for TANG, even though relief of heroin craving would seem to be an extremely positive stimulus (see Rozin and Zellner 1985, 195).

Maturation

Maturation can be defined as a situation in which preferences change in a systematic fashion as a function of time:

$$\frac{\partial^2 u_t(c)}{\partial c\, \partial t} \neq 0.$$

Although these changes are most dramatic in infancy and early childhood, when nutritional needs and preferences develop in a highly predictable manner, they continue into adulthood. For example, puberty brings about significant changes in sexual and other preferences. Similarly, young adults often acquire tastes for substances such as coffee, whiskey, and cigarettes, and shed other preferences, such as that for extremely sweet breakfast cereal.[5] That younger people tend to be more radical and older people more conservative may also be true, though the evidence on this point is ambiguous (see Glenn 1980, 619ff.).

The field of marketing, for obvious reasons, is vitally concerned with the question of how tastes and consumption patterns change with age, and marketing researchers have observed an especially interesting pattern of maturation for certain kinds of preference. Holbrook and Schindler (1989) found that adults tend to like whatever music was popular when they were in their mid-twenties, and that preferences in music tended to decline in a tentlike fashion around the music of this period. In more recent studies, the researchers found closely related patterns in preferences for fashion models (Schindler and Holbrook 1993), photographs of movie stars (Holbrook and Schindler 1994), and motion pictures (Holbrook and Schindler 1996). Despite the similarity in qualitative pattern, however, the specific age at which preferences peak appears to vary by stimulus. For popular music, that age is roughly twenty-four, for fashion models thirty-three, for pictures of movie stars fourteen, and for motion pictures twenty-seven (Holbrook and Schindler 1996, 34). Thus different types of preferences tend to become "frozen" at different critical periods in one's life.

A similar pattern has emerged in research on political preferences. In particular, party identification tends to be fairly stable during one's adult years (Green and Palmquist 1990, 1994). Many researchers see this as evidence that "once partisan or other social identifications take root in young adulthood, they tend to persist even amid changing political circumstances" (Gerber and Green 1998, 795). The traditional explanation suggests that party identification becomes part of one's self-concept, which serves as an impediment to subsequent change.

Many of the preference changes that take place over a lifetime may be due to physiological effects associated with aging. For example, there is evidence that the sense of smell is transformed over time. Seifert and colleagues (1997, 595) report that the ability to recognize a wide variety of foods decreases over the adult years. Similarly, Doty and colleagues (1984, 1441) conclude that the "average ability to identify odors reaches a peak in the third and fourth decades of life, and begins to decline monotonically after this time." This, they argue, explains why elderly people often complain that their food lacks flavor (Doty et al. 1984, 1443), and it could explain why older people are more tolerant of foods with an unpleasant smell (Pelchat 2000).

Maturation and aging affect preferences in part *indirectly*, by changing our susceptibility to external influences. Again this is particularly clear in children, where younger children aged three to four are far more vulnerable to suggestion than are older children aged five to six (Ceci and Huffman 1997). Yet the progressive stabilization of preferences with aging seems to continue well into adulthood, as the research of Holbrook and Schindler confirms. Glenn (1980, 602) finds that research largely confirms the truism that "attitudes, values and beliefs tend to stabilize and become less likely to change as persons grow older." For better or worse, over time we appear to become increasingly inoculated against external influences.

Social Influence

Social factors clearly have a powerful influence on tastes. As attested to by international differences and historical changes, people are capable of forming diverse tastes for food, attire, architecture, styles of furniture, manners, and so on. While good functional reasons may exist for why certain tastes become widespread in certain cultures at certain points, no doubt social transmission is the main mechanism by which such tastes are disseminated.

Social influences can be as subtle as they are powerful. The literature on *co-action effects* indicates that eating and drinking behavior is strongly affected by the presence of others, though few people seem to be aware of the effect. Watson and Sobell (1982) found that males participating in a beer taste test drank significantly more—on average about twice as much—when paired with a heavily drinking companion than when paired with a companion who was not drinking at all. Roth (1999, ii) reports that subjects ate fewer cookies when in the presence of a noneating observer than when alone, and that they tried to match the intake of the companion when both were eating. Roth explains observed behavior as the result of two social norms—one in favor of minimal eating and one in favor of matching the food intake of the other—ultimately driven by a concern for impression management (Roth 1999, 114ff.). Animals show co-action effects as well. Zajonc (1965) reviews research showing that rats, chickens, and puppies eat significantly more when coupled with other hungry individuals. An apparently fully sated chicken, he reports, will eat up to two-thirds as much again when introduced to a hungry companion chicken.

Though a tendency to conform can lead to erroneous judgments, overeating, and so on, conformity can also be good for you. Deutsch and Gerard (1955, 629) identify two important functions that may be served by conforming. First, conformity may satisfy a desire to live up to the expectations of others. Second, conformity may be a useful heuristic in cases of uncertainty about fact or value. Economists recently have become interested in social influence and have formulated models that incorporate both of these effects. For example, Gale (1996) proposes a model of *herd behavior*, in which people imitate others because they provide valuable information about the utility of actions. Models of *conspicuous consumption* (Veblen 1899) see consumption as driven in part by a desire to project a favorable image and to achieve social status (Frank 1985; Corneo and Jeanne 1997). Bernheim (1994) develops a model in this spirit in which agents care not only about "intrinsic" utility (that is, utility they derive directly from consumption) but also their social status, which they take to be influenced in part by their market choices. The model implies conformity, since agents "recognize that even small departures from the social norm will seriously impair their status" (Bernheim 1994, 841).

To say how exactly the social context affects behavior is often difficult. If you invite your friends for dinner but decline to drink wine yourself, they likely will drink less than they otherwise would have. Why is that? Perhaps they think you will not like it if they become uninhibited when you remain sober. Perhaps they assume some social norm that prohibits drinking in this situation. Perhaps—knowingly or not—they adopt what they take to be your current attitude in favor of sobriety. Perhaps they infer that something may be wrong with the wine. As the example suggests, social influences on consumption commonly operate through a mixture of mechanisms, some but perhaps not all of which should properly be counted as causing changes in tastes.

Motivated Taste Change

The famous song "Love the One You're With" performed by the 1960s rock group Crosby Stills Nash and Young highlights the benefits of motivated taste change. If one could only learn to love what one has, or what no one else wants, most people would lead exceptionally fulfilled lives. Unfortunately, humans are not generally constituted in this fashion (which is why we need songs to encourage us to try nevertheless). Quite the opposite, as suggested by research on social influences, we often seem predisposed to want exactly what everyone else wants. This means that we often value what is scarce and expensive.

There are probably good evolutionary reasons for the limited sway we seem to have over our preferences. If people could make their preferences conform to their current attainments, then humans—for better or worse—would have undoubtedly made a lot less progress during our brief time on the planet.

Nevertheless, evidence shows that in some cases people can shift their preferences in favor of what they possess. The oldest demonstrations of what seems to be motivated taste change were produced by cognitive dissonance researchers. Cognitive dissonance was hypothesized to be a negative affective state experienced when one's beliefs are inconsistent with one another or when actions are out of line with beliefs or preferences. Dissonance researchers believed that avoidance or elimination of dissonance motivated people to shift their beliefs or preferences into line with one another. Consistent with their predictions, dissonance researchers demonstrated that people tended to increase their preference for objects they had chosen and to decrease their preference for objects they had rejected (for example, Brehm 1956; Festinger 1964).[6]

Dissonance researchers postulated and found that changes in preference occurred only when people had freely chosen objects, and not when the objects were simply given to them. Subsequent research, however, has found similar effects on liking even when ownership did not depend on subjects' decisions. Beggan (1992), for example, found that simply possessing an object caused subjects to rate it more positively in terms of attractiveness, value, and quality of design (but see Barone, Shimp, and Sprott 1997 for competing findings). Gibbs (1992) found that subjects who expected to sample a bitter-tasting solution twenty times rated the first taste as less aversive than did subjects who expected to taste it only once. Gibbs concluded that subjects who expected to consume the substance had manipulated their tastes for self-protective purposes to diminish the aversiveness of the event that they expected to be repeated so many times. The effect was relatively small, however, and an analogous effect was not obtained for a positive experience.[7]

Several researchers have observed a positive relationship between the perceived likelihood of outcomes (manipulated experimentally) and the desirability of those outcomes, as would be predicted if people attempt to make the best of whatever outcome they expect to occur (Kay, Jimenez, and Jost forthcoming; McGuire 1960; Pyszczynski 1982). For example, on the eve of the 2000 presidential election, Kay and colleagues (forthcoming) found that supporters of both leading presidential candidates rated their preferred candidate more favorably if they were given information that suggested he was likely to win, and rated their dispreferred candidate less harshly if they were given information that made them pessimistic that he would win.

Temporal Proximity

A form of preference change that has received considerable attention in the economic literature is *hyperbolic time discounting* (see Angeletos et al., chap. 18 herein; O'Donoghue and Rabin, chap. 7 herein). Models of hyperbolic discounting have the property that people are much more impatient when it comes to trade-offs between immediate and slightly delayed gratifications than they are between delayed and slightly more delayed gratifications. Thus, for example, an individual might prefer one apple today to two apples tomorrow, but prefer two apples in a year and a day to one apple in a year (Thaler 1981). Hyperbolic discounting can produce systematic changes in preference (preference reversals).

Hyperbolic time discounting is somewhat different from the other determinants of preference change just discussed. Each of the other sources of preference change—habit formation, satiation, visceral factors, maturation, conditioning, social influences, and motivated taste change—leads to changes in hedonic experience at given points in time—that is, to changes in "instantaneous utilities." Hyperbolic time discounting, though, is about changes in how a person trades off hedonic experiences at different times—that is, about changes in "intertemporal utilities."

Predicting Preferences

Knowing how people's preferences change over time will go some way toward explaining and predicting their behavior. Yet many kinds of behavior cannot be understood without considering the extent to which people are able to predict the direction and magnitude of such change. To understand precommitment behavior, for example, we need to know not only what preferences the agent has at the time of the decision but also what preferences he or she expects to have at later points. Thus an adequate descriptive theory of choice cannot escape the question of how people predict future preferences.

Research on predicting preferences began with a 1990 paper by Kahneman and Snell. Subjects in that study ate ice cream and listened to music for ten days in a row and predicted how they would feel about the experience. Subjects' preferences changed over time, although not in any obviously consistent fashion, and subjects predicted that their preferences would change, but the correlation between predicted and actual changes in preferences was close to zero.

Since publication of that study, research on predictions of future preferences has mushroomed. This section provides a broad overview of the literature, touching on what we view as some of the most robust and important findings. We organize the literature according to plausible underlying mechanisms that can lead to mispredictions. As should become evident from our discussion, note that many of the most robust phenomena may well be multiply determined.

Sources of Error in the Prediction of Future Preferences

Misconstrual   One cause of people's mispredictions is that they are mistaken about the objective qualities of the objects or events over which they have preferences. Wilson and Gilbert (forthcoming) refer to this phenomenon as the *misconstrual problem*. Clearly, if potential parents believe that having kids will be a continuously joyful experience, they will be disappointed when they find out that children get sick and keep their parents up all night. Similarly, people who buy lottery tickets may not know about the disadvantages to winning the lottery, and overlook the fact that they are likely to feel harassed by tax collectors, charities, and so on (Kaplan 1978). Misconstrual is likely to be a bigger problem when the decision concerns an unusual event. As Gilbert, Driver-Linn, and Wilson (forthcoming) note, "Many important events, such as marriage, the birth of a child, and terminal illness, are experienced just once or rarely, and thus we predictably mispredict how such novel events will unfold." Since misconstrual is unlikely to lead to any systematic biases, however, we will have little to say about it further.

Underprediction of Adaptation   The first studies to document a systematic bias in the prediction of future preferences were conducted by Loewenstein and Adler (1995). The studies differed from that of Kahneman and Snell (1990) in that they focused on *preferences* for an *object* as opposed to *feelings* about an *experience*.[8] The studies examined whether people could anticipate changes in their preferences produced by the "endowment effect," which is a very rapid form of taste change documented in the behavioral decision research literature (see, for example, Kahneman, Knetsch, and Thaler 1991). The endowment effect captures the observation that people become attached to objects in their possession and are reluctant to part with them, even if they had not particularly desired them in the first place. The endowment effect is an ideal form of preference change to examine because it occurs so rapidly—virtually instantly upon possession of an object.[9]

Loewenstein and Adler (1995) report the results of two studies. In the first, subjects were shown a coffee mug, told that they were going to be given it in the near future, and that they then would have the opportunity to sell it back to the experimenter for cash. Subjects were asked to state the minimum price at which they thought they would be willing to do so. Subjects underestimated their own selling prices substantially, as if they failed to appreciate the fact that they would become attached to the object once they were endowed with it. In the second study, subjects were given an incentive for accurately predicting their own postendowment price. They were told that there was a 50 percent chance (based on a coin flip) that they would win a coffee mug, and that if they did win one, they would have a chance to exchange it for cash. Before flipping the coin, subjects stated a minimum selling price that would apply if they won the coin flip.[10] Again, subjects who did not possess mugs substantially underestimated their own subsequent selling prices.

The most coherent explanation for the endowment effect is that it stems from adaptation and loss aversion—people adapt to ownership of the object, then are averse to losing it (Strahilevitz and Loewenstein 1998). Underappreciation of the endowment effect thus reflects underappreciation of adaptation to ownership. Subsequent studies suggest that underappreciation of adaptation applies to far more than ownership of objects. Thus, for example, Loewenstein and Frederick (1997) asked people to predict how much different types of environmental and personal changes would affect their well-being, and also to recall how much matched changes had affected their well-being in the past. Subjects expected future changes to affect their well-being substantially more than they reported that past changes had actually affected their well-being. The authors attributed this disparity in part to underappreciation of adaptation. Although the subjects had adapted to these changes in the past (which is why the changes had had little hedonic impact), they did not appreciate the degree to which the same process would occur in the future.

Gilbert and colleagues (1998) observed a similar pattern that they attributed to people's underappreciation of their own psychological "immune systems." In one study, they elicited assistant professors' forecasts of how they would feel at various points after their tenure decision, and compared these forecasts to the self-reported well-being of others whose tenure decision had been made in the past. Current assistant professors predicted that they would be happier for a prolonged period following a positive decision and less happy after a negative decision, though they recognized that the long-term impact of the tenure decision would be minimal. In fact both groups converged to baseline levels of happiness shortly after the decision. In another study, Texas voters predicted how they would feel in the days after the gubernatorial election if their candidate (or the opposing candidate) won the election. Again, people overestimated the duration of both positive and negative feelings.[11]

Also consistent with underappreciation of adaptation, Sieff, Dawes, and Loewenstein (1999) asked people who came to a clinic for an AIDS test to predict how they would feel approximately five weeks after obtaining a favorable or unfavorable test result. Respondents overestimated how good they would feel five weeks after obtaining a favorable result and (more tentatively, given the low rate of positive results) how bad they would feel five weeks after getting an unfavorable result.

Focalism   A second possible explanation for observed mispredictions of future tastes and feelings is what Schkade and Kahneman (1998) refer to as a *focusing illusion* and Wilson and colleagues (2000) call *focalism*. This is the tendency, as Loewenstein and Frederick (1997, 66) expressed it, to "overestimate the impact of any one factor on . . . quality of life . . . . Clearly, quality of life depends on a wide variety of different things, any one of which is likely to have only a small impact. However, perhaps when a respondent's attention is focused on a particular type of change—e.g., in opportunities for fishing— they exaggerate its overall importance."

The most compelling evidence for focalism comes from two sets of studies. In one, Schkade and Kahneman (1998) showed that mid- western college students believed students in California to be happier, and California students believed midwestern students to be less happy, despite the fact that both groups reported similar levels of happiness. The authors attributed this discrepancy to a focusing illu- sion based on the observation that those subjects who expected the greatest discrepancy were also those who, in subjective ratings of the importance of different aspects of life, put the greatest weight on weather as a determinant of happiness. In the other study, Wilson and colleagues (2000) had sports fans who watched a college basketball game predict how they would feel at various intervals after the game if the team they supported won or lost, then followed them up and measured their actual feelings in the ensuing days. Respondents over- estimated how long they would feel bad if their team lost and how long they would feel good if their team won, but consistent with fo- calism this tendency was reduced when they were asked to think about other events in their lives.

Distinguishing Between Focalism and Underappreciation of Adaptation One potentially important instance of misprediction of future prefer- ences is the discrepancy between patients' and nonpatients' evalua- tions of quality of life (QOL) associated with different medical condi- tions. In recent years, policy makers have sought to allocate scarce health-care resources in a rational fashion by taking account of how bad it is to have different conditions (and hence how important it is to treat them). With the goal of providing inputs into such policy mak- ing, researchers have sought to measure the quality of life associated with different medical conditions. Repeatedly, however, it has been found that people who have various conditions judge their quality of life to be much higher than the general public anticipates their own quality of life would be if they had the same conditions.

Such discrepancies could result from either of the two causes of misprediction discussed here. Members of the public could be exaggerating the negative impact of medical conditions because their attention is being focused on them (a focusing illusion), or they could be underestimating their own ability to adapt to having such conditions. In a recent series of studies, Ubel and colleagues (2001) attempted to test these two explanations of the cause of the discrepancy between patients' and nonpatients' assessments of patients' QOL. In some studies, they attempted a wide range of defocusing interventions, including one that was virtually identical to the one employed by Wilson and colleagues. For example, before being asked to estimate the quality of life with paraplegia, nonpatient respondents were asked to think of five aspects of their life that would change if they had paraplegia and five aspects that would not change. This and other interventions failed to raise nonpatients' estimates of the quality of life of patients and rather tended to decrease them. In another study, Ubel and colleagues (2001) tested whether underprediction of adaptation could explain part of the discrepancy by having respondents think about times in their lives when they had suffered setbacks and about what had happened subsequently. Consistent with the idea that underprediction of adaptation is at least partially responsible for the discrepancy, thinking about their own experiences of adaptation indeed caused respondents to raise their QOL estimates significantly. While focalism appears to be important in some domains, it does not seem to contribute significantly to the discrepancy in QOL ratings between patients and nonpatients.

Hot-Cold Empathy Gaps   At any point, one's preferences depend not only on stable factors (such as long-lasting individual differences in tastes) but also on transient "visceral factors" (Loewenstein 1996). When visceral factors become elevated, they have a dual impact on preferences: they decrease one's momentary well-being and they increase one's preference for (and pleasure from) specific activities. Hunger, for example, is inherently miserable, and increases one's immediate preference for food. Likewise, pain increases one's desire for relief, sexual arousal for sex, and anger for aggression.

Again, when it comes to visceral factors, research has identified a systematic error in predicting changes in tastes (see Loewenstein 1996, 2000). When people are in a cold state—for example, not hungry, angry, sexually aroused, and so forth—they underappreciate what a hot state will feel like in the future and how such a state will affect their behavior. They make an analogous mistake when in a hot state and predicting how they will feel or behave when the heat dissipates (that is, when they are in a cold state). Such "hot-cold empathy gaps" occur not only prospectively—when people predict their own past or future feelings and behavior—but also retrospectively, as in the infamous morning after syndrome, in which a cold morning self struggles to make sense of a hot past self's evening escapades (Loewenstein 1996; Loewenstein and Schkade 1999). Visceral states for which hot-cold empathy gaps have been documented include hunger (Read and van Leeuwen 1998), anxiety (Sieff, Dawes, and Loewenstein 1999), pain (Read and Loewenstein 1999), sexual arousal (Loewenstein, Nagin, and Paternoster 1997) and embarrassment (VanBoven et al. 2001). In the study of sexual arousal, for example, researchers found that male youths exposed to sexually arousing materials reported substantially higher likelihoods of behaving aggressively in a hypothetical date scenario than did youths not exposed to arousing material (Loewenstein, Nagin, and Paternoster 1997). Hot-cold empathy gaps also occur interpersonally: people have difficulty predicting the behavior of others who are in a different visceral state (VanBoven, Dunning, and Loewenstein 2000; VanBoven and Loewenstein forthcoming).

Projection Bias

Many of the findings in the literature on predictions of preferences, regardless of the mechanism postulated to cause them, appear to fit a simple pattern that Loewenstein, O'Donoghue, and Rabin (2001) label *projection bias*. People behave as if their future preferences will be more like their current preferences than they actually will be—as if they project their current preferences onto their future selves. Projection bias is analogous to a wide range of judgmental biases in which people's current state of knowledge contaminates their judgments of their own prior (or other persons') state of knowledge. Examples are the hindsight bias (Fischhoff 1975), in which people project their own current knowledge on themselves in the past (believing that they must have known in the past what they know now), and the curse of knowledge (Camerer, Loewenstein, and Weber 1989), in which, when people know something, they overestimate the likelihood that other people know it too.

In the paper introducing the concept of projection bias, Loewenstein, O'Donoghue, and Rabin (2001) model changing preferences as a matter of shifting state variables, as discussed earlier. Thus, for example, s could represent an individual's level of hunger and c their consumption of food, with

$$\frac{\partial u(c,s)}{\partial c} > 0;\ \frac{\partial u(c,s)}{\partial s} < 0;\ \text{and}\ \frac{\partial^2 u(c,s)}{\partial c \partial s} > 0.$$

Projection bias says that when an individual attempts to predict the utility of future consumption c_t at a time when his or her actual state will be s_t, that person's prediction will be biased by his or her current level of hunger, s_0:

$$\hat{u}_0(c_t,s_t/s_0) = (1 - \alpha)u(c_t,s_t) + \alpha u(c_t,s_0).$$

In words, the individual's predicted level of utility will lie between the actual level of utility he or she will experience in the future and the utility the person would experience with c_t given the current level of his or her state. People are then assumed to use these biased predictions to make decisions that affect the future, maximizing their biased prediction of their own future utility, instead of their true future utility.

In the case of hunger, this would mean that people who are not hungry who predict their preference for food at a point in the future when they can expect to be hungry would underestimate both their enjoyment of and desire for food at that time. Such a pattern is consistent with the folk wisdom that one should not shop on an empty stomach (see Gilbert, Gill, and Wilson 2002; Nisbett and Kanouse 1968) and has been demonstrated explicitly in research by Read and van Leeuwen (1998). In that study, office workers were asked to choose between healthy snacks and unhealthy snacks that they would receive in one week, either at a time when they could expect to be hungry (late in the afternoon) or satiated (immediately after lunch). Some were approached and asked to make this choice right after lunch, and some were asked to make it in the late afternoon. Not surprisingly, those who expected to receive the snack at a time when they were likely to be hungry were more likely to opt for the unhealthy snack, presumably reflecting an increased taste for unhealthy snacks in the hungry state. In addition, however, those who were hungry when they made the choice were also more likely to opt for unhealthy snacks than those who were satiated. People who were hungry when they made the decision seem to have anticipated being more hungry when they actually received the snack a week later—as if they projected their current hunger onto their future self.

The concept of projection bias can unify most of the misprediction results just discussed and many more; it can also make specific predictions in areas that have not yet been studied. Consider, for example, all of the different determinants of taste change (other than hyperbolic time preference and motivated taste change) discussed earlier. These comprise habit formation, satiation, refinement, visceral influences, maturation, and social influences.

Projection bias makes specific predictions for each of these forms of preference change. When it comes to habit formation, projection bias predicts that people will underestimate the impact of current consumption on utility from future consumption. Thus, for example, projection bias predicts that people will expect to enjoy increases in income for longer than they actually do. For satiation, the prediction is analogous. People will underpredict their own future of satiation, which will cause them to order too much of anything that they currently like—too much food at a restaurant if they begin their meal in a hungry state, or too many books or CDs by their favorite author or artist. Refinement is somewhat trickier, but projection bias again would imply that people underappreciate its effects. Perhaps the best application of this phenomenon is interpersonal; according to this story, boors with crude tastes will tend not to appreciate the pleasures and nuances of experience conferred by refinement.

Turning to visceral influences, projection bias predicts that people who are in different visceral states—angry or not angry, hungry or not hungry, and so on—will have remarkably little empathy for or understanding of themselves (or others) in the different state. Such lack of empathy was demonstrated in a recent study by VanBoven and Loewenstein (forthcoming), in which people who had just exercised (or were about to) read a story about three hikers lost in the woods. Subjects were asked to write an essay about how the hikers felt, to predict whether the hikers would be more bothered by hunger or thirst, and to predict whether they themselves in that situation would be more bothered by hunger or thirst. The results were as predicted. Subjects who had exercised—and who could therefore be assumed to be thirsty but not hungry—mentioned thirst earlier in their essay and predicted that they and the hikers would be more bothered by thirst than did those who had not yet exercised.

The pattern is very much the same for maturation. Projection bias implies that people will underestimate the extent to which their preferences will change as a result of aging, and that this bias will be most pronounced when tastes are most in flux. Many children, for example, find kissing scenes in movies disgusting and are unable to imagine that they would ever find kissing pleasurable to watch, much less do themselves. At the opposite extreme, one of the authors of this chapter observed that with age, his grandfather preferred sweeter wine, eliciting much amusement and contempt from his father. The author had the same reaction when his father's taste in wine underwent the same shift at about the same age. (He is convinced of course that he will always prefer the dry wines that he currently enjoys.)

Projection also makes specific predictions about social influences.

First, people will underestimate the impact of future social influences (they will view their own tastes as more autonomous than they truly are). Second, they will exhibit a systematic bias when choosing whether to be a big fish in a small pond or a small fish in a big pond—they will tend to prefer bigger ponds than are actually optimal for their well-being (see Loewenstein et al. 2001). Imagine a faculty member at Podunk U. who is contemplating a move to Ivy U. According to projection bias, such a person will correctly imagine the impressed reactions of his Podunk colleagues but will underappreciate that his reference group will quickly become the new colleagues at Ivy, who will be much less impressed with the fact that he is at Ivy.

Yet projection bias is not consistent with all of the preference-prediction biases documented in the literature. Phobics, for example (who are not currently experiencing fear of the thing they dread), do not project their calm onto their future self but exaggerate the fear they will experience if faced with the object of their phobia. While some teenagers underestimate the effects of maturation and falsely believe they will remain punk rock rebels for the rest of their lives, others overestimate the same effects and believe that they will adopt more mature tastes earlier than they actually do. In the latter case, people are aware that maturation is a determinant of taste change but exaggerate its effects. The "impact bias" of Gilbert, Driver-Linn, and Wilson (forthcoming) and Wilson and Gilbert (forthcoming) can account for such patterns. This bias is defined as a tendency to overestimate the enduring impact that future events will have on our emotional reactions. The relation between projection bias and impact bias is complex and the conditions under which we should expect projection bias or impact bias (or both) to be observed remains to be specified. One hopes that this will be explored by future research.

The generality of the phenomenon of projection bias is uncertain in part because predictions of future preferences have only been studied for a narrow range of sources of preference change. No researchers to our knowledge have examined prediction accuracy for the types of changes in preferences caused by maturation or conditioning, and no research we know of has tested whether people's attempts to refine their preferences are successful (let alone whether doing so actually makes people happier). Moreover, researchers studying predictions of taste change have not selected their domains at random. Indeed one could conjecture that researchers have focused on domains of behavior where they expected to observe bias (which is always more interesting than its absence). A useful role will be played by skeptical researchers who attempt to discredit (or provide evidence for the opposite) of the documented effects.

Honoring and Resisting Changes in Preferences

A theory of how people expect preferences to change over time will certainly help predict and understand their behavior. Such a theory, though, needs to be coupled with an account of when people choose to honor their current preferences, or, when they choose to honor preferences they expect to have when they experience the consequences of the decision. Take, for instance, a woman's decision to eschew anesthesia during childbirth even though she expects to request it once labor begins. To understand such a pattern, one needs to explain why she wants to honor her immediate preferences rather than those she expects to have when the decision goes into effect. Thus a descriptively adequate theory of choice must also include an account of conditions under which people tend to go with current preferences and conditions under which they tend to go with future preferences. Similarly, a useful normative theory of choice would include an account of when we *should* honor current or future preferences.

On the descriptive side, existing literature reflects seemingly conflicting assumptions. As noted in the introduction, much of the literature on changing preferences consistently assumes that people aim to honor future preferences. This is particularly true of the literature on endogenous changes in tastes. Yet the literature on hyperbolic time discounting assumes throughout that people want to honor current rather than future preferences (for example, Laibson 1997). In the work of O'Donoghue and Rabin (2000), for example, it is assumed that, to the extent that people are *sophisticated* (that is, can predict the changes in their own future preferences wrought by hyperbolic time discounting), they will attempt to take actions that impose their current preferences on the future.

Of course a wide range of cases exist in which people attempt to satisfy future preferences. When grocery shopping on an empty stomach, we are often at least partly aware of the fact that we are likely to overestimate future consumption, and we decide to buy a little less than we would otherwise deem appropriate. When choosing an education, we think about how we will feel about the implicit career choice after graduation. To the extent that we do not take actions that satisfy our future preferences, often this is because we misestimate them, not because we do not want to satisfy them. At the same time, there are many situations in which we aim to honor current rather than future preferences.

This state of affairs raises the important question of when and why people sometimes aim to satisfy their current preferences rather than the preferences they expect to have when the consequences of the decision are experienced. Casual introspection points to two kinds of situation in which such a pattern occurs. The first (more common) situation occurs when people anticipate that they will not act in accord with their perceived self-interests, even though at some level they want to. This situation has received a tremendous amount of attention in the self-control literature, much of which focuses on strategies people use to ensure that their current preferences over future events will not be overridden by their future self (for example, Ainslie 1975; Hoch and Loewenstein 1991; Schelling 1984). The second situation involves cases in which one holds specific values with great conviction but worries that one will lose one's current perspective—in effect becoming "corrupted" from the vantage point of one's current perspective. This latter situation has received little if any attention in the empirical literature but has been of some interest to philosophers.

Why should people fear that they won't act in their best self-interest? Perhaps the most common explanation of such failures involves the activation of visceral factors (Loewenstein 1996). Although visceral factors are essential mechanisms designed to produce specific behaviors (such as eating, drinking, fighting, flight, and copulation), when they become too intense they can override cognitive deliberations about self interest. A wide range of self-destructive behaviors (for example, unsafe sex, dieting problems, road rage, drug addictions, and so on) seem to stem from the activation of intense visceral factors. Most people are well aware of the power of visceral factors. Even at the moment of acting, people indeed may recognize that visceral factors are propelling them to behave self-destructively.[12] Such awareness is, however, often insufficient to produce a correction in behavior, because self-control can require a prohibitive exertion of effort. Baumeister and colleagues (see Baumeister and Vohs, chap. 6 herein) have conducted numerous studies supporting the thesis that exercising self-control draws on some type of mental resource (sometimes referred to as *willpower* or *ego strength*) that is limited in quantity. Moreover, a wide range of situations—from alcohol consumption to sleep deprivation to immersion in a mob—seem to interfere with self-monitoring of behavior and hence with the exertion of self-control (Carver and Scheier 1998; Schelling 1984). In sum, if people expect future visceral factors to interfere with the pursuit of their own self-interest, we should not be surprised if they choose to reject such transient shifts in preference in favor of those that they currently hold.

Another situation in which people may favor their present over anticipated future preferences occurs when they are afraid of *corrup-*

tion—of abandoning values that they currently cherish. In some cases, people suspect that their preferences will change in ways that they find distasteful. Adolescents worry that they will become stodgy. Political radicals worry that they will become more conservative. Entering law students and medical students fear that the professional education they are about to receive will stamp out their idealism and focus them on the goal of making money. In these types of situations, one sometimes observes people taking efforts to commit to their current preferences.

We suspect that this kind of situation is much less common than the previous. Perhaps one reason is that when a preference is so strongly held that one would consider committing oneself to act on it in the future, to imagine that the preference will change over time is especially hard. Moreover, people rarely commit themselves to their current preferences in these situations. Perhaps we realize that dramatic action now—though in accord with current values—may make us unhappy in the future. While getting sterilized may be an effective means to prevent oneself from ever contributing to overpopulation, there is a significant probability that the procedure will lead to regretful misery later.

On the normative side, philosophers have worried about which preferences indeed should be honored in cases of conflict. The considerations proposed in this literature appear to provide rational underpinnings for the observed tendency to discount preferences due to visceral factors. The literature does not, however, unambiguously justify dismissing future preferences due to a general fear of corruption over time.

In the history of philosophy, David Hume is famous for arguing that preferences cannot be rationally criticized. In *A Treatise on Human Nature* (Hume 2000 [1739–1740], 267), he wrote,

> 'Tis not contrary to reason to prefer the destruction of the whole world to the scratching of my finger. 'Tis not contrary to reason for me to choose my total ruin, to prevent the least uneasiness of an Indian or person wholly unknown to me. 'Tis as little contrary to reason to prefer even my own acknowledg'd lesser good to my greater.

Even a follower of Hume, however, can argue that to act on preferences due to visceral factors may be unreasonable. Hume himself adds that a passion "can be call'd unreasonable" when it is "founded on false suppositions" (267). Suppose, for example, that a first drink induces the (false) belief that a second drink would make me more attractive, or increase my chances of befriending the person at the other end of the bar. Knowing that my preference for a second drink is based on a false supposition induced by the first, I may quite rationally dismiss that preference.

In more recent works, philosophers such as Richard Brandt seek to expand the range of desires that can be legitimately dismissed. Brandt (1998) provides a whole list of conditions under which preferences may legitimately be subjected to what he calls "rational criticism." His view is that preferences are rational only if they would survive exposure to logic and the facts. Whether preferences can be rationally criticized, therefore, depends in part on whether they would go away if the subject clearly visualized the consequences of acting on them. Some preferences, Brandt argues, are due to a weakness of imagination, such as an inability to estimate the hedonic impact of alternative acts (Brandt 1998, 63). After playing tennis on a hot day, Brandt explains, a person may feel like drinking a couple of vodka and tonics; but if he made the effort to remember what happened the last time he succumbed to that particular desire, the desire would diminish dramatically (Brandt 1998, 67). Hence the preference can be rationally criticized. Also, in Brandt's view, whether preferences can be rationally criticized depends on their causal history. *Authentic* preferences, on Brandt's account, are acquired "from personal experience with liked/disliked examples of the target object" (1998, 71). Preferences that lack authenticity may be the result of "temporary emotional and motivational states," of conditioning that took place under atypical environments such as a psychologist's lab, or of imitation of someone mistakenly considered a proper role model (1998, 70–71). In Brandt's view, then, to reject preferences due to visceral preferences if they are not "authentic" or would go away if certain consequences were made clear to the agent is perfectly legitimate.

Other considerations could potentially help us to determine which preferences deserve honoring in particular cases. Kusser (1998, 85) argues that one can legitimately discount "unhappy" preferences, by which she means preferences that are obstacles to happiness. Brandt (1998, 75) hints at this possibility: "For instance, you may have acquired an aversion to enjoying yourself, say by boating on a Sunday, because you have been taught to believe that a loving God wants the Sabbath day to be kept holy. Here a false or unjustified belief is the source of an attitude preventing happiness and desire-satisfaction." Bykvist (1999, 51), like Brandt, suggests that the length of time that a desire is entertained matters: "There are cases to suggest that we should give more weight to long-lasting desires than to short ones." If a newly acquired preference, perhaps expected to be fleeting, conflicts with a long-standing one, to honor the long-standing one is rationally justified. These considerations too can be used to dismiss preferences due to visceral factors. If such preferences tend to be of brief duration, even fleeting, or if having them tends to make one unhappy—all of which seems plausible—they are open to rational criticism.

Yet philosophical considerations do not unambiguously support dismissing future preferences due to the mere possibility of corruption over time. As Derek Parfit (1986, 155) points out, while it may be true that my judgment will deteriorate over time, so that I "should give greater weight to what I used to value or believe," it may also be true that my judgment will improve over time, as increasing knowledge and experience will help me make better decisions. Parfit (1986, 155) writes, "On this assumption, I should give to my *future* evaluative desires *more* weight than I give to my present evaluative desires, since my future desires will be better justified." As Parfit notes, which of the two assumptions is better justified and under what conditions corruption is more likely than edification is unclear. For example, whether increasingly conservative politics results from a deeper understanding of the harsh realities of the world or from a decay in one's moral and intellectual faculties remains an open question. So long as we do not know when to expect corruption or edification, the mere possibility of corruption does not give us grounds to rationally criticize future preferences.

Conclusions

In this chapter, we have discussed three interrelated issues: (1) how and why preferences change over time; (2) whether people can accurately predict how their preferences will change, and in what ways those predictions fail; and (3) when future tastes are expected to differ from current tastes, under what conditions people choose to indulge their current tastes or those they expect to prevail in the future. While discussion of these issues is relegated to separate sections of the paper, we have attempted to draw connections which are worth reiterating here in a more explicit fashion.

First, the errors people make in predicting their own preferences (issue 2) are likely to depend on the source of preference change (issue 1). To predict the effects of maturation, for example, people rely in part on intuitive theories of how tastes change over the life cycle. The accuracy of predictions will then depend on the correctness of the theories, as well as on the degree to which they apply to the person making the prediction. To predict one's future appetite at a time when one is ravenously hungry, on the other hand, is likely to involve an attempt to remove from one's prediction the effect of one's immediate hunger. Thus, the processes invoked, and the types of errors one should expect to observe, depend on the nature of the underlying processes producing a change in preferences. Given this observation, it is perhaps somewhat surprising that many of the errors that have been observed in research on prediction of preference can be summarized by the simple pattern referred to as "projection bias."

Second, whether people choose to indulge their immediate or their future preferences (issue 3) will again depend on the source of preference change (issue 1). As noted, people are much more likely to want to go with their future preferences when they reflect the influence of cumulated experience (for example, satiation or habit formation) than when they arise from the influence of intense but transient visceral factors. Our discussion of these issues was necessarily speculative because there has been remarkably little research on when and why people choose to indulge or deny anticipated preferences.

Third, decisions about whether to indulge or deny future preferences (issue 3), and the success of strategies designed to impose current preferences on the future, will depend on the accuracy of an individual's predictions of future preferences (issue 2). Clearly, one can better take immediate measures to satisfy future preferences if one can predict what they will be. But predicting future preferences is also important when one wants to resist such change and satisfy one's current preferences. One is much more likely to successfully practice safe sex in the heat of the moment, defy social pressures by "saying no" to drugs, or resist acting on angry feelings if one can predict when such feelings will arise.

A better understanding of changing preferences could shed light on the proper role of public policy. Economists typically assume that the correct role of government is to create and enforce rules under which people can maximally satisfy their desires (that are assumed to be fixed). This framework is inadequate if, as Sunstein (1993) notes in an essay titled "Democracy and Shifting Preferences," preferences are not fixed but rather depend on public policies. "If the rules of allocation have preference-shaping effects," Sunstein writes (1993, 202), "it is hard to see how a government might even attempt to take preferences 'as given' in any global sense, or as the basis of social choice. When preferences are a function of legal rules, the rules cannot be justified by reference to the preferences."

The possibility that preferences may change as a result of public policy makes the Pareto criterion, as normally applied, inappropriate to evaluate government policies. Taking shifting preferences into account, we may in fact be able to support policies that would not otherwise be justifiable. For example, consistent with the notion of refinement introduced earlier, the government might want to institute policies intended to expose people to (or make it cheap or easy for them to expose themselves to) things that they might not initially appreciate. This could explain why, as Sunstein observes, people "support nonentertainment broadcasting even though their own consumption patterns favor situation comedies" (Sunstein 1993, 207).

Sunstein's essay focuses not only on problems for public policy caused by shifting preferences but also on those that result from failure to accurately predict or to honor future changes in preferences. For example, regulation of drugs could be justified by the observation that people don't seem to accurately predict the effect of addictive drugs on their own subsequent preferences. Likewise (and analogous to the idea that people do not always endorse anticipated changes in their tastes), government might be concerned about not honoring or creating in the first place certain types of preferences—for example, "those that have resulted from unjust background conditions and that will lead to human deprivation or misery" (Sunstein 1993, 203). Yet government action only can be justified by reference to changing preferences if the government itself can make accurate judgments about such changes, something which—as this chapter has argued—is easier said than done.

Governmental policy in the face of shifting preferences is likely to confront some of the same issues that face decision makers themselves—specifically, which preferences one should act on. The problem can be seen in the domain of health care policy, where predictable changes in preferences abound. Whose preferences should we honor when it comes to allocating scarce resources to preventing serious chronic health conditions—that of patients or nonpatients, given that, as we have already discussed, they differ systematically? In a different health-related domain, healthy people often state that they are not interested in receiving "heroic measures" if they become ill—chemotherapy, life-support systems, resuscitation—but sick people are far more interested in receiving such care (Slevin et al. 1988). Whose preferences should we act on? What if someone when healthy expresses a desire to precommit to not receiving heroic measures? If such a desire reflects a correct perception that powerful emotions evoked by sickness will distort his or her decision making, then perhaps we should allow the individual to precommit. Yet what if this is simply a hot-cold empathy gap—a failure of someone in a cold state who can be cavalier toward the prospect of death because he or she is not facing it—to empathize with the true preferences the person will have once he or she becomes sick?

Some economists have argued that economics should not be concerned with issues of preference formation and change. Hayek, for example, wrote, "If conscious action can be 'explained,' this is a task for psychology but not for economics" (1948, 67). As Hodgson (1993, 154) writes in a discussion of this passage, "Hayek's statement . . . amounts to saying that we should not try to explain individual preferences and purposes simply because such explanations are deemed outside social science." Becker (1976, 133) appears to concur with Hayek's judgment; he writes,

> For economists to rest a large part of their theory of choice on differences in tastes is disturbing since they admittedly have no useful theory of the formation of tastes, nor can they rely on a well-developed theory of tastes from any other discipline in the social sciences, since none exists. . . . The weakness in the received theory of choice, then, is the extent to which it relies on differences in tastes to "explain" behavior when it can neither explain how tastes are formed nor predict their effects.

In Becker's view, because of the lack of a theory of preference formation we should assume that tastes are stable over time and identical across people.

We agree that no well-developed, useful theory of preference formation and change exists as of yet, and there is remarkably little rigorous data on which to construct such a theory. Yet we would advocate that economists respond to this not by leaving the task to psychologists or by pretending that preferences remain stable but by making the effort to study and model changes in preferences. A deeper understanding of how preferences are formed and how they change over time could increase the descriptive adequacy of economic models of human behavior; so would a better account of how people predict future preferences, and under what conditions they choose to honor current rather than future preferences.

This research was supported by NSF Grant SBR-9521914 to the Center for Integrated Study of the Human Dimensions of Global Change at Carnegie Mellon University, and by Jan Wallander and Tom Hedelius' Foundation. We thank Krister Bykvist, Shane Frederick, Niklas Karlsson, Ted O'Donoghue, Daniel Read, Paul Rozin, and Timothy D. Wilson for helpful comments and suggestions.

Notes

1. Gilbert and Gill (2000, 394) argue that when we confront stimuli, we initially assume that our first reaction is veridical, then sometimes we elaborate and change our view. As they write,

    [C]ognitive activities may normally be characterized by an initial moment of realism that is quickly followed by an idealist correction. According to this *correction model*, when people attempt to understand the objective properties of a stimulus, they automatically assume that their subjective experience of the stimulus is a factual indicator of its properties, and then—if they have the time, energy, and ability—they rapidly "undo" that assumption by considering the possibility that extraneous factors may have shaped their experience.

2. Whether modeled with diminishing marginal utility or changing state variables, satiation is generally assumed to be a continuous process. That is, marginal increments to consumption are assumed to lead to, at most, marginal changes in the marginal utility of further consumption. Yet this assumption has rarely (if ever) been tested. Contrary to this assumption, our experience has often been that satiation is discontinuous. We will listen to the same CD over and over with no discernible decline in liking until, with no warning, we reach a point where the idea of listening to it even one more time is distinctly aversive. Likewise at various times we have become enamored of a particular kind of food and have indulged our new preference for it repeatedly but found that from one day to the next we go from loving the food to hating it. Such discontinuities in satiation, if verified by systematic empirical investigation, would help to explain why people find it so difficult to predict changes in their own tastes.

3. This problem may be possibly avoided by assigning low- and high-quality goods to separate mental categories. Zellner, Kern, and Parker (2002) gave experimental subjects samples of full-strength and diluted fruit juices. Diluted juices were rated worse by subjects who were told that all of the stimuli were "fruit juices" than by those who were told that the diluted fruit juices were "commercial drinks." (No such effect of labeling was observed by subjects who rated only diluted juices.) In other studies reported in the same paper, consumers of premium coffee and beer who spontaneously assigned premium and low-grade items to separate mental categories rated the inferior-quality products more highly than those who did not.

4. See Carver and Scheier (1998) and Wilson, Gilbert, and Centerbar (forthcoming) for a further discussion of these issues.

5. Maturation is often difficult to distinguish from habit formation, since as one ages one often acquires experience with consumption in a fairly pre-

dictable fashion. For example, perhaps the general (though by no means universal) decrease in taste for candy as people enter adulthood results from satiation rather than biological changes associated with aging. Casual introspection suggests, however, that many of these changes are more tightly linked with age than they are to cumulative consumption experiences.

6. Yet in a seminal paper, Bem (1967) argues that many of the results that had been adduced in support of dissonance theory also could be explained in terms of what he called "self-perception theory." Self-perception theory is based on the idea that people have imperfect knowledge of their own beliefs and tastes, and that they sometimes infer their own beliefs and tastes from their own actions, much as one would infer the beliefs and tastes of other persons by observing their actions. Self-perception theory would say that people increase their evaluations of things they choose, not to make themselves feel better about those things but because they naturally infer that they like the things they choose. Note that such a self-perception theory account of the taste-change phenomena produced by dissonance researchers would not qualify as an instance of motivated taste change.

7. Gibbs's finding may help to explain why experimental subjects who were made to expect to suffer (for example, by eating a worm or receiving an electric shock) were subsequently more likely to choose to suffer (by voluntarily eating the worm or taking the shock) than those who did not initially expect to suffer (for example, Aronson, Carlsmith, and Darley 1963; Comer and Laird 1975).

8. In the literature on predicting tastes, studies dealing with predictions of feelings are often discussed interchangeably with studies that focus on predictions of preferences. The two are certainly related—how much one wants something is likely to be related to how much one expects to enjoy it—but they are not synonymous (for example, Berridge and Robinson 1995).

9. The endowment effect is virtually instantaneous in the sense that people become attached immediately upon possession of an object. Yet this attachment intensifies over time as a function of how long the object is owned (Strahilevitz and Loewenstein 1998). Indeed one can think of the endowment effect as a special case of a more general influence of the history of object ownership on valuation. Valuation of an object increases as a function of whether one has owned it in the past, how long one owned it (either in the present or the past), and potentially (though not yet documented) as a function of how long ago one lost it (if one did) (Strahilevitz and Loewenstein 1998).

10. The study employed the Becker-Degroot-Marschak "truthful revelation" procedure that gives subjects an incentive for revealing their true valuations.

11. Wilson, Gilbert, and Centerbar (forthcoming) explain such phenomena in terms of sense making. They argue that humans have a strong tendency to make sense of events that actually occur, and that the process

lowers the intensity of emotional reactions. *Ordinization neglect* is the term used to denote the failure to anticipate the effects of such sense making (Wilson and Gilbert forthcoming).

12. Visceral factors also can distort people's perception of self-interest through a process sometimes known as rationalization.

References

Ainslie, George. 1975. "Specious Reward: A Behavioral Theory of Impulsiveness and Impulse Control." *Psychological Bulletin* 82(4): 463–96.

Akerlof, George A., and Rachel E. Kranton. 2000. "Economics and Identity." *Quarterly Journal of Economics* 115(3): 715–53.

Aronson, Eliot, Merrill J. Carlsmith, and John M. Darley. 1963. "The Effects of Expectancy on Volunteering for an Unpleasant Experience." *Journal of Abnormal and Social Psychology* 66: 220–24.

Barone, Michael J., Terance A. Shimp, and David E. Sprott. 1997. "Mere Ownership Revisited: A Robust Effect?" *Journal of Consumer Psychology* 5(3): 257–84.

Becker, Gary S. 1976. *The Economic Approach to Human Behavior.* Chicago: University of Chicago Press.

Becker, Gary S., and Kevin Murphy. 1988. "A Theory of Rational Addiction." *Journal of Political Economy* 96: 675–700.

Beggan, James K. 1992. "On the Social Nature of Nonsocial Perception: The Mere Ownership Effect." *Journal of Personality and Social Psychology* 62(2): 229–37.

Belk, Russell W. 1988. "Possessions and the Extended Self." *Journal of Consumer Research* 15(2): 139–68.

Bem, Daryl J. 1967. "Self-Perception: An Alternative Interpretation of Cognitive Dissonance Phenomena." *Psychological Review* 74(3): 183–200.

Bernheim, B. Douglas. 1994. "A Theory of Conformity." *Journal of Political Economy* 102: 841–77.

Berridge, Kent C., and Terry E. Robinson. 1995. "The Mind of an Addicted Brain: Neural Sensitization of Wanting Versus Liking." *Current Directions in Psychological Science* 4: 71–76.

Bouton, Mark E. 1994. "Conditioning, Remembering, and Forgetting." *Journal of Experimental Psychology* 20: 219–31.

Bouton, Mark E., Susan Mineka, and David H. Barlow. Forthcoming. "A Modern Learning Theory Perspective on the Etiology of Panic Disorder." *Psychological Review.*

Bouton, Mark E., and Dale Swartzentruber. 1991. "Sources of Relapse After Extinction in Pavlovian and Instrumental Learning." *Clinical Psychology Review* 11: 123–40.

Brandt, Richard B. 1998. "The Rational Criticism of Preferences." In *Preferences*, edited by Christoph Fehige and Ulla Wessels. Berlin: Aldine de Gruyter.

Brehm, Jack W. 1956. "Postdecision Changes in the Desirability of Alternatives." *Journal of Abnormal and Social Psychology* 52: 384–89.

Brendl, Miguel, Arthur Markman, and Julie Irwin. 2001. "Suppression and Activation of Competing Goals." INSEAD.

Bykvist, Krister. 1999. "All Time Preferences?" *Theoria* 65: 36–54.

Camerer, Colin, George Loewenstein, and Martin Weber. 1989. "The Curse of Knowledge in Economic Settings: An Experimental Analysis." *Journal of Political Economy* 97: 1232–54.

Carver, Charles S., and Michael F. Scheier. 1998. *On the Self-Regulation of Behavior*. Cambridge: Cambridge University Press.

Ceci, Stephen J., and Mary Lyn Crotteau Huffman. 1997. "How Suggestible Are Preschool Children? Cognitive and Social Factors." *Journal of the American Academy of Child and Adolescent Psychiatry* 36: 948–58.

Comer, Ronald, and James D. Laird. 1975. "Choosing to Suffer as a Consequence of Expecting to Suffer: Why Do People Do It?" *Journal of Personality and Social Psychology* 32: 92–101.

Corneo, Giacomo, and Olivier Jeanne. 1997. "Conspicuous Consumption, Snobbism and Conformism." *Journal of Public Economics* 66: 55–71.

De Houwer, Jan, Sarah B. Thomas, and Frank Baeyens. 2001. "Associative Learning of Likes and Dislikes: A Review of 25 Years of Research on Human Evaluative Conditioning." *Psychological Bulletin* 127: 853–69.

Deutsch, Morton, and Harold B. Gerard. 1955. "A Study of Normative and Informational Social Influences upon Individual Judgment." *Journal of Abnormal and Social Psychology* 51: 629–36.

Doty, Richard L., Paul Shaman, Steven L. Applebaum, Ronita Giberson, Lenore Siksorski, and Lysa Rosenberg. 1984. "Smell Identification Ability: Changes with Age." *Science* 226: 1441–43.

Duesenberry, James S. 1952. *Income, Saving and the Theory of Consumer Behavior*. Cambridge, Mass.: Harvard University Press.

Dyer, Geoff. 1997. *Out of Sheer Rage*. London: Little, Brown.

Elster, Jon. 1979. *Ulysses and the Sirens: Studies in Rationality and Irrationality*. Cambridge: Cambridge University Press.

Festinger, Leon. 1964. *Conflict, Decision, and Dissonance*. Stanford: Stanford University Press.

Fischhoff, Baruch. 1975. "Hindsight ≠ Foresight: The Effects of Outcome Knowledge on Judgment Under Uncertainty." *Journal of Experimental Psychology: Human Perception and Performance* 1: 288–99.

Frank, Robert H. 1985. "The Demand for Unobservable and Other Nonpositional Goods." *American Economic Review* 75: 101–16.

Gale, Douglas. 1996. "What Have We Learned from Social Learning?" *European Economic Review* 40: 617–28.

Gerber, Alan, and Donald P. Green. 1998. "Rational Learning and Partisan Attitudes." *American Journal of Political Science* 42: 794–818.

Gibbs, Brian J. 1992. "The Self-Manipulation of Tastes: Experiments on Expedient Utility." Ph.D. diss., Graduate School of Business, University of Chicago.

Gilbert, Daniel T., E. Driver-Linn, and Timothy D. Wilson. Forthcoming. "The

Trouble with Vronsky: Impact Bias in the Forecasting of Future Affective States." In *The Wisdom of Feelings*, edited by L. Feldman-Barrett and P. Salovey.

Gilbert, Daniel T., and Michael J. Gill. 2000. "The Momentary Realist." *Psychological Science* 11: 394–98.

Gilbert, Daniel T., Michael J. Gill, and Timothy D. Wilson. 2002. "The Future Is Now: Temporal Correction in Affective Forecasting." *Organizational Behavior and Human Decision Processes* 88: 430–44.

Gilbert, Daniel T., Elizabeth C. Pinel, Timothy D. Wilson, Stephen J. Blumberg, and Thalia P. Wheatley. 1998. "Immune Neglect: A Source of Durability Bias in Affective Forecasting." *Journal of Personality and Social Psychology* 75(3): 617–38.

Glenn, Norval D. 1980. "Values, Attitudes, and Beliefs." In *Constancy and Change in Human Development*, edited by Orville G. Brim Jr. and Jerome Kagan. Cambridge, Mass.: Harvard University Press.

Green, Donald P., and Bradley Palmquist 1990. "Of Artifacts and Partisan Instability." *American Journal of Political Science* 34: 872–902.

———. 1994. "How Stable Is Party Identification?" *Political Behavior* 43: 437–66.

Hammond, Peter J. 1976. "Endogenous Tastes and Stable Long-Run Choice." *Journal of Economic Theory* 13(2): 329–40.

Hayek, Friedrich A. 1948. *Individualism and Economic Order*. Chicago: University of Chicago Press.

Hoch, Stephen J., and George Loewenstein. 1991. "Time-Inconsistent Preferences and Consumer Self-Control." *Journal of Consumer Research* 17: 492–507.

Hodgson, Geoffrey M. 1993. *Economics and Evolution*. Cambridge: Polity Press.

Holbrook, Morris B., and Robert M. Schindler. 1989. "Some Exploratory Findings on the Development of Musical Tastes." *Journal of Consumer Research* 16: 119–24.

———. 1994. "Age, Sex, and Attitude Toward the Past as Predictors of Consumers' Aesthetic Tastes for Cultural Products." *Journal of Marketing Research* 31: 412–22.

———. 1996. "Market Segmentation Based on Age and Attitude Toward the Past: Concepts, Methods, and Findings Concerning Nostalgic Influences on Consumer Tastes." *Journal of Business Research* 37: 27–39.

Hume, David. 2000 [1739–1740]. *A Treatise of Human Nature*, edited by David Fate Norton and Mary J. Norton. Oxford: Oxford University Press.

Kahneman, Daniel, Jack L. Knetsch, and Richard Thaler. 1991. "Anomalies: The Endowment Effect, Loss Aversion, and Status Quo Bias." *Journal of Economic Perspectives* 5: 193–206.

Kahneman, Daniel, and Jackie Snell. 1990. "Predicting Utility." In *Insights in Decision Making: A Tribute to Hillel J. Einhorn*, edited by Robin M. Hogarth. Chicago: University of Chicago Press.

Kaplan, H. Roy. 1978. *Lottery Winners: How They Won and How Winning Changed Their Lives*. New York: Harper and Row.

Kay, Aaron C., Maria Cristina Jimenez, and John T. Jost. Forthcoming. "Sour

Grapes, Sweet Lemons, and the Anticipatory Rationalization of the *Status Quo*." *Personality and Social Psychology Bulletin.*

Kusser, Anna. 1998. "Rational by Shock: A Reply to Brandt." In *Preferences*, edited by C. Fehige and U. Wessels. Berlin: Aldine de Gruyter.

Laibson, David. 1997. "Golden Eggs and Hyperbolic Discounting." *Quarterly Journal of Economics* 112: 443–77.

LeDoux, Joseph. 1996. *The Emotional Brain.* New York: Simon & Schuster.

Loewenstein, George. 1996. "Out of Control: Visceral Influences on Behavior." *Organizational Behavior and Human Decision Processes* 65: 272–92.

———. 2000. "Emotions in Economic Theory and Economic Behavior." *American Economic Review: Papers and Proceedings* 90: 426–32.

Loewenstein, George, and Daniel Adler. 1995. "A Bias in the Prediction of Tastes." *Economic Journal* 105: 929–37.

Loewenstein, George, and Shane Frederick. 1997. "Predicting Reactions to Environmental Change." In *Environment, Ethics, and Behavior*, edited by Max H. Bazerman, David M. Messick, Ann E. Tenbrunsel, and Kimberly A. Wade-Benzoni. New York: Russell Sage Foundation.

Loewenstein, George, Daniel Nagin, and Ray Paternoster. 1997. "The Effect of Sexual Arousal on Predictions of Sexual Forcefulness." *Journal of Research in Crime and Delinquency* 34: 443–73.

Loewenstein, George, Ted O'Donoghue, and Matthew Rabin. 2001. "Projection Bias in Predicting Future Utility." Unpublished paper. Carnegie Mellon University, Pittsburgh.

Loewenstein, George, and David Schkade. 1999. "Wouldn't It Be Nice? Predicting Future Feelings." In *Foundations of Hedonic Psychology: Scientific Perspectives on Enjoyment and Suffering*, edited by Ed Diener, Norbert Schwartz, and Daniel Kahneman. New York: Russell Sage Foundation.

McCauley, Clark, Paul Rozin, and Barry Schwartz. 2002. "The Nature and Origin of Preferences and Values." Unpublished manuscript, University of Pennsylvania, Department of Psychology.

McGuire, William J. 1960. "A Syllogistic Analysis of Cognitive Relationships." In *Attitude Organization and Change*, edited by Milton J. Rosenberg, C. I. Hovland, W. J. McGuire, R. P. Abelson, and J. W. Brehm. New Haven: Yale University Press.

Nisbett, Richard E., and David E. Kanouse. 1968. "Obesity, Hunger, and Supermarket Shopping Behavior." *Proceedings of the American Psychological Association Annual Convention* 3: 683–84.

O'Donoghue, Ted, and Matthew Rabin. 2000. "The Economics of Immediate Gratification." *Journal of Behavioral Decision Making* 13: 233–50.

Öhman, Arne. 1986. "Face the Beast and Fear the Face: Animal and Social Fears as Prototypes for Evolutionary Analyses of Emotion." *Psychophysiology* 23, 123–45.

Parfit, Derek. 1971. "Personal Identity." *Philosophical Review* 80(1): 3–27.

———. 1982. "Personal Identity and Rationality." *Synthese* 53: 227–41.

———. 1986. *Reasons and Persons.* Oxford: Oxford University Press.

Pelchat, Marcia L. 2000. "You Can Teach an Old Dog New Tricks: Olfaction and Responses to Novel Foods by the Elderly." *Appetite* 35: 153–60.

Pollak, Robert A. 1970. "Habit Formation and Dynamic Demand Functions." *Journal of Political Economy* 78(4): 745–63.

Pyszczynski, Thomas. 1982. "Cognitive Strategies for Coping with Uncertain Outcomes." *Journal of Research in Personality* 16: 386–99.

Read, Daniel, and Barbara van Leeuwen. 1998. "Predicting Hunger: The Effects of Appetite and Delay on Choice." *Organizational Behavior and Human Decision Processes* 76: 189–205.

Read, Daniel, and George Loewenstein. 1999. "Enduring Pain for Money: Decisions Based on the Perception of Memory of Pain." *Journal of Behavioral Decision Making* 12(1): 1–17.

Ross, Lee, and Andrew Ward. 1996. "Naive Realism in Everyday Life: Implications for Social Conflict and Misunderstanding." In *Values and Knowledge*, edited by Edward S. Reed, Elliot Turiel, and Terrance Brown. Mahwah, N.J.: Erlbaum.

Roth, Deborah A. 1999. "The Influence of Norms on Eating Behavior: An Impression Management Approach." Ph.D. diss., University of Toronto.

Rozin, Paul, and Deborah Zellner. 1985. "The Role of Pavlovian Conditioning in the Acquisition of Food Likes and Dislikes." In *Experimental Assessments and Clinical Applications of Conditioned Food Aversions*, edited by Norman S. Baverman and Paul Bronstein. New York: New York Academy of Sciences.

Ryder, Harl E., and Geoffrey M. Heal. 1973. "Optimal Growth with Intertemporally Dependent Preferences." *Review of Economic Studies* 40: 1–33.

Schelling, Thomas C. 1984. "Self-Command in Practice, in Policy, and in a Theory of Rational Choice." *American Economic Review* 74(2): 1–11.

Schindler, Robert M., and Morris B. Holbrook. 1993. "Critical Periods in the Development of Men's and Women's Tastes in Personal Appearance." *Psychology and Marketing* 10: 549–64.

Schkade, David A., and Daniel Kahneman. 1998. "Does Living in California Make People Happy? A Focusing Illusion in Judgments of Life Satisfaction." *Psychological Science* 9(5): 340–46.

Seifert, Kelvin L., Robert J. Hoffnung, and Michele Hoffnung. 1997. *Lifespan Development*. Boston: Houghton Mifflin.

Sieff, Elaine M., Robyn M. Dawes, and George Loewenstein. 1999. "Anticipated Versus Actual Reaction to HIV Test Results." *American Journal of Psychology* 112: 297–311.

Simon, Herbert A. 1981. *Sciences of the Artificial*. 2d ed. Cambridge, Mass.: MIT Press.

Slevin, Maurice L., H. Plant, D. Lynch, J. Drinkwater, and W. M. Gregory. 1988. "Who Should Measure Quality of Life, the Doctor or Patient?" *British Journal of Cancer* 57: 109–12.

Smith, Adam. 2000 [1759]. *The Theory of Moral Sentiments*. Amherst, N.Y.: Prometheus Books.

Stigler, George J., and Gary S. Becker. 1977. "De Gustibus Non Est Disputandum." *American Economic Review* 67: 76–90.

Strahilevitz, Michal, and George Loewenstein. 1998. "The Effects of Ownership History on the Valuation of Objects." *Journal of Consumer Research* 25: 276–89.

Sunstein, Cass R. 1993. "Democracy and Shifting Preferences." In *The Idea of Democracy*, edited by David Copp, Jean Hampton, and John Roemer. New York: Cambridge University Press.

Thaler, Richard H. 1981. "Some Empirical Evidence of Dynamic Inconsistency." *Economic Letters* 81: 201–7.

Ubel, Peter, George Loewenstein, Jack Hershey, Jonathan Baron, Tara Mohr, David A. Asch, and Christopher Jepson. 2001. "Do Nonpatients Underestimate the Quality of Life Associated with Chronic Health Conditions Because of a Focusing Illusion?" *Medical Decision Making* 21: 190–99.

VanBoven, Leaf, David Dunning, and George Loewenstein. 2000. "Egocentric Empathy Gaps Between Owners and Buyers." *Journal of Personality and Social Psychology* 79: 66–76.

VanBoven, Leaf, and George Loewenstein. Forthcoming. "Social Projection of Transient Visceral Feelings." *Personality and Social Psychology Bulletin.*

VanBoven, Leaf, George Loewenstein, Edward Welch, and David Dunning. 2001. "The Illusion of Courage: Underestimating Social-Risk Aversion in Self and Others." Working paper. Pittsburgh: Department of Social and Decision Sciences, Carnegie Mellon University.

Veblen, Thorstein. 1899. *Theory of the Leisure Class.* New York: Macmillan.

Watson, Donnie W., and Mark B. Sobell. 1982. "Social Influences on Alcohol Consumption by Black and White Males." *Addictive Behaviors* 72: 87–91.

Wilson, Timothy D., and Daniel T. Gilbert. Forthcoming. "Affective Forecasting." *Advances in Experimental Social Psychology.*

Wilson, Timothy D., Daniel T. Gilbert, and D. B. Centerbar. Forthcoming. "Making Sense: The Causes of Emotional Evanescence." In *Economics and Psychology*, edited by Juan Carrillo and Isabelle Brocas. New York: Oxford University Press.

Wilson, Timothy D., Thalia Wheatley, Jonathan Meyers, Daniel T. Gilbert, and Danny Axsom. 2000. "Focalism: A Source of Durability Bias in Affective Forecasting." *Journal of Personality and Social Psychology* 78: 821–36.

Zajonc, Robert B. 1965. "Social Facilitation." *Science* 149: 269–74.

Zellner, Deborah A., B. B. Kern, and S. Parker. 2002. "Protection for the Good: Subcategorization Reduces Hedonic Contrast." *Appetite* 38: 175–80.

PART IV

Applications

· 13 ·

Time Discounting of Health Outcomes

Gretchen B. Chapman

Research on the psychology of intertemporal choice typically employs a choice between a small immediate outcome and a larger delayed outcome. The decision maker makes a series of choices or gives a judgment to indicate how much larger the delayed outcome would need to be to make it just as attractive as the immediate outcome. This indifference point can be used to compute the temporal discount rate, or the percentage increase in magnitude that is needed to offset a given time delay. For example, if someone said that $100 to be received now was just as attractive as $110 to be received in one year, that would indicate a 10 percent annual discount rate. Sometimes the purpose of a study is simply to compute the discount rate. Other times, the purpose of the study is to examine whether the discount rate varies as a function of nonnormative factors.

Early research on time preferences employed hypothetical choices made about monetary outcomes. For example, Thaler (1981) asked college students what amount of money to be received in three years was just as attractive as receiving $250 now. In recent years, however, investigations have used not only monetary choices but also choices in other domains, most notably health (for example, Cairns 1992; Chapman 1996a; 1996b; Chapman and Elstein 1995; Chapman et al. 1999; Cropper et al. 1992, 1994; MacKeigan et al. 1993; Olsen 1993; Redelmeier and Heller 1993; van der Pol and Cairns 2001). Normative theory (for example, Keeler and Cretin 1983) dictates that the same discount rate be used for health and money when the two are exchangeable. Thus normatively, studies of health time preferences should yield the same results as similar studies using money. Empirical study of time discounting of health outcomes reveals that this is not always the case.

The study of intertemporal choice in health domains is important for three reasons. First is that time preference research has the potential to explain many problematic health behaviors (Critchfield and Kollins 2001). Self-control behaviors such as exercising, eating a healthy diet, and refraining from smoking represent intertemporal choices between small immediate rewards (for example, sleeping in rather than exercising, or eating a tempting dessert) and long-term health. Similarly, preventive medical treatment, such as taking medication to control high blood pressure, represents an investment in future health. These health behaviors are likely influenced by a number of factors, including the perceived risk of the health outcome and perceived effectiveness of the health behavior. Time preferences for the delay between the cost and benefit of the health behavior should be one of the influential factors. If so, understanding how intertemporal choice operates in health domains could help to explain why people frequently do not engage in these behaviors and may have implications for how to encourage such behaviors. For example, manipulations that affect time preferences in experimental studies might also be used to alter preventive health behavior in field studies.

A second motivation for the study of intertemporal choice in health domains is the potential for applications in public policy decisions. Public policy makers frequently make decisions about delayed health outcomes (see Caplin, chap. 15 herein). Medical experts must decide what preventive health care to advocate in clinical practice guidelines, insurers must decide what services to pay for, and safety officials must decide what regulations to implement. These decisions sometimes involve decision analyses that explicitly incorporate a discount rate. Recent recommendations (Gold et al. 1996) advocate using the same discount rate for both health outcomes and monetary costs. One may ask whether the preferences of actual decision makers conform to these recommendations. Research on intertemporal choice in health domains can address this question.

A final reason for studying discounting of health outcomes is that a comparison across domains can serve as a tool for uncovering the psychological processes that underlie intertemporal choice. Parallels between intertemporal choice for health and money outcomes would point to generalizability of monetary findings and a common mechanism. Alternatively, if intertemporal choice for health differs from choice for money, the nature of the differences can illuminate the ways in which decision processes are context sensitive.

Methodological Issues

In studies of monetary time preferences, decision makers are presented with choices between larger and smaller amounts of money to be obtained at different points. The size of the monetary outcomes and the time of their occurrence can be easily manipulated independently. This same flexibility is not always present in studies of health time preferences, and consequently the study of intertemporal choice in health domains poses some methodological challenges to measuring pure time preferences (Dolan and Gudex 1995; Gafni 1995). Health outcomes by necessity have a time duration, and manipulation of time of occurrence sometimes faces limitations. Owing to these constraints, some studies of health time preferences (for example, Ganiats et al. 2000; Redelmeier and Heller 1993; van der Pohl and Cairns 2001) have as their primary purpose simply to demonstrate a new method for measuring discount rates for health outcomes.

A key challenge faced in measuring time preferences in the health domain is separating time and quantity effects. Time preferences and decreasing marginal utility can have similar effects on choice, making the distinction between the two difficult. Consider, for example, life expectancy as a health outcome. Added life expectancy is an important outcome in many health decisions. Indeed such decisions are employed as preference measurement methods. For example, the time trade-off technique for assessing utility asks participants how much added life expectancy they would demand in exchange for a specified decrease in quality of health. Additional years of life expectancy of course are added to the end of life. Thus an increase in life expectancy is always a delayed outcome. Consequently, the magnitude of the life expectancy outcome is confounded with the timing of the outcome, making it difficult to separate time preferences from quantity effects such as diminishing marginal utility (Chapman 1997). Suppose, for example, a twenty-year-old feels that eighty-five years of life expectancy is not much better than eighty years. This may indicate temporal discounting of the last five years, due to the sixty-year delay (analogous to $1,000 in sixty years being preferred to $1,000 in sixty-five years). Alternatively, this may indicate diminishing marginal utility (analogous to $1,100 being only slightly better than $1,000). Gafni and Torrance (1984) showed that both time preference and diminishing marginal utility result in similar patterns (often interpreted in terms of risk preference). Separating time preferences for longevity from quantity effects therefore is problematic. Only a few empirical studies have examined time preferences for years of life expectancy (Dolan and Gudex 1995; Enemark et al. 1998; Moore and Viscusi 1990b; Viscusi and Moore 1989).

Many studies of time preferences for health consequences instead use health quality outcomes (Berndsen and van der Plight 2001; Bleichrodt and Johannesson 2001; Cairns 1992; Cairns and van der Pol 1999; Chapman 1996a, 1996b, 1998, 2000, 2002; Chapman et al. 2001; Chapman and Coups 1999; Chapman and Elstein 1995; Chapman et al. 1999; Dolan and Gudex 1995; Ganiats et al. 2000; Kahneman et al. 1993; Lipscomb 1989; MacKeigan et al. 1993; Moore and Viscusi 1990a; Olsen 1993; Redelmeier and Heller 1993; van der Pol and Cairns 1999, 2000, 2001). For example, Redelmeier and Heller (1993) presented scenarios describing a four-month episode of depression, temporary blindness, or hernia necessitating a temporary colostomy. Each episode was described as occurring at each of several delays.

Most health quality outcomes have a duration (for example, four months of depression). In contrast, monetary amounts can be delivered at a single point. Consumption of money takes place over time, similar to the consumption of health outcomes. An important distinction, however, is that for monetary outcomes the magnitude of the outcome can be separated from the time course of consumption. One can consume a large amount of money in a short period of time (for example, a deluxe vacation) or a small amount of money over a long period of time (for example, a pair of shoes).

For health outcomes, the magnitude of the outcome is not so easily disentangled from the duration of the outcome. The magnitude of health outcomes is often manipulated by adjusting the duration of the target health state. Chapman and Elstein (1995) examined whether different discount rates were used for large and small magnitude health outcomes. To manipulate magnitude, they presented short and long intervals of a target health state, for example, one versus four years in perfect health, relative to a poor health baseline. Four years of perfect health is not only better (higher magnitude) than one year of perfect health, it also extends further into the future. The duration of the health state has consequences for examining choice biases (for example, Bleichrodt and Johannesson 2001).

Due to the differences between monetary and health outcomes, any observed differences in empirical results for the two domains could be attributed to the temporal structure of the outcome, rather than to differences between health and money per se. One solution to this confound is to use consumer products that, like health outcomes, have a time duration, such as vacations (Chapman and Elstein 1995). Another solution is to give the monetary outcomes the same temporal structure as the health outcomes. Chapman and her colleagues (1999) and Chapman (1998) presented monetary outcomes that occurred in a stream (for example, $10 per week for a given number of weeks) just as the health outcomes did. Magnitude of both health and money outcomes were manipulated by adjusting the length of the stream. These studies noted differences between time preferences for health and money even after equating the temporal structure of outcomes in this way. For example, health discount rates were higher than monetary discount rates, and the two were not well correlated (as will be discussed).

A final type of health outcome frequently used in time preference research is number of lives saved (Cairns 1994; Cairns and van der Pol 1997a, 1997b; Chapman 2001; Cropper et al. 1992, 1994; Cropper and Portney 1990; Cropper and Sussman 1990; Horowitz and Carson 1990; Johannesson and Johansson 1996; Moore and Viscusi 1990b; Olsen 1993; Poulos and Whittington 2000; Svenson and Karlsson 1989). This outcome is critical for many public health decisions about delayed consequences, but differs from monetary outcomes in several respects. First, decisions made about lives saved are by definition made on behalf of other people. Monetary decision, though, can be made either on behalf of other people or on one's own behalf, but studies of time preferences have focused on personal monetary decisions. A second distinction is that decisions about lives saved are always made about a group of people, whereas monetary decisions can be made about a group of people or a single person. Studies of time preferences have focused on monetary decisions made about a single person (oneself). Studies comparing temporal discounting of lives saved to discounting of money consequently need to hold these factors constant (Chapman 2001).

Similarities Between Health and Money Discounting Results

Research on temporal discounting of health outcomes has identified a number of findings that parallel those from research on monetary outcomes. A large number of intertemporal biases appear in both monetary and health decisions. Contrary to normative prescriptions, decision makers tend to use different discount rates in different situations. Many of these context effects occur for both health and money decisions. These similarities between health and money provide cues as to the mechanisms underlying intertemporal biases.

High and Variable Rates

One result from discounting research is that people demonstrate discount rates that are extremely high, often on the order of 50 percent annually or more. High rates occur both in monetary choices (for example, Benzion et al. 1989; Thaler 1981) and in health choices (for example, Chapman 1996b; Chapman and Elstein 1995; Ganiats et al. 2000). Although such high discount rates do not technically violate normative theory, they do radically differ from those used in decision analyses (Gold et al. 1996). Extremely high discount rates for health outcomes are not ubiquitous. Redelmeier and Heller (1993) found low average discount rates but a high degree of variability. In addition, zero or negative discounting of health outcomes occurs with some frequency (Chapman et al. 2001, Study 1; Chapman and Coups 1999; Redelmeier and Heller 1993; van der Pol and Cairns 2000).

Delay Effect

Discount rates tend to be higher for short delays than for long delays. This effect has been demonstrated in both monetary decisions (for example, Benzion et al. 1989; Thaler 1981) and health decisions (Bleichrodt and Johannesson 2001; Cairns 1994; Chapman 1996b; Chapman and Elstein 1995; Redelmeier and Heller 1993).

The delay effect can result in preference reversals (Green et al. 1994; Kirby and Herrnstein 1995). Someone may prefer a large headache relief eight years from now to a small headache relief six years from now, but six years later the same person would prefer the small headache relief right away to the large headache relief two years from now. Note that both questions involve whether one wishes to delay relief for two years in order to receive the better outcome, but the second decision takes place six years after the first decision. Since both delays are longer in the first question, the subjective discount rate is lower and the person is willing to wait for the larger reward.

Christensen-Szalanski (1984) demonstrated such a preference reversal in women deciding whether to have anesthesia for childbirth. One month before labor and one month postpartum, the women preferred to avoid using anesthesia during labor. During active labor, their preferences suddenly shifted toward using anesthesia to avoid pain. Anesthesia offers immediate pain relief but also the risk of long-term side effects. At short delays (during labor), the women showed a stronger preference for immediate relief.

The fact that the delay effect and resulting preference reversals occur in both health and money decisions suggests that the delay effect is a result not of the value function for health or money but rather depends on how decision makers treat the time dimension. As further support for this proposal, the size of the delay effect in the monetary domain is correlated across subjects with the size of the delay effect in the health domain (Chapman and Weber forthcoming). The delay effect and resulting preference reversals can be modeled with a particular discount functional form—specifically, a hyperbolic discount function rather than the exponential function specified by normative theory (Kirby and Marakovic 1995). Unlike exponential discount functions, hyperbolic functions for a large and small reward can intersect, indicating a preference reversal. Ainslie (1975, 1982, 1984, 1986, 1991) suggests that to solve the self-control problem introduced by these preference reversals, decision makers must bind themselves to their earlier preferences to prevent a preference reversal from occurring during the "window of temptation."

Prelec and Loewenstein (1991) explain the delay effect by proposing the property of decreasing absolute sensitivity for time, which means that the difference between zero and two years seems larger than the difference between six and eight years. In the choice between small headache relief in six years versus large headache relief in eight years, the additional two years required for the larger prize does not seem very large. As a consequence, discounting of the larger outcome is not as extreme as in the choice between small headache relief now and large headache relief in two years. This account is equivalent to hyperbolic discounting in that a common difference between delays has more influence on choice when the delay is between two short delays than between two long delays.

An alternative account of the delay effect (Read, chap. 10 herein) is subadditive discounting, whereby discounting over a long delay is more extreme when the delay is divided into separate intervals. Thus the discount factor applied to an eight-year delay is less than four times the factor applied to any two-year interval contained within the delay. This account can explain the delay effect (higher discount rates for short delays) but not preference reversals (Christensen-Szalanski 1984; Green et al. 1994; Kirby and Herrnstein 1995).

Both the psychophysical and subadditivity explanations attribute the delay effect to a property of time delay. These accounts therefore make the prediction that the delay effect should occur for health, money, and other domains. Since the bias is not due to the value dimension (for example, the utility function for money), the effect should not be dependent on which value dimension (for example, health or money) is used. This prediction is consistent with empirical evidence showing the delay effect for both health and money.

Magnitude Effect

Subjective discount rates vary not only with the delay to the outcome, but also with the magnitude of the outcome. Smaller outcomes tend to elicit larger discount rates. Someone may prefer one day of perfect health now to one and a half days of perfect health in three years, but also prefer one and a half *years* of perfect health starting in three years to one year of perfect health starting now, even though both choices offer a 50 percent return for waiting three years. This effect has been demonstrated both for monetary (Benzion et al. 1989; Chapman and Winquist 1998; Green et al. 1997; Kirby and Marakovic 1996; Thaler 1981) and health decisions (Bickel and Johnson, chap. 14 herein; Chapman 1996b, 1998; Chapman and Elstein 1995).

Loewenstein and Prelec (1992) (Prelec and Loewenstein 1991) explained the magnitude effect by positing a value function with the property of increasing proportional sensitivity, such that the ratio between the values of 0.5 years and 1.0 years is larger than the ratio of the values of 0.5 days and 1.0 days. Thus the added 50 percent seems like a larger ratio when choosing between 1 year of perfect health now versus 1.5 years of perfect health starting in 3 years than between 1 day of perfect health now and 1.5 days of perfect health starting in 3 years.

Chapman and Winquist (1998) (see also Green et al. forthcoming) found an analogous magnitude effect in decisions about tipping at a restaurant. Subjects indicate they would give a larger percent tip on a smaller restaurant bill. The fact that a magnitude effect occurs in settings other than intertemporal choice suggests that, consistent with Loewenstein and Prelec's account, this is a result of the shape of the value function for money (or other outcomes).

Since the magnitude effect is explained via a property of the value dimension, one might expect that some value dimensions (say, money) might have this property while others (say, health) might not. Consequently, one would not necessarily expect the magnitude effect to occur for both health and money decisions. That it does implies that both health and money dimensions have the property of increasing proportional sensitivity, perhaps because the increasing proportional sensitivity property is a very general characteristic of numerical scales.

Sign Effect

Discount rates for losses are lower than discount rates for gains. Thus someone may view a gain of $10 right away to be equal in value to a $20 gain in one year (a 100 percent discount rate) but also see a loss of $10 right now to be equal in value to a $15 loss in one year (a 50 percent discount rate). This effect has been demonstrated in both health decisions (Chapman 1996b; MacKeigan et al. 1993) and money decisions (Benzion et al. 1989; Shelley 1993, 1994) as well as decisions about consumer products (Loewenstein 1988). Like the magnitude effect, the sign effect can be explained in terms of the value function for money (or whatever outcome is being delayed). Loewenstein and Prelec (1992) (Prelec and Loewenstein 1991) proposed the property of loss amplification—that is, the ratio of the subjective values of gains is smaller than the ratio of values of equivalent losses. Thus the ratio between $20 and $10 seems larger if the two outcomes are losses than if they are gains. That the sign effect occurs in both health and money decisions implies that both dimensions have this property.

Preferences for Sequence

Preferences for sequences of outcomes often differ from choices for individual outcomes. Loewenstein and Prelec (1993) showed that 80 percent of their subjects preferred dinner at a French restaurant in one month to dinner at a French restaurant in two months—that is, they preferred the better outcome sooner rather than later. When outcomes were imbedded in a series, however, preferences reversed. While all preferred French food to Greek food, 57 percent preferred dinner at a Greek restaurant in one month and dinner at a French restaurant in two months over the reverse order. Subjects no longer preferred to have the attractive French meal as soon as possible. Instead they showed a slight preference for an improving sequence with the better outcome delayed until the end of the sequence.

Whereas choices between individual outcomes usually display a positive time preference (that is, a preference for good events sooner rather than later), choices among sequence often demonstrate a negative time preference, a preference for improving sequences. Negative time preferences for sequences have been demonstrated for monetary (Loewenstein and Sicherman 1991) and health outcomes (Chapman 1996a, 2000), and also for hedonic experiences (Loewenstein 1987; Loewenstein and Prelec 1993). One explanation for the preference for improving sequences is that decision makers anticipate adapting to their current position in the sequence and, because of loss aversion, are averse to decreases in their position. In other words, later outcomes in the sequence are evaluated in contrast to earlier outcomes. An improving sequence offers a series of gains and is seen as more attractive than a declining sequence, which offers a series of losses, even if both sequences include the same total amount of money (or restaurant meals). Since loss aversion is a general property of value functions that should be present for both health and money dimensions, preferences for improving sequences should and are observed for both health and money. The sequence effect is reconsidered in the next section, where differences between health and money sequence effects are discussed.

A related phenomenon is duration neglect (Fredrickson and Kahneman 1993; but see Ariely and Loewenstein 2000). When evaluating an affective episode, decision makers appear to ignore the duration of the episode, such that a longer period of pain may be preferred to a shorter period (Kahneman et al. 1993). Evaluative judgments instead are based on salient features of the episode, such as whether it ends with a good or bad level (Ariely and Carmon 2000; see Ariely and Carmon, chap. 11 herein). Consequently, decision makers may prefer an improving episode over an alternative that is objectively superior (Kahneman et al. 1993). Duration neglect has important applications to painful medical procedures, such as colonoscopy (Redelmeier and Kahneman 1996).

Spreading Effect

Loewenstein and Prelec (1993) found that, in addition to a preference for improving sequences, decision makers also prefer outcomes that are spread evenly across the sequence interval. They found that 84 percent of subjects preferred to have a fancy French restaurant dinner on the second rather than the first of three weekends when it was specified that they would eat at home on the remaining weekends. Yet when it was specified that they would eat an exquisite lobster dinner on the third weekend, 54 percent of subjects preferred to have the fancy French dinner on the first rather than the second weekend. That is, the preference for having the French dinner sooner versus later was influenced by the event occurring on the third weekend. When a lobster dinner was scheduled for the third weekend, subjects were more likely to schedule the French dinner for the first weekend, so that the positive events would be spread across the three-week interval. This pattern violates the independence or separability axiom.

Chapman (1998) replicated this spreading effect in some additional scenarios about money (either winning a prize or paying a fine), health-related events (a painful trip to the dentist or a pain-relieving trip to the chiropractor), and restaurant meals (a pleasant meal with one's spouse or guest, or an unpleasant meal with an irritating co-worker). All types of scenarios showed a spreading effect. That is, preference for scheduling an event on the second or third of four weekends depended on what was scheduled for the first and fourth weekends. Thus the preference for spreading appears to generalize to multiple outcomes, including health.

In summary, a number of intertemporal decision biases occur in health decisions just as they do in decisions about money or other outcomes. These parallels point to the generality of these biases and suggest that the same mechanisms underlying monetary decisions can also account for health decisions.

Differences Between Health and Money Discounting Results

Not all studies have found consistency between health and money time preferences. Three differences between time preferences for health and money are next discussed.

Differences in Mean Discount Rates

Most studies that have compared time preferences for health and monetary outcomes have found discount rates to be higher for health than for monetary outcomes (Berndsen and van der Plight 2001; Cairns 1992; Chapman et al. 2001, Study 2; Chapman and Elstein 1995; Chapman et al. 1999). In the Chapman and colleagues (2001) study, the mean annual discount rate for a monetary scenario was 265 percent, whereas the mean discount rate for a heart disease scenario was 1125 percent. Madden and colleagues (1997) (see also Bickel and Johnson, chap. 14 herein) found that among heroin addicts, discount rates for heroin were higher than discount rates for money. This is especially interesting considering that money can be exchanged for heroin. Although most studies have found health discount rates to be higher, a few studies (Chapman 1996b, 1998; Chapman and Coups 1999) have found no difference between health and money discount rates. Few studies (Cairns 1992) have found discount rates to be higher for money than for health. When and why discount rates for health are higher than are those for money is currently not clear. One possibility is that decision makers infer uncertainty in the health outcome from the delay, but are less likely to infer this for monetary outcomes.

Domain Independence

Several studies have demonstrated domain independence (Cairns 1992; Chapman 1996b; Chapman and Elstein 1995; Chapman et al. 1999), which is the phenomenon that discount rates are not well correlated across domains such as health and money. Chapman and Elstein (1995) gave subjects a number of monetary discounting questions and an equal number of health discounting questions. The intradomain correlation between pairs of money questions or pairs of health questions was much larger than the interdomain correlation between health-money pairs. In one experiment, for example, the mean correlation between pairs of money questions was 0.81 and the analogous correlation for health was 0.82. Subjects thus were quite consistent in their time preferences within a domain. In contrast, the mean between-domain correlation was much lower, 0.26.

Domain independence represents a violation of normative discounted utility theory because normatively, decision domain should not influence discount rates. This bias does not consist of differences in mean discount rates across domain. Instead the bias consists of a lack of correlation across subjects between domains, indicating that individual subjects do not use the same discount rate for health and money. Much as other decision biases, domain independence may be a clue as to the psychological processes underlying intertemporal choice. Specifically, factors that differ between money and health and that influence time preferences could account for domain independence. Several potential causes of domain independence have been considered.

Chapman (1996b) assessed the possibility that domain independence might be the result not of different time preferences for health and money but of different utility functions for health and money. Matching health and money outcomes in terms of utility, however, did not eliminate domain independence. Similarly, computing discount rates in terms of utility (rather than in dollar or years of good health) also did not eliminate the domain differences.

Domain independence also does not appear to be due to differential familiarity with the health and money domains. Chapman and her colleagues (1999) compared discount rates for familiar and unfamiliar health domains. Patients with migraine headaches and patients with inflammatory bowel disease responded to intertemporal choice scenarios about both disorders. All patients made choices about a familiar domain (choices relating to their own disorder) and an unfamiliar domain (choices relating to the other group's disorder). In addition, all patients made intertemporal choices about money, a domain that is presumably familiar to everyone. Discount rates were highly correlated between the two health domains, despite their difference in familiarity. Monetary discount rates were only weakly correlated with either health domain. Domain independence thus appears not to be caused by differential familiarity with the health and money domains, and familiarity is not a strong determinant of time preferences.

A more viable account of domain independence concerns perceptions of tradability of health for money. The reason normative theory prescribes the same discount rate for both health and money is that violation of this prescription leads to anomalies in trading health for money. For example, if health is discounted at a lower rate than money, then any public health program that spends money now to gain health benefits now would be more cost effective if both the costs and benefits were delayed (indefinitely) into the future (Keeler and Cretin 1983). Thus the normative prescription to use the same discount rate in the two domains holds only under the assumption of fungibility. Fungibility is a reasonable assumption in health policy settings, where health benefits can be increased by spending more money and money can be saved by scaling back health benefits. Fungibility may be a less realistic assumption in some personal choices. In cases where money cannot be traded for health, no paradoxes or inconsistencies will result if different discount rates are used for health and money. Perhaps decision makers do not view health and money as tradable and as a consequence do not use consistent discount rates.

Chapman (2002) presented participants with a scenario in which money and health (a headache treatment) were either tradable (that is, headache treatment available for sale) or not tradable (that is, headache treatment available free of charge, but not for sale). Both versions of the questionnaire then asked participants to express their time preferences for health and money. In the nontradable condition the correlation between health and money discount rates was near zero, but in the tradable condition the correlation was moderate and significant. Thus decision makers were at least partially sensitive to the prescription that discount rates be consistent across decisions when the relevant domains are fungible.

Preferences for Sequences

Another difference between time preferences for health and money appears in preferences for sequences. As discussed previously, decision makers often express a preference for improving sequences, demonstrating a negative time preference. Chapman (1996a) found that negative time preferences for sequences were not ubiquitous. Preferences for sequences instead were influenced by expectations about how sequences are usually experienced. Subjects rated their preferences for sequences that described how their health or monetary income could change over their entire lifetime. Whereas subjects preferred increasing monetary sequences, they preferred declining health sequences. Furthermore, these preferences were in line with their stated expectations about how health and money would change over their lifespan. When evaluating short sequences (one year or twelve days), expectations about changes in health and money were similar to one another, and preferences also were similar in the two domains, with improving sequences preferred. Domain (health versus money) thus interacted with sequence length such that health and money preferences differed for long sequences but not for short sequences. Finally, ratings of expectations mediated this interaction.

The effect of expectations on preferences for sequences can produce different preferences for health and money outcomes. In addition, expectations can produce different preferences across health outcomes. Chapman (2000) found that college women were more likely to prefer an improving sequence of facial acne over a worsening sequence than to prefer an improving sequence of facial wrinkles over a worsening sequence. These preferences were in line with their expectations that acne improves but wrinkles worsen with age.

These results suggest that preferences for sequences are governed by at least two processes. One process involves adjustment to the current level of money or health, and interpretation of future levels as either gains or losses, relative to the current level. Because of loss aversion, decision makers prefer the series of gains provided by an increasing sequence to the series of losses provided by a decreasing sequence (Loewenstein and Prelec 1993). A second process involves expectations about how sequences usually occur and a preference for sequences that match expectations (Chapman 1996a). When expectations are strong (as with lifetime sequences of health), they can overpower the loss aversion mechanism, and when expectations for health differ from those for money, sequence preferences can differ across the two domains. When expectations are absent or weak (as with many short sequences), the loss aversion mechanism alone guides preferences, and thus preferences are similar for health and money.

Note that whereas the delay, magnitude, and sign effects discussed previously are all consistent across decision domains, the sequence effect is influenced by the decision domain. Preferences for sequences appear to be governed by mechanisms, such as expectations, that do not play such an important role in other intertemporal choice phenomena. Multiple mechanisms may be employed in intertemporal choice (Frederick et al., chap. 1 herein). Differences between health and money domains (or between different health domains) can help to uncover these mechanisms.

Time Preferences and Health Behavior

One of the rationales for studying intertemporal choice in the health domain is the possible application to preventive health behaviors. That is, understanding how decision makers make intertemporal health choices may illuminate the mechanisms behind preventive health behavior (Critchfield and Kollins 2001). Preventive health behaviors instantiate a choice between a small immediate reward (for example, eating a tasty dessert now) and a larger delayed reward (for example, being thin and healthy later). Thus a potential explanation for why many people fail to take preventive health measures is that they have very high discount rates. A failure to engage in preventive health behaviors is not in itself evidence of a high discount rate, because the behavior may have been rejected for other reasons, such as the belief that it would not be effective in improving future outcomes. High subjective discount rates instead provide one possible explanation for a failure to take preventive measures. Furthermore, intertemporal biases could account for inconsistent intentions to take preventive action. For example, the delay effect is a potential explanation for why people make resolutions to diet, exercise, or quit smoking but later fail to live up to these intentions (see Herman and Polivy, chap. 16 herein).

A strong relationship between time preferences and preventive health behaviors would suggest methods for encouraging these health behaviors. Specifically, manipulations that decrease discount rates should increase preventive health behaviors. Framing a health decision as a choice between losses rather than gains should decrease discount rates and thus increase the tendency to select the behavior with the better long-term outcome. Integrating multiple decisions about small-magnitude outcomes into one decision about large-magnitude outcomes should have a similar effect, as should framing a decision in terms of a sequence of outcomes rather than individual outcomes.

Despite the conceptual appeal of the temporal discounting account of preventive health behavior, relatively little evidence supports it. Several studies have examined the correlation between discount rates as measured with hypothetical choices and real-world health behavior. These studies assess whether individual differences in discount rates on the hypothetical-choice task correspond to individual differences in the health behavior. Overall, these studies have found little relationship.

In one such study, Fuchs (1982) compared monetary discount rates to self-reports of several health behaviors. He asked 508 community members ages twenty-five to sixty-four a series of monetary time-preference questions such as "Would you choose $1,500 now or $4,000 in five years?" The monetary amounts and delays varied across questions so as to identify each respondent's discount rate. Fuchs also asked about several health behaviors: smoking, exercise, seat belt use, dental exams, and being overweight. Discount rates had a small relationship to smoking. In addition, exercise was related to discount rate for men, but in the opposite direction to that expected (men with lower discount rates exercised less). Discount rate was not significantly correlated with any of the other health behaviors, although these relationships were in the expected direction. A measure of health status did show a small correlation with time preference, suggesting that those with low discount rates may engage in more health-improving behaviors. Thus time preferences were related to some but not all measures of health behavior, and the observed correlations were quite small.

Chapman (1998) reported two studies in which measures of time preference were unrelated to preventive behavior. One study examined two measures of adherence to hypertension treatment: pharmacy records of prescription refills and medical appointments kept. Neither measure was related to a hypothetical-choice measure of discount rate. The second study examined exercise behavior, which was unrelated to multiple time-preference measures (with one measure showing a small correlation in the counterpredicted direction).

Chapman and Coups (1999) examined the relationship between responses to hypothetical intertemporal trade-offs and acceptance of an influenza vaccine. They found a small but significant relationship between vaccine acceptance and a hypothetical monetary choice measure of time preferences. The same relationship did not hold for two measures of health time preference. Their results indicate some correspondence between hypothetical-choice time preferences measures and preventive health behaviors (such that people who show lower discount rates are more likely to engage in such behaviors), but that the relationship was quite small and was found with some measures but not others.

Chapman and her colleagues (2001) replicated the small but significant correlation between monetary (but not health) discount rates and flu shot acceptance. They also examined the relationship between discount rates and adherence with medication to control hypertension and high cholesterol. A health-choice measure of discount rates showed no relationship with cholesterol medication adherence. Ten correlations between discount rates and adherence with hypertension medication adherence were examined (two discount rate measures times five adherence measures), and only one was significant (and even that one was weak).

The aforementioned studies detected correlations between discount rates and preventive health behaviors for a minority of the measures examined, and when detectable, correlations were quite small. Thus they provide only very weak support for an association between time preferences and preventive health behavior.

In contrast to the studies reviewed thus far, strong evidence for the relationship between time preferences measures and health behavior comes from several studies of addictive behaviors (Bickel et al. 1999; Kirby et al. 1999; Madden et al. 1997; Vuchinich and Simpson 1998) neatly summarized in Bickel and Johnson (chap. 14 herein). Addictive behavior can be understood as an instance of intertemporal choice in that the user chooses whether to engage in an immediately pleasurable activity (using the substance) that carries a long-term cost (sustained addiction with negative consequences for health, job, and so forth) (Herrnstein and Prelec 1992). In several studies, addicts and matched controls were presented with choices between immediate and delayed sums of money. Participants' choices indicated their indifference points for each of several temporal delays, and discount functions were fit to the indifference points. The resulting discount rates were higher for heroin addicts than for matched non-drug-using controls (Kirby et al. 1999; Madden et al. 1997), higher for heavy social drinkers and problem drinkers than for light social drinkers (Vuchinich and Simpson 1998), and higher for current cigarette smokers than for ex-smokers and never-smokers (Bickel et al. 1999; see also Cairns 1994). Chesson and Viscusi (2000), however, used a somewhat different hypothetical measure of time preferences and found that discount rates were higher for nonsmokers than for smokers, contrary to expectation.

Addiction may bear a special relationship to time preference. Why substance abuse shows a reliable relationship to hypothetical-choice measures of time preference when other behaviors do not is currently unclear. One possibility is that substance abuse, rather than simply reflecting time preferences, actually influences them (see Bickel and Johnson, chap. 14 herein). A second possibility is that the association between time preference measures and addiction is an artifact of the case-control design used in these studies—specifically, addicts and controls may have differed in factors other than their addiction status. An alternative possibility is that some classes of behaviors reflect time preferences but not others. For example, "hot" emotional or impulsive behaviors might reflect time preferences more so than "cool" considered or habitual behaviors (for example, Metcalfe and Mischel 1999; Mischel et al., chap. 5 herein).

In summary, several previous studies have examined the relationship between health behavior and hypothetical measures of time preference. Fuchs (1982), Chapman (1998), Chapman and Coups (1999), and Chapman and colleagues (2001) found small or nonexistent relationships between discount rates and health behavior. Chesson and Viscusi (2000) found results in the contrapredicted direction. In contrast, Bickel and colleagues (Bickel et al. 1999; Kirby et al. 1999; Madden et al. 1997; also Vuchinich and Simpson 1998) found reliable and consistent associations between time preferences and addictive behaviors.

Given that time preferences vary so much from situation to situation, it is not surprising that discount rates measured with hypothetical choice scenarios do not predict real-world health behaviors that represent intertemporal trade-offs. Even when the hypothetical scenario describes a choice similar to the health behavior (for example, Chapman and Coups 1999; Chapman et al. 2001), enough contextual differences may exist between the two that different time preferences are applied to each. Thus, it may be that both hypothetical choices and health behaviors reflect time preferences but that time preferences vary sufficiently from situation to situation that the two are not related to each other. This position is consistent with data on intertemporal biases. It cannot explain, however, why addiction behaviors, unlike other health behaviors, show a strong relationship to discount rates measured via hypothetical choices. Differences between addiction and other health behaviors in relation to time preferences await future research.

Conclusion

Three rationales motivated the study of time discounting of health outcomes. First, it was hoped that an understanding of intertemporal choice would shed light on why people often fail to engage in preventive health behaviors—behaviors that exemplify a trade-off between short-term and long-term rewards. Recent studies have found surprisingly little relationship between discount rates and preventive health behavior, perhaps because discount rates are very sensitive to context. These findings suggest that time preference research may not be as helpful as once thought in understanding and encouraging preventive health behavior. That is, decision makers apparently do not have a consistent time preference trait that can be measured or manipulated in one setting and used to predict or influence health behavior in another.

The second rationale is the application of discount rates to health policy decisions. Health policy recommendations specify that the same discount rate be applied to both health and money outcomes. Empirical studies show that individual decision makers do not adhere to this prescription. This finding could have implications for how willing members of the public are to endorse health policies developed using the same discount rate for health and money.

The final rationale for studying time discounting of health outcomes is to use similarities and differences between health and money results as a clue to the underlying decision processes. As discussed, the pattern of results suggests that psychophysical functions, expectations, and context sensitivity underlie time preferences.

References

Ainslie, George. 1975. "Specious Reward: A Behavior Theory of Impulsiveness and Impulse Control." *Psychological Bulletin* 82(4): 463–509.

———. 1982. "A Behavioral Economic Approach to the Defense Mechanisms: Freud's Energy Theory Revisited." *Social Science Information* 21(6): 735–79.

———. 1984. "Behavioral Economics II: Motivated Involuntary Behavior." *Social Science Information* 23(1): 47–74.

———. 1986. "Beyond Microeconomics: Conflict Among Interests in a Multiple Self as a Determinant of Value." In *The Multiple Self*, edited by Jon Elster. New York: Cambridge University Press.

———. 1991. "Derivation of 'Rational' Economic Behavior from Hyperbolic Discount Curves." *American Economic Review* 81(2): 334–40.

Ariely, Dan, and Ziv Carmon. 2000. "Gestalt Characteristics of Experiences: The Defining Features of Summarized Events." *Journal of Behavioral Decision Making* 13(2): 191–202.

Ariely, Dan, and George Loewenstein. 2000. "When Does Duration Matter in Judgment an Decision Making?" *Journal of Experimental Psychology: General* 129(1): 508–23.

Benzion, Uri, Amon Rapoport, and Joseph Yagil. 1989. "Discount Rates Inferred from Decisions: An Experimental Study." *Management Science* 35(3): 270–84.

Berndsen, Mariëtte, and J. Joop van der Plight. 2001. "Time Is on My Side: Optimism in Intertemporal Choice." *Acta Psychologica* 108(2): 173–86.

Bickel, Warren K., Amy L. Odum, and Gregory J. Madden. 1999. "Impulsivity and Cigarette Smoking: Delay Discounting in Current, Never, and Ex-Smokers." *Psychopharmacology* 146(4): 447–54.

Bleichrodt, Han, and Magnus Johannesson. 2001. "Time Preference for Health: A Test of Stationarity Versus Decreasing Timing Aversion." *Journal of Mathematical Psychology* 45(2): 265–82.

Cairns, John A. 1992. "Health, Wealth and Time Preference." *Project Appraisal* 7(1): 31–40.

———. 1994. "Valuing Future Benefits." *Health Economics* 3(4): 221–29.

Cairns, John A., and Marjon M. van der Pol. 1997a. "Constant and Decreasing Timing Aversion for Saving Lives." *Social Science and Medicine* 45(11): 1653–59.

———. 1997b. "Saving Future Lives. A Comparison of Three Discounting Models." *Health Economics* 6(4): 341–50.

———. 1999. "Do People Value Their Own Future Health Differently from Others' Future Health?" *Medical Decision Making* 19(4): 466–72.

Chapman, Gretchen B. 1996a. "Expectations and Preferences for Sequences of Health and Money." *Organizational Behavior and Human Decision Processes* 67(1): 59–75.

———. 1996b. "Temporal Discounting and Utility for Health and Money." *Journal of Experimental Psychology: Learning, Memory, and Cognition* 22(3): 771–91.

———. 1997. "Risk Attitude and Time Preferences." *Medical Decision Making* 17(3): 355–56.

———. 1998. "Sooner or Later: The Psychology of Intertemporal Choice." In *The Psychology of Learning and Motivation,* edited by Douglas L. Medin. Vol. 38. New York: Academic Press.

———. 2000. "Preferences for Improving and Declining Sequences of Health Outcomes." *Journal of Behavioral Decision Making* 13(2): 203–18.

———. 2001. "Time Preferences for the Very Long Term." *Acta Psychologica* 108(2): 95–116.

———. 2002. "Your Money or Your Health: Time Preferences and Trading Money for Health." *Medical Decision Making* 22(5): 410–16.

Chapman, Gretchen B., Noel T. Brewer, Elliot J. Coups, Susan Brownlee, Howard Leventhal, and Elaine A. Leventhal. 2001. "Value for the Future and Preventive Health Behavior." *Journal of Experimental Psychology: Applied* 7(3): 235–50.

Chapman, Gretchen B., and Elliot J. Coups. 1999. "Time Preferences and Preventive Health Behavior: Acceptance of the Influenza Vaccine." *Medical Decision Making* 19(3): 307–14.

Chapman, Gretchen B., and Arthur S. Elstein. 1995. "Valuing the Future: Temporal Discounting of Health and Money." *Medical Decision Making* 15(4): 373–86.

Chapman, Gretchen B., Richard Nelson, and Daniel B. Hier. 1999. "Familiarity and Time Preferences: Decision Making About Treatments for Migraine

Headaches and Crohn's Disease." *Journal of Experimental Psychology: Applied* 5(1): 17–34.

Chapman, Gretchen B., and Bethany J. Weber. Forthcoming. "Decision Biases in Intertemporal Choice and Choice Under Uncertainty: Testing a Common Account."

Chapman, Gretchen B., and Jennifer R. Winquist. 1998. "The Magnitude Effect: Temporal Discount Rates and Restaurant Tips." *Psychonomic Bulletin and Review* 5(1): 119–23.

Chesson, Harrell, and W. Kip Viscusi. 2000. "The Heterogeneity of Time-Risk Tradeoffs." *Journal of Behavioral Decision Making* 13(2): 251–58.

Christensen-Szalanski, Jay J. J. 1984. "Discount Functions and the Measurement of Patients' Values: Women's Decisions During Childbirth." *Medical Decision Making* 4(1): 47–58.

Critchfield, Thomas S., and Scott H. Kollins. 2001. "Temporal Discounting: Basic Research and the Analysis of Socially Important Behavior." *Journal of Applied Behavior Analysis* 34(1): 101–22.

Cropper, Maureen L., Sema K. Aydede, and Paul R. Portney. 1992. "Rates of Time Preference for Saving Lives." *American Economic Review* 2: 469–72.

———. 1994. "Preferences for Life Saving Programs: How the Public Discounts Time and Age." *Journal of Risk and Uncertainty* 8(3): 243–65.

Cropper, Maureen L., and Paul R. Portney. 1990. "Discounting and Evaluation of Lifesaving Programs." *Journal of Risk and Uncertainty* 3(3): 369–79.

Cropper, Maureen L., and Frances G. Sussman. 1990. "Valuing Future Risks to Life." *Journal of Environmental Economics and Management* 19(2): 160–74.

Dolan, Paul, and Claire Gudex. 1995. "Time Preference, Duration and Health State Valuations." *Health Economics* 4(4): 289–99.

Enemark, Ulrika, Carl H. Lyttkens, Thomas Troëng, Henrik Weibull, and Jonas Ranstam. 1998. "Implicit Discount Rates of Vascular Surgeons in the Management of Abdominal Aortic Aneurysms." *Medical Decision Making* 18(2): 168–77.

Fredrickson, Barbara L., and Daniel Kahneman. 1993. "Duration Neglect in Retrospective Evaluations of Affective Episodes." *Journal of Personality and Social Psychology* 65(1): 45–55.

Fuchs, Victor R. 1982. "Time Preference and Health: An Exploratory Study." In *Economic Aspects of Health*, edited by Victor R. Fuchs. Chicago: University of Chicago Press.

Gafni, Amiram. 1995. "Time in Health: Can We Measure Individuals' 'Pure Time Preferences'?" *Medical Decision Making* 15(1): 31–37.

Gafni, Amiram, and George W. Torrance. 1984. "Risk Attitude and Time Preference in Health." *Management Science* 30(4): 440–51.

Ganiats, Theodore G., Richard T. Carson, Robert M. Hamm, Scott B. Cantor, Walton Sumner, Stephen J. Spann, Michael D. Hagen, and Christopher Miller. 2000. "Population-Based Time Preferences for Future Health Outcomes." *Medical Decision Making* 20(3): 263–70.

Gold, Marthe, Joanna Siegel, Louise Russell, and Milton C. Weinstein, eds. 1996. *Cost Effectiveness in Health and Medicine.* New York: Oxford University Press.

Green, Leonard, Nathanael Fristoe, and Joel Myerson. 1994. "Temporal Discounting and Preference Reversals in Choice Between Delayed Outcomes." *Psychonomic Bulletin and Review* 1(3): 383–89.

Green, Leonard, Joel Myerson, and Edward McFadden. 1997. "Rate of Temporal Discounting Decreases with Amount of Reward." *Memory and Cognition* 25(5): 715–23.

Green, Leonard, Joel Myerson, and R. Schneder. Forthcoming. "Is There a Magnitude Effect in Tipping?" *Psychonomic Bulletin and Review.*

Herrnstein, Richard J., and Drazen Prelec. 1992. "A Theory of Addiction." In *Choice Over Time*, edited by George Loewenstein and Jon Elster. New York: Russell Sage Foundation.

Horowitz, John K., and Richard T. Carson. 1990. "Discounting Statistical Lives." *Journal of Risk and Uncertainty* 3(3): 403–13.

Johannesson, Magnus, and Per-Olov Johansson. 1996. "The Discounting of Lives Saved in Future Generations—Some Empirical Results." *Health Economics* 5(4): 329–32.

Kahneman, Daniel, Barbara L. Fredrickson, Charles A. Schreibner, and Donald A. Redelmeier. 1993. "When More Pain Is Preferred to Less: Adding a Better End." *Psychological Science* 4(6): 401–5.

Keeler, Emmett B., and Shan Cretin. 1983. "Discounting of Life-Saving and Other Non-Monetary Effects." *Management Science* 29(3): 300–6.

Kirby, Kris N., and Richard J. Herrnstein. 1995. "Preference Reversals Due to Myopic Discounting of Delayed Reward." *Psychological Science* 6(2): 83–89.

Kirby, Kris N., and Nino N. Marakovic. 1995. "Modeling Myopic Decisions: Evidence for Hyperbolic Delay-Discounting Within Subjects and Amounts." *Organizational Behavior and Human Decision Processes* 64(1): 22–30.

———. 1996. "Delay-Discounting Probabilistic Rewards: Rates Decrease as Amounts Increase." *Psychonomic Bulletin and Review* 3(1): 100–4.

Kirby, Kris N., Nancy M. Petry, and Warren K. Bickel. 1999. "Heroin Addicts Have Higher Discount Rates for Delayed Rewards than Non-Drug-Using Controls." *Journal of Experimental Psychology: General* 128(1): 78–87.

Lipscomb, Joseph. 1989. "Time Preferences for Health in Cost-Effectiveness Analysis." *Medical Care* 27(3): s233–s253.

Loewenstein, George. 1987. "Anticipation and the Valuation of Delayed Consumption." *Economic Journal* 97(387): 666–84.

———. 1988. "Frames of Mind in Intertemporal Choice." *Management Science* 34(2): 200–14.

Loewenstein, George, and Drazen Prelec. 1992. "Anomalies in Intertemporal Choice: Evidence and Interpretation." *Quarterly Journal of Economics* 107(2): 573–97.

———. 1993. "Preferences for Sequences of Outcomes." *Psychological Review* 100(1): 91–108.

Loewenstein, George, and Nachum Sicherman. 1991. "Do Workers Prefer Increasing Wage Profiles?" *Journal of Labor Economics* 9(1): 67–84.

MacKeigan, Linda D., Lon N. Larson, JoLaine R. Draugalis, J. Lyle Bootman, and Lawton R. Bruns. 1993. "Time Preference for Health Gains Versus Health Losses." *Pharmacoeconomics* 3(5): 374–86.

Madden, Gregory J., Nancy M. Petry, Gary J. Badger, and Warren K. Bickel. 1997. "Impulsive and Self-Control Choices in Opioid-Dependent Patients and Non-Drug-Using Control Participants: Drug and Money Rewards." *Experimental and Clinical Psychopharmacology* 5(3): 256–62.

Metcalfe, Janet, and Walter Mischel. 1999. "A Hot/Cool-System Analysis of Delay Gratification: Dynamics of Willpower." *Psychological Review* 106(1): 3–19.

Moore, Michael J., and W. Kip Viscusi. 1990a. "Discounting Environmental Health Risks: New Evidence and Policy Implications." *Journal of Environmental Economics and Management* 18(2): S51–S62.

———. 1990b. "Models for Estimating Discount Rates for Long-Term Health Risks Using Labor Market Data." *Journal of Risk and Uncertainty* 3(3): 381–401.

Olsen, Jan Abel. 1993. "Time Preferences for Health Gains: An Empirical Investigation." *Health Economics* 2(3): 257–65.

Poulos, Christine, and Dale Whittington. 2000. "Time Preferences for Life-Saving Programs: Evidence from Six Less Developed Countries." *Environmental Science and Technology* 34(8): 1445–55.

Prelec, Drazen, and George Loewenstein. 1991. "Decision Making over Time and Under Uncertainty: A Common Approach." *Management Science* 37(7): 770–86.

Redelmeier, Donald A., and Daniel N. Heller. 1993. "Time Preferences in Medical Decision Making and Cost-Effectiveness Analysis." *Medical Decision Making* 13(3): 212–17.

Redelmeier, Donald A., and Daniel Kahneman. 1996. "Patients' Memories of Painful Medical Treatments: Real-Time and Retrospective Evaluations of Two Minimally Invasive Procedures." *Pain* 66(1): 3–8.

Shelley, Marjorie K. 1993. "Outcome Signs, Question Frames, and Discount Rates." *Management Science* 39(7): 806–15.

———. 1994. "Gain/Loss Asymmetry in Risky Intertemporal Choice." *Organizational Behavior and Human Decision Processes* 59(1): 124–59.

Svenson, Ola, and Gunnar Karlsson. 1989. "Decision-making, Time Horizons, and Risk in the Very Long-term Perspective." *Risk Analysis* 9(3): 385–99.

Thaler, Richard H. 1981. "Some Empirical Evidence on Dynamic Inconsistency." *Economic Letters* 8: 201–7.

van der Pol, Marjon M., and John A. Cairns. 1999. "Individual Time Preferences for Own Health: An Application of a Dichotomous Choice Question with Follow-up." *Applied Economics Letters* 6(10): 649–54.

———. 2000. "Negative and Zero Time Preference for Health." *Health Economics* 9(2): 171–75.

———. 2001. "Estimating Time Preferences for Health Using Discrete Choice Experiments." *Social Science and Medicine* 52(9): 1459–70.

Viscusi, W. Kip, and Michael J. Moore. 1989. "Rates of Time Preference and Valuation of the Duration of Life." *Journal of Public Economics* 38(3): 287–317.

Vuchinich, Rudy E., and Cathy A. Simpson. 1998. "Hyperbolic Temporal Discounting in Social Drinkers and Problem Drinkers." *Experimental and Clinical Psychopharmacology* 6(3): 292–305.

· 14 ·

Delay Discounting: A Fundamental Behavioral Process of Drug Dependence

WARREN K. BICKEL AND MATTHEW W. JOHNSON

> Thence is imposed the task of everywhere seeking out in the natural phenomena those elements that are the same, and that amid all multiplicity are ever present.
>
> —Ernst Mach (1893)

ERNST MACH states one of the basic goals of all sciences: to discover the commonalities or fundamental elements that provide a parsimonious account of the subject matter. In the science of drug dependence, these fundamental elements, or underlying behavioral processes, are generally not well understood. To date only two such processes—drug reinforcement and drug craving—have been conclusively identified. From our perspective, drug dependence is unlikely to result from merely one or two behavioral processes. If those were the only processes involved, we would have expected greater success in the prevention and treatment of drug dependence than has been observed to date. In contrast to viewing drug dependence as composed of one or two behavioral processes, we propose here (and to our knowledge for the first time in the field) that drug dependence is a complexly determined self-organizing system.

Self-organizing systems are characterized by an essential property of robustness (Kitano 2002). Robustness entails the ability to cope

419

with environmental change, insensitivity to a wide variety of parameter values of the comprising processes, and absence of catastrophic failure following damage to the system (Kitano 2002). These characteristics of self-organizing systems in biology are certainly shared by drug dependence. If drug dependence were such a self-organizing system, then robustness may result from control systems (for example, negative feedback), redundancy (multiple components serving similar functions), structural stability (mechanisms to specifically support stability), modularity (the system contains subsystems that can sustain damage and not propagate damage to other subsystems), or some combination thereof (Kitano 2002).

If drug dependence is such a system, then an important research goal is to identify any additional behavioral processes (that is, modules) that may contribute to drug dependence. This should be followed by exploration of how they operate (for example, negative feedback) and how one behavioral process interacts with others in a potentially self-reinforcing manner to produce the phenomenon of drug dependence. The behavioral processes in which we are interested do not necessarily contribute to drug dependence in an additive sense, but rather interact dynamically to form the complex, self-sustaining system of drug dependence. Such behavioral processes therefore should not be viewed as independent risk factors predisposing drug dependence, but rather as interdependent components or modules that have a specific role (perhaps multiple specific roles) in the system. We are not interested in long enduring factors such as personality traits, which may be important predisposing factors. Rather, we are interested in dynamic behavioral processes that are presumably available to our species because of their value to survival and reproduction, but that come to be employed in the process of drug dependence.

The task that follows from our proposal is to specify criteria with which we can identify candidate behavioral processes. Herein we propose criteria that drug reinforcement and drug craving meet and, as we will show, delay discounting meets. These criteria, as we employ them, may not be definitive and perhaps could result in false positive identifications; but because no such criteria for identifying candidate behavioral processes exist, proposing our criteria here may foster debate that may lead to widely accepted criteria.

One potential approach to developing such criteria is to start with widely replicated and accepted empirical findings that are considered important in drug dependence. One such widely accepted observation is that drug dependence results from the interaction of drugs of abuse with evolutionarily old regions of the brain (Nestler and Landsman 2001). These regions, such as the limbic system, regulate an organism's response to reinforcers such as food, drink, and sex (Robbins and Everitt 1999). Expanding on this observation, Nestler and Landsman (2001, 834) state, "the loss of control that addicts show with respect to drug seeking and taking may relate to the ability of drugs of abuse to commandeer these natural reward circuits and disrupt an individual's motivation and drive for normal reinforcers."

Our first criterion therefore states that drugs of dependence interact with—or to use Nestler and Landsman's term, *commandeer*—evolutionarily old brain regions, and we should expect a candidate behavioral process to be conserved across species (qualitatively fixed), including humans, due to common descent. That is, the same functional process should be observed across species, although quantitative differences may exist as might be expected with homologous processes. Our second criterion states that we should observe quantitative differences in this behavioral process when the drug-dependent are compared with non-drug-dependent controls if the drug or some aspect of dependence is affecting the process. Our third criterion states that if the drug use has commandeered the behavioral process, then decreasing drug use to a nondependent status should produce a quantitative reversal in the behavioral process (quantitatively flexible). Experimental evidence therefore must be used to evaluate each of these three criteria for a viable behavioral process to be considered a module of drug dependence.

We suggest that delay discounting is a behavioral process that meets these three criteria. Delay discounting describes an important aspect of behavior—that is, delaying a reinforcer decreases its effect on behavior (Rachlin, Raineri, and Cross 1991). In other words, the value of a delayed reward is discounted (reduced in value or considered to be worth less) compared to the value of an immediate reward. Indeed the notion of delay discounting is intuitive in the sense that most people would prefer a reward now rather than later (Kirby 1997).

Criterion 1. Cross-Species Generality

Studies of delay discounting typically employ procedures similar to those used in psychophysical experiments (Richards et al. 1997). Psychophysical procedures typically present a participant with a standard stimulus and another stimulus that is adjusted until the two stimuli are considered equivalent by the participant (Stevens 1975). Similarly, procedures used in delay-discounting experiments present subjects with a choice between a standard larger, later reward (for example, food pellets in seconds, or $1,000 delivered months later for nonhumans and humans, respectively) and an immediate reward whose magnitude is adjusted until the participant considers the two rewards to be of approximately equal worth (for example, Green, Fry, and Myerson 1994). This procedure is referred to as the adjusting magnitude procedure (Richards et al. 1997). This point of equivalence is referred to as the *indifference point* for a particular delay interval. When indifference points are obtained for a variety of delays, an *indifference curve* may be plotted. The shape of the indifference curve may then be expressed and evaluated as a *discounting function*, which expresses the shape of the indifference curve mathematically and allows the discounting rates to be quantified.

The shape of the indifference curve is fundamental because it helps in understanding the delay discounting process and in turn allows predictions of derivative phenomenon (for example, preference reversals: see Frederick, Loewenstein, and O'Donoghue, chap. 1 herein; Green, Fristoe, and Myerson 1994). Traditional economic models, including the Rational Theory of Addiction (Becker and Murphy 1988), assume that indifference curves are *exponential* (for example, Fishburn and Rubinstein 1982; Lancaster 1963; Meyer 1976). That is, for each additional unit of time that constitutes delay until delivery, the present value of a reward decreases (or is discounted) by a fixed proportion (Kirby 1997). Exponential discounting, however, has *not* been empirically supported by behavioral research conducted in nonhuman and human subjects. Instead these studies demonstrate that delay discounting is hyperbolic. *Hyperbolic discounting* refers to the devaluation of delayed rewards proportional to their delay (Ainslie 1992); that is, for each additional unit of time that constitutes delay until delivery, the reward's present value decreases by an increasingly smaller proportion (Kirby 1997). Although not the only hyperbolic equation capable of modeling delay discounting, the following equation with a single free parameter developed by Mazur (1987) has been used successfully to accurately model indifference curves.

$$v_d = \frac{V}{(1 + kd)} \tag{14.1}$$

In equation 14.1, v_d is the present, discounted value of a delayed reward (that is, the indifference point), V is the objective amount (or undiscounted value) of the delayed reward, k is an empirically estimated constant expressing the degree of delay discounting (that is, discounting rate), and d is delay duration. Given this equation, consider what would be necessary to increase the present value of a reinforcer. The value of a reinforcer (v_d) can be increased by either increasing its objective amount (V), decreasing its delay (d), or by decreasing the delay discounting rate (k), if discounting rate can be directly manipulated.

Using such methods, the cross-species generality of delay discounting can be considered. Figure 14.1 shows discounting functions that describe the delay discounting of three different species, all with a high degree of accuracy. The upper-left panel shows the discounting function obtained from pigeons in Mazur's original study (1987). In that study, Mazur used an analogous procedure to that described in the foregoing. Specifically, Mazur used a smaller, immediate and a larger, delayed food reinforcer and adjusted the time interval between them until the pigeons were indifferent (adjusting delay procedure). The upper-right panel shows the discounting function obtained from a study by Richards and colleagues (1997) that used an adjusting magnitude procedure with water as the reinforcer in rats. The bottom panel shows the discounting function obtained from a study by Rachlin and colleagues (1991) that used an adjusting magnitude procedure with a hypothetical $1,000 reward in human research participants. Collectively, these data demonstrate that the discounting function of a variety of different reinforcers across these three species is hyperbolic in form (see Tobin and Logue 1994 for a comparable demonstration). Note, however, that along with that generality in the function form, quantitative differences exist: in these experimental procedures the discounting rates of food and water for pigeons and rats were best expressed with seconds, and those of money for humans were best expressed with months. Moreover, the fact that humans can discount money suggests that humans may employ this process with a wide range of consequences. Nonetheless, these and other data conclusively demonstrate that the indifference curves are accurately modeled with the hyperbolic function expressed in equation 14.1 (typically accounting for more than 85 percent of the variance) when food and water are used with nonhumans (Mazur 1988, 2000; Richards, Sabol, and DeWit 1999; Rodriguez and Logue 1988; Wade et al. 2000) and real and hypothetical money are used with human subjects (Green, Fry, and Myerson 1994; Kirby 1997; Kirby, Petry, and Bickel 1999; Johnson and Bickel 2002; Madden et al. 1997; Myerson and Green 1995; Rachlin, Raineri, and Cross 1991).

The first criterion specified that behavioral processes underlying drug dependence should have cross-species generality, given that drugs of dependence interact with evolutionary old-brain regions. As reviewed here, the discounting of delayed reinforcers was found to

Figure 14.1   Discounting Functions for Pigeons, Rats, and Humans

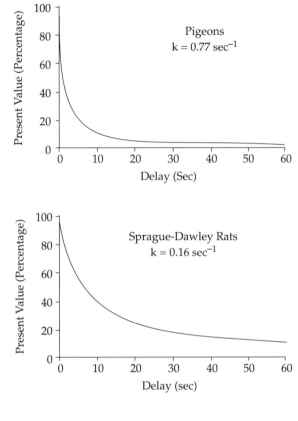

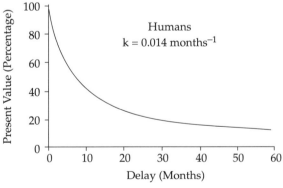

Source: Mazur (1987); Richards et al. (1997); and Rachlin et al. (1991), respectively.

have cross-species generality. Moreover, a recent report using rats as subjects examined brain regions that may contribute to delay discounting. Lesions to the nucleus accumbens in the limbic system produced persistent increases in the preference of smaller immediate food reinforcers over larger delayed ones, but lesions to two of its afferents in the evolutionarily newer cortex—the anterior cingulate cortex and medial prefrontal cortex—produced no such change (Cardinal et al. 2001; see Manuck et al., chap. 4 herein, for a review of the limbic system's role in delayed reinforcement). Thus this study empirically demonstrated that evolutionarily old-brain regions mediate or contribute to discounting of delayed reinforcers. In conclusion, delay discounting is a behavioral process that has cross-species generality, and as such meets the first criterion.

Criterion 2. Quantitative Differences in Discounting Between Drug Dependents and Controls

For delay discounting to meet the second criterion, quantitative differences must be observed between the discounting of drug-dependent individuals and matched control individuals. Examination of delay discounting in the drug dependent has been increasingly investigated. Overall, these findings demonstrate that the drug-dependent discount delayed reinforcers more so than controls. We are aware of fourteen studies that examined this topic, which we will categorize by drug of dependence.

Opioid-dependent individuals have been examined in four studies. The first study reviewed here was our initial study on delay discounting. In that study, we compared the delay discounting of opioid-dependent patients and community volunteer controls matched on age, education, gender, income, and IQ (Madden et al. 1997). Participants chose between hypothetical monetary rewards available immediately or following a delay. Delayed rewards were $1,000, and the immediate reward amount was adjusted until choices reflected indifference. This process was repeated at each of seven delays (ranging one week to twenty-five years). The opioid-dependent participants were also given a second series of choices between immediate and delayed hypothetical heroin, using the same procedures (the amount of heroin was adjusted using street values such that the dollar amount of the delayed heroin was $1,000). Figure 14.2 shows the results from this study. Across the opioid-dependent and control participants, the hyperbolic discounting function expressed in equation 14.1 accounted for between 80 percent and 99 percent of the variance. The rate of delay discounting for monetary rewards was significantly greater for the opioid-dependent than normal participants. For example, to reduce the subjective value of $1,000 by approximately 50 percent required an average delay of one year for the opioid dependents and an average delay of five years for the controls (a fivefold difference). Within the opioid-dependent sample, the discounting of heroin was significantly greater than the discounting of money; heroin lost nearly 60 percent of its value at one week (more than fifty-two-fold difference compared to their monetary choices). This demonstrates that the magnitude of discounting is not invariant but rather is dependent on the type of reinforcer. Moreover, these results demonstrate that we can successfully modify commonly used money procedures to estimate the delay discounting of drugs. Most important, this study demonstrates that there is a large quantitative difference between the two groups in this behavioral process.

The second study systematically replicated the preceding one by using a procedure in which subjects actually received one of their monetary choices, chosen randomly from all choices made (Kirby, Petry, and Bickel 1999). Opioid-dependent participants were found to discount significantly more than controls. This study also examined more than one monetary amount, and was therefore able to demonstrate the magnitude effect. The magnitude effect refers to the inverse relationship between the magnitude of the delayed reward and the degree of delay discounting in humans (Chapman 1996): for example, $10 would be discounted proportionally more than a $1,000 reward. Evidence for the magnitude effect in humans comes from a variety of experiments employing real (for example, Kirby 1997; Kirby and Marakovic 1996) and hypothetical monetary rewards (for example, Myerson and Green 1995; Raineri and Rachlin 1993; Thaler 1981). This study is the first to examine the magnitude effect in the drug dependent. Interestingly, the magnitude effect was observed in both the opioid dependents and the controls, even though the opioid-dependent individuals discounted more than the controls. Of equal importance, this study confirms that the same findings observed with hypothetical rewards could be replicated with actual monetary outcomes (see Johnson and Bickel 2002 for a within-subject comparison of the delay discounting of real and hypothetical rewards across several magnitudes).

The third study examining opioid dependents compared the hyperbolic and exponential discounting functions in their ability to account for the discounting of delayed hypothetical money and heroin (Madden, Bickel, and Jacobs 1999). The hyperbolic form accounted for significantly more variance than the exponential model. The fourth

Figure 14.2   Delay Discounting

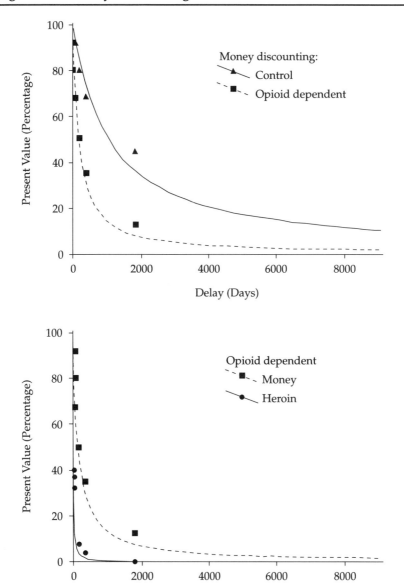

Source: Madden et al. (1997).
Note: The top panel describes the discounting of money by opioid-dependent individuals and controls. The bottom panel describes the discounting of money and heroin by opioid-dependent individuals.

study addressed heterogeneity among opioid-dependent individuals by comparing the discounting of opioid-dependent individuals who do and do not share injecting equipment (Odum et al. 2000). Patients who did not share needles replicated the general observation that opioid-dependent individuals discount heroin significantly more than money. In contrast, opioid-dependent individuals who shared needles discounted both heroin and money extremely, with no difference between the discounting of money and heroin. This study illustrates that the delay-discounting behavioral process is related to risky behavior even among the drug dependent. Perhaps this effect of increased discounting of money, but not heroin, among needle sharers is a result of a ceiling effect for heroin discounting among opioid-dependent individuals regardless of needle-sharing status. In other words, perhaps needle sharers are generally more impulsive than nonsharers, but this was only evident for money because heroin discounting is already near a maximum even for nonsharers, which is evident in the bottom panel of figure 14.2.

The next three studies compared the delay discounting of cigarette smokers and matched controls. Bickel, Odum, and Madden's (1999) results were consistent with the observations made with opioid-dependent individuals. Results are shown in figure 14.3. Cigarette smokers discounted a hypothetical $1,000 reward more than matched controls, and cigarette smokers discounted hypothetical cigarettes ($1,000 worth) more than hypothetical money. Mitchell (1999) replicated part of these results by showing that smokers discounted real money more than controls. In the third study, Baker, Johnson, and Bickel (forthcoming) comprehensively compared the delay discounting of cigarette smokers and matched controls. This study examined the discounting of hypothetical money gains and losses at three magnitudes ($10, $100, and $1,000), real money at two magnitudes ($10, $100), gains and losses in hypothetical health at all three magnitudes (amounts subjectively equivalent to $10, $100, and $1,000), and, in the smokers only, gains and losses of cigarettes at these three magnitudes (also amounts subjectively equivalent to $10, $100, and $1,000). This study replicated each of the within-subject measures at a one-week interval to assess their stability. Thus this study allowed a comparison of real versus hypothetical money, an assessment of the reliability of the measures, the magnitude effect (described earlier) and the sign effect. The sign effect refers to the observation that rewards are discounted more than comparably valued losses (for example, Thaler 1981). This loss aversion phenomenon has been empirically demonstrated in normal human populations. For example, Loewenstein (1988) found that subjects were indifferent to gaining $100 now and

Figure 14.3   Delay Discounting of Cigarette Smokers

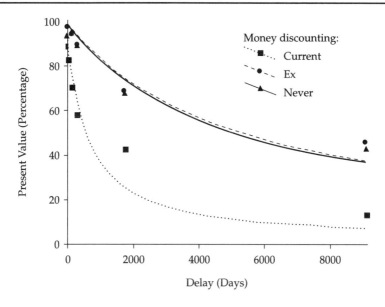

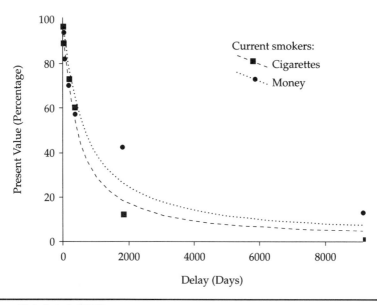

Source: Bickel et al. (1999).
Note: The top panel describes the discounting of money by current, never-, and ex-smokers. The bottom panel describes the discounting of money and cigarettes by current smokers.

gaining $157 a year from now, while they were indifferent between losing $100 now and losing $133 a year from now; that is, gains were discounted 68 percent more than losses. Our results were consistent with these other previously observed phenomena. First, cigarette smokers discounted all magnitudes and signs of all commodities more than matched controls. Second, there were no significant differences between real and hypothetical money (replicating Johnson and Bickel 2002). Third, the results were reliable when subjects were retested one week later (replicating Simpson and Vuchinich 2000, who examined delay discounting of money at a one-month interval in nondependent individuals). Fourth, the magnitude and sign effects were observed across commodities and subject groups. Fifth, this study demonstrated that health outcomes are delay discounted, demonstrating the same functional relationships observed with other rewards (hyperbolic in form, magnitude effect, sign effect). This finding supports the notion that humans delay discount a wide variety of consequences, and these can be studied with methods analogous to money. Together these results suggest that the increased delay discounting observed in the drug dependent is systematic—that is, the group differences were apparent across commodities, magnitudes, and signs, even though the typical magnitude and sign effects were observed in both groups. This indicates that differences in discounting in the drug dependent are better described by a generalized quantitative shift in the normal delay-discounting process, rather than by a separate process.

Four studies examined the association between delay discounting and alcohol. Two studies examined delay discounting of hypothetical monetary rewards in heavy- versus light-drinking participants, and participants classified as problem drinkers versus light-drinking participants (Vuchinich and Simpson 1998). The heavy and problem drinkers were college students not in treatment. Relative to the light drinkers, heavy and problem drinkers showed higher rates of delay discounting; that is, heavy and problem drinkers devalued delayed money more than light drinkers. Moreover, the hyperbolic equation described in equation 14.1 accounted for significantly more variance than the exponential function developed via economic approaches. Petry (2001) compared the discounting of money and alcohol (each at two magnitudes) among alcohol-dependent individuals and matched control subjects. Alcoholics discounted hypothetical money more than controls, and alcoholics discounted alcohol more than money. In addition, subjects in both groups showed the magnitude effect. Finally, Petry and colleagues (2002) examined the association between paternal history of alcohol dependence and delay discounting of real monetary rewards by comparing nondependent individuals with and without a father with a history of alcohol dependence. Although the researchers found no difference in discounting rates between males with and without paternal histories of alcohol dependence, they did find that females with a paternal history of alcohol dependence had higher rates of discounting compared with females without a paternal history of alcohol dependence. Although no effect was found for males, these results suggest the possibility that increased discounting may be a risk factor for alcohol dependence that is susceptible to familial transmission.

Three studies looked at more heterogeneous groups of drug-dependent individuals. The very first study of this type compared the delay discounting of hypothetical monetary outcomes of a heterogeneous group of substance-abusing inpatients versus employees of that inpatient unit (Ainslie and Haendel 1983). The substance abusers discounted hypothetical monetary rewards to a greater extent than did employees. Another study found the same profile of results comparing a heterogeneous group of heroin and amphetamine injectors versus controls in Norway (Bretteville-Jensen 1999). Lastly, Petry (2000) has examined the discounting of heterogeneous substance abusers that do and do not gamble. Intriguingly, her data suggest that the comorbid disorder of gambling contributed to greater discounting than observed among substance abusers who did not gamble.

The second criterion specified that quantitative differences should be observed between normal and drug-dependent individuals on the candidate behavioral process. Substantial quantitative differences were observed in comparisons of the drug dependent and controls on measures of the discounting of delayed reinforcers. This growing body of research demonstrates that there are quantitative differences in the discounting of delayed reinforcers when the drug dependent are compared to non-drug-dependent controls. These data provide substantial evidence that discounting meets the second of the three criteria.

Criterion 3. Decreases in Drug Use or Changes in Drug-Dependence Status Produces Quantitative Changes in Discounting

The third criterion is that discounting will change when drug-use or drug-dependence status changes. Evidence in support for discounting of delayed reinforcers meeting this criterion can be obtained by: cross-sectional studies comparing the discounting of individuals who are currently drug dependent with individuals who have a history of dependence but are not currently dependent on drugs; and prospective studies where drug use is actively manipulated.

Several of the foregoing studies also examined discounting individuals who were no longer drug dependent. For example, in the study described earlier where we examined the discounting of current and never-smokers, we also examined the discounting of ex-smokers (abstinence for one year or longer) who were matched on the same demographic characteristics as current and nonsmokers (Bickel, Odum, and Madden 1999). Ex-smokers were found to discount money in a fashion identical to nonsmokers. Petry (2001) examined delay discounting in recently abstinent alcohol-dependent individuals (abstinence for one month or longer) and found that their discounting of money was intermediate between current alcoholics and controls. In a study of heroin and amphetamine injectors, Bretteville-Jensen (1999) also examined ex-injectors of heroin and amphetamine in comparison to current and never heroin and amphetamine users and found that the ex-injectors' discounting of money was intermediate between the current and never groups. Allen and colleagues (1998) compared a heterogeneous group of current and ex-drug-dependent individuals and found differences between the groups on a behavioral measure of impulsivity with real monetary reinforcers. This procedure shares some similar elements to the discounting procedure. Collectively, these studies are consistent in that they find that individuals who are no longer dependent or have a period of abstinence discount less than current drug users.

These studies must be interpreted with care, given that they are cross-sectional comparisons. Specifically, these studies may be interpreted in at least two ways. First, these data would be consistent with the notion that individuals who discount less find it easier to become abstinent (less discounting leads to abstinence). Second, these data are also consistent with the notion that individuals who stop using drugs in turn discount less (abstinence leads to less discounting). Of course, a test of these competing interpretations requires prospective studies. In developing these studies, we hypothesized that abstinence leads to less discounting. Yet in formulating these studies, we also hypothesized that duration of abstinence may be an important modulator. Specifically, we hypothesized that an initial period of abstinence may lead to greater discounting (analogous to responding during the immediate imposition of extinction in operant arrangements). Also, we hypothesized that after a longer period of abstinence (analogous to an extended sequence of extinction) discounting would decrease to a level below that observed when drug use was ongoing. This latter hypothesis, if proved, would confirm the third criterion.

To address these hypotheses, we conducted two prospective studies. In the first study, using a within-subject design, we examined the effects of brief abstinence and correspondingly mild opioid withdrawal in the discounting of opioid-dependent individuals who were maintained on buprenorphine (Giordano et al. forthcoming). Specifically, these individuals discounted small, medium, and large magnitudes of hypothetical heroin and money under conditions of brief buprenorphine deprivation and satiation. To participate, subjects had to demonstrate abstinence from opioids other than buprenorphine under all conditions. Across conditions, hyperbolic functions provided a good fit for the discounting data. Degree of discounting across commodity and magnitudes was significantly higher when subjects were opioid deprived than satiated. Consistent with previous findings, degree of discounting was higher for heroin than money and inversely related to the magnitude of the reinforcers. Opioid deprivation thus increased the degree to which dependent individuals discounted delayed heroin and money.

In the second study using a random-assignment parallel group design, we examined a longer period of abstinence (Bickel et al. forthcoming). Specifically, we randomly assigned cigarette-dependent individuals to two groups. Both groups performed a procedure measuring temporal discounting for money and cigarettes on a Friday. During the following Monday through Friday, the experimental group came to our laboratory and provided a carbon monoxide (CO) breath sample (an indicator of recent smoking) three times daily (for example, morning, afternoon, and evening). If the reading indicated that a participant had not smoked, he or she was immediately reinforced with $10 in cash. Control group members were only asked to follow their regular smoking patterns during this time. On the Friday of this week (one week after initial discounting assessment), delay discounting was again measured for money and cigarettes in both groups. Figure 14.4 shows the results from the study by plotting the resulting k parameter obtained with equation 14.1. No changes were observed in the control group on measures of discounting taken prior to and after the seven-day period, while discounting of money and cigarettes were significantly less after the week of abstinence in the experimental group. No differences were detected between groups on measures of discounting prior to the intervention, but the abstinent group was more self-controlled than the control group at the end session. These findings suggest that increased temporal discounting may be a reversible consequence of cigarette smoking in this case and, if replicated, this observation may pertain to drug dependence in general.

The third criterion specified that delay discounting changes when drug use or drug dependence status changes. Cross-sectional studies

Figure 14.4   Delay Discounting for Money and Cigarettes

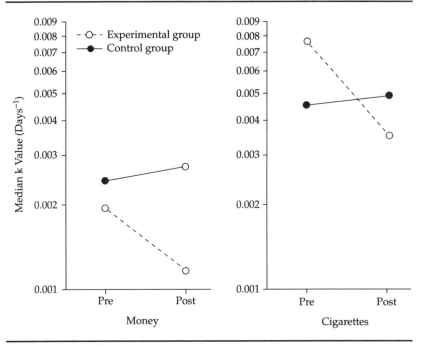

Source: Bickel et al. (forthcoming).
Note: Median discounting parameters (k from equation 14.1) from Bickel et al. (forth-coming) for the experimental group, which was paid money for abstinence, and the control group who smoked normally. The left panel shows discounting for money and the right panel shows discounting for cigarettes. Note the logarithmic scale for the y-axis.

demonstrated that ex-dependent individuals or individuals who have some degree of abstinence discount less than current drug-dependent individuals and approximate controls who were never dependent. Prospective studies demonstrated that discounting is quantitatively flexible or dynamic in that discounting can increase and decrease de-pending on conditions related to drug use. Specifically, during initial periods of brief abstinence, discounting increased in opioid-depen-dent individuals, while a longer period of abstinence resulted in less discounting in cigarette smokers. Interestingly, some of these changes are not only evident across drug reinforcers but money as well. In conclusion, the data on the topic support that the discounting of de-layed reinforcers meets the third criterion.

Conclusion

We conclude that delay discounting meets the three criteria set forth at the beginning of the chapter for a fundamental behavioral process of drug dependence. First, evidence suggests that evolutionarily, old-brain regions may be central in the delay-discounting process, which corresponds to the quantitatively fixed hyperbolic discounting function observed in a wide variety of species and a variety of reinforcers. Second, study after study has demonstrated that the drug dependent discount more than the nondrug dependent, across a wide range of drug-dependent populations and across different commodities, magnitudes, and signs (reward or loss) of consequence. Third, results in our laboratory have demonstrated that the extreme discounting among the drug dependent may be modulated by present manipulations of drug deprivation. Therefore, to the degree that these criteria are appropriate, delay discounting appears to be a fundamental behavioral process underlying drug dependence.

If extreme delay discounting is a fundamental behavioral process of drug dependence, what implication does this have for the prevention and treatment of drug dependence? For prevention, it would indicate that individuals with sufficient experience in pursuing and accomplishing relatively long-term goals may be less susceptible to allowing the brief, intense reinforcing effects of drugs to commandeer a large portion of their behavior. Education, exercise, athletics, religious activities, and a variety of recreational activities may provide such opportunities for realizing long-term goals. Therefore an environment rich with such temporally extended activities may serve to condition lower rates of delay discounting, and thus provide a protection against the initiation of drug use, or the development of dependence upon initiation of drug use. An environment rich in nondrug stimuli that are likewise brief and intense without long-term goals, however, may serve to increase delay discounting (or perhaps simply prevent the development of decreased delay discounting during development). Examples of such stimuli could be television, a diet rich in calorie-dense foods, and video games. Environments rich in these activities to the exclusion of more temporally extended activities may provide fertile ground for the development of drug dependence once drugs are encountered later in life.

For drug-dependence treatment, such an account would suggest two points. First, it indicates what is to be expected on the part of the drug-dependent individual during treatment. Hyperbolic discounting, particularly the steep discounting seen in drug-dependent individuals, predicts the phenomenon of preference reversals (Frederick, Loewenstein, and O'Donoghue, chap. 1 herein; Green, Fristoe, and Myerson 1994). Preference reversals may be manifest in treatment when an individual expresses interest in drug abstinence while in the context of treatment but exhibits a sharp reversal of preference days or perhaps hours later, when he or she encounters drugs in his or her normal environment. This reversal may not be evidence of deception in treatment, but simply a genuine reversal of preference due to hyperbolic discounting of an extreme rate.

Second, one would not expect treatments that exclusively rely on extended, long-term reinforcers to be effective. Perhaps this is one reason for the success of contingency management treatments in drug dependence (for example, Higgins 1997). In these treatments, drug-dependent participants submit frequent urinalysis samples, and drug-free samples are reinforced with vouchers exchangeable for socially acceptable reinforcers such as recreational activities. Viewed from the perspective of delay discounting, these treatments have taken the normally very delayed reinforcing consequences of drug abstinence, such as improved health, a fulfilling career, and a stable family life, and supplemented them with near-immediate reinforcers that are within the dependent individual's shortened time horizon. With continued abstinence, perhaps the long-term, naturalistic consequences of drug abstinence may be realized and serve to maintain further abstinence.

The thorough examination of any scientific phenomenon requires a search for those common elements that define the subject matter. The history of science is full of examples where the identification of fundamental elements set the stage for a proliferation of research and theory. Pioneering work in the physical sciences by such individuals as Dalton and Rutherford led to the acceptance of the atom as a fundamental element of matter. Similarly in biological sciences, Mendel's discovery that inheritance was transmitted through fundamental units (genes) allowed genetics to flourish (although thirty-five years passed before others realized the importance of his work). In the history of psychology, the identification of Pavlovian and operant conditioning as fundamental forms of learning were essential for the exploration of behavioral phenomena.

We believe that this review supports our contention that delay discounting is a dynamic behavioral process that underlies drug dependence. As noted, whether such criteria prove useful will await other behavioral phenomena shown to conform to these notions. In this regard, a recent study by Perkins and colleagues (2001) provide such data. They examined the reinforcing properties of nicotine in current, ex-, and nonsmokers. Consistent with the proposed criteria, nicotine was more reinforcing in current smokers than in ex- and nonsmokers. Importantly, ex- and nonsmokers were not different from each other. These criteria, if supported with additional data and with other behavior phenomena, could be one potential benefit of this research beyond the scope of the specific studies reviewed herein.

Nonetheless, delay discounting appears to be a behavioral process underlying drug dependence, and understanding more about discounting may provide a better scientific understanding of drug dependence. Such information indeed may suggest new molecular targets for study, new agents for candidate medications, and perhaps new approaches to developing psychotherapies. A broader potential contribution of this work on discounting is that it may suggest the utility of identifying additional behavioral processes that contribute to or underlie drug dependence. If these other behavioral processes are identified, perhaps they may be found to affect or be affected by discounting. Such interaction in turn may suggest that drug dependence is a manifestation of these dynamic interacting processes.

This research was supported by National Institute on Drug Abuse Grants R01 DA11692 and T32 DA07242. The authors thank Amy Prue for assistance in manuscript preparation.

References

Ainslie, George. 1992. *Picoeconomics: The Strategic Interaction of Successive Motivational States Within the Person.* Cambridge: Cambridge University Press.

Ainslie, George, and Varda Haendel. 1983. "The Motives of the Will." In *Etiology Aspects of Alcohol and Drug Abuse,* edited by Edward Gottheil, Keith Druley, Thomas Skodola, and Howard Waxman. Springfield, Ill.: Charles C. Thomas.

Allen, Terry J., F. Gerard Moeller, Howard M. Rhoades, and Don R Cherek. 1998. "Impulsivity and History of Drug Dependence." *Drug and Alcohol Dependence* 50: 137–45.

Baker, Forrest, Matthew W. Johnson, and Warren K. Bickel. Forthcoming. "Delay Discounting Differs Between Current and Never-Smokers Across Commodities, Sign, and Magnitudes." *Journal of Experimental Psychology: General.*

Becker, Gary S., and Kevin M. Murphy. 1988. "A Theory of Rational Addiction." *Journal of Political Economy* 96: 675–700.

Bickel, Warren K., Matthew W. Johnson, Louis A. Giordano, and Gary J. Badger. Forthcoming. "Decreasing Impulsivity: The Effect of Abstinence on Delay Discounting in Cigarette Smokers."

Bickel, Warren K., Amy L. Odum, and Gregory L. Madden. 1999. "Impulsivity and Cigarette Smoking: Delay Discounting in Current, Never, and Ex-Smokers." *Psychopharmacology* 146: 447–54.

Bretteville-Jensen, Anne L. 1999. "Addiction and Discounting." *Journal of Health and Economics* 18: 393–407.

Cardinal, Rudolf N., David R. Pennicott, C. Lakmali Sugathapala, Trevor W. Robbins, and Barry J. Everitt. 2001. "Impulsive Choice Induced in Rats by Lesions of the Nucleus Accumbens Core." *Science* 292: 2499–2501.

Chapman, Gretchen B. 1996. "Temporal Discounting and Utility for Health and Money." *Journal of Experimental Psychology: Learning, Memory and Cognition* 22: 771–91.

Fishburn, Peter C., and Ariel Rubinstein. 1982. "Time Preference." *International Economic Review* 23: 677–94.

Giordano, Louis A., Warren K. Bickel, Eric A. Jacobs, George Loewenstein, Lisa Marsch, and Gary J. Badger. Forthcoming. "Mild Opioid Deprivation and Delay to Outcomes Affect the Reinforcing Efficacy of an Extra Maintenance Dose of Buprenorphine in Opioid Dependent Outpatients."

Green, Leonard, Nathaniel Fristoe, and Joel Myerson. 1994. "Temporal Discounting and Preference Reversals in Choice Between Delayed Outcomes." *Psychonomic Bulletin and Review* 3: 383–89.

Green, Leonard, Astrid F. Fry, and Joel Myerson. 1994. "Discounting of Delayed Rewards: A Life-Span Comparison." *Psychological Science* 5: 33–36.

Higgins, Steve T. 1997. "The Influence of Alternative Reinforcers on Cocaine Use and Abuse. A Review." *Pharmacology, Biochemistry, and Behavior* 57: 419–27.

Johnson, Matthew W., and Warren K. Bickel. 2002. "Within-Subject Comparison of Real and Hypothetical Money Rewards in Delay Discounting." *Journal of Experimental Analysis of Behavior* 77: 129–46.

Kirby, Kris N. 1997. "Bidding on the Future: Evidence Against Normative Discounting of Delayed Rewards." *Journal of Experimental Psychology: General* 126: 54–70.

Kirby, Kris N., and Nino N. Marakovic. 1996. "Delay-Discounting Probabilistic Rewards: Rates Decrease as Amounts Increase." *Psychonomic Bulletin and Review* 3: 100–4.

Kirby, Kris N., Nancy M. Petry, and Warren K. Bickel. 1999. "Heroin Addicts Discount Delayed Rewards at Higher Rates than Non-Drug Using Controls." *Journal of Experimental Psychology: General Processes* 128: 78–87.

Kitano, Hiroaki. 2002. "Systems Biology: A Brief Overview." *Science* 295: 1662–64.

Lancaster, Kelvin. 1963. "An Axiomatic Theory of Consumer Time Preference." *International Economic Review* 4: 221–31.

Loewenstein, George. 1988. "Frames of Mind in Intertemporal Choice." *Management Science* 34: 200–14.

Mach, Ernst. 1893. *The Science of Mechanics: A Critical and Historical Account of Its Development*. LaSalle: Illinois: Open Court.

Madden, Gregory J., Warren K. Bickel, and Eric A. Jacobs. 1999. "Discounting of Delayed Rewards in Opioid Dependent Outpatients: Exponential or Hyperbolic Discounting Functions." *Journal of Experimental and Clinical Psychopharmacology* 7: 284–93.

Madden, Gregory J., Nancy Petry, Gary Badger, and Warren K. Bickel. 1997. "Impulsive and Self-Control Choices in Opioid-Dependent Subjects and Non-Drug-Using Controls: Drug and Monetary Rewards." *Experimental and Clinical Psychopharmacology* 5: 256–62.

Madden, Gregory J., Nancy Petry, Warren K. Bickel, and Gary Badger. Forthcoming. "Delay Discounting in Heroin-Dependent Individuals and Controls: Effects of Commodity Type." *Journal of Clinical and Experimental Psychopharmacology.*

Mazur, James E. 1987. "An Adjusting Procedure for Studying Delayed Reinforcement." In *Quantitative Analysis of Behavior. Vol. 5. The Effect of Delay and of Intervening Events on Reinforcement Value,* edited by Michael L. Commons, James E. Mazur, John A. Nevin, and Howard Rachlin. Hillsdale, N.J.: Erlbaum.

Mazur, James E. 1988. "Estimation of Indifference Points with an Adjusting-Delay Procedure." *Journal of the Experimental Analysis of Behavior* 49: 37–47.

———. 2000. "Trade-offs Among Delay, Rate, and Amount of Reinforcement." *Behavioural Processes* 49: 1–10.

Meyer, Richard F. 1976. "Preferences over Time." In *Decisions with Multiple Objectives: Preferences and Value Trade-offs,* edited by R. L. Keeney and H. Raiffa. New York: Wiley.

Mitchell, Suzanne H. 1999. "Measures of Impulsivity in Cigarette Smokers and Nonsmokers." *Psychopharmacology* 146: 455–64.

Myerson, Joel, and Leonard Green. 1995. "Discounting of Delayed Rewards: Models of Individual Choice." *Journal of the Experimental Analysis of Behavior* 64: 263–76.

Nestler, Eric J., and David Landsman. 2001. "Learning About Addiction from the Genome." *Nature* 409: 834–35.

Odum, Amy L., Gregory J. Madden, Gary J. Badger, and Warren K. Bickel. 2000. "Needle Sharing in Opioid Dependent Outpatients: Psychological Processes Underlying Risks." *Drug and Alcohol Dependence* 60: 259–66.

Perkins, Kenneth A., Debra Gerlach, Michelle Broge, Carolyn Fonte, and Annette Wilson. 2001. "Reinforcing Effects of Nicotine as a Function of Smoking Status." *Experimental and Clinical Psychopharmacology* 9: 243–50.

Petry, Nancy M. 2000. "Psychiatric Symptoms in Problem Gambling and Non-Problem Gambling Substance Abusers." *American Journal on Addictions* 9: 163–71.

———. 2001. "Delay Discounting of Money and Alcohol in Actively Using Alcoholics, Currently Abstinent Alcoholics, and Controls." *Psychopharmacology* 154: 243–50.

Petry, Nancy M., Kris N. Kirby, and Henry R. Kranzler. 2002. "Effects of Gender and Family History of Alcohol Dependence on a Behavioral Task of Impulsivity in Healthy Subjects." *Journal of Studies on Alcohol* 63: 83–90.

Rachlin, Howard, Andres Raineri, and David Cross. 1991. "Subjective Probability and Delay." *Journal of the Experimental Analysis of Behavior* 55: 233–44.

Raineri, Andres, and Howard Rachlin. 1993. "The Effect of Temporal Constraints on the Value of Money and Other Commodities." *Journal of Behavioral Decision Making* 6: 77–94.

Richards, Jerry B., Suzanne H. Mitchell, Harriet de Wit, and Lewis S. Seiden. 1997. "Determination of Discount Functions in Rats with an Adjusting-Amount Procedure." *Journal of the Experimental Analysis of Behavior* 67: 353–66.

Richards, Jerry B., Karen E. Sabol, and Harriet de Wit. 1999. "Effects of Methamphetamine on the Adjusting Amount Procedure: A Model of Impulsive Behavior in Rats." *Psychopharmacology* 146: 432–39.

Robbins, T. W., and B. J. Everitt. 1999. "Interaction of the Dopaminergic System with Mechanisms of Associative Learning and Cognition: Implications for Drug Abuse." *Psychological Science* 10: 199–202.

Rodriguez, Monica L., and Alexandra W. Logue. 1988. "Adjusting Delay to Reinforcement: Comparing Choice in Pigeons and Humans." *Journal of Experimental Psychology: Animal Behavior Processes* 14: 105–17.

Shelley, Marjorie K. 1994. "Gain/Loss Asymmetry in Risky Intertemporal Choice." *Journal of Studies on Alcohol* 59: 124–59.

Simpson, Cathy A., and Rudy E. Vuchinich. 2000. "Reliability of a Measure of Temporal Discounting." *Psychological Record* 50(1): 3–16.

Stevens, Stanley S. 1975. *Psychophysics.* New York: Wiley.

Thaler, Richard. 1981. "Some Empirical Evidence on Dynamic Inconsistency." *Economic Letters* 8: 201–7.

Tobin, Henry, and Alexandra W. Logue. 1994. "Self-Control Across Species." *Journal of Comparative Psychology* 108: 126–33.

Vuchinich, Rudy E., and Cathy A. Simpson. 1998. "Hyperbolic Temporal Discounting in Social Drinkers and Problem Drinkers." *Experimental and Clinical Psychopharmacology* 6: 292–305.

Wade, Tammy R., Harriet de Wit, and Jerry B. Richards. 2000. "Effects of Dopaminergic Drugs on Delayed Reward as a Measure of Impulsive Behavior in Rats." *Psychopharmacology* 150: 90–101.

· 15 ·

Fear as a Policy Instrument

ANDREW CAPLIN

$\mathbf{M}$ANY OF the most important decisions that we make depend
on the extent of our orientation toward the future. Our long-term financial fitness depends on how much we save in our early and middle years. Our long-term physical fitness depends on the extent that
we adopt healthy habits of life when young. Despite their common
dependence on future orientation, academic analyses of savings behavior and of preventive health care draw on entirely different intellectual traditions. Savings behavior has been almost the exclusive domain of economists, while health psychologists have dominated the
research on preventive health care.

Differences in intellectual tradition between economists and psychologists influence not only the direction of scientific investigation
but also the design of public policies. Economic incentives are front
and center in discussions of savings policy, while psychological interventions dominate in the case of preventive health care. This chapter
develops a hybrid approach to future orientation that incorporates
psychological hypotheses into an otherwise traditional economic
model. The model is applied to issues of policy design, with central
emphasis on the field of health care. The ultimate goal of this line of
research is to develop a framework in which the social value of both
economic and psychological health interventions can be understood.

The analysis here focuses on two questions: the "positive" question
of whether policy makers can increase future orientation among private citizens, and the "normative" question of whether or not they
should. Both questions highlight differences in approach between

economists and psychologists. With respect to the positive question, economists generally treat future orientation as a fixed individual characteristic that cannot be influenced by policy, while health psychologists spend a great deal of time devising messages precisely to influence future orientation (for example, Rothman and Salovey 1997; Witte 1998). With respect to the normative question, economists generally argue against using up scarce resources changing tastes, while health psychologists generally assume that such interventions are socially desirable, provided they produce improvements in health. This chapter analyzes how these questions are answered in my hybrid approach.

Fear Appeals in Health Communication

Many public health campaigns seek to frighten individuals into changing their behavior. Among the best known of these *fear appeals* are those that try to discourage the use of illegal drugs, to encourage smokers to stop smoking and nonsmokers not to start, and to discourage youngsters from becoming habitual criminals ("scared straight"). Evidence shows that some of the more recent campaigns in the tobacco arena have had success at least in raising awareness (Hafstad and Aaaro 1997). Yet other programs, including scared straight, appear to have failed in all dimensions (Finckenauer and Gavin 1999). The critical job for psychological theorists interested in this area is to identify when and how such campaigns can be successfully incorporated into a broader public health campaign.

A recent survey of the fear appeals literature (Witte and Allen 2000) divides the history of the field into several distinct phases. The earliest approaches were grounded in learning theory, and interpreted fear as a drive that motivated action; the nature of the response, however, was seen as different depending on the level of fear provoked. Janis (1967) proposed that the behavioral response to fear would depend on its intensity—that low levels of fear would lead to inaction, moderate levels would produce self-protective behavior, and high levels would result in counterproductive defensive responses. This early research ground to a halt when the evidence failed to support the hypothesized U-shaped response of self-protective behaviors to the level of fear aroused.

In an effort to revive the model, Leventhal (1971) proposed the parallel processing model. Just as in the earlier work, this model divided the response to any frightening message into two types: danger control responses that lead to preventive activity, and fear-control responses that lead to avoidance, including in particular defensive inattention. Yet this model allowed this tension to be present in response to all messages, and was far less specific about what might trigger one type of response to dominate another.

In line with the changes happening in the general field of psychology, the next stage of research was essentially cognitive. The protection motivation theory of Rogers (1975) and the more general subjective expected utility model portrayed the choice of preventive actions as depending only on those logical factors that make it good or bad to undertake prevention. How bad is the underlying health threat? How likely is one to suffer if action is not taken? How medically effective is the proposed prevention? How able is one to follow through on the proposed set of preventive acts? Rogers labeled these four dimensions severity, susceptibility, response efficacy, and personal efficacy. The higher the outcome in any of these dimensions, the more likely one was presumed to be to undertake the preventive act.

These cognitive models portray emotional responses as irrelevant to message efficacy. Yet the models failed to explain why some messages conveying identical information seemed to work better than others, and why some even appeared to backfire. In 1992, Witte proposed an integrative model that was designed to address these issues. Her extended parallel processing model (EPPM) follows Leventhal (1971) in proposing that the fundamental question is whether a given fear appeal triggers additional vigilance and danger control through prevention, or instead promotes inattention and avoidance as fear control mechanisms (Witte 1992). Yet she follows the cognitive theorists in making the distinction depend on rational features of the preventive act itself, in particular, beliefs about response efficacy and personal efficacy. A recent presentation of the complete model and the level to which its various hypotheses have found experimental support can be found in Witte (1998).

The EPPM represents the state of the art in the field of fear appeals. In applications, it suggests that one should always pair a frightening message about the consequences of inaction with an upbeat message about the efficacy of a proposed program of prevention. The theory allows for individual differences, whereby some are more prone to defensive responses than others. The model is used to design a number of different campaigns with such diverse goals as reducing smoking (Council for a Tobacco-Free Ontario 2000), preventing genital warts (Witte et al. 1998), and preventing skin cancer (Stephenson and Witte 1998; Sunsmart 2000).

The Model

The first step in building an economic model is to strip away details that are deemed inessential to the question at hand.[1] Since my theoretical model is closely based on the EPPM, the issue on which I focus in this section is how to capture the potential for fear-inducing messages to modify behavior. To isolate this issue, I begin by making the highly artificial assumption that private citizens are perfectly informed about medical matters. The only question for policy makers is one of propaganda: how can they communicate in a manner that motivates change, even when that communication conveys no new facts about the world? Of course, in practice, policy makers are often interested in providing the public with improved information on their medical risks. For this reason, issues of information transmission are added to the model later in the chapter.[2]

How to treat the passage of time? Since the key issue is the trade-off between current and future welfare, I conceptualize the individual as having but two periods of life. Continuing with the process of simplification, I assume that the health state in period 2 can be either good or bad. The state of health, however, can be influenced only by actions taken in period 1. Again, only two choices are available to the individual, involving a simple yes or no decision on whether to undertake preventive care. Taking the preventive action is referred to as choice P, not taking it as choice N.

What is the trade-off in deciding whether to undertake the preventive act? On one hand, this act has current costs measured at $K > 0$ in some standard unit of measurement, such as thousands of dollars. On the other hand, it may impact period-2 health. I assume that it lowers the probability of bad health from to b_N to b_P. To translate this probability measure into a utility measure, I fix the utility advantage of certain good health in period 2 over certain ill health at $H > 0$, measured in the same units as the prevention costs K. The precise value of H reflects both the absolute importance of the health problem, and the importance of period-2 welfare from the perspective of period 1. Using the classical economic model of choice under uncertainty—the expected utility model—the relative costs and benefits of the preventive act may be calculated. The preventive act will be undertaken if and only if the expected health benefit exceeds the cost of prevention.

$$(b_N - b_P)H \geq K. \tag{15.1}$$

The classical economic model is remarkably similar to the protection motivation theory of Rogers (1975). The severity of the health threat is H. The individual's susceptibility is measured by b_N. Response efficacy is measured by the difference $b_N - b_P$. Personal efficacy is analogous to the inverse of the personal cost of the preventive act $1/K$. Just as proposed by Rogers, inequality 15.1 shows that increases in any of these factors increase the prevention incentive.

How must the framework be changed to allow for fear, and for policy makers to use propaganda to influence choice? The first necessary amendment is to include fear itself as a contributor to decision making, as in Akerlof and Dickens (1982). I assume that in period 1 the individual under threat experiences a certain level of fear, $F \geq 0$, associated with the health threat. As with H and K, fear is measured using a monetary equivalent.[3]

What exactly is it that makes a particular health threat frightening? I make the natural assumption that a central determinant of fear is the actual danger posed by the health threat. I treat this level of danger in the simplest possible fashion, as reflecting the direct impact on current welfare of the actual bad outcome, much in the spirit of Jevons (1905) and Loewenstein (1987). The level of danger resulting from action P is assumed to be $b_P H$, which is the expected health cost resulting from the given choice of action. Similarly, the (higher) danger from action N is $b_N H$.

While danger and fear are related, they are not identical. One reason for differentiating between them is to allow for differences in magnitude between fear and the actual health threat. Thinking about a future car accident is frightening, but it is surely not as unpleasant as the accident itself. A second reason for differentiating between danger and fear is to allow a role for the level of *attention* demanded by the health threat. Even if one is in danger, the level of fear may be very low if one is able to provide oneself with adequate distraction. Conversely, a relatively low level of danger may be experienced as very unpleasant if it becomes a subject of obsession.

The following simple equations formalize the distinction between fear and danger:

$$F_P = A_P b_P H;$$

$$F_N = A_N b_N H.$$

The only restriction I impose is that A_P and A_N are both positive, since negative values appear nonsensical. Given the connection with attention, I refer to A_P and A_N as *attentional multipliers*.

Attentional multipliers connect this framework with the fear-appeals literature summarized in the foregoing. The key question in that literature is how and why health messages influence fear, and thereby change the calculus of prevention. The multipliers allow me to follow the fear-appeals literature in conceiving of health messages as operating through an attentional channel. I assume that many different health messages can be communicated, varying in their intensity, m. Higher levels of intensity represent ever more forceful methods of drawing attention to the future threat. In practical terms, this corresponds to such measures as placing gruesome pictures of the impact of the health threat in ever more intrusive locations. Higher levels of intensity always succeed in provoking attention, and thereby make the subject more upset about the dangers involved in failing to undertake preventive activities. These indeed will be fear-inducing messages.

What is it that determines the precise level of the attentional multipliers? I view the level of attention as a function of the health threat, the message intensity, and whether or not the preventive act is undertaken. I use the notation $A_P(m,H)$ and $A_N(m,H)$ to reflect the levels of attention given to a health threat of type H given a message of intensity m, conditional, respectively, on undertaking and on not undertaking the preventive act. Naturally, I assume that more intense messages and worse health threats make the danger ever more attention grabbing.

What is the impact of the preventive act itself on attention? The interesting cases analyzed in the EPPM—in which fear avoidance causes the preventive act to be rejected—require that prevention is more stressful than neglect. Psychologically, this may occur if the effort to battle a future threat involves an effort of concentration that connects it with the source of fear. An example is breast self-examination, a setting in which heightened susceptibility has been found to be a disincentive to preventive care (Kash et al. 1992). To capture this effect, I make the qualitative assumption that to engage in the preventive activity necessitates giving higher attention to the threat:

$$A_P(m,H) \geq A_N(m,H).$$

The model is now complete, at least in conceptual terms. Given the presence of fear, the decision whether or not to take preventive action depends not only on the net discounted health benefits but also on the level of fear associated with the two options. Prevention will be undertaken if and only if,

$$(b_N - b_P)H + (F_N - F_P) \geq K. \tag{15.2}$$

The new term $(F_N - F_P)$ in inequality 15.2 is the "fear differential": it represents the difference in the level of fear depending on whether or not the preventive act is undertaken. If the fear differential is positive, then taking the preventive action decreases fear. If the fear differential is negative, then the preventive action increases fear. The precise value of the fear differential reflects the combination of actual danger, and the amount of attention that danger receives. Equation 15.3 summarizes the operation of these two forces.

$$F_N - F_P = H[b_N A_N(m,H) - b_P A_P(m,H)] \tag{15.3}$$

Important Cases

Equations 15.2 and 15.3 represent the complete solution to the model, at least in conceptual terms. What is missing is detail on how the prevention incentive is impacted by the presence of fear, and how this incentive depends on the intensity of the health messages. Rather than trying to provide unequivocal answers to these questions, it seems more appropriate to explore possibilities using simple, special cases.

Proportionality and the EPPM

One particularly simple case arises when the preventive act has a fixed proportionate impact on the prevention incentive,

$$A_P(m,H) = (1 + \lambda)A_N(m,H). \tag{15.4}$$

Here, $\lambda \geq 0$ can be interpreted precisely as the incremental impact of prevention on attention. Higher levels of λ make the preventive act more costly in terms of attention. With this assumption, the condition for prevention to raise the level of fear is,

$$\lambda > \frac{b_N - b_P}{b_P}. \tag{15.5}$$

If this inequality is valid, the fear differential is negative, so that fear acts as a disincentive to prevention. Precisely this same condition ensures that increases in message intensity are a disincentive to prevention, since they further expand the fear-based incentive to inaction.

Yet if the inequality is reversed, increases in message intensity expand the fear-based incentive to undertake the preventive act.

Inequality (15.5) indicates how well this simple proportional case captures the current state of the art in the fear appeals literature. As outlined earlier, the central hypothesis of this literature is that a fear appeal is far more likely to incentivize the positive danger-reducing outcome if it is combined with a strong efficacy message. If one stirs up fears, however, but the individual does not believe that prevention is all that effective, the message may be counterproductive. In the model, the natural efficacy measure is precisely $\frac{b_N - b_P}{b_P}$. It measures the impact of the treatment in reducing danger as compared with the extent of the danger that remains even if the treatment is undertaken. With high efficacy, fear is reduced if the preventive act is undertaken, and more intense message transmission serves to expand this fear-based differential. With low efficacy, the opposite statements are true: prevention raises fear, and intense message transmission serves only to further discourage prevention.

Obsession and Avoidance

What happens if attention depends in a more intricate manner on the preventive act than in the simple proportional case? This section outlines two entirely opposite possibilities to make a general point. I believe that the impact of messages on the prevention incentive needs to be analyzed on a case-by-case basis, and that it may depend on rich details of given health settings and character types. One valuable role of psychological research in this area would be to develop a more detailed inventory of the characteristics of different health settings and of different personality types to pin down conditions under which fear can be fruitfully used to motivate prevention.

Case 1. Creating an Obsession   Consider an individual who at some point becomes almost totally preoccupied with health status, either due to complete saturation with messages, the objective nature of the health threat, or personality type. If the health authorities believe that they can induce complete preoccupation merely by sending highly intense messages (for example, plastering all walls with horrific images), then fear can certainly be an effective policy instrument. If the subject becomes completely preoccupied with the health threat regardless of whether or not he or she undertakes the preventive act, the resulting high level of fear further motivates the preventive act.

The case of unconditional preoccupation produces the possibility that ever more intense messages become more and more productive in terms of the prevention incentive, by making it harder to avoid contact with the danger, even if one does not undertake the preventive act. We now describe the converse case in which this strategy would completely backfire.

Case 2. Provoking Avoidance   Suppose that there was a costly form of distraction in which the subject could engage, provided he or she did not undertake the preventive act (for example, refusing to watch any television because of constant messages about the implications of drinking and driving). If such a form of costly avoidance were available, the end result would be a nonlinearity in the impact of message intensity. As soon as the level of attention associated with the health threat became too unpleasant to bear, the individual would be completely unwilling to engage in the preventive act. Messages that triggered this form of complete avoidance would clearly be counterproductive as incentives to prevention.

Information Provision

This section explores several new issues that arise when messages may contain both information and propaganda. In terms of the model, messages may not only induce fear, they may also change subjective beliefs about the extent of the health threat, and the value of the preventive act in reducing risk.

Fear and the Provision of Information

In a world without fear, what types of information give rise to an additional prevention incentive is clear. If the public health authorities provide information indicating that the treatment is more effective than is believed by private agents, the private prevention incentive is raised. The prevention incentive is similarly increased if they provide information that the danger of inaction is greater than believed, or that the actual damage to health is greater than expected. In terms of the model, a fall in b_p, and an increase in either b_N or H all act to increase the purely economic incentive to undertake preventive care.

Do the same conclusions concerning the impact of new information on b_P, b_N, and H follow when one allows for the presence of fear? Clearly a fall in b_P is all to the good as a prevention incentive: it improves the actual outcome associated with prevention, and lowers the level of danger associated with prevention, and thereby the level of fear. Similarly, an increase in b_N both causes the actual outcome associated with inaction to deteriorate, and raises the level of fear associated with such inaction. An increase in H has a more intricate impact on the prevention incentive, since the change in the fear differential is less clear-cut. An example, albeit somewhat extreme, indicates that an increase in H can raise the fear differential, and thereby be a disincentive to prevention.

Case 3. A U-Shaped Response   Consider an individual who is able, absent propaganda, to ignore the health threat completely unless he or she undertakes the preventive act, $A_N(0,H) = 0$ (the zero in the first argument corresponds to the absence of propaganda). Assume also that the level of attention in the case of prevention is precisely equal to the health threat, $A_P(0,H) = H$. In this case, it turns out that there is a U-shaped response of the prevention incentive to the extent of the health threat. This can be confirmed by noting that the fear differential in this case is,

$$F_N - F_P = -b_P H^2.$$

Substitution into equation 15.3 reveals that the preventive act is undertaken if and only if,

$$b_N H - b_P H - b_P H^2 \geq K.$$

The left-hand side of this equation is first increasing in H, then decreasing. This means that increases in H up to a threshold raise the prevention incentive, but that further increases beyond this threshold lower it. For low levels of H, danger reduction motivates prevention. For high levels of H, fear prevention motivates avoidance.

In this example, providing negative information on the health threat may produce perverse incentives when that threat is already perceived as dangerously large. Rather than encouraging the subject to adopt the preventive measure, further adverse information induces him to bury his head yet further into the sand. The U-shaped effect of negative information and fear on the prevention incentive in this case is very reminiscent of the initial hypothesis of Janis (1967). This suggests that it may be more appropriate to view his theory as a special case valid in particular circumstances rather than as completely mistaken. Note that his case is more likely to be valid when efficacy is low, since low efficacy reduces the actual health benefits of action, while leaving the remaining risk still frighteningly high.

Information and Propaganda

In what manner do information provision and propaganda interact? How should message content and message intensity interact? These issues are far too rich to address in detail in the current context. The following case shows that the direction in which information provision influences the prevention incentive may depend on the intensity with which propaganda messages are being pushed.

Case 4. Using Intrusive Messages to Overcome Resistance This example combines case 1 and case 3. As in case 3, I assume that when there is no propaganda, there is a U-shaped relationship between the extent of the health threat and the incentive to undertake the preventive act. As in case 1, however, I assume that with enough propaganda, there is complete obsession with the health threat. This means that in the absence of propaganda, bad news about the health threat acts as a disincentive to prevention if H exceeds a critical threshold just as in case 3. Once message intensity is so high that the subject becomes completely obsessed with the health threat, increases in danger are a pure incentive to prevention, just as in the purely economic model.

In this example, bad news about the health threat is a disincentive to prevention if there is low propaganda, yet a positive incentive if there is a high level of propaganda. With low propaganda, avoiding the preventive act aids greatly in fear reduction. The propaganda is able to break through this type of avoidance, however, forcing the dangers to mind even when the preventive act is not taken. At this point, the best decision is clearly to take the preventive act and thereby reduce the actual health risk.

Feedback Effects

In the foregoing examples, I have treated the news on a "once-off" basis. If the health authorities happen to know something that they can convey to the public, is this information going to encourage or discourage the preventive act? Yet such a piecemeal analysis is not fully satisfactory. In the long run, policies *themselves* have feedback effects. In particular, the policies will influence how the public interprets any information it receives, an issue addressed by Caplin and Leahy (1999) in a particularly simple setting.

One important feedback effect concerns credibility. If people know that the health authority is trying to increase preventive behavior, then their communications may lack credibility. Only "hard evidence" will be seen as anything other than propaganda. If hard evidence is the only valid form of information, then the next step in public skepticism might be to wonder what are the implications of a lack of such information. Given that the public health authorities are scouring the scientific news for evidence that certain behaviors are damaging, the absence of such information may be seen as conveying the good news that the danger is not as severe as was previously believed. Once this stage is reached, lack of information transmission itself becomes a policy instrument, and may influence both the prevention decision and the level of fear. Going one step further, public health messages may ultimately reduce the private incentive to gather information. If there is an expert organization filtering information for relevance, why should any individual expend energy assessing the future health implications of his or her current choices? Important as are these questions, they lie beyond the scope of the present analysis. I hope that others will deem them worthy of thought, thereby further enriching our practical knowledge of when and how fear appeals may be effective in inducing preventive behavior.

Policy

Economic model building allows one to study not only positive but also normative aspects of policy. While a policy of provoking fear may be effective in raising the incentive to undertake preventive acts, is such a policy ever a good thing from the welfare perspective? Since my interest is primarily methodological, I restrict attention to the case of purely propagandistic messages and to the case of proportionality, as defined in equation 3. In this case, to understand whether or not messages can raise the overall level of utility, two different cases must be considered, depending on the validity of inequality 15.5:

$$\text{CASE 1: } \lambda > \frac{b_N - b_P}{b_P}.$$

This is the case in which additional messages are a disincentive to prevention. In this case, publicity is only a bad thing. If an individual chooses to undertake the preventive act in spite of the disincentive provided by the message, then all that has happened is that his or her level of fear has been needlessly raised. Similarly, nothing is accomplished except the raising of fear if the individual would not engage in the preventive act even absent the message. Finally, if the message induces the private agent to no longer undertake the preventive act that he or she would otherwise have undertaken, then the person ends up in an even worse position: the individual is worse off than he or she would have been were there no publicity, and had he or she chosen the worse option at that point of not undertaking the preventive act.

$$\text{CASE 2: } \lambda \leq \frac{b_N - b_P}{b_P}.$$

In this case, publicity is able to alter the incentive in favor of prevention. The only possible benefit occurs when an individual who would not otherwise have undertaken the preventive act is induced to do so by the additional publicity. Here preventive measures are not undertaken at $m = 0$, yet are undertaken at some cutoff level of $\overline{m} > 0$. Immediately, increases in intensity above this critical level are a bad idea, since they raise fear without changing the decision. For the same reason it is clear that $m = 0$ is the best policy among those that do not induce the preventive act. So is it better to entirely refrain from sending any message, or to hit $\overline{m}$ exactly? A little thought shows that from the viewpoint of the decision maker, sending no message is definitely superior. At the cutoff point, $\overline{m}$, the decision maker is indifferent between prevention and nonprevention, and is certainly worse off in the case of nonprevention than with the lower level of fear when no message is sent.

These arguments show that it is always in the best interests of the private decision maker to set $m = 0$, even if it is costless to send messages. This conclusion appears somewhat at odds with the recommendations of experts in health communication, who generally measure their success by the extent that they reduce target behavior. Why are propagandistic messages that promote prevention damaging to welfare, even if they succeed in their goal? One part of the answer is that the view that future health is all that is at stake here is simply too narrow. Fear is also important, and to provoke fear for its own sake is definitely not a good idea. In a richer setting, this caveat to a one-dimensional view of the problem may be even more important. If one stops a troubled teen from smoking, what will be the second-best outlet for rebellious instincts—and can one be sure that this will not be even more dangerous to future well-being?

Does adoption of a multidimensional approach to utility imply that one must accept the economic argument that $m = 0$ is the best policy? To the contrary, I believe this argument to be vulnerable to attack on the grounds that it is excessively present-based. If an individual chooses to put his head in the sand, should a benevolent policy maker leave him to get run over by a bus, or should he or she try to force him to pay attention to the danger? In intuitive terms, such situations point to a conflict of interest between present and future self. That such conflicts are close to universal has recently been argued (Kahneman et al. 1997; Caplin and Leahy 2000; O'Donoghue and Rabin 2001). The fundamental argument is that utility functions summarize personal welfare *only at the moment of decision making in period 1.* This may not be the same as the view of welfare either from earlier periods (as in O'Donoghue and Rabin 2001), or from later periods (as in Caplin and Leahy 2000).

In the simple two-period model of the study, the argument of Caplin and Leahy is particularly easy to illustrate. There are present costs of the preventive act, both economic and psychological. What gets set against this is a future health benefit. Caplin and Leahy argue that this future benefit in period 2 will be viewed as more important relative to period-1 costs than it is in period 1. That health in old age is especially important when one is old seems intuitively reasonable. If so, and if the social planner's objective is to maximize a weighted sum of welfare in the two periods, policy should be oriented more toward prevention than is the first-period choice. Even if head-in-the-sand behavior is currently attractive, the social planner may have reason to intervene if he or she believes that the subject will later be grateful for intervention.

While recent research in welfare theory has produced valuable insights, many unanswered questions remain. Is there any reason for differential treatment of economic and psychological costs? How does period-1 fear impact the utility function in period 2? The answers to these questions rest on a deeper understanding of how and why future and past matter to current decision makers. Indeed to distinguish between "Samuelsonian" forces—reflecting the cognitive weight of the future in the present, and "Jevonian" forces—reflecting immediate rewards and punishments based on anticipations of the future, may be important (Loewenstein 1992).

Conclusion

The chapter began with two questions, one positive and one normative. Is there anything that policy makers can do to increase future orientation among private citizens? If so, should they? To answer these questions, I describe a simple model of health communication that places psychological insights into an economic framework. The model provides an affirmative answer to the positive question, and a more evenhanded answer to the normative one. Policies that promote fear can be used to change future orientation, and there are some cases in which such policies may be socially beneficial.

I view this model as merely the first step in a larger agenda-to develop a framework in which the social value of both economic and psychological health interventions can be understood. Caplin and Eliaz (2002) take a further step in this direction, by analyzing the potential for psychologically inspired policy interventions to reduce the spread of AIDS. More generally, the potential payoffs would seem to be enormous if economists and psychologists interested in health care were able to unite around a common analytic framework. The need for such a framework will grow ever more pressing, given the rapid advances in medical technology. Indeed Caplin and Leahy (2002) suggest some specific policy questions growing out of the genetic revolution that appear to require just such a framework.

In addition to health care, the hybrid approach to future orientation proposed here connects with broader streams in the fields of psychology and economics. With respect to psychology, I believe that the model would be greatly enriched by incorporating the ideas of Metcalf and Mischel (1998) on delay of gratification.[4] There are also interesting connections with the theory of cognitive dissonance, which suggests that beliefs themselves be somewhat flexible.[5] With respect to economics, to explore the extent to which the current framework generalizes to the financial arena is important. Many households pay very little attention to their financial future in light of its importance in later life. In turn, this low level of attention is connected with low levels of savings and wealth accumulation (Lusardi 1999; Ameriks et al. 2002). In what circumstances can fear be used as a policy instrument to increase the savings rate, and when are such interventions beneficial?

Notes

1. Separating essential from inessential elements is a highly personal art form. I view a model as successful provided it delivers—or at least promises to deliver—insights of potential value to practitioners. Crude as it is, the current model achieves this standard.

2. In the case of AIDS prevention, the first-order task is to convey information on behaviors in the sexual and other arenas that can reduce risk. In the case of tobacco, the propaganda element dominates. Indeed evidence shows that most people overestimate the dangers of smoking (Viscusi

1992), so that a purely informational campaign might reduce fear rather than raise it. The fear appeal is based not on presenting novel information but rather on putting the case against smoking in a form that motivates more individuals to quit.

3.   The very idea that one can find such a simple equivalence between emotional stress, health problems, and monetary costs is open to question. In the future, to develop richer models of the emotions will be increasingly important, with the more general model in Caplin and Leahy (2001) serving as one possible starting point.

4.   The fear appeals literature implies that one way to increase future orientation is to use fear to "heat up" future payoffs. Metcalf and Mischel (1999) argue for the converse approach of "cooling down" factors that promote shortsightedness, using such techniques as diverting attention from objects of immediate desire. Given that the ideas are so complementary, it should be relatively straightforward to develop an integrative model encompassing both.

5.   Models of dissonance have been constructed both by Akerlof and Dickens (1982) to explain underinvestment in future health, and by Dickens (1986) to explain possibly perverse effects of increased punishments on the incentive to commit crime.

References

Akerlof, George, and William Dickens. 1982. "The Economic Consequences of Cognitive Dissonance." *American Economic Review* 72: 307–19.

Ameriks, John, Andrew Caplin, and John Leahy. 2002. "Wealth Accumulation and the Propensity to Plan." Working paper no. 8920. Cambridge, Mass.: National Bureau of Economic Research.

Caplin, Andrew, and Kfir Eliaz. 2002. "AIDS Prevention and Psychology: A Theoretical Approach." Research Report 02-44. C. V. Starr Center, New York University.

Caplin, A., and J. Leahy. 1999. "The Supply of Information by a Concerned Expert." Research report 99-08, C. V. Starr Center, New York University.

———. 2000. "The Social Discount Rate." Working paper no. 7983. Cambridge, Mass.: National Bureau of Economic Research.

———. 2001. "Psychological Expected Utility Theory and Anticipatory Feelings," *Quarterly Journal of Economics* 116: 51–80.

———. 2002. "Behavioral Policy." In *The Psychology of Economic Decisions*, edited by Isabelle Brocas and Juan D. Carrillo. New York: Oxford University Press.

Council for a Tobacco-Free Ontario. 2000. "Fear Appeals for Tobacco Control." *Center for Health Promotion*, University of Toronto.

Dickens, William. 1986. "Crime and Punishment Again: The Economic Approach with a Psychological Twist." *Journal of Public Economics* 30: 97–107.

Finckenauer, James, and Patricia Gavin. 1999. *Scared Straight: The Panacea Phenomenon Revisited*, Prospect Heights, Ill.: Waveland Press.

Hafstad, A., and L. Aaaro. 1997. "Activating Interpersonal Influence Through Provocative Appeals—Evaluation of a Mass Media-Based Anti-Smoking Campaign Targeting Adolescents." *Health Communication* 7: 122–27.

Janis, Irving. 1967. "Effects of Fear Arousal on Attitude Change: Recent Developments in Theory and Experimental Research." In *Advances in Experimental Social Psychology*. Vol. 3, edited by L. Berkowitz. New York: Academic Press.

Jevons, William. 1905. *Essays on Economics*. London: Macmillan.

Kahneman, Daniel, Peter Wakker, and Rakesh Sarin. 1997. "Back to Bentham: Explorations of Experienced Utility." *Quarterly Journal of Economics* 112: 375–406.

Kash, K., J. Holland, M. Halper, and D. Miller. 1992. "Psychological Distress and Surveillance Behaviors of Women with a Family History of Breast Cancer." *Journal of the National Cancer Institute* 84: 24–30.

Leventhal, Howard. 1971. "Fear Appeals and Persuasion: The Differentiation of a Motivational Construct." *American Journal of Public Health* 61: 1208–24.

Loewenstein, George. 1987. "Anticipation and the Valuation of Delayed Consumption." *Economic Journal* 97: 666–84.

———. 1992. "The Fall and Rise of Psychological Explanations in the Economics of Intertemporal Choice." In *Choice Over Time*, edited by G. Loewenstein and J. Elster, New York: Russell Sage Foundation.

Lusardi, Annamaria. 1999. "Information, Expectations, and Saving for Retirement." In *Behavioral Dimensions of Retirement Economics*, edited by H. Aaron. New York: Russell Sage Foundation.

Metcalfe, Janet, and Walter Mischel. 1999. "A Hot/Cool-System Analysis of Delay of Gratification: Dynamics of Willpower." *Psychological Review* 106: 3–19.

O'Donoghue, Ted, and Matthew Rabin. 2001. "Risky Behavior Among Youths: Some Issues from Behavioral Economics." In *Risky Behavior Among Youths: An Economic Analysis*, edited by Jon Gruber. Chicago: University of Chicago Press.

Rogers, Ronald. 1975. "A Protection Motivation Theory of Fear Appeals and Attitude Change." *Journal of Psychology* 91: 93–114.

Rothman, Alexander J., and Peter Salovey. 1997. "Shaping Perceptions to Motivate Healthy Behavior: The Role of Message Framing." *Psychological Bulletin* 121: 3–19.

Stephenson, M., and K. Witte. 1998. "Fear, Threat, and Perceptions of Efficacy from Frightening Skin Cancer Messages." *Public Health Review* 26: 147–74.

Sunsmart. 2000. *Report and Prospectus for 2000–2003*. Melbourne: Anti-Cancer Council of Victoria.

Viscusi, W. Kip. 1992. *Smoking: Making the Risky Decision*. New York: Oxford University Press.

Witte, Kim. 1992. *Putting the Fear Back into Fear Appeals: The Extended Parallel Process Model. Communication Monographs* 59. Available at: *www.msu.edu/symbol{126}wittek/fearback.htm*.

————. 1998. "Fear as Motivator, Fear as Inhibitor: Using the Extended Parallel Process Model to Explain Fear Appeal Successes and Failures." In *Handbook of Communication and Emotion: Research, Theory, Applications, and Contexts*. New York: Academic Press.

Witte, K., and Mike Allen. 2000. "A Meta-Analysis of Fear Appeals: Implications for Effective Public Health Campaigns." *Health Education and Behavior*, 27: 591–615.

Witte, K., J. Berkowitz, K. Cameron, and J. Mckeon. 1998. "Preventing the Spread of Genital Warts: Using Fear Appeals to Promote Self-Protective Behaviors." *Health Education and Behavior* 25: 571–85.

· 16 ·

Dieting as an Exercise in Behavioral Economics

C. Peter Herman and Janet Polivy

IT'S EASY to decide to go on a weight-loss diet. The benefits of such a diet are obvious enough. During a confrontation with the bathroom scale or mirror, we can see the long-term advantages of dietary restraint and how they outweigh the fleeting advantages of caloric indulgence. The problem of course is that we can't stay in the bathroom forever. We find ourselves all too often in the kitchen, the dining room, or a restaurant. The food that was so easy to forgo as an abstraction in the bathroom is not so easy to forgo when it's right in front of you. What we have here is a classic instance of what decision researchers refer to as *dynamic inconsistency,* with eating forbidden food (or quantities) being ranked lower than dieting in those resolute bathroom moments but rising to the top of the behavioral hierarchy when it really matters. Indeed the resolution to refrain from eating forbidden (fattening) foods, followed by the collapse of this resolution when the forbidden food is actually encountered, is a perfect example of dynamic inconsistency, if the repeated references to the dynamics of dieting in several other chapters in this volume are any indication. The Laibson group (chap. 18 herein) doesn't get through the first paragraph without noting that "When planning for the long-run, we *intend* to . . . eat healthfully. Yet in the short-run, we have little interest in . . . skipping the chocolate soufflé à la mode."[1] Chapman (chap. 13 herein) throws a "tempting dessert" our way in her third paragraph.

This chapter will examine the research literature on weight-loss dieting as an instance of behavioral economics. Although this research was not conducted from a behavioral-economic perspective, dieting does involve many features of intertemporal choice, especially hyperbolic discounting and dynamic inconsistency.[2] Still, a closer look at dieting reveals that it may not be the perfect example of these phenomena that many social scientists make it out to be. An examination of how dieting fails to fulfill the exemplar role it has been asked to play raises several interesting issues for diet researchers as well as for researchers from far afield who would use dieting as an easily understood example of what they are trying to explain.

How Dieting Works

The dieter makes an agreement with herself to give up some or most of the gratifications of food in exchange for a slimmer physique. Unfortunately, the slimmer physique appears, if at all, at the end of a lengthy series of encounters with tempting food. On each encounter, the dieter must withstand the temptation of appetizing food; but denying oneself appetizing food is not something that comes naturally or easily to humans. To assist in this effort, the dieter has at her disposal various tricks, such as redirecting her attention, engaging in self-exhortation, conjuring up images, and so on; but none of these tricks is especially reliable. They must overcome the sensory allure of palatable food, which is tough enough to resist under the best of circumstances and even tougher when one has been depriving oneself for an extended period. The diet itself of course is an elaborate trick: it is a set of stratagems and rules for staying within one's caloric quota. If one adheres to these rules, then one will succeed (perhaps). Yet the sensory allure of appetizing food often overwhelms one's resolve. The diet may break down, as when the dieter succumbs to irresistible food, acknowledges that the diet has collapsed, and takes some solace in her firm resolve to begin the diet again, perhaps with even greater fortitude, tomorrow morning. Alternatively, the dieter may succumb to the food even while convincing herself that the diet remains intact. This bit of sophistry usually involves a legalistic exploitation of dubious loopholes in the diet, such that certain types of eating "don't count" (because you are eating off someone else's plate, you are just "tasting" the food, you are eating standing up, and so on).

Succumbing to appetizing food represents a dynamic inconsistency. When the food is encountered, the immediate pleasure of eating leapfrogs over the long-term benefits of dieting; these benefits, in the absence of tempting food, are themselves very appealing and motivating. Indeed when one is not in the immediate presence of appetizing food, one tends to discount the value of such food, to the point where the long-term payoff of the diet exceeds the value of indulging in the food. The forceful presence of the food, however, reinstates its value, and has a corresponding negative effect on the perceived value of dieting, which in some cases is discounted to zero. In this sense, the terms of reference of intertemporal choice may be applied directly to the dieting enterprise, and the dieter may be seen as fully engaged in economic calculations.

This analysis has only one major empirical flaw: the laboratory data suggest that dieters do not, as a rule, succumb to the allure of tempting food. In our lab, offering dieters tempting food—up to and including cookies, cake, and ice cream—is the *control* condition. By and large, dieters do not eat a lot under these circumstances, even though, in addition to providing them with very tempting food, we go out of our way to ensure that they are not self-conscious. We have them eat without being observed—or so they think—and we arrange the food so that it will not be obvious to the observer, after the fact, how much was eaten.[3] Still, they tend to eat less than do nondieters, effectively validating their status as dieters. This is not to say that dieters never eat the tempting food; in fact they often do. Yet rarely is the food in and of itself enough to undermine the dieter's resolution to abstain. In most cases, some other disinhibitory factor—emotional arousal, intoxication, or another form of motivational disruption—is required. When the dieter encounters tempting food and at the same time experiences a disruption in her motivation to abstain, then she becomes likely to display the disinhibited eating that wipes out the accumulated "gains" of all those hours of self-imposed deprivation.

From the outside, it may appear that the food itself has defeated the dieter's resolve. To the external observer, the attractive food is the most (or only) salient stimulus in the dieter's environment and thus the obvious candidate to explain the dieter's lapse. Food alone, however, is never the true culprit. Even in those cases where no other specifically disinhibitory influence is operating (that is, the only thing that appears to have changed is that a favorite food is now available to be eaten), to explain the breakdown of restraint solely in terms of the presence of food is not quite accurate. When we spy a favorite food and decide that our diet can be suspended for a few minutes, we do in fact make a decision: our behavior is controlled by our cognitive, decision-making apparatus and not just by the food. Obviously, the allure of the food affects our decision, but this allure will not necessarily trump the resolution to abstain. It is always a question of how our mental apparatus copes with the "threat," and not a simple matter of food inexorably driving us to eat. Under all but the most extreme conditions, to resist temptation is always possible; indeed in our lab studies, unless some additional factor intervenes to disrupt their ability or motivation to resist temptation, dieters usually do resist.

Cognitive and motivational shifts that accompany the breakdown of dietary restraint serve as a fertile domain for the exploration of dynamic inconsistencies. Such research is not new, of course. Mischel's work on delay of gratification over many years (see Mischel, Ayduk, and Mendoza-Denton, chap. 5 herein) has provided some interesting ideas for research on dieting.[4] These studies emphasize that it isn't the objective circumstances (for example, the mere presence of tempting food), but rather the subjective state of mind (for example, how the food is construed) that determines the outcome. By the same token, research on dieting suggests some interesting ideas for other domains in which resistance to temptation is a challenge.

Our analysis of how dieting works represents a challenge to simple hyperbolic discounting models. As far as we can tell, to maintain that temporal proximity to forbidden food renders the food irresistible and thus eliminates dietary restraint is not accurate. More congenial to our view is the position articulated by Loewenstein (for example, Hoch and Loewenstein 1991; Loewenstein 1996), which emphasizes fluctuations in desire for certain "forbidden" items or activities. Temporal proximity is often associated with increased desire for such consumables, but it will affect behavior only insofar as it activates a common visceral (desire) pathway that is subject to all sorts of other influences as well. Loewenstein's broad analysis of consummatory behavior opposes impulsivity to willpower, much as we (Herman and Polivy 1980) have done in the narrower domain of inhibited and disinhibited eating, and he incorporates various factors that enhance and impair each of these battling elements. To give a simple example, physical proximity is likely to be more powerful than is temporal proximity in inflaming desire. Knowing that it's "time for dessert" is nowhere near as powerful an influence on desire (and eating) as is the actual presence of the dessert.[5] The hyperbolic discounting approach distinguishes between resolutions to diet when the encounter with tempting food is temporally distant versus immediate; but from Loewenstein's desire perspective, the critical feature is not time but physical vividness (often—but not necessarily—confounded with time). To a large extent, Loewenstein bases his model on research from the delay-of-gratification literature, but the dieting literature that he mentions in passing would suit his purpose just as well.

Many of the factors that have been shown to impair delay of gratification or reduce resistance to temptation in general apply to dieting specifically. Mischel (for example, Mischel et al. 1992) has emphasized what he calls *hot cognitions*, a focus on the most appealing aspects of the to-be-resisted objects. We have noted likewise that a focus on the most attractive sensory properties of the forbidden food is likely to undermine one's resistance (Herman and Polivy 1993). Loewenstein (1992, 6) quotes Rae to the effect that "the prospects of future good, which future years may hold out to us, seem at such a moment dull and dubious, and are apt to be slighted, for objects on which daylight is falling strongly, and showing us in all their freshness just within our grasp." This pre-Victorian formulation captures nicely what happens when one's earnest plans to achieve slimness through dietary restraint are shattered by "daylight falling strongly" on a slab of chocolate cake "in all its freshness."

Mischel has thoroughly investigated the distinction between hot and cold cognitions. Thus the dieter might reduce the allure of the slab of chocolate cake by reconstruing it as something else, say as mud rather than chocolate cake. Our own recommendation is to pursue a slightly different tack. Instead of trying to convince oneself that the cake is something other than what it truly is, one may distinguish among its actual properties. The trick for the dieter is to emphasize the cake's caloric aspect at the expense of its sensory aspect. One needn't misrepresent the stimulus to remind oneself of its fattening qualities, which are conceptually distinct from its wonderful taste.[6] There is no guarantee that the dieter will succeed in keeping the negative caloric aspect of the cake more prominently in mind than the positive gustatory aspect. Yet neither is there a guarantee that the dieter will succeed in maintaining the fiction that the piece of cake is not truly a piece of cake.

Manipulations of attentional focus have had mixed effects on eating. We were able to increase or reduce hunger by turning people's attention toward or away from food-related material on videotape (Herman, Ostovich, and Polivy 1999), but that study explored only hunger, not eating, and in any case was confined to nondieters. As we already noted, Fedoroff and colleagues (1997) induced greater hunger and eating in dieters by having them focus on the smell or thoughts of food for ten minutes before eating. (Nondieters were less responsive to these manipulations.) Rogers and Hill (1989) likewise found that dieters exposed to food (and pictures of food) and told to imagine any food (and focus on its flavor, texture, and smell) ate more when subsequently given access to cookies. Yet nondieters actually ate less under these conditions, and the correlation between hunger and intake was negligible for both dieters and nondieters. As is so often the case, our theorizing is not unequivocally supported by the few data that exist.

Although the delay-of-gratification literature has focused on how cognitions (and individual differences in cognitive style) impair or enhance delay, mostly by affecting how strong the temptation is, the dieting literature has tended to focus on situational factors that undermine the ability to resist a temptation of a given strength.[7] Fortunately for us, all sorts of circumstances—we are sometimes inclined to believe that almost *any* unusual circumstance—can disinhibit eating in dieters.

Consider distress. The physiological effects of emotional upset ought by rights to inhibit eating, and in nondieters emotional distress does just that. In dieters, however, emotional distress increases eating, even if the food is not particularly palatable (Polivy, Herman, and McFarlane 1994). Dozens of experiments have examined the effects of manipulated emotions on eating, and the evidence is clear (Herman, Polivy, et al. forthcoming): distress suppresses eating in nondieters and disinhibits eating in dieters.[8] Several explanations have been offered for why distress makes dieters eat more. (Remember, these explanations cannot simply be a matter of asserting, for instance, that eating is comforting. If eating were comforting, then it should be comforting for everyone, nondieters included; but nondieters eat less when they're upset. The explanation must relate somehow to the dieter's prior inhibition.) These explanations are all fairly complicated. Briefly, they include: subtler versions of the comfort explanation, consistent with Tice and Bratslavsky's (2000) recent finding that if dieters are led to believe that eating will not improve their mood, then they do not eat more when distressed; the masking hypothesis (Herman and Polivy 1988), in which overeating creates its own problems for the dieter, conveniently masking more fundamental and intractable sources of distress; and externality hypotheses (Heatherton and Baumeister 1991; Slochower 1983), in which emotional arousal has the effect of narrowing attention to the most perceptually salient stimuli (for example, food) and drawing attention away from broader and more abstract concerns such as dieting. One further possible hypothesis is suggested by Kacelnik's work (chap. 3 herein) demonstrating that changes in one's state (including one's mood state?) may add uncertainty to the value of future rewards, and raise the aversive possibility of high opportunity costs if one doesn't pursue other, shorter-term rewards while waiting for the longer-term one. Negative mood thus may call into question the value of future weight loss, and make more attractive the current, short-term reward of eating attractive food.

These various hypotheses as to why distress unleashes eating in dieters force us to address another issue: Does distress undermine dieters' motivation to diet or their ability to diet? Our long-held assumption, dating to our first study of distress and eating in dieters (Herman and Polivy 1975), has been that the distressed dieter displays a dynamic motivational inconsistency, although we have until now never used that term (and will try never to use it again). The serene dieter ranks the long-term goal of slimness ahead of short-term gratification and is thus prepared to resist temptation. The distressed dieter, however, undergoes a motivational shift and no longer cares so much about distant and doubtful goals. Short-term gratification replaces long-term objectives at the top of the motive hierarchy, and the result, especially in the presence of attractive food, is indulgence.[9] More recently, self-regulatory strength theory (Baumeister et al. 1998; Baumeister and Vohs, chap. 6 herein; Muraven, Tice, and Baumeister 1998) has argued that we have only a limited amount of energy available to cope with trouble and conflict. The implication, for dieters (Vohs and Heatherton 2000; Kahan, Polivy, and Herman forthcoming), is that they remain motivated to diet even when upset, but cannot summon the strength to simultaneously cope with distress and resist temptation in the form of food. Something has to give, and more often than not, resistance to temptation is what suffers. The motive to diet remains intact but cannot be executed for lack of resources. We imagine that these different views of how distress releases inhibited eating will produce some interesting critical experiments in the next few years.

One further twist to this particular issue concerns the effects of positive emotions on eating. Some evidence (Cools, Schotte, and McNally 1992) shows that feeling good also disinhibits dieters.[10] The motivational inconsistency view can easily accommodate this finding by arguing that the happy dieter no longer has as much motive to diet: because dieting itself is basically just a way to improve one's life, if one is already feeling good, then why bother dieting? The self-regulatory strength view may have more difficulty explaining why positive mood disinhibits eating.

One should note that the disinhibition of eating in distressed dieters is probably just a specific case of a more general phenomenon: distress releases inhibited behavior in everyone. For dieters, the inhibited behavior is eating, and so—especially when our dependent measure is amount eaten—what we notice is increased eating. Nondieters may not eat more when upset but will probably display disinhibition in other behavioral domains, specifically those domains (for example, smoking, drinking, aggression) in which they are chronically trying to hold themselves in check. Both the motivational inconsistency perspective and the self-regulatory strength–depletion perspective could usefully address this topic.

Intoxication is another factor that disinhibits eating in dieters (Polivy and Herman 1976). Our initial interpretation of this effect was motivational: tipsy dieters simply don't care about the future as much as they care about the present. The cognitive narrowing interpretation of alcohol effects (Steele and Josephs 1990) argues that alcohol has the effect of focusing one's attention on the most salient stimuli (much as distress does in the accounts by Heatherton and Baumeister 1991 and Slochower 1983). Whether this narrowing is more compatible with a motivational or an SRS interpretation remains to be determined.

Social influence is often nominated as a source of disinhibition. In a group setting—and we usually eat with others—how one dieter capitulating to temptation could bring other dieters along with her is easy to see. Dieters certainly are committed to their diets, but they also appear to be constantly on the lookout for an excuse to cheat.[11] The example of others may serve this purpose nicely. Dieter *A* may gain "superiority points" if she maintains her diet even as her companion, Dieter *B*, breaks down and boards the Jamaican Banana Boat.[12] Dieter *A*, however, is just as likely to join Dieter *B* for the guilty but thrilling ride. Sometimes *B* will actively pressure *A* into breaking *A*'s diet so that *B* can gain some social support for breaking her own diet. These observations, interestingly, do not find a great deal of support in the experimental literature (see Herman, Roth, and Polivy 2002 for a review). The problem is not that *A* doesn't follow the lead of *B*; the literature is very decisive in support of modeling effects. Rather the problem is that nondieters appear to be just as influenced by the example of others as are dieters. The ubiquity of social-influence effects suggests that social influences drive behavior directly, irrespective of prior inhibitions and not necessarily as a reflection of or an excuse for cheating. Social influence then may well make dieters eat more, mimicking the effect of known disinhibitors. Yet this effect may be only as an incidental consequence of social influence as a general facilitator of eating in almost everyone.[13]

Preloading and the Diurnality of Dieting

Perhaps the most well-explored trigger for the disinhibition of dieters' eating—at least in the laboratory—is *preloading*, or forcing the dieter to consume food that is disallowed by the diet and then allowing her to eat ad lib. Whereas the nondieter tends to eat less in direct proportion to the size of the preload, the dieter tends to eat more after a high-calorie preload than after a low-calorie preload or none at all.[14] We stumbled on this effect inadvertently (Herman and Mack 1975), but it has proved to be relatively robust (Polivy and Herman forthcoming), although several limiting conditions for the effect certainly exist (for example, Herman, Polivy, and Esses 1987; Herman, Polivy, et al. 1987; Herman, Polivy, and Silver 1979; Polivy et al. 1986). Again, we have favored a motivational interpretation of the preloading–counterregulation effect. The dieter, having consumed a preload (for example, a large milkshake) that is clearly disallowed by her diet— either because it is calorically excessive or because it is a type of food forbidden in any amount—finds herself in a position in which continued dieting seems to have no point. The diet is "blown" and ("what the hell!") she might as well be hanged for a sheep as for a lamb (or for two large milkshakes and half a pie as for one small milkshake). Note that this interpretation argues that the effect of the preload is not to increase the desirability of the food on which the disinhibited dieter splurges. Rather the preload acts to undermine resistance to temptation. The food's allure is constant, but the dieters' resolve is weakened.

Note that the diet-breaking preload does not have to be all that significant calorically. For one thing, what counts is the perceived size of the preload, not its actual size. If the dieter is misled to believe that a low-calorie preload is actually high in calories, it will disinhibit eating (Polivy 1976; Spencer and Fremouw 1979). Also, even if the preload is perceived to be high in calories, it need not contain more calories than the dieter might otherwise have eaten during the remainder of that day, even while adhering to the diet. As was just noted, some foods are simply not allowed by the diet in any amount, and consuming even a small portion of such disallowed food may violate the diet and thereby undermine motivation to continue dieting, since the diet has already been ruined.

At this point, one should stop to consider the fundamental irrationality that characterizes many of the dieter's calculations. First consider the notion that particular foods are forbidden in any quantity. Chocolate fudge might be an example of a food disallowed by any self-respecting diet. If the dieter, however, were to consume a square of fudge under pressure from an experimenter or from her own grandmother, what sense does it make to conclude that the diet is ruined? Obviously, the goal of the diet would be more easily achieved had the fudge not been eaten, but why exactly has the diet been ruined?

The ruination of the diet reflects its rigidity. If the point of dieting is to cut back on calories by eating little or none of certain fattening foods and perhaps less food overall—and if this project is intended to reduce one's weight by a significant number of pounds—then the diet will necessarily take days, weeks, even months to achieve its goal. So how can a single square of fudge ruin the diet? In the grand scheme of things, the square of fudge is trivial, and could easily be compensated for by cutting back on intake by a handful of calories per day for a few days, or by just extending the diet for an additional day. Yet dieters don't think like that. The big picture is too difficult to see; or rather regulating one's intake in terms of weekly or monthly caloric quotas is too difficult and complicated. Most diets—except for the so-called all-you-can-eat diets, in which the prescribed foods are those of which a human can eat only a limited amount—are based on a daily caloric regimen. The day is a unit of time according to which we find it relatively easy to organize our behavior. Thus most dietary allowances are diurnal, and the consequences would be amusing were they not so pathetic.

Dieters are not the only ones drawn to diurnal budgeting. Examination of taxi drivers' trip sheets indicates that they tend to set a daily income target and quit for the day when they reach this target (Camerer et al. 2000). Thus on a day when earnings are higher (for example, when it is raining and demand for cabs increases), instead of working their usual hours and maximizing earnings, drivers (especially inexperienced ones) work shorter hours, quitting as soon as they reach their goal amount.

If the dieter thought in monthly terms, it would be difficult to sustain the notion that a square of fudge could ruin her diet. If the diet is construed in terms of a single day, however, is more plausible that the fudgy culprit could ruin things. Four hundred calories does not make much of a dent in a 50,000-calorie monthly allotment, but it certainly poses a threat to a 1,700-calorie daily allotment. The daily diet quota makes calculations easier then, but at the cost of making infractions much more serious.

Taking a longer perspective would avoid certain pitfalls, but apparently no strategy is foolproof (or temptation-proof). When they set themselves a weekly quota, Camerer and colleagues' (2000) taxi drivers were often sorely tempted early in the week to quit before making an adequate amount for the day, convincing themselves that they would be able to make up the difference later in the week. If the dieter therefore were to establish a weekly or monthly calorie quota, one wonders how she would resist the temptation to overeat early on, all the while planning to compensate by dieting furiously later in the cycle. This problem with longer time intervals is what makes taxi drivers incline toward setting daily quotas for themselves; dieters too may appreciate the advantages of daily diet quotas, even though such quotas cause problems of their own.

A further problem of the daily diet quota stems from the fact that each day may be considered independently of each other day. This consideration is crucial in understanding the bizarre behavior of dieters. Remember, when the dieter concludes that her diet has been blown on account of an experimental preload or grandmotherly fudge square, the reason is that the diet is such a short-term (daily) event. This short-term perspective on the diet, however, has its compensations; most notably, it permits the dieter to begin dieting again almost immediately, tomorrow morning. Thus overindulgence today can be "recouped" soon. The proximity of a possible fresh start, however, causes trouble of its own, for it means that the dieter can convince herself fairly easily that salvation for her sins is near at hand. Such a conviction in turn makes sinning all the more attractive—and probable.

Let us return to our fudge eater. Since her diet quota is established on a daily basis, chances are good that the fudge will jeopardize her diet; even if the calories in the fudge square don't push her over her allowance, the mere fact that she ate *chocolate fudge* may be ruinous. Yet because her diet quota is established on a daily basis, she can restart her dietary clock as early as tomorrow. So what does she do when she realizes that she has blown her diet? In most cases, she continues to overeat as long as palatable food is available. The diet dictates to her how much she is allowed to eat, but it does not dictate how much more than that she can eat if she decides to forget about the diet. Once she abandons the diet all bets are off; the day is lost, so she might as well enjoy herself, especially since she has been depriving herself of her favorite foods for lo these many days. The way in which diets are structured—with dieters either under quota or over quota, succeeding or failing and generally thinking in dichotomous terms—corresponds to inhibition or disinhibition of eating, with no apparent limit on how much gets eaten once disinhibition occurs. From a strictly caloric standpoint, whether the dieter who fails to adhere to her 1,700-calorie diet for the day ends up consuming 1,800 calories or 3,800 calories makes all the difference in the world; but dieters don't see it that way. A blown diet is an excuse for effectively unlimited indulgence, accompanied by assurances to self and others that tomorrow will be different.

Nowadays, therapists often recommend incorporating some "cheating" into the diet. Cheating is going to happen anyway, so we might as well anticipate it, and yoke it to a clear understanding that an instance of cheating does not provide license for total disinhibition, even for just the rest of the day. In the realm of drinking, Marlatt (1985) has identified an "abstinence violation effect," in which a small slip tends to turn into a major binge. For this very reason some experts (Rosenberg 1993; Sobell and Sobell 1995) have called for a less stringent goal for problem drinkers. If abstinence is too difficult to sustain and failure to maintain perfect abstinence represents unmitigated failure, then adopting a less demanding criterion for success will lessen the chances of failure and unregulated binge drinking that ensues. Likewise in the political sphere Elster (1992) has argued for the value of maintaining a balance between rigidity and flexibility in designing a constitution. A system for governing a country must not allow passions of the moment to overcome long-term stability, yet some alterations of the rules must be permitted (after due consideration) or the nation will be unable to adapt to changed circumstances. In the personal sphere too much flexibility is tantamount to not really dieting at all, whereas too much rigidity often leads to frequent self-regulatory collapses and out-of-control eating.

Before we leave the topic of disinhibition and diurnality, let us turn our attention briefly to some variations on the basic preloading–counterregulation effect. In the original version, dieters were preloaded and then given access to palatable food ad lib. Overeating was attributed to a belief that their diet for the day had already been ruined.[15] Yet what if the dieter were convinced that today's diet would be ruined, not now but later on? What would be the effect on current eating? If the belief that today's diet cannot succeed is what triggers disinhibited eating, then it should matter little whether the failure of the diet occurs now or will with certainty occur later in the day. Indeed such is the case. Dieters overeat earlier in the day when they are convinced that they will consume forbidden food later in the day (Ruderman, Belzer, and Halperin 1985; Tomarken and Kirschenbaum 1984).

Another variation hinges on the connection between overindulgence today and renewed restraint tomorrow. Lowe (1982) has proposed that the opportunity to begin dieting again as early as tomorrow morning is a factor in the dieter's willingness to abandon restraint today. The dieter eases the burden of overindulgence with bracing self-statements about how well she will behave in the morning. This intimate connection between sin and penance can work both ways, though. If one is absolutely committed to dieting conscientiously tomorrow, one may be inclined to overindulge today. ("Eat, drink, and be merry, for tomorrow we diet.") Lowe (1982) and Ruderman and colleagues (1985) obtained equivocal results in their attempts to demonstrate this effect, but Urbszat, Herman, and Polivy (2002) recently provided clear support for the contention that anticipating a diet tomorrow disinhibits eating today.[16] Thus, although it is true that a lengthy period of deprivation may provide justification for a postdeprivation feast (as when Jews "break the fast" of Yom Kippur with an excessive meal), it is equally true that anticipating deprivation also provides a justification for a feast (as when Catholics overindulge at Mardi Gras celebrations before Lent). Why Jews resort to excess after deprivation and Catholics do so before deprivation is an issue that goes beyond the mandate of this chapter. Further questions, such as how an anticipated diet-breaking event tomorrow affects eating today, or how anticipating a period of deprivation later in the day affects eating earlier in the day, remain to be explored.

Factors That Enhance Delay

Laboratory research has focused on factors that interfere with dieters' resolve to diet. Somehow, it seems to be more interesting to study dieters' failures rather than their successes, but what is the ultimate goal of such studies? For the most part, both the public and granting agencies assume that our goal is to learn enough about the factors that make diets fail so that we can construct better diets, or better dieters. By the same token, much of the literature on intertemporal choice appears to be concerned with why people act imprudently (for example, Bickel and Johnson, chap. 14 herein). The assumption is that the choice made in the cool light of reason (usually some sort of abstinence) is the correct choice, and that the choice made in the heat of the moment (usually some form of indulgence) is the erroneous choice. As far as dieting is concerned, however, we are not convinced that dieting is a particularly worthwhile goal; we are happy to point out the difficulties and dangers of dieting (Polivy 1996; Polivy and Herman 1983, 2000). Our research on dieting is not intended to make dieting more effective; more often we are interested in highlighting the difficulties of dieting, to suggest that these very difficulties are "nature's way" of indicating that dieting may not be worth pursuing. Certainly in evolutionary terms (Kacelnik, chap. 3 herein), abstaining from available, high-calorie food has little or no survival value (Beller 1978). More generally, we are interested in the costs of behaving "prudently" (Polivy 1998). Is it possible that the imprudence—the focus of the intertemporal choice literature—is something that we are working too hard to eradicate? From our engaged perspective, if dieting is to serve as a perfect example of anything, perhaps it is a perfect example of how people set out to achieve the impossible, and in failing, reveals that people are not designed to achieve perfection, and that perfection—perfect restraint at least—in fact is not desirable, as our own experience tries to tell us.

Still, value judgments aside, we may consider what factors make it easier for dieters to resist attractive food, just as Mischel has drawn our attention to factors that enhance delay of gratification. The concern with helping dieters resist tempting food and stay on their diets is naturally more prevalent among therapists than among experimentalists, especially since therapists are less likely than are experimentalists to share our conviction that dieting is on balance a bad idea. Tips for helping aspiring dieters avoid or conquer temptation emerged initially decades ago from the behavior therapists (for example, Mahoney and Mahoney 1976; Stuart 1967), who made commonsensical recommendations based on the unproven (see Herman and Polivy 1993) notion that exposure to food cues makes it difficult to sustain a diet. The simplest version of this approach is to recommend that dieters distance themselves from food cues, either by removing cues from sight (for example, storing food in opaque containers, keeping only a minimal amount of food in one's home) or by removing themselves from food cues (for example, going for long walks, or at least staying out of the kitchen). Distancing oneself from cues that threaten one's resolve is recommended by Hoch and Loewenstein (1991) as a general tactic for enhancing one's willpower. Other simpleminded first-generation behavioral techniques include binding oneself contractually.[17] Schelling (1992, 168) suggests "joining a coalition to lose weight in which the members who fail to reach target must publicly acknowledge defeat by paying token, or perhaps substantial, financial penalties to their partners."[18]

Mischel, representing a more cognitive generation of behaviorists, recommends various mental interventions to keep yourself from succumbing to immediate gratification. We have already discussed reconstruing the tempting object as something less tempting (cold cognitions), to which may be added self-devised distractions (instead of thinking about the piece of cake as mud, think of something else altogether). One can focus on the negative features of the cake (its calories) or the benefits of resisting it ("If I get thin . . .") or the dangers of not resisting it ("If I stay fat . . ."). None of these recommended tactics has proven itself in the crucible of actual weight loss, but then again, none has been implemented and tested in a serious way.

The literature on behavioral economics has emphasized the distinction between present and future selves (Loewenstein 1992). Contemplating one's future self appears to be a favorite activity among dieters. Imagining oneself in one's new, slimmer body appears to serve as an important motivator for dieters. Recent research has opened up a number of fascinating questions pertaining to such motivation. For instance, is one better off putting a picture of a fat individual or a slim individual on the refrigerator door as a means of keeping that door shut? It is widely believed that exposure to slim models makes young women feel bad about themselves and thereby motivates them to diet to feel better. Our own research (Mills et al. forthcoming) suggests that exposure to slim models does not necessarily make young women feel bad about themselves. Under certain circumstances in fact it makes them feel better, apparently by promoting fantasies in which these young women take on the (slim) properties of the idealized models. Whether exposure to a slim model makes these young women eat less is another question. On the one hand, the prospect of looking like the model would seem to require eating less; on the other hand, the fantasy of oneself as slim may undermine dieting by short-circuiting the need to actually do something to become thin. If one is slim (at least in one's addled mind), then dietary restraint is not required. The empirical data are mixed. (Mills and colleagues found that exposure to idealized models made young women eat more.)

Contrast with Delay-of-Gratification Paradigm

Mischel has suggested (Mischel, Ebbesen, and Zeiss 1972) that one way to enhance delay is to focus on a photograph of the delayed reward. This suggestion corresponds in a way to the suggestion to look at a photograph of a slim model. In another respect, though, this suggestion highlights the contrasts between the traditional delay-of-gratification paradigm and the situation confronting the dieter. In Mischel's studies, the subject must decide between a small reward now versus no reward now but a large reward later. Typically, though, the immediate and delayed rewards differ only in magnitude. For the dieter, however, the rewards differ in other important ways. For the dieter, the question is not one cookie now versus no cookies now and two cookies later, but rather one cookie now (and possibly six cookies now, on account of disinhibition) versus no cookies now and no cookies later (but having a slim waistline, due to forgoing all those cookies).

The difference in the reward structure facing dieters is crucial to understanding dieting, and why dieting may be more difficult than are normal delay-of-gratification situations. Mischel's subjects for one thing are guaranteed the delayed reward; they know that if they wait, they'll get their extra cookie. The dieter, however, has no such guarantees. She can resist that tempting plate of cookies, but there's no certainty that she will become slim as a result. The stubborn fact is that weight loss is only vaguely connected to food intake. For one thing, energy output is as essential a part of the equation as is energy input. If the dieter—perhaps unwittingly, or perhaps owing to processes over which she has no control, such as a slowed metabolism—expends less energy, then her consummatory sacrifices may go for naught. By the same token, if she deliberately steps up her energy output, she could perhaps move in the direction of slimness without cutting back on cookies at all. Moreover, how much weight she can lose depends critically on her starting point. The slimmer she is to begin with, the less the marginal loss in weight that can be expected from a given caloric shortfall or a given energy expenditure; body weight is defended, at least roughly (Polivy and Herman 1983). Even if the connection between eating less and becoming slim is inexorable, how long will it take? Mischel's subjects know how long they must wait. For the dieter, the process is normally slow; she could diet forever and still not reach her weight goal.

The reward that the dieter is after also could be something more than slimness. For some dieters, slimness may be an end in itself; but for many other dieters, slimness is simply a means to an end. Being slim is how one becomes attractive; being slim is how one becomes healthy; being slim is how one displays one's virtue.[19] Just as eating less does not guarantee slimness, though, becoming slim does not guarantee that one will become attractive, healthy, or a paragon of virtue. Those few dieters who actually achieve their weight goals are often worse off than those who don't. Those who don't can at least hold out hope that the next diet will make them slim and thereby produce desirable friends, lovers, and a better job. For those who do succeed in losing weight, the result is often a more profound disappointment; after all that sacrifice, life remains essentially unchanged.[20] Whatever other difficulties they face, Mischel's subjects rarely encounter existential despair.[21]

How Costly Is Dieting?

So far, our discussion of dieting, like most discussions of this subject, has focused on the cost of dieting (abstaining from immediate gratification) as payment for the eventual gain (slimness and its attendant rewards). This traditional view of dieting—a view that makes it a "perfect example" of delay of gratification and short-term economic sacrifice—is premised on the assumption that denying oneself the pleasures of immediate consumption is in fact unpleasant. Dieters certainly complain about having to forgo all that tempting food and how difficult it is to resist, but a careful analysis suggests that things are not so simple, hedonically. As Jevons noted (cited in Loewenstein 1992), denying oneself immediate gratification is likely to occur only if this sacrifice is offset—indeed exceeded—by anticipation of future gratification. If one were not convinced that long-term benefits outweighed short-term costs, one would presumably not undertake dieting in the first place. The question thus arises as to whether the pain of sacrifice actually exceeds the pleasure of anticipation. Important to remember, though, is that it this is not necessarily a matter of current pain exceeding future pleasure; it is more a matter of current pain exceeding current (pleasurable) anticipation of future pleasure. Both of these hedonic events occur in the present virtually simultaneously and may be directly compared on the same metric. From this perspective, the conclusion seems unavoidable that the pleasure of anticipated weight loss (and other pleasures of the self-improvement crusade) exceeds the pain of current and anticipated abstinence. Dieters feel virtuous, superior—especially in the presence of self-regulatory weaklings who succumb to temptation—and may luxuriate in the anticipation of their soon-to-be-realized thinner self and better life. Indeed the very hunger pangs that signal abstention and that are allegedly so difficult to bear provide a clear signal of success. Going to bed hungry is usually regarded as an aversive experience; for the dieter, however, it may provide a sense of accomplishment. This hedonic dialectic—in which pain confers pleasure, and dieting is an exercise in masochism—makes the application of standard behavioral economic calculations questionable. How much are dieters truly suffering when they turn aside a delectable morsel? In all probability, at least some of the suffering comes much later, when all that sacrifice turns out to have been for naught, the diet lies in ruins, and hopes of a better self and life are dashed (once again). Only then do all the forgone treats evoke true regret. As long as one retains hope, then sacrifice is a precursor of reward and takes on the pleasant aspect of reward foreshadowed.

This dialectic is perhaps most pronounced in the case of those with anorexia nervosa. Anorexics would seem to be the ones who suffer most in pursuit of slimness; after all, they eat the least. Yet anorexics seem to enjoy their asceticism mightily, and feel a clear superiority to the rest of us (who do not display their iron will). Debate continues as to whether anorexics suffer from (or even experience) hunger. They

often claim that they don't, and some theories of the origin of anorexia are based on the assumption that absence of hunger is what
leads anorexics to refrain from eating. After therapy, anorexics will
sometimes admit that they have been ravenously hungry all along,
but these admissions are just as deserving of skepticism as are the
prior denials. Most anorexics display an eerie disregard for their own
plight. Either their suffering is overrated (by those of us who find
even minor instances of food deprivation agonizing) or their suffering
is more than offset by the pleasures of self-denial.

Very Short-Term Diets

Another anomaly concerning dieting is the *very short-term diet*. We
refer here to situations in which the individual—not necessarily a
chronic dieter—abstains from food for a brief period for a purpose
other than losing weight. Sometimes—for religious reasons, or when
you are scheduled for a fasting blood test—you have no choice but to
abstain. On other occasions, people abstain in an attempt to increase
their net pleasure. The classic instance is the individual who eats minimally (or not at all) during the day in anticipation of a feast in the
evening.[22] What purpose is served by this gratuitous deprivation? Perhaps ensuring that the total intake for the day does not exceed a certain level; and given that the food at the feast promises to be special,
then saving one's calories so that one will have more to "spend" on
the feast makes sense. This caloric-quota approach, however, makes
sense only if one is counting calories. Nondieters shouldn't bother
with it, and ironically, dieters are the ones who are *less* likely to deprive themselves in anticipation of a same-day feast. So what other
motive might one have for anticipatory deprivation? Possibly, the
eater is "making room" for the anticipated feast; but this is really just
another version of the caloric-quota argument. One hears occasionally
that the food will taste (even) better if one is (very) hungry when one
eats it, so by depriving oneself during the day one may enjoy the
banquet even more. This argument boils down to the contention that
pain (hunger) enhances pleasure (eating) and thus becomes an "economic" issue, with the current cost of deprivation increasing the future benefit of eating. Given that the anticipated food is likely to be
above average in quality to begin with, how much better it could get
as a result of the deprivation effect is not entirely clear. Indeed, there
is not a great deal of evidence that hunger significantly affects the
palatability of good-tasting food.[23] "Hunger is the best sauce" sup-
posedly, but empirical evidence for that proposition is weak.[24] In our

lab, hungry subjects did not find good-tasting food (milk shakes) to be any more pleasant than did nonhungry subjects (Kauffman, Herman, and Polivy 1995), although they did consume more of it.[25] Even were hunger to enhance the palatability of good-tasting food—which seems doubtful—it is not clear whether skipping breakfast and lunch will necessarily increase hunger enough to make a difference. The connection between hours since last meal and reported hunger is positive, but not very positive.[26] We are doubtful of the claim that deprivation makes the feast any better. We suspect that people enjoy the anticipation of the feast, and hunger may promote a forceful focus on food, enhancing the anticipation (Herman and Polivy 1993). That actual enjoyment of the feast is not enhanced by prior deprivation matters little; the entire day may be pleasantly occupied in drooling anticipation. Note that the marginal pleasure in this case occurs not in the evening but during the day, anticipating the evening.[27]

Another version of the very short-term diet occurs when the young woman cuts back on her eating on Friday and Saturday so that her stomach will not protrude in the slinky dress she plans to wear on Saturday night. The notion that food deprivation (or indulgence) manifests itself visibly in the gut is widely accepted, but is notably short on empirical documentation.[28]

Who Diets?

So far we have neglected an issue that in some ways takes precedence over the dynamics of dieting: Who becomes a dieter in the first place? Not everyone diets.[29] The literature on economic choice may help us to understand why some people choose to diet and others don't. The most obvious reason for dieting (or not)—one's current weight or extent of overweight—is not as powerful a predictor of dieting as one might imagine. Lots of slim people diet and lots of fat people don't. Why doesn't the amount of weight that you "need" to lose strictly determine your likelihood of dieting? Most obviously, because the chances of losing a significant amount of weight are not a simple function of initial weight. The likelihood of losing a given amount of weight is a direct function of one's initial weight. This means that the fat person has a better chance of losing twenty pounds than does the slim person. Yet the advantage of losing this weight is an inverse function of one's initial weight—meaning that losing twenty pounds might make a negligible difference to the appearance of the fat person but a huge difference to the appearance of the slim person. So the fat person has a better chance of losing weight but is unlikely to lose enough to make a noticeable difference, whereas the slim person's weight loss is likely to be noticeable but at the same time extremely difficult to achieve. Thus from the economic or rational perspective, initial weight is not a clear determinant of who will diet.

Another undoubtedly significant factor in determining the likelihood of dieting—a factor of prominence in the behavioral economics literature—is temporal perspective. In general, those with a more distant temporal horizon are more likely to diet than are those who think only in the short term. This generalization is captured nicely in the recommendation to "Eat, drink, and be merry, for tomorrow we die." People who don't expect to live much longer have no reason to deprive themselves of immediate satisfactions in exchange for rewards that they will not be around to enjoy. We are not aware of any systematic research on the composition of "last meals" ordered on death row, but we would be surprised if those certain to die on the morrow bothered to restrain their intake or eat in a health-conscious fashion.[30] Do people diet in a war zone?

Many people diet in anticipation of their vacations so that they can look suitably svelte in their beachwear. One of us (J.P.), though, had a patient who would give up dieting just before her planned vacation. The thing was, she was deathly afraid of flying; looking good on the beach didn't mean much, given that she was fairly sure she would not survive the flight to get to the beach (and owing to the carnage associated with air crashes, she was confident that she would have a closed-coffin funeral, further undermining the need to diet).

Rae (cited in Loewenstein 1992) refers to the "brevity and uncertainty" of life. In our society, life has become longer and more certain. Dieting has become more prevalent as well. Although young women remain most likely to diet, the "appropriate" age for dieting in women has been extended, along with life expectancy. Dieting requires confidence that one will live long enough to enjoy the benefits of slimness (or that life will be miserable if one is not slim). A lengthy time horizon makes dieting a good—maybe even a necessary—investment.

One immediate consequence of the September 11, 2001, terror attacks in the United States was a retraction of the time horizon, and the *Wall Street Journal* (Barnes and Petersen 2001) reported that Americans were abandoning their diets. As one twenty-five-year-old woman in Los Angeles put it, "life is too short to suffer again through . . . celery sticks." (She confessed that she had fudge for breakfast.) Jenny Craig, Inc., reported a "sharp wave of cancellations." According to the cashiers at Kopp's Frozen Custard in Milwaukee, "people are skipping the low-calorie vanilla and heading straight for varieties swirled with fudge and pecans." Diet guru Richard Simmons summed up the situation as follows: "Who wants to be measuring out four-ounce portions of chicken at a time like this?" Time alone will tell whether the war on terrorism will allow American dieters to resume the war on fat.[31]

Another way to capture this connection between dieting and temporal perspective would be to classify individuals of the same chronological age in terms of their "time orientation." Humanistic psychology suggests that people may be categorized as present oriented, as opposed to past or future oriented.[32] This categorization presumably would be at least partially independent of health and social condition. We are not aware of any research linking dieting to future orientation, but one would have to predict that those who are firmly anchored in the present are less likely to diet than are those who are thinking ahead.[33] Certainly there are cultural and subcultural differences in the extent to which people are concerned about maintaining a slim physique (Polivy and Herman 2002a). Are the groups least concerned about slimness also the groups least concerned with planning for the future and least likely to delay gratification?

The temperamental characteristic of "impulsivity" has been linked to eating, and specifically to the bingeing at the heart of the clinical conditions of bulimia nervosa and binge eating disorder. Impulsivity does not conduce to successful dieting for either the bulimic or the normal dieter. Dieters passing a bakery may impulsively stop in for a freshly baked treat; bulimics struggle to control their impulses to binge but often succumb. To compensate for their binges, bulimics are forced to engage in purging (most notably in the form of vomiting, but also through laxatives, diuretics, and strenuous exercise). Once the purging becomes entrenched in their routine, things may turn around, with purging serving to excuse or even encourage bingeing.[34]

Substantial research indicates that the impulsivity of the bulimic extends to domains other than eating, including drinking and drug taking, promiscuity, shoplifting, and other problematic behaviors. Indeed impulsivity may be a general trait, with binge eating representing just one salient manifestation. The notion that impulsivity may be consistent across domains raises interesting questions regarding dieting. For instance, does restraint—the opposite of impulsivity and the presumptive key to successful dieting—also extend to other domains? Do successful dieters save more money than do nondieters? Are they more abstemious with respect to drugs and liquor and sex? In short, are people who are restrained (or low in impulsivity) as a general personality style more likely to become dieters? Logically, the answer would seem to be in the affirmative. Yet at the same time, research on dieters (as we have already seen) highlights the extent to which their impulsivity sabotages their diets; indeed many or most people who adopt dieting perhaps do so as a corrective to their basic impulsivity.

The proposal that restraint or self-control may be a general trait figures prominently in recent speculation (Baumeister et al. 1998; Baumeister and Vohs, chap. 6 herein; Muraven, Tice, and Baumeister 1998) about self-regulatory strength (SRS). SRS researchers argue that we all possess a modicum of SRS. If we expend SRS on one activity (for example, resisting a particular temptation), then we may deplete our SRS resources and have less strength available for some other challenge (for example, resisting another temptation). This model suggests that people who exert a great deal of self-control in one domain (for example, dieting) may have less SRS available in other domains. Thus we would expect that dieters might be particularly self-indulgent when it comes to, say, shopping, sex, or other sins. SRS theorists, however, have suggested that SRS can be cultivated—just as muscular strength can be developed—so that repeated exercises of self-control in one domain (such as dieting) may make future displays of self-control easier, both in the domain of dieting and in other domains. Unfortunately, SRS predictions are contradictory: people who spend a lot of time resisting the temptation of food may find their ability to resist further culinary temptations weakened (by depletion) or strengthened (by practice). Likewise people who exert a great deal of effort to control, say, their sexual urges, may find that their ability to control their urge to eat is either enhanced or impaired. Clarification of these matters awaits further research exploring how depletion, repletion, practice, and exhaustion affect self-regulatory strength. Reconciling the contradictory aspects of SRS theory will undoubtedly entail a closer consideration of temporal aspects of how strength is created and expended.

SRS theory focuses on factors that affect one's ability to regulate one's behavior "properly," either by doing the right thing or by not doing the wrong thing. Loewenstein's visceral theory, however, focuses not on changes in the capacity to resist temptation so much as on changes in the strength of temptation. Our own unsystematic speculations, as noted, focus on the relative strength of the desire to eat and the desire to resist, with disinhibition occurring when the desire to eat becomes stronger than the desire to resist. Our analysis of relative strength, however, has not attended sufficiently to the question of whether disinhibition arises from an increase in the strength of the desire to eat or from a decrease in the desire (or ability) to resist eating, or both.[35] Further complications arise when we consider whether it is better to think about impulsivity (the desire to eat) and restraint (the desire to not eat) as traits, states, or hybrids. This issue ultimately will bear on the question of whether enduring, temporally stable personality constructs such as impulsivity and restraint are well-suited to understanding the origins and dynamics of dieting (and analogous motivational conflicts), or whether we would be better served by focusing not on broad traits but on dynamic inconsistencies in behavioral control.

Meanwhile, distinguishing between the "individual difference" question ("Who diets?") and the more traditional economic questions pertaining to restraint and indulgence is important. For the most part, such economic questions are designed to apply to everyone, and we may assume that we are all beset by conflicts as to whether to refrain from temptation or indulge our impulses. Approaching the question from an individual-difference perspective is not incompatible with approaching it from a more "nomothetic" angle. Indeed traitlike individual differences in a domain may illuminate the role of more variable, short-term factors as they affect everyone (Underwood 1975). By the same token, a more situationist approach, emphasizing factors that apply to everyone, may help us to understand the development and dynamics of chronic individual differences.

Concluding Remarks

Dieting is a neat example of an economic calculation in the behavioral sphere; it is also a neat example of how such calculations can go astray. Perhaps dieting is not typical of the sorts of bargains that people make with themselves, but it is certainly typical of the way in which such bargains unravel. Certain unusual aspects of dieting—such as its diurnal structure and extremely loose connection between dietary ambitions and achievements—render dieting a less-than-optimal model of behavioral economics. Still, perhaps these idiosyncratic aspects of dieting make it a perfect test case for behavioral economic theories. Any theory that can account for the complexities of dieting is a theory worthy of our attention.

Notes

1. The economist David Laibson echoes the economist Robert Frank, who, in his essay on intertemporal choice in the previous volume in this series (1992, 275–77), noted that "[a]s every dieter knows, it is one thing to calculate a rational plan for meeting caloric requirements, but quite an-

other to implement it [because] the immediacy of the . . . reward is, for many subjects, just too vivid to ignore. It floods their consciousness and overwhelms their judgment."

2. The models of eating explored in this literature—even when they concern themselves with quantities of food ingested—are themselves mostly nonquantitative. Predictions regarding the dynamics of the inhibition and disinhibition of eating rarely go beyond "more" or "less." The sorts of mathematical formulae favored by economists and even some psychologists are largely absent in the eating literature.

3. We normally surreptitiously weigh the food before and after the experimental participants eat, and simply calculate the difference. Only rarely do people stuff their pockets with our cookies.

4. "As efforts at self-reform so often attest, however, decisions to forgo immediate gratification for the sake of later consequences (e.g., by dieting) are readily forgotten or strategically revised when one experiences the frustration of actually having to execute them. . . . Intentions to practice self-control frequently dissolve in the face of more immediate temptations" (Mischel, Shoda, and Rodriguez 1992, 150).

5. Knowing that it's time for dessert may involve both cognitive and physiological cues. One may deduce that it is time for dessert from the waiter's removal of the tableware used for the main course; and completing the main course also may serve as a conditioned signal for anticipation of dessert, complete with physiological correlates (for example, increased anticipatory insulin secretion). Expecting dessert, however, is unlikely to arouse desire as effectively as is the actual sight, smell, and initial taste of the Jamaican Banana Boat. (For more on the Jamaican Banana Boat, keep reading.) This is not to say that physiological correlates do not contribute to the experience. Fedoroff, Polivy, and Herman (1997) found that dieters ate more when they smelled or thought about the food for ten minutes before eating it (compared to encountering the food without a ten-minute preexposure period). We believe that the enhancing effect of preexposure is mediated by the buildup of cravings, the subjective correlative of anticipatory physiological adaptations. Still, it must be remembered that the salient sensory presence of desirable food itself is crucial to the entire process.

6. The humorist Dave Barry disputed this point, defining a calorie as a unit of measurement that scientists use to determine how good something tastes.

7. In Loewenstein's terms, these factors promote eating not by increasing the desirability of the food but by reducing the dieter's will or ability to resist.

8. The type of distress further moderates the effect: in general, ego threats lead to more eating than do physical threats, in both dieters and non-dieters.

9. Dieters usually come to regret this decision, once the food is eaten and guilt is added to whatever distress obtained initially. Knowing that re-

gret will follow does not seem to inhibit dieters' distress-induced eating, however. "I know I'm going to regret this, but . . ." seems to be our human family motto, especially when we are upset. According to the masking hypothesis, of course, adding guilt and regret to one's other negative emotions is the whole point of overeating.

10. This is reminiscent of the can't-lose situation of the saloon owner: when times are good, people celebrate by drinking more; when times are bad, people drown their sorrows by drinking more. Indeed some evidence shows that both negative and positive mood states provoke relapse in alcoholics and drug abusers, possibly through the mechanism of conditioned craving linked to both negative and positive emotion cues. (We thank George Loewenstein for this suggestion.)

11. As Ainslie and Haslam (1992, 70–71) note, "[p]eople do not seem to outgrow in any general sense their tendency to form temporary preferences, but rather selectively apply the impulse-avoiding skills that they have acquired." This formulation captures the essence of cheating on one's commitment to resist temptation. Dieters are notorious for finding reasons why their diet does not apply in the current situation, which is construed as a special occasion: one has recently exercised vigorously, it's a party, and the like. Does a special occasion trigger the binge? Or do tempting foods and other disinhibitory factors lead the dieter to declare the occasion special and therefore bingeworthy?

12. The recipe for this delicious concoction may be obtained from the second author.

13. The social influence to which we refer of course is a facilitative influence. Sometimes inhibited or minimal eating by one person will rub off on his or her eating companion(s) (Goldman, Herman, and Polivy 1991; Herman, Koenig, et al. 2002). Social influence therefore can increase or decrease food intake, although group eating generally seems to swing in the direction of increased intake (de Castro and de Castro 1989).

14. We say that nondieters display *regulation* and that dieters display *counterregulation*.

15. Logically, a given preload ought to be more likely to disinhibit dieters' eating if administered later in the day, when fewer calories are "left in the diet," than if administered early in the day, when plenty of caloric room is still "left in the diet." To the best of our knowledge this experiment has never been attempted.

16. A diet starting tomorrow did not lead to increased eating today in nondieters. We believe for them the connection between overindulgence today and restraint tomorrow is not so well established.

17. The problem is to make oneself behave as one has resolved to behave, especially in moments of crisis or whenever the resolve may lapse, and the tactic is to structure incentives so that even if the original motivation for behaving as resolved should fade or be rationalized away, there remains a forbidding consequence of misbehavior to provide the necessary discipline (Schelling 1992, 167).

18. One variation on this contract has the dieter who fails to lose (enough) weight making a substantial gift to an organization with whose purpose he or she vehemently disagrees.

19. Displaying one's virtuousness by dieting represents a form of self-signaling (Prelec and Bodner, chap. 9 herein). To paraphrase Prelec, however, the dieter not only displays her virtue by dieting, but may also discount her own perceived virtue to the extent that she understands that her dieting is at least partially motivated by the desire to signal virtue. To regain the moral high ground, she must redouble her efforts, but self-awareness may undercut the attempt, creating a spiral—ever more abstinence in an increasingly desperate quest for virtue—that finds its ultimate expression in anorexia nervosa.

20. "In this world there are only two tragedies. One is not getting what one wants, and the other is getting it" (Oscar Wilde, *Lady Windermere's Fan*).

21. The intrinsic difficulty of losing weight and keeping it off, along with the slim chance that weight loss, even if achieved, will deliver on its promise of an improved life, has led us to conclude that for most people dieting represents a false hope of self-change (Polivy and Herman 2000, 2002b).

22. This situation contrasts sharply with that of the dieter who abandons the diet early in the day in anticipation of a feast in the evening (see earlier discussion).

23. Sweets ordinarily decline in palatability thirty to forty-five minutes after a caloric load. This phenomenon (negative alliesthesia) is counteracted by weight loss, though, such that the underweight individual maintains a stronger preference for sweets, even at the end of a meal (Cabanac 1979). So being hungry might serve to make desserts at the feast especially attractive, but unfortunately, it is significant weight loss (perhaps 10 percent of normal weight), not just a few hours of deprivation, that produces the effect (Cabanac, Duclaux, and Spector 1971).

24. Loewenstein (personal communication), on the basis of his camping experiences, insists that deprivation makes food taste better. By his own admission, however, he and other ravenous campers "devour food that we wouldn't go near at home, but which we find more delicious than the fanciest food we eat at home." That hunger may enhance the allure of mediocre food is possible, but that it would enhance gourmet delights to the same extent, if at all, is doubtful.

25. Strangely, hungry subjects consumed *less* bad-tasting (that is, quinine-adulterated) milk shake than did nonhungry subjects. See Kauffman, Herman, and Polivy (1995) for a consideration of various possible explanations for this seemingly paradoxical effect.

26. Our own (unpublished) survey of the published research found a median correlation of 0.22 between hours of deprivation and reported hunger.

27. That the reality of the feast does not live up to heightened expectation also matters little. Anticipated pleasures rarely live up to their billing in fantasy, but this does not stop us from spending our fondest moments in anticipation. The best year is the year *before* your sabbatical.

28. Maybe whether her stomach is really concave on Saturday night doesn't matter. As long as she *feels* beautiful, perhaps she will be beautiful; let's just hope she doesn't faint.

29. Determining whether or not an individual should be classified as a dieter is not a simple matter. Debate has raged over assessment issues for almost thirty years (see Heatherton et al. [1988] for a typically heated discussion).

30. Still, for his final meal on death row, drug lord and murderer Juan Raul Garza ordered steak, French fries, onion rings, bread—and Diet Coke ("Drug Kingpin Executed in Indiana Federal Prison." *New York Times*, June 19, 2001).

31. Short-term effects of domestic terror were evident in other domains. Barnes and Petersen (2001) reported (anecdotally) less abstinence in the realms of smoking and drinking. Although consumer confidence in the economy fell, some indices of consumer spending (although not those associated with travel and tourism) were above normal in the month following the attack. Shopping is often regarded as just another appetitive behavior, subject to the same exigencies of control and disinhibition.

32. See Caplin (chap. 15, herein) for a discussion of chronic time orientation from an economic perspective.

33. Those who think ahead would presumably display what Rae (cited in Loewenstein 1992) calls "prudence." The humanists tend to argue that many of us are too future oriented, and waste our lives worrying about the future instead of enjoying the present. This may be a philosophical argument against dieting. Paul Rozin and his colleagues have argued in a similar vein that North Americans worry too much about what they eat, and that the French enjoy better health not because their diet is intrinsically healthier but because their more relaxed attitude toward food and eating imposes less stress on them (Rozin et al. 1999).

34. Those with binge eating disorder are not known for their compensatory purging and tend to be correspondingly heavier. Those with anorexia nervosa are not at all impulsive; they have much less difficulty resisting temptation and therefore have little need for purging (although excessive exercising remains popular among anorexics).

35. We thank Roy Baumeister for this suggestion.

References

Ainslie, George, and Nick Haslam. 1992. "Hyperbolic Discounting." In *Choice Over Time*, edited by George Loewenstein and Jon Elster. New York: Russell Sage Foundation.

Barnes, B., and A. Petersen. 2001. "As Priorities Change, Some Question Why They Eschew the Fat." *Wall Street Journal*, October 5, 2001, A1, 4.

Baumeister, Roy F., Ellen Bratslavsky, Mark Muraven, and Dianne M. Tice.

1998. "Ego Depletion: Is the Active Self a Limited Resource?" *Journal of Personality and Social Psychology* 74: 1252–65.

Beller, Anne Scott. 1978. *Fat and Thin: A Natural History of Obesity*. New York: Farrar, Straus and Giroux.

Cabanac, Michel. 1979. "Sensory Pleasure." *Quarterly Journal of Biology* 54: 1–29.

Cabanac, Michel, R. Duclaux, and N. H. Spector. 1971. "Sensory Feedback in the Regulation of Body Weight: Is There a Ponderostat?" *Nature* 229: 125–27.

Camerer, Colin F., Linda Babcock, George Loewenstein, and Richard H. Thaler. 2000. "Labor Supply of New York City Cab Drivers—One Day at a Time." In *Choices, Values, and Frames*, edited by Daniel Kahneman and Amos Tversky. New York: Cambridge University Press.

Cools, J., D. E. Schotte, and R. J. McNally. 1992. "Emotional Arousal and Overeating in Restrained Eaters." *Journal of Abnormal Psychology* 101: 348–51.

de Castro, J. M., and E. S. de Castro. 1989. "Spontaneous Meal Patterns of Humans: Influence of the Presence of Other People." *American Journal of Nutrition* 50: 237–47.

Elster, Jon. 1992. "Intertemporal Choice and Political Thought." In *Choice Over Time*, edited by George Loewenstein and Jon Elster. New York: Russell Sage Foundation.

Fedoroff, I. C., Janet Polivy, and C. Peter Herman. 1997. "The Effect of Pre-Exposure to Food Cues on the Eating Behavior of Restrained and Unrestrained Eaters." *Appetite* 28: 33–47.

Frank, Robert H. 1992. "The Role of Moral Sentiments in the Theory of Intertemporal Choice." In *Choice Over Time*, edited by George Loewenstein and Jon Elster. New York: Russell Sage Foundation.

Goldman, S. J., C. Peter Herman, and Janet Polivy. 1991. "Is the Effect of a Social Model on Eating Attenuated by Hunger?" *Appetite* 17: 129–40.

Heatherton, Todd F., and Roy F. Baumeister. 1991. "Binge Eating as Escape from Self-Awareness." *Psychological Bulletin* 110: 86–108.

Heatherton, Todd F., C. Peter Herman, Janet Polivy, G. A. King, and S. T. McGree. 1988. "The (Mis)Measurement of Restraint: An Analysis of Conceptual and Psychometric Issues." *Journal of Abnormal Psychology* 97: 19–28.

Herman, C. Peter, S. Koenig, J. B. Peterson, and Janet Polivy. 2002. "Individual Differences in Conformity?" Unpublished manuscript, University of Toronto.

Herman, C. Peter, and D. Mack. 1975. "Restrained and Unrestrained Eating." *Journal of Personality* 43: 647–60.

Herman, C. Peter, J. M. Ostovich, and Janet Polivy. 1999. "Effects of Attentional Focus on Subjective Hunger Ratings." *Appetite* 33: 181–93.

Herman, C. Peter, and Janet Polivy. 1975. "Anxiety, Restraint, and Eating Behavior." *Journal of Abnormal Psychology* 84: 666–72.

———. 1980. "Restrained Eating." In *Obesity*, edited by Albert J. Stunkard. Philadelphia: Saunders.

———. 1988. "Restraint and Excess in Dieters and Bulimics." In *The Psychobiology of Bulimia Nervosa*, edited by D. Ploog, Karl Martin Pirke, and Walter Vandereycken. Heidelberg: Springer.

———. 1993. "Mental Control of Eating: Excitatory and Inhibitory Food Thoughts." In *Handbook of Mental Control*, edited by Daniel M. Wegner and James W. Pennebaker. Englewood Cliffs, N.J.: Prentice-Hall.

Herman, C. Peter, Janet Polivy, and V. M. Esses. 1987. "The Illusion of Counter-Regulation." *Appetite* 9: 161–69.

Herman, C. Peter, Janet Polivy, C. Lank, and Todd F. Heatherton. 1987. "Anxiety, Hunger, and Eating Behavior." *Journal of Abnormal Psychology* 96: 264–69.

Herman, C. Peter, Janet Polivy, D. A. Roth, and Todd F. Heatherton. Forthcoming. "Effects of Distress on Eating: A Meta-Analysis of the Experimental Literature."

Herman, C. Peter, Janet Polivy, and R. Silver. 1979. "Effects of an Observer on Eating Behavior: The Induction of 'Sensible' Eating." *Journal of Personality* 47: 85–99.

Herman, C. Peter, D. A. Roth, and Janet Polivy. 2002. "Social Influences on Eating: Eating as Impression Management." Unpublished manuscript, University of Toronto.

Hoch, Stephen J., and George F. Loewenstein. 1991. "Time-Inconsistent Preferences and Consumer Self-Control." *Journal of Consumer Research* 17: 492–507.

Kahan, D., Janet Polivy, and C. Peter Herman. Forthcoming. "Conformity and Dietary Disinhibition: A Test of the Ego Strength Model of Self-Regulation."

Kauffman, N., C. Peter Herman, Janet Polivy. 1995. "Hunger-Induced Finickiness in Humans." *Appetite* 24: 203–18.

Loewenstein, George. 1992. "The Fall and Rise of Psychological Explanations in the Economics of Intertemporal Choice." In *Choice Over Time*, edited by George Loewenstein and Jon Elster. New York: Russell Sage Foundation.

———. 1996. "Out of Control: Visceral Influences on Behavior." *Organizational Behavior and Human Decision Processes* 65: 272–92.

Lowe, M. G. 1982. "The Role of Anticipated Deprivation in Overeating." *Addictive Behaviors* 7: 103–12.

Mahoney, Michael J., and Kathryn Mahoney. 1976. *Permanent Weight Control*. New York: Norton.

Marlatt, G. Alan. 1985. "Relapse Prevention: Theoretical Rationale and Overview of the Model." In *Relapse Prevention*, edited by G. Alan Marlatt and Judith R. Gordon. New York: Guilford.

Mills, J. S., Janet Polivy, C. Peter Herman, and M. Tiggemann. Forthcoming. "Effects of Thin Body Images on Eating Behavior, Mood, and Self-Perception in Restrained and Unrestrained Eaters." *Personality and Social Psychology Bulletin*.

Mischel, Walter, E. B. Ebbesen, and A. R. Zeiss. 1972. "Cognitive and Attentional Mechanisms in Delay of Gratification." *Journal of Personality and Social Psychology* 21: 204–18.

Mischel, Walter, Yuichi Shoda, and Monica L. Rodriguez. 1992. "Delay of Gratification in Children." In *Choice Over Time*, edited by George Loewenstein and Jon Elster. New York: Russell Sage Foundation.

Muraven, Mark, Dianne M. Tice, and Roy F. Baumeister. 1998. "Self-Control as Limited Resource: Regulatory Depletion Patterns." *Journal of Personality and Social Psychology* 74: 774–89.

Polivy, Janet 1976. "Perception of Calories and Regulation of Intake in Restrained and Unrestrained Subjects." *Addictive Behaviors* 1: 237–43.

———. 1996. "Psychological Consequences of Food Restriction." *Journal of the American Dietetic Association* 96: 589–94.

———. 1998. "The Effect of Behavioral Inhibition: Integrating Internal Cues, Cognition, Behavior, and Affect." *Psychological Inquiry* 9: 181–204.

Polivy, Janet, and C. Peter Herman. 1976. "Effects of Alcohol on Eating Behavior: Influences of Mood and Perceived Intoxication." *Journal of Abnormal Psychology* 85: 601–6.

———. 1983. *Breaking the Diet Habit: The Natural Weight Alternative.* New York: Basic Books.

———. 2000. "The False Hope Syndrome: Unfulfilled Expectations of Self-Change." *Current Directions in Psychological Science* 9: 128–31.

———. 2002a. "Causes of Eating Disorders." In *Annual Review of Psychology* 53: 187–213.

———. 2002b. "If at First You Don't Succeed: False Hopes of Self-Change." *American Psychologist* 57: 677–89.

———. Forthcoming. "Experimental Studies of Dieting." In *Eating Disorders and Obesity: A Comprehensive Handbook.* 2d ed., edited by Christopher Fairburn and Kelly D. Brownell. New York: Guilford.

Polivy, Janet, C. Peter Herman, R. Hackett, and I. Kuleshnyk. 1986. "The Effects of Self-Attention and Public Attention on Eating in Restrained and Unrestrained Subjects." *Journal of Personality and Social Psychology* 50: 1253–60.

Polivy, Janet, C. Peter Herman, and Traci McFarlane 1994. "Effects of Anxiety on Eating: Does Palatability Moderate Distress-Induced Overeating in Dieters?" *Journal of Abnormal Psychology* 103: 505–10.

Rogers, P. J., and A. J. Hill. 1989. "Breakdown of Dietary Restraint Following Mere Exposure to Food Stimuli: Interrelationships Between Restraint, Hunger, Salivation, and Food Intake." *Addictive Behaviors* 14: 387–97.

Rosenberg, Harold. 1993. "Prediction of Controlled Drinking by Alcoholics and Problem Drinkers." *Psychological Bulletin* 113: 129–39.

Rozin, Paul, Claude Fischler, Sumio Imada, Allison Saruban, and Amy Wrzesniewski. 1999. "Attitudes to Food and the Role of Food in Life in the U.S.A., Japan, Flemish Belgium and France: Possible Implications for the Diet-Health Debate." *Appetite* 33: 163–80.

Ruderman, A. J., L. J. Belzer, and A. Halperin. 1985. "Restraint, Anticipated Consumption, and Overeating." *Journal of Abnormal Psychology* 94: 547–55.

Schelling, Thomas C. 1992. "Self-Command: A New Discipline." In *Choice Over Time*, edited by George Loewenstein and Jon Elster. New York: Russell Sage Foundation.

Slochower, Joyce Anne. 1983. *Excessive Eating: The Role of Emotions and Environment.* New York: Human Sciences Press.

Sobell, Mark B., and Linda C. Sobell. 1995. "Controlled Drinking After 25 Years: How Important Was the Great Debate?" *Addiction* 90: 1149–53.

Spencer, J. A., and W. J. Fremouw. 1979. "Binge Eating as a Function of Restraint and Weight Classification." *Journal of Abnormal Psychology* 88: 262–67.

Steele, Claude M., and R. A. Josephs. 1990. "Alcohol Myopia: Its Prized and Dangerous Effects." *American Psychologist* 45: 921–33.

Stuart, R. B. 1967. "Behavioral Control of Overeating." *Behavior Research and Therapy* 5: 357–65.

Tice, Dianne M., and Ellen Bratslavsky. 2000. "Giving in to Feel Good: The Place of Emotion Regulation in the Context of General Self-Control." *Psychological Inquiry* 11: 149–59.

Tomarken, Andrew J., and Daniel S. Kirschenbaum. 1984. "Effects of Plans for Future Meals on Counter-Regulatory Eating by Restrained Eaters." *Journal of Abnormal Psychology* 93: 458–72.

Underwood, B. J. 1975. "Individual Differences as a Crucible in Theory Construction." *American Psychologist* 30: 128–34.

Urbszat, Dax, C. Peter Herman, and Janet Polivy. 2002. "Eat, Drink and Be Merry, for Tomorrow We Diet: Effects of Anticipated Deprivation on Food Intake in Restrained and Unrestrained Eaters." *Journal of Abnormal Psychology* 111: 396–401.

Vohs, Kathleen D., and Todd F. Heatherton. 2000. "Self-Regulatory Failure: A Resource-Depletion Approach." *Psychological Science* 11: 249–54.

· 17 ·

Self-Rationing: Self-Control in Consumer Choice

KLAUS WERTENBROCH

Betcha can't eat just one.
—Bert Lahr, advertising Lay's Potato Chips, 1963

MOST OF the decisions in our lives as consumers are recurring over time. How much television should we watch tonight? How many potato chips should we eat tonight (while watching television)? How much money can we afford to spend on taking our date out to dinner? A normative analysis of such repeated choices to expend a resource (health, leisure time, earnings, goodwill, and so on) makes all these choices subject to the same global constraint. Our cholesterol level imposes a global constraint on deciding how many chips to eat on a given night. Our expected life expectancy imposes a global constraint on the time-allocation decision of when to stop watching television and go to bed. Our lifetime budget constraint imposes a global constraint on the purchase decision of whether to take our date to a fancy restaurant or to a neighborhood diner.

Global Constraints and Local Resources in Consumer Choice

An example of such a normative analysis is provided by Ando and Modigliani's (1963) life-cycle hypothesis of saving, which says that consumers maximize utility subject to their available resources, expressed as the sum of their current and discounted future earnings in addition to their current wealth. At any given time, consumers plan to spread consumption of their total resources evenly over the remainder of their life span. Such consumption smoothing occurs even though current assets and income may fluctuate over time. Borrowing thus allows consumers with lower initial assets but higher expected future income to make utility-maximizing consumption choices within the overall lifetime budget constraint. For example, if you expect to be able to pay off your credit card debt from future income, you can charge a dinner with your date at a fancy restaurant that you cannot afford to pay for out of your current assets or income.

In contrast to this normative analysis, however, intuition as well as empirical observation suggest that consumers are not very capable of taking lifetime budget constraints into account when making repeated consumption choices that are distributed over time (see Herrnstein and Prelec 1992). The sheer computational complexity and uncertainty involved in the required present-value calculations suggest that the life-cycle hypothesis does not provide a realistic description of intertemporal consumer choice (Shefrin and Thaler 1988). For example, the surge in personal bankruptcies in the 1990s hints that many consumers take on more debt than they can afford. Experimental data show that consumers often undervalue future relative to current resources, resulting in excessive current consumption (Kotlikoff et al. 1988). In particular, recent experimental results by Soman and Cheema (2002) suggest that consumers overspend when their lifetime budget constraint is not salient to them.

Thus global resource constraints (for example, a lifetime budget constraint) may not be tenable as a guide for consumers' spending and consumption decisions because they often are too abstract, not salient enough, and difficult to compute or gauge. Here I propose that consumers whose preferences are dynamically inconsistent—as much of the work in this volume suggests (Frederick, Loewenstein, and O'Donoghue, chap. 1 herein; Kacelnik, chap. 3 herein; Manuck et al., chap. 4 herein)—will consume excessively when faced with such intangible *global constraints* because nothing limits their consumption at the "local" level. These consumers don't know when to say when. Instead they seem to consume at a rate that is a monotonic function of their immediately available and salient *local resources*. These local resources often are independent of consumers' global constraints: for example, the size of the bag of potato chips from which consumers are eating; the possibility of sleeping in with impunity on Sunday after a late night watching television; or the credit limit on a credit card (Soman and Cheema 2002). This chapter explores how consumers with self-control problems (that is, with dynamically inconsistent preferences) cope with choice situations in which normative constraints are global and intangible while locally available resources are abundant and salient. (For a related conceptualization in terms of temporal construal of outcomes see Liberman and Trope, chap. 8 herein.) I argue that consumers often have enough insight into these problems to employ self-rationing strategies that induce more tangible, localized constraints to control their choices. While framing choices in narrow, local terms may induce suboptimal behavior (Read, Loewenstein, and Rabin 1999), the local constraints employed by self-rationing help consumers to partially compensate for their inability to stick to imperceptible global constraints.

This chapter proceeds as follows: The next section presents empirical evidence that (relatively loose) local rather than (relatively tight) global constraints drive many repeated purchase and consumption decisions. In particular, I examine the effect on buying and consumption of relaxing three forms of local resource constraints, of (monetary) liquidity, of goods in inventory, and of time. Relaxing these local constraints can induce self-control problems of overconsumption. Evidence from the marketing literature suggests that marketing tactics can enhance these effects. I then provide evidence that consumers are often sophisticated enough to address these problems by rationing themselves. Consumers actively and strategically try to keep themselves from consuming resources excessively by self-imposing limits where marketers or policy makers do not provide any. Finally, I conclude the chapter by showing why evidence of self-rationing is important for research on intertemporal choice and self-control and what constitutes such evidence.

While the focus here is on self-control problems in the context of intertemporal consumer choice, note that time also plays an important role in other areas of consumer research and marketing. Some are relatively specific (for example, the effect of diurnal variation on advertising effectiveness; Hornik 1988). Others transcend marketing (Jacoby, Szybillo, and Berning 1976) and are covered elsewhere in this volume, including consumer perceptions of experiences of waiting (for example, waiting for service, say, at a cash register; see Ariely and Carmon, chap. 11 herein), and the development and self-prediction of consumer preferences (for example, Loewenstein and Angner, chap. 12 herein).

Marketing, Resource Effects, and Self-Control Problems

While consumption resources are usually exogenous, consumer choice of how to allocate these resources is not. Moreover, in their attempts to create and manage mutually beneficial trades with consumers, marketers often try to influence that allocation. What follows is how some of their attempts may lead to or exacerbate consumer self-control problems.

Impulsive Buying and Consumption: Self-control problems arise from impulsive behavior. Marketing researchers' interests in impulsive behavior have long focused on impulse buying (for example, Bellenger, Robertson, and Hirschman 1978; Clover 1950; Kollat and Willett 1967; Pollay 1968; Stern 1962; West 1951). Early investigations defined impulsive purchases simply as unplanned purchases in a given product category. This definition, however, was fraught with conceptual and operational problems (Kollat and Willett 1967) and did little to illuminate the consumer's decision processes. Rook (1987) lamented the lack of compelling theorizing about impulse buying and impulse control, which characterized consumer research at the time. In response, Rook and Hoch (1985) asked consumers to describe their experiences of impulse buying episodes, typically characterized by product emanations, spontaneous urges to consume, and sometimes-intense inner conflict about the purchase. Marketing researchers also began to develop personality scales to measure consumer impulsiveness as a trait (Puri 1996; Rook and Hoch 1985; Rook and Fisher 1995) and began to explore the concepts of willpower and desire (Baumeister and Vohs, chap. 6 herein; Hoch and Loewenstein 1991; Loewenstein 1996).

In contrast, economic and behavioral analyses of impulsive consumer choice have typically focused on exploring the implications of models of dynamically inconsistent consumer preferences. (See, for example, Ainslie 1975; Angeletos et al., chap. 18 herein; Loewenstein and Prelec 1992; O'Donoghue and Rabin 2000; Pollak 1968; Prelec and Loewenstein 1997; Thaler and Shefrin 1981; Strotz 1956.) Yet besides stable consumer characteristics such as traits and preferences, two other elements are implicated in impulsive consumer choice: the intertemporal distribution of the costs and benefits of consumption (O'Donoghue and Rabin 1999a; Wertenbroch 1998) and the resource constraints under which consumers make choices (Wertenbroch and Carmon 1997).

As Hoch and Loewenstein (1991) point out, not all goods, activities, or resources prompt dynamically inconsistent preferences. Self-control problems occur when the benefits of consuming one choice option arise earlier and the costs later (as in having a juicy steak high in cholesterol for lunch) than those of another choice option (as in having bland broccoli high in fiber for lunch). Self-control problems also occur when some of the costs or benefits are particularly imminent or salient (Loewenstein 1996). Wertenbroch (1998) provides a formal analysis of how the intertemporal distribution of the consequences of consumption may create self-control problems for so-called vice and virtue goods and activities (for related conceptualizations see, for example, Giner-Sorolla 2001; O'Donoghue and Rabin 1999a; Read, Loewenstein, and Kalyanaraman 1999).[1] Vices pose a greater potential need for self-control because they are relatively more likely to be consumed on impulse (considering only immediate consequences) than comparable virtues in the absence of constraints. Virtues, however, such as castor oil or savings are subject to self-control problems of relative underconsumption.

Marketing Tactics That Exacerbate Self-Control Problems: While dynamically inconsistent preferences and the distribution of costs and benefits of consumption have received focal attention in research on self-control, most analyses place less emphasis on how constraints on resources allow for or limit impulsive buying and consumption. Basic consumer decisions fall into three classes, for which research in consumer behavior and related disciplines suggests that relaxing resource constraints leads to increased spending and consumption.

The first class of consumer decision problems is whether or not to make a purchase given one's budget constraint, and how to pay for the purchase. Loosely speaking, spending can be seen as a vice, while saving represents virtuous behavior. Recent consumer research suggests that the provision of consumer credit can have positive liquidity effects on purchase rates and spending levels (for example, Feinberg 1986; Laibson 1997; Prelec and Simester 2001; Shefrin and Thaler 1988; Soman 2001).

Another basic decision that consumers make every day is which goods to consume from inventory—that is, from among those goods they have stocked up in their pantry, refrigerator, and so on. A recent stream of research in marketing has shown that consumer stockpiling in response to price promotions can lead to positive inventory effects of supply on consumption rates (for example, Ailawadi and Neslin 1998; Assunçao and Meyer 1993; Bell, Chiang, and Padmanabhan 1999; Chandon and Wansink 2002; Folkes, Martin, and Gupta 1993; Nijs et al. 2001; Wansink 1996). This may occur in part because consumers seem to depreciate the costs of goods they have in inventory (Gourville and Soman 1998; Prelec and Loewenstein 1998) and partly because vice goods are more tempting to consume than are virtue goods.

A third type of decision that consumers make on a daily basis is how to allocate, value, or consume their time (for example, Leclerc, Schmitt, and Dubé 1995). Casual observation suggests that consumers often use up the time they have available to complete a task. For example, students usually hand in term papers when they are due rather than earlier. Indeed even their professors seem subject to similar procrastination effects: peer reviews of papers submitted to academic journals tend to be completed around the time of the deadline, no matter how many months reviewers have available for their reviews. Procrastination is a vice, while completing a task on time is virtuous.

What these three types of resources (supplies of money, goods, and time) have in common is that they are consumed at higher rates when available in larger, less bounded quantities—that is, under more global constraints. To see why, consider an analogy to moral hazard problems. These occur when, for example, an insurance company cannot properly monitor the risky behavior it is insuring (for example, driving). The insured then have an incentive to engage in riskier behavior (for example, driving faster) than they would otherwise because the cost of that behavior (losses from accidents and resulting premium increases) will be spread across all insured. So by lowering the price that individuals pay for a good, moral hazard causes them to demand more than the efficient level of the good. Similarly, lifting constraints on resources or making constraints less salient or more difficult to monitor lowers the perceived cost of consuming these resources and may thus induce excessive consumption.

Effects of Consumer Credit on Liquidity, Spending, and Consumption

According to Shefrin and Thaler's (1988) behavioral life cycle hypothesis, consumers' propensity to spend on current consumption increases with the liquidity of their available funds, contrary to normative theory. Consistent with this hypothesis, researchers have suggested that the use of consumer credit and financing tools (for example, in the form of credit cards) enhances consumer spending because consumer credit temporarily lifts liquidity constraints (compare with Ausubel 1991; Gross and Souleles 2001; Laibson 1997). Such enhanced spending, however, implies a reallocation of consumption from the future to the present as the liquidity boost from financing does not affect the consumer's real budget constraint. Perhaps that is why furniture retailers such as Seaman's often provide extended credit terms to furnish consumers with enough liquidity to enable purchases that they might otherwise not make owing to budget constraints.

What is the evidence that consumer financing enhances spending, as would be expected if the provision of credit removes liquidity constraints? Evidence shows that credit card financing in particular increases purchase likelihood (Soman 2001) and willingness to pay (Feinberg 1986; Hirschman 1979; Prelec and Simester 2001; Soman 2001). In an early field study at the point of sale, Hirschman (1979) found that credit card usage was associated with higher spending, although her results could be explained by differences between users and nonusers of credit cards or differences among products, which are bought with or without a credit card. Feinberg (1986) experimentally examined subjects' spending levels for consumer products and charitable donations in the presence or absence of credit card–related stimuli. Although payments were not even made by credit card, he found that the presence of credit card cues enhanced the probability, speed, or magnitude of spending, a finding for which he proposed a conditioning explanation. Soman (2001) showed with hypothetical scenario-based data that past credit card payments enhance current willingness to pay because the budgetary impact of making a credit card payment is not immediately realized in full. Consumers do not encode the paid amount as well when paying by credit card as when they pay cash and they do not immediately book the expense against their objective budget constraint. As a result, they make current purchase decisions as if their available budget had not been depleted by the prior expense. Soman and Cheema (2002) show across a series of experiments and surveys that consumers use the size of the available credit limit as an indicator of future earnings potential. That is, consumers interpret their credit line as indicative of their objective budget constraint, even though the relationship between credit limits and future earnings is highly uncertain and the decision of allocating future income to present consumption is difficult to make in a normatively appropriate manner. Finally, Prelec and Simester (2001) showed experimentally under incentive-compatible conditions (compare with Wertenbroch and Skiera 2002) that willingness to pay is higher when paying by credit card than when paying cash. Specifically, they randomly allocated consumers to a credit card or cash payment condition, controlling for possible differences between consumers in the two conditions. They also ensured that there were no liquidity constraints. They found a large credit card premium: in one study, for instance, consumers in the credit card condition were willing to pay more than 100 percent more than consumers in the cash condition to see a National Basketball Association regular season game between the Boston Celtics and the Miami Heat.

Effects of Promotional Stockpiling and Inventory on Consumption

Over the last decade or so, marketing researchers have begun studying the impact of sales promotions on household stockpiling. A key question in this regard is whether sales promotions increase only secondary demand, through enhanced brand switching, or whether they can also increase primary demand (Bell, Chiang, and Padmanabhan 1999). Do consumers who buy additional units of a good that is on sale simply forward buy and then stay out of the market when price returns to its higher regular level? Or does promotion-induced stockpiling result in greater consumption? While early work on promotion effects assumed a constant usage rate (for example, Gupta 1988), evidence is scant of postpromotion dips that would be expected if sales promotions simply resulted in forward buying without enhancing consumption (Blattberg and Neslin 1990). More recent work with scanner data analyses has shown that category consumption varies with the level of promotion-induced household inventory (Ailawadi and Neslin 1998). Yet the extent to which sales promotions accelerate consumption differs across a variety of consumer packaged goods categories. For example, bacon, potato chips, soft drinks, and yogurt have been shown to exhibit consumption acceleration, while bathroom tissue, coffee, detergents, and paper towels do not (Bell, Chiang, and Padmanabhan 1999).

Aside from these econometric analyses, experimental evidence also suggests inventory effects on consumption. Folkes and colleagues (1993) demonstrated experimentally that the product supply (for example, of household cleaning products) that consumers have on hand on a given usage occasion boosts the quantity consumed. Specifically, they found that usage decreases with diminishing supply in an effort to make it last but only when the supply can be assessed visually. The effect of supply on usage disappears when the bottles holding the supply are opaque. Folkes and colleagues (1993) suggested that the supply effects they showed may lead to overconsumption but could not conclusively demonstrate such overconsumption. Wansink (1996) showed in a number of experimental studies that not only supply but also package size influences usage. This effect is mediated by perceptions of unit costs, which are usually lower for larger package sizes. Similarly, price promotions entail lower unit costs and thus enhance usage. Wansink (1996) found an interesting exception to these effects:

package size and perceived lower unit cost did not enhance the usage of Clorox bleach, which can hardly be described as a tempting vice subject to overconsumption.

More recently, Chandon and Wansink (2002) outlined and tested a conceptual framework that explains stockpiling effects on consumption as a function of consumption incidence and quantity. Specifically, the salience of items in inventory, moderated by the effect of how conveniently the product can be consumed (for example, ready-to-eat food products), drives *consumption incidence* rates. For example, food items in unusual package designs or items left openly on the counter are more likely to prompt consumers to consume them than items out of sight and hence out of mind (see Herman and Polivy, chap. 16 herein). Hoch and Loewenstein (1991) suggest similarly that physical proximity can induce consumption impulses. This may be one reason why retailers saliently display popular magazines and small packages of candy near the cash register, so that customers waiting in line with no distractions will find themselves (or their children) unable to resist the temptation to buy and consume these items (compare with Mischel, Ayduk, and Mendoza-Denton, chap. 5 herein).

While inventory effects on consumption incidence are moderated by consumption convenience and inventory salience, Chandon and Wansink's (2002) framework suggests that inventory effects on *consumption quantity* are triggered by a decline in the cost of consumption due to higher inventory levels. Specifically, stockpiling may entail storage costs as it uses up pantry space and involves the risk of perishability. Thus Assunçao and Meyer (1993) argue that normative reasons exist for why promotional stockpiling should accelerate consumption. This happens because of stock pressure effects from inventory holding costs and because higher inventories provide consumers with more flexibility in consumption without having to worry about replacing the product at a high price. Yet not only the actual cost but also the psychological impact of the cost of consumption declines as inventory increases. Work by Gourville and Soman (1998) and Prelec and Loewenstein (1998) shows that the negative hedonic impact of paying for a purchase that may discourage consumption recedes as payment and consumption are temporally dissociated. The more time elapses since a consumer has bought an item, the more he or she will adapt to having made that payment and will mentally depreciate it (Heath and Fennema 1996). Hence the net benefits from consumption should appear bigger for goods kept in inventory in large quantities and packages.

Procrastination

A third class of resource that consumers use up is time. A lot of anecdotal and introspective evidence suggests that people use too much of it when they have it—that is, they procrastinate. For example, people often use up the time allotted to a task, no matter whether a lot of time or only a little time is allotted, in line with what's popularly known as Parkinson's Law. Accordingly, procrastination has been the subject of much theoretical analysis (for example, Akerlof 1991; O'Donoghue and Rabin 1999a, 1999b, 2001). Yet empirical research to demonstrate procrastination and possibly people's attempts to curb it is scarce.

Suggestive evidence about procrastination comes from Hayes-Roth and Hayes-Roth (1979), who show that subjects often overestimate what they can achieve in a given period, despite repeated feedback. Similarly, Buehler, Griffin, and Ross (1994) show that people underestimate how long it takes them (but not others) to complete tasks (see also Buehler et al. 1997). Does this mean that consumers procrastinate? If so, are consumers sophisticated enough to be aware of their own procrastination (compare with O'Donoghue and Rabin 1999a)? Trope and Fishbach (2000) provide evidence that suggests self-control in preventing procrastination. Specifically, they show that subjects precommit to paying penalties if they fail later to take an agreed-on medical test with unpleasant short-term consequences and useful delayed consequences (that is, an absolute virtue). This type of precommitment may be interpreted as an attempt to prevent indefinite procrastination—that is, not taking the test at all. By precommitting, subjects behave as if they were afraid of procrastinating.

Evidence of Self-Rationing in Addressing Self-Control Problems

Below, I discuss evidence of consumer self-control in response to these three types of resource effects.

Self-Rationing Liquidity

Consumer Credit and Overconsumption   The research discussed earlier on the effects of payment mechanisms demonstrates that perceived liquidity enhances spending. This research does not show, however, whether and when the temporary liquidity boost that consumer credit provides induces *over*spending and *over*consumption in excess of consumers' real (lifetime) budget constraints. After all, it might just be that the effect of consumer credit on spending is in line with a normatively appropriate reallocation of consumption from the future to the present. Yet the pervasiveness of consumer borrowing coupled with the ease with which one can obtain consumer loans, the currently negative savings rate, and the record number of personal bankruptcies in the United States seem to suggest that consumers borrow too much. How can we demonstrate that borrowing leads to overspending and overconsumption? Do consumers try to prevent or minimize such an effect?

Initial evidence comes from Wertenbroch, Soman, and Nunes (2001), who propose that relaxing constraints on purchasing and consumption (for example, by providing additional liquidity) is likely to lead to overconsumption of more tempting hedonic products than of less tempting utilitarian goods (see Dhar and Wertenbroch 2000; O'Curry and Strahilevitz 2001).[2] Therefore consumers with a need for self-control avoid going into debt for hedonic goods in an attempt to control their hedonic consumption. The authors show in several experiments and in field data from a consumer panel they created that consumers with a stronger need for self-control prefer not to finance current consumption or, alternatively, self-impose stricter payment terms.[3] For example, respondents in a hypothetical scenario study were more likely to prefer a shorter but more expensive car loan to a longer, less expensive one (measured as the net present value of the loan payments) when considering the purchase of a hedonic car rather than a utilitarian car. While Prelec and Loewenstein's (1998) work suggests similar preferences for prepayment for goods with short consumption streams, consumers' willingness to pay premia for limiting their own liquidity implies that their behavior is strategically directed at self-control. Note that such a *self*-imposition of constraints suggests that consumers are worried that they would otherwise (that is, without self-rationing) risk overspending and overconsuming.

Mental Budgeting   In addition to debt aversion, consumers have been shown to impose (economically) nonbinding limits on their spending behavior by imposing mental budgets (Heath and Soll 1996; Henderson and Peterson 1992; Thaler 1985, 1999). Mental budgeting entails allocating expenditures to specific spending categories (such as entertainment) such that each category is characterized by a spending limit, much like budgets used in organizations to limit expenditures. Some budgets are more accessible than others, depending on their liquidity (Shefrin and Thaler 1988) or their origin (O'Curry 1997). For example, Shefrin and Thaler (1988) propose that consumers are most easily tempted to spend out of what they call *current assets* (for example, cash and checking accounts), followed by *current wealth* (for example, savings and stock), and lastly, *future income* (for example, designated retirement savings accounts). Note that, unlike the deliberate avoidance of consumer financing described earlier—a precommitment device that imposes actual constraints on overspending—mental budgeting does not entail automatic imposition of a penalty or binding constraint. This is because tracking expenditures against a budget is a malleable process that requires that expenditures are first noticed ("booked") and then assigned to the proper account ("posted"). Booking requires attention and memory, and posting requires similarity judgments and categorization processes (Heath and Soll 1996), all of which make mental budgeting flexible. Nonetheless, mental budgeting appears to be a useful self-control device in that it allows consumers to partition and ration their financial resources, whose real constraints may otherwise not be salient enough to prevent excessive spending.

Self-Rationing Inventories

The earlier section on stockpiling showed that not only do normative reasons exist for inventory effects on consumption (lower cost per unit consumed), but also psychological effects on consumption incidence (inventory salience and consumption convenience) and quantity (mental payment depreciation). In addition, Bell and colleagues' (1999) and Wansink's (1996) findings on differences in inventory effects on consumption suggest that product characteristics such as the intertemporal distribution of the costs and benefits of consumption may affect inventory effects as well. Chandon and Wansink's (2002) concept of consumption convenience suggests as well that inventory effects are stronger when immediate costs of consumption (such as the transaction costs of preparing a tempting dinner) are low or removed. This raises the possibility that at least some inventory effects on consumption or part of these effects are impulsive. How can we tell whether these effects of varying the external (inventory) constraints encourage dynamically inconsistent consumption behavior?

We can infer dynamic inconsistency and the operation of strategic self-control from consumers' self-imposition of constraints on their consumption choices (see O'Donaghue and Rabin 1999a). Wertenbroch (1998) provided the first empirical evidence of this sort, showing that consumers' attempts to control their consumption impulses influence many everyday purchases. I proposed that consumers ration their purchase quantities of vice goods by buying them in small quantities per purchase occasion. This imposes transactions costs and

Table 17.1   Numbers of Buyers Intercepted at the Point of Sale and Endorsing Specific Reasons for Buying Different Package Sizes

Reasons	Small Size[a]		Large Size[b]	
	Cigarettes	Vitamin C	Cigarettes	Vitamin C
Self-control	21	—	—	6
Price	13	4	3	20
Convenience	—	—	—	12
Other	6	3	—	2
Buyers[c]	28	7	3	26

Source: Wertenbroch (1994).
[a]Smallest package size (pack of cigarettes, 50 milligrams of vitamin C).
[b]Any larger package size (carton of cigarettes, more than 50 milligrams of vitamin C).
[c]Column totals may exceed numbers of buyers due to endorsement of multiple reasons.

possibly associated feelings of guilt on additional consumption. Consider table 17.1, which contains the unpublished results of an informal point-of-purchase survey of cigarette (vice) buyers at a large convenience store and vitamin C (virtue) buyers at a nearby health food store in Chicago. Ninety percent of the cigarette buyers bought single packs of cigarettes rather than cartons, while only 21 percent of the vitamin C buyers bought the smallest package size (50 milligrams) available in the store. When asked about their reasons for choosing the particular package sizes that they had just purchased, they listed budget constraints, perceived quantity discounts, and convenience (that is, lower transaction costs). Yet 75 percent of those who bought cigarettes by the pack also endorsed self-control as a reason, and 24 percent of those who purchased larger vitamin C containers did so. Typically, cigarette buyers claimed to try to control their smoking by having only a small inventory of cigarettes available at any given time.

To provide more controlled evidence of purchase quantity rationing, Wertenbroch (1998) conducted two experiments and two field studies comparing sales of products that corresponded to the definition of relative vices and (otherwise matched) relative virtues given earlier. A choice experiment showed that consumers are more likely to forgo quantity discounts for a large package size to ration their purchases of a relative vice (fatty potato chips) compared with a relative virtue (fat-free potato chips). The results are shown in figure 17.1. Using an incentive-compatible measure of reservation prices (see Wertenbroch and Skiera 2002), a second choice experiment showed similarly that consumers with a higher need for consumption self-control exhibit less price-sensitive demand for Oreo cookies than consumers with a lower need for self-control. Specifically, when situ-

Figure 17.1   Probability of Choosing Large-Purchase Quantity over Small-Purchase Quantity, Given Discounts

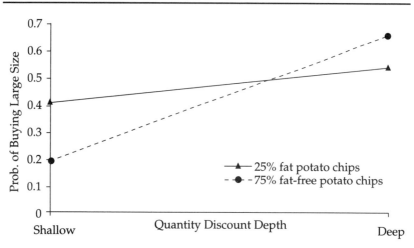

Source: Reprinted by permission, Wertenbroch, Klaus, "Consumption Self-Control via Purchase Quantity Rationing of Virtue and Vice." *Marketing Science* 17(4): 317–37. Copyright 1998, the Institute for Operations Research and the Management Sciences, 901 Elkridge Landing Road, Ste. 400, Linthicum, M.D. 21090.
Note: Observed probability of choosing a large purchase quantity of potato chips (three six-ounce bags) instead of a small purchase quantity (one six-ounce bag), given a purchase and a shallow (7 percent) or a deep (40 percent) quantity discount for the large size (adapted from Wertenbroch 1998).

ational temptation (being offered regular rather than reduced-fat Oreos) and trait impulsiveness combined to enhance temptation and a corresponding need for self-control, respondents showed a steeper decline in their reservation prices per pack when offered two rather than one package of Oreos than when these factors were not both present. That is, the higher respondents' need for self-control (driven by an interaction of both situational and trait impulsiveness), the less likely they were to buy more in response to unit price reductions.

Two field studies provided external validity to these experimental results. The first field study showed that retail quantity discounts are deeper for relative vices than for relative virtues, suggesting the less price-sensitive demand that reflects purchase quantity rationing of vices. The study compared quantity discount depths within thirty pairs of consumer product categories (listed in table 17.2) that were matched with respect to production technology, retailer and consumer inventory holding and handling costs, and frequency and expandability of consumption. Across the top ten pairs with the strongest vice-virtue distinction, the average quantity discount was 25.7 percent

Table 17.2   Relative Vice and Virtue Product Categories in Field Study 1 (Adapted from Wertenbroch 1998)

Relative Vices	Relative Virtues	Mean Vice Rating[a]	N
Regular salad dressing	light salad dressing	2.95****	130
Regular fat cream cheese	light cream cheese	2.93****	122
Regular processed cheese	light processed cheese	2.77****	125
Regular mayonnaise	light mayonnaise	2.74****	125
Ice cream	frozen yogurt	2.69****	134
Regular yogurt	light yogurt	2.37****	125
Alcoholic beer	nonalcoholic beer	2.20****	107
Regular ice tea	low calorie ice tea	1.71****	105
Sugared cereal	low sugar cereal	1.64****	134
Regular chewing gum	sugarless chewing gum	1.50****	131
Dunkin' Donuts munchkins	Dunkin' Donuts muffins	1.44****	115
Regular soft drinks	diet soft drinks	1.35****	127
Regular coffee	decaffeinated coffee	1.34****	98
Whole milk	low fat milk	1.18****	133
Butter	margarine	1.17****	133
Beef bologna	turkey bologna	0.96****	95
Regular tea	decaffeinated tea	0.91***	116
Regular cigarettes	light cigarettes	0.68	28
Hairspray (aerosol)	hair spray (pump)	0.53	75
Dexatrim	Slimfast	0.53	30
Snacks with preservatives	snacks w/out preservatives	0.51**	136
White rice	brown rice	0.43****	134
Sugared fruit drinks	fruit juice	0.40**	134
Bleached flour	whole-wheat flour	0.23	128
Pornographic magazines	news magazines	0.22*	128
White bread	wholegrain bread	0.17	128
Deodorant (aerosol spray)	deodorant (roll-on)	0.16	123
Seltzer water	natural spring water	0.14	125
Sugar	brown sugar	0.11	133
Vegetable shortening	vegetable oil	−0.15[b]	126

Source: Reprinted by permission, Wertenbroch, Klaus, "Consumption Self-Control via Purchase Quantity Rationing of Virtue and Vice." *Marketing Science* 17(4): 317–37. Copyright 1998, the Institute for Operations Research and the Management Sciences, 901 Elkridge Landing Road, Ste. 400, Linthicum, M.D. 21090.
[a]See Wertenbroch (1998) for details of vice-virtue rating scales.
[b]Mean vice rating was counter to hypothesized vice-virtue distinction ($p < 1$).
*$p < .05$, **$p < .01$, ***$p < .001$, ****$p < .0001$ in two-sided t-test.

for doubling the purchase quantity of the virtue, compared with a much deeper 36.4 percent for doubling that of a corresponding vice. A second field study used scanner data of actual sales records to show that store-level demand for relative vices is less price-sensitive than demand for virtues, again in line with purchase quantity rationing. This study analyzed a year's worth of data from a major supermarket chain with eighty-six stores and a 20 percent market share in metropolitan Chicago.

The consistent finding across multiple methods and data sources was a characteristic crossover in demand schedules for vices and virtues. Vice demand increased less in response to price reductions than did virtue demand, although consumers did not generally prefer virtues to vices. Hence inventory constraints on vices appeared self-imposed and strategic rather than driven by simple preferences. By restricting their inventory of vices at the time of purchase, consumers can limit subsequent consumption. As a result of purchase quantity rationing, vice buyers forgo savings from price reductions via quantity discounts, effectively paying a premium as the price of self-control.

These findings offer marketing practitioners in many consumer goods industries new opportunities to increase profits through segmentation and price discrimination based on consumer self-control. They can charge premium prices for small sizes of vices relative to the corresponding quantity discounts for virtues. All else equal, virtue consumers or vice consumers who do not engage in purchase quantity rationing tend to buy in larger amounts anyway, even at shallow quantity discount levels. Yet companies that want to induce vice consumers to stockpile must offer deeper discounts. Public policy makers may (or perhaps should) show concern about firms charging consumers a premium for "virtuous" or self-constrained consumption behavior.

Lemon and Wertenbroch (2000) advance a similar rationing argument for the self-control of service consumption (see also Della-Vigna and Malmendier 2001). They examine strategic consumer behavior in response to usage-sensitive pricing plans in services, in which consumers pay a total cost that has two parts: a prepaid, fixed access fee (independent of the usage rate) and a concurrently paid, variable usage fee (cost per unit consumed). If the service is one that consumers are tempted to underconsume ("virtue" services such as health clubs), consumers can instrumentalize the prepaid (sunk) fixed fees to self-impose a strategic incentive to consume by amortizing them across consumption episodes. Variable fees only add to the immediate costs of virtue consumption that deter usage. If the service is one that consumers are tempted to overconsume, however ("vice" services such as video rentals), sunk fixed fees would mitigate the effect of self-control. Variable per-unit fees can be used to self-impose a strategically desirable constraint on each consumption occasion. In support of this reasoning, Lemon and Wertenbroch (2000) show experimentally that consumers given a choice between pricing schedules are less likely to prepay vice services than virtue services, apparently based on the intuition that they will more easily consume services when these are already in "inventory" (that is, services already paid for).

Additional evidence consistent with purchase quantity rationing of virtues and vices comes from Read, Loewenstein, and Kalyanaraman (1999), albeit in a context in which rationing may more directly help mitigate *under*consumption. In a study of simultaneous versus sequential choices, they found that consumers who rent multiple movies simultaneously for delayed consumption choose a higher total proportion of virtue movies ("highbrow," such as *Schindler's List*) relative to vice movies ("lowbrow," such as *Four Weddings and a Funeral*) than do consumers who rent only one movie at a time for immediate consumption.[4] These choices are in line with what would be predicted if consumers tried to reduce constraints on virtue consumption by making virtue movies easily accessible, by carrying them in inventory. For example, the authors report that in one small sample of consumers, the share of *Schindler's List* was increased thirteenfold in simultaneous choice—that is, when subjects rented movies "in bulk" (Read, Loewenstein, and Kalyanaraman 1999). At the same time, a strategy of filling up their inventory with virtue movies limits the share of vice movies consumers can watch.

Finally, an interesting attempt to control consumption by strategically *creating* rather than limiting an inventory is shown by Kivetz and Simonson (2002). They explore situations in which consumers underconsume nonessential luxuries because spending money on these is often painful and difficult to justify. Spending also may be difficult to allocate optimally on luxuries vis-à-vis necessities because consumers often avoid luxuries completely so as not to be tempted to overconsume them. Given this allocation difficulty, Kivetz and Simonson (2002) hypothesize that consumers often precommit to hedonic consumption as a means to curb underconsumption of luxury goods. They show that consumers in precommitment situations prefer hedonic luxuries to cash payments (for example, when choosing among prizes; see O'Curry and Strahilevitz 2001), even when the luxuries are of lower monetary value than the cash payments, suggesting strategic behavior.

Self-Rationing Time

A self-control device in the face of procrastination is a deadline. For instance, organizations often impose deadlines with penalties on their members to motivate them not to procrastinate. These deadlines increase and boost the salience of the costs of putting off a task (O'Donoghue and Rabin 1999b). Yet in the absence of such external deadlines, are people sophisticated enough to strategically impose *costly* deadlines on themselves, as much well-meaning advice suggests they should?

Ariely and Wertenbroch (2002) provide the answer to this question by showing direct evidence of self-imposed binding deadlines. In one study, they show that people impose deadlines on themselves in tasks in which performance may deteriorate with procrastination, even when missing these deadlines entails penalties. In a world without procrastination such behavior seems nonnormative. A rational decision maker with time-consistent preferences would not self-impose constraints on his or her choices. If people procrastinate, however, and if they are aware of that, self-imposing costly deadlines as a binding mechanism appears strategic and makes sense (O'Donoghue and Rabin 1999a). The authors also demonstrate experimentally that self-imposed deadlines do not enhance performance as much as externally imposed deadlines unless they are evenly spaced—some people apparently are not sophisticated enough to space their deadlines for maximum performance. Further, Ariely and Wertenbroch (2002) show that performance is better under self-imposed early deadlines than under externally imposed late deadlines—that invite the highest degree of procrastination, measured as performance-diminishing delays. Overall their findings show that people are sophisticated enough to understand the value of binding themselves to overcome procrastination, despite strong normative reasons for setting deadlines as late as possible. What is clear from their data is that procrastination is a real behavioral problem. If consumers have a relatively unlimited amount of time on their hands to complete a task, they self-impose costly deadlines to impose boundaries where none (or not enough) existed.

The Role of Empirical Evidence of Self-Rationing

The evidence reviewed here suggests that consumers are ill equipped to make distributed, moment-to-moment choices subject to the global constraints that normative theory calls for. This leads to nonnormative resource effects on consumption. Impulsive consumers will end up overconsuming their inventories of money, time, and goods if they try to evaluate these inventories assuming the normatively required lifetime horizon or some other global constraint. The less locally bounded tempting resources (inventories of vice goods, money, time) are that consumers have available when making consumption choices, the more likely impulsive consumers are to encounter self-control problems, as shown by their attempts to solve these problems. To make the overconsumption problem more manageable, consumers scale down their spending and consumption decisions by self-imposing relatively narrow rule-based (for example, mental budgeting) or physical (for example, costly deadline) constraints on their choices—they ration themselves. The evidence of resource effects and self-rationing reviewed here suggests three key implications and possible areas for future research.

Marketing to Lose Control

This chapter has shown that marketers have come up with mechanisms to boost consumers' resources and, inadvertently or not, put at least the more impulsive ones at risk of excessive consumption. Among marketing forces that enhance consumer self-control problems in this way are price promotion-induced stockpiling and the provision of consumer credit to temporarily boost consumer liquidity. Stockpiling has been shown to accelerate consumption, and consumer credit boosts spending.

Partial Sophistication

Self-rationing is a form of binding behavior. What characterizes binding behaviors in general is that, to prevent themselves from giving in to the temptation to consume, people voluntarily impose constraints on their future choices that are costly to overcome, and they sometimes even pay a premium for binding themselves (Wertenbroch 1998). The defining characteristic of effective binding (precommitment) behaviors is that a lapse triggers the automatic self-imposition of costs (that is, a penalty). If, as in the case of Ulysses tying himself to the mast to avoid steering his ship closer to the dangerous shores of the Sirens, precommitment completely precludes giving in to temptation, the cost is infinite. The literature is replete with anecdotal evidence of precommitment (for example, Hoch and Loewenstein 1991; Schelling 1992; Thaler 1980; Thaler and Shefrin 1981; Wertenbroch and Carmon 1997). Drug addicts, for example, write self-incriminating letters to be held in trust, to be opened and sent out in case they relapse into drug use (Schelling 1992). Academics precommit to giving conference presentations to keep themselves from procrastinating on important research projects (Thaler 1980), and so forth. Controlled empirical evidence of self-rationing and of its implications is rare, however, and only now is beginning to emerge in the literature on consumer choice. Such controlled evidence is necessary not only to validate the anecdotal evidence but also to bolster and advance economists' theoretical attempts to model dynamic inconsistency and self-control.[5]

Empirical evidence of self-rationing plays a key role in research on intertemporal choice because it provides researchers with an assessable criterion to distinguish between consuming *a lot* (but within a consumer's unobserved objective resource constraint) and *too much* (more than is feasible given this constraint). Being overweight, for example, does not necessarily imply time-inconsistent preferences for eating; we cannot rule out that the person simply likes to eat a lot in a time-consistent, rational way. Strategic self-rationing of eating, however (for example, by visiting a fat farm), cannot be explained by time-consistent preferences and constitutes what O'Donoghue and Rabin (1999a) have called "smoking gun" evidence of dynamic inconsistency. More generally, we can infer overconsumption from consumers' attempts to self-ration their consumption. If they ration themselves, then they must be aware of their self-control problems (Bénabou and Tirole 2002) and have at least partial insight into how to solve them. Ariely and Wertenbroch's (2002) findings on performance under self-imposed deadlines provide direct empirical evidence that consumers exhibit varying degrees of sophistication in dealing with self-control problems.

Inefficiencies

How successful are consumers' attempts to ration their own consumption in curbing their self-control problems? Self-rationing prevents decisions that maximize marginal utility and therefore entails inefficiencies. Heath and Soll (1996) showed experimentally that consumers are less willing to buy tickets to a play when they have spent $50 on a basketball ticket than when they have spent $50 on a parking ticket that same week. Consumers drop their reluctance to buy the ticket to the play when the basketball ticket is free. From a normative perspective, they should consider the ticket-purchase decision solely based on the marginal utility to be derived from the play. This may depend on whether they have seen the basketball game earlier in the week but not on whether or not they had to pay for it. Similarly, Leclerc, Schmitt, and Dubé (1995) show that consumers' willingness to pay money to avoid standing in line doubles when waiting for a $45 purchase compared with waiting for a $15 purchase. The normative view implies that consumers' marginal value of saving time should be independent of the purchasing context. More generally, rationing in its various forms (for example, mental budgeting) can create distortions if rations cannot be exceeded when this would yield greater marginal utility, violating fungibility (Thaler 1999). Consumers, for example, may spend the night watching an undelightful TV show if their mental entertainment budget keeps them from going to the play, once they have sufficiently drawn down the available funds by attending the basketball game. Apparently the inefficiencies entailed by self-rationing are the price consumers must pay to "have the cake and eat it"—that is, to partially give in to their spending and consumption impulses rather than refrain from consumption altogether (Carrillo 2000). Thus smokers who buy cigarettes by the pack can tell themselves that they are curbing their addiction, yet at the same time, they continue their addictive behavior. How much consumption is too much and how much too little will always remain an open question. The only thing we can infer from self-rationing is that consumers are afraid that they would consume excessively in the absence of such self-rationing.

Notes

1. Following Wertenbroch (1998), let $X >_I Y$ denote a strict preference for good X over a comparable, matched good Y when the consumer considers only concurrent or immediate consequences of consumption (for example, taste) and ignores delayed consequences (for example, long-term health effects). Let $X >_D Y$ denote a strict preference for X over Y when the consumer considers only delayed consequences and ignores immediate ones. X is a vice relative to Y, and Y is a virtue relative to X, if and only if, at the margin, $X >_I Y$ (maximizing immediate pleasure) and $Y >_D X$ (maximizing delayed utility). Nonconstant (for example, nonexponential) discounting can lead to time-inconsistent preferences such that $Y >_D X$ at $t < T$ when the consequences of one's choice are all delayed, but $X >_I Y$ at $t = T$ when at least some of the consequences are immediate (Strotz 1956).

2. The distinction between hedonic and utilitarian goods is similar to that between vices and virtues, except that the latter are more formally defined in relation to each other (see earlier discussion). The intertemporal distribution of the costs and benefits of consumption of hedonic and utilitarian goods renders hedonic goods more tempting to consume than utilitarian goods. Specifically, hedonic goods are those whose consumption is primarily characterized by an immediate affective and sensory experience of aesthetic or sensual pleasure, fantasy, and fun, whereas utilitarian goods are those whose consumption is more cognitively driven, oriented

toward achieving a delayed goal, and accomplishes a functional or practical task (Dhar and Wertenbroch 2000).

3. The empirical evidence of self-rationing discussed in this chapter is obtained under conditions in which the situation (for example, being faced with a vice or hedonic good) or respondents' trait impulsiveness pose a risk of tempting respondents to act impulsively. These conditions invoke a *potential* need for self-control, and the findings are consistent with strategic, self-regulatory behavior. The data, however, do not address the extent to which consumers actually experience that need for self-control and feel motivated and competent to exercise control.

4. To get people into the theater to watch a movie such as *Schindler's List* is difficult, although they are glad to have watched it in hindsight and recommend it to their friends (Read, Loewenstein, and Kalyanaraman 1999). This suggests that consumers are tempted not to watch the movie when faced with an immediate opportunity to see it, despite its long-term benefits. This makes the film a virtue according to our earlier definition.

5. One reason why research has been slow to provide controlled evidence of self-control may be that, as Read, Loewenstein, and Kalyanaraman (1999) note, serious self-control problems are difficult to observe under controlled conditions, often for ethical reasons, as researchers may not experimentally manipulate drug or alcohol addiction or unprotected sex.

References

Ailawadi, Kusum, and Scott A. Neslin. 1998. "The Effect of Promotion on Consumption: Buying More and Consuming It Faster." *Journal of Marketing Research* 35(August): 390–98.

Ainslie, George. 1975. "Specious Reward: A Behavioral Theory of Impulsiveness and Impulse Control." *Psychological Bulletin* 82: 463–96.

Akerlof, George A. 1991. "Procrastination and Obedience." *American Economic Review* 81(2): 1–19.

Ando, Albert, and Franco Modigliani. 1963. "The Life Cycle Model: Aggregate Implications and Tests." *American Economic Review* 53(1): 55–84.

Ariely, Dan, and Klaus Wertenbroch. 2002. "Procrastination, Deadlines, and Performance: Self-Control by Precommitment." *Psychological Science* 13 (May): 219–24.

Assunçao, Joao, and Robert J. Meyer. 1993. "The Rational Effect of Price Promotions on Sales and Consumption." *Management Science* 39(5): 517–35.

Ausubel, Lawrence M. 1991. "The Failure of Competition in the Credit Card Market." *American Economic Review* 81: 50–81.

Bell, David R., Jeongwen Chiang, and V. Padmanabhan. 1999. "The Decomposition of Promotional Response: An Empirical Generalization." *Marketing Science* 18(4): 504–26.

Bellenger, Danny, D. H. Robertson, and Elizabeth C. Hirschman. 1978. "Impulse Buying Varies by Product." *Journal of Advertising Research* 18(December): 15–18.

Bénabou, Roland, and Jean Tirole. 2002. "Self-Knowledge and Self-Regulation." In *Collected Essays in Psychology and Economics*, edited by Isabelle Brocas and Juan D. Carrillo, Oxford: Oxford University Press.

Blattberg, Robert, and Scott Neslin. 1990. *Sales Promotions: Concepts, Methods, and Strategies.* Englewood Cliffs, N.J.: Prentice-Hall.

Buehler, Roger, Dale Griffin, and Heather MacDonald. 1997. "The Role of Motivated Reasoning in Optimistic Time Predictions." *Personality and Social Psychology Bulletin* 23(March): 238–47.

Buehler, Roger, Dale Griffin, and Michael Ross. 1994. "Exploring the 'Planning Fallacy': Why People Underestimate Their Task Completion Times." *Journal of Personality and Social Psychology* 67(3): 366–81.

Carrillo, Juan D. 2000. "Self-Control, Moderate Consumption, and Craving." Center for Economic Policy Research discussion paper no. 2017.

Chandon, Pierre, and Brian Wansink. 2002. "When Are Stockpiled Products Consumed Faster? A Convenience-Salience Framework of Post-Purchase Consumption Incidence and Quantity." *Journal of Marketing Research* 39(August): 321–35.

Clover, Vernon T. 1950. "Relative Importance of Impulse Buying in Retail Stores." *Journal of Marketing* 25(July): 66–70.

DellaVigna, Stefano, and Ulrike Malmendier. 2001. "Self-Control in the Market: Evidence from the Health Club Industry." Working paper. Cambridge, Mass.: Harvard University.

Dhar, Ravi, and Klaus Wertenbroch. 2000. "Consumer Choice Between Hedonic and Utilitarian Goods." *Journal of Marketing Research* 37(February): 60–71.

Feinberg, Richard A. 1986. "Credit Cards as Spending Facilitating Stimuli: A Conditioning Interpretation." *Journal of Consumer Research* 12: 304–56.

Folkes, Valerie S., Ingrid M. Martin, and Kamal Gupta. 1993. "When to Say When: Effects of Supply on Usage." *Journal of Consumer Research* 20(December): 467–77.

Giner-Sorolla, Roger. 2001. "Guilty Pleasures and Grim Necessities: Affective Attitudes in Dilemmas of Self-Control." *Journal of Personality and Social Psychology* 80 (2): 206–21.

Gourville, John T., and Dilip Soman. 1998. "Payment Depreciation: The Behavioral Effects of Temporally Separating Payments from Consumption." *Journal of Consumer Research* 25 (2): 160–74.

Gross, David B., and Nicholas S. Souleles. 2001. "Do Liquidity Constraints and Interest Rates Matter for Consumer Behavior? Evidence from Credit Card Data." National Bureau of Economic Research working paper no. 8314.

Gupta, Sunil. 1988. "Impact of Sales Promotions on When, What, and How Much to Buy." *Journal of Marketing Research* 25: 342–55.

Hayes-Roth, Barbara, and F. Hayes-Roth. 1979. "A Cognitive Model of Planning." *Cognitive Science* 3: 275–310.

Heath, Chip, and M. G. Fennema. 1996. "Mental Depreciation and Marginal Decision Making." *Organizational Behavior and Human Decision Processes* 65(November): 95–108.

Heath, Chip, and Jack Soll. 1996. "Mental Budgeting and Consumer Decisions." *Journal of Consumer Research* 23: 40–52.

Henderson, Pamela W., and Robert A. Peterson. 1992. "Mental Accounting and Categorization." *Organizational Behavior and Human Decision Processes* 51(February): 92–117.

Herrnstein, Richard, and Drazen Prelec. 1992. "Melioration." In *Choice Over Time*, edited by George Loewenstein and Jon Elster. New York: Russell Sage Foundation.

Hirschman, Elizabeth C. 1979. "Differences in Consumer Purchase Behavior by Credit Card Payment System." *Journal of Consumer Research* 6(June): 58–66.

Hoch, Stephen J., and George F. Loewenstein. 1991. "Time-Inconsistent Preferences and Consumer Self-Control." *Journal of Consumer Research* 17(4): 492–507.

Hornik, Jacob. 1988. "Diurnal Variations in Consumer Response." *Journal of Consumer Research* 14 (March): 588–91.

Jacoby, Jacob, George J. Szybillo, and Carol Kohn Berning. 1976. "Time and Consumer Behavior: An Interdisciplinary Overview." *Journal of Consumer Research* 2(March): 320–39.

Kivetz, Ran, and Itamar Simonson. 2002. "Self-Control for the Righteous: Toward a Theory of Pre-Commitment to Indulgence." *Journal of Consumer Research* 29(September): 199–217.

Kollat, David T., and R. P. Willett. 1967. "Consumer Impulse Purchasing Behavior." *Journal of Marketing Research* 4(February): 21–31.

Kotlikoff, Laurence, William Samuelson, and Stephen Johnson. 1988. "Consumption, Computation Mistakes, and Fiscal Policy." *American Economic Review* 78(2): 408–13.

Laibson, David. 1997. "Golden Eggs and Hyperbolic Discounting." *Quarterly Journal of Economics* 62: 443–77.

Leclerc, France, Bernd Schmitt, and Laurette Dubé. 1995. "Decision Making and Waiting Time: Is Time Like Money?" *Journal of Consumer Research* 22: 110–19.

Lemon, Kay, and Klaus Wertenbroch. 2000. "Consumer Self-Control and the Two-Part Pricing of Services." Working paper. Fontainebleau: INSEAD.

Loewenstein, George. 1996. "Out of Control: Visceral Influences on Behavior." *Organizational Behavior and Human Decision Processes* 65(March): 272–92.

Loewenstein, George, and Drazen Prelec. 1992. "Anomalies in Intertemporal Choice: Evidence and an Interpretation." In *Choice Over Time*, edited by George Loewenstein and Jon Elster. New York: Russell Sage Foundation.

Nijs, Vincent R., Marnik G. Dekimpe, Jan-Benedict E. M. Steenkamp, and Dominique Hanssens. 2001. "The Category Demand Effects of Price Promotions." *Marketing Science* 20(winter): 1–22.

O'Curry, Sue. 1997. "Income Source Effects." Working paper. Chicago: DePaul University.

O'Curry, Sue, and Michal Strahilevitz. 2001. "Probability and Mode of Acquisition Effects on Choices Between Hedonic and Utilitarian Options." *Marketing Letters* 12(February): 37–49.

O'Donoghue, Ted, and Matthew Rabin. 1999a. "Doing It Now or Later." *American Economic Review* 89(1): 103–24.

———. 1999b. "Incentives for Procrastinators." *Quarterly Journal of Economics* 114(3): 769–816.

———. 2000. "The Economics of Immediate Gratification." *Journal of Behavioral Decision Making* 13(2): 233–50.

———. 2001. "Choice and Procrastination." *Quarterly Journal of Economics* 116(1): 121–60.

Pollak, Robert. 1968. "Consistent Planning." *Review of Economic Studies* 35: 201–8.

Pollay, Richard. 1968. "Customer Impulse Purchasing Behavior: A Reexamination." *Journal of Marketing Research* 5(August): 323–25.

Prelec, Drazen, and George Loewenstein. 1997. "Beyond Time Discounting." *Marketing Letters* 8: 97–108.

———. 1998. "The Red and the Black: Mental Accounting of Savings and Debt." *Marketing Science* 17(1): 4–28.

Prelec, Drazen, and Duncan Simester. 2001. "Always Leave Home Without It: A Further Investigation of the Credit-Card Effect on Willingness to Pay." *Marketing Letters* 12(February): 5–12.

Puri, Radhika. 1996. "Measuring and Modifying Consumer Impulsiveness: A Cost-Benefit Accessibility Framework." *Journal of Consumer Psychology* 5: 87–113.

Read, Daniel, George Loewenstein, and S. Kalyanaraman. 1999. "Mixing Virtue and Vice—Combining the Immediacy Effect and the Diversification Heuristic." *Journal of Behavioral Decision Making* 12(4): 257–73.

Read, Daniel, George Loewenstein, and Matthew Rabin. 1999. "Choice Bracketing." *Journal of Risk and Uncertainty* 19: 171–97.

Rook, Dennis W. 1987. "The Buying Impulse." *Journal of Consumer Research* 14(September): 189–99.

Rook, Dennis W., and Robert Fisher. 1995. "Normative Influences on Impulse Buying Behavior." *Journal of Consumer Research* 22(December): 305–13.

Rook, Dennis W., and Stephen J. Hoch. 1985. "Consuming Impulses." In *Advances in Consumer Research.* Vol. 12, edited by Morris B. Holbrook and Elizabeth C. Hirschman. Provo, Utah: Association for Consumer Research.

Schelling, Thomas C. 1992. "Self-Command: A New Discipline." In *Choice Over Time,* edited by George Loewenstein and Jon Elster. New York: Russell Sage Foundation.

Shefrin, Hersh M., and Richard H. Thaler. 1988. "The Behavioral Life-Cycle Hypothesis." *Economic Inquiry* 26(October): 609–43.

Soman, Dilip. 2001. "Effects of Payment Mechanism on Spending Behavior: The Role of Rehearsal and Immediacy of Payments." *Journal of Consumer Research* 27(March): 460–74.

Soman, Dilip, and Amar Cheema. 2002. "The Effect of Credit on Spending Decisions: The Role of the Credit Limit and Credibility." *Marketing Science* 21(winter): 32–53.

Stern, Hawkins. 1962. "The Significance of Impulse Buying Today." *Journal of Marketing* 26(April): 59–62.

Strotz, Robert H. 1956. "Myopia and Inconsistency in Dynamic Utility Maximization." *Review of Economic Studies* 23: 165–80.

Thaler, Richard H. 1980. "Toward a Positive Theory of Consumer Choice." *Journal of Economic Behavior and Organization* 1: 39–60.

———. 1985. "Mental Accounting and Consumer Choice." *Marketing Science* 4(3): 199–214.

———. 1999. "Mental Accounting Matters." *Journal of Behavioral Decision Making* 12(3): 183–206.

Thaler, Richard H., and Hersh M. Shefrin. 1981. "An Economic Theory of Self-Control." *Journal of Political Economy* 89: 392–406.

Trope, Yaacov, and Ayelet Fishbach. 2000. "Counteractive Self-Control in Overcoming Temptation." *Journal of Personality and Social Psychology* 79(4): 493–506.

Wansink, Brian. 1996. "Can Package Size Accelerate Usage Volume?" *Journal of Marketing* 60(July): 1–14.

Wertenbroch, Klaus. 1998. "Consumption Self-Control via Purchase Quantity Rationing of Virtue and Vice." *Marketing Science* 17(4): 317–37.

Wertenbroch, Klaus, and Ziv Carmon. 1997. "Dynamic Preference Maintenance." *Marketing Letters* 8 (1): 145–52.

Wertenbroch, Klaus, and Bernd Skiera. 2002. "Measuring Consumer Willingness to Pay at the Point of Purchase." *Journal of Marketing Research* 39(May): 228–41.

Wertenbroch, Klaus, Dilip Soman, and Joe Nunes. 2001. "Debt Aversion as Self-Control: Consumer Self-Management of Liquidity Constraints." Working paper. Fontainebleau: INSEAD.

West, John C. 1951. "Results of Two Years of Study into Impulse Buying." *Journal of Marketing* 15(January): 362–63.

· 18 ·

The Hyperbolic
Consumption Model:
Calibration, Simulation, and
Empirical Evaluation

George-Marios Angeletos, David Laibson,
Andrea Repetto, Jeremy Tobacman,
and Stephen Weinberg

O ur preferences for the long run tend to conflict with our short-run behavior. When planning for the long run, we *intend* to meet our deadlines, exercise regularly, and eat healthfully. Yet in the short run we have little interest in revising manuscripts, jogging on the stairmaster, and skipping the chocolate soufflé à la mode. Delay of gratification is a nice long-term goal, but instant gratification is disconcertingly tempting.

This gap between long-run intentions and short-run actions is apparent across a wide range of behaviors, including saving choices. A 1997 survey found that 76 percent of respondents believe they should be saving more for retirement. Looking only at respondents who believed they were at an age where "you should be seriously saving already," the survey found that 55 percent reported being "Behind" in their savings and only 6 percent reported being "Ahead" (Farkas and Johnson 1997). The report on the survey concluded: "[T]he gaps between people's attitudes, intentions, and behavior are troubling and threaten increased insecurity and dissatisfaction for people when they retire. Americans are simply not doing what logic—and their own reasoning—suggests they should be doing."

A 1993 Luntz Webber–Merrill Lynch survey found similar answers when baby boomers were asked, "What percentage of your annual household income do you think you should save for retirement?" and "What percentage of your annual household income are you now saving for retirement?" The median reported shortfall was 10 percent of income and the mean gap was 11.1 percent (Bernheim 1995).

Such survey evidence resonates with popular and professional financial planning advice. Financial planners seem to recognize self-control limits when they advise consumers to "use whatever means possible to remove a set amount of money from your bank account each month before you have a chance to spend it" (Rankin 1993).

These observations suggest that households have self-control problems, but this conclusion is tempered by doubts about the quality of the evidence. Most of the data described in the foregoing is either anecdotal or based on attitudinal survey questions. By contrast, almost all mainstream economic analysis focuses on consumer *behavior*, not consumer *attitudes* about ambiguous concepts like what people believe they should be doing.

In this chapter, we report new behavioral evidence that self-control problems importantly influence savings choices (see also Thaler and Shefrin 1981, Thaler 1990, and Wertenbroch 1998). We adopt a conceptual framework that integrates a standard economic theory of life-cycle planning with a psychological model of self-control. This integrated model provides a parsimonious formal framework in which to evaluate the quantitative effects of self-control problems.

We build our modeling framework on three principles. First, our model adopts the standard assumptions of modern consumption models, including the ideas that consumers have uncertain future labor income and face liquidity constraints in the sense that they have limited ability to borrow against this future labor income (Carroll 1992, 1997; Deaton 1991; Zeldes 1989b). Second, we extend the consumption literature by allowing our simulated consumers to borrow on credit cards and by including a partially illiquid asset in the consumers' menu of investment options. Third, we assume that consumers have both a short-run preference for instantaneous gratification and a long-run preference to act patiently. This combination of time preferences is usually called *hyperbolic discounting* (Ainslie 1992), since generalized hyperbolas were first used to capture such intertemporal preferences (Chung and Herrnstein 1961).

Hyperbolic discounting generates the self-control problem that motivates our analysis. When two rewards are both far away in time, decision makers act relatively patiently. For example, a worker prefers a twenty-minute break in 101 days, rather than a fifteen-minute break in 100 days. Yet when both rewards are brought forward in time, preferences exhibit a reversal, reflecting more impatience; the same person prefers a fifteen-minute break right now, rather than a twenty-minute break tomorrow. Far in advance, the consumer prefers to be patient between t and $t + 1$, waiting the extra day for the extra five minutes of break time. Yet, when date t actually arrives, the consumer's preferences have switched, and the consumer now prefers to act impatiently, taking the shorter break immediately.

This type of preference "change," or dynamic inconsistency, is reflected in many common experiences. Such reversals should be well understood by everyone who willfully sets the alarm clock the night before, only to repeatedly press the snooze button the morning after—and even better understood by anyone who goes out of their way to put their alarm clock on the other side of the room. Hyperbolic consumers will report a gap between their long-run goals and their short-run behavior. They will not achieve their desired level of "target savings," since short-run preferences for instantaneous gratification undermine the consumers' efforts to implement patient long-run plans.

The hyperbolic discounting model generates numerous empirical predictions that distinguish the model from the standard model with exponential discounting. First, households with hyperbolic discount functions will hold their wealth in an illiquid form, since such illiquid assets are protected from consumption splurges. Second, households with hyperbolic discount functions are very likely to borrow on their credit cards to fund instant gratification. Thus households with hyperbolic discount functions are likely to have a high level of revolving debt, despite the high cost of credit card borrowing. Third, since hyperbolic households have little liquid wealth, they are unable to smooth consumption, generating a high level of comovement between income and consumption. Indeed, hyperbolic households will even exhibit a high level of comovement between predictable changes in income and changes in consumption. Fourth, this comovement between income and consumption will stand out around retirement, when labor income falls and the lack of liquid wealth generates a necessary fall in consumption.

These rich empirical predictions enable us to distinguish between the standard exponential discounting model and the hyperbolic discounting model. In this chapter we calibrate the exponential and hyperbolic models so that both models match available evidence on the level of retirement savings. We then show that the hyperbolic discounting model better matches available consumption and asset allocation data from the Panel Study of Income Dynamics and the Survey of Consumer Finances.

Hyperbolic Discounting

Robert Strotz (1956) first suggested that people are more impatient when they make short-run trade-offs than when they make long-run trade-offs. Since then dozens of formal experiments have shown that decision makers are more impatient in the short-run than in the long-run. Time preference experiments have been done with a wide range of real rewards, including money, durable goods, fruit juice, sweets, video rentals, relief from noxious noise, and access to video games.[1] Most of these experiments elicit the values of rewards at different time horizons. Then, experimenters deduce the shape of the "discount function," which measures the value of utility, as perceived from the present, at each future time period.

Figure 18.1 plots examples of discount functions, which are normalized to take a value of 1 at 0 delay. The horizontal axis represents the duration of delay, τ, and the vertical axis represents the value of a util delayed by τ periods. The downward slope of the discount functions implies that delaying a reward reduces its values.

Economists usually assume that discount functions are exponential. Specifically, a util delayed τ periods is worth δ^τ times a util enjoyed immediately ($\tau = 0$). Typically, economists assume that δ is less than 1, capturing the fact that future utils are worth less than current utils. In figure 18.1, δ is set at 0.944, which is the annual discount factor used in our exponential simulations herein. In this exponential case, the discount function declines at a constant rate over time—5.6 percent per year.[2]

The experimental evidence implies, however, that the actual discount function declines at a greater rate in the short run than in the long run. In other words, delaying a short-run reward by a few days reduces the value of the reward more in percentage terms than delaying a long-run reward by a few days. When researchers estimate the shape of the discount function based on choices by experimental subjects, the estimates are better approximated by generalized hyperbolic functions than by exponential functions. In the original psychology literature, researchers used hyperbolic discount functions such as $1/\tau$ and $1/1 + \alpha\tau$, with $\alpha > 0$ (Chung and Herrnstein 1961, Ainslie 1992). The most general hyperbolic discount function (Loewenstein and Pre-

Figure 18.1   Discount Functions

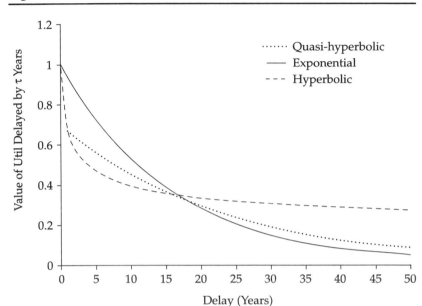

Source: Authors' configuration.
Note: Exponential: δ^τ, with $\delta = 0.944$; hyperbolic: $(1 + \alpha\tau)^{-\gamma/\alpha}$, with $\alpha = 4$ and $\gamma = 1$; and quasi-hyperbolic: $\{1, \beta\delta, \beta\delta^2, \beta\delta^3, ...\}$, with $\beta = 0.7$ and $\delta = 0.957$.

lec 1992) weights events τ periods away with factor $1/(1 + \alpha\tau)^{\gamma/\alpha}$, with $\alpha, \gamma > 0$. Figure 18.1 plots such a generalized hyperbolic discount function. Note that the generalized hyperbolic discount function declines at a faster rate in the short run than in the long run, matching the key feature of the experimental data.

To capture this qualitative property, Laibson (1997a) adopted a discrete-time discount function, $\{1, \beta\delta, \beta\delta^2, \beta\delta^3, ...\}$, which Phelps and Pollak (1968) had previously used to model intergenerational time preferences. This "quasi-hyperbolic" function reflects the sharp short-run drop in valuation measured in the experimental time preference data and has been adopted as a research tool because of its analytical tractability. The quasi-hyperbolic discount function is only hyperbolic in the sense that it captures the key qualitative property of the hyperbolic functions: a faster rate of decline in the short run than in the long run. Laibson (1997a) adopted the term *quasi-hyperbolic* to emphasize the connection to the hyperbolic discounting literature in psychology (Ainslie 1992). O'Donoghue and Rabin (1999a) call these preferences *present biased*, and Krusell and Smith (1999) call them *quasi-geometric.* Akerlof (1991) used a similar discount function to model the salience of the present: $\{1,\beta,\beta,\beta, \ldots\}$.

Figure 18.1 plots the particular parameterization of the quasi-hyperbolic discount function used in our simulations, $\beta = .7$ and $\delta = .957$. Using annual periods, these parameter values roughly match experimentally measured discounting patterns. Delaying an immediate reward by a year reduces the value of that reward by $1 - \beta\delta \approx 1/3$. By contrast, delaying a distant reward by an additional year reduces the value of that reward by a much smaller percentage: $1 - \delta$.

All forms of hyperbolic preferences induce dynamic inconsistency.[3] Consider the discrete-time quasi-hyperbolic function. From the perspective of time 0, the value of a util at time 11 relative to the value at time 10 is $\beta\delta^{11}/\beta\delta^{10} = \delta$. *From the perspective of time 10,* however, the value of a util at time 11 (1 period in the future) relative to the value at time 10 (right now) is $\beta\delta/1 = \beta\delta$. Since δ is close to 1, the period 0 perspective implies that utils in periods 10 and 11 are close in value. So self 0 wishes to be *patient* when considering trade-offs between periods 10 and 11. Since β is much less than 1, the time 10 perspective implies that a util in period 10 is worth a lot more than a util in period 11. So self 10 wishes to be *impatient* between periods 10 and 11.

This dynamic inconsistency forces the hyperbolic consumer to grapple with intrapersonal strategic conflict. Early selves wish to force their preferences on later selves. Later selves do their best to maximize their own interests. Economists have modeled this situation as an intrapersonal game played among the consumer's temporally situated selves (Strotz 1956). Recently, hyperbolic discount functions have been used to explain a wide range of anomalous economic choices, including procrastination, contract design, drug addiction, self-deception, retirement timing, and undersaving (see, for example, Akerlof 1991; Barro 1999; Bénabou and Tirole 2000; Carrillo and Mariotti 2000; Diamond and Koszegi 1998; Laibson 1994, 1996, 1997a; O'Donoghue and Rabin 1999a, 1999b, 2000). We focus here on the implications for life-cycle savings decisions.

In the analysis that follows, we analyze the hyperbolic model with "sophisticated" consumers. These consumers correctly predict that later selves will not honor the preferences of early selves. Thus the early selves take actions that seek to constrain their future selves.

An appealing alternative is to assume that consumers make current choices under the false belief that later selves will act in the interests of the current self. Such "naifs" have optimistic forecasts in the sense that they believe that future selves will carry out the wishes of the current self. Under this belief, the current self constructs the sequence of actions that maximizes the preferences of the current self. The current self then implements the first action in that sequence, expecting future selves to implement the remaining actions. Of course, those future selves conduct their own optimization and therefore implement actions that potentially do not maximize earlier selves' preferences. This naif assumption was first proposed by Strotz (1956) and has been studied by Akerlof (1991) and O'Donoghue and Rabin (1999a, 1999b, 2000), who show that naifs and sophisticates sometimes behave in radically different ways. In the particular economic setting that we simulate, however, the choices of naifs and sophisticates are nearly identical, so we focus only on the sophisticates. Details of analogous naif simulations are available in a longer working paper, Angeletos and colleagues (2001).

A Model of Consumption over the Life Cycle

We analyze a special case of a model of hyperbolic discounting developed in Laibson, Repetto, and Tobacman (2000). This model is based on the simulation literature pioneered by Carroll (1992, 1997), Deaton (1991), and Zeldes (1989b) and extended by Hubbard, Skinner, and Zeldes (1994, 1995), Engen, Gale, and Scholz (1994), Gourinchas and Parker (2002), and Laibson, Repetto, and Tobacman (1998). The model of Laibson, Repetto, and Tobacman (2000) incorporates most of the features of previous life-cycle simulation models and adds new features, including credit cards, variation in household size over time, and the ability to invest in illiquid assets. We summarize the key features of the model herein and refer interested readers to Laibson, Repetto, and Tobacman (2000) for details and for extensions, including an option to declare bankruptcy and an ability to borrow against illiquid collateral (for example, mortgages on housing).

In the simulations presented here, households live for a maximum of ninety years, beginning economic life at age twenty, and retiring at age sixty-three. Household composition—number of adults and non-adults—varies over the life cycle. Labor income is autocorrelated over time, but can be affected by stochastic shocks. The level of labor income and the size of the shocks are calibrated to match empirical data. Here we focus only on households the head of which has only a high school degree, which accounts for roughly half of U.S. households. Laibson, Repetto, and Tobacman (2000), however, analyze households across three different levels of education attainment.

Households in our simulations may hold both liquid assets and illiquid assets, and they may borrow up to a credit limit equal to 30 percent of average labor income for their age group. The real after-tax interest rate received from liquid assets is 3.75 percent. We chose this return because it corresponds to the return realized by a household with two-thirds of its assets in stocks and one-third in risk-free bonds, assuming an average tax rate of 25 percent. The real interest rate on credit card loans is 11.75 percent, two percentage points *below* the mean debt-weighted real interest rate reported by the Federal Reserve Board. This low value is chosen to implicitly capture the impact of bankruptcy and default, which lower consumers' effective interest payments. The credit limit—30 percent of income—is calibrated from data on credit limits in the Survey of Consumer Finances. The illiquid asset, which can be thought of as housing, generates annual consumption flows equal to 5 percent of the value of the asset. Hence the return on illiquid assets is considerably higher than the return on other assets. The illiquid asset can only be sold, however, with a transaction cost equal to $10,000 plus 10 percent of the value of the asset.

These asset market assumptions imply that the household has an implicit crude "commitment" technology. Since sales of the illiquid asset generate transaction costs, wealth invested in the illiquid asset is partially protected from future splurges. This transaction cost enables consumers to constrain themselves *imperfectly* by investing wealth in the illiquid asset. Had we assumed that *perfect* commitment technologies existed, then the sophisticated consumer with a hyperbolic discount function would behave much as a consumer with an exponential discount function. With a perfect commitment technology, the sophisticated hyperbolic consumer would be able to commit to future actions that maximize the young self's preferences for the future.

We assume that households have preferences toward risk characterized by a coefficient of relative risk aversion of two.[4] Households have either an exponential discount function ($\delta^\tau_{exponential}$) or a quasi-hyperbolic discount function ($\beta\delta^\tau_{hyperbolic}$). For the hyperbolic case, we fix $\beta = .7$, corresponding to the one-year discount factor typically measured in laboratory experiments.

We assume that the economy is either populated exclusively by exponential households or exclusively by hyperbolic households. We pick $\delta_{exponential}$ and $\delta_{hyperbolic}$ to match empirical levels of retirement saving. Specifically, $\delta_{exponential}$ is picked so that the exponential simulations generate a median wealth to income ratio of 3.2, for individuals between ages fifty and fifty-nine. The median of 3.2 is calibrated from the Survey of Consumer Finances (SCF).[5] The hyperbolic discount factor, $\delta_{hyperbolic}$, is also picked to match the empirical median of 3.2.

The discount factors that replicate the SCF wealth to income ratio are $\delta_{exponential} = .944$ and $\delta_{hyperbolic} = .957$. Since hyperbolic consumers have two sources of discounting—β and δ—the hyperbolic δ lies above the exponential δ. Recall that the hyperbolic and exponential discount functions are calibrated to generate the same amount of preretirement wealth accumulation. In this manner the calibrations "equalize" the underlying willingness to save between the exponential and hyperbolic consumers. The calibrated long-term discount factors are sensible when compared to discount factors that have been used in similar exercises by other authors. Finally, note that these discount factors do not include age-dependent mortality effects, which reduce the respective discount factors by an additional 1 percent on average per year. The underlying question is how this generally similar willingness to save is translated into actual patterns of consumption over a lifetime.

When a household has a hyperbolic discount function, the household will have dynamically inconsistent preferences. So the problem of allocating consumption over time cannot be treated as a straightforward optimization problem. A sophisticated hyperbolic consumer realizes that selves at later points will not implement the policies that are optimal from the perspective of selves at earlier points.

Following the work of Strotz (1956), we model a sophisticated consumer as a sequence of rational players in an *intra*personal game. Selves {20, 21, . . . , 90} are the players in this game. Taking the strategies of other selves as given, self t picks a strategy for time t that is optimal from its perspective. At an equilibrium, all selves choose optimal strategies given the strategies of all other selves. We numerically compute the equilibrium strategies using a backward induction algorithm.

Results of the Exponential and Hyperbolic Simulations

Figure 18.2 plots the mean consumption profile for households with an exponential discount function and households with a hyperbolic discount function. The figure also plots the calibrated mean labor income profile that is fixed by the data and hence is the same for both types of consumers. The exponential and hyperbolic consumption profiles roughly track the labor income profile. This comovement is driven by two factors. First, low income early in life holds down con-

Figure 18.2   Simulated Mean Income and Consumption

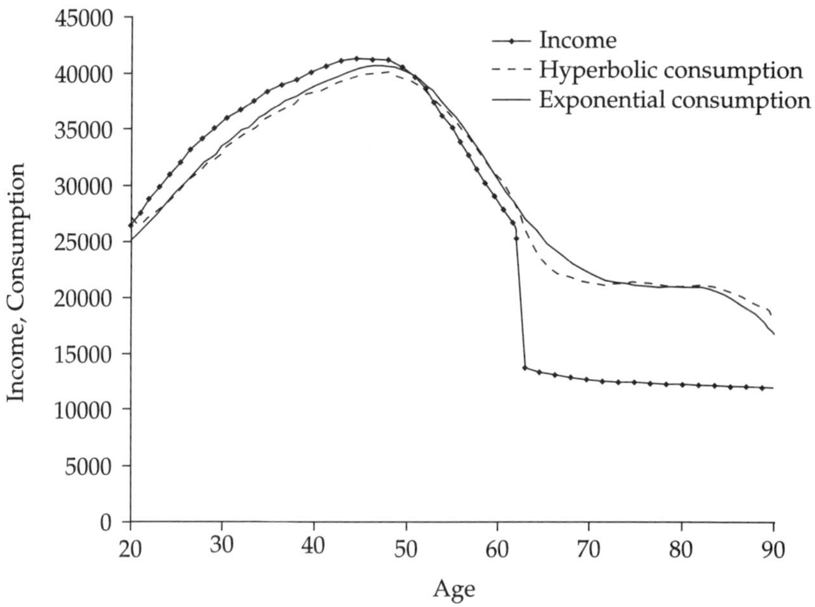

Source: Authors' simulations.
Note: The figure plots the simulated mean values of consumption and labor income for five thousand simulated households with high school graduate heads. The labor income process is identical for households with either exponential or hyperbolic discount functions. The income process is calibrated from the Panel Study of Income Dynamics and includes a deterministic component and both persistent and transitory shocks. Income includes government transfers and pensions, but does not include asset income. Consumption includes both direct consumption and indirect consumption flows of 5 percent of the value of the household's illiquid asset holdings.

sumption, since consumers cannot borrow much against future income. After all, in this model the credit card borrowing limit is 30 percent of one year's income, which is not enough to smooth consumption over the life cycle. Second, consumption needs peak in mid-life, as the number of children increases. The number of children in the household reaches a peak of 2.09 when the household head is thirty-six years old. As the number of children declines, the household begins to support more and more adult dependents (that is, the grandparents of the children), reaching a peak of .91 adult dependents at age fifty-one.

Figure 18.2 also compares the consumption profile of exponential households with the profile of hyperbolic households. These two con-

Figure 18.3   Simulated Total Assets, Illiquid Assets, Liquid Assets, and Liquid Liabilities for Households with Exponential Discount Functions

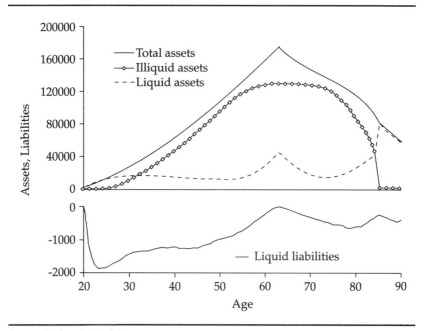

Source: Authors' simulations.

Note: The figure plots the mean level of liquid assets (excluding credit card debt), illiquid assets, total assets, and liquid liabilities (that is, credit card debt) for five thousand simulated households with high school graduate heads and exponential discount functions.

sumption profiles are almost indistinguishable, with small differences arising at the very beginning of life, around retirement, and at the very end of life. At the beginning of life, consumers with hyperbolic preferences go on a spending spree financed with credit cards, leading to higher consumption than households with exponential preferences.[6] Around retirement, hyperbolic consumption falls more steeply than does exponential consumption, since hyperbolic households have most of their wealth in illiquid assets, which they cannot cost-effectively sell to smooth consumption. At the end of life, hyperbolic consumers have more illiquid assets to sell, supporting a higher level of late-life consumption.

The top panel of figure 18.3 plots the mean levels of liquid assets, illiquid assets, and total assets for our simulated exponential households. Liquid assets include year-end liquid financial assets and 1/24 of annual labor income. The latter term adjusts for the fact that our annualized discrete time model doesn't contain any motive to hold cash. If labor income is paid in equal monthly installments, $Y/12$, and consumption is smoothly spread over time, then average cash inventories resulting from monthly income will be $Y/24$.

Liquid wealth is held as a buffer against income shocks and against the fall in income at retirement. As a result, liquid wealth has a local peak just before retirement. Illiquid wealth is accumulated up until retirement and is then sold off after age seventy. Most households sell all of their illiquid wealth in one transaction, thereby minimizing transaction costs, which include proportional and fixed components. A small proportion of wealthy households, however, continue to hold illiquid wealth through the end of life because of a bequest motive. The sell-off in illiquid wealth generates a late-life jump in liquid wealth as assets are shifted from one account to the other.

Liquid financial assets accumulate until they reach a temporary plateau at age thirty. This buffer stock of liquid wealth is used to ride out transitory shocks during working life. More liquid wealth is accumulated in the decade before retirement (ages fifty-three to sixty-three) to smooth out the drop in labor income at retirement. Illiquid accumulation begins at age thirty and peaks at age sixty-three. Late in life, illiquid wealth is sold, transformed into liquid wealth, then consumed.

The bottom panel of figure 18.3 plots the mean level of liquid liabilities—in this model, credit card debt on which interest is paid—for our simulated households with an exponential discount function. This panel shows that credit card borrowing grows quickly early in life. It then remains fairly steady between ages thirty and forty, and then is paid off between ages forty and sixty.

Before comparing the wealth accumulation of simulated exponential and simulated hyperbolic households, note that the total assets accumulated—including liquid and illiquid assets—are almost identical. This similarity is built into the simulation framework, since after all, the time preference parameters for the exponential and hyperbolic discount functions were calibrated to match observed levels of preretirement wealth holding. The only noticeable difference between the simulated total asset profiles occurs after retirement. Households with exponential discount functions spend down their retirement savings much more quickly than those with hyperbolic discount functions, since those with exponential discount functions hold less of their assets in illiquid form

Figure 18.4 illustrates this point by plotting the average illiquid asset holdings of exponential and hyperbolic households. Households with hyperbolic discount functions begin accumulating the illiquid

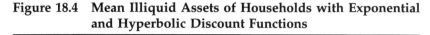

Figure 18.4   Mean Illiquid Assets of Households with Exponential and Hyperbolic Discount Functions

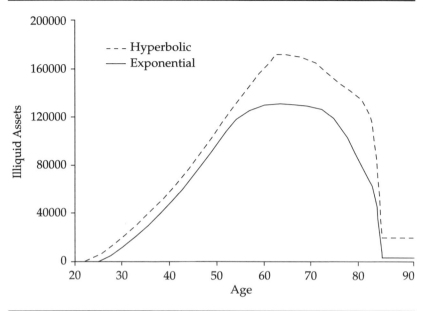

Source: Authors' simulations.
Note: The figure plots mean illiquid assets for five thousand simulated households with high school graduate heads with exponential or hyperbolic discount functions.

asset earlier and continue actively accumulating longer. Households with hyperbolic discount functions are more willing to hold illiquid wealth for two reasons. First, they view illiquid assets as a commitment device, which they value since it prevents later selves from splurging their saved wealth. Second, illiquid assets have the same property as the goose that laid golden eggs (Laibson 1997a). The asset promises to generate substantial benefits, but these benefits can only be realized by holding the asset for a long time. Trying to extract value quickly—by slaughtering the goose or selling the illiquid asset—reduces the value of these assets. Such illiquid assets are particularly valuable to hyperbolics, since hyperbolics have a relatively low *long-run* discount rate.[7]

Hyperbolics and exponentials dislike illiquidity for the standard reason that illiquid assets can't be used to buffer income shocks, but this cost of illiquidity is partially offset for hyperbolics since they value commitment and they more highly value the long-run dividends of illiquid assets. Hence on net, illiquidity is more costly for an

Figure 18.5   Mean Liquid Assets and Liabilities

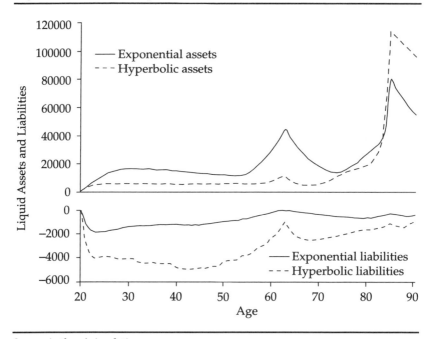

Source: Authors' simulations.
Note: The figure plots mean liquid assets and liabilities over the life cycle for five thousand simulated households with high school graduate heads with exponential or hyperbolic discount functions. Liquid assets include year-end liquid financial assets and 1/24 of annual labor income, representing average cash inventories resulting from monthly income.

exponential household than for a hyperbolic household, explaining why hyperbolics hold a higher share of their wealth in illiquid form.

Conversely, households with hyperbolic discount functions tend to hold relatively little liquid wealth. Figure 18.5 plots the average liquid financial assets and credit card debt for the two types of simulated households. Households with hyperbolic discount functions hold far more credit card debt and lower levels of liquid assets than households with exponential discount functions. The hyperbolic households end up holding relatively little liquid wealth and high levels of liquid debt because liquidity tends to be used to satisfy the hyperbolic taste for instant gratification. Households with hyperbolic discount functions view credit cards as a mixed blessing. Credit cards enable future selves to splurge (which is viewed as a cost) but credit cards also provide liquidity when income shocks hit the household.

Empirical Evaluation of the Simulation Results

This section evaluates empirically the predictions of the simulation models just presented. We focus on simulation predictions about liquid and illiquid wealth accumulation, credit card borrowing, and consumption-income comovement. Relative to households with exponential discount functions, households with hyperbolic discount functions hold less liquid wealth, hold more illiquid wealth, borrow more aggressively on credit cards, and smooth consumption less successfully over the life cycle. As we will argue, the hyperbolic model can make sense of a wide range of facts about the life-cycle choices of U.S. households.

Wealth Accumulation and Asset Allocation

We begin by considering the percentage of households with high levels of liquid wealth. Using our simulated data, we calculate the ratio of liquid assets to annual labor income for every household at every age. We then report the percentage of households that have liquid asset holdings that are at least as large as one month of labor income. The results of this analysis of simulated data and survey data are reported in table 18.1. For example, from ages forty to forty-nine, 72 percent of simulated households with exponential discount functions hold liquid assets greater than one month of labor income. The analogous number for households with hyperbolic discount functions is only 38 percent. For comparison, depending on the definition of liquid assets adopted, between 26 percent and 42 percent of households aged forty to forty-nine in the Survey of Consumer Finances hold liquid financial assets greater than one month of labor income. The narrowest definition of liquid assets is just cash and checking and savings accounts. An intermediate definition of liquid assets includes those items plus money market accounts. Our most inclusive definition of liquid assets includes the previous items plus call accounts, certificates of deposit, bonds, stocks, and mutual funds. Our results change very little as we vary the liquid assets definition. The proportions of households in the Survey of Consumer Finances with liquid assets greater than one month of income, based on these three definitions, are shown in the final three columns of table 18.1.

Consider our intermediate definition of liquid financial assets. Using this definition, on average 43 percent of actual households hold liquid assets greater than one month of household income. This percentage rises over the life cycle. The simulated exponential model

Table 18.1 Percentage of Households with Liquid Assets Greater than One Month of Income

Age Group	Simulated Data		Survey of Consumer Finances		
	Exponential	Hyperbolic	Definition 1	Definition 2	Definition 3
All ages	0.73	0.40	0.37	0.42	0.52
20 to 29	0.52	0.34	0.18	0.19	0.26
30 to 39	0.72	0.39	0.21	0.24	0.36
40 to 49	0.72	0.38	0.26	0.31	0.42
50 to 59	0.76	0.43	0.35	0.41	0.50
60 to 69	0.91	0.42	0.58	0.58	0.76
70 +	0.77	0.46	0.62	0.71	0.78

Sources: Authors' simulations and 1995 Survey of Consumer Finances.
Note: The table reports the fraction of households who hold more than a month's income in liquid wealth. Three different definitions are used for liquid assets.
Definition 1 includes cash, checking and savings accounts.
Definition 2 includes definition 1 plus money market accounts.
Definition 3 includes definition 2 plus call accounts, CDs, bonds, stocks and mutual funds.

does a poor job of approximating this survey data. The exponential profile lies *everywhere* above the empirical profile, with a decade-by-decade mean square difference of 11 percentage points. The simulation of households with hyperbolic discount functions does a much better job of approximating the empirical measures of liquid wealth holding. The hyperbolic profile intersects the empirical profile, with a decade-by-decade mean square difference of only 3 percentage points. Yet the hyperbolic simulations do not predict the sharp empirical rise in liquid wealth holding over the life cycle.

In table 18.2 we evaluate the theoretical models by analyzing the simulated quantity of liquid assets as a share of total assets, what we call the *liquid wealth share*. In the data from the Survey of Consumer Finances, the average liquid wealth share is only 10 percent (using the intermediate definition of liquid wealth). Neither the exponential nor the hyperbolic simulations come close to matching this number, though the hyperbolic simulations are a bit closer to the mark. This failure may arise because illiquid assets in the real world are less illiquid than illiquid assets in our simulations. By lowering the transactions costs of our simulated illiquid assets we can increase our simulated consumers' willingness to hold illiquid assets. In addition, liquid assets in the real world may provide a lower rate of return than liquid assets in our model. If most liquid assets are checking account balances—instead of stocks and corporate bonds—then the liquid re-

Table 18.2   Share of Assets in Liquid Form

| Age Group | Simulations | | Survey of Consumer Finances | | |
	Exponential	Hyperbolic	Definition 1	Definition 2	Definition 3
All ages	0.50	0.39	0.07	0.08	0.15
20 to 29	0.97	0.86	0.10	0.11	0.16
30 to 39	0.65	0.46	0.05	0.06	0.11
40 to 49	0.35	0.24	0.04	0.05	0.08
50 to 59	0.20	0.13	0.04	0.05	0.09
60 to 69	0.27	0.12	0.09	0.10	0.20
70 +	0.57	0.56	0.09	0.12	0.24

Sources: 1995 Survey of Consumer Finances and authors' simulations.
Note: Liquid asset share is liquid assets divided by total assets.
Three different definitions are used for liquid assets.
Definition 1 includes cash, checking accounts, and savings accounts.
Definition 2 includes definition 1 plus money market accounts.
Definition 3 includes definition 2 plus call accounts, CDs, bonds, stocks and mutual funds.
Three complementary definitions are used for illiquid assets.
Illiquid assets includes all assets not included in the corresponding liquid wealth definition, plus IRAs, DC plans, life insurance, trusts, annuities, vehicles, home equity, real estate, business equity, jewelry, furniture, antiques, and home durables.

turn may be lower than 3.75 percent. A lower *liquid* return would increase the relative appeal of the *illiquid* asset.

Revolving credit—that is, credit card borrowing—represents an important form of liquidity. Low levels of liquid net assets are naturally associated with high levels of credit card debt. At any point, only 19 percent of simulated consumers with an exponential discount function borrow on their credit cards compared with 51 percent of those with a hyperbolic discount function. By comparison, in the 1995 Survey of Consumer Finances, 70 percent of households with credit cards report that they did not fully pay their credit card bill the last time that they mailed in a payment. Both of the simulated results are low relative to this empirical benchmark, but hyperbolic simulations do come closer to matching the available data.

Analogous results arise when we measure the average amount borrowed on credit cards. On average, simulated households with exponential discount functions owe $900 of interest-paying credit card debt, *including* the households with no debt. By contrast, simulated households with hyperbolic discount functions owe $3,400 of credit card debt. Empirically, the actual amount of credit card debt owed per household with a credit card is over $5,000 (*including* households with no debt, but *excluding* the float).[8] Again, the hyperbolic simulations provide a better approximation than do the exponential simulations.

Comovement of Consumption and Labor Income

Since Hall's (1978) pathbreaking work, the core of the empirical consumption literature has been based on tests of comovement between consumption and income. Hall argued that if current consumption is based on asset wealth and the net present value of future income flows, then changes in consumption will only occur if news arrives that changes wealth or expectations of future income. As a result, the standard model of consumption, in which consumers face no liquidity constraints, implies that the marginal propensity to consume out of predictable changes in income should be zero.

By contrast, empirical estimates of the marginal propensity to consume out of predictable changes in income lie generally between 0 and .5, with typical estimates between .1 and .3. For example, Altonji and Siow (1987) report a statistically insignificant coefficient of .091; Attanasio and Weber (1993) report an insignificant coefficient of .119; Attanasio and Weber (1995) report an insignificant coefficient of .100; Hall and Mishkin (1982) report a significant coefficient of .200; Hayashi (1985) reports a significant coefficient of .158; Lusardi (1996) reports a significant coefficient of .368; Shea (1995) reports a marginally significant coefficient of .888; and Souleles (1999) reports a significant coefficient of .344. Deaton (1992) and Browning and Lusardi (1996) discuss the literature on the excess sensitivity of consumption to income.

We have replicated the standard comovement regressions using the 1978 to 1992 surveys from the Panel Study of Income Dynamics. We use a range of definitions of consumption and several different assumptions on the measurement error in income (Angeletos et al. 2001). We predict expected income growth with a range of instruments: lagged income, lagged hours worked by the head and spouse, and race and marital status dummies. Our empirical estimates of the marginal propensity to consume out of predictable changes in income lie between .19 and .33 and most are significant at the 5 percent level.[9]

We have also estimated the standard comovement regression using our *simulated* households with exponential discount functions. For these households, the estimated marginal propensity to consume out of predictable changes in income is only 0.03. This estimate lies slightly above zero owing to liquidity constraints. Yet liquidity constraints do not bind or come close to binding often enough in the calibrated exponential model to push the marginal propensity to consume far above zero. Remember that the calibration of the exponential discount function, based on the actual level of retirement wealth, yields a discount factor $\delta_{exponential}$ = .944, implying an exponential discount rate of .056. This discount rate is not high enough to make the liquidity constraints matter. Hence consumption comoves only weakly with predictable changes in income. With higher discount rates the implied comovement would be stronger, but such higher discount rates are inconsistent with the observed empirical level of retirement wealth accumulation.

We have also estimated the marginal propensity to consume out of predictable changes in income using the simulated households with hyperbolic discount functions. For our hyperbolic households we estimate a marginal propensity to consume of 0.166. This estimate compares well with the available empirical evidence. Households with hyperbolic discount functions hold more of their wealth in illiquid form than do households with exponential discount functions. So households with hyperbolic discount functions are more likely to hit liquidity constraints, raising their marginal propensity to consume out of predictable changes in income.

We also use our simulations to investigate income-consumption comovement around the time of retirement. Banks, Blundell, and Tanner (1998) and Bernheim, Skinner, and Weinberg (1997) argue that consumption falls particularly steeply as consumers enter retirement. From the standpoint of the standard theory of consumption, this decline appears anomalous; rational consumers should anticipate retirement and should smooth their consumption even though their income is falling.

Using data from the Panel Study of Income Dynamics, we confirm the results of Bernheim, Skinner, and Weinberg (1997) and estimate a statistically significant excess drop in consumption of 11.6 percent in the four-year window around retirement (Angeletos et al. 2001).[10] We then ran analogous regressions on our simulated data. For households with an exponential discount function, we estimate an excess drop in consumption of 3.0 percent around retirement. For households with a hyperbolic discount function, the analogous drop is 14.5 percent, close to the corresponding estimate from the Panel Study of Income Dynamics. The underlying reason for the difference is that hyperbolic consumers hold relatively little liquid wealth. Therefore a drop in income at retirement translates into a substantial drop in consumption, even though retirement is an exogenous, completely predictable event. Naturally, this is just one explanation for the empirical drop in consumption at retirement. Consumption may also fall because of leisure-consumption substitution and because retirement correlates with negative health or labor supply shocks. Banks and colleagues (1998) and Bernheim and colleagues (1997) do argue, however, that leisure-consumption substitutability effects and "bad news" effects cannot explain the drop in consumption within a rational expectations framework. Neither of these potentially important effects is present in our model.

Conclusions

All in all, a model of consumption based on a hyperbolic discount function consistently better approximates the data than does a model based on an exponential discount function. The hyperbolic discount function turns out to be useful in helping to explain why households hold relatively low levels of liquid wealth, measured either as a fraction of labor income or as a share of total wealth. The model also helps to explain why households borrow so aggressively with their credit cards. In addition, because the households with hyperbolic discount functions have relatively low levels of liquid assets and relatively high levels of credit card debt, they are less able to smooth their consumption paths in the presence of predictable changes in income. As a result, their consumption responds to predictable changes in income, matching well-documented empirical patterns of consumption-income comovement. For similar reasons, the hyperbolic discount function helps to explain why consumption drops around retirement.

Future work should enrich the life-cycle modeling framework. Expanding the number of assets and sources of uncertainty pose important challenges. Such extensions would overwhelm the current generation of computers. As computers get faster, however, richer simulations will become possible. We are also intrigued by analysis that examines the high-frequency behavior of decision makers with hyperbolic discount functions. To economize on computer resources, the model in the current chapter analyzes a model with annual decisions. Yet self-control problems arise from moment to moment—think of the chocolate soufflé à la mode. A complete understanding of self-regulation will require high-frequency analysis of intertemporal choices, including models embedded in continuous time (Barro 1999; Harris and Laibson 2001; Luttmer and Mariotti 2000). Other interesting extensions include analysis of "mixed" economies populated by different types of consumers—both exponential and hyperbolic (Laibson, Repetto, and Tobacman 1998). To understand the role of sophistication in the savings and asset allocation decisions of hyperbolic consumers will also be important (O'Donoghue and Rabin 2000). Researchers should also endogenize the menu of contracts provided by profit-maximizing firms to hyperbolic consumers (O'Donoghue and Rabin 1999b; DellaVigna and Malmendier 2001).

Future work also should attempt to estimate time preference parameters using field data. In preliminary work along these lines, we have empirically evaluated the model described here using the method of simulated moments (Pakes and Pollard 1989). Following this approach we have tightly estimated the hyperbolic preference parameters: $\beta = .55$ (standard error .05) and $\delta = .96$ (standard error .01). This inference joins a nascent literature in which structural hyperbolic models are estimated with field data, as in DellaVigna and Paserman (2000).

We believe that the model of consumption based on a hyperbolic discount function will prove useful because it provides a parsimonious framework that makes sharp empirical predictions. Naturally, we expect such empirical predictions to identify both the strengths and failings of the hyperbolic approach. We predict that the failings will reflect the fact that the hyperbolic model is a reduced form that captures a more complicated underlying preference structure. For now, the hyperbolic model represents an empirically useful parsimonious representation of our self-control problems. Future authors will undoubtedly uncover the deeper cognitive subcomponents of the struggle for self-command.

This chapter was reprinted with the permission of the American Economic Association. It was originally published in 2001 as "The Hyperbolic Consumption Model: Calibration, Simulation, and Empirical Evaluation." *Journal of Economic Perspectives* 15(3): 47–68. Laibson acknowledges financial support from the National Science Foundation (SBR-9510985), the National Institute on Aging (R01-AG-16605), the MacArthur Foundation and the Olin Foundation; and Repetto, from DID-Universidad de Chile, FONDECYT (1990004), Fundación Andes and an institutional grant to CEA from the Hewlett Foundation.

Notes

1. See Solnick et al. (1980); Thaler (1981); Navarick (1982); Millar and Navarick (1984); King and Logue (1987); Kirby and Herrnstein (1995); Kirby and Marakovic (1995, 1996); Kirby (1997); Read et al. (1996). See Ainslie (1992) and Frederick et al. (2002) for partial reviews of this literature. See Mulligan (1997) for a critique.
2. The rate of decline of the discount function is given by $-f'(\tau)/f(\tau)$,

where $f(\tau)$ is the discount function. For the exponential case, $f(\tau) = \delta^\tau$, the rate of decline is $-\ln(\delta) \simeq 1 - \delta$.

3. *Dynamic inconsistency* refers to preferences that contradict the decision maker's own preferences at a later date. For example, imagine that on Monday I prefer to quit smoking on Tuesday but that on Tuesday I change my mind (with no new information) and now prefer to quit smoking on Wednesday. Then I would hold preferences that are dynamically inconsistent. A distinct kind of dynamic inconsistency sometimes arises in strategic interactions between distinct agents. For example, a durable goods manufacturer may wish to commit to a permanently high price for a good, thereby encouraging customers to buy the good immediately instead of waiting for subsequent price declines. Yet if this early buying were to take place, the manufacturer would then wish to subsequently lower the price to attract buyers who weren't willing to buy at the original price (Coase 1972; see also Kydland and Prescott 1977; Barro and Gordon 1983).

4. Typically, the coefficient of relative risk aversion is set between one and five. If a household has a coefficient of relative risk aversion of two, then a household is indifferent between sure consumption of \$66,667 and a fifty-fifty gamble between \$50,000 and \$100,000 of consumption.

5. Wealth does not include social security wealth and other defined benefit pensions, which are already built into the model in the form of post-retirement "labor income."

6. See Gourinchas and Parker (2002) for empirical evidence on an early-life consumption boom.

7. The long-run discount rate of a hyperbolic consumer, $-\ln(\delta_{\text{hyperbolic}}) = -\ln(.957) = .044$, is calibrated to lie below the long-run discount rate of an exponential consumer, $-\ln(\delta_{\text{exponential}}) = -\ln(.944) = .058$. To see these effects graphically, note that in figure 18.1 the exponential curve eventually falls below both hyperbolic curves.

8. This average balance includes households in all education categories. It is calculated on the basis of aggregate information reported by the Federal Reserve. This figure is consistent with values from a proprietary account-level data set assembled by Gross and Souleles (1999a, 1999b, 2000). See Laibson, Repetto, and Tobacman (2000) for a much more detailed analysis of credit card borrowing.

9. Specifically, we estimate,

$$\Delta \ln(C_{it}) = \alpha E_{t-1}\Delta \ln(Y_{it}) + X_{it}\beta + \epsilon_{it}.$$

Here X_{it} is a vector of control variables. The standard consumption model (without liquidity constraints) predicts $\alpha = 0$; the marginal propensity to consume out of predictable changes in income should be zero.

10. Specifically, we estimate,

$$\Delta \ln(C_{lt}) = I_{it}^{\text{RETIRE}}\,\gamma + X_{it}\beta + \epsilon_{it},$$

where I_{it}^{RETIRE} is a set of dummy variables that take the value of 1 in periods $t - 1, t, t + 1$ and $t + 2$ if period t is the age of retirement, and X_{it} is a vector of control variables, including mortality and household composition. By summing the coefficients on the four dummy variables (and switching signs), we get an estimate of the "excess" drop in consumption around retirement.

References

Ainslie, George. 1992. *Picoeconomics*. Cambridge: Cambridge University Press.

Akerlof, George A. 1991. "Procrastination and Obedience." *American Economic Review (Papers and Proceedings)* 81: 1–19.

Altonji, Joseph, and Aloysius Siow. 1987. "Testing the Response of Consumption to Income Changes with (Noisy) Panel Data." *Quarterly Journal of Economics* 102(2): 293–328.

Angeletos, George-Marios, David Laibson, Andrea Repetto, Jeremy Tobacman, and Stephen Weinberg. 2001. "The Hyperbolic Buffer Stock Model: Calibration, Simulation, and Empirical Evaluation." Working paper. National Bureau of Economic Research.

Attanasio, Orazio. 1999. "Consumption." In *Handbook of Macroeconomics*, edited by John Taylor and Michael Woodford. North Holland: Elsevier.

Attanasio, Orazio, and Guglielmo Weber. 1993. "Consumption Growth, the Interest Rate, and Aggregation." *Review of Economic Studies* 60(3): 631–49.

———. 1995. "Is Consumption Growth Consistent with Intertemporal Optimization? Evidence from the Consumer Expenditure Survey." *Journal of Political Economy* 103(6): 1121–57.

Banks, James, Richard Blundell, and Sarah Tanner. 1998. "Is There a Retirement Puzzle?" *American Economic Review* 88: 769–88.

Barro, Robert J. 1999. "Laibson Meets Ramsey in the Neoclassical Growth Model." *Quarterly Journal of Economics* 114(4): 1125–52.

Barro, Robert J., and David B. Gordon. 1983. "A Positive Theory of Monetary Policy in a Natural Rate Mechanism." *Journal of Political Economy* 91(4): 589–610.

Bénabou, Roland, and Jean Tirole. 2000. "Willpower and Personal Rules." Mimeograph, Princeton University/University of Toulouse.

Bernheim, B. Douglas. 1995. "Do Households Appreciate Their Financial Vulnerabilities? An Analysis of Actions, Perceptions, and Public Policy." In *Tax Policy for Economic Growth in the 1990s* (1–30). Washington, D.C.: American Council for Capital Formation.

Bernheim, B. Douglas, Jonathan Skinner, and Steven Weinberg. 1997. "What Accounts for the Variation in Retirement Wealth Among U.S. Households?" Working paper no. 6227. Cambridge, Mass.: National Bureau of Economic Research.

Blundell, Richard, Martin Browning, and Costas Meghir. 1994. "Consumer

Demand and the Life-Cycle Allocation of Household Expenditures." *Review of Economic Studies* 61: 57–80.

Brocas, Isabelle, and Juan Carrillo. 2000. "The Value of Information When Preferences Are Dynamically Inconsistent." *European Economic Review* 44: 1104–15.

Browning, Martin, and Annamaria Lusardi. 1996. "Household Saving: Micro Theories and Micro Facts." *Journal of Economic Literature* 32: 1797–1855.

Carrillo, Juan, and Thomas Mariotti. 2000. "Strategic Ignorance as a Self-Disciplining Device." *Review of Economic Studies* 67: 529–44.

Carroll, Christopher D. 1992. "The Buffer Stock Theory of Saving: Some Macroeconomic Evidence." *Brookings Papers on Economic Activity* 2: 61–156.

———. 1997. "Buffer-Stock Saving and the Life Cycle/Permanent Income Hypothesis." *Quarterly Journal of Economics* 112: 1–57.

Chung, Shin-Ho, and Richard J. Herrnstein. 1961. "Relative and Absolute Strengths of Response as a Function of Frequency of Reinforcement." *Journal of the Experimental Analysis of Animal Behavior* 4: 267–72.

Coase, Ronald H. 1972. "Durability and Monopoly." *Journal of Law and Economics* 15(1): 143–49.

Deaton, Angus. 1991. "Saving and Liquidity Constraints." *Econometrica* 59: 1221–48.

———. 1992. *Understanding Consumption*. Oxford: Oxford University Press.

Deaton, Angus, and John Muellbauer. 1986. "On Measuring Child Costs: With Applications to Poor Countries." *Journal of Political Economy* 94(4): 720–44.

DellaVigna, Stefano, and Ulrike Malmendier. 2001. "Self-Control in the Market: Evidence from the Health Club Industry." Mimeograph, Harvard University.

DellaVigna, Stefano, and M. Daniele Paserman. 2000. "Job Search and Hyperbolic Discounting." Discussion paper no. 00.15. Jerusalem: Maurice Falk Institute for Economic Research.

Diamond, Peter, and Botond Koszegi. 1998. "Hyperbolic Discounting and Retirement." Mimeograph, Massachusetts Institute of Technology.

Engen, Eric, William Gale, and John Karl Scholz. 1994. "Do Saving Incentives Work?" *Brookings Papers on Economic Activity* 1: 85–180.

Farkas, Steve, and Jean Johnson. 1997. "Miles to Go: A Status Report on Americans' Plans for Retirement." Public Agenda.

Frederick, Shane, George Loewenstein, and Ted O'Donoghue. 2002. "Time Discounting and Time Preference: A Critical Review." *Journal of Economic Literature* XL(June): 351–401.

Gourinchas, Pierre-Olivier, and Jonathan Parker. 2002. "Consumption over the Life-Cycle." *Econometrica* 70: 47–89.

Gross, David, and Nicholas Souleles. 1999a. "An Empirical Analysis of Personal Bankruptcy and Delinquency." Mimeograph, University of Pennsylvania.

———. 1999b. "How Do People Use Credit Cards?" Mimeograph, University of Pennsylvania.

———. 2000. "Consumer Response to Changes in Credit Supply: Evidence from Credit Card Data." University of Pennsylvania, Mimeograph.

Hall, Robert E. 1978. "Stochastic Implications of the Life-Cycle/Permanent Income Hypothesis: Theory and Evidence." *Journal of Political Economy* 96: 971–87.

Hall, Robert E., and Frederic S. Mishkin. 1982. "The Sensitivity of Consumption to Transitory Income: Estimates from Panel Data on Households." *Econometrica* 50(2): 461–81.

Harris, Christopher, and David Laibson. 2001. "Dynamic Choices of Hyperbolic Consumers." *Econometrica* 69(4): 935–57.

———. 2001. "Instantaneous Gratification." Mimeograph, Harvard University.

Hayashi, Fumio. 1985. "The Permanent Income Hypothesis and Consumption Durability: Analysis Based on Japanese Panel Data." *Quarterly Journal of Economics* 100(4): 1083–113.

Hubbard, Glenn, Jonathan Skinner, and Stephen Zeldes. 1994. "The Importance of Precautionary Motives in Explaining Individual and Aggregate Saving." *Carnegie-Rochester Conference Series on Public Policy* 40(June): 59–125.

———. 1995. "Precautionary Saving and Social Insurance." *Journal of Political Economy* 103: 360–99.

King, G. R., and A. W. Logue. 1987. "Choice in a Self-Control Paradigm with Human Subjects: Effects of Changeover Delay Duration." *Learning and Motivation* 18: 421–38.

Kirby, Kris N. 1997. "Bidding on the Future: Evidence Against Normative Discounting of Delayed Rewards." *Journal of Experimental Psychology* 126: 54–70.

Kirby, Kris N., and Richard J. Herrnstein. 1995. "Preference Reversals Due to Myopic Discounting of Delayed Reward." *Psychological Science* 6(2): 83–89.

Kirby, Kris N., and Nino N. Marakovic. 1995. "Modeling Myopic Decisions: Evidence for Hyperbolic Delay-Discounting Within Subjects and Amounts." *Organizational Behavior and Human Decision Processes* 64(1): 22–30.

———. 1996. "Delayed-Discounting Probabilistic Rewards Rates Decrease as Amounts Increase." *Psychonomic Bulletin and Review* 3(1): 100–4.

Krusell, Per, and Anthony A. Smith Jr. 1999. "Consumption-Savings Decisions with Quasi-Geometric Discounting." Mimeograph, University of Rochester.

Kydland, Finn E., and Edward C. Prescott. 1977. "Rules Rather than Discretion: The Inconsistency of Optimal Plans." *Journal of Political Economy* 85(3): 473–91.

Laibson, David I. 1994. "Self-Control and Savings." Ph.D. diss., Massachusetts Institute of Technology.

———. 1996. "Hyperbolic Discounting, Undersaving, and Savings Policy." Working paper no. 5635. Cambridge, Mass.: National Bureau of Economic Research.

———. 1997a. "Golden Eggs and Hyperbolic Discounting." *Quarterly Journal of Economics* 62(2): 443–78.

———. 1997b. "Hyperbolic Discount Functions and Time Preference Heterogeneity." Mimeograph, Harvard University.

———. 1998. Comments on "Personal Retirement Saving Programs and Asset Accumulation," by James M. Poterba, Steven F. Venti, and David A. Wise.

In *Studies in the Economics of Aging*, edited by David A. Wise. Cambridge, Mass.: National Bureau of Economic Research and University of Chicago Press.

Laibson, David I., Andrea Repetto, and Jeremy Tobacman. 1998. "Self-Control and Saving for Retirement." *Brookings Papers on Economic Activity* 1: 91–196.

———. 2000. "A Debt Puzzle." Mimeograph, Harvard University.

Loewenstein, George, and Drazen Prelec. 1992. "Anomalies in Intertemporal Choice: Evidence and an Interpretation." *Quarterly Journal of Economics* 107: 573–98.

Lusardi, Annamaria. 1996. "Permanent Income, Current Income, and Consumption: Evidence from Two Panel Data Sets." *Journal of Business and Economic Statistics* 14: 81–90.

Luttmer, Erzo, and Thomas Mariotti. 2000. "Subjective Discount Factors." Mimeograph, London School of Economics.

Millar, A., and D. J. Navarick. 1984. "Self-Control and Choice in Humans: Effects of Video Game Playing as a Positive Reinforcer." *Learning and Motivation* 15: 203–18.

Mulligan, Casey. 1997. "A Logical Economist's Argument Against Hyperbolic Discounting." Mimeograph, University of Chicago.

Navarick, D. J. 1982. "Negative Reinforcement and Choice in Humans." *Learning and Motivation* 13: 361–77.

O'Donoghue, Ted, and Matthew Rabin. 1999a. "Doing It Now or Later." *American Economic Review* 89(1): 103–24.

———. 1999b. "Incentives for Procrastinators." *Quarterly Journal of Economics* 114(3): 769–816.

———. 2000. "Choice and Procrastination." Mimeograph, University of California, Berkeley.

Pakes, Ariel, and David Pollard. 1989. "Simulation and the Asymptotics of Optimization Estimators." *Econometrica* 57(5): 1027–57.

Parker, Jonathan A. 1999. "The Reaction of Household Consumption to Predictable Changes in Social Security Taxes." *American Economic Review* 89(4): 959–73.

Phelps, Edward S., and Robert A. Pollak. 1968. "On Second-Best National Saving and Game-Equilibrium Growth." *Review of Economic Studies* 35: 185–99.

Rankin, Deborah M. 1993. "How to Get Ready for Retirement: Save, Save, Save." *New York Times*, March 13, 1993, 33.

Read, Daniel, George Loewenstein, Shobana Kalyanaraman, and Adrian Bivolaru. 1996. "Mixing Virtue and Vice: The Combined Effects of Hyperbolic Discounting and Diversification." Working paper. Carnegie Mellon University.

Runkle, David. 1991. "Liquidity Constraints and the Permanent-Income Hypothesis: Evidence from Panel Data." *Journal of Monetary Economics* 27(1): 73–98.

Shapiro, Matthew D., and Joel Slemrod. 1995. "Consumer Response to the Timing of Income: Evidence from a Change in Tax Withholding." *American Economic Review* 85(1): 274–83.

Shea, John. 1995. "Union Contracts and the Life-Cycle/Permanent Income Hypothesis." *American Economic Review* 85(1): 186–200.

Simmons Market Research Bureau. 1996. *The 1996 Study of Media and Markets.* New York: Simmons Market Research Bureau.

Solnick, Jay V., et al. 1980. "An Experimental Analysis of Impulsivity and Impulse Control in Humans." *Learning and Motivation* 11(1): 61–77.

Souleles, Nicholas. 1999. "The Response of Household Consumption to Income Tax Refunds." *American Economic Review* 89: 947–58.

Strotz, Robert H. 1956. "Myopia and Inconsistency in Dynamic Utility Maximization." *Review of Economic Studies* 23: 165–80.

Thaler, Richard H. 1981. "Some Empirical Evidence on Dynamic Inconsistency." *Economic Letters* 8: 201–7.

———. 1990. "Saving, Fungibility, and Mental Accounts." *Journal of Economic Perspectives* 4(1): 193–205.

Thaler, Richard H., and Hersh M. Shefrin. 1981. "An Economic Theory of Self-Control." *Journal of Political Economy* 89: 392–410.

Wertenbroch, Klaus. 1998. "Consumption Self-Control by Rationing Purchase Quantities of Virtue and Vice." *Marketing Science* 17(4): 317–37.

Zeldes, Stephen P. 1989a. "Consumption and Liquidity Constraints: An Empirical Investigation." *Journal of Political Economy* 97(2): 305–46.

———. 1989b. "Optimal Consumption with Stochastic Income: Deviations from Certainty Equivalence." *Quarterly Journal of Economics* 104(2): 275–98.

Index

Numbers in **boldface** refer to additional figures or tables

Abelson, Robert P., 28
abstinence, as delay of gratification, 16–17
academic performance: educational attainment and delay ability, 6, 179, 190, 202; improvement preferences and dynamic gestalt characteristics, 328
accommodation dilemma and delay ability in hot-cool model, 192–93
accumulation. *See* consumption
adaptation underprediction in preference prediction, 368–71
addiction: habit-formation models, 36; hyperbolic discounting and time preferences, 33–34; mean discount rates and, 405; priority of present time, 214; self-awareness and self-control, 233–35; time preference, 33–34, 411; visceral influences on utility function, 39. *See also* health and drug dependence, delay discounting in
additive discounting, 305, 306–7

additive duration effect, 331–32
additive duration neglect, 332
additivity, 8, 305
Adler, Daniel, 368–69
affect. *See* emotion and affect
age effects: delay of gratification ability, 187; maturation and preference change, 362–63, 363, 374; selves, similarity of past to future, and measure of psychological connectedness, 94–101, **96, 100, 102, 103,** 104; temporal discounting and life expectancy, 397–98
aggression and serotonin, 153–54
Ahlbrecht, Martin, 310, 312
Ainslie, George, 401
Akerlof, George A., 231, 445, 522, 523
Albrecht, Martin, 23, 53
alcohol: alcohol-dependent discounting, 430–31; dieting and self-control, 466; priority of present time, 214. *See also* health and drug dependence, delay discounting in

alleles and MAO transmission, 158
Allen, Terry J., 432
Altonji, Joseph, 534
amino acid tryptophan, 151
amygdala, 5, 145, 146–47, 181
Anderson, Dack, 118
Ando, Albert, 491
Angeletos, George-Marios, 11, 33, 117–18, 232–33
Angner, Erik, 8
animals: aggressive behavior and CSF 5–HIAA levels, 154; brain lesions and reward response, 147–48; co-action effects and preference choices, 364; delay discounting and cross-species generality criterion, 421–25, **424**; economics of impatience, 118–19; evolution of time discounting, 4–5, 115–17; hot-cool model of delay of gratification across species, 183, 187; neurotransmitters and behavior, 147–48, 154, 162; self-control in, 118, 201; temporal discounting in, 117–18; utility maximization with variable choice and variable outcome options, 119, 122–36
anorexia nervosa, 475–76, 485n34
anticipation: delay of gratification, historical origins of, 16–17; dieting, 476–77; discount rate estimation, 54; and dread, construal level theory (CLT), 266–67; duration underweighing and summary assessment, 334–36; models incorporating utility from, 31, 38–39; of threat and rejection sensitivity (RS) in hot-cool model, 193–95
appetite and preference change, 358–60
arbitrage, intertemporal, 51–52
Ariely, Dan, 8, 34–35, 508, 510
assets and asset allocation: current budget constraints, self-rationing and consumption, 501–2; hyperbolic consumption model simula-tion results, 525–36; pricing and habit-formation models, 36
assumption of additivity, 8
assumption of separability, 8
Assunçao, Joao, 499
Attanasio, Orazio, 534
attention control: attentional focus and dieting, 463–64; attentional multipliers, danger vs. fear in health communication, 445–46; flexible deployment of, 189–90; ideation of, 145. *See also* hot-cool model
automatization in hot-cool model, 188–89
avoidance and fear as policy instrument, 448, 449
awareness, basic principles of, 221–30; activity timing, 222–26; "one-shot" decisions, 221–22; in richer environments, 226–27; and self-signaling model, 7, 292–95; welfare implications, 227–30. *See also* self-awareness and self-control
axons, neuron, 149–50, 151, 163
Ayduk, Ozlem, 5, 6

Bailey, Samuel, 163
Bain, Alexander, 162–63
Baker, Forrest, 428
Banks, James, 535
Barrett Impulsiveness Scale, 155–58
Baumeister, Roy F., 6, 208, 210, 213, 377
Bautista, L. M., 127–28
Bechara, A., 145
Becker, Gary S., 36, 354, 355, 383
Beggan, James K., 366
behavioral economics. *See* psychology
Bell, David R., 502
Bem, D. J., 280
Benabou, Roland, 34, 235
Benartzi, Shlomo, 41
Benzion, Uri, 28, 54

bequest motive and intertemporal choice, 15
Bernheim, B. Douglas, 40, 364, 535
Bickel, Warren K., 9, 117, 411, 428, **429**
Bing delay of gratification studies, 194
binge eating disorders, 485n34
Bizot, J. C., 160–61
Blundell, Richard, 535
Bodner, Ronit, 7
Böhm-Bawerk, Eugene von, 17, 18
boundedly rational incomplete awareness, 236–38
Bowman, David, 37
brain: drug commandeering and delay discounting, 420–25, **424**; structure and development, human, 5, 140–48
Brandt, Richard, 379
Bratslavsky, Ellen, 213, 464
Bretteville-Jensen, Anne L., 432
Brocas, Isabelle, 235
Broca's area, brain, 142
Brown, Judson S., 264
Browning, Martin, 534
budget constraints and consumption, 495, 501–2
Buehler, Roger, 500
bulimia, 479, 485n34
Bushman, Brad J., 213
Bykvist, Krister, 379

Camerer, Colin F., 468
Capital and Interest (Böhm-Bawerk), 17
Caplin, Andrew, 9–10, 39, 451–54, 455
Carmon, Ziv, 8
Carrillo, Juan D., 33–34, 233, 235
Carroll, Christopher D., 36, 56, 523
Carter, Samuel R., 204
categorization, level of construal and temporal distance, 246–47, 248
causality: and habit-formation models, 36; motivation without, and self-control, 7, 277–79

cerebral cortex and functions, 142–43, 151
cerebral spinal fluid, 5-hydroxyindoleacetic acid (CSF 5-HIAA), 152–54
Chandon, Pierre, 499, 502
Chapman, Gretchen B., 9, 29, 53, 63, 329, 459
Cheema, Amar, 492, 497, 501
Chesson, Harrell, 411, 412
children. *See* hot-cool model
choice. *See specific topics*
choice bracketing, 42–43
Choice Over Time (Loewenstein and Elster), 3
choice tasks: SS/LL ratios, 302–3; in subadditive discounting, 307, 308, 314–15
Christensen-Szalanski, Jay J. J., 400
cigarette-dependent discounting, 428, **429,** 430, 432, 434, 436–37. *See also* health and drug dependence, delay discounting in
CLT. *See* construal level theory (CLT)
co-action effects and preference choices, 364
cognitive approach: cognitive performance and time preference, 63; dieting and self-control, 461–66, 472; fear appeals in health communication, 442–43; futuremindedness and delay of gratification, 210–111; human brain evolution, 140; "know" cognitive system, 180–81; mechanisms to voluntarily delay goal during time interval, 178–91; psychological research on intertemporal choice, 2; strategic ignorance and hyperbolic discounting, 34; theories of self control, 202–7; value, level of construal and temporal distance, 253–56. *See also* construal level theory (CLT); hotcool model
cognitive dissonance, 208, 365–66, 455

cohesiveness of experience as gestalt characteristics moderator, 330

Coller, Maribeth, 60–61

Combe, George, 141

commitment, preference for: initial choice and motivation in goal commitment, 176–78; and self-awareness, 34–35; visceral influences on utility function, 40

comovement of consumption and labor income, hyperbolic consumption model simulations, 534–36

comparative brain anatomy, 140–41

comparative evaluation and duration neglect, 333–34

concave utility, discount rate estimation, 52–53

concern for future self and psychological connectedness, measure of, 94–101, **96, 100, 102, 103**

conditioned stimulus (CS), conditioning as source of preference change, 360–62

conditioning: conditioned place preference, 360–62; and delay discounting, 422–23; as source of preference change, 360–62

conflict theories, level of construal and temporal distance, 253

conformity and preference choices, 364–65

confounding factors in time discounting measurement, 50–55; about, 46, 54–55; anticipatory utility, 54; changing utility expectations, 54; concave utility, 52–53; consumption reallocation, 50–51; habit formation, 54; inflation, 53–54; intertemporal arbitrage, 51–52; uncertainty, 53; visceral influences, 54

connectedness: and hot-cool model, 180; of time problems and activity planning, 222–26. *See also* psychological connectedness

conservation vs. exhaustion in willpower, choice and self-control, 207–8

conspicuous consumption and preference choices, 364–65

constant discounting, and discounted-utility (DU) model, 22–23

construal, defined, 6

construal level theory (CLT), 245–76; about, 6–7, 245, 249–50; affirmative and cognitive sources of value, 253–56; conclusion, 270–71; construal, intertemporal changes in, 247–49; construal, level of, 245–47; controlling intertemporal variations in evaluation and choice, 261–62; dread-savoring hypothesis, 266–67; dynamic inconsistency in hyperbolic consumption model, 318; feasibility and desirability, 256–59; gambling, probabilities and payoffs in, 259–61; intertemporal changes in value, 249–61; motivational intensity gradients over temporal distance, 263–66; other perspective-dependent construals, 262–63; preference reversals, 267–69; primary vs. secondary sources of value, 250–53; self-control, 269–70; theories of intertemporal evaluation and choice, 263–70

consumer choice. *See* self-rationing, self-control in consumer choice

consumers, hyperbolic vs. exponential, 11

consumption: abit-formation models, 36; comovement with labor income in hyperbolic consumption model simulations, 534–36; conspicuous, and preference choices, 364–65; consumer credit effects on, 233, 496–98; consumption-saving decisions and self-awareness, 232–33; historical origins of intertemporal choice and accumulation, 15–16; independence of, and discounted-utility (DU) model, 21, 30, 31; inventory effects on, 499; over life-cycle model, 523–25, 531, 533; marketing and impulsive, 494–95, 509; patterns of, and habit-formation models, 36; Permanent Income Hypothesis and reference-point model, 37–38; promotional stockpiling and inventory effects on, 498–99; reallocation of, discount rate estimation, 50–51. *See also* hyperbolic consumption model

contingent pledges, 296*n*6

contingent resolutions, salience and self-control, 291–92

control beliefs and goal commitment, 177

convergence, neural, 149–50

corruption and resistance to preference change, 377–78

Coups, Elliot J., 63, 410, 412

cranial variations and phrenology, 141–42

credibility and health communication, 451–52

credit, consumer: consumption and self-control problems, 495, 496–98; hyperbolic consumption model, 518, 519; marketing and consumer self-control, 496–98; self-rationing liquidity and overconsumption, 233, 500–502; simulations, exponential and hyperbolic, results of, 530

credit attribution and learning processes, 132

cross cultural view, initial choice and motivation in goal commitment, 177

CS (conditioned stimulus), conditioning as source of preference change, 360–62

CSF 5-HIAA (cerebral spinal fluid, 5-hydroxyindoleacetic acid), 152–54

cue management, visceral influences on utility function, 40

Damasio, Antonio R., 5, 145, 146

danger vs. fear in health communication, 445

Darwin, Charles, 140

Dawes, Robyn M., 369

"De Gustibus Non Est Disputandum" (Stigler and Becker), 354

deadlines. *See* procrastination

Deaton, Angus, 523, 534

decision fatigue, 208–9

decision-making. *See specific topics*

decision utility, visceral influences on, 40

declining discount rate. *See* hyperbolic discounting

defensive system regulation in hot-cool model, 192–95

delay discounting. *See* health and drug dependence, delay discounting in

delay effect: health vs. monetary discounting, 400–402, 408; subadditive discounting, 303–5, 306–10, **311**, 314–15, 401–2

delay interval: and initial choice to delay, 178; subadditive discounting, 303–5, 306–10, **311**, 314–15, 401–2

delay of gratification, 175–200; about, 5, 175–76; conclusion, 195–96; and dieting, 463, 472, 473–76; vs. enhance delay, 473–74; evolution of, 5; fear and health communication, 455; goal pursuit processes, 178–79; historical origins of intertemporal choice, 16; hot-cool model, 179–95; individual differences in, 190–91; initial choice and motivation in goal commitment, 176–78; psychologi-

delay of gratification (*cont.*)
  cal research on intertemporal
  choice, 2; serotonin enhancement
  of, 159–60; willpower to, 175,
  188–89
"Delay-Speedup" asymmetry as discounted utility model anomaly, 28,
  37
DellaVigna, Stefano, 537
"Democracy and Shifting Preferences" (Sunstein), 381–83
dendrites, neuron, 149–50
deprivation and dieting, 484n24
descriptive validity of discounted-
  utility model, 4, 14, 19
desirability, level of construal and
  temporal distance, 256–59
destructive behavior and serotonin,
  153–54. *See also* visceral influences
Deutsch, Morton, 364
diagnostic motivation, and self-
  signaling, 285, 295–96
diagnostic reward, 7, 279
diagnostic utility and self-signaling
  model, 280–84, 288–90
Dickens, William, 445
dieting as behavioral economics exercise, 459–90; about, 10, 459–60;
  anomalies in, 474–81; conclusion,
  481; degree of cost, 474–76; dieting determination, 477–81; dieting
  process, 460–66; factors that enhance delay, 471–74; preloading
  and diurnality of dieting, 466–71;
  self-regulation and delay of gratification, 209, 210; very short-term
  diets, 476–77
diminishing marginal utility and
  positive time preference, 23–24
direct-acting agonist, neurotransmitter, 160
discomfort and pain. *See* summary
  assessment of experience
discount rate: concave utility, 52–53;
  consumption reallocation, 50–51;
  decline with increased time horizon, across studies, 25–26, **27,**
  218–19; empirical variation in, 14;
  estimation and confounding factors, 46; in exponential discounting formulation, 301; as function,
  7, 22–23; health vs. monetary discounting, 405–6; intertemporal arbitrage, 51–52; normative theory,
  395–96, 400; similarity of past to
  future, and measure of psychological connectedness, **98, 99, 101,
  102, 103;** as situation dependent,
  399–400; smaller-sooner (SS) vs.
  larger-later (LL) reward in hyperbolic discounting, 25; and subadditive discounting, 7
discount rates: and hyperbolic
  models, 32–34; measurement with
  experimental studies, 55, 57–61;
  measurement with field studies,
  55–57; time discounting, measurement of, 45–46, **47–50, 51**
discounted utility (DU) model, 18–
  45; about, 18–20; alternative
  models, 14, 31–45; anomalies and
  alternative models to, 27–45; assumptions, 27; and basic research
  on intertemporal choice, 2; constant discounting and time consistency, 22–23; consumption
  independence, 21; deficiencies in,
  7, 302; descriptive validity of, 4,
  14, 19; diminishing marginal utility and positive time preference,
  23–24; duration neglect and
  additive duration effect, 331–32;
  historical origins of, 13–18; independence of discounting from
  consumption, 22; integration of
  new alternatives with existing
  plans, 20; intertemporal choice,
  18–24, 65–67; introduction and explanation of, 18–20; with one-shot
  choice and two fixed outcome options, 119–24; stationary instantaneous independence, 21;

temporal delay vs. interval in, 303–5. *See also* subadditive discounting; time discounting and time preference, critical review of
discounted utility (DU) model, anomalies and alternative models to, 27–45; "Delay-Speedup" asymmetry, 28, 37; effects as errors, 30–31; hyperbolic discounting, 24–26, **27**; instantaneous utility function enrichment models, 35–45; magnitude effect, 28, 31; preference for improving sequences, 28–29, 31, 45; self-awareness, 34–35; sign effect, 27–28, 31; violations of independence and preference for spread, 29–30. *See also* hyperbolic discounting
discounting: cross-species, 117–18, 421–25, **424**; dieting and delay of gratification, 463, 472, 473–76; hyperbolic, in hyperbolic consumption model, 520–23; independence from consumption and discounted-utility (DU) model, 22; real vs. hypothetical rewards, 60–61; terms describing, 73*n*42; value of reward and initial choice to delay, 178; zero, historical origins of intertemporal choice, 16. *See also* health discounting outcomes
distraction in hot-cool model, 184–85
distress: dieting and self-control, 464–66; priority of present time, 213–14
diurnality of dieting, 466–71
divergence, neural, 150
dollar discount rate in concave utility, 52–53
domain independence, health vs. monetary discounting, 406–7
dopamine, 150
Doty, Richard L., 363
dread-savoring hypothesis, construal level theory (CLT), 266–67
Dreyfus, Mark K., 56

Driver-Linn, E., 368, 375
drug dependence. *See* health and drug dependence, delay discounting in
DU model. *See* discounted utility (DU) model
Dubé, Laurette, 510
Duesenberry, James, 35
duration neglect, 330–34; defined, 331; gestalt characteristics of, 330–32; health vs. monetary discounting, 404; response effect mode on, 332–34
duration weighting in summary evaluations of experience, 330–36; conditions influencing, 336; gestalt characteristics and duration neglect, 330–32; response effect mode on duration neglect, 332–34; underweighing duration as error, 334–36
Dyer, Geoff, 351
dynamic gestalt characteristics of experience, 326, 327–28
dynamic inconsistency and hyperbolic discount model: and dieting, 459–60, 461; hyperbolic consumption model, 519, 522, 538*n*3; impulsive consumption and marketing, 494–95; and self-rationing, 510; and subaddivitiy, 10, 316–18, 538*n*3

ecological validity in discount rate measurement, 57
economics: basic research on intertemporal choice, 2, 3; defined, 1; on discounted utility (DU) model, 7–8, 19–20; historic interest in intertemporal choice, 13, 15–18; hyperbolic discounting, 520; modeling and health communication, 452–54; multiple-motives approach to discounting and time preference, 66–67; and preference change, 353, 383; subadditive dis-

economics (*cont.*)
counting, 26; time-consistent preferences assumption, 218; utility maximization and temporal neutrality, 89–90
"The Economics of Impatience" (Fehr), 118–19
The Economics of Welfare (Pigou), 67*n*1
educational attainment: and delay ability, 6, 179, 190, 202; improvement preferences and dynamic gestalt characteristics, 328
Efficiency model, 128
ego-depletion and theories of self-control, 205–6, 208–9, 211
Eliaz, Kfir, 455
Elstein, Arthur S., 63, 398, 406
Elster, Jon, 32, 93–94, 470
emotion and affect: and amygdala in brain, 146; dieting and self-control, 464–66; ego-depletion and theories of self-control, 205–6; "go" hot system, 180–81; mechanisms to voluntarily delay goal during time interval, 178–91; and preference change, 358–60; priority of present time, 213–14; psychological research on intertemporal choice, 2; self-regulation and time perception, 212–13; self-signaling, 280–81; suppression, and retrospective time perception, 212; value, level of construal and temporal distance, 253–56. *See also* hot-cool model
empirical research and methodology: Barrett Impulsiveness Scale, 155–58; brain damage and brain function, 140–48; delay discounting and drug dependence, 421–34, **424, 427, 429**; discount rates measurement, 55, 57–61; gambling experiments and neurochemistry, 145–46, 164; hot-cool model, 183–90; hyperbolic consumption model, 519–20; impulsivity measurement, 154–61; pattern of correlation in implied discount rates, 64; psychological connectedness, measure of, 94–101, **96, 100, 102, 103**; self-control problems and self-awareness, 218–30; self-rationing, 508–11; self-signaling, 279–81; time preference and discount rates, 63–64. *See also* discounted utility (DU) model; subadditive discounting
end state, gestalt characteristics of experience, 326, 329, 341–43
endogenous factors: taste preference change, 356–58; visceral influences on utility function, 39–40
endowment effect, and preference prediction, 368–69
energy level: decision fatigue, 208–9; temptation resistance and willpower, 207–8; and theories of self-control, 202–7
Engen, Eric, 523
enhance delay: vs. delay-of-gratification paradigm, 473–74; factors in dieting, 471–73
An Enquiry Concerning the Principles of Morals (Hume), 91
EPPM (extended parallel processing model) and fear as policy instrument, 443–48
equity-premium puzzle (EPP): anticipatory utility, 39; and habit-formation models, 36; mental-accounting models, 42
error in preference prediction. *See* preference, error in prediction of future
errors, discounted utility (DU) model anomalies as, 30–31
Euler equation in discount rate measurement, 57
evolution: of brain size, 140–48; delay of gratification as adaptive, 209–14; dieting, 471; of subjective experience, 323–24

evolution of patience, 4, 115–38; application to discounting in humans, 136–37; case 1: one-shot choice with fixed outcome, 119–124; case 2: repeated choice with fixed outcome, 124–30; case 3: repeated choice with multiple outcome, 130–36; choice bracketing, 42–43; nature-based (nonhuman) intertemporal examples, 115–17; research background on intertemporal choice, 117–19

exhaustion vs. conservation in willpower, choice and self-control, 207–8

expectancy-value mechanism, 176

expectation of experience as gestalt characteristics moderator, 329

expected-utility theory: anticipatory utility, 39; discount rate estimation, 54; discounted-utility (DU) model, 21, 301; extended parallel processing model (EPPM), 444

experience, summary assessment of. See summary assessment of experience

experience profile, defined, 323–25

experienced utility, visceral influences on utility function, 40

experimental research. See empirical research and methodology

exponential discounting, from normative theory: delay discounting and drug dependence, 422; formulation of, 301; vs. hyperbolic discounting, 11, 25, 32, 218, 401; life-cycle hyperbolic consumption model, 524–25; utility maximization and evolution of patience, 123–30

extended parallel processing model (EPPM) and fear as policy instrument, 443–48

factors affecting intertemporal choice, 61–62

failures of rate maximization with repeated choices and multiple outcomes, 131–36

fear as policy instrument. See health, and fear as policy instrument

fear differential, 447, 450

feasibility, level of construal and temporal distance, 256–59

Fedoroff, I. C., 463

feedback effects and fear as policy instrument, 451–52

Fehr, Ernst, 118–19

Feinberg, Ricahrd A., 497

fenfluramine, 156, 159, 160

Ferrier, David, 144–45

field studies for measuring of discounting rates, 55–57

Fischer, Carolyn, 231

Fishbach, Ayelet, 500

Fisher, Irving, 17–18, 33

fitness, biological, 116

flexible attention deployment, hot-cool model, 189–90

The Fly (film), 90

focalism (focusing illusion), and preference prediction, 370–71

Folkes, Valerie S., 498

foraging studies, utility maximization with repeated choice and fixed outcome, 128–30

formulations: anticipatory utility, 38; danger vs. fear in health communication, 445; delay discounting, 422–23; discount function, 22–23; discounted utility (DU) model development, 18–20; endogenous change in taste, 356–58; expected-utility theory, EPPM, and fear as policy instrument, 444–47; exponential discounting, 301; fear differential, 447, 450; homeostatic mechanism in taste determination, 359; hyperbolic discounting, 32, 422–23; intertemporal utility function, 219; life-cycle hyperbolic consumption model, 524–25; long-

formulations (*cont.*)
    term utility and self-control, 228;
    maturation and preference change,
    362; projection bias, 372–73; self-
    signaling model, 283, 284
Frank, Robert, 481*n*1
Frederick, Shane, 4, 118, 119, 369,
    370
Frederickson, Barbara L., 326–27,
    331
Freud, Sigmund, 142, 183
frontal lobe and frontal lobe syn-
    drome, 5, 143, 144, 163, 180
Fuchs, Victor R., 51, 410, 412
Fuhrer, Jeffrey, 36
future, approach to: income and
    budget constraints, self-rationing
    and consumption, 502; interest
    rate in exponential discounting,
    301; naive extrapolation hypoth-
    esis and summary assessment,
    338–39; optimism and temporal
    distance, 258–59; research on sum-
    mary assessment of experience,
    341–45; welfare and psychological
    connectedness, measure of, 94–
    101, **96, 100, 102, 103**. *See also* pref-
    erence change, prediction and in-
    dulgence of
futuremindedness: and delay of
    gratification, 210–111; dieting,
    472–73

GABA (gamma-aminobutyric acid),
    150
Gafni, Amiram, 397–98
Gage, Phineas, 143–44
Gale, Douglas, 364
Gale, William, 523
Gall, Franz Joseph, 141, 142
gambling: improvement preferences
    and dynamic gestalt characteris-
    tics, 328; level of construal and
    temporal distance, 259–61; and
    neurochemistry, 145–46, 164; prob-
    abilities and payoffs, 259–61

gamma-aminobutyric acid (GABA),
    150
Gerard, Harold B., 364
gestalt characteristics: of duration
    neglect, 330–32; of experience,
    325–30, 336–39; memory effi-
    ciency, 337–38; prediction of fu-
    ture states, 338–39; and sequence
    preference, 8
gestalt characteristics of experience,
    326–30. *See also* summary assess-
    ment of experience
Gibbs, Brian J., 366
Gilbert, Daniel T., 368, 369, 375
Glenn, Norval D., 363
global resource constraints, intertem-
    poral consumer choice, 491, 492–93
glutamate, 150
"go" hot system, 180–81. *See also*
    hot-cool model
goals: futuremindedness and delay
    of gratification, 210–111; mecha-
    nisms to voluntarily delay goal
    during time interval, 176–91; re-
    sponse mode and duration ne-
    glect, 332–34
Gollwitzer, Peter M., 188, 211
Gourinchas, Pierre-Oliver, 56, 523
Gourville, John T., 499
gratification. *See* delay of gratifica-
    tion; impulsivity and immediate
    gratification
Green, Leonard, 131, 132–34, 302–3,
    317
Griffin, Dale, 500
Gross Rate model, 128
growth and discounted utility,
    119–24
Gruber, Jonathan, 33, 233, 234
Gul, Faruk, 45

h-discounting in subadditive dis-
    counting experiments, 312–13,
    316–18
habit formation: changing prefer-
    ences, 353; discount rate estima-

tion, 54; endogenous change in taste, 356; as instantaneous utility enrichment models, 35–36; practice breaking habits, 206
Hall, Robert E., 534
harm generated by impulsivity, 228–30, 234, 239–40
Harman, C. Peter, 471
Harvey, Charles M., 312
Hayashi, Fumio, 534
Hayek, Friedrich A., 383
Hayes-Roth, Barbara, 500
Hayes-Roth, F., 500
Heal, Geoffrey M., 36
health, and fear as policy instrument, 441–58; about, 9–10, 441–42; cases of, 447–49; conclusion, 454–55; economic model of (formula), 443–47; feedback effects, 451–52; health communication appeals to, 442–43; information, provision and propaganda, 449–52; policy aspects, 452–54
health and drug dependence, delay discounting in, 419–40; about, 9, 419–21; changes in drug-use and quantitative changes in discounting, 431–34; conclusion, 435–37; criteria for, 421–34; cross-species generality criterion, 421–25, **424**; and neurotransmitters, 161–62; quantitative discounting differences between drug dependents and control criterion, 425–31, **427, 429**
health and pain. *See* summary assessment of experience
health discounting outcomes, 395–418; about, 8–9, 395–97; conclusion, 412–13; differences to money discounting outcomes, 405–9; discounting large vs. small effects, 9; methodological issues, 397–99; vs. monetary discounting outcomes, 9, 395–409; similarities to money discounting outcomes, 399–405;

time preferences and health behavior, 409–12
Heath, Chip, 510
Heatherton, Todd F., 205, 210
Hebl, Michelle, 189–90
hedonic vs. utilitarian goods, 511n2
Heller, Daniel N., 398, 400
herd behavior and preference choices, 364
Herman, C. Peter, 10, 278–79
heroin addiction, 9
Herrnstein, Richard, 63
heuristics and choice bracketing, 43
Hier, Daniel B., 63
high choice and decision fatigue, 208
high-level construal and temporal distance, 246–53, 256–59, 270–71
Hill, A. J., 463–64
hippocampus, 5, 145, 151, 180
Hirschman, Elizabeth C., 497
Hoch, Stephen J., 317, 472, 494, 499
Hodgson, Geoffrey M., 383
Holbrook, Morris B., 362–63
Holcomb, J. H., 26
homeostatic mechanism in taste determination, 358–60
honoring preference change, 352, 353–55, 376–80
hope and futuremindedness, 210–111
hot-cool model, 179–200; about, 179–81; and brain structures, 5; changing preferences, 353; conclusion, 195–96; defensive system regulation, 192–95; defined, 5, 180–81; and dieting, 463, 472; empathy gaps and preference prediction, 371–72; interactions between, 181–83; value, level of construal and temporal distance, 253–56; visceral influences on utility function, 40
hot-cool model, and delay of gratification analysis, 183–90; about, 183; across species, 187; age effects on delay ability, 187; distraction, role of, 184–85; flexible attention

hot-cool model, and delay of gratification analysis (*cont.*)
deployment, 189–90; regulatory strength and automatization, 188–89; rewards, alternative representations of, 185–86; rewards, effects of attention to, 183–84; stress effects, 188
household consumption. *See* hyperbolic consumption model
Hsee, Christopher K., 28
Hubbard, Glenn, 523
Hume, David, 91, 378–79
hunger. *See* visceral influences
Huxley, Thomas Henry, 141
hyperbolic consumption model, 517–44; about, 11, 517–20; conclusions, 536–37; dynamic inconsistency in, 10, 316–18, 538*n*3; empirical evaluation of simulation results, 531–36; hyperbolic discounting, 520–23; model of consumption over life cycle, 523–25; simulations, exponential and hyperbolic, results of, 525–36
hyperbolic discounting: defined, 3, 24–25, 518–23; delay discounting and drug dependence, 422–23, 435–36; dieting and self-control, 462–163; and discounted utility (DU) model, 24–26, **27**, 302, **303**; vs. exponential discounting, 11, 25, 32, 218; and individual differences in delay of gratification, 190–91; models of, 32–34, 45; monetary vs. drug dependence delay discounting, 425–31, **427, 429**; in subadditive discounting experiments, 307, 310, **311,** 311–14; utility maximization and learning process, 128, 136–37. *See also* preference change, prediction and indulgence of; problems of self-control

"I" as personal identity, 23–24, 90–91

identity, personal. *See* time preference and personal identity
immediate gratification. *See* impulsivity and immediate gratification
impact bias and projection bias, 375
implementation plans, self-regulation and delay of gratification, 188–89
improving sequence. *See* sequence preference
impulsivity and immediate gratification: defined, 139; dieting and self-control, 479–80; harm generated by, 228–30, 234, 239–40; historical origins of intertemporal choice, 16; hyperbolic discounting as explanation of, 317–18; marketing and consumer self-control, 494–95, 509; measurement of, 154–61; neurochemistry of, 5, 148–62; pattern of correlation in implied discount rates, 64; and psychological problems, 152; psychological research on intertemporal choice, 2; and self-signaling, 284–90; and serotonin, 5, 151–58; willpower theories of self control, 204–5. *See also* problems of self-control
income: budget constraints and self-rationing, 502; labor, comovement with consumption in hyperbolic consumption model simulations, 534–36; and life-cycle consumption model, 523–25; Permanent Income Hypothesis and reference-point model, 37–38; simulations, exponential and hyperbolic, results of, 525–36
independence of variables, and discounted-utility (DU) model, 21–22
indifference point and curve, delay discounting and drug dependence, 422–23, **424**
indulgence. *See* impulsivity and immediate gratification

inefficiencies as evidence of self-rationing, 510–11
inflation and discount rate estimation, 53–54
information: acquisition decisions and self-control, 235–36; and fear as policy instrument, 449–52
ingroups and level of construal, 262–63
inhibition and correlation in implied discount rates, 64
initial choice in goal commitment, hot-cool model, 176–78
inside perspective on decision and construal level theory (CLT), 269–70
instantaneous utility function enrichment models, 35–45; in alternative models, 31; choice bracketing, 42–43; habit-formation models, 35–36; mental-accounting models, 41–42; models incorporating utility from anticipation, 38–39; multiple-self models, 43–45; projection bias, 40–41; reference-point models, 36–38; self-control problems and self-awareness, 218–19; temptation utility, 45; visceral influences, 39–40
instrumental self-signaling, 281, 284–90
intelligence and time preference, 63
intensity in experience profile, defined, 323–25
interdependence theory and delay ability in hot-cool model, 192
interpersonal relationships, quality of, and delay ability, 5
intertemporal arbitrage, 51–52
intertemporal choice: defined, 2, 13, 17, 139; and discounted utility (DU) model, 18–24, 65–67; examples from nature, 115–17; historical origins of, 15–18; psychological processes, 396–97; research by psychologists and economists, 2–

3, 395–96; self-regulation and delay of gratification, 209–14; terms describing, 73n42; and time preference, 17–18; and uncertainty, 15–16, 118–19; utility function formulation, 18–19. See also specific topics
interval. See time interval
intrinsic self-signaling, 281, 284–90
inventory issues: inventory effects and marketing and consumer self-control, 495, 498–99; self-rationing inventories, 502–7
isomorphic discounting, utility maximization and learning process, 136–37

James, William, 178, 181
James-Lange theory of emotion, 280
Jamison, Kay Redfield, 152
Janis, Irving, 442, 450
Jevons, Herbert S., 16, 17, 38
Jevons, William S., 16, 17, 445, 475
Johnson, Matthew W., 9, 117, 411, 428
Josephs, Robert A., 214

k-discounting, in subadditive discounting experiments, 312–13, 316–18
Kacelnik, Alex, 4–5, 264, 464–65
Kagel, John H., 134
Kahneman, Daniel, 29, 30, 40, 42, 269–70, 326–27, 331, 366, 368, 370
Kalyanaraman, S., 507
Kay, Aaron C., 366
Keren, Gideon, 53
Kirby, Kris N., 60, 302, 317
Kivitz, Ran, 507
"know" cognitive system, 180–81. See also hot-cool model
Koopmans, Tjalling C., 19, 21, 65
Koszegi, Botond, 33, 39, 233, 234
Krusell, Per, 521
Kruskall-Wallis test, **97,** 98
Kundera, Milan, 326
Kusser, Anna, 379

labor income, comovement with consumption in hyperbolic consumption model simulations, 534–36
Lahr, Bert, 491
Laibson, David I., 11, 32–33, 218, 232–33, 459
Landsman, David, 421
Lange, James C., 181
larger-later (LL) reward: in hyperbolic discounting, 25, 267–69, 302–3; preference reversals and construal level theory (CLT), 267–69; in subadditive discounting experiments, 302–3, 308, 310, 312–31–315; utility maximization and pigeon learning process, 133–36
Leahy, John, 39, 451–54, 455
learning processes: conditioning as source of preference change, 360–62; fear appeals in health communication, 442; practice breaking habits, 206; utility maximization with repeated choices and multiple outcomes, 130–36
Leclerc, France, 510
LeDoux, Joseph, 149
Lemon, Kay, 506–7
Lenventhal, Howard, 442, 443
"Levels of Personal Agency" questionnaire, 247–18
Lewis, David, 91
Liberman, Nira, 6–7, 248, 256, 259, 318
life-cycle model and consumption, 491–92, 523–25
limbic system, 145, 421
liquid wealth share, 532
liquidity: consumer credit effects on, 233, 496–98; consumption and self-control problems, 495, 496–98; hyperbolic consumption model, 518; self-rationing, 500–502
lives saved as health outcome measurement, 399

local resource constraints, intertemporal consumer choice, 491, 492–93
Loewenstein, George F., 182, 255–56, 263, 312, 317, 330, 331, 332–33, 339–40, 341, 344, 353, 368–69, 370, 372, 374, 401, 402, 403, 404, 428, 430, 445, 462–63, 472, 494–95, 499, 501
Logue, A. W., 152
loss, utility with one-shot choice and two fixed outcome options, 119–24
loss aversion: health vs. monetary discounting, 404; myopic, mental-accounting models, 42; and preference prediction, 369; in value function of prospect theory, 37–38
loss effect in health vs. monetary discounting, 403
Lovallo, Dan, 269–70
low choice and decision fatigue, 208
low-level construal and temporal distance, 246–53, 256–59, 270–71
Lowe, M. G., 470
Luntz Webber—Merrill Lynch survey, 518
Lusardi, Annamaria, 534

Mach, Ernst, 419
Madden, Gregory, 405, **427**, 428
magical self-signaling, 281–82
magnitude effect: as discounted utility model anomaly, 28, 31; dynamic inconsistency in hyperbolic consumption model, 318; health vs. monetary outcomes, 398–99, 402, 408; monetary vs. drug dependence delay discounting, 428, 430; preference prediction and projection bias, 8, 41, 353, 372–75, 381
Manuck, Stephen, 5
MAO (monoamine) neurotransmitters, 150, 151, 157–58, 159, 163
Marakovic, Nino M., 60

marginal utility, diminishing, and positive time preference, 23–24

Mariotti, Thomas, 34, 235

marketing and consumer self-control, 493–500; about, 493–94; consumer credit effects on, 496–98; impulsivity, 494–95, 509; maturation and preference change, 362–63; procrastination, 500; promotional stockpiling and inventory effects, 498–99; tactics that exacerbate problems, 495–96

Marlatt, G. Alan, 470

matching tasks: discount rate measurement, 58–59; sooner-smaller/larger-later (SS/LL) ratios, 302–3; in subadditive discounting experiments, 307, 314–15

maturation and preference change, 362–63, 374

Mazur, James E., 131, 312, 422, **424**

Mccrae, Sean, 248

memory: in brain, 145; duration underweighing and summary assessment, 334–36; effects, of, and gestalt characteristics of experience, 343–44; efficiency, and summary assessment, 337–38; gestalt characteristics of experience, 326–30, 339–41; information acquisition decisions and self-control, 235–36; and level of construal, 262

Mendoza-Denton, Rodolfo, 5, 6

mental representations: budgeting and self-rationing liquidity, 501–2; mental-accounting models, 41–42; and sequence preferences, 8. *See also* construal level theory (CLT)

Metcalf, Janet, 179–80, 182, 256, 455

methodology. *See* empirical research and methodology

Metzner, Ralph, 178

Meyer, Robert J., 499

Minehart, Deborah, 37

Mischel, Walter, 5, 6, 202, 256, 261, 291, 455, 463, 472–73

misconstrual problem, preference, error in prediction of future, 367–68

mistakes, discounted utility (DU) model anomalies as, 30–31

Mitchell, Suzanne H., 428

Mobini, S., 161

models. *See specific models*

Modigliani, Franco, 491

monetary discounting outcomes: vs. drug dependence delay discounting, 425–31, **427, 429**; vs. health discounting outcomes, 9, 395–409; improvement preferences and dynamic gestalt characteristics, 328

monoamine (MAO) neurotransmitters, 150, 151, 157–58, 159, 163

mood. *See* emotion and affect

Moore, Bert, 186

Moore, Michael J., 56

motivation: diagnostic, and self-signaling, 285, 295–96; dieting and self-control, 461–66, 467; in goal commitment and delay of gratification, 176–78; multiple-motives approach to discounting and time preference, 65–66; temporal discounting of, construal level theory (CLT), 263–66; without causality and self-control, 7, 277–79

multiperson strategic interactions, 44

multiple-self models, instantaneous utility function enrichment models, 43–45

Munasinghe, Lalith, 63

Muraven, Mark, 207

Murphy, Kevin M., 36

Murray, Charles, 63

Myerson, Joel, 317

myopic choice: alcoholic myopia, 214; brain damage, 146; of health and risk, 9–10; hyperbolic discounting as explanation of, 317–18; mental-accounting models, 42; multiple-self models, 43–44; neurology and time preference, 64–65;

myopic choice (*cont.*)
visceral influences on utility function, 39

naïfs and naive state of awareness and self-control: about, 6, 34–35, 220; and activity planning, 223–25, 228–29; addiction and consumption, 234–35; boundedly rational incomplete awareness, 236–38; hyperbolic discounting, 522–23; information acquisition, 235–36; preference change, 376; procrastination, 231–32; and self-awareness, 220, 238–40
naive extrapolation hypothesis and summary assessment, 338–39
naive realism, 352
natural environment and evolution of time discounting, 4–5, 115–17
natural selection, 140
negative habits, 356
Nelson, P. S., 26
Nelson, Richard, 63
Nestler, Eric J., 421
net present value (NPV), 46
neurobiology of intertemporal choice, 139–72; about, 5, 139–40; brain development and capacity, 140–48; conclusion, 162–65; neurochemistry of impulse control, 148–62; time preference, 64–65
neurochemistry of impulse control, 148–62; about, 148–49; neurons, neurotransmitters and neuro-modulators, 5, 149–51; serotonin, 5, 151–62
neuromodulators, 150–51
neuron anatomy, 149–50
neurotransmitters, synaptic transmission of, 5, 149–65
non-planning impulsiveness, Barrett Impulsiveness Scale, 155–58
norepinephrine, 150
normative theory: consumer self-rationing, 491–92; health outcome discounting, 395–96, 400. *See also* exponential discounting, from normative theory

"A Note on Measurement of Utility" (Samuelson), 18
Nozick, Robert, 110*n*7
NPV (net present value), 46
Nunes, Joe, 501

obsession, and fear as policy instrument, 448–49
O'Donoghue, Ted, 4, 6, 8, 35, 40–41, 292, 372, 510, 521, 523, 535
Odum, Amy L., 428
OFT (optional foraging theory), 126–27
"one-shot" decisions as basic principle of awareness, 221–22, 226
opioid-dependent discounting, 425–28, **427**, 433, 434. *See also* health and drug dependence, delay discounting in
optimism, future, and temporal distance, 258–59
optional foraging theory (OFT), 126–27
outcome expectations and goal commitment, 177
outcome utility and self-signaling model, 280–84, 288–90, 291–92
outgroups and level of construal, 262–63
outside perspective on decision and construal level theory (CLT), 269–70
overconsumption: and consumer credit, 233, 500–501, 500–502; inventory and promotional stockpiling effects on consumer self-control, 498–99; purchase quantity rationing, 11
overindulgence and resuming dieting, 470–71
Overland, Jody, 36
Owen, Sir Richard, 141

ownership: endowment effect, and preference prediction, 368–69; and motivated taste change, 365–66

package size and self-rationing inventories, 502–7
pain. *See* summary assessment of experience
Panel Study of Income Dynamics (survey), 520, 534–36
para-Chlorophenylalanine (*p*CPA), 160
parallel processing model, fear appeals in health communication, 442–43
Parfit, Derek, 4, 23–24, 90–104, 380
Parker, Jonathan, 56, 523
Parkinson's Law on procrastination, 500
partial models: naivete and self-control, 35, 220, 223–24; sophistication as evidence of self-rationing, 509–10
Paserman, M. Daniele, 537
patience, in exponential discounting formulation, 301–2. *See also* evolution of patience; subadditive discounting
*p*CPA (*para*-Chlorophenylalanine), 160
peak state, gestalt characteristics of experience, 326
Peake, Philip, 189–90
percent biased hyperbolic discounting, 521–22
Perkins, Kenneth A., 436
Permanent Income Hypothesis and reference-point model, 37–38
Perry, John, 109n5
personal identity. *See* time preference and personal identity
persons vs. selves, as terms, 109n2
Pesendorfer, Wolfgang, 45
Petry, Nancy M., 430–31, 432
Phelps, Edward S., 32, 218, 521
Phillips, Coleen M., 213

philosophical view of personal identity and intertemporal choice, 90–94, 101–2, 109n6
phobias and projection bias, 375
phrenology, 141–42, 162–63
Pigou, Arthur, 67n1
place preference, conditioned, 360–62
"planner-doer" model and multiple-self models, 44
Plato, 90–91
pleasure, self-regulation and time perception, 212–14. *See also* self-signaling model; summary assessment of experience
Pleeter, Saul, 56
Polivy, Janet, 10, 278–79, 471
Pollak, Robert A., 32, 34, 36, 218, 239, 521
positive habits, 356–57
possession: endowment effect, and preference prediction, 368–69; and motivated taste change, 365–66
Powell, Melanie, 329
prediction of future preference. *See* preference change, prediction and indulgence of
preference: for commitment and self-awareness, 34–35; for improving sequences, and dynamic gestalt characteristics, 328; for improving sequences, discounted utility model anomaly, 28–29, 31, 45. *See also* summary assessment of experience
preference, error in prediction of future, 367–72; about, 352–53; adaptation underappreciation, 370–71; adaptation underprediction, 368–69; conclusions, 380–83; focalism, 370–71; hot-cold empathy gaps, 371–72; misconstrual problem, 367–68
preference change, prediction and indulgence of, 351–92; about, 8, 351–54; conclusions, 380–83; error

preference change, prediction and
indulgence of (*cont.*)
    in prediction of future preference,
    367–72; honoring changes in, 376–
    78; prediction, 367–75; projection
    bias, 372–75; resisting changes in,
    376–78; sources of, 354–67. *See also*
    hyperbolic discounting
preference change, sources of, 354–
    67; conditioning, 360–62; emotions
    and visceral influences, 358–60;
    habit formation, 356; maturation,
    362–63; refinement, 357–58, **359**;
    satiation, 357; social influence,
    364–65; stability vs. change in,
    354–55; taste changes, endo-
    genous, 356–58; taste changes,
    motivated, 365–66; temporal prox-
    imity, 366–67
preference reversals: and delay ef-
    fects, health vs. monetary dis-
    counting, 400–401; hyperbolic
    consumption model, 519; and hy-
    perbolic discounting, 25, 267–69,
    318; and self-control problems,
    218–19; utility maximization and
    pigeon learning process, 134–35
prefrontal cortex, 5, 143, 144–46
Prelec, Drazen: 7, 29, 30, 37, 42–43,
    45, 231, 263, 312, 330, 401, 402,
    403, 404, 497, 499,
preschoolers. *See* hot-cool model
present value in exponential dis-
    counting, 301
pricing tasks in discount rate mea-
    surement, 59–60
problems of self-control: about, 217,
    238–40; addiction, 233–35; bound-
    edly rational incomplete aware-
    ness, 236–38; consumption-saving
    decisions, 232–33; in health issues,
    396; and information acquisition,
    235–36; intertemporal choice and,
    218–19; marketing tactics that
    exacerbate, 495–96; personal and
    social problems as, 202; procras-

tination, 231–32; savings choices,
    518; and self-rationing, 500–508;
    temptation and preference rever-
    sals, 401; and theories of self-
    control, 205. *See also* impulsivity
    and immediate gratification
procrastination: hyperbolic discount-
    ing and time preferences, 33; mar-
    keting and consumer self-control,
    500; naïfs and sophisticates in ac-
    tivity planning, 223–26; practice
    breaking habit of, 206–7; self-
    awareness and self-control, 231–
    32; and self-rationing time, 507–8;
    and sophisticated vs. naive state
    of awareness, 6, 35; as vice, 496
product evaluation, level of con-
    strual and temporal distance,
    251–52
projection bias: instantaneous utility
    function enrichment models, 40–
    41; preference prediction magni-
    tude effect, 8, 41, 353, 372–75, 381
promotional stockpiling, 495, 498–99
proportion and model of fear as pol-
    icy instrument, 447–48
proportional-discounting in subaddi-
    tive discounting experiments,
    312–13
prospect theory and reference-point
    models, 36–37
protection motivation theory, fear
    appeals in health communication,
    443
psychological connectedness: appen-
    dix questionnaire, 105–8; defined,
    110n7; final remarks, 101, 104;
    measure of, 94–101, **96, 100, 102,
    103**
psychology: basic research on inter-
    temporal choice, 2–3; changing
    preferences, 353; defined, 1; on
    discounted utility (DU) model, 7–
    8; historical origins of intertem-
    poral choice, 15–16, 18; hyperbolic
    discounting, 520–23; life-cycle

model and consumption, 491–92, 523–25; mental-accounting models, 41–42; processes of intertemporal choice, 396–97; self-regulation and delay of gratification, 209–14; subadditive discounting, 26; and time preference, 18; utility maximization and temporal neutrality, 89–90. *See also specific topics*

public policy: discounted-utility (DU) model as standard for, 14; drug dependence and delay discounting, 428, 435–37; health decisions and intertemporal choices, 396; naive vs. sophisticated state of awareness, 35; preference change, 381–82; welfare implications of self-regulation and awareness, 227–30. *See also* health, and fear as policy instrument

purchase quantity rationing, 11

quasi-geometric hyperbolic discounting, 522

quasi-hyperbolic discounting, 521, 524–25

Quattrone, G. A., 280, 293

queuing events, improvement preferences and dynamic gestalt characteristics, 328–29, 345

Rabin, Matthew, 6, 8, 35, 37, 40–41, 292, 353, 372, 510, 521, 523

Rachlin, Howard, 269, 423, **424**

Rae, John, 13, 14, 15–16, 17, 18, 463

Rangel, Antonio, 40

raphe nuclei, 151

Rapoport, Amnon, 28, 54

rating tasks in discount rate measurement, 59–60

Read, Daniel, 7, 25–26, 31, 59, 329, 373, 507

reappraisal, self-regulation and time perception, 212–13

Redelmeier, Donald A., 327, 398, 400

reference-point utility models, 36–38, 52–53

refinement and sources of preference change, 353, 357–58, **359**

regret and dieting, 482n9

regulatory strength and automatization, hot-cool model, 188–89

reinforcement, conditioning and delay discounting, 423, 425, 436

rejection sensitivity (RS) and delay ability in hot-cool model, 193–95

Repetto, Andrea, 11, 33

research. *See* empirical research and methodology

resisting changes in preference, 376–78

responses, ability to change initial. *See* willpower, choice and self-control

retrospective recall experience. *See* summary assessment of experience

retrospective time perception, 212

reuptake of neurotransmitters, 150, 151, 159–60, 163

reversals, preference, 25, 267–69

rewards: brain damage and gambling experiments, 145–46, 164; delay of gratification, 176; diagnostic vs. causal, and self-signaling model, 279; for dieting, 473–74; hot-cool model, 183–86; real vs. hypothetical rewards, 60–61; and self-signaling model, 7; serotonin-enhanced preference for, 159–60; utility maximization with one-shot choice and two fixed outcome options, 119–24; utility maximization with repeated choice and fixed outcome, 124–30; value of, initial choice and motivation in goal commitment, 177–78. *See also* larger-later (LL) reward; smaller-sooner (SS) reward

Richards, Jerry B., 423, **424**

risk-free rate puzzle, 39

robustness in self-organizing systems, 419–20
Roelofsma, Peter, 53, 59
Rogers, P. J., 463–64
Rogers, Ronald, 443, 445
Rook, Dennis W., 494
Ross, Lee, 352
Ross, Michael, 500
Roth, Deborah A., 364
RS (rejection sensitivity) and delay ability in hot-cool model, 193–95
Ruderman, A. J., 470–71
Ryder, Harl E., 36

Sagristano, Michael, 248, 259
salience and self-control, 291–92
Salovey, Peter, 28
Samuelson. Paul, 13–14, 18, 19, 21, 65
Samwick, Andrew, 56
SAT scores and delay ability, 179, 190
satiation and preference change, 357
savings: and habit-formation models, 36; hyperbolic discounting and, 11; incentives for, 233; intentions vs. actions, 517–18
SCF (Survey of Consumer Finances), 520, 524–25, 531, 533
Schelling, Thomas C., 472
schemas and level of construal, 246–47
Schindler, Robert M., 362–63
Schkade, David A., 370
Schmeichel, Brandon J., 212
Schmitt, Bernd, 510
Schneider, David J., 204
Scholz, John Karl, 523
Seifert, Kelvin L., 363
self-awareness and self-control, 217–44, 218–19; about, 6, 217; addiction, 233–35; awareness, basic principles of, 221–30; boundedly rational incomplete awareness, 236–38; consumption-saving decisions, 232–33; discounted utility

(DU) model, alternatives to, 34–35; discussion, 238–40; information acquisition, 235–36; and intertemporal choice, 219–21; intertemporal choice and self-control problems, 218–19; procrastination, 231–32
self-control: and construal level theory (CLT), 269; defined, 277; and intertemporal choice, 209–14; nature of, and willpower, 202–7; neurobiology of, 141–42; resisting preference changes, 377; self-signaling promotion of, 290. *See also* self-rationing, self-control in consumer choice; willpower, choice and self-control
self-control and self-signaling, 277–98; about, 7, 277; as human virtue, 277; intrinsic and instrumental, 284–90; in lab and everyday life, 279–82; motivation without causality, 277–79; salience and self-control, 291–92; self-signaling model, 282–84; self-signaling without awareness, 292–95; summary, 295–96
self-efficacy beliefs and goal commitment, 177
self-perception theory, 280, 283
self-rationing, self-control in consumer choice, 491–516; about, 10–11, 491; empirical evidence, role of, 508–11; global constraints in, 491–93; local resources in, 491–93; marketing and resource effects on, 493–500; in self-control problems, 500–508
self-rationing inventories, 502–7
self-rationing time, 507–8
self-regulation. *See* willpower, choice and self-control
self-regulatory strength (SRS) and dieting, 480–81
self-restraint and intertemporal choice, 15

self-signaling model: about, 7, 282–84; diagnostic vs. outcome utilities, 286–90; indulgence vs. abstinence, 284–86; inferential problem examples, 286–88; intrinsic and instrumental, 284–90; in lab and everyday life, 279–82; without awareness, 292–95

selves: vs. persons, as terms, 109n2; similarity of past to future, and measure of psychological connectedness, 94–101, **96, 100, 102, 103,** 104

Senior, N. W., 16, 17

separability, assumption of, 8

separate evaluation and duration neglect, 333–34

September 11, 2001, terror attacks and dieting, 478–79

sequence preference: discounted utility theory application to, 8; in health vs. monetary discounting, 403, 404, 407–9; improved, and discounted utility model anomalies, 28–29, 31, 45; improved, and dynamic gestalt characteristics, 328

serotonin: and impulse control, 5, 150–58; and intertemporal choice, 158–62; and suicide, 152–54

serotonin transporter, 151

set-point, homeostaic mechanism in taste determination, 359

sexual activity. *See* visceral influences

Shea, John, 38, 534

Shefrin, Hersh M., 44, 496

Shelley, Marjorie K., 28

Sherman, Steven J., 248

Shizgal, Peter, 334

Shoemaker, David, 110n7

short term perspective. *See* myopic choice

Sicherman, Nachum, 31, 63

Sieff, Elaine M., 369

sign effect: as discounted utility model anomaly, 27–28, 31; health

vs. monetary discounting, 403, 408, 428, 430

Simester, Duncan, 497

Simmons, Richard, 479

Simon, Herbert, 354–55

Simonson, Itamar, 507

simulations, hyperbolic consumption model: comovement of consumption and labor income, 534–36; empirical evaluation of results, 531–36; exponential and hyperbolic, results of, 525–36; wealth accumulation and asset allocation, 531–33

single outcome preference, discounted utility theory application to, 8

Siow, Aloysius, 534

skill and strategy theories of self control, 202–7

Skinner, Jonathan, 523, 535

smaller-sooner (SS) reward: in hyperbolic discounting, 25, 267–69, 302–3; preference reversals and construal level theory (CLT), 267–69; in subadditive discounting experiments, 302–3, 308, 310, 312–15; utility maximization and pigeon learning process, 133–36

Smith, Adam, 13, 15, 352, 362

Smith, Anthony A., Jr., 521–22

smoking-dependent discounting, 428, **429,** 430, 432, 434, 436–37. *See also* health and drug dependence, delay discounting in

Snell, Jackie, 366

Snyder, C. Richard, 210

Sobell, Mark B., 364

social influences: dieting and self-control, 466, 478–81; and goal commitment, 177; and level of construal, 262–63; and preference change, 364–65; projection bias, 374–75

The Sociological Theory of Capital (Rae), 15

Soll, Jack, 510
Soman, Dilip, 492, 497, 499, 501
somatic markers, 145
Sonnenschein, Bonnie H., 334
sophisticated state of awareness and
    self-control: about, 6, 34, 35; and
    activity planning, 223–26; addic-
    tion and consumption, 234;
    boundedly rational incomplete
    awareness, 236–38; hyperbolic dis-
    counting, 522–23; information ac-
    quisition, 235–36; and preference
    change, 376; procrastination, 231–
    32; and self-awareness, 220,
    238–40
Souleles, Nicholas, 534
spending: consumer credit effects
    on, 233, 496–98; patterns of, and
    habit-formation models, 36. See
    also consumption
spread of experience as gestalt char-
    acteristics moderator, 330
spreading effect, health vs. monetary
    discounting, 404–5
Spurzheim, Johann, 141
Spurzheim-Combe system, 141
SRS (self-regulatory strength) and
    dieting, 480–81
SS reward. See smaller-sooner (SS)
    reward
state management, visceral influ-
    ences on utility function, 40
static gestalt characteristics of expe-
    rience, 326–27
stationary instantaneous utility, and
    discounted-utility (DU) model, 22
Staub, Ervin, 177
Steele, Claude M., 214
Stephens, David W., 118
Stigler, George J., 354, 355
strategic ignorance and hyperbolic
    discounting, 34
strategies to aid delay of gratifica-
    tion. See hot-cool model
stress effects, hot-cool model, 188
Stroop task, 206

Strotz, Robert H., 32, 34, 91, 520, 523,
    525
On the Study of Character (Bain), 162
subadditive discounting, 301–22;
    about, 7–8, 301–5; choice vs.
    matching, 314–15; defined, 305;
    and delay effect, 401–2; discount
    rate decrease with increased time
    horizon, across studies, 25–26, 27;
    discussion, 313–14; dynamic in-
    consistency processes, 10, 316–18,
    538n3; experiments, 307–9; hyper-
    bolic discounting predictions and
    matching results, 311–13; hypoth-
    eses, 305–7; results, 309–10, 311
subliminal conditioning as source of
    preference change, 361–62
substance abuse. See health and drug
    dependence, delay discounting in
suicide, serotonin and impulsivity,
    152–54
summary assessment of experience,
    323–50; about, 8, 323–25; conclu-
    sions, 345–46; duration weighting
    in evaluation of, 330–36; ending
    effects on memory of experience,
    341–43; evaluated dimensions of
    experience, 344–45; evolution of,
    323–25; future research, directions
    for, 341–45; gestalt characteristics
    of, 325–30; memory effects and
    temporal aspects of experience,
    343–44; retrospective memories vs.
    actual experience of events, 339–
    41; types of experience, 345
Sunstein, Cass R., 381–82
Survey of Consumer Finances (SCF),
    520, 524–25, 531, 533
Swedenborg, Emanuel, 141
Symposium (Plato), 90–91
synapse, 149–50
synaptic self, 149

Tanner, Sarah, 535
taste preference change: endo-
    genous, 356–58; and habit forma-

tion, 8, 35–36, 356; honoring and predicting, 352, 353–55, 376–80; motivated, 365–66; refinement, 357–58, **359**; satiation, 357; visceral influence on, 358–60

temporal construal theory, 6

temporal proximity, preference change, sources of, 366–67

temptation: and dieting, 461–62; indulgence and self-signaling, 284–90; instantaneous utility function enrichment models, 45; level of construal and controlling variations in choice, 261–62; and preference reversals, 401; resistance and willpower, 6, 207–8; and temporal discounting, 119; transcendence and futuremindedness, 210–111

terminal buttons, neuron, 149

testicular cancer self-examination. *See* health, and fear as policy instrument

Thaler, Richard H., 25, 27, 28, 41, 44, 302, 316, 395, 496

threat anticipation and rejection sensitivity (RS) in hot-cool model, 193–95

threshold level of desire and self-signaling, 285, 289–90

Tice, Dianne M., 210, 213, 464

time: consistency in, and discounted-utility (DU) model, 22–23; in experience profile, defined, 323–25; inconsistency in, anticipatory utility, 38–39; self-rationing, 507–8

time discounting, defined, 14

time discounting, measurement of, 45–62; confounding factors, 46, 50–55; discounting rates, procedures for measuring, 55–61; discounting rates and discount factor, 45–46, **47–50**, 51

time discounting and time preference, critical review of, 13–86; about, 4, 13–15; alternatives to dis-

counted utility model, 31–45; anomalies in discounted utility model, 24–31; conclusions, 65–67; defined, 61–62; discounted utility model, described, 18–24; historical origins of discounted utility model, 15–18; psychological and economic conceptions of, 62–65; time discounting measurement, 45–62, **47–50**

time interval: cognitive mechanisms to voluntarily delay goal during, 178–91; in subadditive discounting, 303–5, 306–10, **311**, 314–15

time preference: choice bracketing, 42–43; defined, 14–15, 17–18, 61–62; diminishing marginal utility and positive, 23–24; disagreement on study measurement of, 51, 61–62; health behavior, 409–12; historical origins of, 16, 17–18; independence discounting from consumption and discounted-utility (DU) model, 22; monetary vs. health discounting, 409–12; psychological and economic conceptions of, 61–65; weak research on discount rates and, 63–64

time preference and personal identity, 87–114; about, 13, 89–90; appendix questionnaire, 105–8; critiques of Parfitian view, 91–94; discussion, 94; final remarks, 101, 104; personal identity, 90–91; psychological connectedness, measure of, 94–101, **96, 100, 102, 103**

Tinbergen, Joost, 127–28

Tirole, Jean, 34

Tobacman, Jeremy, 11, 33

Torrance, George W., 397–98

total utility and self-signaling model, 280–84

transcendence and futuremindedness, 210–111

A Treatise on Human Nature (Hume), 378–79

Trope, Yaacov, 6–7, 248, 256, 259, 500
true increasing patience in subadditive discounting, 307
tryptophan, 151, 164
Tversky, Amos, 30, 42, 280, 293
Tykocinski, Orit E., 340, 344
type of experience as gestalt characteristics moderator, 328–29,
   345

Ubel, Peter, 371
uncertainty: discount rate estimation, 53; and intertemporal choice,
   15–16, 118–19
unconditioned stimulus (US), conditioning and preference change,
   360–62
underestimation of future desires, 17
Urbszat, Dax, 471
US (unconditioned stimulus), conditioning and preference change,
   360–62
utilitarian vs. hedonic goods, 511n2
utility discount rate and concave
   utility, 52–53
utility independence, and
   discounted-utility (DU) model, 21
utility maximization: with one-shot
   choice and two fixed outcome options, 119–24; with repeated
   choice and fixed outcome, 124–30;
   with repeated choices and multiple outcomes, 130–36; and temporal neutrality, 89–90

vacations, improvement preferences
   and dynamic gestalt characteristics, 328
Vallacher, Robin R., 247
value: of choice, and decision fatigue, 208–9; consumption and
   self-control problems, 496; function of, and prospect theory, 37–
   38; primary vs. secondary sources
   of, 250–53; of rewards, initial
   choice and motivation in goal

commitment, 177–78. See also construal level theory (CLT)
van Leeuwen, Barbara, 373
VanBoven, Leaf, 374
Varey, Carol A., 29, 331
ventromedial prefrontal cortex,
   145–46
visceral influences: discount rate estimation, 54; dynamic inconsistency in hyperbolic consumption
   model, 318; hot-cool empathy
   gaps and preference prediction,
   371–72; and hot-cool model, 182–
   83; hyperbolic discounting as explanation of, 317–18; instantaneous utility function
   enrichment models, 39–40; pattern
   of correlation in implied discount
   rates, 64; and preference change,
   358–60, 377–80; projection bias,
   374; value, level of construal and
   temporal distance, 255–56
Viscusi, W. Kip, 56, 411, 412
Vohs, Kathleen D., 6, 205, 210–11,
   212

Wachsberg, Milton, 91
waiting for reward. See delay of
   gratification
Wall Street Journal, 478–79
Wallace, Alfred Russel, 140
Wansink, Brian, 498–99, 499
Ward, Andrew, 352
Warner, John T., 56
Watson, Donnie W., 364
wealth accumulation, exponential
   and hyperbolic, results of, 501–2,
   525–36
wealth of nations and intertemporal
   choice, 13, 15
Weber, Guglielmo, 534
Weber, Martin, 23, 53, 310, 312
Wegner, Daniel M., 204, 247
weight loss. See dieting as behav-
   ioral economics exercise
Weil, David, 36

Weinberg, Stephen, 11
welfare implications of self-
regulation and awareness, 227–30
Wernicke' area, brain, 142
Wertenbroch, Klaus, 10–11, 34–35
White, Teri L., 204
Whiting, Jennifer, 109–10n5
Williams, Bernard, 92
Williams, Melonie B., 60–61
willpower, choice and self-control,
201–16; about, 6, 201–2; conclusion, 214; decision fatigue, 208–9;
dieting, 462–163; exhaustion vs.
conservation, 207–8; and hot-cool
model, 175, 188–89; nature of self-
control, 202–7; resistance to pref-

erence change, 377; self-regulation
and intertemporal choice, 209–14;
willpower theories of self control,
202–7
Wilson, Timothy D., 368, 370, 375
Winquest, Jennifer R., 402
Witte, Kim, 443
working memory, 145

Yagil, Joseph, 28, 54

Zajonc, Robert B., 364
Zauberman, Gal, 339
Zeiss, Antonette R., 186
Zeldes, Stephen P., 523
Zemach, Eddy, 91